MUSIC IN AMERICAN LIFE

A list of books in the series appears at the end of this book.

The Hank Snow Story

Photo by Les Leverett.

The Hank Snow Story

Hank Snow, the Singing Ranger,

with

Jack Ownbey and Bob Burris

Published in association with the
Canadian Country Music Hall of Fame

UNIVERSITY OF ILLINOIS PRESS
Urbana and Chicago

Published simultaneously in Canada by arrangement
with the Canadian Country Music Hall of Fame
Manufactured in Canada
C 5 4 3 2 1

This book is printed on acid-free paper.

Unless otherwise noted, illustrations are from
the Hank Snow Collection. Used by permission.

Library of Congress Cataloging-in-Publication Data

Snow, Hank.
The Hank Snow story / Hank Snow with Jack Ownbey and Bob Burris.
p. cm. — (Music in American life)
Includes index.
ISBN 0-252-02089-8 (cloth : acid-free paper)
1. Snow, Hank. 2. Country musicians—United States—Biography. I. Ownbey, Jack, 1933- . II. Burris, Bob. III. Title. IV. Series.
ML420.S674A3 1994
782.42'1642'092—dc20 93-34476
[B] CIP
MN

To Min

My sincerest critic

My best friend

My loving wife

Contents

Introduction

Jack Ownbey

THE RED VELVET CURTAIN rolls back and the concert hall falls very quiet as the audience anticipates the show. The singer, short in stature, dressed in a white suit studded with sparkling rhinestones and colored sequins, stands tall before the microphone. Then the familiar words begin to ring:

> That big eight-wheeler rollin' down the track
> Means your true-lovin' daddy ain't comin' back.
> I'm movin' on. . .

Cameras flash, and many in the capacity crowd leap to their feet and clap enthusiastically as they recognize this classic song. The singer continues with complete concentration, looking straight ahead as his deep melodic voice resonates through the large state-of-the-art speakers. His eyes are intense and compelling as he delivers another flawless performance. When the song concludes, his eyes soften and he humbly expresses his appreciation for being invited to this concert hall where royalty is often entertained by the world's most renowned artists.

This is Hank Snow, the Singing Ranger, and this is the London Palladium.

However, this could be any city in the United States or one of a number of cities throughout the world. From small-town taverns, schoolhouses, theaters, military bases, outdoor stadiums, the Grand Ole Opry, television studios, the Hollywood Bowl, or the London Palladium, Hank has touched the hearts of people in all walks of life. Whether they come dressed in tuxedos, blue jeans, or the latest London fashions, members of the audience can relate to Hank as he sings of disappointment, lost love, a mother's love, humor, abuse, inspiration, happy times, the good and the bad. The audience will sometimes laugh and sometimes cry. Hank sings about situations that touch people's feelings. He tells about life in song.

On this night, like any concert night, his songs are special. Every one has been chosen carefully, and every word is enunciated precisely and sung as if an important message is being communicated to each person in the audience. That has always been the Hank Snow way. "I never record a song," says Hank, "unless it is a song that I like and is not suggestive and doesn't go in depth about drinking, and I will never sing any song referring to narcotics of any kind."

Those are important ingredients in Hank's influence in country music. Many consider him to be one of America's most important goodwill ambassadors for traditional country music. Hank has maintained his popularity throughout the music world since he began recording nearly six decades ago. This longevity is a message in itself.

In recognition of Hank's talent and achievements, he has received many awards throughout his illustrious career, and he is proud of each and every one of them. In April, 1979, at a special dinner and during the Canadian Juno Awards, Hank was inducted into the Canadian Academy of Recording Arts and Sciences Hall of Fame for his contribution toward the greater international recognition of Canadian artists and music. This honor was conferred by the prime minister of Canada, Pierre Trudeau.

In 1985 Hank was inducted into the Canadian Hall of Honor. This presentation was made on the Nashville Network in Nashville, Tennessee, when Hank and his band were appearing there on a televised show. Then on November 1, 1989, Canada honored Hank again by electing him into the Canadian Country Music Hall of Fame.

On September 25, 1963, at the rodeo in Omaha, Nebraska, he was inducted into the Nebraska Western Hall of Fame, AK-SA-RB-EN (Nebraska spelled backwards). In 1953, during the Jimmie Rodgers Festival in Meridian, Mississippi, Hank became a member of the Jimmie Rodgers Hall of Fame, and in 1978 he was inducted into the Songwriters' Hall of Fame in Nashville.

In 1979 Hank was inducted into the Country Music Hall of Fame by his peers during the Country Music Association's national awards show, televised live on CBS. The CMA plaque reads:

> Canada's Hank Snow is one of country music's most prominent and influential entertainers. His determined motivation and talent as a singer, songwriter and guitar player have earned him innumerable hits and awards. Career milestones for the Singing Ranger include

joining RCA Victor in 1936, making him the longest-term artist on any label; holding *Billboard*'s #1 chart position for an unequaled 29 consecutive weeks for self-penned "I'm Movin' On"; joining the Grand Ole Opry in 1950; and founding the Hank Snow Child Abuse Foundation.

Because of his uncommon talent, it's not surprising that Hank survived the ups and downs of show business. What is surprising is the fact that he survived the ups and downs of his early life. There were lots of obstacles along the way. Fate dealt Hank heartaches and sorrow. But surely this background has conditioned his creative genius, and fortunately for us, fate also gave us the fruits of those hardships. Somewhere along life's highway many of us have received inspiration from his perseverance.

❧ ❧ ❧

In December, 1976, Hank Snow came to Cleveland, Tennessee, to headline a benefit show raising money to fight child abuse. This event was prompted by the tragic death of a local girl, little Melisha Gibson. At that show Hank told how he also had been severely abused as a child. Bob Burris, my brother-in-law, was at the concert and was impressed with Hank's sincerity and commitment to fight abuse wherever it existed.

Bob discovered that the story of Hank's abuse had never been fully told in print. Believing that Hank's experiences could be a great inspiration to others, Bob contacted me about the possibility of our cowriting Hank's biography. I was definitely interested. I'd been an avid fan of Hank's since 1950, when I first heard his monster hit "I'm Movin' On." I've also been a collector of Hank's records and have read everything I could find on his life. In 1977 Bob wrote Hank. Even though he had been approached by several others to write his story, Hank agreed to work with Bob and me, provided that his book be an extensive account and properly reflect the most important events in his life.

However, since Hank was then heavily involved in his foundation for the prevention of child abuse, he didn't know when he'd have time to concentrate on the research. Bob and I were willing to wait. Over the next several years Bob met with Hank many, many times in Nashville and gathered data for the book. He sent this abundance of material, along with his ideas, to me in San Diego. Via the mail and over the telephone I worked with Hank in putting the manuscript together.

One of our biggest challenges came from the fact that Hank's memories could easily fill three books. He had so many inspirational and well-told stories! We've included as many of these as possible, in Hank's own words, just as he remembered them. Our efforts were a labor of love, and our hope is that we've helped capture the essence of this great artist and humanitarian.

1

The Snow Family

What a strange world we're living in, oh what a shame!
Someone's always quarrelling, the marriage don't remain.
Divorces by the thousands; is the human race insane?
I always thought that marriage should be a sacred thing.

"Married by the Bible, Divorced by the Law,"
by Johnny Rector, Neva Starns, and Pee Wee Truehitt

❦

FIVE HUNDRED SPECIAL GUESTS attended the dinner in Halifax in 1986 hosted by the premier of Nova Scotia, the Honorable John M. Buchanan, at which I was being honored for my fifty years in show business. After several speeches of tribute, a letter of commendation was read to the audience and me from the prime minister of Canada, Brian Mulroney. During all of these high praises, my mind kept wandering back to my early years of poverty and abuse. I remember telling my wife that this seemed like a dream and that the Good Lord sure has been good to this boy who never even finished the fifth grade.

❦ ❦ ❦

Friends, I'll start in the beginning and tell you about the events in my life that seemed most important to me. I was born on May 9, 1914, in a small sawmill town in eastern Canada called Brooklyn, located in Queens County in the province of Nova Scotia. Fishing is a major industry in the province and colorful fishing villages are located all along its foggy Atlantic coast. Brooklyn lies 423 miles from the state of Maine in the United States.

In 1914 Brooklyn had a population of about seven hundred people, and this little country town had two sawmills, two grocery stores, two churches—English and Baptist—and a two-room schoolhouse. Indoor plumbing was uncommon in those days, and there was no electricity. The streets were unpaved and were lighted by four or five gas lamps. An old gentleman by the name of Howard Godfrey went around each night at dusk to pump air into those lamps, light them, and hoist them on posts about twenty-five feet in the air. It was a typical little town and very picturesque—something you might see in a Canadian or American movie in the early 1900s.

I was the fifth of six children. My dad was George Lewis Snow, and my mother was Marie Alice Boutlier. The first two children, Max and Olive, died in their first year, both from natural childhood diseases. They're buried in Mount Olive, a private cemetery on a little hill in northeastern Brooklyn. I have three sisters. The oldest is Lillian Mae and the second is Nina Elizabeth. Both of them have now passed away. The youngest is Marion Victoria.

For some reason my schoolmates started calling me "Jack," and after that my family did, too. The name stuck with me until I entered the recording field in 1936.

My dad was a rugged and healthy-looking man who took great pride in being neat and well dressed. I've always had a striking physical resemblence to him, and as I grew into manhood, I guess it was normal that I developed the same pride in neatness and being well dressed. Dad had a lot of interests. One was ice skating, and I was told that he could actually skate his name in the ice. He loved to sing, although in an amateurish way. His singing was very pleasing to the ear, and he'd sing to us kids at night. The oil lamps would not be lit, and his voice would be so soft. Dad sang with such feeling, and after a few of the old songs we would all get sleepy and go to our beds. He was a pretty happy man back in those early years before Mother and he started to drift apart.

Dad loved to do little things to please my sisters and me. One Christmas Eve, after we had gone to bed, we heard something like the door opening and heavy footsteps. In an unusual voice he said, "Ho, ho, ho," and then he rang sleigh bells. We took for granted that this, without a doubt, was the real Santa Claus. We giggled and laughed and just had us a ball talking about it, and then we went off to sleep.

My mother was a lady of many talents and a successful entertainer in her own right. She was a very attractive brunette, well dressed, and the center of attraction at parties and group get-togethers. She had a beautiful singing voice and was actually an accomplished singer. She played piano in the silent picture days at the local theater, and sometimes she worked in a minstrel show, back when minstrel shows were all the rage. Mother played the organ well, and in later years she became especially adept at playing the Hawaiian guitar. Even though she was a professional entertainer, she turned down a number of offers to join traveling shows. Mother had the talent to be a commercial success, but she was dedicated completely to her family.

Our family was pretty typical of poor working people in Canada and the United States at that time. We had severe trouble in making ends meet, but so did the other folks around us. Our house was quite small and had tiny rooms. Dad had built it with the help of neighbors, as it was common practice back then for neighbors to help each other by swapping work. All four of us kids had our regular chores to do around the house, and if they were not done, we were punished in some way like other kids.

Dad worked at many jobs, but his main trade was working in sawmills as a millwright or mill foreman. To find work he had to be away from home a lot. He had several mill jobs in Nova Scotia, New Brunswick, and the state of Maine. The work was hard and the pay was poor, but we managed.

Dad loved to hunt moose and deer in the fall when the season was open. He also acted as a guide for other hunters, and he would always be sure they got a moose before going home. Dad fascinated the hunters with his hunting skills and his marksmanship. He was a crack shot, and he always used his old .30-30 Winchester rifle.

At an early age Dad had learned from other hunters how to make a moose call from birch bark. It was actually a horn, but it was referred to as a moose call. This was made of pieces of birch bark in different lengths, each rolled up into the shape of a regular horn. These horns made various sounds to attract the moose. When the moose heard them, they would find their way to where the sounds were coming from. Dad would be out in the open when he made the call, and the moose would be a clear target for the hunter. Dad also had another way of attracting the moose. He'd beat on an old stump or tree trunk with an axe handle or large piece of wood. This would not only bring the moose into the open, it would anger the animal for some reason, so you had to be ready with your rifle and react quickly. Dad thought it disturbed the moose during the mating season, but whatever the reason, he was very successful, and he became famous with the hunters in Nova Scotia and elsewhere. Many hunters came back each fall to ask for Dad's professional help.

Several hunters who had witnessed the incident told me this story. One day when Dad used the old axe-handle trick, he was charged by a moose weighing almost two thousand pounds. The tourists were terrified, since Dad was the only one who had his rifle by his side at that moment. As the moose came closer and closer, Dad calmly bent down on one knee and waited until the moose was only about fifty yards away—and then he shot him. Several such stories helped Dad to get his reputation for courage.

For a time when I was about six years old, Dad worked at Corcum and Ritchy, a wholesale grocery store in Halifax, about ninety-six miles from Brooklyn. Dad usually came home by train on the weekends, and when it was time for his train, my sisters and I would huddle close to the window and watch for the train lights through the trees, about a mile away. We would get excited, knowing he would bring us candy or some other inexpensive gifts. I remember well when Dad often teased me by saying, "I'm going to take you to work with me someday, Jack. I have a whole barrel of candy right under my desk, and you can reach for it any time you want some." I really believed he would, and I'd continue to ask him when I could go, but he never did take me.

Also, when I was about five or six years old, I have a vivid memory of saying to Mother, "Someday when I get rich I'll buy you a sixty-dollar sweater!" Since then, I've heard Mother mention that many, many times. I had a lisp as a child, and she would tell friends exactly what I said and say it with a lisp. She got the biggest kick out of that!

Mother loved her children very much. She was a good mother and an excellent cook. We had rough times financially, though, and she had to be away from home a lot to help support us four children. She worked for several rich families, washing and ironing clothes, scrubbing floors, and keeping their houses clean and tidy. But she always maintained a wonderful disposition. She was also an outstanding seamstress. She could take any hand-me-downs and make them into practical and pretty clothes for us kids. And Mother always found time to work with the Salvation Army, and she maintained strong Christian beliefs throughout her life.

I did well in school for the first few years and have fond memories of my school playmates and teachers. I distinctly remember Lillian Parks and Ethel Vogal, two favorite teachers. One of my schoolmates, Constance Gardner, was a sweet, pretty little girl about my age, and I liked her very much. There were many Gardners in Brooklyn, and her family lived next door to us and were fine people. Constance and I often walked to school together, played together, and ran store errands for our parents. Whenever we got candy or cookies we'd always share them.

Some of my other school buddies were Gordon Gregory, Lee Smith,

Randolph Rhyno, and Ernie Croxen. In July, 1987, we got together during the official opening of the new Hank Snow Playground for the Brooklyn children, donated by the Mersey Papermill. We had a great time reminiscing, and they still called me Jack.

I guess I was a typical kid—and mischievous at times. During school vacation, my buddies and I often went to our favorite swimming place, which was located right beside our school. One day after swimming we were in a devilish mood and decided to break a school window out. We made a small bet as to who could break it first. This was such a thrill that we didn't stop until we broke out every window in the school! As if that wasn't enough, we went up on the roof and removed the loose chimney bricks and threw them down inside the chimney. We were all severely punished for this episode, and it was damn well deserved.

Here's a story I've never forgotten because it made such a strong impression on me. Each year our teacher would take the school children on a picnic in some field or place by the ocean. Each child was supposed to take a food basket from home and trade food, such as a piece of cake or an apple, with the other kids. One year on the day of the picnic our family had nothing to eat in the house except bread and molasses. We were too embarrassed to take this food to the picnic because we didn't want the other kids to know just how poor we really were. But we had our picnic anyway. We stayed at home and made bread-and-molasses sandwiches and had just as much fun.

My grandmother lived less than three hundred yards away from our house. She had married twice, first to a Snow, and then to Curtis Godfrey. Mother was against us going to her house, but she wouldn't say too much if we went there occasionally. I loved Grandfather Godfrey, and sometimes I'd help him put up hay in the barn for his milk cow. He'd mow hay in the field nearby with his hand scythe and haul it to the barn on a small wagon. As he forked the hay through the upstairs shutter, I'd stack it in the back of the barn loft. Granddad also had a job hewing huge oars out of long logs, which were shipped to the West Indies for the black folks to row those big boats they use there, eight men to a boat.

Even though I hardly ever visited Grandmother, I'll never forget what happened at her place one day after school. She was away visiting friends, and Granddad was away at work. I crawled up into the hayloft and was looking out of the big shutter when all of a sudden I heard what sounded like a cat meowing. We didn't have any cats, but I thought it might be a strange cat that had come around, and I called as if calling a kitty. When the meows got louder, I climbed down from the loft and went to the house, which was only a few feet away, and peered into the window. Everything looked peaceful and quiet inside. Still, the sounds got louder and changed to a high-pitched groan. By then I knew it couldn't be a cat, and I was so scared that I began shaking. I ran down to the road, about two hundred yards away, as fast as I could. The noise got louder, and it sounded exactly like people throwing huge pieces of lumber down the stairs.

About this time my sister Nina came by and she also heard the eerie noise. Soon my grandmother appeared, and when we told her about what we had heard, she started walking toward the house, thinking we were imagining things. Then, suddenly, we all heard a series of loud groans. Grandmother turned white as a sheet! At this time Cil Godfrey, an elderly neighbor, came along. Grandmother told him what we had heard, but the sounds had stopped. He laughed and said, "There are no such things as ghosts, but I'll go inside with you and look around." We entered the kitchen and everything was in place, except for some black soot from the stove on the floor and three wooden blocks that no one had ever seen before. The story got around the neighborhood, and it had everybody baffled. I heard ghostly sounds, even though I've never believed in ghosts. Or do I?

My memories of family life were quite pleasant until I was six or seven years old. Then the happy and normal times got fewer as my parents began to have serious marital problems. I felt the tension of this "cold war" for almost two years, and when the separation came, it was to have profound effects on my life. Even before the legal split, my sisters and I were in constant fear of being taken away to an orphanage. The Overseers of the Poor was an organization that could remove kids from their parents' home if an investigation showed they were being seriously abused because of their parents' problems.

Jabe Gardner was the official representative of the Queens County Overseers of the Poor Commission. He was a big man, and with his bushy white beard that reached almost down to his waist, he looked like Santa Claus. He came out several times to talk to my parents before the separation, and I had a sick feeling every time I saw him. I was sure he was coming to take me away. I would peer from behind the house until he had driven off in his horse and buggy.

I'll never forget the day my dad left home. I can remember it as if it was yesterday. He borrowed a small four-wheel cart from my step-grandfather Godfrey, and I helped Dad load his trunk on the wagon. As I was pulling the wagon down to the train station about a mile away, Dad didn't say a word, and I was wondering where he was going and if he would ever come back. At the station he patted me on the back and gave me a nickel. I remember his exact words: "Well, good-bye, Son. I may see you again, and I may never see you again."

Dad boarded the train and waved good-bye.

Shortly thereafter, the court approved a legal separation between Mother and Dad, and Mother was prohibited from keeping any of the children because she was financially unable to do so. According to the court, my grandmother on my father's side was to be my legal guardian.

So I moved into Grandmother Godfrey's home. I had eluded old Jabe Gardner, and I felt confident that I would not be sent to an orphanage, but I had no idea what would happen to my sisters. In a few days, while I was sitting on Grandmother's veranda, Jabe drove by again. I watched sadly as he took Nina and Marion away in his horse and buggy. I heard later that they were taken to separate foster homes. Lillian, the oldest, was also rescued, and since she was about sixteen years old, she went to board with my aunt Cecile, one of Mother's three sisters. She got a job in a shoe factory in Stewiacke, a small town in Colchester County, Nova Scotia.

It was barely dusk a few days later as I watched our parents' furniture being hauled away in a horse-drawn wagon. The last piece of furniture to go was Mother's old pump organ. This was an old-fashioned instrument with wind bellows that you had to pump with your feet in order to get air to work the organ keys. Mother loved this old organ and had played it many hours for us. It was a pity to see it taken away, as it was such an important part of our family.

The family was broken up. The furniture was gone. And I cried my eyes out. Being only eight years old, I didn't understand what was going on, and I wasn't prepared for all these changes that were taking place.

But my problems were only beginning. On the first day I moved in, Grandmother told me never to mention Mother's name in her presence—ever. Can you imagine that? My own mother! Actually, I didn't know my grandmother very well before the breakup of the family. Occasionally I'd overheard someone say she was an unhappy old woman. Supposedly she was bitter because her son had married a Boutlier, and for unknown reasons she detested Mother and never accepted her in the family. But one thing for sure—that woman scared the hell out of me. I studied her very carefully, and even though she was short and thin, she looked like a giant to me. Her hair was pulled back and tied in a bun, and she always wore a checkered apron. I can see her now looking down at me, without the slightest appearance of a smile, and bawling me out for something.

I can't believe the military could ever be as strict as my grandmother. Every time I completed the household chores, she would inspect them. If they were not done exactly right, and if I opened my mouth to explain, she would give me a lecture. She had a lot of different ways to punish me for the least little thing that I might have done wrong. If I didn't get home from school right on the minute, she wouldn't let me go swimming with my playmates or allow me out of the yard on the following Saturday. Often she would lock me in my room on a hot summer afternoon and keep me there the entire day. She even deprived me of meals. Occasionally I'd deliberately slip away and go down to the swimming location with some of the boys or down to the wharfs where some of them were fishing. But I always knew I'd get a good lashing when I got back, and I hated to go into that unhappy house.

My poor old granddad was scared to open his mouth. She dominated his life completely, and I felt sorry for him, as he was a quiet and beautiful man. On many occasions I saw her beat him over the head with a broom handle. Granddad often stayed out of the house just to avoid her. At times he got so depressed that he went into the woods and stayed for days with nothing to eat and with no warm clothes, even in the coldest weather. Grandmother would send neighbors to look for him and bring him home again. It was crystal clear to me that the woman hated both of us.

During the time I lived with my grandmother I was a bed-wetter. Every morning when I woke up, she would turn the covers back to see if I had wet the bed. This humiliated me. The bed was always wet, and she would always take a leather strap and beat me. She thought this would be a deterrent. It was not. I tried not drinking any liquid after 3:00 P.M., as well as other possible remedies, but nothing worked, and I continued to wet the bed until I was about twelve years old. I sincerely hope that all parents will be tolerant of this problem. Children don't wet the bed on purpose, and I've read that there may be psychological reasons for bed-wetting. I don't know, but I do know that kids can't help it, and they will eventually outgrow it.

When I did something wrong, I expected Grandmother to punish me—like the time I "borrowed" the neighbor boy's set of bobsleds. These were two sleds tied one behind the other with a chain crossed over in the form of an X. One late afternoon I took the sleds from the boy's yard, and instead of trying to carry them, I pulled them through the snow to Grandmother's house. I put them in the coal bin in the barn and was planning to play with them the next day. But soon after I got into the house, here came the neighbor boy after his sleds. All he had to do was follow the sled tracks through the snow! When he asked Grandmother where I had put the sleds, I thought, "Oh boy, here goes another thrashing." I got a stern lecture about stealing and going to jail, but I didn't understand why I didn't get a beating. This time it was deserved.

One of the more touching stories I remember was concerning little Alfred Gardner. The Gardner family lived in Brooklyn, not too far from us. They were friends of my grandparents and were good people. Alfred was their only son, and they loved him dearly. He and I were about the same age and about the same size, and occasionally we played together. I was around nine years old when the Gardners moved to Boston. During their first Christmas they gave their little boy a child-size, two-wheeled bicycle. Alfred was so excited that he took it outside on Christmas day and was trying to learn how to ride it. There was a lot of ice on the streets, and he got in the way of a car coming around a curve in front of the house. He was struck and died instantly. The family was crushed. They moved back to Brooklyn to have Alfred buried there. In those days there were no funeral parlors, so after the undertaker prepared Alfred's body, he was brought to the Gardners' home and placed in the living room to be viewed. Many people from the community came to pay their final respects and to console the parents the best they could.

My grandparents took me to see Alfred. This was the first time I had ever seen a dead person. I'd played with him a few months prior to this, and I was having a tough time understanding death. I can still see him lying there in his coffin with a Bible in his little hand. That touched me as much as anything I've experienced in my whole life. That night I had a nightmare and woke up crying bitterly. I got out of bed and went to Grandmother. I was scared. I was trembling. And I needed comforting. But Grandmother was angry because I had awakened her, and she lashed out at me and demanded I go back to bed.

As I look back, I can't remember a single time when my grandmother held me or spoke to me in a tender way. I was craving tenderness on that particular night, and I was thinking how much I needed my mother. If I could only be in her arms, everything would be all right. But that was impossible. I didn't know where Mother was or if she was even alive.

I felt completely alone.

Through a relative, Grandmother acquired little Alfred's clothes for me, and they didn't even have to be altered. But it felt very strange to wear them—the jackets and pants and the high-top laced boots.

I had been living with Grandmother for about a year and a half when a schoolmate came to me where I was playing in the yard. "Jack," he said, "your mother is waiting up the road. She wants to see you, and she has a gift for you." I couldn't believe this was really my mother! Had she come back to take me with her and away from my mean grandmother? I hadn't seen her since the breakup, and I had no idea where she was living, but she was forever on my mind. I knew if Grandmother was aware that Mother was anywhere near, she would lock me in my room immediately. I was afraid, but nothing in this world would keep me from going to my mother. I ran up the dirt road as fast as I could go, and sure enough, Mother was waiting for me with open arms. She was dressed so pretty and looked so beautiful. She grabbed me in her arms and kissed me, and I don't know who was crying more—her or me. But for sure they were happy tears.

Mother took a small package from her purse and told me to unwrap it. This was better than any Christmas could ever be. It was a pretty brown belt with a beautiful silver buckle on it—the first belt or buckle I'd ever seen. I was really thrilled. She showed me how it buckled and said, "Jack, whenever you wear it, always remember that my love is with you." Then she explained why I could not come to live with her at the present time, as I had been placed with Grandmother by order of the court. She told me not to mention her visit to Grandmother and she would keep in touch with me somehow. She kissed me good-bye, and I watched her as she walked away and disappeared up the old dirt road. I was so homesick that night that I couldn't stop crying and didn't sleep a wink.

I was proud of my belt and buckle, but I didn't dare wear it, because if Grandmother saw it, she would question me as to where it came from. So I hid it in the barn. Every chance I got, I'd sneak out, put it on, and wear it before I left for school. But I became afraid that Grandmother would see where I'd hid it, so I eventually put it in a little box and hid it in the woods on my way to school. When no one was looking, I'd sneak into the woods, get the belt, and put it on. I really thought I was a big shot. I'd say to myself, "Mother gave me this belt and she loves me. Someday I will go live with her again." That became my burning desire.

I learned that Mother had a job in Liverpool, located about two miles from Brooklyn. She was working as a live-in housekeeper for a Mr. Balcom, a kind gentleman, as I would later find out. He was about eighty years old and was still running his livery stable. He had established a good business over the years. Every day Mr. Balcom or his drivers would meet the trains that ran between Halifax and Yarmouth. They would transport passengers to and from the station in rubber-tired buggies, and they would pick up and deliver suitcases and trunks with their freight wagons.

Mother had warned me never to come to her place. She was afraid they would put me in a reform school since I was not supposed to see her. But one Saturday afternoon I felt I just had to see her again. So I walked the railroad tracks from Brooklyn to Liverpool, feeling confident that no one would see me, since there were woods between the tracks and the highway. Besides, there wasn't much traffic on the roads in those days. If Grandmother did question me when I got back, I'd simply say I was playing with my friends down at the wharf. Oh, I'd get a beating, but it would be worth it to see Mother again.

After searching for a long time, I finally found Mr. Balcom's house, and when I knocked on the door, Mother was so surprised. "Jack, what are you doing here? Don't you know you'll get in trouble?" But I could see beyond her words. Her eyes sparkled, and I knew she was glad to see me. It was the first time I'd seen her since the day she gave me the cherished belt and buckle.

I also met Guy White, her boyfriend. He was kind and very friendly. He made me feel special, and I liked him right away. Guy lived a few miles up the road from Mother and visited her quite often. That afternoon I just enjoyed their company and wished it would never end.

About eight o'clock that night, after Mother had fixed us a delicious meal and a dessert, she said, "Well, dear, we'll drive you back to your grandmother's house. I'm afraid she'll have a search party out looking for you, and this could cause both you and me a lot of trouble."

I watched as Guy harnassed up one of Mr. Balcom's horses and hitched up the rubber-tired buggy, and we were soon on our way. But before we reached Brooklyn, the horse got too far over on the side of the graveled road in the darkness and turned the buggy half over in the ditch. Mother had her hand outside the buggy, holding one of the braces that supported the buggy top, and her arm was caught between the buggy post and the bank. It's a wonder she didn't break her arm. But you know, the poor old horse seemed to know what had happened, as he stood there very still and waited until Guy finally got the buggy back on the road again.

They left me off a short distance from Grandmother's house. Mother kissed me good-bye and said we would get together again as soon as it was legally possible.

As they drove away, I started thinking about the beating I'd get when I walked into the house. Now, I could have gone to the door and knocked, and Grandmother would have let me in, but I had funny ways about approaching her, so I decided I'd go down into the cellar until I got up enough courage to go to the door. You entered the cellar from the outside of the house, through two big doors that opened upward. The cellar had a mud floor, and I spent the whole night in that damp, cold cellar. I was chilled to the bone and didn't sleep a wink all night. I was so hungry the next morning that I feasted on apples that Grandmother had put in barrels and stored away for the winter. I went into the house the next morning scared to death, but for some strange reason I didn't get a beating. Perhaps my grandfather had told Grandmother not to beat me for going to see my own mother. I don't know.

Anyway, I made a vow to myself that nothing—I mean absolutely nothing—would ever prevent me from going to see Mother again. These visits continued every week. Grandmother knew I was going to disappear on Saturday afternoon, and I usually got a beating when I returned. She was the only person I can remember who ever called me "Clarence" at that time, and I felt like I was a total stranger to her as she lectured me over and over again. Questions about my disappearances seemed endless, but she finally accepted the fact that she couldn't control me, and she stopped locking me in my room or even asking me where I went on Saturdays. She knew where I was, and the beatings continued, but I never gave her the satisfaction of admitting where I'd been.

Leaving Grandmother's and going to see Mother was like leaving hell and going into heaven.

By the summer of 1925 Mr. Balcom had moved into a larger home with an extra bedroom and a huge cellar. His health had been steadily failing, so he sold his white cottage home and livery stable, except for one horse and buggy, and Mother continued keeping house for him.

It was around this time that I started doing something very weird. I don't understand it. Maybe a psychologist would. I began to feel a sense of love—even if I was in the same town with Mother. Even if I wasn't at Mother's place, I could feel her love just as long as I was in Liverpool, where she lived.

After my Saturday visits Guy would borrow Mr. Balcom's horse and buggy, and he and Mother would drive me back to Grandmother's place. But just as soon as they were out of sight, I'd walk the railroad tracks again and head back to Liverpool. Sometimes I'd get back to her place before they did. I'd lift the big double doors from the outside (just like at Grandmother's place), and I'd crawl down into the dark cellar. It also had a mud floor, and it was just as cold and damp as Grandmother's cellar, but I would manage to get a little sleep in spurts.

One night shortly after I entered the cellar, it became so cold that I went outside and got a pole from the clothes line to reach up to Mother's upstairs bedroom window. I scratched on the window to get her attention, and it's a wonder she didn't have a heart attack. No matter what weird things I did, she would always put on her gown and come down, and I'd be standing there very shy and sorry for scaring her.

Another time I beat on the washtub in the cellar to get Mother's attention. If Mr. Balcom had not been in the house, I guess she would have panicked. No matter what I did, Mother was always kind to me. I think she well understood what I was going through to be with her. My little bed was always ready for me. I could never go to sleep, though, until she sat on the side of my bed and we talked for a while. Then she would kiss me goodnight, tuck me in, put out my light, and I'd be asleep in no time.

You might know that I could hardly wait for the weekends. Well, I began doing a stupid thing. I started playing hookey from school so I could go see Mother during the weekdays. She would say things like, "Oh, Jack, what am I going to do with you? People will blame me for keeping you away from school and harboring you. This could make for a lot of trouble, or they may put you in a reform school."

Mother had often talked to me about the importance of a good education and planning for my future. She knew at Grandmother's house I could get proper physical care, and she was praying that things would eventually work out for me to stay with her. She never criticized Grandmother, at least in front of me, but she also knew that kids need love, and she was caught in the middle.

Nevertheless, these visits got more frequent, and some weeks I'd go see Mother almost every day. Usually I'd follow the tracks to Liverpool, but sometimes for kicks I'd steal someone's rowboat and row across the Mersey River to the shore on the other side. It would only be a short walk of about a mile to Mother's house. When I was ready to go back to Grandmother's, Guy and Mother would drive me to where the boat was left and watch me row to the other side to make sure I made it okay. Rowing could be quite dangerous, so I'd only take this chance in the summer weather.

One day I stole a sailboat. Since I'd seen other people sail, I thought it would be easy, but I really knew nothing about sailing. The heavy mast, which held the sail, had to be lifted up and set in a certain place. I struggled but finally managed that. When I started out, there was a good breeze blowing, but when I got about halfway out in the middle of the river, the winds began blowing much stronger. I was really frightened when the sail started flapping and the boat drifted toward a rocky shore in a small settlement called Sandy Cove. I pulled the boat up on the beach as far as I could get it, but I couldn't find anything to tie it to, so I just rolled a big rock over the tie rope, or painter, and left it there. The next day I discovered that the storm had broken the boat in a million pieces on the big rocks. Worse yet, and being my luck, the boat was owned by Howard Godfrey, who was a close relative of my grandfather. Grandfather, bless his heart, saved me by paying the thirty dollars to replace the boat. And I wondered how he convinced my grandmother not to send me away to reform school.

When I didn't sleep overnight in Liverpool, I'd head for Grandmother's cellar. But sometimes the cellar doors would be locked, and instead of waking Grandmother up and getting another beating, I'd sleep on the floor of the outside toilet. During real cold nights, I felt like I was almost freezing to death.

To be in the same town as Mother, sometimes I'd stay in Mr. Balcom's cellar. Most of the time I slept wherever I could find some protection from the rain or the cold. Often, when it was freezing cold, I'd walk to the tiny Canadian National railroad station in Liverpool, and I'd go inside where it was warm and I'd sleep on one of the benches.

One night on my way to Mother's house, a heavy rain came, and I was wearing a thin sweater over my shirt and a thin pair of knee pants. Plus, I was barefooted. I climbed into the middle of a thorn hedge that ran along the edge of the sidewalk. I pulled my sweater up over my head and doubled my knees up, in a fetal position, and the leaves kept some of the rain off me. But I had to be careful how I moved, and I can't understand how I got in the hedge without putting my eyes out or getting serious scratches. I was so tired that I got some sleep, even though I was in that cramped position. The pounding of feet of the people passing by on the way to work the next morning woke me up, and no one even noticed me in the hedge.

On another night it started to rain while I was in Liverpool. The rain got heavier, and I took cover at a sawmill. This time I was really in a dangerous place. The mill had a huge pile of lumber to dry out, and in the middle of the pile there was a space about three feet by three feet. This was done so the lumber would dry on the inside of the pile. So I crawled into the small space, and although there was a cold draft coming through the opening, I managed to get some sleep through the night. I was awake early the next morning, and when I left the lumber pile, I noticed something that nearly took my breath away. The lumber pile had a very bad slant to the one side, and if it had fallen in the night those tons of lumber would have crushed me to death! My heart started beating really fast just thinking about the whole thing.

One cold winter night Mother and Guy drove me to Grandmother's in a sleigh pulled by one of Mr. Balcom's horses. The moonlight glistened on the snow, and the sleigh bells were ringing. It was a typical winter night. Again I walked back to Liverpool along the old faithful railroad tracks. This time I went to the local bowling alley, hoping to go inside and warm myself, but since I was underage, I couldn't go in. I went to the back of the building, where there was a window open to let the cigarette smoke out, and I leaned in the window. This gave me much-needed heat from the inside. I was warm, but not for long, as the bowling alley closed at 11:00 P.M. Again I was out in the cold. Imagine this, friends: With a warm bed at Grandmother's and Mother's, why was I going through such an ordeal?

When the place closed I did another daring thing. I went back to the sawmill and climbed inside near a huge three-feet-wide saw. There was a big pile of sawdust under the saw. I squeezed in back of the saw to half lie down on the sawdust floor. This left me pressed against the saw teeth, where I fell asleep. If I had been sleeping when the mill started the next morning, the saw would have caught in my sweater and I would have been cut in two.

During one June night after my visit, I went back to Mother's house and noticed that the front door was partially opened, but the screen door, which let the summer breeze blow through the house, was hooked. It was about 11:00 P.M., and I knew Mother would be in bed. I could see through the dining room and into the kitchen, where Mr. Balcom was reading his newspaper. He was sitting at an angle with his back to the door, and he couldn't see me. In the dining room was a huge cabinet, like a china closet that held shelves with glasses and dishes. On the bottom of the cabinet were two doors that opened out, where Mother kept tablecloths, napkins, and odds and ends. I was very tired and sleepy, so I wanted to try my idea. I put a small straw through the screen door and unhooked the hook. I crept inside, and since old Mr. Balcom was hard of hearing, he didn't hear what was taking place. I hooked the door behind me and tiptoed to the china closet. I opened the cabinet doors, crawled inside, and slept in the cabinet, curled up like a ball.

The next day Mother went out to a small garden in front of the house. When I heard her shut the door behind her, I crawled out of the cabinet. Then I went to the door, and to get her attention I scratched on the screen door. Can you imagine how she must have felt when she saw me standing inside? "We took you home last night, Jack, and I know that screen door was locked. How in the world did you get in? Do you know this almost gave me a heart attack?" It was spooky. She thought I was a ghost, and I felt sorry for scaring her.

You can see that as a kid I did a lot of crazy things just to be near my mother.

2

Nobody's Child

I'm nobody's child, I'm nobody's child,
I'm like a flower just growing wild.
No mommy's kisses and no daddy's smile,
Nobody wants me, I'm nobody's child.

"Nobody's Child," by Cy Coben and Mel Foree

AS THE MONTHS WENT BY, THE CONFLICT between Grandmother and me got even worse. She locked me in my room. She wouldn't let me play with the other children. She beat me, and she lectured me about what a bad woman my mother was. She tried so hard to turn me against my own mother that I couldn't stand to look at Grandmother. She made it perfectly clear that the divorce was strictly my mother's fault and not my dad's. Actually, my sisters and I never did know what caused the breakup between our parents. I don't remember either one of them stepping out on the other. They just couldn't get along. Maybe the big problem was Dad's mother constantly brainwashing him to the point that he turned against Mother. That's the only answer I have.

Grandmother's next method was to try to get the courts to send me to a reform school, since she considered me to be completely unruly. She even had me put in jail. Can you believe that? I was scarcely ten years old, and I had run away again and was at Mother's house. On a Saturday afternoon about 1:00 P.M. George Wright, the town policeman, came for me. Officer Wright was a scary-looking character who wore the typical blue suit, the cap, and the badge. He had a big black mustache, and he looked like one of the Keystone Kops in the silent movies. He came to the door and said, "Mrs. Snow, I'm George Wright, police officer, and I'm here to take the boy. The boy's grandmother has been after us a dozen times because the boy is not going to school. I have been advised to put your son in jail until his grandfather comes for him."

Mother fell apart. She cried, and she pleaded with the policeman. But he took me anyway. He put me on the handlebars of his bicycle and I went to jail. I sat in jail about four hours until Grandfather came to get me. Jail was no deterrent. If anything, it made me worse. I hated my grandmother, and I felt so bad for poor Grandfather having to face this embarrassment. I know according to the Bible that we're not supposed to hate anyone, and I probably should not use the word "hate," but that's exactly the way I felt. I don't believe that woman is in heaven. She tried to keep me from seeing my own mother, whom I dearly loved. I believe what Grandmother did was strictly against the Good Book.

Well, the day finally came when the courts told Grandmother, "Mrs. Godfrey, we've done all we can do. The boy doesn't deserve to be sent to a reform school. He loves his mother very much, and he should be with her. It's a sin for us to go any further with this problem."

Boy, I was the happiest person in the whole world! Love had finally won out. I remember Grandmother putting my clothes in a burlap bag, and I ran all the way to Liverpool. No words under heaven could describe the beautiful expression on Mother's face when she knew I was free. Leaving my grandmother had been my nightly dream for almost three years. Dreams really do come true!

I moved in with Mother and Mr. Balcom. Within a very short time, though, Mr. Balcom's health began to fail. He moved in with some of his relatives, and his house was sold.

In the meantime, Lillian, my oldest sister, had met Wilbert Risser. Wilbert was a fisherman, and they dated only a few months when he asked her to marry him. Drifting around as she had done, following our parents' divorce, I guess she was glad to say yes, if only for security reasons. She did some investigating as to his character, and on the surface he seemed okay. I later learned that the Risser family were fine people, but out of a large family of mostly boys it seemed that Wilbert was the black sheep.

After living with Mother for a few months, Lillian invited Mother and me to come live with Wilbert and her as soon as they could get married and find a place to live. The timing was good, since the new owner of Mr. Balcom's house was anxiously waiting to move in. A few weeks later we got the word to come to Lunenburg for the wedding. Mother and I took the train to Lunenburg from Liverpool, and Lillian met us at the station. To save the price of a taxi, we walked to Wilbert's family home, where the wedding was to take place. Wilbert had hired Teemy Thompson, who owned one of the few cars in town, and after a very brief ceremony he took Lillian, Wilbert, Mother, and me for a ride in his big new car. This was really a treat. We came back and had a nice lunch that Mother had made, and that was the end of what was called a honeymoon.

The next day we proceeded to our new home, about five miles from Lunenburg. What little furniture the newlyweds had was sent on ahead in a small truck. The house looked like an old square box, and it was located in a little village that had two names. Some called it Black Rocks and some called it Stonehurst. I can see where it got the names, because it was an area with a whole lot of rocks. It had a population of about fifty families scattered throughout the village. The crumbly old house was built on top of a cliff on a big flat rock with barren space all around, except for a little cove that ran up to the back of the house. That flat rock served as a foundation for the weather-beaten house, which was the coldest damn house I had ever been in! Sleeping in the cold damp cellar, hedges, and sawmills was much better.

I'll bet the old place had been built by pioneers at least a hundred years earlier. It had two bedrooms upstairs, a small kitchen, a living room, and one bedroom downstairs. Everything was falling apart, and it was truly a rat trap. Many of the windows were broken, and you could see outdoors in several places through the cracks in the walls. My bedroom was upstairs on the north side of the house, where the cold north wind whistled around the corners and blew right through the cracks and into my bones. There was no bed. I slept on an old broken-down couch, which had been left there by whoever moved out of the house a long time before we moved in. The one leg was broken, so it was sitting on a slant. It had holes in the cloth top, and one of the old coil springs stuck up through the top. The only bedclothes I had were mat rags—old rags that people used for hooking rugs—and old coats and sweaters. Many nights I lay in bed shivering and wishing the morning would soon come before I froze to death.

About this time, I learned that my grandparents had moved to a small town in Massachusetts. I'm speaking about the Godfreys, the kind old gentleman who was married to the meanest woman in the world. Grandfather had two daughters. Blanche lived in Massachusetts and Irene still lived in Brooklyn. I referred to each of them as "aunt."

One day Mother got a letter from Aunt Irene saying that Aunt Blanche wanted me to come live with her and her husband, just outside of Boston. Aunt Blanche and Aunt Irene were wonderful ladies, and everybody thought this would be a great opportunity for me to live in the United States. That might have been okay, but my grandmother lived there with them, too, so I didn't cherish the idea.

By this time I knew that Wilbert did not want me around. It had been Lillian's idea in the first place for Mother and me to live with them. He had two more mouths to feed, and living in that dump made matters worse. He turned his anger on me, and I received a daily dose of his filthy language and his constant complaining about having to feed me. I helped out all I could by doing a lot of chores around the house, running errands, cutting firewood for the stove, and washing the wooden floors for Mother. Mother was busy trying to fix the old place up to look like something.

Mother and I discussed Aunt Blanche's offer for several days, and we agreed that I'd never amount to anything staying in Stonehurst. We talked about me getting a good education and learning a trade to make a good living. When I had the money, I could come back to Canada and make Mother a good home. We had big dreams—both of us. We made up our minds and advised Aunt Irene that I was ready to make the big move. The plan was for me to walk the five miles from Stonehurst to Lunenburg and board the train for Brooklyn. Aunt Irene had mailed me the ticket, and she was to meet me at the train station. She would put me on the train to Yarmouth, Nova Scotia, and give me a ticket to go aboard the steamer leaving for Boston.

I'll never forget the morning I left Mother, not knowing whether we would ever see each other again. It reminded me of the sad moment when Dad told me good-bye, and I didn't know if I'd see him again. I was outside, almost ready to leave, when she said, "Aren't you forgetting something?" I remembered immediately. Mother had had several pictures taken a couple of years earlier, and among them was an enlarged one that was my favorite of all. "Oh, yes," I said, "my picture!" Mother went inside and got it for me. She had wrapped it in brown paper and tied it with twine, and she handed me my special twelve-by-fourteen framed picture. We both cried. Leaving that morning was, I guess, the hardest thing for both of us that we had ever experienced. Oh, how I hated to leave her. She kissed me good-bye, and I walked across the field, out to the main road of mud and gravel, with her picture under one arm and an old beat-up suitcase, tied with a piece of rope, under the other arm. I was only a kid, on my way to another country, leaving my mother and wondering what the future would bring.

As planned, Aunt Irene was at the Brooklyn station to meet the train. I went to her house and spent the night. The next morning she took me back to the station, and I boarded the train to Yarmouth.

When I arrived there, a friend of Aunt Irene's was waiting for me at the station. It was about 7:00 P.M. in the fall of the year, so it was dark and quite cold. Snow on the ground had turned partly to slush and made walking difficult. There were holes in the bottom of my shoes, and my feet were soaked and freezing. Since we had an hour before the passenger steamer would leave for the overnight trip, Aunt Irene's friend took me downtown to a shoe store and bought me a pair of stockings and a pair of rubbers to cover my shoes. I changed my soaking-wet socks, and the warm socks certainly did feel good. These were bought out of the money Aunt Irene had given me to buy food on the boat. The rubbers cost one dollar and the socks cost twenty-five cents.

My aunt's friend took me down to the passenger steamer to Customs and Immigration, where we were startled to learn that I was too young to travel by myself. I was not twelve years old yet, and the immigration laws were such that any child under twelve couldn't travel unless accompanied by a parent or a relative. So the gentleman had no choice but to drive me back to his house, where I spent the night. I was really happy, though, since I didn't want to go in the first place. The next day the gentleman called Aunt Irene to explain the situation, and I took the train back to Brooklyn, where my aunt met me at the station. I gave her the train ticket so she could get a refund, and the following day, I boarded the train to Lunenburg and walked the five miles back to Stonehurst.

Was I glad to see Mother again! It seemed like I had been gone to the other end of the world for a year. Mother was just as glad to see me and said, "Everything happens for the best, Jack." And I never forgot that philosophy.

Mother and I continued to live with Lillian and Wilbert, but life for me got worse, not better. Shortly after I returned, Charles Enos Tanner, a friend and working partner of Wilbert's, came into the picture. He dropped by one Sunday afternoon and invited all of us to go for a ride in his boat. It was just an ordinary small fishing boat with a motor and small cabin-like structure built up on the bow to protect you from harsh weather. Before the afternoon was over, I noticed that Charlie and Mother became quite close in their conversation. It wasn't long until they began dating, and Charlie started hanging around the house quite often. Although I didn't know it then, this was to be the worst thing that could ever happen to me.

Charlie was about five feet nine and weighed around 170 pounds. He was big boned with ham-like hands, and when he looked at me with his jet-black eyes, he scared the hell out of me.

About two or three times that year, Guy White came to see Mother. I heard Guy plead with her to come back to Liverpool and marry him, and he would make a good home for the three of us. But I guess Charlie had his clutches in too deep, because Guy could never persuade her to go with him. I really felt bad for Guy, as he and Mother were a perfect couple, and he was so good to me. The difference between Charlie Tanner and Guy White was the difference between night and day. Charlie was a highly ignorant person with no schooling. He couldn't write his own name and had to mark an *X* as his signature. Guy White had class. He was a kind, sensitive, and handsome gentleman.

The old saying is "Love is strange." How true!

George Whynot came into the picture not long after Mother started dating Charlie. He was the captain of an ocean liner—a passenger ship that sailed to the Caribbean, France, Italy, and other interesting places. Mother met him one day when she and Lillian were shopping. After a few casual meetings the captain told Mother, "If you'll come with me, I'll gladly show you my credentials, and you can investigate me in any way you choose. I'll be glad to take your son with me, and if he desires, I'll teach him a career in navigation and help him mature into a fine young man."

I'd like to know how my life would have turned out had Mother married either Captain Whynot or Guy White, or if I had boarded that ship and gone to Boston. God only knows. The Good Lord laid out the master plan for me, and He knew exactly where I was going. But I suppose if He wanted me to know, He would have told me.

For reasons unknown to me and beyond my comprehension, Mother liked Charlie Tanner. Maybe it was because they were thrown together by circumstances. He lived about a mile and a half away from us and owned the fishing boat that he and Wilbert used for their livelihood. When they were not on the boat, they were at the house talking about silly things that only they could understand. They constantly used the Lord's name in vain with filthy talk and would fire crude slurs at me. Many nights I lay upstairs on the old broken couch and heard Charlie and Wilbert making fun of me. They were two of a kind.

With Charlie it was hate at first sight. Every time he looked at me, I could feel his jet-black eyes piercing right through me. The first time he yelled at me was when I walked through the kitchen as he was talking to Mother. I stopped to ask her a question and he suddenly yelled, "Get the hell out of here. Don't you see we're talking?" I saw the fire in his eyes. Mother tried to correct him, but it made no difference. From that day on, I tried to keep out of his way as much as I could.

It wasn't long before Charlie began spending the night and staying around for meals, and I noticed he watched every mouthful I ate. I'd always take small portions of food and never ask for a second helping. He made me feel like a stranger who had no right to live there. I was even afraid to reach for a piece of bread. I was constantly under severe tension. I couldn't understand how someone as kind and as beautiful as Mother could be attracted to such an idiot. Maybe she thought if they got married she could change him, and after they were married, perhaps she could have both Nina and Marion released from their foster homes and we could become a family again.

Moving from Grandmother's house and moving in with Wilbert was like "jumping from the frying pan into the fire." I thought Grandmother was bad, but she was a saint compared to the treatment I got daily from Wilbert and Charlie. I was constantly called "little bastard," "son of a bitch," and other names too filthy to put in print. I'm sure Charlie was trying to force me to leave home. I didn't want to hate him so much, as I always believed it was against the Bible to do so, but I just couldn't stop this burning fury I felt toward him.

Charlie was extremely jealous of Mother whenever I was near. He wanted her undivided attention at all times. During the day Charlie, especially, would make me feel guilty by saying over and over again, "Why in the hell don't you get out and find a job somewhere? You're too damn lazy. All you want to do is hang around the house and eat up the food. If you had any respect for your mother you'd go to work." Now, can you imagine a man telling a frail twelve-year-old boy to go find a job? He knew that was impossible. Canada was going through a severe depression, and there were not many jobs available even for skilled and robust men, let alone an eighty-pound boy in poor health. Charlie wanted Mother, but he sure wanted no part of me.

During this time Mother saw an advertisement in a magazine for a Hawaiian guitar. Along with the instrument you would receive fifty-two free lessons accompanied by 78 rpm gramophone records. You could put these records on the old Victrola, wind it up, and play the guitar right along with the records. Mother ordered the guitar, and in a few weeks it came through the mail. She really prized that instrument. I think it helped to relieve her tension, because when she was upset, she'd take out the guitar to play and sing. I loved her voice and the beautiful music she played. But Mother gave me strict orders never to touch her guitar, and I think it was months before she would even let me pick it up. However, every once in a while when she was gone, I'd sneak it out of the case and fool around with it. I'd always put it back, though, before she found out.

In time, Mother let me try my hand with it, and she was fascinated by the various sounds that I could get from the instrument. I used the regular Hawaiian steel bar, and I'd slide it up and down over the strings to get different chords and tones. As I played, Mother's eyes would light up and she used to say, "Jack, I think you have a good ear for music, and I believe you'll be a professional singer someday, as well as a good guitar player." I sure loved those compliments! She told me she didn't mind me getting the guitar out once in a while to practice as long as I didn't play it when Charlie was around and provided, of course, that I'd take good care of it.

After I mastered a few chords and a few songs, she would sometimes ask me to play and sing something special for her, and she'd always praise me. Later on she said, "If you want to play and sing when Charlie's around, I don't see why he should say anything. I'd like to see what happens. But don't play it after he goes to bed because he has to get up early each morning." When I had gotten pretty good with the guitar, I was excited when I got it out to play for Charlie, but he sure put an end to that real fast. "It's a wonder you don't do something that's going to make you a living. Or do you plan living off someone else all your life?" I should have known that was the kind of response I'd get from him.

One night Mother let me take her guitar over to our neighbors, Mr. and Mrs. Demone, and I sang and played for them. They were very pleased and clapped for me in a big way. They gave me cookies and their comments gave me a big lift, particularly after Charlie's remarks. The word soon got around the neighborhood, and I was being invited out somewhere just about every night.

So it was through Mother's mail-order guitar that I became interested in music, God bless her. Looking back now, maybe Mother bought the guitar for me, thinking that music would help me endure the frustrations in a house that could never be a home. I wonder.

No matter what I did or what Mother did or said, there was no way I could escape the Tanner punishment. For no good reason he would twist my frail arms and hit me with his fists. Many times he knocked me on my back onto the bare floor. Then one day I heard of a possible way out of this violent situation. Someone told me about a job one of his friends got aboard a fishing schooner sailing out of Lunenburg. The job didn't pay anything, but he said you got the best of food and a clean, dry bed to sleep in. When I heard this, I immediately fantasized about escaping to sea and getting away from Charlie and Wilbert's constant torture. Maybe I would even become a captain someday and earn enough money to buy a big house for Mother and reunite all the family. I would save Mother from Charlie!

I began asking a lot of questions. I found out that a fishing vessel usually carries a crew of twenty-two men, plus a flunky (also called a cabin boy). A flunky is a young boy who does a variety of jobs aboard the ship in addition to his many chores for the cook and captain. When he has the time, the flunky can fish on his own off the deck and sell whatever he catches when the vessel gets back into port from the fishing trip. This all sounded good to me. But was I old enough and strong enough to handle the work? Would a captain hire me as a flunky?

In the middle of my problems and my thoughts about the fishing idea, I received a tragic blow. One afternoon, when I noticed that Charlie and Wilbert had not gone fishing that day, I knew something unusual was about to take place. Mother and Charlie had put on their best clothes and hired one of the two cabs in the little village of Bluerocks. Lillian told me, as the taxi pulled away, they had gone to get married. I didn't want to believe it. I hoped Lillian was wrong, or maybe Mother would change her mind at the last minute before doing such a foolish thing. If she were going to get married, I knew she would have told me, but the only thing she said before they left was, "We won't be gone too long. I'll see you all later."

They returned late that night, but nothing was said about marriage. About a week later Mother told me they had been married by a justice of the peace. I was upset but tried not to show it. I only asked one question. "Mother, why didn't you marry Guy White?" She didn't answer.

I had acquired a stepfather, but I knew he would never be any real father to me. I wished many times that I had never laid eyes on him. I tried to avoid him at all costs. I tried not to speak to him because he would go into a fit over most anything. His fanatical rages got more frequent, and during these times I'd leave the house and sneak back in after he was in bed, so I wouldn't have to see him.

Mother was always like herself when Charlie was away. She could tell lots of interesting stories about us kids before the family broke up—some funny and some sad. And I'd say or do things to make her and Lillian laugh at me. Certain things were funny to us, but others might not see any humor in them. I treasured those moments. But when Charlie came in, everything would get deathly quiet.

Mother was crushed every time Charlie cursed or hit me. She'd lash out at him, but this didn't do any good. She tried to be the peacemaker in these difficult situations, and she even threatened to leave him if he continued his attacks on me. She did leave him on a couple of occasions, but after she married him, it was not so easy to walk away.

During this time Mother's health was deteriorating, and she began getting mysterious seizures. I'll never forget the first time I saw her in one of those spells. One day I came into the house and couldn't find her, so I dashed upstairs and was shocked to see her lying on the bed. Her eyes were wide open, but she wasn't moving. She was staring straight ahead, and I thought she was dead. Charlie was sitting on the side of the bed by her, white as a sheet. He kept slapping Mother on the face trying to get her to talk. Suddenly she went limp and it seemed like she wasn't breathing. Then all of a sudden she started taking cold chills, and her whole body began to shake beyond anything I had ever seen. I could even hear her teeth chatter. She managed to ask for blankets, and I ran through the house grabbing blankets, coats, anything I could find to keep her warm. She continued to shake. I was scared to death. After about fifteen minutes of these chills and horrible shaking, Mother's body went limp, and again I thought she was dead. Charlie began slapping her again to snap her out of it. The doctor told us later that if he hadn't done this, she would not have survived, because each time her body went limp, her heart had stopped beating.

These spells continued off and on. The doctor told us they were caused by stress and nerves. He said the spells could happen anytime, and they could get worse, or she might not even survive them. He did emphasize the importance of slapping her face and shaking her when this condition occurred. The doctor called these unusual spells "ague chills." He explained that the most important thing we could do to help her was to reduce any family conflicts. This was easier said than done. If he had only known the situation between Charlie and me, he would have had the answer right there.

These spells scared the hell out of me. I could almost tell when one was coming on, and I'd immediately leave the house and walk and pray to God that Mother would be alive when I got back home. I felt guilty, thinking that I was the cause of the stressful turmoil, and if something were to happen to Mother, I'd have to live with this the rest of my life. I tried real hard after her first seizure to get along with Charlie, but when I'd speak to him in a pleasant voice, he would have nothing to do with me except to say something like, "Why don't you get the hell away from here and leave us alone? Don't you care about your mother?"

All of this was helping me make up my mind to get away somewhere, somehow. I would try to get a job on one of the fishing schooners. But if I couldn't, where could I go?

A few days later I headed to Lunenburg to see about signing on as a flunky. I walked around all afternoon just looking at the many schooners and checking the storefronts. I was really impressed by the big signs I saw on the buildings, such as Zwicker and Co., W. C. Smith & Co., Robin, Jones, and Whitman Supplies, Scott Corkum Co., and Adams and Knickle. These were outfitting companies that owned the vessels and supplied the crews with a complete line of foods and equipment for their fishing expeditions. As I looked up at the big signs, I thought about the stories I'd heard concerning these companies and schooners. The cook ordered an abundance of food from the firms to make sure there was plenty for all the fishermen. Fishing gear was provided for each man, plus enough coarse salt to salt down the summer's catch as the fish were cleaned and stored in the hold of the vessel.

As I thought about all of this, I said to myself, "What do I know about the sea? How could a frail twelve-year-old boy do the job of a grown man?" I knew it would be scary leaving home, not knowing what lay ahead. I decided to go back home and forget about the whole idea, at least for now. But with a cursing from Charlie as soon as I got in the door, raising hell because I hadn't cut up any wood for the kitchen stove, I changed my mind. This gave me renewed courage to go back to Lunenburg and try desperately to get a job on a schooner.

I felt I had no other choice.

3

First-Class Flunky

There's a place I'll always cherish 'neath the blue Atlantic skies,
Where the shores down in Cape Breton bid the golden sun to rise.
And the fragrance of the apple blossom sprays the dew-kissed lawn
Back in dear old Nova Scotia, the place where I was born.

"My Nova Scotia Home,"
by Hank Snow

THE NEXT MORNING I GOT UP EARLY and walked back to Lunenburg. After making several inquiries about some of the vessels, I got a job as a flunky aboard the *Grace Boehner.* (Sometimes these ships are called vessels and other times schooners. Either term is correct.) The captain was Lapene Crouse, a big, kind-looking man. He told me to go to the store and get fitted out for the trip and to be ready to sail Monday morning.

That night I hardly slept. I was excited about going aboard the big vessel and somewhat worried, knowing I'd be among complete strangers. Although I didn't know it at the time, my sister Nina's future husband, Richard Tanner, was assigned to the same schooner. We called him "Ritchie." He was in no way related to Charlie Tanner. He was a friend of Wilbert and Charlie, and he came to the house now and then to chat. I took a liking to him the first time I saw him, and I believe the feeling was mutual. He called me "Jack," which made me feel closer to him. Later I heard he had spoken to Captain Crouse about me and indicated that he knew part of my family and would look out for me during the trip.

I hadn't mentioned going to sea as yet, but a few days later when Mother, Lillian, and I were alone I told them of my plans. Mother seemed shocked at first, but when I told her the name of the captain and the vessel she exclaimed, "Oh, Jack, that's the same sailing ship that Ritchie's going on. This makes me feel better, because I know Ritchie will see to it you receive good care." "Mother," I said, "I'll have good food and a warm place to sleep, and I'll be away from Charlie and Wilbert. I won't make any wages, but I was told that I can fish some of the time on my own, and I'll get to keep all the money I make from selling my fish."

I was really pleased when Mother reassured me, "It will be a great experience for you, Jack, and I'm really proud that you have the courage to try this new venture. A mother could never ask for a better son. You've already been through a lifetime of pain with both your grandmother and Charlie. I haven't been much help to you, but my prayers have been that God would strengthen you to help you endure all your hardships. In a way my prayers have been answered, because you have more determination than any person I've ever known. So, Jack, I won't interfere with your plans. If you want to go to sea, you have my blessings. My love and prayers will be with you every minute of every day." I should have known that Mother would make it easy for me, and I'll never forget her words of encouragement.

The next day I made the trip again to Lunenburg to get clothes for the trip. As I entered the store, I saw a clerk standing back of a long counter. I told him who I was and that I was going on the *Grace Boehner* as their flunky. I explained that this spring trip would last around five or six weeks, and we would be running into some very cold weather. "Oh, I know about all that," he said. "I'm just the man you need to see. I'll fit you out with exactly what's necessary." He collected clothes from the shelves and said, "Son, I'm giving you the smallest size we have. Everything will still be too big, but that's the best I can do." He handed me the clothes and wrote down the prices on paper and had me sign it. The total cost was a little over seventeen dollars. I was concerned that I might not make enough money to pay the bill, but I reasoned that if the company wasn't worried about it, why should I be.

I had long underwear, two flannel jackets, two pairs of heavy work pants, two pairs of woolen socks, one pair of rubber hip boots, a pair of oil pants with straps that went over my shoulders like overalls, an oil hat, an oil jacket, and two pairs of cotton gloves. The oil-treated material was like raincoat material that the crew and I would wear when dressing down the fish, whether rain or shine.

When I got home, I went upstairs to try everything on. Mother came in and couldn't stop laughing. My clothes were at least three sizes too big, and I must have looked real funny as I paraded around acting like a clown.

When I got up real early on Monday morning, both Charlie and Wilbert were gone, so that was a blessing. But it was hard telling Mother good-bye, not knowing how this adventure would work out.

And so it was that in 1926, at the age of twelve, I began an adventure at sea that would give me some of the happiest—and some of the most terrifying—times of my life.

As soon as we went aboard, Ritchie took me to meet the captain in his cabin. He was nice to me and said he hoped I'd enjoy life at sea, and he warned me about seasickness, since this was my first trip on the ocean. The crewmen were still loading supplies, and the captain said it would be late that afternoon before we could depart for the open sea.

I felt completely out of place, but I was anxious to learn everything possible about the vessel and the work of each crew member, so I walked around the deck watching every move the crew made. It was all so interesting to me, and I felt better when many of the men stopped and talked for a bit and tried to make me feel at home. They showed me the parts of the schooner and told me the nautical names that sailors always use. The front of the ship was called the forecastle, and about two-thirds of the ship's crew slept in that area. The galley (kitchen) was in the forecastle, and there was a long table the whole length of the forecastle where the fishermen ate their meals. The hold, midway in the schooner, held the cargo of fish as it was salted down daily. Another compartment held the supplies for the cook and our meals. Ice was kept in appropriate bins, and the coarse salt was stored in a separate compartment. The captain had a small private stateroom in the stern of the vessel, partitioned off from the main cabin where the remainder of the crew slept.

The *Grace Boehner* was like most of the other Lunenburg schooners. She was about 125 feet long, had no engines, and was powered by sails only. Only two or three vessels had a generator for electric lights. Most used kerosene lamps. The name of the sails were mainsail, foresail, jib, jumbo jib, and staysail. Maximum speed with a good sailing breeze was between twelve and fourteen knots. Each schooner usually carried seven dories and usually a crew of twenty-two men, which included the fishermen, captain, salter, cook, header, throater, and flunky. The crew came from many places in the province, and some from Newfoundland, which at that time was not a separate province of Canada but in later years became the tenth province. A few men were from neighboring villages close to Lunenburg.

The fishing schooners made three kinds of trips, depending on the season. The first was the frozen-bait trip, which began early in March and lasted about four weeks. Here only frozen herring for bait was used.

The second was the spring trip. It started in April and was about five to six weeks long. On this trip mostly frozen bait was used. But now and then the men got fresh bait in some of the ports. They used fresh or frozen herring and a small fish, like a sardine, called caplin.

The third was the summer trip. It was about three months long and called for mostly fresh bait. Every two weeks or so the crew would hoist the anchor and set sail for land. The port might be Sydney in Cape Breton or Canso or Queensport in Nova Scotia. The vessels usually stayed in port two or three days and then sailed back out to sea for another two or more weeks to look for another good fishing ground.

In the late afternoon, we were ready to get under sail for the spring trip. Since fishing schooners back then had no engines, a tugboat had to tow us from the wharf. Tom Nauss, the captain of a little tugboat named the *Mascot,* had this important job. He not only towed each vessel out to the open sea, he also had to meet each one at the entrance to the harbor when it arrived home, to dock it to the wharf. So he towed us out and then cast us off. We hoisted the ship's sails—and we were under way!

Soon the *Grace Boehner* was sailing on her own. It was just about dark, and Lunenburg was slowly disappearing in the dusk. There was no turning back. I guess the unknown is always frightening, and I remember thinking, "What are the dangers out in this vast ocean? If I can't do the job as flunky what will happen to me? Where will I live? How can I survive?" I watched the land fade in the distance. As the cold, lonely, dark night surrounded me, I became more homesick and wished I had never left home. At that time, I would have gladly taken the cruel punishment from Charlie Tanner, if only I could be back home with Mother. We were heading straight for the western fishing banks. As the schooner was tossed to and fro, I was beginning to feel a little nauseated, so I went to my bunk and turned in.

On the first morning at sea I was awakened by the men talking while they were getting dressed in their fishing clothes. They had finished breakfast, and it was only 4:30 in the morning. I was feeling much better after a good night's sleep. I jumped right out of bed and ate a big breakfast just like the other members of the crew. The breakfast table was long with a red and white checkered tablecloth, and it was loaded with fried eggs, bacon, biscuits, and anything you could imagine as breakfast food.

After breakfast I walked around on deck and talked to some of the crewmen. They told me about the fishing grounds, which were known to be the best in the world for codfish, haddock, and halibut. The captains usually fished on the western part of the Atlantic in the spring when the weather was cold and went to the Grand Banks off Newfoundland much of the time during the summer months.

There's a wide continental shelf that in some places extends hundreds of miles from the shore. Large areas of this shelf rise to form underwater plateaus called banks—the Grand Banks of Newfoundland, the Western Banks, and Quero Banks. The Grand Banks is still one of the best fishing spots in the entire world, and trawlers come there from many foreign countries, even Russia. It is composed of a five-hundred-mile stretch of shallow water off the southeast coast of Newfoundland. It curves in a two-hundred-mile area around the Newfoundland coast and extends as far as three hundred miles out into the Atlantic Ocean. The waters in these areas are as much as one thousand feet deep and are crowded with fish, especially the popular codfish. Other desirable fishing grounds are Cape North, which is off Cape Breton Island, Bonaventure Island around the Quebec coast, and St. Pierre and Miquelon islands between Nova Scotia and Newfoundland. Fishing ships from Gloucester, Boston, and other ports along the United States Atlantic coast come here.

After we had been under sail for thirty-six or more hours, we were on the Western Banks. A crewman threw the dipsey lead overboard to test the depth and the kind of ocean floor. This was a five-pound lead weight fastened to a lengthy, strong hemp line. The lead was countersunk on the bottom and filled with soap, to which the mud or gravel would stick. A graveled bottom indicated a good fishing area. Then the crew dropped the huge anchor. The sails were lowered, rolled up, and tied into place, and the triangular-shaped mutton or storm sail was raised. This sail helped steady the vessel in heavy seas or swells.

Fishing vessels out of Lunenburg followed similar trawl-line fishing procedures. The schooner would anchor, the crew would lower the dories into the water, and the fishermen would row out a certain distance to set the trawls. The dories were painted a light tan so they could be easily seen from the schooner when they were setting or hauling the trawl. It depended, of course, on whether there was fog or not—which there was most of the time. The dories were about twenty feet long, with seats and flat bottoms. When they were hoisted in, they were stacked on deck like drinking cups, one inside the other, and stored on each side of the schooner. Two men were assigned to each dory, which carried emergency supplies, such as a compass, flashlight, survival food in a sealed kit, two sets of oars, and most important, water. The dories had a small mast and sail that could be used to sail to and from the schooner. After the dories were hoisted over the side, the dress-down crew (except the captain) held the dory's rope, called a painter. One man would be down in the dory, and another would pass the trawl tubs down to him. It was rough trying to hold the dory lines with the vessel rocking and putting a strain on the lines, but it didn't take long until I could handle this job.

While the men were out with the dories, the captain called me aside on deck and explained my work as a flunky. "Your most important job will be to help the dress-down crew after the dories return each time with their catch. The dorymen will fork the fish onto the deck with a two-pronged pitchfork." The captain gestured with his hands as he explained. "You can see there are two bins or compartments, and they sit about three feet off the deck. You'll throw the fish in this first compartment. The throater will take the fish out. He'll hold them on the side of the bin and cut their throats, and he'll slit the fish down the belly almost to the tail. Then he'll slide the fish into the other compartment. The header will take the slit fish out, put them on the edge of the dressing table, and snap the heads off before sliding them across the table to me."

I was all ears as the captain continued. "I'll cut the backbones out and throw most of them overboard, but I'll save some from the larger fish, and later on I'll show you how to take the piece of skin from the backbone. These skins are called sounds. Son, these are a delicacy to some people. I like them myself. When they're fried in butter and bread crumbs, they are delicious. Next I'll slide the fish, which are now flat, into this huge tub. The salter will fork the fish down into the ship's hold from the tub, and then he'll go down inside the hold and salt the fish down. The salting procedure is like shingling a roof of a house. The salter puts a layer of coarse salt on top of a layer of fish and continues until all the fish are covered. This preserves the fish until the vessel gets back to the home port in Lunenburg." The captain also informed me that if I had time to cut out any fish tongues, I could sell them in port and keep the money.

Well, I knew I'd have to work fast in order to keep the throater's bin full of fish so it would not slow him down or slow the dress-down crew. As I was thinking about this, the dories came sailing toward the schooner, so the dress-down crew, including myself, put on our regular oilskin suits. The dories pulled alongside one by one, loaded with codfish so heavy they looked as if they might sink any minute. I thought to myself, "How in the world can I fork that many fish into the throater's bin and have any time to cut out the fish tongues, which is the only way I can make any money on the trip, except catching the fish off the deck?"

I struggled somewhat in the beginning. The deck was constantly slick from the fish lying all around and the vessel rocking and rolling. It was a real hassle. I'd fall down among the fish, get up, slide, and fall again. I know I was a funny sight in my much-too-big oil suit. The men sure got a big kick out of me, but actually I did quite well until I came to a really big codfish. The codfish were usually eighteen inches to four or five feet long. I couldn't handle the big fish by myself, so the throater would fork the big ones into the bin for me. My job wasn't as hard as I had expected, because the throater couldn't do his job very fast, and that gave me enough time to fill his bin. While he was preparing the fish for the header, I could cut the tongues out easily and quickly.

Since the fish tongues are a delicacy, the price for a regular-size bucketful was fifty cents. I'd put a big barrel on the deck and lash it down with a rope so it wouldn't turn over when the vessel rocked or was under sail. I discovered that if I could fill one barrel with tongues, and if I could catch a good amount of codfish off the deck of the vessel, I'd make a fair sum of money. Later on I was able to have extra time to do my own fishing. Whenever I caught fish, I'd tie a gangion line around their tail to mark them, then throw them into the hold of the vessel with the other fish. The salter would salt mine with the rest of them.

This first day turned out to be a good fishing day. The dories continued to come back loaded with fish, trip after trip. We were working until way after dark, dressing the fish down and salting them.

The men told me I had done well. I don't know how many fish I forked that first day, but it seemed like a million to me. When we were through, I went to my bunk in the bow of the ship and fell fast asleep and missed the evening meal. I didn't wake up until the loud bell rang the next morning. I believe I could have stayed in the bunk for a week. My whole body was just as sore as it could be, since I was not used to the hard work yet.

On the second day we all got up at the same time and went for breakfast. The cook had all the food hot and on the table, with huge pots of tea ready for us. When each man took his place, it looked like some big convention setting. I listened to the crew to learn all I could about sea life, and I was already feeling a closeness and acceptance that I had never felt before.

The cook served four meals every day except Sunday, when we had three meals. There were two sittings at each meal, since there were too many in the crew to all be seated at one time. After the first table gang finished, the cook would prepare for the next group. He knew exactly what he was doing and could clear the table and reset it in less than ten minutes. I had never eaten or even seen such fine food before in my whole life. In addition to the fish, we ate beef and pork. We were able to have fresh meat since we carried big blocks of ice in the bins of the ship. We had cream, excellent homemade pies, fruitcake, and canned fruits such as pears, bananas, and strawberries. There was a huge closet, called the snack locker, that the cook always kept full of food in case any of the crew wanted to snack between meals—which was quite often. This food was a treat from the usual bread and molasses I got at home!

After my first day at sea I pretty well knew the procedures. Each dory crew was responsible for laying out one trawl. These were not nets. We didn't do net fishing. Our trawls consisted of a main line, one mile long, with smaller lines attached, called gangions. They were about two feet in length and hung down from the main line, about six feet apart, with a regular codfish hook attached to the end. These lines were made from regular hemp. Altogether there were about seven miles of trawl.

The fishermen always followed a certain pattern so the trawls wouldn't get tangled up with each other. When setting them out, one dory started from the starboard or right bow and rowed straight out. Another rowed straight out from the port or left bow. Two more dories rowed out from the starboard and the port beam, that is, from the middle of the ship. The next two dories set out from the port and starboard rear quarters, and the seventh dory rowed straight out from the stern. This pattern looked like the spokes in a wagon wheel, with the schooner as the hub.

The trawls were usually started about a half mile from the schooner and extended out one mile. One doryman rowed while the other set the trawl. These lines had been carefully coiled in huge tubs, and it took four tubs full of trawl to make the one mile of the main line. The doryman flipped the trawl from the tub and threw it in the ocean, using a "throw stick" so he wouldn't get stuck by the hooks on the gangion lines. Both ends of the main trawl line were anchored to the ocean's bottom with small anchors, and a brightly colored buoy about the size of a five-gallon keg, with a bright flag on top, marked each end of the trawl.

If the fishing was good in that first spot, we would usually stay there for two weeks before shifting to another spot or going to the nearest port to get bait. It was not customary to anchor close to another vessel that was anchored for fishing. The usual distance to keep from each other was around five miles or more.

I had the job of helping the one doryman row, if he was headed into the wind as the other doryman set out the trawl. If there was no headwind, one doryman could handle this job by himself. I enjoyed doing this every once in a while, because it got me away from the ship and broke the monotony.

Boy, I remember the waves were very high that first morning, and I'd brace myself when I saw them coming. But the dory just rolled over the top of the waves like a roller coaster going up and down. After I got over my initial fear, I loved to ride the waves. And do you know, never in my years at sea did I ever once get seasick. I'd get a little squeamish, but that was all.

After the trawls were set, the dories came back to the vessel. This part of the job usually took an hour and a half to two hours, and if the sea was rough, the dories had to be hoisted back on the deck to keep them from pounding against the side of the vessel and breaking up. However, if the sea was calm, the crew tied the dories to the stern. The men would come aboard and rest an hour or so, then go back and haul the trawl. If the fishing spot turned out to be a good one, they would return with their load of codfish sometimes within an hour. If the fishing was bad, I've seen them come back with only one, two, or three fish in the bottom of the dory. This was rough on them, because they would still have to haul the whole mile of trawl set by each dory, to be sure they got all the fish on the line.

Mainly these Lunenburg vessels caught codfish, but also a few halibut and a few haddock. We cleaned the halibut and put them in the ice bins to keep fresh until our next trip to land for bait. Then they would be sold to the fish plant. The other fish would be salted down and unloaded in port when the trip was over.

The trawls were checked three or four times a day, depending on the weather and how the good fishing held up. Each time before the dorymen went to haul the trawl, they had to cut more bait to replace what was missing on the hooks. Either the hooks had fish on them or the bait was gone—probably some of the other fish had eaten it off but didn't get hooked. We were fortunate that the fishing was good where we had first anchored, and we stayed in the same spot for the two weeks.

Each day except Sunday, we followed pretty much the same routine. We ate breakfast about four o'clock in the morning. Then the dorymen would go out, haul the trawl, and come back to the vessel. The men would eat lunch around 9:30 or 10:00 A.M. Usually supper was served about three o'clock in the afternoon. When the trawl was hauled for the last time of the day, the crew would help dress down the fish, clean the deck, and put everything in place to be ready for the next morning. We had our last meal of the day, the late snack, around eight at night.

Sunday was a day of rest. Everybody worked hard six days a week and looked forward to Sunday. We all slept in and ate breakfast around 8:00 A.M. Some wrote letters to be mailed on the first trip to land and others read, but it was usually conversation or sleep all day. I got homesick all over again on Sundays. When I was working, I didn't have time to think, and at night I was so tired I just wanted to sleep. But on Sundays I thought a lot about Mother.

There were times during the four years I went to sea when I longed for the good old land so much that I got sick to my stomach. Several times on those Sundays when I was so homesick and when the ocean looked exactly like glass, I had strong thoughts of doing a stupid thing. On calm days the dories were always tied to the stern, and I took a notion, while the men were asleep, to slip into one of them and row and sail for land. What a horrible idea! We were hundreds of miles from land, and the first slight gale would have sunk the dory. I didn't know anything about how to handle a dory, and thank God I didn't act on those foolish thoughts.

On those lonely Sundays I kept thinking that if I had Mother's Hawaiian guitar, I could pass the time away and entertain the crew, who I knew would enjoy it. That didn't happen, but later on I did find ways to entertain the crew.

After being anchored on the Atlantic for the two weeks, we set sail for the mainland and anchored in the harbor of Canso, Nova Scotia. We unloaded our fresh halibut and took on ice, fresh bait, and a few miscellaneous supplies. In a few days we were headed back to sea again. I was beginning to get very excited, because after one more trip for bait our trip would be over, and we would be on our way home.

This time the captain charted our course to the fishing grounds off St. Pierre and Miquelon islands. The Atlantic waters were freezing cold and it was snowy, but the fishing was excellent, and we stayed anchored for the usual two-week run. Then we sailed for St. Pierre for bait.

In St. Pierre a few of the men rowed ashore after we finished loading bait and supplies, and they took me with them. This port was known for the finest liquors and every kind of American cigarettes. In the stores the men were allowed to go down into the cellar, where there was barrel after barrel of liquor, and test each brand. The barrels were strapped to the wall and had wooden taps. Some men stayed by the barrels, drank as much as they could, and got really high before we left. They bought quite a supply for themselves. Since I did not drink but smoked cigarettes, I bought me a couple of cartons of good American Camels, one dollar a carton. There was quite a party on the ship that night, and some mighty big hangovers the next morning.

Then we were on our way back to the fishing banks, a couple hundred miles from St. Pierre. On our way we spotted a couple of icebergs, but they were in the far distance. The weather was very foggy and dreary when the vessel dropped anchor in the middle of the frozen Atlantic. I was concerned about the fog because I'd heard stories that big steamers had been known to cut a 125-foot schooner right in half. Icebergs and raging storms were dangers, too. In fog or at night the crew had to keep a strict, continuous watch for icebergs and other ships. One man at a time would stand watch on deck, four hours on and then eight hours off.

If I was fishing off the deck, I'd stop immediately if it became foggy. Fog could move in quickly on the finest sunshiny day. If that happened when the men were out in their dories hauling trawl, I was assigned a job that I didn't like very much. Each schooner carried its own foghorn, which was like a big square box driven by a wind bellows, much like an old-fashioned pump organ. The big lever used to pump the wind bellows was located on the right side of the box. So in foggy weather my job was to sit straddling the box and push and pull the handle back and forth. This made an extremely loud sound that could be heard a couple of miles away if the wind was not blowing too hard. The only consolation I got from this job was the possibility of guiding the men back to the ship if they were to get lost.

Sometimes the fog was so thick and heavy that you couldn't see more than ten or fifteen yards away. The mist would collect on the schooner's halyards and roll like ice down my neck. To break the boredom I'd sing to myself. One day I created an instrument to help the boredom. I drove a small nail near the front corner of the foghorn box, on the same side where the handle was located. I put a rubber band around the nail and stretched it over the handle, which was located in the middle of the side. I could move the handle back and forth slowly (so it wouldn't blow the horn), and I'd pick the rubber band with my finger like you would a string on a guitar. Stretching the band would change the sounds, and I was in business with my own instrument—my foghorn music box! I learned to play tunes on it and sometimes got so involved that I'd forget to blow the horn as often as I was supposed to.

Someone was on watch from the minute it got dusk until daylight. The watchman always had to be alert for steamers crossing the Atlantic, because we could be anchored right in the path of these big ocean liners and freight steamers. Of course, this was before the days of radar detectors. These big ships, such as ocean liners and freighters, were going back and forth constantly from England, Ireland, Halifax, New York, France, and other major ports. Fishing vessels were forever in danger. We were, in other words, a sitting duck for the traffic of the sea.

When the visibility was good, we could see the ships way off in the distance. At night they would sail within a few miles of us. If it was clear, they looked like a big city all lit up, and they were beautiful. In clear weather a collision was pretty unlikely. However, fog was very common, especially at certain times of the year. Ocean liners were also alert to the dangers, and they kept a sharp lookout, too, for the fishing vessels. They would blow their big foghorn every minute and a half or two minutes.

Our man on watch had to judge the danger primarily by listening to the ship's horn to determine what direction it was coming from, and he tried to judge its distance by following the sound of the horn. If it sounded like the ship was heading in our direction, the man on watch would not take any chances. He'd come to the companionway (the steps down to the forecastle where everyone was sleeping) and yell at the top of his voice, "Steamer, all hands on deck!" Since the schooner was so long, some men were responsible for yelling the order to the cabin area where the rest of the men were sleeping. Those words were frightening, especially when we were awakened from a sound sleep in the wee hours of the morning. When we heard those commanding words, we jumped out of our bunks and were on deck in a flash.

It was customary for all the crew to sleep in their pants, socks, and shirts, so this saved time getting on deck. If the steamer seemed to be getting closer, we carried out the following procedure. One of the men started blowing our big square foghorn, and we sent up bright flares that penetrated the fog in the night, lighting up the sky. We hoped the men on watch on the other ship would see our flares and alter its course temporarily. Then one of our men would ring the huge bell continually. I think this bell was about the size of the Liberty Bell in Philadelphia. It hung in the bow of the vessel and had a huge clapper with a rope hanging from it. The sound could be heard for a long distance. If the ship continued to come closer, the final thing was to fire the swivel cannon. This looked like a typical cannon, about two feet long, with the rear end about the size of a table saucer, and tapered so the front end was smaller. It was loaded with gunpowder only, like the old-fashioned muskets were. The powder was crammed into the cannon from the front opening. It had a regular dynamite cap with a fuse, that extended three or four feet from the cannon. A crewman would light the end of the fuse, and when the fuse burned to the cap, it exploded the gunpowder. The cannon was anchored with heavy ship chains to keep it from flying overboard from the force of the explosion.

If all these sounds didn't cause the other ship to alter course, it was time to abandon ship! In such a case, we were supposed to lower the dories into the water quickly and leave the ship. Fortunately, I never had to experience that part of it, but I have seen ships come so close to us that it was pure pleasure to hear the sound of the ship's foghorn get weaker. Then we knew they heard our warning or had seen our flares.

One afternoon, when we had run out of frozen bait, the captain told the men to get under way and sail for Sydney. "Get under way" was a slang phrase for getting the ship's anchor pulled up, setting all the sails, and heading for port. That always sounded good to me, knowing I was going to see land again and get a chance to go ashore.

While on our way to Sydney, we spotted trouble. We ran into miles of ice during the night. This was not the iceberg type, it was the regular flat drift ice, but it was dangerous, too. The ice patterns blocked our way so we couldn't get into port. We'd sail down a lane for three or four miles, hoping that we would be able to get out of the miles of ice drifts. But every time, we'd run into a dead end and have to angle the ship around and sail down another opening. This dead-end sailing went on all night and into the next afternoon. The whole crew was totally frustrated, but finally, thank the Lord, we found an opening and were on a steady course again.

That afternoon we saw several big icebergs. This was terrifying. They looked to be as high as mountains. Yet that's only about one-third of them, because two-thirds were below the surface of the ocean. The saying "It's only the tip of the iceberg" has a special meaning to sailors. The salt sea air will cause an iceberg to become honeycombed and fragile, and just a rifle shot or a loud clap of thunder can cause it to fall completely apart. When an iceberg collapses and hits the ocean, a ship close by could easily be sucked under and destroyed. We saw a lot of icebergs, but luckily we were always able to avoid them. Ice drifts were a more common problem.

One of the most beautiful sights I have ever seen came while we were trapped in those miles of drift ice. The sun was coming above the horizon, and the men called me on deck to witness something I'll probably never see again. There were thousands of seals sunning themselves as far as the eye could see. This panoramic view of little seals lying on the ice with their mothers made a calm and peaceful scene. The morning sun cast a silver light on the ice as the seals lazily rested in the sun. It looked like the whole ocean was silver.

We continued sailing toward Sydney Harbor. I knew this would be our last time in port for bait, and after the two weeks were gone, we would be setting the sails for home. In ports like Sydney we lowered the big anchor, which was held by big steel-link chains that we used only in port. On the fishing grounds we used a huge hemp cable, which was about ten inches in circumference and was coiled up in a huge circle on the deck of the ship near the bow.

Then bad luck caught us again. Suddenly we noticed, to everyone's astonishment, that the ice that had drifted in from the sea was starting to enter the mouth of the harbor. Immediately the captain had to have a tugboat come and tow us in and dock us at one of the large wharfs. We had planned to stay in port for only two or three days, but we were iced in in Sydney for eighteen long days. I was disappointed. This would make us spend an additional eighteen days on top of our two weeks, if the captain decided to stay the two weeks to fish.

I had a lot of fun, though, while we were in Sydney. Since we were tied up to the wharf, I could come and go whenever I liked. My future brother-in-law, Ritchie, was on this trip, and he gave me a lot of guidance. He and I would go ashore at night and browse around and enjoy the town.

When the captain thought it was safe to go back to sea, a government icebreaker, a big steamer that was built for rescues, towed us through the ice and out into the open waters. We anchored and fished for about a week on the fishing grounds, and then the captain decided it was time to pull up anchor and set sail for home. After setting sail, I don't believe I slept one single night, I was so excited. I can still remember the morning when I was on deck and saw Lunenburg harbor ahead of us. Spring was beautiful with the green grass and the trees with new leaves. The weather was warm. It was a perfect day. I knew before long I would be seeing Mother, and I could hardly wait.

4

Adventures at Sea

My ship set sail to Bluebird Island
And slowly drifted out to sea,
Her silver sails to cross the ocean,
My lover's lonely heart set free.

"Bluebird Island,"
by Hank Snow

THE SALTER HAD PUT AWAY ON ICE a small halibut for each of the crew to take home, and I felt so proud walking the five miles to Stonehurst carrying my halibut by the gills. When Mother saw me, she welcomed me like royalty. Her eyes sparkled as she gave me a big hug and kiss. I had so much to tell her about my experiences that I couldn't stop talking. I made sure that I complimented Ritchie. He had been a great companion to me and had explained some of the procedures aboard the schooner. She was pleased, too, that I'd received such excellent treatment from Captain Crouse and the crew.

After a while I had to return to the dock because the crew would be unloading the codfish cargo, and I had to be there to pick out my catch, which I had marked from the rest of the fish. I'd have to take my fish home to Stonehurst and cure them for the market. Curing meant soaking all the salt out of them and laying them out to dry. In Lunenburg the companies had dozens of specially built racks for curing the fish. They looked like long tables, about three feet off the ground, with netting over them. The fish lay on top of the netting so the breeze could blow up through them, and they would dry in no time.

I didn't have a way to get my fish to Stonehurst. No way would I ask Charlie Tanner. I knew he would have turned me down, and I didn't want to give him that satisfaction. Luckily, I found a gentleman with a boat who transported them for me. I rigged up a table and net, and soon they were ready for market.

I sold my fish and the barrel of fish tongues for a total of $24.65. I thought this fortune was more than I could ever spend. The first thing I did was pay off my debt to the supply company for my clothes, and I still had money left. But I had one big problem. When I wasn't at sea, where would I live? Of course Mother wanted me to stay with her, and since I would be going to sea again soon, I figured I could tolerate Charlie and Wilbert for a while. I gave Mother half of my money to buy something for herself and to buy groceries. I hoped this might ease the pressure. If Charlie knew I was helping, surely he would be nicer to me. Fortunately, Charlie and Wilbert were away a lot during the day, fishing in Charlie's boat, and they didn't get home until way after dark.

While I had been away at sea, Mother had scraped up two dollars and bought a second-hand Victrola and several Vernon Dalhart records, including "The Wreck of the Old '97" and "The Prisoner's Song." While Charlie and Wilbert were at work, I'd play those records over and over again.

One day, after returning from Lunenburg, I got the surprise of my life. Nina, my second-oldest sister, was there. I couldn't believe what I was seeing! I was overjoyed, but I hardly recognized her, since I hadn't seen her for years. She had matured into a very fine young lady. Mother was thrilled, too, and said, "Well, here we are together now, except for Marion. One of these days the Good Lord will let us all be together again as a family."

When Charlie and Wilbert came home late that night, they both gave Nina and me a hateful look and went right to the table to eat supper. After they had gone to bed, Mother, Lillian, Nina, and I talked until the wee hours of the morning—or I should say we whispered as we reminisced, so that we wouldn't wake up the wild man.

Nina had been released from the foster home and had gotten a job in Halifax as a house servant for Mr. and Mrs. Kennedy. She spoke of how well they had treated her. It was like a real home. Nina and Mother had been corresponding, and Mother took the chance to invite her, believing that Charlie would at least be good to Nina. Mother also hoped this might ease his pressure on me.

That didn't happen. A short time after Nina moved in, it started—the hateful looks, the jokes between Wilbert and Charlie, the curse words. Nina said to me, "I made a big mistake. I knew it the moment I moved in. I should have only come for a visit and not given up my job, but I wanted to be with all of you, Jack. I sure moved into a hornet's nest. Now I know how you feel." Nina was certainly in a bind. Charlie treated her like dirt, and it was obvious to her, as it had been with me, that Charlie wanted Mother only. He was jealous if Nina and I made over Mother in the slightest way. Poor Mother. She was right in the middle of it all. All she ever wanted was to reunite her family. None of us ever blamed Mother for marrying the "beast." Even though she never admitted it, we all thought she was sorry she did.

One morning before Charlie went to work, he told me to cut up a certain amount of firewood for the kitchen stove and stack it in the woodbox behind the stove. I did exactly as he directed. The first thing Charlie did when he came home from work was check to see if I had filled the woodbox. Then he checked the woodpile outside. I was sitting at the kitchen table when he came back in. "Where in the hell is the wood you were supposed to cut up and leave at the woodpile?" This time I was going to stick up for my rights. "You never told me to cut more wood other than to fill the woodbox behind the stove. I did that." "You bastard, you," he yelled, "don't you talk back to me, or call me a liar."

I remember what happened next as if it was yesterday. Charlie grabbed me, and with all his strength he literally pushed me through the door. I landed on my back, on that big flat rock upon which the old house was built. With the terrible pain in my back, I was sure it was broken. I lay there for several minutes. My head was cut open and bleeding. Nina came running to help me, and when she saw the blood, she was so furious with Charlie that I honestly believe she would have shot him if she had had a gun. Mother came rushing, too, when she heard Nina screaming. She warned Charlie, "If you ever lay a hand on Jack or any of my children again, I'll leave you, and I will never see you again." Knowing Mother, she meant it, I can assure you. As it turned out, my pride and body were badly bruised, but I had no broken bones. However, this incident caused Nina to lose any respect she might have ever had for Charlie.

Here's a funny story that involved Nina and me. I was just twelve years old, and like most kids, I enjoyed pulling little practical jokes occasionally. This time the victim was Nina. One morning, a few days before I was to go back to sea, Mother had an 8:00 A.M. appointment with a dentist in Lunenburg, and she asked Nina to go with her to ease the boredom on the five-mile walk. They had to get up before daylight. Nina kept going up the darkened stairs to ask Mother questions like "What time should I be ready? How do I look?" I took my old black oil hat that I had worn at sea, and I tied it to a piece of kite line. Then I put the line around a doorknob at the top of the stairs and hooked the end of the line on something downstairs so that it made an endless loop. I was downstairs behind the kitchen door waiting for Nina to make another trip upstairs. When she was partway up, I pulled the kite string and the hat followed her. She screeched at the top of her voice and ran upstairs—with the oil hat chasing her. She was so scared that she turned around and started running down again—and that hat was right behind her! She was yelling and going on, and her face was snow white. It also upset Mother, who gave me a stern and well-deserved reprimand.

One day, when Wilbert was away from home on a fishing trip, I decided to see what it felt like to dress up in a real suit. Wilbert had only one suit of clothes, which he kept for special occasions. It was not by any means a church suit, because I'm sure he never knew what the word church meant. Wilbert was about five feet, eight inches tall and weighed around 160 pounds. When I put on his two-piece blue serge suit, you can imagine how I looked! The pants came way up under my arms. The coat sleeves were several inches too long, and the coat went way around me. It was as long as a three-quarter-length coat. It had black braid on the cuffs and looked like something you would wear to a funeral. I found the only dress shirt he had and an old half-worn-out tie. I had to laugh at myself when I looked in the mirror. But away I went, walking to Lunenburg. I thought I was a big shot when the people smiled at me as I proudly showed off my borrowed clothes.

I was embarrassed about being so poor and having no clothes, so I thought if people saw me dressed up, they might figure I must be from a middle-class family. I walked through town as if I was the richest kid in Lunenburg, even though I must have looked like Charlie Chaplin in my funny garb. One good thing, the trousers covered my feet so no one could see my worn-out shoes with holes on the bottom. Often I would cut pieces of cardboard and put several layers inside the shoes. But that didn't last long, because as soon as the first raindrops came, that was the end of my shoe soles. I would joke with my family that I had to walk on my heels to save my sole. Sometimes I wore Lillian's stockings when they were full of holes and she could no longer wear them. I'd cut the tops off, fold the toes back under my feet and put my old shoes on. Both the stockings and the cardboard were good for only a few miles, and then I was walking on human leather again.

Friends, even back then I was putting on a front.

Mother insisted that I stay with her until the next fishing trip. But after a few days I couldn't be around Charlie or Wilbert any longer. I tried, but I couldn't control my deep-seated anger toward them, especially Charlie. I got terrible stomach pains just at the sight of him, and since Mother was still having those uncontrollable spells, I blamed Charlie. So I decided to leave, which was exactly what he and Wilbert wanted. But at least I got to see Mother, Lillian, and Marion. Mother understood and said, "Jack, why don't you go stay with Grandmother Boutlier until I can get things straightened out with Charlie, or until I decide to leave him for good." Poor Mother was the eternal optimist, but I knew she meant it at the time. It was hard to leave her again. I never knew, with her poor health, if I would ever see her again.

Grandmother Boutlier, Mother's mother, was a beautiful lady. If there ever was an angel in heaven I know she's there. Mother had two sisters, Cecile and Grace, and three brothers, Carl, Hastings, and Wilford, all delightful people. They were always kind to me. As I was growing up, it never ceased to amaze me why some people in this world could be so decent and others so damn mean. Anyway, I stayed with my good grandmother until I was ready to go back to sea. Grandmother lived in a little country village called Western Head, about four miles from Liverpool and close to the shore of the Atlantic Ocean. When I left, she made it clear that I was always welcome at her home.

About the middle of June I went into Lunenburg and strolled along the waterfront looking for a schooner called the *Marie A. Spindler.* I went aboard and asked one of the crew if they needed a flunky for the trip. "I believe we do, young man, but you'll have to talk to the captain. He should be coming aboard in about two hours." I waited. When Captain Willard Spindler came aboard, I noticed he was a pretty stout, middle-aged man with a kind face. He was very pleasant to me. "Yes, we need a boy for the trip. Have you ever been to sea before?" When I told him of my trip with Captain Crouse on the *Grace Boehner,* he replied, "Good. You've been initiated. We sail in three days."

This was the longest of the three yearly fishing trips. We followed the same routine we did on the spring trip. We sailed straight to the Grand Banks of Newfoundland, found a good fishing spot, and anchored for the next two weeks. Then we sailed to port to get another supply of fresh bait. Through his navigation skills our captain always searched for the best fishing grounds on either the Grand Banks, the Western Banks, or the Quero Banks. Sometimes he sailed up around Cape North off Sydney, Nova Scotia, or even Bonaventure Island.

Whenever we had any leisure time, especially on Sundays, I found something to do to pass the time away. I had a good singing voice in an amateurish way. I knew several songs that I had learned from Mother, including "Was There Ever a Pal like You" and "The Wreck of the

Altoona," as well as songs I learned from records played on our old Victrola. I would sing to the crew, and to my surprise, they really liked my singing and would give me pieces of homemade fudge they had brought from home. I got an occasional nickel, too. I also played the mouth organ and danced a little bit, a sort of tap dance that I had taught myself. But I didn't spring all of this on the men at one time. I'd save some of it to build my act to keep it entertaining. Occasionally I would play the mouth organ and dance at the same time.

The praise I received from the crew was worth a million dollars! It sure gave me confidence. I believe to this day that it was their great encouragement that helped shape my career later on.

I began to feel very close to the men. I knew they really cared for me, and I wanted them to respect my work as a member of the crew. I did all the chores a flunky was supposed to do, as well as duties I was not assigned. I helped the cook peel potatoes, clean the galley, and do anything else that needed doing.

Captain Spindler gave me a lot of good advice about the sea as well as practical knowledge about life. I've always been a good listener and willing to learn. By sitting around listening to the crew tell tales, I learned about growing up, honesty, and morality, and much about human nature. These were among the most memorable events of my life. I believe these men and life at sea had a profound effect on the kind of person I was becoming.

There were always lots of sharks cruising around and under the schooner, looking for fish heads or whatever the cook might throw overboard. Those ugly things were anywhere from three to ten feet long. Their big top fin sticking above the water looked like the tail of an aircraft. Sharks were a real menace to the fishermen. They were forever getting tangled in the trawl, and they were always preying on smaller fish.

The men taught me how to catch sharks from off the deck, but they wanted me to try this only while they were on board, so they could watch in case I fell overboard. I'd make a loop like a lasso in a long one-inch rope and drop this over the side of the vessel. Then I'd take a small line, tie a fish head on it, and hold it down on one side of the loop. The shark would naturally swim through the loop after the fish head, and when he got halfway through the loop, I'd pull up and tighten the lasso. When I had the shark, some of the men would rush over and hoist it aboard with a dory hook. Next, they would cut the shark into pieces and throw it over the side. This may sound cruel, but these sharks are dangerous things. They could tear you to pieces in seconds if you fell overboard.

There was something about sharks that always puzzled me. I observed that a pilot fish traveled with each shark. These fish ranged in length from four to eight inches and had tiny stripes around them with all colors of the rainbow. But out of the water they became jet black. They swam about three or four inches above the shark's head, and wherever the little fish turned, the shark would also turn, like it was guided. I heard that without the little pilot fish the shark would become completely lost.

The bottom of the ocean yielded some beautiful colored objects that fascinated me. Sometimes they were brought up with the trawls. In color and shape they looked exactly like real strawberries, raspberries, grapes, pineapples, watermelons, squash—you name it, same color, same size. They made me crave good fresh fruit every time I saw them. I don't know if they would kill a person to eat them, but they sure would give your skin a fit if you touched them.

Occasionally Captain Spindler let the dorymen set the trawls and fish under sail. We wouldn't anchor but would fish while the vessel was moving. Whenever the captain had doubts about how good the fishing might be in certain areas, he would try this. As the schooner was sailing five to six knots, the dories were launched. The trawl was set out while the vessel sailed around in the area, and the men stayed out in their dories until they hauled in their trawls, in an hour or so. One at a time the dories sailed back to the vessel, where their catch was forked aboard the schooner. In order to hoist the dories safely on board, the captain would slow the vessel down by turning the schooner's nose into the wind. The men then threw a rope, or painter, to one of us on board, and we pulled the dory to the side of the vessel to be hoisted aboard. If the haul indicated a good fishing ground, the captain decided whether the tests warranted anchoring the vessel for a two-week stay. Fishing under sail called for special skills, as there was always a chance of running into one of the dories and possibly drowning the men.

Toward the end of the summer trip a huge sea turtle got tangled in the trawl line of one of our dories, and the men wanted to bring it to the schooner and hoist it aboard. It looked exactly like a land turtle but measured about five feet in length and four feet across. It weighed around a hundred pounds, and the men had a tough job towing it back to the vessel. Sea turtles, I was told, can't live out of the water for very long at one time. So one of the crewmen bored a hole in the rear end of its shell, where he tied a long trawl line so we could drop the turtle into the water. We brought it aboard at night to feed, and then we'd drop it into the ocean again. It would swim part of the day, and then we would bring it aboard to roam around on deck and sleep in the sun. We kept it until we went to land for bait. After showing it off to several people, we put it back into the water and let it return to its natural sea life again. The turtle was a nice diversion and gave us a lot of pleasure for a few days at sea.

As soon as land came into sight, it seemed like it took our vessel forever to get there. If we were on our way to land, and the wind was calm and the ocean looked like glass, the men would do something unusual to hurry the schooner into port. They would hoist all the dories overboard, tie them together in a straight line, get into the dories, and row like crazy to tow the vessel. For about the first ten minutes the vessel barely moved, but it would slowly gain momentum, and we'd be going at least two knots faster! This happened on my first summer trip when we were about fifteen miles from Lunenburg harbor. After three months at sea the men were all very anxious to get to their homes.

When the summer's catch was unloaded and cured, each man made around four hundred dollars, which was great money back then. After I sold my fish and barrel of fish tongues, I made around fifty-eight dollars. Again, I thought I was rich.

This was the last fishing trip until spring, and the men had to make their summer cash last until then. Often they stocked up on foods, which they bought from the outfitting firms, so they could eat when they had no money coming in. When spring came around, most of the men would return to Lunenburg and be off to sea again. Some would sail on the same schooner, while others signed up to fish on a different one. It was a hard life, but it was the only life that most of the men knew.

Whenever our schooner sailed into our home port of Lunenburg, the first thing I did was to go see Mother. Sometimes it was for a brief visit. Sometimes I stayed longer, depending on the attitude of Charlie.

The second thing I did after this trip was send for my own guitar! I ordered a T. Eaton Special for $5.95 through a mail-order catalog. I was as proud of that guitar as if it was the most expensive one in Canada.

I hadn't been home long when Nina and I got caught up in the middle of an almost tragic situation. I shall never forget this as long as I live.

Mother wanted to visit Wilbert's father, who was near death with yellow jaundice, and she asked Nina and me to go with her for company. We walked the five miles from Stonehurst to Lunenburg, and while they were visiting, I took a walk around the waterfront. It had been arranged that Charlie would come to get us in the boat late that afternoon so that Mother would not have to walk the five miles back. I was to watch for Charlie and go tell Mother and Nina when he came to pick us up.

About four in the afternoon Charlie arrived. He tied his boat up to the wharf and told me to go get them. I didn't know that Mother and Charlie had had an argument the previous night, and she was still very upset. She said, "Jack, you go back there and tell him I'm in no hurry. Tell him I will come when I'm good and ready." Well, I took the message back to Charlie, and dumb me, I repeated her exact words. Charlie lashed out, "Okay, when she does come, you tell her I said the same thing. I'll be back when I'm good and ready." Then he stalked off.

When Charlie finally came back to the boat, he was drinking rum and his bottle was half empty. His black eyes had that murderous look, and it scared me half to death. When Mother and Nina showed up, about an hour later, not one word was spoken between them and Charlie until we were on the boat and speeding away from the dock.

That afternoon Charlie took us on a horror trip. The distance between Lunenburg and Stonehurst, by boat and through the different channels, was a good six and a half miles. Some of this area was extremely dangerous because it was filled with reef, ledges, and narrow channels. Charlie continued to plague Mother and curse her until she got so worked up she made a desperate attempt to jump overboard. Charlie grabbed her and hauled her back into the boat, but she made another attempt to jump. While he was trying to prevent this tragedy, the boat was running on its own, so I grabbed the helm and steered the boat directly to the shore. We were fairly close to land, and my intention was to ditch the boat. But Charlie grabbed the helm from me and aimed the boat back on its course. Poor Nina was terrified. She crawled up into the small shed-like space in the bow of the boat, shaking like a leaf. Charlie pounded his fists on the engine house. He continued to curse Mother and threatened to throw Nina overboard. I think all the shouting made him tired, because all of a sudden he slumped over the engine house and lay still for several minutes.

It was almost dark as we approached the most dangerous area, and with Charlie being drunk and trying to steer, I knew we all would be drowned. But the Good Lord was with us. Soon we were passing a tiny island, just a stone's throw from the mainland, called Mason's Island, when Charlie started to slow the boat down. He shouted, "I'm going ashore to see an old friend of mine and have a drink with him." This was a godsend to us. Charlie tied the boat up to the wharf and tried to climb the five-step ladder to the top of the wharf, but he lost his hold and fell back into the boat. It's a wonder he didn't break his back or neck—which I hoped he would. He passed out, and we three climbed the ladder and left Charlie in the boat. We soon found the house where his friend, John Tanner, lived. (He was no relation to Charlie.)

We told the people who we were, and they gave us hot tea and doughnuts while we related our trip of horror. They could not believe what we had gone through. By this time it was completely dark. There was no moon, and the weather had turned very cold and windy. The folks very kindly invited us to stay for the night, knowing that the next morning Charlie would be sober and perhaps he could be reasoned with. However, John was obliging and said, "I've lived here for many years, and I've traveled these same shoals and reefs many times. If you think you should get Charlie home tonight, I can steer the boat blindfolded. I'll be glad to take you. I can stay with my brother in Stonehurst overnight, and he'll bring me back in the morning." Mother was pleased and decided we should go home.

John had us on our way in the black night, through the perilous narrow passages. Soon Charlie woke up freezing, and he went crazy again. I've heard that these drunken fits are called the horrors and that a person in this condition can easily kill himself or other people. Charlie was trying to jump overboard, but John grabbed him on every attempt and let his head drag through the cold water, hoping this would sober him up. Being about six feet, four inches tall and very strong, John was still able to steer the boat safely. I was hoping Charlie would drown.

At Stonehurst, John walked us the mile and a half to our house, to make sure Charlie didn't start raving again. John hadn't left the house but a few minutes, when Charlie jerked a piece of nickel-trimmed metal off the front of the kitchen stove and made a swipe at me. "I'll kill you yet, you bastard—and the whole damn family with you," he shouted as he continued to swing. After several misses he hit the wall and broke the metal bar in a dozen pieces. Finally he fell down on the floor and went to sleep.

Friends, this sort of thing is what made the life at sea so attractive to me—being away from this constant pressure and madness. I hope the Good Lord will forgive me for the way I despised Charlie. I should have had some time to enjoy a young boy's life, to go to school, to have playmates. Instead I was tortured both physically and emotionally, and I still have body scars from the effects of his ham-like hands.

My next sea trip was the spring trip on a schooner named the *J. H. St. Clair.* The captain was St. Clair Tanner. This trip lasted five or six weeks, but it was not too successful because we were constantly anchored in poor fishing grounds. I remember the cold weather, snow, ice, and icebergs that we encountered.

After a couple of weeks at home I struck it lucky and found another captain looking for a flunky. This time it was Captain Albert "Dob" Selig. The name of his vessel was the *Jean Smith.* He was a very short, stubby little man with big round eyes. The first time I saw him after we got to sea and anchored, I had to laugh. We were putting on our dress-down clothes, preparing to dress down the fish as the men came in from the trawls. Instead of wearing regular oil pants for this job, which had suspenders going over the shoulders like regular farmers' overalls, he wore an oil skirt, like a woman's skirt. He had on this funny-looking oil hat, and he looked like a little old woman.

During the three-month trip that summer we came close to a real disaster. We were sailing into Belleoram, Newfoundland, for fresh bait. Captain Selig liked to drink, and it was quite obvious he had been drinking a lot. I was terrified of being around anyone who was drinking because of my experiences with Charlie Tanner.

It was a strict marine law that all vessels over a certain size or length must have a licensed marine pilot to guide the vessel into port. Belleoram was a tricky harbor to get in and out of. It was filled with small reefs and shoals, and in some places it was very shallow.

In the harbor there were eight dories ahead on our starboard bow. They were tied together, each to the stern of the next, and the men in each dory were all jigging squid. On the other side, just ahead on our port bow, was a huge shoal. The local pilot was up in the bow of our schooner, fully aware of this critical situation. He was giving orders to the man at the wheel to steer between the shoal and the eight dories. Our man at the wheel was doing fine until our captain interfered. As soon as the pilot yelled to the man at midship, who was relaying the message to our man at the wheel to keep her hard to the right, the captain, being drunk, yelled, "Keep her to the left, keep her to the left!" Our man got so thoroughly mixed up that he steered right into the middle of the eight dories. Four dories went to the right side of our vessel and the other four went to the left. Our vessel was sailing at a reasonable speed, and it dragged the small dories in all directions and knocked the men overboard. Some of the dories capsized. Others became a tangled mess, and several men in the water were struggling to keep from drowning.

One skinny old man with a long white beard down to his waist, wearing his oil suit and hat, was standing on the bow of one of the dories, crying out, "Save me, save me, somebody save me." Bless his heart, it was really sad. A big husky fellow reached over the bow of the vessel, grabbed him by the collar, and dragged him onto the deck. The old fellow was in a state of shock, but after a while he stopped shaking and seemed much better.

In the meantime, the other men in the water were pulled out and brought on deck. But one of them nearly drowned. I saw the men rolling him over a barrel to get the water out of his lungs. Then he was taken ashore to a doctor, who worked on him for a long time. The harbor personnel demanded that the captain be brought to the police station, where he was questioned for over an hour. Since no one died, the captain was not charged with anything.

In the many ports I enjoyed meeting people and visiting the towns like Sydney and Canso in Nova Scotia. We also sailed into several ports in the province of Newfoundland, such as Belleoram, Aquaforte, Cape Royal, Burin, Harbour Grace, and St. John's. We would drop anchor in the middle of the harbor and usually stay for a couple of days to get fresh bait. In the evening after supper, and sometimes in the afternoon if time permitted, some of the men would row ashore in the dories. Often we would write and mail letters home and receive mail at these ports. It was always a thrill getting a letter from home.

Occasionally I'd meet a pretty little gal about my age. On one of our trips into Canso some of the men took me to an old-fashioned square dance in a tiny dance hall, where I met a very pretty girl. I remember her name was Juanita Monroe, and her girlfriend's name was Amy Strider.

Before I go any further with my sea stories, I want to mention the famous *Blue Nose*. She was a schooner built in Lunenburg. As soon as she was launched, it was apparent this was no ordinary vessel. She became known as the Queen of the Atlantic—the fastest schooner in the history of all sailing vessels in Canada. Captain Angus Walters, brother to Captain Sonny Walters, who I sailed with later, was the skipper of the *Blue Nose*. During the 1920s and 1930s, Canada and the United States had a competition each summer to see who had the fastest sailing ship. The *Blue Nose* won the International Fisherman's Trophy Cup and never lost it for seventeen straight years. So it was only natural that all of Canada was very proud of this schooner.

There is some sadness about the famous *Blue Nose*. The owner in Lunenburg sold her to a foreign country, and this was a bad blow to the people across Canada. I think they should have put the *Blue Nose* up on a high mountaintop and painted her with gold paint, so everyone could see her and appreciate her as a national monument. She became an emblem in Canada, as did the maple leaf, and the *Blue Nose* likeness is on the Canadian dime. Unfortunately, in 1946 she was pounded to pieces on the cruel reefs of Haiti. Because of this great disappointment, *Blue Nose No. 2* was built. She was also a beautiful vessel, identical to the famous *Blue Nose,* but she didn't have the speed of the original.

Since I had started dabbing around with different colors of old house paint, I tried painting a picture of the *Blue Nose* racing with the *Gertrude L. Tebeau,* one of the fastest vessels that competed for the Marine Cup. I couldn't afford canvas so I painted it on cardboard. Believe it or not, it won first prize in the Lunenburg Fisheries Exhibition! I was on cloud nine. I still have the painting, and it reminds me of those lean but nostalgic days when I went to sea.

5

Disaster!

The lights were burning low and Mister Midnight made his way,
Old Father Time had trudged along to close another day;
The old clock ticked and seemed to say,
"Your heart is sad and blue,
But just remember, pal, there's others broken, too."

"A Message from the Tradewinds,"
by Hank Snow

❖

WHEN THE SUMMER TRIP WAS OVER, I was wondering where I could stay. Well, like they always say, "The Good Lord always provides." My blessing came from Nina and Ritchie when they invited me to stay with them. Nina and Ritchie had dated for a short time, fallen in love, and suddenly gotten married. I'm sure Charlie was partly responsible for such a quick wedding, and maybe this was Nina's way of getting out of that hornet's nest.

Ritchie always signed up for all three fishing trips each year, as did most of the fishermen. When the fishing season was over, he needed work since he now had a wife to support. He took a job in Halifax at Boutlier's Fish Plant, a major company that bought all kinds of fresh fish from the numerous offshore vessels sailing in and out of Halifax during the winter season.

Nina and Ritchie rented an attic on the third floor of a house owned by a Mr. and Mrs. Fenerty. As soon as they got settled, Nina mailed Mother a letter inviting me to come and live with them for the winter. Nina thought I could get a job in Halifax until it was time for me to leave for the spring trip. I was pleased to go. Nina and Ritchie were happy, carefree people and fun to be around. Mother gave me fifty cents for the train ride from Lunenburg to Halifax, which was approximately seventy-five miles.

But I had one big problem. A friend had given me a two-year-old boxer by the name of Spot, and I had become attached to him. He was very affectionate toward me and followed me everywhere I went. Even Charlie and Wilbert liked my dog. Mother told me I wouldn't be able to take him on the train without a crate or cage. She suggested that I make one for him, but I didn't have the time to do this. Besides, I didn't have a red cent to my name to buy one. The money I had made on the summer trip was spent on clothes and a dozen other things before I could wink an eye. However, the ticket agent at the train station had an idea. "I know a young man who works in Powers Hardware Store downtown, and I'll bet if you tell him your story, he'll make a muzzle for your dog and you can tie him in the baggage car. You don't have to have a cage if you have him on a leash and have a muzzle on him. We can't take a chance that he might bite someone. You've got time to go there—if you hurry." I took Spot, and away we went to Powers Hardware Store as fast as we could go.

A pleasant young clerk by the name of Ralph listened while I explained my problem and told him that I had no money. He took some leather scraps, and in a few minutes he had a muzzle riveted together as good as any you could buy. "This is a little gift from me," he said as I thanked him over and over again. "They say a man's best friend is his dog, and I can see that your dog loves you, and you love your little dog. I'm an animal lover, too. Now, you have a good trip." Spot wasn't really overjoyed with his muzzle, but I knew he would get used to it.

We made it back in time to catch the train. Spot rode in the baggage section, and I rode in the passenger car. Nina and Ritchie were waiting for me at the station, and they looked surprised when they saw Spot. Nina said, "My glory, Jack, we didn't know you were bringing a dog. We have a little white Pomeranian, and I don't know whether or not they'll get along." "Don't worry about it," Ritchie said. "We'll work something out." When we got to their place, I saw their little dog was as cute as a button, with a red ribbon tied around its neck. We were afraid to leave the two dogs alone in case they might fight, but after they got acquainted, they got along just fine. I put Spot in the basement where there was a furnace so he would stay warm.

Nina and Ritchie had a real cozy three-room apartment that had been converted from the attic. I had only been there about three weeks when Ritchie got me a job at the fish plant where he was working, but he wasn't sure I could handle the heavy work. I punched the time clock, the same as the men. I helped carry boxes of fresh fish and stack them one box on top of the other, three boxes high. These large boxes held around one hundred fifty pounds of fish and had two handles on each end. We had to swing the boxes back and forth a couple of times and make a big swing to put them up on top of each other. I often dropped my end of the heavy box, and each time one of the men would run over and cover for me so I wouldn't get fired. Several times I saw the boss looking at me out of the corner of his eye, and I knew my job wouldn't last much longer. But he didn't fire me until the end of the week. Then he said, "Son, you're a frail little boy and you try as hard as any man we have working here, but this work is too heavy for you. I'm sorry to have to let you go." I was glad in a way because I was feeling pain in my side from the heavy lifting.

A few days later, Ritchie and I were walking by the *Halifax Herald* newspaper office and saw a sign that read, "Why not go into business for yourself—sell newspapers." Since I had not been paid for my week's work at the fish plant yet, Ritchie loaned me enough money to buy twenty newspapers. I tried to sell my papers on the corner of Hollis Street. By noon I gave it up. I couldn't sell the first paper. I gave my newspapers to an old man who was also selling them on another corner, and I went home.

Luck was with me again, because in a few days I met Carl, a likeable boy about my age and my size. He was clean cut and polite, and we began to chum around together. He was working at Faders Pharmacy as a delivery boy, and he told me they needed to hire another boy to help him. I went to see Mr. Fader the next day, and I got the job, making three dollars a week. People would call on the telephone for prescriptions and personal products, and Carl and I took the streetcar to deliver the products to their homes. Every day I traveled all over Halifax, waiting for streetcars in all kinds of weather, but I still loved it. It was clean work, and I was out in the fresh air a lot. Even on the coldest and snowiest days I never got as cold as I did on the cold Atlantic Ocean. Mr. Fader trusted me to take large sums of money to the bank for deposit, and often I'd bring back change for the store. I carried a leather folder loaded with cash, with sometimes as much as $300, which was a lot of money in the late 1920s.

One day as I was on my way to the bank, swinging this bank folder back and forth in my hand, a gentleman stopped me on the sidewalk and said, "Sonny, I'm going to give you a little tip. One of these days while you're walking along, someone will come up to you and say, 'Hey, look at that airplane,' and while you're distracted, he will relieve you of your bank folder." That was good advice, and from that time on I carried the bank folder inside my shirt.

When I got home from work, Spot was always eager to see me and go for a walk. One day I took him for a long walk down Hollis Street. He was on a leash, but I let him loose from the leash so he could use the telephone pole. Before I knew it, he had run across Hollis Street, into a big office building. How he got through those revolving doors without getting jammed, I don't know. I ran inside to the lobby, where a lady told me she had seen a dog take the elevator. I had to snicker to myself. I looked all over the five floors and couldn't find him anywhere. So I sat down to rest for a bit, and it wasn't long before Spot came down on the same elevator with several people, with his tail between his legs. He slowly walked over to me, and those big, sad eyes told me he was sorry. As I was taking Spot home, an elderly man, a typical Englishman with a wide gray mustache curled up on both sides, stopped me on the street. "Young fellow," he said, "I'd like to buy your dog. Here's a five-dollar bill for him. This should be more than enough. You can buy yourself another dog for about a dollar, and you'll have four dollars left to spend as you choose." Well, this seemed like a lot of money, especially since I was only making three dollars a week at the drug store, but my reply was, "No sir, all the money in the world couldn't buy my dog." He smiled and said, "Young man, you're very wise. Already you've learned something that most people never learn in a lifetime. When you find love, you should never sell it for any price. God bless you." This lesson stayed with me throughout my life.

During my winter stay in Halifax, Nina, Ritchie, and I attended Sunday night meetings at the Salvation Army, and we loved the inspirational songs they sang. One night when we were attending a meeting, I was converted. I can still remember some of the lines in one of the beautiful hymns they sang:

> Those hands are outstretched to you,
> Those hands with the nails pierced through,
> On the cross where He died with His arms opened wide,
> And those arms are outstretched to you.

This is a beautiful hymn, especially the way it was sung during the meeting. It is still a favorite of mine. Whenever I attended services after my conversion, I felt especially close to Mother since she received so much spiritual comfort in the Salvation Army. Through her influence I've also become a strong supporter and advocate of their love and charitable work.

I liked living in Halifax. Nina and Ritchie were very good to me, but when it was almost time to depart for the spring trip, I took the old train south and went to stay with Mother again. I walked into

Lunenburg, anxious to get back to sea, and signed up with the schooner *Gilbert B. Walters,* commanded by Captain Sonny Walters.

Besides almost hitting an iceberg on two occasions, the most memorable thing that happened was me being promoted from flunky to throater on this trip. Here's how it happened. Borg, a Swede about sixteen years old, was staying in the small Hillside Hotel in Lunenburg, and somehow he got to know Captain Walters. Borg claimed he had been a throater on schooners sailing out of Sweden, and the captain hired him as a throater on this schooner in which I would be the flunky. Being a throater, he'd be paid wages, and as a flunky I wouldn't, but that was no problem with me.

We set sail for the fishing banks and anchored in what the captain thought would be a good fishing spot. I'll never forget the look on the captain's face when the first codfish were forked on board. Borg handled the fish in the most awkward way, and all of us knew he didn't know the first thing about the job. He had only been bluffing. However, the captain tried to show him how it was done and gave him a week or so to learn. But it was no use. Borg couldn't handle it. The crew was upset because when one man can't do his job, it slows everyone else down.

Captain Walters asked me if I'd take over the throater's job in Borg's place. "You're a damn good flunky. You do your job well, and you learn fast. We'll pay you the regular wage, and you can fish on your own whenever you have free time. Is that okay with you?" You bet it was! I had watched the throaters on other vessels, and I had learned how fish were supposed to be dressed down, so I knew I could be a good throater.

The captain told Borg in a kind reprimand that since he couldn't handle the throater's job, he wanted him to become the flunky, but assured him he would still be paid a throater's wages. As the throater, I am proud to say the men, including the captain, complimented me. But every time I walked past Borg, he mumbled something hateful, and if looks could kill, I would have been dead.

I wish this were the end of the story—but it's not. About nine o'clock one night in Lunenburg, long after the fishing trip was over, I was walking along the sidewalk with a friend, Cecil Dorey. Suddenly, here came Borg with a knife in his hand, straight toward me. "I'll teach you to take my job," he said. "I'm going to slash you in a hundred places." I tried to explain that I hadn't asked for his job, but you don't argue with someone who has a knife. I'd seen Borg display his violent temper several times aboard the schooner. With that evil look in his eyes, he slashed at me several times and cut my left hand. I ran like hell, with Cecil beside me, and we lost Borg in an alley.

About a week later, in the middle of the afternoon, I ran into Borg again. This time he had a pistol. I said, "Feet, if you ever did your duty, do it now. Don't fail me!" My feet never stopped until we reached the police station in Lunenburg. When I told Chief Gardner about the incident with the gun, he replied, "Son, we can't do anything unless he harms you in some way, sorry." I never did lay eyes on Borg again, and thank God for that.

Since I had much respect for Captain Walters, I decided to sail again on the *Gilbert B. Walters*. Besides the regular dangers of being at sea, this trip was about the same as the others. I earned the regular wages for being the throater, and since I didn't have to deal with Borg, the trip was even more pleasant.

When this trip ended, I had no idea where I was going to stay. I had made about seventy dollars, but after I paid the firm for my fishing clothes, I had thirty-nine dollars left. Nina and Ritchie asked me to stay with them for the three weeks before the upcoming summer trip. In the meantime, they had moved to Lunenburg and rented part of a big old yellow house across from a company known as the Bailey Brothers, a firm where I would later work. Nina had the place neat and comfortable, and the meals were so good. Like Mother, she was a great cook. Ritchie was sailing on a different vessel, but he would return home about the same time as me. They made it clear they wanted me to stay with them again after the next trip was over.

Of all the interesting events at sea, nothing was more important to me than listening to the ship's radio. Some of the vessels had the first radios made, battery operated, of course. These early radios looked like a small box and had a tiny dial—with plenty of static. There was a small station, with 150 watts or so, in Louisburg, Cape Breton. It gave the marine weather reports and told where fresh bait was available and in which ports. If we were close enough, we'd pick up this station. During these reports, the station played country music, and I'd almost get into the radio to listen to every word.

It was during 1927 or 1928 when I first heard a broadcast aboard a schooner. Certainly radio was a big source of entertainment during the 1920s and the 1930s for those who could afford one. These programs came on the air at noon every day for one hour. Rest assured, I would always be ahead of my work so I could listen. The announcer played records of different artists such as Vernon Dalhart and Carson Robison. I still remember Dalhart singing "The Prisoner's Song," and "The Wreck of the Old '97." These songs gave me a great lift. I loved them.

I'd try to sing them exactly like the artist did, word for word, and with the same voice style.

I began entertaining the crew with my mouth organ and my dancing and singing. They applauded me like I was really something! Yes sir, their approval was one of the reasons I became more involved in music as time went by. Many of my story songs I later wrote reflect the disappointment and sensitivity of a young man being blown about like a ship without a sail. My situation made those songs true to life.

For the summer trip I lined up a job as a throater with Captain Leo Corkum. His ship was the *Maxwell F. Corkum*. He was a super gentleman, and I took a liking to him right away. I went to Corkum's firm and purchased the clothes I needed for the three months at sea.

Up to this point, I had experienced several dangerous situations at sea. Our vessel was almost run down by a steamer in the fog. We were nearly destroyed by icebergs. We were stuck in an ice blockade. We were tossed around the sea by gale-force winds on several occasions. But in spite of all this danger, I was more afraid of Charlie Tanner than I ever was at the treacherous times I spent at sea—that is, until a near-tragic situation developed that scared me from ever wanting to go to sea again.

Our trip started out in the usual way. Tom Nauss came alongside in his tugboat. The men let the lines go from the post on the dock, and we were towed out to the mouth of the harbor. We entered the open sea about dusk and were on our way to the Grand Banks of Newfoundland and the Western Banks. We had beautiful weather, and the crew seemed quite happy. They were busy doing their jobs getting the trawls ready, painting the buoys, and taking care of a dozen things that needed to be done before we reached the fishing banks. After a couple of days and nights we anchored on the Grand Banks and were ready to start the summer's work.

When I wasn't working as a throater and when it wasn't too foggy, I'd go back to the aft deck and fish for cod. One sunny, warm afternoon when I was fishing and sort of daydreaming about the future, I got something on my line that I couldn't pull up. I called for the salter, and he came running to help me. He had a terrible time with whatever I had hooked. "I believe it's a halibut," he said. "And them damn things don't come up nose first. They come up sideways and swim right and left, and it's like pulling a big flat object up against the pressure of the water." As the salter was struggling, the cook ran to see what was going on and to help. They finally got the fish on board by using the vessel's block and tackle, which was there to lower and raise the dories over the side of the vessel.

It was a halibut—and a big one! Unfortunately, as they were trying to get the huge fish aboard, the hook tore a hole in its side about four inches long. It was funny the way the crew made bets as to who weighed the most, me or the fish. They put the fish in the ship's ice bin to keep it fresh until we got to Canso, Nova Scotia, in a week or so. I was very excited about hooking this big one and could hardly wait to find out how much I'd get from this catch.

Every once in a while squid would be schooling across the fishing banks during the summer. The captain told me to use my squid jig and line often, and he promised me a dollar if I were the first of the crew to jig a squid, but I wasn't that lucky. One of the men jigged one while standing watch one night. Then all hands hit the deck, including me, to jig as many as we could. We needed them for fresh bait. They were excellent for catching codfish or haddock. One thing about them that I didn't like was the terrible black ink they'd squirt on you the moment you pulled them out of the water. If you didn't turn your head, they'd squirt you right in the face—which they did to me several times. This was their protection and served as a smoke screen if fish were after them. This black substance was not poison, but if you didn't wash it off right away, it would make small sores on your skin. If we continued to catch squid, it usually meant they were swimming across the fishing banks in schools. Sometimes we would jig them throughout the night. If we were lucky, we could catch enough squid that we could delay our trip into port.

During my trips at sea I spent a lot of time sitting on the side of the rails, nearly falling asleep trying to jig squid. Then some of the men would make me stop and go below, as they were afraid I'd fall overboard.

Some people eat squid. They're a delicacy in some parts of the world, Japan being one of them. Squid are ugly, about five to ten inches long, and have a lot of tentacles around the head. They look like an octopus. You jig them with a small red jig that has many small sharp pins curling upward from the bottom.

A bunch of men jigging squid is a very funny thing to watch. Back in the late 1950s I recorded a song entitled "Squid-Jiggin' Ground," written by Arthur R. Scammel of Canada. This record turned out to be one of the biggest hits I had in Canada in all my recording years there. These lyrics will show you how much fun it can be jigging squid:

> Oh, this is the place where the fishermen gather,
> In oilskins and boots and Cape Anns battened down;

All sizes of figures, with squid lines and jiggers,
They congregate here on the squid-jiggin' ground.

Some are workin' their jiggers while others are yarnin',
There's some standin' up and there's more lyin' down,
While all kinds of fun, jokes, and tricks are begun,
As they wait for the squid on the squid-jiggin' ground.

There's men of all ages and boys in the bargain,
There's old Billy Cave and there's young Raymond Brown;
There's a red-rantin' Tory out here in a dory,
A-runnin' down squires on the squid-jiggin' ground.

There's men from the harbor, there's men from the tickle,
In all kinds of motorboats, green, gray, and brown;
Right yonder is Bobby and with him is Nobby,
He's chawin' hardtack on the squid-jiggin' ground.

God bless my sou'wester, there's a skipper John Chaffey,
He's the best hand at squid jiggin' here, I'll be bound.
Hello! What's the row? Why, he's jiggin' one now,
The very first squid on the squid-jiggin' ground.

The man with the whisker is old Jacob Steele,
He's getting' well up but he's still pretty sound,
While Uncle Bob Hawkins wears six pairs of stockin's
Whenever he's out on the squid-jiggin' ground.

Holy smoke! What a scuffle, all hands are excited,
It's a wonder to me that there's nobody drowned;
There's a bustle, confusion, a wonderful hustle,
They're all jiggin' squids on the squid-jiggin' ground!

Says Bobby, "The squids are on top of the water,
I just got me jiggers 'bout one fathom down."
But a squid in the boat squirted right down his throat,
And he's swearin' like mad on the squid-jiggin' ground.

There's poor Uncle Billy, his whiskers are spattered
With spots of the squid juice that's flyin' around;
One poor little boy got it right in the eye,
But they don't give a darn on the squid-jiggin' ground.

Now, if you ever feel inclined to go squiddin',
Leave your white collars behind in the town;
And if you get cranky, without your silk hankie,
You'd better steer clear of the squid-jiggin' ground.

Throughout each trip, fog was always a concern. Each dory had its own compass, but the dorymen could still get lost. So it was extremely important to keep the horn blowing all the time when the men were out hauling their trawls in the fog. And wouldn't you know it, a serious problem developed one foggy afternoon. One of the dories didn't return with the others. The captain ordered the men to start the signal procedures—blowing the horn, sending up flares, firing the swivel cannon, and ringing the loud ship's bell. All of this was done, well into the night. We were afraid the dory had been hit by a passing steamer or had capsized and the men had drowned. But if it was a steamer, we reasoned, we would have heard their loud signal.

Into the second day we still had no sign of the dory and the two men. The captain then decided we should head for Canso to see if the men had been found and to notify the Coast Guard if they hadn't. As soon as we dropped anchor in the harbor, a man came on board and notified us that the men had been picked up by another vessel and had gone on to their homes since it was getting pretty late in the summer. We were all relieved, to say the least.

In Canso the first thing I wanted to do was to get my big halibut ashore to the fish plant and sell it. Some of the men took it ashore for me, and I was stunned when they told me the fish weighed eighty-seven pounds and sold for seventy-four dollars. I couldn't believe it! And if the hook had not torn the fish on the side, it would have brought even more money.

We spent about two days in Canso and returned to sea. Soon thereafter I experienced the most terrifying situation in my life. Had it not been for this near disaster when I was sixteen years old, I might still be a seaman.

The year was 1930. And it was August, when the storms are most dangerous. We were sailing to another fishing spot west of Sable Island about seven o'clock. It was almost dark. We noticed that the clouds overhead were flying by so fast we could hardly follow them with our eyes. I could tell by listening to the crew that something big was about to take place. The captain's orders were to stand by on deck as the storm came, in case the winds got stronger.

Believe me, they did. It got much worse. About nine o'clock the men lowered the foresail and put a single reef in it. I'll try to explain how this is done. There are reefing points on both the foresail and the mainsail. These are two rows of rope, each approximately three feet long, that go horizontal across the sail. Reefing a sail meant the sail would be lowered to the first reefing point and secured to the boom, a horizontal bar that holds the bottom of the sail. Doing this causes the sail to become at least a quarter smaller than its original size, which would help keep the wind from tearing the sail or stripping it from the vessel entirely.

Since we were on a lengthy passage from one fishing bank to the other, the mainsail, the biggest sail, had also been raised. This is seldom done on short sailing trips. So the captain ordered the single reef in the mainsail also. About two hours later the storm had gotten so much worse, the captain ordered a double reef in the foresail and the mainsail, bringing both down about a third smaller than their original sizes. Then he put us on a course sailing into the wind. After that there was nothing else we could do. Nothing at all. We were strictly at the mercy of the August gale. Our only hope was that the storm wouldn't last much longer and that we could weather it out.

But by midnight the winds got even stronger—the strongest I had ever seen—and this was the biggest I had ever seen the seas (they're called seas when they become big and dangerous). They were mountains high! Our vessel seemed so small as it was battered by these enormous seas. The crew didn't want me on deck, so you can imagine just how scared I was. However, I took a chance and climbed up the ladder in the galley and took a peek outside. When I stuck my head out, the open force of the gale spun my head around so fast it was a wonder it didn't break my neck. I went below as quick as lightning. My quarters were way up in the bow of the ship, which was the worst part to be in during a storm. I felt like I was trapped in a coffin.

Our schooner would rise to the top of those huge waves, then slide down until it struck the bottom of the waves. It felt like going down on a fast elevator and suddenly coming to a stop. Every time the ship rose to the top, I held my breath, wondering when we would hit bottom, fully expecting our vessel to break into a million pieces. When we hit bottom, the whole ship trembled. It seemed like the waves would hold her steady for a split second, and then water would come streaming down the companionway as the big seas continued to break over the ship. The lamp that hung down by a chain over the long table in the galley went out, and it looked like a dungeon down there. It was black as coal. I was terrified.

One of the men came down the companionway to try to light the lamp, but the water had soaked it and he couldn't light it. Then, to make things even worse, another crewman came down and said, "We've got two men lashed to the wheel, trying to keep our vessel headed straight into the wind. If she turns sideways, these big seas will break her in two." One of the seaman who had been tied to a rope was washed overboard on the front of the ship, then picked up by another wave and washed back onto the aft deck. It was a miracle he wasn't hurt. He could easily have been thrown against the side of the vessel and killed.

About midnight another of the crew came down and announced, "This is the worst hurricane I've ever seen in all my forty years at sea. We better all start saying some very well-meant prayers." Friends, you can bet I said mine!

Soon the foresail blew away, and the men said later that it flew into the air like a silk handkerchief. By then the winds had almost stripped the deck clean, except for the dories, which had been lashed down with heavy ropes. Our vessel had been thrown around so much I didn't think it could take much more of this beating.

It was deathly quiet except for the frightening sounds from the storm. When I heard the men talking again, I didn't miss a word. They said the wind was blowing us directly toward Sable Island. Someone exclaimed, "Oh, no!" And you could feel the fear in the air. Every one of the crew knew exactly what that meant. Sable Island is known worldwide as the Ocean's Graveyard. It's about two hundred or two hundred fifty miles from the eastern tip of Nova Scotia, about twenty miles long and a mile wide, with long quicksand bars running off each end in different directions. Since the 1700s, many ships have been shipwrecked by these submerged sandbars, and countless sailors have lost their lives there. Ships never go near the island by choice because it is a death trap. When a ship is blown on the island by a severe storm, the vessel and the crew rarely survive. The men said we were on our way to the Ocean's Graveyard, and there was absolutely nothing we could do about it. We had no control over our schooner. None whatsoever.

But when we were only about fourteen miles from the island, the Good Lord reached out His hand and changed the wind. Saved by the grace of God! The men cheered and offered prayers. When the wind changed, we were blown completely in the opposite direction from the treacherous island, and our vessel limped into Canso a few days later. It looked like a tornado had hit the ship. The deck was beaten up, and the living quarters were a tangled mess.

The captain had decided we'd go back to sea and head for the Western Banks again, since this would be on our way home. But my mind was made up. I would not go back to the open sea on that vessel or any other vessel. I was finished. No more fishing trips for me. I was on the first dory that went ashore after we anchored in the harbor, and I stayed on shore. I didn't say a word to any of the crew that I wasn't going back to the schooner. I sat on the bank, watching to see when our vessel left. I knew I'd feel better when the schooner pulled up anchor and was under way, but I was worried when it didn't leave at the time it was supposed to. Later I heard that when the captain found out I wasn't aboard, he held the vessel at anchor for several more hours, waiting for me to return. As soon as I found a vessel going to Lunenburg, I was on it.

A day after the tragedy, the grim news came that six vessels within a hundred-mile radius of us had been lost in the storm, drowning 132 men. Most of these men came from the village of Bluerocks. This was one of the greatest sea disasters in Canada's history, and it nearly wiped out the male population in that little village.

During October of each year, when all the fishing schooners were home for the winter, Lunenburg had a big fair known as the Fisheries Exhibition. This fair was for the benefit of all the fishermen and their families and any outsiders who wanted to attend. It featured a carnival, owned and operated by Bill Lynch. Included were rides and games. Prizes were awarded in the competitive events, such as diving and other water contests, and in boat, dory, and swimming races.

These diversions offered the men a little enjoyment and recreation after their long months at sea. The celebration was fun, but it had its serious side, too. It lasted four or five days, and on the last day, Sunday, a memorial service was held for those who had lost their lives at sea. Priests and preachers conducted appropriate services on the waterfront, and the loved ones dropped wreaths of memory into the water from the wharfs where the ceremony took place.

Although I knew I'd never go to sea again, I wouldn't trade those memories for all the money in the world. The sea was my home—the only real home I knew after my mother was divorced from my father. The fishermen were my family. They gave me a sense of belonging. The sea and the men were my education. The sea was my adventure.

They say sea life gets in your blood. It sure got in mine. I experienced real-life situations of excitement and danger that most people only learn through books and movies. I never even finished the fifth grade. I was held back in that grade and left school altogether in the middle of the second year because I was too embarrassed to return. Nevertheless, because of the many types of people I met and the many experiences I had, my education was probably more extensive than any of us can get inside a classroom. I humbly believe these real-life experiences shaped me into a very understanding and appreciative person.

Later on I had many good offers to sail on ocean liners as well as on merchant marine ships. During the days when rum-running boats were smuggling rum and other liquors from St. Pierre and Miquelon islands and other places, the merchant marine jobs paid extremely well. I could have taken several of those jobs if I had been interested, but I decided against any of that. My ocean sailing was over.

6

Struggling

Traveling the lonely road of sorrow,
Heartaches are all I've ever known.
Time has turned a million pages,
Fate has dealt and I'm alone.

"Somewhere along Life's Highway,"
by Hank Snow

❧

NOT GOING BACK TO SEA MEANT I had no real home, no job, and no money. Jobs were hard to find during the depression. Even men with families were unemployed.

Once again I moved in with Nina and Ritchie. Since Ritchie didn't have a job during the winter, he and I chummed around, and these were happy times for me. I had earned a little money, and Ritchie gave me the rest to buy a .22 rifle. I hunted rabbits, partridges, and other small game so we could have meat during the winter months.

Dad's skill with the rifle apparently rubbed off on me. I became an expert marksman. But I did something very stupid, and I'm almost too embarrassed to tell it. I hope, though, someone may learn a valuable lesson from this. I was sitting in the kitchen cleaning my rifle and had the barrel pointed toward the ceiling while I checked to make sure it was not loaded. Now, you know what I'm going to say, because you all have heard this story before. Yes, the supposedly unloaded rifle went off, and the bullet barely missed Nina's head! Neither of us could speak for a full minute. Nina turned as white as a sheet, and I was shaking like a leaf to think I almost killed my sister.

As a teenager I was naturally interested in girls, and I needed money to dress up like the other boys to impress the girls. When I couldn't find a job, I became a teenage bootlegger to make some money. A lot of bootlegging was going on, and I'm sure drinking increased as people wanted some relief from the daily worries of economic problems. Rum was the popular drink, at least in Bluerocks.

A gentleman friend in Stonehurst, whose name I won't mention, owned a large sea-going vessel. He'd go out to the twelve-mile limit to meet the rum-running boats and buy a load. These boats brought the rum from places like St. Pierre, Miquelon, and Barbados. This was risky business, because anything inside the twelve-mile limit was definitely illegal, and government coast guard boats were constantly searching these waters day and night. When this gentleman brought his rum into shore, his regular buyers would immediately meet him and make their purchases.

I borrowed possibly the only dollar that Nina had, and I bought my first quart of raw rum from the gentleman. This undiluted rum was 200 proof. I was not a drinker, but a friend told me how much to cut it, in which one quart should make three pints. But I diluted it to four pints. By adding more water, I could get another pint and make more money. I would sell each pint for one dollar and make three dollars on my investment.

The Royal Canadian Mounted Police were forever driving around, trying to catch bootleggers, and I was always scared they might discover my scheme. I wanted to store the rum completely away from the house and sell it secretly. I walked up over the hill from Nina's house and found an abandoned well across from the Baptist church. I reached inside the top of the well and hid the rum under the edge of some rocks that served as a wall for the well. The next day someone asked for a pint of rum, and I told him I'd be back in about thirty minutes. I walked to the old well, and surprise! My rum was gone. Somebody evidently had seen me hide it and probably stole it as soon as I left the well. Anyway, that was my first venture into bootlegging, and it seemed so easy that I wanted to do it again.

When I came up with another dollar, I bought a quart and diluted it into three pints. I went to the store where I would find guys who were potential buyers. Now, several months previous to this, while walking back and forth to Lunenburg, I had become acquainted with three mounted police. On several occasions they had stopped me to ask where certain people lived, in their efforts to investigate people suspected of bootlegging.

On that afternoon I stuck the three pint bottles in my belt and pulled my sweater down over them. That made me look like I weighed about one hundred fifty pounds. On my way over to Bluerocks from Nina's place I spotted the Royal Canadian Mounted Police's car coming over the hill. I was sure they had heard about me and were coming to arrest me. My heart started pounding, and I was shaking all over. I couldn't run. They had already seen me, and if I had run, the three bottles would have been strewn all over the dirt road. They pulled up beside me and stopped. Right away I saw they were in a pleasant mood. They asked how things were going. Back then the cars had running boards. This was a plus for me. I put my foot on the running board, because I was afraid the bottles would slip down my leg and go on the ground. But I tried to keep my smile and acted as unconcerned as I could. They asked me where a certain person lived, and if I knew him. I knew him, all right. He was a good friend of mine, but I pretended I only knew him casually. I said I'd heard that he had moved away and I didn't know where. I was certainly relieved when they thanked me and drove away. I immediately went to my friend's house and told him what had happened. We both decided to stop bootlegging. But this venture did produce enough money for me to buy some brand-new clothes—the best I'd ever had.

I got so desperate for money a short time later that I did squeal on another bootlegger. Nina and Ritchie had moved again, into a larger place on the Atlantic shore, and another family lived on the other side of the house. With only a thin partition between the two apartments you could hear every sound made in the other one.

One night when I couldn't get to sleep, I heard what sounded like jugs and bottles rattling around. As a former bootlegger myself, I recognized this sound immediately. I was sure they were diluting rum and bottling it to sell. And I knew the Canadian government was paying twelve dollars to anyone who turned in a bootlegger.

The next day I walked to Lunenburg, into the Mounted Police office, and reported my suspicions. The police came that night and caught the bootlegger red-handed. To make it look like it was not a setup, the three policemen first came to our apartment. They whispered to us what they were going to do, then talked real loud to make the neighbors think they were searching our place. I was glad they did this, because I didn't want the neighbors to think I had turned them in.

Soon thereafter I had my first experience with a halfway house. In Canada a halfway house is a house of prostitution. Three friends, John, Carl, and J.T., and I decided to visit one on a weekend. I told Nina and Ritchie I was going to visit friends in Bridgewater. I put on my new clothes that I'd bought with my bootlegging money: gray flannel pants, light green sweater, and black-and-white summer oxfords.

The halfway house was way back in the woods on a dirt road, about ten miles from Bluerocks. Carl had an old beat-up car and he drove us there.

I was nervous going in, but the lady of the house, the madame, a big woman with a happy personality, made us feel right at home. We had a couple of drinks of rum, which I was definitely not used to. We giggled, made suggestive remarks, and enjoyed the atmosphere. After an evening of unusual fun, Carl drove home that night because he had to work the next day. Of course, this left us without transportation, and way out in the woods, about two miles from the main highway. The next day we had a few more drinks and a good time. After supper we tried to figure out a way to get back home. There was no phone to call a friend, but I remembered that Mr. Zink, an elderly gentleman, lived about two miles away in the tiny village of First South. He operated a general store, post office, and one or two gas pumps. He also had an old car he used for a taxi in an emergency.

John said, "Let's get the old man out of bed and have him drive us to Bluerocks." We walked to his door and knocked. Mr. Zink opened the upstairs window, and when we told him we needed to be driven to Bluerocks, he said he'd be right down. Before we could leave, he had to open the pump and get gasoline. The nice old man had been crippled in one leg and hip for many years, and he had a bad limp.

Mr. Zink was quite uncomfortable trying to drive through the rain and fog. But he was friendly and asked questions like where we had been and where we were from. Well, I never heard such wild tales as John and J.T. made up. When these guys began whispering to themselves, I realized that just like me they had no money. When we got to the edge of Bluerocks, J.T. asked Mr. Zink to let us out in front of the home of Alex Knickle and said, "My uncle lives here, and we'll be staying here for the night. I'll have to get some money from him to pay you, so wait right here. I'll be back in a jiffy." John and J.T. got out and walked toward the darkened house. They had no intention of paying the man. They were long gone, leaving me to face the music.

I didn't want to be alone with Mr. Zink when he learned about their trick. After about ten minutes, I said I'd go see what was taking them so long. I climbed over the fence and stood at the corner of the house, wondering what I should do, when I heard Mr. Zink calling, "Boys, you'll have to hurry, I can't wait much longer. I need to get back home before it gets too late." Nina only lived about a mile from Mr. Knickle's house, so I was trying to decide whether or not to traipse through the tall, wet bushes and swamp, or to wait until Mr. Zink was gone and then take the road.

All of a sudden I heard the bushes rattle as if someone were coming through them. I thought Mr. Zink was trying to find us! I took off and ran through the bushes with the speed of a deer. All of a sudden my feet left the ground and I landed in a huge swamp well filled with frog slime. It came up nearly to my neck, and it smelled terrible. I was gasping for breath and thought I heard all kinds of strange noises. I was sure snakes were swimming around me, and I was trying like hell to get out of there. After several desperate attempts I climbed out. Well, I ruined my new clothes and new shoes. My best sweater and pants had been shredded by the bushes and thorns. So you see, friends, what goes around comes around, doesn't it?

As I stood there with the dirty water running off my clothes, I heard Mr. Zink's car drive away. I was relieved but felt bad about the dirty trick. I walked back to the road and proceeded to Nina's place, feeling guilty with every step.

The next day I went to the general store to find John and J.T. bragging and laughing about what they had done. But my conscience bothered me. Even with his handicap, Mr. Zink had been nice enough to drive us the long distance in bad weather. Throughout the years I've had a soft place in my heart for anybody with a physical handicap.

Now, friends, I must tell you about the most embarrassing moment in my entire life. This is crystal clear in my mind today. How could I ever forget it? Bluerocks had three country stores where folks would hang out and spread some gossip and the men would tell a lot of fishing stories. Each of these general stores had an old potbellied coal stove sitting in the middle of the floor and benches around it. One of these was the main store for the teenagers to hang out, make dates, and just talk.

One cold winter night a bunch of us boys and girls were sitting around in the store. We were laughing and the boys were trying to impress the gals as usual. I was stuck on Sheila. She was very pretty, with jet-black hair and eyes to match. I believe she liked me, too, but she was very bashful. Whenever I could, I'd try to catch her eye and do things to impress her.

Well, I impressed her all right! Not only her, but everyone in the entire store. Kenny Knickle, a good friend of mine and a real character, was sitting next to me on one of the benches back of the big coal stove. Sheila and some of the other girls were sitting on the other bench across from us. Kenny must have been eating beans or something else that filled him full of gas. When things got real quiet for a few seconds, Kenny let the biggest and longest fart I have ever heard! Then he jumped up and started shaming me with his one index finger over his other index finger. He said, "Shame on you, Jack. I never thought you'd do anything like that, especially in front of these young ladies." I was devastated. I was helpless. There was nothing I could do or say. I must have turned a thousand colors. I tried to defend myself, but no words came out. I just sat there for a minute—then I got the hell out of there.

Some things seem so big at the time, especially to a teenager, that you never forget them. Only when you look back do they become humorous.

There weren't many exciting things to do in those days, but we boys found ways of getting together with the girls. In addition to meeting in the stores, we'd walk up and down the country lanes, wearing our best clothes. We'd talk and giggle, and if there was no moon, we'd carry our flashlights to see who the girls were and to look them over. We did this almost every night, including Sundays.

Bluerocks had two churches, Baptist and English. Most of the young people looked forward to attending Sunday night services. We made that a social event, and the boys and girls would again try to impress each other.

The following story was told to me by many people, who swear it's true. One of the boys involved was Abraham, "Abey" for short, and the other was George. They would choose the back seat because they would take a "bully" of rum to church. The bully was about the same size as a pint bottle. Abey carried it in his inside coat pocket. They would take a few nips during church services. One night during the meeting Abey slouched way down in the seat and was just about to take a drink. The minister's sermon was built on the topic "Abraham, what hast thou in thy bosom?" When Abey heard these words, he jumped straight up and poked George and said, "Here, George, you take it, he knows I've got it!" That was the end of taking rum to church.

Bluerocks was definitely known for its beautiful girls. During the time I lived there, I guess I was in love with a dozen pretty ones. But I was embarrassed because I didn't have the best of clothes, though what I did have were always clean and pressed. Nevertheless, I treated the young ladies with the utmost respect, and it made me feel good to know that many of them liked me, in spite of the fact that I didn't have any money to spend on them.

Among the social events I loved the most were the pie or cake socials. These were usually sponsored by the churches or by a ladies' fund-raising club. On the day of the social the church congregation would take the benches, chairs, and tables outside and put them on the lawn, and the girls would display their pies and cakes on the tables. One of the men acted as the auctioneer, and the boys bid on the baked goods. Whoever bid the highest price got to eat the pie or cake with the girl who made it. Unfortunately, I never had any money to buy one, but I'd bid sometimes anyway if I knew that certain boys would outbid me. When the eating began, there was plenty of pie and cake to go around. Everybody had a real good time, and I've seen several romances blossom at these social events.

Another popular social occasion was the summertime garden party, also sponsored by a church or a charitable organization. Booths were built on the church grounds for selling merchandise and playing games for prizes. The women made quilts and various other articles to sell and raise money for the churches. Good fun and fellowship were in abundance during these events.

Bluerocks received a good many Canadian and American tourists, as well as a few from other countries. The wharfs and fishing boats were a popular attraction for visitors. Many artists came here to paint pictures, especially to create landscapes, seascapes, and marine paintings of boats and the fishhouses. Coves extended inland from the Atlantic Ocean, and fishhouses were built along the shores of these little coves, where the boats were tied up. The unique lay of the land, with its trees and flowers, along with the blue skies and the white-capped ocean waves, made this a beautiful setting for creating paintings. When I lived in Bluerocks and wasn't working, I spent much of my time around the wharfs watching the artists at work. I observed them closely to learn about different techniques of oil painting.

Along with a friend I'd go swimming in the area. To impress the tourists we'd dive off the wharf and swim underwater as long as we could. Sometimes the tourists would throw a nickel or dime in the water, and we were so good at diving, we could catch the money and bring it back up. There wasn't much danger to us as long as we stayed on the inside of the cove where the wharf could shield us from the big Atlantic waves. On the ocean side of the wharf the sea was very dangerous because of the strong undertow.

One time I got very brave and ventured over to the ocean side of the wharf. Almost immediately I was caught up in a swirling undertow that dragged me away from the wharf. I had no control whatsoever over my body. I was tossed all around by the waves, and I screamed for someone to save me. But nobody had a rope to throw, and nobody could help me unless they also jumped into the fierce undertow. I thought I was drowning. Then suddenly a huge wave picked me up and drove me against the side of the wharf. I felt like every bone in my body was broken. Several of the boys pulled me out, and thanks to the Good Lord I was safe again. I had done a dumb thing in trying to show off, and I nearly lost my life over it.

The word got around Bluerocks that I had almost drowned, but you know how stories get blown out of proportion as they pass from one to another, and it wound up that I had drowned. In Lunenburg, where Mother was living, she heard the rumor and nearly had a heart attack. But thankfully, she soon got the corrected story. However, a Mrs. Schwartz, whose son was taking guitar lessons from Mother, said she heard I was dead, and she had already bought a wreath for my funeral.

Since childhood I've had chronic bronchial trouble. During a time when I was living with Nina and Ritchie, I began to cough a lot and was afraid I'd develop pneumonia. But I had no money, neither did Nina or Ritchie, for me to pay a doctor. As the cough got worse I went to Lunenburg and saw Dr. Creighton. He treated people whether they could pay or not, and he even made house calls in emergencies. After he examined my throat, he shook his head. "My dear boy, those tonsils need to come out. They're honeycombed and have yellow blisters. The poison could go through your whole system and cause you a serious problem."

He wrote me a prescription and said to be sure to take the pills for one week, then come back for the operation. The purpose of the pills was to thicken my blood so I wouldn't bleed to death during and after the operation. I've always had a problem with excessive bleeding whenever I cut myself, so I knew the importance of the medication. Although Nina, Ritchie, and I didn't have any money, I went to the drugstore and was told the prescription would cost fifty cents. I tried several ways to get the money but to no avail. I asked one of Ritchie's brothers, who had a steady job, but he couldn't or wouldn't help me. I was beginning to panic because I wasn't getting better. Dr. Creighton was a caring person, and I knew he would take my tonsils out without being paid, but I couldn't even get the money for the prescription.

I was in a dilemma. I was afraid I'd bleed to death if I didn't take the pills, and I was afraid I'd die from the serious coughing problem if I didn't have the operation. What could I do? During the next couple of days I made several trips to Lunenburg, eight miles round trip, to see if I could catch Dr. Creighton going in or out of his office. I hoped I could muster enough courage to ask him if it were really necessary that I take the pills. But I couldn't get up the courage to ask him. I know in my heart that he would have taken care of it because he was such a kind and understanding man.

But what bothered me the most was Ritchie's brother going around the neighborhood telling everybody I had asked him for the money, as well as several other boys, and that no one would lend it to me. After that, every night when I was around those general stores or walking up and down the roads, someone would yell to the others, "Hey, give me fifty cents to get my tonsils out. Poor little guy don't have fifty cents to get his tonsils out. Let me have fifty cents to buy medicine. Poor thing, he might bleed to death." This was not funny to me at all. It was real embarrassing, especially since all the girls were hearing it, too. Now I believe they made fun of me because I had become popular with many of the girls, and some were their girlfriends.

About a week and a half after my throat exam, I returned at 9:00 A.M. for my operation. Dr. Creighton didn't ask if I had taken the pills. I'm sure he assumed I had, since he had emphasized their importance. The doctor had me sit in a regular straight chair, and he sat down facing me. He numbed my throat with some sort of spray and gave me a shot. He asked, "Would you like me to put something over your eyes so you can't see what's going on?" I told him no. I thought to myself that if I were going to bleed to death, I wanted to see it. Fortunately, I didn't have to worry about excess bleeding. I never saw one drop of blood. Dr. Creighton was kind enough to drive me back to Nina's house. My throat was a little tender for about a week, and then I was as good as new.

The good doctor never did send me a bill for his services. Bless his heart. I'm sure he knew of my poor circumstances, and I've never forgotten him for his kindness. Some years later I wrote a letter to him in Lunenburg, offering to pay him, but my letter came back unopened.

Once I was cutting kindling wood and almost cut the end of my middle finger off. The blood spurted out, and I wrapped my handkerchief around it, but I was afraid the bleeding might not stop. When Nina saw it, she said I should go to the doctor in Lunenburg as soon as I could. I began the four-mile walk, but it was getting dark and cold, and the road was real muddy. After I'd gone about a mile, I stopped and thought to myself, "Why am I walking all the way into Lunenburg to see a doctor? I'll be okay." By then most of the bleeding had stopped, and I returned home. I didn't realize it at the time, but I could have lost my finger. However, in a couple of weeks it had nearly healed, but it did form proud flesh around the cut, which had to be taken off. Usually the doctor does this with a special instrument, but Ritchie heated a piece of haywire to sterilize it, and he burned this flesh completely off.

I thank the Good Lord for saving my finger. Otherwise I might never have been able to pick my guitar like I've always done on my records and on stage. My music career might never have happened.

While living with Nina and Ritchie, I saw a picture in the T. Eaton catalog advertising a new guitar for $12.95. I still owned my first guitar, the T. Eaton Special I had bought for $5.95, including a chord book. But it was hard to chord because the strings were so high above the neck. I was sure this new and more expensive one would be easier to play. Every few days I'd get the catalog out and look at the picture of the beautiful guitar.

And I would dream, dream, dream!

But how could I ever come up with that kind of money? I didn't have a penny, and I didn't have a job. However, I figured if I could sell my first guitar for five dollars I might find a way to get the additional $7.95.

Sure enough, good fortune came by way of Charlie Knickle. Charlie and his sweet wife, Sue, owned and operated the store in Bluerocks in which the local post office was located. Charlie had just purchased a beautiful, classy new dark-blue car, with yellow pinstripes on the body. The blue wooden spokes on the wheels were the same shade of blue, and I thought they would look better if they also had thin yellow stripes. I told Charlie I could paint pinstripes on the spokes to match those on the body. He knew I'd done some painting before. "Great idea!" he said, "I'll be glad to pay you two dollars per wheel." I jumped for joy! With eight dollars, and if I could sell my first guitar, I'd be able to order the new one. I was timid about painting the thin stripes because I hadn't done anything this tedious before. But I was determined to do a good job, and I was determined to get that guitar.

Charlie took the wheels off one at a time, and I sat on the ground with my can of house paint. I took my time and worked about two weeks off and on, making sure that the tiny yellow lines were perfect. Both Charlie and Sue were well pleased with my project, and he paid me immediately.

I took my old guitar into Lunenburg and asked the gentleman who owned Himmelmon's Optical Studios if he'd put it in his window. He was courteous and happy to do that for me. He put a five-dollar price tag on it, and it was sold the next day to Lorraine Mason.

Hooray! I had the money. I ordered my new guitar immediately, and I was like a little kid waiting for Christmas. When it finally arrived at the post office, Sue sent word to me, and I was there in no time. Some of the boys were hanging around the store and tried to get me to open the box and show them my prize. But I didn't. I never liked to open something new in front of people. It always seemed more special to me to open a package in private. This way, I could examine it slowly and enjoy that moment of pleasure myself. I was on cloud nine as I hurried home. When I opened the box, the guitar was even more beautiful than its picture! Its tone was much superior to my first guitar. The new one had a thinner neck and the strings were lower, which made it easier to play.

I found myself picking it up just about every free moment I had, and I experimented with guitar runs and chord progressions that sounded like Jimmie Rodgers. Jimmie had become my idol the moment I first heard his record of "Moonlight and Skies," and I wanted to play and sing just like him.

Before I even bought my first guitar, one of the boys in Bluerocks had purchased a cheap guitar, and we used to gather in an old fishhouse where the men stored their fishing gear, and I'd sing and play for them. They liked it, even though at that time I could only play by sliding a steel bar across the strings, Hawaiian style, like Mother had showed me. When I bought my first guitar, I started mastering the chords and began playing Spanish style.

Both Nina and Ritchie bragged about me to everyone. Whenever Ritchie was home from the fishing banks, we'd take my guitar and go to people's houses, and I'd play and sing for them. He would enthusiastically say to the neighbors, "You've got to hear Jack. He can play and sing just like Jimmie Rodgers, and he's going to be a big star someday."

Every time I learned a new song I couldn't wait to sing it to the neighbors. Gradually I built quite a catalog of songs. I had begun to believe some of the good things Ritchie and Nina were saying about me, and when the neighbors bragged on me, too, this was tremendous encouragement. Soon I bought a mouth organ, which I placed in a frame that clamped on the top of my shoulders, and I could play the mouth organ and the guitar chords together.

I began to daydream about singing on the radio and making records just like Jimmie Rodgers. These dreams began to overwhelm me so much that I started making plans in my mind to go to Halifax to get on radio station CHNS. On the back of a scribbler cover I drew a picture of a record and a microphone at radio station CHNS. The title of the song on the record was "My Blue-Eyed Jane," by Clarence E. Snow. Of course, this was a Jimmie Rodgers song, but eventually, when my dreams came true, I recorded the song Hank Snow style.

I was not comfortable staying with Nina and Ritchie, eating their food every day and not being able to add a few dollars to help out. So I moved in with Lillian for a while. She and Wilbert had rented a small, weather-beaten house in the middle of Lunenburg. Again I was back to bread and molasses and sleeping on a very hard, broken-down couch. This was the kind of reality that I hoped my musical dreams would take me from.

One day when I came home after unsuccessfully looking for a job, Lillian cheered me up with a big surprise. She said some people had come by and invited me to take part in a minstrel show in Bridgewater to help raise money for a charity fund. This was a happy moment for me. Somebody besides family thought I had talent as a singer! I was walking on air. The show was being staged by a Mr. Moss, who had heard about me and had tracked me down at Lillian's house. The folks said they would check back in about a week to see if I was interested. I remember thinking they had come to the right place to find charity, and I thought about asking them to put on a show for me. I needed money worse than any charity I could think of. Of course I was interested.

On the night of the show, a chauffeur came for me in a new car to drive me the twelve miles to Bridgewater. He carried my guitar to the car, opened the door, and ushered me in. Sitting in the back seat of this big car, I really felt important. When we got to Bridgewater, the driver took me to the Moss Jewelry Store to meet Mr. Moss and two of his sons. They took me home with them, and I met Mrs. Moss, who was just as wonderful as the rest of her family. We sat down to a fine supper, with a variety of food that I hadn't eaten since being on my last schooner.

After supper we drove to the big gym hall for the show. The closer we got, the more nervous I got. Blackface comedy was big in those days, and minstrel shows were popular just about everywhere. Somebody blackened my face with black polish and put white rings around my eyes and lips. This was a funny show with an interlocutor who introduced each act and had jokes going back and forth with the performers on stage. When I was introduced, I went on stage and sat down in a chair, and the interlocutor handed me my guitar. I proceeded to play and sing a song entitled "I Went to See My Gal Last Night." My debut was a big success! I even got a standing ovation. When the Moss family drove me back home, they said I had stolen the show. Maybe they were just being nice, but I sure appreciated the compliment. This was definitely one of the proudest moments of my younger life. It gave me more encouragement to pursue my musical dreams.

While staying with Lillian, I'd often go downtown in Lunenburg and hang out during the day until late at night. I'd stand on the corner watching the sights, but mainly I just wanted to keep away from Wilbert as much as I could. Then one day I discovered that one of my friends, Cecil Dorey, was working in a livery stable owned by an older gentleman, Solly Knickle. Cecil told me they needed another worker, and I was hired right away. This turned out to be one of the most enjoyable jobs I ever had.

I was working not far from where Mother was living at the time. She and Charlie had moved into a big old white house on the outskirts of Lunenburg, and Mother invited me back to stay with her. I wanted to give it another try. I reasoned that as long as I was able to contribute some money, Charlie might not be so mean to me.

I loved the idea of working with horses. Mr. Knickle had six horses and several rubber-tired buggies, as well as regular freight wagons for hauling trunks of all sizes. My job was the same as Cecil's. He and I'd pick up and deliver passengers and freight to and from the train station in Lunenburg. This was the same kind of business that Mr. Balcom had when Mother worked for him, but Mr. Knickle kept at least two cars and drivers on hand for taxi service in case people preferred to ride in cars. Most of the customers, though, preferred to ride in the buggies.

This job carried a lot of responsibilities. Cecil and I took care of the horses, buggies, and wagons. We fed and groomed the horses daily, kept them shod, and cleaned the stables every day. Mr. Knickle paid us six dollars in cash at the end of each week. This was pretty good money.

The facilities at the livery stable were also quite good. The big three-story barn was so large inside you could park several wagons on both the first and second floors. I got very attached to the horses—Kitty, Harry, Fred, Prince, Polly, and Maude—and I can still picture in my mind how the barn looked, each horse's position in the stalls, and their personalities.

Maude was a little brown mare. She was my favorite. Cecil and I made a makeshift saddle so I could ride her, and I rode her every day to Mother's place for lunch. Maude was fast, and I could be home in no time.

Once I rode Fred bareback to the blacksmith's shop to be freshly shod. He was exceptionally fast, and we had to be real careful with him because he would calk himself. This meant he'd kick the inside of his ankle with the shoe from his opposite foot, and this kept his ankle constantly raw. Blacksmiths tried to shoe him in different ways to prevent this, but they couldn't stop it. If we ran Fred too much, his foot would become very painful, and he'd start to limp when he was trotting. Therefore, we usually walked him rather than let him trot.

After Fred was shod, I was riding him back to the livery stables, when I saw some teenage girls. I started showing off. The road was paved, and pavement is hard on a horse's hoofs, especially if he trots or gallops. Well, to impress the girls, riding bareback, I put Fred into a gallop. About that time someone yelled my name, and I turned around to see who it was. With a slight sway from Fred, I slid right off his back on the hard pavement and knocked the enamel off three of my teeth and cut a large gash on the bottom of my chin. I still carry the scar, but most of all I was thoroughly embarrassed. And Fred was long gone. When I walked back to the stable, Cecil had already put the horse in his stall.

Now, friends, I have to confess something. Cecil and I were a little dishonest with Mr. Knickle, even though he was fair and always kind to us. Sometimes fishermen would come from Newfoundland to take a job aboard a fishing schooner in Lunenburg. They would travel from Newfoundland to Sydney, Cape Breton, Nova Scotia, via an overnight steamship, then take the train to Lunenburg. Cecil or I would meet the men at the train station and take them and their chests or trunks to the particular vessel they were going to sea on. Sometimes there would be three or four men with their chests. In this case we'd haul the chests only, and the men would walk or hire one of Mr. Knickle's taxis. Usually, though, we were sent to the station for one man and his chest, and we'd take the pay from the other three and put it in our pockets. The cost was fifty cents per man. We did the same thing when the fishermen returned from their fishing trips. We'd take the chests back to the station to be sent to their homes. Sometimes we'd give Mr. Knickle part of what we made, and sometimes we wouldn't. He was never the wiser. This was dishonest. We were cheating a fine old man, and I feel guilty about that to this day.

When I started the job working with horses, I didn't even know how to put a collar on or put a bit in a horse's mouth, but it didn't take me long to learn. I developed a great love for horses, and I became a very good rider. All my life, and especially since I had my dog Spot, I've loved all kinds of animals.

During this time, Mother and my sisters met two neighborly families. One couple, Mr. and Mrs. Donald Legag, lived in one side of a double house, and the Lohnes family lived in the other side. The Lohnes family was large, with six or seven boys and a beautiful daughter named Myrtle. The Legags had an old pump organ, and every Sunday night, and some nights through the week, the families would all get together and sing hymns while Mother played the organ. At some of those gatherings Mother played the Spanish guitar and sometimes the ukelin. The ukelin was an unusual instrument. It had several rows of strings to pick and also a bow to play while you were picking the strings. Mother looked forward to these get-togethers, and she loved singing the old hymns most of all. These times were among the most precious of my teenage years.

Charlie took a job on the waterfront for the summer. Mother and he moved from the outskirts of Lunenburg into the center of town and lived in one side of a house owned by Mr. and Mrs. Charlie Loye.

In the meantime, Mr. Knickle's health was failing, and the poor old gentleman passed away. After he was laid to rest, the horses and the stable were sold. Being unemployed, I was beginning to get the same ugly looks from Charlie again. But luck was with me. Captain Robert Garrett, a former captain on one of the fishing schooners, opened a new fish and meat market. He hired me for six dollars a week. I learned how to meet customers, weigh meat and fish, make change, and perform other duties of a clerk. Captain Garrett trusted me to work in the store by myself, which gave me another good feeling. But as hard as he tried, business was never very good because of the stiff competition from other well-established businesses. I worked there for several months, but finally he had to let me go, and he handled the business by himself.

Since I was without a job, Charlie's broken record began. "Go easy on the sugar. Go easy on the butter. Go easy on this. Go easy on that." Or "Why in the hell don't you go looking for another job?" It was one insult after another. To get away from this static, I'd walk the streets of Lunenburg daily, hoping I'd get lucky and find a job.

I heard that a big three-masted square-rigger ship was coming from Turk's Island with a shipload of salt to be unloaded at the Scott Corkum Company. Salt, of course, was used to preserve fish in the fish plant as well as on the fishing vessels. I went to the company and asked the boss if he would hire me when the ship arrived. He gave me a funny look—just as everyone did when I asked for a job. "You're kind of puny and pale," he said. "What makes you think you can do a man's job?" I told him I'd worked on fishing schooners for over four years and had done a man's job many times before. "Well, young man," he said, "since you're so determined, you can give it a try. The job will last three to four weeks, and we'll pay you fifteen cents an hour, the same as we're paying the rest of the men—if you can do the work."

The only time Charlie ever talked to me was about a job or when he criticized me. So I was surprised when I told him I had a new job, and he never cracked a smile or said one word. But I just wanted him to know I would give him some money to help out with groceries like I always did.

I watched daily for the big ship, and I was happy when I saw it heading into port. That meant we would start unloading the salt the next morning. At seven o'clock the men and puny little me began our long day. This was the procedure. Huge tubs were lowered down into the hold of the ship by a derrick. Several men would shovel the salt into the tubs, and the derrick would hoist the filled tubs up and over the ship and onto the wharf to be dumped into hand-pushed two-wheeled carts. These carts looked like barrows with two rear handles on them. Each cart held one tub of salt, which weighed around one hundred fifty pounds. They had to be pushed approximately two hundred feet over the rough planks on the wharf, up a slight ramp into the warehouse, and dumped. My job was to push one of those carts.

I did this from 7:00 A.M. until 6:00 P.M. except for the hour for lunch. Man, I never would have believed there was that much salt in the whole world! I did my best to handle these heavy loads, but it was difficult. Occasionally my cart would hit an uneven plank on the wharf and tilt forward, and being so small, I'd be lifted right up into the air. That must have been a funny sight. I was afraid the boss would see this and fire me for spilling the salt, but anytime this happened, some of the men would rush to my rescue and shovel the spilled salt back into the cart. The boss never saw any of my accidents, and I was able to stick it out until all the salt was unloaded. I felt proud when I stood in line with those husky men to be paid for the three and a half weeks' work. I collected about thirty dollars.

I ran home and gave Mother twenty-five dollars to help with expenses. I knew she'd be anxious to tell Charlie to keep his filthy mouth shut and that I was doing everything I could to help out. As expected, Charlie didn't acknowledge my help. He never gave me a compliment. Never. But whenever I lived under his roof, I always gave him my earnings, except for a small amount that I'd keep for shoes or roll-your-own cigarette tobacco.

My next job was trying to sell Rogers silverware from door to door. Then I tried to sell men's wristwatches. This kind of work was difficult during the depression, but after trying to sell several products from door to door, I found a product that did well. I had heard about a unique hand-cleaner product, and I wrote to the company about a job. They sent a man to check me out and hired me on the spot. This sand-like cream was called Hanslic. It had a beautiful smell and removed grease and tough dirt from your hands and under your fingernails in seconds. It truly worked. I sold a whole pile of it for fifty cents a can and made a dime profit on each one. Again, I was giving most of the money to Charlie.

After the Hanslic job was over, I rented a bicycle, with a basket attached to the handlebars, for twenty cents a day. I'd go down to the fish firm on the waterfront, buy fresh haddock, clean them at the plant, then ride my bike door to door to sell them. I'd get to the plant early in the morning, pay for my fish supply, and ride to as many homes as possible before the housewives started to prepare lunch for their families. When they answered the door, I'd make my sales pitch. My sales were good. I usually doubled my selling price over what I paid for the fish, but I still sold them for less than customers had to pay at the markets. Usually I'd make about $1.25 each morning. The problem was, of course, that the people couldn't eat fish every day. The return got pretty scanty, and I started looking elsewhere for my next job.

In the meantime I heard about a big steamer coming into Lunenburg with a load of coal for the Scott Corkum Company, and I knew the company would need men to unload it. I applied for the job and was hired. The coal would be loaded on the dock in the same fashion the salt was, but the coal had to be hauled by a truck to the retail coal dealers in Lunenburg. My job was to work in the hold of the steamer, helping to fill the big tubs as they were lowered down into the hold of the ship. This was extremely dirty work, and it was as bad as working in a coal mine. We inhaled coal dust all day long, despite the fact that we'd spray the coal with water when the dust got extremely bad. Working hours were 7:00 A.M. to 5:00 P.M.

I'd walk through Lunenburg after work, and I looked like the blackest man in Africa. When I got home, I'd sponge bathe. We had no showers or bathtubs in any of the places where I had ever lived, but I had a secret weapon in addition to soap—Hanslic. That stuff would remove anything. So each morning I'd go to work looking as clean as I could be, with not even the hint of black on me.

After work I'd get all cleaned up, put on the best old clothes I had, and go downtown with my friends to stand on the corner and try to line up a date. One summer night, when I had the job unloading this coal steamer, I had a special date with a pretty girl, but my only pair of shoes was falling apart. They had holes in the bottoms, and I discovered that this old saying was true, "I could step on a dime and tell if it was heads or tails." I had a pair of gray flannel pants, a V-neck sweater, and an old shirt, but I was embarrassed about my shoes and didn't have money to buy new ones. The money I'd made from selling the Hanslic was gone. Furthermore, I wouldn't be paid for unloading the coal steamer until after the job was finished.

Here's what I did. I went to a small clothing store, Thomas and Ferris, on one of the back streets in Lunenburg to see if I could buy a pair of shoes on credit. The store manager explained, "We would like to help you, young man, but we don't know if your story is correct or not. However, if you'll bring a note from your boss indicating that he, or his firm, will pay for the shoes if you don't, then we can sell you the shoes on credit." I thanked the man and said I'd be back.

After I left, I wrote a note and it said something like this: "It is perfectly okay to give Clarence Snow the pair of shoes he requests. He is a fine young man and he will pay you, but if for any reason he does not, I will make good whatever he owes you." I signed it Scott Corkum and put down the date. I went back to the store manager and gave him the note. He looked at me a little suspiciously, but I walked out of the store with a cheap pair of shoes. However, I was tempted to take them back before I got a block away from the store because of the terrible guilt I was feeling. During my date with the young lady I kept thinking about the note I had written. I was so scared that I couldn't keep my mind on the girl at all!

I found out later that somebody at the clothing store had contacted the Scott Corkum Company and asked about the note. I heard reports that I was going to be sent to a reform school. That scared me, but nothing bad happened, except the rumor sure taught me a damn good lesson.

When the coal job was finished, I received my pay along with the other men, and you can bet the first place I went was back to pay for those shoes.

7

Unwanted Signs

A rainy day is always followed by the sun up in the sky,
So when you're down, you'll find that silver lining if you try.
But if you can't find it, then catch a shooting star
And bid your blues good-bye.

"I'm Gonna Bid My Blues Good-bye,"
by Hank Snow

MOTHER AND CHARLIE MOVED NEXT to a home owned by Julia Loye in Lunenburg and closer to the waterfront where Charlie kept his boat tied up. He and Wilbert started shore fishing again.

Friends, you're probably wondering by now why the people in my family were always moving. Sometimes it was to be closer to a job. Sometimes it was to find a place with cheaper rent. Sometimes it was for reasons I didn't know and never asked about.

While living in Lunenburg, Mother continued to correspond with the foster-home people and the authorities in hopes of getting my youngest sister, Marion, released. Just when it appeared this would happen, another problem developed. Marion had had tuberculosis of the bone, which required several serious operations on one of her legs. Consequently, she had been in the hospital several times during the previous two years. Then, when we thought Marion was ready to come home, she had another unexpected surgery. This delay caused Mother to get very depressed, since she had been trying for so long to reunite the family.

By 1931 the economic depression had worsened and I took any job I could find. It was just one struggle after another. But I continued to dream about making it big in music—somewhere along life's highway.

Having no money was embarrassing to a seventeen-year-old. My friend Leon could sometimes borrow his dad's car, and several of us boys would go girl hunting. I'd be invited, even when I couldn't help buy the gas. One night Leon drove us to Bridgewater, twelve miles away, to meet girls and drive around the town. I was dating a pretty little girl at the time by the name of Leone Kemp.

After we left our dates, the boys wanted to get something to eat. We went to a Chinese restaurant and everybody ordered food but me. Leon asked me if I was going to order something. I said, "Boy, that banana cream pie sure looks good." He smiled and told me to go ahead and order a slice. I thought he knew I had no money and that he would pay for it. We finished eating and the waiter brought the bill. Each boy figured up how much he owed and put his money on the table. The waiter, who was one of the owners, waited for me to pay my part, and finally I had to admit I had no money. I was wearing a green peak cap, and the Chinaman grabbed it off my head and said, "Solly, no money, no cap. Good-bye." I sat there stunned. I didn't know what to do. Finally one of the boys paid the dime for me. I'm sure the Chinaman would have kept my cap if nobody had paid my share.

One night after walking down Main Street, eyeing and talking to the girls, I came home to a big surprise. I went down to the basement kitchen to have a snack, and each cabinet had a padlock on it. Locked up tight. This was the work of you-know-who, but unknown to Mother. The next day when Mother found out about this, she was fit to be tied. She warned Charlie, "This does it! When you lock food from my children, my own flesh and blood, it shows you don't have much respect or love for me. I'll tell you right now, Charlie Tanner, if this ever happens again I'll leave you, and I'll never see you again. Ever." When Mother threatened to leave him, Charlie knew she meant it. And those locks came off those cabinet doors real fast.

I was feeling guilty again because Mother wouldn't have had those problems if it weren't for me being around. About this time, one of my friends, Harry Lohnas, talked me into going to Halifax with him to look for a job. Naturally, I asked where we'd get the money to pay our way up there. He said, "Don't worry. The M&L Coaster freighter goes to Halifax from Lunenburg, and if we help steer her the seventy-five miles, we'll get free passage." Anything free sounded like a good deal to me.

Halifax was in the midst of a terrible rainstorm when we arrived. Harry went ashore to stay with some friends, and I immediately went to the Fenertys' home (the family that Nina and Ritchie had previously rented from). Mrs. Fenerty welcomed me, but I had the feeling I was imposing. "Go into the next room," she said, "and take those soaked clothes off. You'll get pneumonia. Here's a blanket to cover yourself up." After I came back into the room, I sat down in a big soft chair, and she asked me all about Nina and Ritchie, but I was having a hard time keeping my eyes open. I was so tired that I fell fast asleep while she was talking. I slept for several hours, and after I woke up, I felt embarrassed.

I thanked Mrs. Fenerty for her hospitality and left. It started pouring again, and I found an old shed to shelter myself and slept all night. The next morning I made some inquiries about jobs, but no luck. I gave up on Halifax and hitched several rides back to Lunenburg.

When I heard that the Bailey firm had another steamer load of coal coming in and would need workers to help unload the cargo, I got lucky and was hired again. This time my job was much harder than working in the hold of the vessel. I was assigned to shovel coal into a huge shed for storing. This shed was about fifty feet in length, and it had a very high ceiling, probably nine feet high or more.

Here's the procedure we followed. Arthur, one of the Bailey sons, drove his truck, which had a large dump box on it, to the wharf. Big tubs of coal were hoisted up and over into the box on Arthur's truck. He drove the coal up to the entrance to the coal shed where I worked, and he dumped it off. I shoveled the coal into the huge shed. My job was to trim the coal. That meant firing the coal as high as possible so it would slide down from the top of the pile. I had to continue building the pile as close to the ceiling as I could. If I didn't toss it near to the top of the shed, I'd wind up with a two-foot-high pile of coal stretching all the way from the back to the front.

I'd shovel the truckload of coal on each trip that Arthur made. I was supposed to have it all shoveled before he got back with the next load, but that was impossible, no matter how fast I worked. The distance from the wharf to the shed was about the length of four city blocks, and it seemed like Arthur was back with a load in no time. But since coal was going to other distributors too sometimes Arthur would have to wait his turn while the other trucks were being loaded. Still, I got behind, and one of the other Bailey sons had to help me out from time to time.

This went on daily from eight o'clock in the morning until five o'clock at night, and the work lasted several weeks. Even though this was one of the hardest jobs I'd ever had, I stayed with it until the job was completed. And since I gave Charlie most of my wages, this helped keep him off my back. After the job was finished, I coughed up the black coal soot out of my lungs for several days.

The whole Bailey family was highly regarded among the Lunenburg people. Mom and Dad Bailey had several sons, and I got to know some of them well in later years. Earl Bailey was special to a lot of folks. He was born in Lunenburg in 1903, and at the age of two he was stricken with polio, which completely deformed his body. His arms and legs never developed. When he was six years old, his father put a pencil in his mouth, and to the family's amazement, he began to draw. Soon he began to paint pictures by holding the brushes between his teeth.

The family had a special wheelchair made for Earl. It had a small table attached over his lap and fastened to the arms of the wheelchair, so he could reach his brushes and pick them up with his teeth. His brother Donnie stayed by his side throughout the years and took him on locations wherever good scenery was found to paint.

Earl loved to paint Nature's beauty, and he won fame and praise from many parts of the world. He was mentioned in the famous "Believe It or Not" column by Ripley. On December 15, 1937, Earl received a nice letter from the White House. Franklin D. Roosevelt thanked Earl for the beautiful seascape he had painted for him. In 1939 King George and Queen Elizabeth were in Halifax, and when Earl was presented to them, he was given the autograph of Queen Elizabeth, which was a very special favor, since royalty rarely give autographs.

Earl was also a fine singer and sang in the church choir. I can't say enough about this great man, who was truly a great inspiration to me. He was the person who announced to me that my oil painting of the *Blue Nose* racing the *Gertrude L. Tebeau* had won first prize at the Lunenburg Fisheries Exhibition. Donnie and I became close friends in later years, and when I went back to Canada in the summer of 1984, he gave me a private tour of Earl's studio. Earl had passed away, but the studio rekindled my admiration and nostalgic feelings for Earl Bailey.

As economic times got even tougher, I began doing what many other poor people were doing. I went from house to house asking the housewives if they had any old clothing to contribute to charity. I didn't tell them I was the charity. People would sometimes throw old shoes or clothing items in big trash cans, and one time I found a good topcoat and a pretty good pair of shoes. I was as happy with them as if they were brand new.

I found another way to earn money. Lunenburg had a militia at the time, and I joined for the summer months. We trained one night a week, for which the government paid us around twelve dollars at the end of the training period. The program was like the army reserve, where participants were issued regular army clothes, or fatigues, and a rifle. We weren't permitted to take the rifles out of the barracks, but we were allowed to wear the uniforms to and from home while in training. However, shoes were not issued, so we had to furnish our own. We were required to keep our shoes shined so that you could see your face in them, and we had to keep the brass buttons and brass things like the maple leaves sparkling clean. I had no shoe polish, so I cleaned my old ordinary laced shoes with lard to shine them up. The militia and I got along fine. I held my breath when the sergeant lined us up for inspection, but I always passed, even with my lard-shined shoes.

Around this time, something very unusual happened. Mother said, "I've got the surprise of your life, Jack, so you'd better sit down. Charlie said if you want to make a little money, he'll take you with him on the boat to help rake scallops. He'll give you a dollar a day." That was the surprise of my life! Charlie would pay me? I didn't know whether to faint and fall down, jump in the air, or what. Mother encouraged me to do it. "Why don't you give it a try? As long as you're working with him, perhaps things will go better at home." There was Mother again being the eternal optimist. I reluctantly agreed.

Charlie and I began working together about the middle of January. We'd leave each morning around five o'clock and walk down to the wharf where he kept his boat. Early in the morning, especially at the cold waterfront on the Atlantic Coast at that time of the year, it could be pretty darn cold. Snow was sometimes on the ground. It was probably about zero weather much of the time. We would travel in the motorboat about four or five miles out of Lunenburg to where Charlie thought we'd find the best bottom for scallops, and we'd drop the rake.

I'll explain the procedures we used. The rakes were about three feet wide and had oval-shaped jaws with steel teeth on the bottom. A large steel wire net, about three feet long, was attached to the jaws. The motorboat dragged this rake with the huge steel teeth along the bottom for a mile or two. Anything in the rake's path was gathered into the basket-like net. Then we'd pull the rake to the side of the boat, remove any big rocks from the net, and dump the scallops into the boat. Sometimes we'd get mostly rocks, and sometimes we'd get a good haul of scallops. Whenever the rakes were nearly full of rocks, the contents might weigh 150 or 175 pounds, and it was hell for the two of us to pull them up. People who could afford it had small engines mounted on their boats to pull the rakes up.

Throughout this ordeal we wore wool mittens. You may not believe this, but after the mittens got soaked in the ice-cold water, our hands stayed warm. Maybe the salt water did something to the wool, like tighten the weaves, I don't know. But when we worked with the rakes, we did keep warm. Charlie and I ate our lunch in the boat, which usually was bread and molasses. On rare occasions we would have a piece of cake or a doughnut. Anything tasted great after pulling those heavy rakes in all morning.

These were meager days. The only money Charlie got was what he received when he sold the scallops to the fish stores or when we went from door to door to sell them when he took a day off from raking. They sold for twenty-five cents a dozen. Each night we would get back to the house around seven o'clock, and Charlie would give Mother the dollar to give to me. Of course, you wouldn't expect him to give it to me himself, now could you? It's hard to believe, but while we were working, he was pretty nice, and he did talk to me a little bit.

One afternoon the rake got caught on something on the bottom as we were raking, and the boat wouldn't move. Whenever the rake got caught, the usual thing was to steer the boat in a circle. This had always cleared the rake before, but it didn't work this time. After wasting about an hour going in circles, Charlie decided that we should try to pull it loose by hand. We pulled inch by inch, and it took us about two hours to pull our catch up to the side of the boat. We had caught an abandoned anchor! I'm sure it weighed four hundred pounds or more. Getting it into the boat seemed like an impossibility, so we tied the line to the boat and headed toward the wharf with the anchor hanging on the side. Later on I heard that Charlie sold the anchor for $200, but I never got a dime of the money.

Around this time, too, Charlie decided to try bootlegging. He bought the rum from one of the suppliers around the area, the same as I had done earlier. Charlie knew what proof the rum should be to satisfy the customers, and he sold it for one dollar a bully, or pint. He told me he'd give me so much a bottle for whatever I sold, and I was surprised that he would even involve me.

One night I was going back to Bridgewater with the regular bunch and decided to take a bully with me. Except for my experience with the halfway house and my bootlegging before, I knew very little about drinking. In Bridgewater one of the boys mentioned that he'd like to have a few drinks and he knew where he could buy bootlegged rum. I quickly spoke up and said I had some with me, which surprised the hell out of everyone, because they knew I didn't drink. I passed the bottle to one of the boys, and they passed it around several times. They tried to get me to drink with them, but I refused—at least for a little while. Then I joined in so as not to be a party pooper.

When I got back to the house in Lunenburg the next morning about two o'clock, I was high as a kite and horribly sick. I got out of the car and staggered across the street to the house. I struggled to open the door, then started the long climb up the three flights of stairs to my straw tick on the floor. I made so much noise that I woke Mother and Charlie, and they came upstairs to see what in the world was wrong. I was lying there too sick to get up, and they both knew right away what had happened. As far as I was from reality, I could still see the look on Mother's face. I knew she was hurt and disappointed in me.

Charlie never asked me for the money for the rum. He never mentioned it again. And Mother, bless her soul, never lectured me, but I know she was devastated. I was so ashamed the next morning when she said, "Here is the scarf you had around your neck. I happened to see it from the kitchen window and went out and picked it up in the street."

I raked scallops with Charlie until the season ended in the early spring. I was out of a job again, and I knew Charlie so well that I could just about tell you to the day when I'd get his usual abusive treatment.

But there has been something on my mind until this very day, and every time I think about it, I shiver. If Charlie hated me so much, why didn't he push me overboard and let me drown? No one would have known. He could have said that I had fallen off the boat accidentally and that he had made every effort to save me. I still wonder.

Luck again! I got a new job with Adams and Knickle, a large fish firm that packed and shipped dried fish, mainly cod, to many parts of the world. They employed a lot of men, and I worked along with them, Monday through Saturday from 8:00 A.M. until 5:00 P.M., with a half day off on Saturday.

Here's a look at the operation. When the Lunenburg vessels came in from their fishing trips each spring and summer, they would unload their salted fish on the wharfs. These fish, of course, had not been cured as yet. They were dressed and salted down at sea in the hold of the vessel. When the schooners tied up, the fish were forked out on the wharfs and hauled away in wagons pulled by yokes of oxen to the countryside for curing.

These wagons had big sides and looked a lot like regular hay wagons. The oxen wore a large yoke made out of a long piece of oak and hewed out in a curve to fit over each ox's head. The yokes had to be a perfect fit so as not to give the animals any discomfort when pulling heavy loads. There was a long wooden tongue that fastened to the center of the yoke and ran back between the oxen and fastened to the center of the wagon in the middle. These oxen could pull unbelievably huge loads of cargo of any kind, from fish to logs.

After the fish were properly dried, they were hauled back to the fish firms, Adams and Knickle being one of them. From these warehouses the fish were prepared for shipping to many other countries. Some of the fish were sealed in barrels and shipped just as they were dried. Other fish were cut in assorted shapes and sizes.

Outside the Adams and Knickle warehouse, which was three stories high, a wide ramp went from the ground level up the outside of the building at about a forty-five-degree angle and extended upward about fifty feet to a small platform. As the wagonloads of dried fish were brought back to the plant, they would stop at the bottom of the ramp, and the fish would be unloaded on barrows. These barrows were about six feet long, with two handles in the back and two in the front. About one hundred fifty pounds of fish were loaded on each one. My job was to work with other men to carry the loaded barrow up and into the building. This was easier said than done.

One man at each end of the barrow would grab the handles and carry the fish up the elevated ramp. We'd set the barrow down on a small bench to take a breathing spell for a minute. Then we'd carry the barrow inside the building, turn to the right, go up another ramp, and turn to the left on the second floor. We'd walk back about forty feet, where another man was stationed by huge scales, and he would cull the fish. Any damaged fish or any under standard size for shipping were taken out. Then we'd dump the ones to keep out on the pile. Two other men would take the fish away to another location. Thereafter, the man that I worked with and I would go on down the two ramps to the ground level for a second barrow of fish. We'd do this all day long. This was hard and heavy work for a frail teenager.

In early July I suddenly took ill. I developed a serious pain in my right side, and for several days my stomach continued to swell bigger and bigger until I thought I was going to burst. When Charlie came home on the first day that I was real sick and saw I hadn't gone to work, he flew into one of his wild rages. He yelled out for anybody in the house to hear, and I can remember it as if it were yesterday, "The only thing wrong with him is he don't do enough work to physic the shit through him."

My pain got so bad that Mother called Nina's doctor. After he examined me, he said, "The boy is constipated. All he needs is a good laxative, and he'll be fine." As I found out later, that was the worst thing in the world for me. When the laxative did no good and the pain and the swelling continued, Mother called her doctor, a distinguished gentleman by the name of Dr. Sanders.

I had been too sick to climb upstairs to my mattress on the floor, so I laid on the living room couch. When Dr. Sanders entered the room, Mother explained my symptoms. The doctor didn't even have to examine me. He said, "Get him ready for the hospital immediately. The boy has appendicitis. We need to get him there before it bursts. It's showing every sign of being to that point now. If it does burst, the poison could go all through his system and it would be very dangerous."

Mother immediately called a taxi to take me to the train station, where I'd be put on the train for the twelve-mile ride to the Dawson Memorial Hospital in Bridgewater. The minute I was helped to my feet I felt my stomach deflate and I had no more pain. I said to Mother, "I feel fine now. Why am I going to the hopsital?" I didn't understand just how bad I was. In fact, my appendix had burst and the poison was going through my system.

At the station I had to wait for the train, and it took about an hour and a half to get to Bridgewater. Dr. Sanders had called ahead to make sure a taxi would be waiting at the station to rush me to the hospital. The doctor, bless his heart, had also called ahead to have nurses and a doctor standing by. When the cab pulled up, they rushed me into the operating room, put me on the operating table, and prepared me for surgery. It was about 4:00 P.M. when the mask was placed over my nose, and I was told to breathe deeply as they administered chloroform. I could feel myself going, going, gone.

I woke up around 7:00 P.M. and was very sick. My violent vomiting could have caused the stitches to break and open the incision. I was told that my entrails had to be taken out on the table in order to have all the poison flushed out of them, and then placed back inside me. The doctor placed a long tube into my side, leaving an inch or so of the tube outside my stomach. A large safety pin was put through the end of the tube so it wouldn't go back inside. The tube was inserted in order to drain all the remaining poison fluid out of my stomach. Each day a small portion of the tube was pulled out, cut off, and the safety pin was put through the end of the tube again. This daily procedure was continued for most of the three weeks I was in the hospital.

Dr. Rafuse, my doctor, was a beautiful old gentleman. His hands were the biggest I'd ever seen, but as gentle as a child's when he was checking the incision. One of the nurses, Miss Walsh, told me when I was recovering that when Dr. Rafuse opened me up to remove my appendix, he found another problem. She said it was a good thing, too, because it would have caused me serious trouble in the future. I asked her what it was, and she said she would tell me before I was released. But I never did find out, and I've always wondered about it.

During my recuperation, I came close to developing pneumonia and had a severe cough for a long time. I knew Mother was concerned throughout this whole ordeal, wondering if I would survive it. She really took good care of me at home. But my greatest concern was Charlie. I can still see and hear him when he came in the front door on my first day home. Of course, I had brought the famous hospital smell home with me. At the top of his voice he cursed, "Goddamn, this place smells like there's been a dozen operations in here." By now, friends, I'm sure you've gathered that this man was a complete idiot.

Dr. Sanders made several trips to the house to check my progress. He told Mother, "Due to the seriousness of the operation, don't let your son do any hard work of any kind for a full year. Since his general health is not good, he could still get a serious infection." But constant pressure from Charlie had me back working at Adams and Knickle's in less than three months, doing the same heavy work I was doing before the operation.

As I look back on my life, there were so many things that happened to me in which I thought I'd never make it through. I'm thoroughly convinced that God was on my side every minute of every day and night. I am a firm believer. He gave me the strength to continue on with Adams and Knickle and to survive once again.

Each payday I gave Charlie my wages until my job ended in the fall when the work at the firm was completed. After Charlie's broken record began to spin again, I just drifted around, spending a few weeks with Nina and a few weeks with Lillian, in the meantime searching for something to make me a little money. But no luck this time.

My good friend Cecil Dorey and I continued to chum around. We joined up with a couple of characters who we knew were in and out of trouble with the law. They were brothers, and I won't mention their real names, but let's just call them Johnny and Harry. Cecil and I ran around with those boys mainly because they were big guys. One looked like a prize fighter. Another reason was that Harry had an old beat-up Studebaker. That stubborn old car only ran when it felt like it, and it had tires to match its personality. But it was transportation—most of the time, anyway.

Harry and Johnny had girlfriends in Bridgewater, as did several of the other boys in the group, including me. We'd travel back and forth as often as we could to see them. And whenever they had money for gasoline, we'd drive to Bridgewater. On one of these trips, we were about four miles on our way when one of the tires blew out. They patched the old bald tire with the last piece of cold patch, pumped it up with a hand pump, and we were on our way again. We drove about three miles and ran out of gas, and none of us had any money. Johnny and Harry grabbed the can they carried for stealing gas, and away they went. These guys would sneak into someone's yard, even into the garage if the car was not outside, and siphon a can of gasoline. They took many chances of getting caught, and many times I've heard the dogs raising hell, but those guys were scared of nothing. Anyway, these boys brought their stolen gas and we were on our way again.

Soon another tire blew out, and we had no more patching material. Rather than mess with it anymore, they decided to push the old car off the road into this field and leave it. We pushed it, but the car didn't stop where it was supposed to. It rolled on its own for a great distance, down to the edge of the woods, before it stopped. We walked back to Lunenburg. I never did find out if the boys ever went back to get the old car or not. I think they just left that pile of junk in the farmer's field.

Another friend of mine, Wilbert Hiltz, who we used to call "Switchel," had the same habit of stealing gas on occasion. He'd rent an old Model A Ford from a friend, and we'd run around in it. One time we started to Halifax and ran out of gas. He took his siphon hose and can and got a few gallons from one of the highway trucks that had been left parked overnight by the highway. This being government property, we could have all gone to the reform school. We stayed in Halifax overnight and got gas from a friend to take us the seventy-five miles back to Lunenburg.

I suppose these adventures were not too uncommon for teenagers during those hard depression days in Canada. Nevertheless, they represented some happy times for me.

I came home from hanging around uptown one day and got my happiest surprise! Marion, my youngest sister, was home. She was about thirteen or fourteen years old. She was neat and well dressed. What a pretty girl! Indeed, she had a striking resemblance to Mother. Mother, Marion, and I had a great reunion, and we carried on like three little kids. We told stories of the past and talked about good times when the whole family was together.

We hadn't seen Marion for years. Mother had tried on several occasions to bring her home, but she had always been disappointed. Besides the complication of Marion's leg operations, I suppose the court was reluctant to let Marion come home to such a poor family situation. Anyway, Marion's leg was now just fine. It was obvious that she had been well treated in her foster home, and she had only good things to say about her foster parents. Even Charlie was extra nice to her in the beginning, and for some reason he was beginning to treat me a little better.

But you know the old saying, "There's always a calm before the storm." How true! Soon the ugly looks started again and the insults followed. Gradually Charlie turned on Marion. I'm sure, with his own insecurities, he was jealous of any time that Mother spent with her.

Charlie decided to take Wilbert to scallop fish and leave me out. That was okay, because the work was too heavy for me anyway. I was in poor health from the pressure and strain after the operation and the hard work that I had struggled with at Adams and Knickle.

Next Charlie tried lobster fishing. There's a large body of water back of Lunenburg that extends out into the Atlantic Ocean. This is ideal for lobster fishing, so Charlie moved his boat over to First Peninsula, a beautiful little village with houses all along the waterfront. We moved from the big three-story house in Lunenburg to a quaint, white wooden house owned by John Rhuland at First Peninsula, about two and a half miles from Lunenburg. This large house had two big bedrooms, plus a smaller bedroom for me, a living room, and a storeroom.

Mother fixed up this old-fashioned house to be really comfortable. I had my own cot, and thanks to Mother, I thought I was living in the finest hotel in Canada. Without a job, I helped her with whatever I could to make things easier for her. I washed dishes, scrubbed the wooden floors, cut up firewood, and ran errands when needed. These times were like heaven to me with Charlie out of the house fishing all day and until after dark each night.

Our landlord, John Rhuland, and his family lived just a stone's throw from our house. One afternoon John's father and his youngest brother, Billy, were leaving to go into Lunenburg. Elderly Mrs. Rhuland, John's mother, wanted to go with them. She hardly ever got to go anywhere. She told Mr. Rhuland and Billy it would only take her a few minutes to get ready, but for some reason they just didn't have the time to wait, so they went without her. Mother and Marion were also in town, and I was home alone and had the flu. I was lying on the bed, when I heard a knock on the door. I slipped on some clothes and went to the door. It was our landlord's wife. "Jack," she said, "can you help me? Billy and his father have gone into town, and there's something radically wrong with Mrs. Rhuland. She's down in the cellar lying on the mud floor, and I can't get no life into her."

We quickly ran to the Rhuland house and down the cellar steps. The poor soul was trying to sit up at the foot of the stairs, mumbling something that was impossible to understand. Her body was weaving back and forth, and she was staring into space, like she didn't know we were there. We wanted to get her upstairs and onto the couch, until we could get a doctor to come. But with me being weak from the flu and fever and John's wife being very tiny, it was like trying to lift dead weight.

We lifted her step by step and finally managed to get her upstairs and onto the couch. Then we called Dr. Zink, their family doctor.

Not long after Dr. Zink came, Mr. Rhuland and Billy arrived home. When Billy saw the doctor's car, he looked like he would pass out. I knew it must have cut Billy and the old man pretty deep, thinking they couldn't wait a few extra minutes to take her to town with them. The doctor said she'd had a serious stroke. She never regained consciousness and passed away in a few days. Poor old soul. She was an angel, one of the sweetest ladies I ever met. She was a hard worker and was always helping other people. Mother and my sisters had been kind to her and had visited her quite often.

Meanwhile, another big salt steamer had docked and needed men, and Charlie landed a job at the Smith and Rhuland Company (no kin to the Rhulands I just mentioned). After Charlie started working, he thought I could get a job there, too. He said he would wake me up at six the next morning, so I could get there early and probably work that same day. He woke me up early as he said he'd do. I walked into town and was hired without being asked any questions about whether I could handle the job. I worked all day until 6:00 P.M. and then walked the two and a half miles home. I was dead tired and every bone in my body was aching. I slept like a baby after that first day.

The next morning Charlie was supposed to wake me up, but he went off without me. When I woke up around 7:30, I was frantic. I jumped into my clothes, and without a bite to eat I ran most of the way to Lunenburg and down to the wharf. But since the workers started work at 7:00 A.M., they had already hired someone to take my place. I felt real bad about oversleeping, and I was scared to death at the thought of seeing Charlie that night.

When he came home after work, the tirade started. "You little bastard, you ain't got sense enough to get out of bed and get to work. You think we don't need the money? You're the laziest damn bastard I ever seen." I tried to reason with him by telling him he was supposed to wake me. He threw up his hands and yelled, "Who in the hell is supposed to wake me?" I figured the best thing for me to do was say nothing more and get away from him. I flew out the door and stayed out of the house until I knew he would be asleep.

I couldn't help but think that Mother was making a hell of a sacrifice to keep her kids together.

Then fate turned favorably in my direction. Mother had sent for her mother, who was an angel, to come stay with us for a while. I knew I was safe, as Charlie wouldn't dare use those filthy words and curse in front of my grandmother. Grandmother really enjoyed herself, especially when Charlie was away. But as soon as he entered the house, things became deathly quiet, and tension was so thick you could cut it with a knife. After a couple of months Grandmother returned to her home in Western Head, four miles from Liverpool.

In the meantime, Nina and Ritchie had moved into an apartment with a Mrs. Herman at First Peninsula. Ritchie was planning a summer trip to the fishing banks, and Nina wanted to be closer to Mother, Lillian, Marion, and me.

It was about this time that Mother received a letter from her sister, Grace. Many years before this, Mother and Grace had a falling out. I never learned what it was about, but they never spoke to each other for years. At any rate, after Mother received Grace's letter, she wrote back and invited Grace to spend a couple of months with us. Soon Aunt Grace arrived, and she and Mother seemed real happy to see each other again. They would sit up half the night talking about old times, and I thoroughly enjoyed listening to them. When Aunt Grace was with us, things ran more smoothly with Charlie, at least for a while.

Aunt Grace liked my paintings, especially the ships, and she asked me to paint her a couple of pictures to take home with her. She was pleased with the results and paid me several dollars.

During this visit Grace said to Mother, "Why don't you, Charlie, Jack, and Marion move to Brooklyn and live with us? The house is big and we've got plenty of room." Her home was in Brooklyn, the same little village where I was born. Mother was interested in the idea and said she would give it a lot of thought. Shortly after Aunt Grace returned home, Charlie became very difficult again, and he attacked Marion, too. When he saw that Mother was interested in Aunt Grace's idea, I guess Charlie wanted to discourage Marion and me from tagging along.

Thank God for the letter I received from my dad. He was living only fourteen miles away in a remote part of the country, back in the woods, in a community called Pleasantville. Dad had married a widowed lady by the name of Fanny Blakney, a middle-aged woman with three children. I was delighted to hear from him, and I mailed a letter back to him the next day, asking if I could come to stay with them for a while. He wrote right back, wanting me to come. He told me to take the train to Bridgewater and he'd meet me at the station.

Mother gave me the few cents for the fare, and I climbed aboard the train. I was quite nervous about seeing Dad after all these years. I hadn't seen him since I was eight years old. That's when I hauled his trunk to the station from my grandmother's place, and he spoke those memorable words, "Well, good-bye, Son. I may see you again, and I may never see you again."

As I rode the bumpy old train, I thought about when we were all together as a family. It seemed as if I could only remember the happy times, like when Dad used to sing and tell stories to us kids, and I recalled how Mother and Dad would talk and laugh together. Now I wondered how he would look. Was he happy? Did he ever think about me? Was there still a feeling somewhere deep down about Mother?

I sure had a lot to tell him. Much had happened to me in my young life. Here I was a teenager and had been to sea for four years and had visited many ports during that time. I had lived in many different towns and villages, had a dozen jobs, had a little money once in a while, and had experienced extreme poverty most of the time. And there was Charlie Tanner. Pleasantville, I thought, was where I needed to be.

As soon as the train pulled into the station, Dad was waiting for me with his horse and buggy. He seemed pleased to see me. He shook my hand and started asking me questions about my sisters and how we were all doing, but he never did mention Mother's name. After I answered his questions, though, there wasn't much conversation. It was sad to me that Dad didn't ask me more about my life. However, as I remember him, he was a quiet man, and he just didn't have much to say.

Actually, I felt like he was a complete stranger to me.

We arrived at the house in the backwoods at Pleasantville, about three miles from the main road—and I mean back in the woods. His second wife, Fanny, was sort of quiet, too, but she was nice. She had three children by her first marriage: Ray, Evelyn, and Jack. In addition, Fanny and Dad had a little girl they named Ethel. My little stepsister had red hair and was very sweet and pretty. She and Ray were living at home, and I liked them both.

When Dad married Fanny, he acquired a small farm that she owned. The house had a big barn attached, and along with the farm was a horse, poultry, a couple of wagons, and many acres of choice timber wood.

I stayed with Dad and his family during the winter. It was very cold, and we had a lot of snow that year. But that didn't matter. At least I was away from Charlie. Dad said I could help him and Ray cut pulpwood, and that was fine with me. I was used to hard work, and I doubted if any job could ever be more difficult than hauling coal, salt, and fish.

We'd get up early in the morning, hitch up the horse to the work wagon, and drive about three miles from the house to the place where we'd cut the wood. We would unhitch the horse and walk another half mile or more to the areas where we'd cut timber for the day. Dad would pick out a spruce or a fir tree that was suitable to be made into pulpwood. Some were from seventy-five to one hundred feet tall and anywhere from six inches to two feet across the butt.

After Dad picked the tree, Ray would cut a notch close to the ground, toward the spot where we wanted the tree to fall. Then I'd help Ray cut down the tree, using a crosscut saw, me on one end and him on the other. In this process the snow would be jarred off the trees and fall down our necks, causing us a lot of distraction. One of the hardest things about this job was the strain on our backs because these trees had to be cut as close to the ground as possible. Bending over and sawing back and forth for hours was not the easiest thing in the world to do.

After the tree had fallen, we'd trim the limbs off its entire length, as close to the trunk as possible, so it wouldn't mess up the log and make it less acceptable to the buyers at the mill. Dad would snake the logs out to the main road. Snaking meant hooking a big chain around the logs and having the horse drag them to the highway. While Dad was snaking, we'd find other trees marked with a notch, and we'd cut as many down as we could until Dad returned for more logs. This went on for about two days. Then Ray and I would spend the next day out at the main road, sawing the logs that Dad had snaked there. They all had to be measured and cut in exactly four-foot lengths for the mill. We would stack them in neat piles between two posts driven in the ground. The piles were about eight feet long and four feet high. The wood had to be piled in so many cords to the pile, and when there were enough piles, the trucks would come along, load them, and take them to the mill.

We worked all winter, off and on, six days a week. But whenever Dad took off a week or two from the pulpwood cutting, Ray and I continued working. Another firm wanted ten cords of hardwood, so Dad gave the job to us. And we'd cut cords of hardwood and split it to be hauled away to private families for burning in their fireplaces and stoves. We were paid ten dollars a cord, and the money was split between Ray and me. Not only was our job hard, it was dangerous as well. We both had double-bitted axes, razor sharp. Double bitted means a sharp edge on each side of the axe. After we sawed the hardwood, which was either birch or maple, into four-foot lengths, Ray and I would face each other to split the wood. I'd sink my axe into the wood as far as I could to start the split. I'd keep the axe in the wood to serve as a wedge until Ray struck the wood near my axe. We would continue, alternating each swing into the wood. With the hardwood this was tough. Sometimes we had to drive steel wedges in the cracks and use a sledgehammer to split them.

We had a little social life in the settlement of Pleasantville, but not much. The houses were spread far apart, but sometimes a family in the countryside would have a square dance on a Saturday night, and we'd take the long walk there to join in the fun. Usually the family would clear the furniture out of the largest room, where we'd dance. The music was scarce, but often we had a fiddler or a guitar player. Sometimes we were lucky and had both. Normally there weren't too many people at these dances, as the rooms at the different houses were quite small. But those who could find space would dance and live it up. They'd dance a while, then sit down and let another crowd in to dance. Cheap wine was the favorite drink, and people drank it by the gallons. I think it cost one dollar per gallon. I witnessed several fights at the places we went.

Pleasantville was not always pleasant, but it was a great experience for me.

8

Out in the Cold

I'm a wand'rer, I'll keep driftin' on,
Can't see, honey, why you did me wrong.
Hard luck sure has got me, I can't sleep a wink,
I'll just have to face it from now on.

"Unwanted Sign upon Your Heart,"
by Hank Snow

WHENEVER THE WEATHER WAS NOT suitable for working in the woods, I'd go out and shoot rabbits. Rabbits and deer were everywhere. Luckily, I had my .22 rifle with me at Dad's, and with the money I made from the firewood, I was able to buy shells. I'd take the rabbits to Bridgewater and attempt to sell them to the meat stores, but it seemed that everybody else was doing the same thing, so I didn't sell too many. But we ate a lot of rabbit, and in those poverty days when food was hard to come by, rabbit stew and rabbit pie tasted mighty good.

Mother used to cook rabbits whenever she could find them in the meat stores and could afford them. They were one of her favorite meals. Around Christmas time, I wanted to take Mother a pair of rabbits. I knew she would be pleased that I was thinking of her and bringing her a special gift. Being away from Charlie Tanner for over two months, I figured he wouldn't say too much to me if I only stayed a couple of days. I asked Ray to go with me. We hitchhiked the fourteen or so miles to Lunenburg, carrying the rabbits with us. Mother was overjoyed to see me, and she made Ray feel welcome, too.

Christmas Eve, 1931, turned out to be the worst Christmas I ever had. This event tore Mother's Christmas apart, too, and I regret that very much. We had a great visit until Charlie showed up about 6:00 P.M. He gave Ray and me his hateful look and in an angry voice said,

"What the hell are you doing back here?" Nobody said anything. There was complete silence as he took his coat off and went to wash his hands. Then he yelled again. I can remember these words as if it was last night: "If you're in this house till tomorrow at dinnertime, I'll walk in blood to my knees." That was it, word for word!

Like me, Ray was dumbfounded. I believed Charlie meant exactly what he said. He was unpredictable, and my mind immediately flashed back to a rumor about his brother George. It was told that George had a girlfriend who was running around on him. One day in downtown Lunenburg George spotted his girlfriend walking on the other side of Main Street, and he fired at her with a .22 rifle. The sound scared the girl and she fell down in the street, although the bullet missed her. But George thought he had killed her, and he ran back of the town to an old graveyard, where he committed suicide with the same rifle.

Ray and I left immediately and went into Lunenburg and reported Charlie's threat to the chief of police, Chief Gardner. I was surprised with his response: "I'm sorry, but the courts can't take any action against Charlie unless he actually harms one of you." Great, I thought, if Charlie shoots me, the police might arrest him. This made no damn sense to me then. It never did, and it never will. We had no place to go except back to Dad's. We hung around the post office and railway station all night to keep warm. Then we hitchhiked back to Dad's place.

I worked with Dad for most of the winter. By the spring of 1932, when the pulpwood cutting was over, it was time to move on again. Dad and his family had been good to me, but there was sort of a distance there. If I didn't feel completely at home, under the circumstances, I guess that was natural.

Once again I moved back with Nina in the two-room apartment with Mrs. Herman. (Mrs. Herman's daughter, Leone, was married to a Frenchman by the name of Prudhomme, who was to be a great help to me later on.) Nina's big old reclining chair became my bed. After sleeping in so many different chairs and makeshift beds, I could sleep standing up in a hammock! However, I did a little improvising. I'd put a straight chair in the front to put my feet up on, lean the chair back as far as it would go, and I'd be fast asleep in no time. Each morning, though, after sleeping in that cramped position, it would take me a few minutes to straighten up.

I enjoyed staying there. Mrs. Herman was a sweet and gentle old lady. She reminded me of my loving Grandmother Boutlier. I used to talk with Mrs. Herman for hours at a time, listening to her stories about her life when she was young. She became very special to me. Nina lived in Mrs. Herman's house for close to a year and a half until the old lady passed away, then we moved again. I lost a very dear friend. I had told her most of my personal problems, and she shared my pain and my loneliness. God bless her.

Whenever I couldn't find a job, I'd practice my painting with my leftover house paints. Usually I couldn't afford to buy canvas to paint on, so I used oilcloth or cardboard. Once I bought a large piece of ordinary everyday canvas, five feet by two and a half feet, and shellacked it first to make it easier to paint. I did a sixteen-by-twenty-inch painting that I was quite proud of and sold it to our neighbors, the Demones family, for five dollars. The scene was a basket of fruit sitting on a table, with a peach cut in half showing half of the pit in the center of the peach and the hole where it came out of in the other half. I added several kinds of fruit around the peach, and I managed to make the colors of the fruit true and natural looking.

The Buckmaster family lived across the field from us. They were neighborly people, and I became friends with the boys, especially with Arthur. He was a fine-looking young man, clean cut, and very tidy. He had done some boxing and could handle himself very well.

Arthur and I would go camping together, hunt rabbits, and practice target shooting. We each owned a .22 rifle, and whenever we had the money, we'd buy a couple of boxes of shells. We'd go into an open field, fire a tin can in the air, and drill it before it hit the ground. We could also lean backwards and look along the barrel of the rifle while standing, line the target up with the forward sight, and hit our targets nearly every shot.

We both got awfully brave. I'd hold a small chip of wood, stretch my arm out away from my body, and Arthur would shoot the chip out of my hand. And vice versa with Arthur. Here's something else we did a few times, but this was utterly foolish. No one should ever try this! I'd put an empty bottle on my head, and Arthur would shoot it off from about fifty feet away. I'd do the same thing to him.

One time Arthur and I planned to go hunting and camp out for a couple of nights. We packed some gear and sandwiches and took our rifles. We paddled his small homemade canoe across to a tiny island. There was a small hay barn on the left, and on top of the hill was a vegetable garden. From the shore up through the field to where the garden was, it was about an eighth of a mile. Arthur walked up the hill to the garden. Then he came back down to me and said, "Jack, how would you like to have some fresh vegetables to go with the sandwiches? Someone has planted corn, tomatoes, lettuce, cucumbers, and green peas, and they're ready for harvesting. Man, we're going to have a feast all weekend with all kinds of fresh food! You keep an eye out for the old man who tends the garden, while I raid it."

I warned Arthur, "That old man will shoot you if he catches you." I made up a story and said, "I've heard about that old man and how dangerous he is. Maybe you ought to forget it." "Hell, I ain't afraid of him," Arthur boasted.

Arthur was at the top of the hill and I was at the bottom, supposedly to be the lookout. I gave him time enough to pick a good armful. Then I yelled in an old man's voice, "What the hell are you doing in my garden? I'm going to shoot your ass off." My voice must have echoed off the barn, because the next thing I saw was Arthur flying down the hill faster than any deer could go. Cucumbers, corn, tomatoes, and lettuce were flying in every direction. He passed me doing a hundred miles an hour, urging in a sort of whispered voice, "Come on, come on, he's going to shoot us. Let's get out of here." I fell to the ground busting with laughter. Arthur kept on going, and he couldn't understand why I wasn't running, too.

We finished our vacation with pouring-down rain and paddled our canoe back to the other side. We didn't do much hunting, but we sure had a lot of fun.

Around this time Mother accepted Aunt Grace's invitation to move in with her and her husband, Horace Lavender, and their children. Mother prepared the furniture and the housewares for moving, but first she wanted to spend a little time with Lillian in Lunenburg. Charlie planned to stay behind for a while and see how the move worked out for Mother. If all went well, Charlie would join Mother later. In the meantime, he would store his boat on dry land, so he could get it in good shape for his next fishing trips. He intended to live on it and sleep in the closed-in cabin area. But if the weather got too cold, he would stay with Wilbert for a short time while he was waiting to join Mother in Brooklyn.

Since Mother was leaving, Nina decided she and Ritchie would move back to Bluerocks from First Peninsula. Naturally, I wanted to stay with Nina and so did Marion. Marion and I didn't know exactly when Mother would be leaving, and we wanted to see her before she moved. One cold night we made the long walk to Lunenburg from Bluerocks. I've always regretted making that visit.

We got to Lillian's house, knocked on the door about 9:00 P.M., and were surprised when there was no answer. We knocked several times. Then slowly the door opened just barely enough for us to see Wilbert's face through the crack. In a hateful voice he said, "What the hell do you want around here this time of the night?" I explained, "We came to see Mother before she leaves for Brooklyn, and we're cold and hungry. Can we come in for a little while?" Wilbert didn't answer. He closed the door in our faces. We just stood there. In about five minutes he cracked the door again and without saying a word passed us two slices of molasses bread. And he shut the door.

Both Marion and I were hurt. We didn't know what was taking place, and we never found out. Mother would have gladly welcomed us if she had known we were there. Where were Mother and Lillian? We were real concerned, but our immediate problem was to find a warm place to sleep.

We were too tired to make the long journey back to Nina's place. I knew where Charlie was keeping his boat in the back harbor at the wharf, and we walked the mile or so from Lillian's place and crawled up in the tiny cubbyhole he had made for a cabin. We found some pieces of old canvas, covered ourselves up, and tried to sleep. But I knew Charlie would come to his boat the next morning between six and seven o'clock, and we certainly didn't want to be there when he arrived. We kept waking up throughout the night, worried that Charlie might come before we left. Being chilled to the bone didn't help either. We were on our way to Bluerocks before six o'clock.

In a few weeks we heard from Mother. She was settled in Aunt Grace's house, and Aunt Grace sent word for Marion and me to come live there also. Now that Mother was back in our little hometown of Brooklyn, this seemed to spur something in both Lillian's and Nina's minds. They started talking about moving back to Brooklyn, where we were born. In spite of Charlie we all wanted to be close to Mother. Marion said, "Jack, let's give it a try. Charlie wouldn't dare give us a rough time with Aunt Grace and her family in the same house. I think we should go." So again another move.

Marion and I hitchhiked on the pulpwood trucks to Brooklyn. We got a royal welcome by everyone except you-know-who. When Charlie came into the house and saw us, his face turned all kinds of colors. I could tell he was dying to cuss us out but didn't dare—not yet. It was just a matter of time until he cut me down. At first he completely ignored me, and my cousins were wondering what was wrong. Aunt Grace knew, because she had seen the beast in him when she visited us in the house at First Peninsula.

The depression got even worse, and this became the worst economic times I've ever lived through. Since Charlie was not working, and after the few dollars Mother had saved was gone, we were destitute. And I mean destitute. It got to the point where we had nothing in the house to eat. We didn't even have a cup of flour. Aunt Grace had no idea in the world how bad off we were. At least we didn't think so, and Mother was too proud to let her know. Aunt Grace would have been more than glad to help us, if she had known.

We finally got so desperate that Mother asked Marion and me to sell ten-cent tickets on her treasured Hawaiian guitar. She would raffle it off. This was the mail-order guitar she had bought with the fifty-two free lessons some years earlier. She treasured this instrument more than anything else she owned, and it hurt me to think she would have to give it up. I remembered when Mother lost her old pump organ after she and Dad separated, and I was deeply saddened when I saw it being hauled away. Now I couldn't bear seeing her guitar go.

But the next morning, strictly against our will, we took the guitar in its canvas case and went to Liverpool to try our luck. It was cold and damp with a heavy overcast sky, and it looked like it would snow any minute. Marion and I knocked on door after door. But we didn't find one single soul who seemed the least bit interested in buying a ticket. Just about everybody was insecure and fearful about the depression. Most people couldn't spend money for a luxury, and a guitar was a luxury in those bleak days. I'm thankful it worked out this way. Marion and I would have rather gone from house to house begging for food than to sell Mother's guitar. The guitar and a few records were about the only luxuries I remember Mother ever having.

Charlie went to Liverpool to Simms Flour and Feed Store to see if he could buy a bag of flour on credit. He took me along. I'm sure he thought the man would know we were starving to death for sure when he saw how thin and sickly I looked. I stood in the store, watching Charlie beg for the credit. He gave the man a sob story. He told about Mother being in bad health, and that we had nothing to eat in the house. Nothing. Charlie even offered to give him a signed paper stating he would give him our furniture if we didn't pay the bill. It didn't work. I suppose the man had heard the same story many times before.

The next afternoon one of Aunt Grace's boys came into the house and said to Mother, "There's a ninety-eight-pound bag of Robin Hood flour sitting out by the front of the house, and it must be yours because it's certainly not ours." Sure enough, I went to check it out, and there it was! I asked Aunt Grace about it, and she said she didn't know where in the world it came from. I've always believed Aunt Grace must have heard some of us talking about our financial condition and had the flour delivered for us. It was sure good to see Mother smile again. In no time Mother had put the ingredients together to make us a pan of biscuits.

Boy, I took some of the dough that Mother had prepared for the biscuits and fried it on top of the stove. I was too hungry to wait until the biscuits baked. Friends, if you've never eaten plain dough, fried to a golden brown on top of a wood stove, you really have a treat coming. That is, of course, if you're weak from hunger.

Mother would usually be able to scrape up something for us to eat. Often she'd stretch and ration the food, and we had to eat small portions many times. I had no money to buy shells for my .22 rifle. Otherwise I would have shot rabbits for food. However, I did make some rabbit snares out of some old wire that I found around the place. I set them back of the house in the tall bushes, and I caught one every now and then.

Charlie made things much worse for Marion and me. He didn't lay a hand on me when we were around Aunt Grace or whenever any of her family was present. But when Grace's family wasn't around, the cursing went on nonstop. He'd call Marion such filthy names that I wouldn't even repeat them. Marion was such a sweet and kind person. There was no way she deserved that kind of treatment. I was Charlie's scapegoat. Everything that was wrong he blamed on me. The depression was my fault. If he didn't have a job, it was my fault. The problems of the world were my fault. That's the way it seemed to me.

Charlie Tanner was, truthfully, a beast in my eyes. When I was younger, I thought something was dreadfully wrong with me, and I felt guilty for causing so many problems. By the time I was eighteen, however, I began to see Charlie for what he was. To me he was an ignorant monster without human compassion, and nothing ever changed my point of view.

It didn't take long for my cousins to see that Charlie was filled with anger. Aunt Grace had three boys, Cyril, Carl, and Freeman, and a daughter named Mary. One afternoon the youngest boy, Freeman, came to me very upset. He said if I promised not to say who told me, he'd tell me something about Charlie that was extremely important. I assured Freeman that I wouldn't tell a soul. Then he said, "I heard that Charlie has a .32 revolver, and he's been carrying it around for three days. That crazy bastard hates you so much he's going to shoot you. I'd report this to the Royal Canadian Mounted Police if I were you."

Believe me, I was going to report it to the police, but before I could get there, someone apparently tipped Charlie off that the news had gotten to me. Supposedly, Charlie had gotten scared that he might be arrested, and he threw the pistol in the well.

I got to Liverpool as soon as I could and informed Corporal Richards of the Royal Canadian Mounted Police at his office. I repeated what I'd heard. Corporal Richards was kind, and he talked to me like a father. But he told me the same thing that I had heard from the chief of police in Lunenburg when I reported an earlier threat. "Clarence, there isn't a thing the law can do unless he harms you in some way. But I'll drive to Brooklyn and visit you and the family members, and we'll talk this out. Maybe counseling will help, and I'll also check out the well for the pistol."

We set a time for his visit, and I was so relieved that finally something was going to be done. I didn't mention to anyone, except Mother, that the police were coming. When Corporal Richards walked into the house the next day, Charlie looked utterly shocked. He turned as white as a ghost. The corporal talked to all of us about the importance of resolving problems, and he looked Charlie straight in the eye and told him he would be in serious trouble if he continued to make threats against me. Charlie listened. Corporal Richards finished his hour or so of counseling all of us, and before he left, he searched the well for the gun, but the search didn't turn up any pistol. I still believe, and so did Freeman, that someone had tipped Charlie off and he had removed the gun from the well.

Charlie was much better, and he seemed very quiet for several weeks after the counseling. Then all hell broke loose! I honestly don't remember what triggered him off this time. But Charlie broke into a sudden rage, and he ordered Marion and me to "get the hell out of the house and never come back again." This rampage could have been heard a mile away—yet nobody came to help us. I suppose they were afraid to butt in, knowing that you can't reason with a crazy person. I thought he might still have the pistol, and since he was so full of clear hell, I was afraid he might shoot both Marion and me.

This was the middle of February, and at least a foot of fresh snow was on the ground. There were no tracks on the road, because nobody in their right mind would even think about walking or driving on that snowy day. It was probably the coldest night of the year, and I'd be safe in saying the temperature was zero degrees, if not colder. Marion and I grabbed our coats and got out the door as fast as we could. This was around nine o'clock at night. Neither of us was dressed for that kind of weather, but we began walking through the snow in the direction of Lunenburg, hoping to get to Nina's place before we froze to death. The nearest house was nine miles away in a little settlement called Mill Village.

Can you believe that we walked through a foot of snow for nine miles? It's hard to believe, but we did. We knocked on the door of this big house that sat way back in the field, and a lady came to the door, looking surprised that we would be out on a night like that, especially since it was about midnight. She invited us in and we told our story. After we were given something to eat, Marion slept upstairs in one of the bedrooms, and I was made a comfortable bed on the living room couch.

I woke up around 7:00 A.M. when the people of the house got up and made breakfast. The food sure smelled good to me, and I was hoping they'd have enough left over for my sister and me. Marion came downstairs, and the lady fed us a good breakfast with orange juice, ham and eggs, toast, jelly—things we certainly were not used to. After breakfast we thanked them and started on our journey to Nina's place.

It was cold, but the sun was shining and the fresh fallen snow was beautiful. We walked along the highway and saw some fresh tracks on the road. After we walked for about two miles, a big truck from a wholesale company stopped and picked us up. I got in the bed of the truck, and the driver let Marion sit in the front with him, where he had a heater that kept them warm. The driver was going to Bridgewater, about fifteen miles away, but he was nice enough to drive us all the way to Lunenburg, another twelve miles. We then walked the other four miles to Bluerocks and to Nina's place. Whenever I was in a helpless situation, I could always count on Nina and Ritchie. Always.

Marion and I stayed with them throughout the winter of 1932 and 1933. I often visited Lillian in Lunenburg, and of course Wilbert always completely ignored me. But Lillian always made me feel comfortable and at home. One thing with Lillian and Wilbert, he was always afraid that Lillian was going to leave him since he was a lot older than she was. So Lillian pretty well did what she wanted.

Lillian was a collector of Jimmie Rodgers records, as was Mother, and I loved to visit Lillian and play her new records. I played them so much that the turntable spring often broke in the old crank-up machine. We'd have to place our index finger close to the spindle and move the turntable with our finger. The sound was a bit wobbly, but we got to where we could turn it pretty evenly. Of course, when any of us had the money for a new spring, we'd buy a new one right away.

These records were inspirational to me. As I listened, I paid strict attention to Jimmie's phrasing and the guitar runs on all of his records. The more music I heard, the more convinced I was that I would also become a top-rated entertainer. I still had my $12.95 guitar at Nina's, and I practiced every chance I got. By Christmas of 1932, Jimmie had many more records available in the record stores across Canada, and between Lillian and Mother, they usually came up with the money to get them all.

Jimmie Rodgers, without a doubt, had become my idol.

More and more, I was able to dismiss Charlie from taking up so much time in my mind. I reasoned that if I wanted to be successful in music, I had to concentrate on positive thoughts and plan a course of action to be able to achieve my dreams. By early 1933, I became determined to go to Halifax. When I was in Halifax on two previous occasions, I heard radio station CHNS play good country music, including the artists Jimmie Rodgers, Vernon Dalhart, Wilf Carter (known to many people in America as Montana Slim), and a few others.

I believed that if I was to have any chance at becoming a performer, I had to get on radio CHNS for my debut. But just thinking about the big step to Halifax made me nervous. My faith would waver a bit and I'd wonder, "How could I, a poor, uneducated, sickly teenager, hope to compete with people trained in music?" However, I kept reminding myself about the success story of Jimmie Rodgers. It was obvious to me that to be successful in the music business, you had to have talent and determination. I felt these were the key ingredients. No doubt, I had determination. Did I have talent? My family and friends said so, but I had to find out for myself if I had commercial talent.

I would go to Halifax. But first I had to earn some money, and I had to have a plan. In early March, 1933, I got the nerve to write a letter to the managing director of CHNS asking for an audition. Boy, was I nervous when Nina told me I had a letter in the mail from the station. It was typed and addressed to Mr. Clarence E. Snow. Here's what it said:

March 14, 1933

Dear Mr. Snow:

We have your letter and I regret to tell you that we are not able to offer you anything at this station. All the artists who appear here are paid by the sponsors of the programs and unless a sponsor was to ask for you, we could not do anything for you. If, however, your services are required, we have your name on file.

Yours very truly,

William Coates Borrett
Managing Director

Even though I figured this was a "Don't call me, I'll call you" letter, I was not discouraged. To think that the managing director of the station would answer my letter personally actually encouraged me. After all, the director didn't say not to come. This letter, written on blue stationery, still has a prominent place in my scrapbooks. If I had received this letter a few years earlier, before I could handle rejection, I would have found a hundred reasons to forget about pursuing a career in music. I filed the letter away, knowing I'd be going to CHNS sometime in the future.

Certainly, I was driven to succeed, in whatever I did, to satisfy this need within me. I wanted to rise above the poverty and lack of a formal education. I wanted people who cared about me to be proud of me in whatever I accomplished. And I guess in the back of my mind I was determined to show Charlie Tanner I was going to be successful—come hell or high water.

On my nineteenth birthday, May 9, 1933, I made up my mind to go for it. I would not be satisfied with my life until I could have an audition to be heard on the radio. My immediate problem was to figure out some way to get enough money to get me to Halifax.

One morning I was walking along the waterfront in Lunenburg, thinking and dreaming, when on the corner I saw a big beautiful Stutz Blackhawk convertible. It had a Massachusetts license plate and the top was down. I was admiring the gorgeous inside, with its many instruments on the mahogany dashboard, the beautiful Spanish leather seats, and all the finery you could imagine. I made my mind up right then that I'd be driving a beautiful, expensive car someday.

While I was admiring the classy car, two well-dressed men came up and started talking to me. They were friendly, and in a New England accent they told me their names and asked if I'd like to sit behind the wheel. As I was sitting in the car, they told me their reasons for being in Lunenburg. They had purchased a big three-mast, square-rigger ship that was anchored in the harbor. They wanted to hire some men to clean it up and paint the decks, cabins, wheelhouse, and so on. In other words, they wanted to get their vessel in shipshape condition. One said, "We need three or four men and you can be one of them. There's no heavy work involved, and I'm sure you can handle the job. Could you use a little extra money?"

You bet I could! This could be my ticket to Halifax. They hired me on the spot, and I started scraping paint that same afternoon. The job lasted about three weeks, and when it was finished, I was pleasantly surprised when one of the gentlemen handed me $32.50 in cash.

Now I figured I had enough money to enable Marion and me to

get to Halifax, so I began to lay out my plan. I wanted to take Marion with me because she had suffered much abuse from Charlie also, and I felt it was partly my responsibility to keep her away from him. Besides, she wanted to go and look for a job, and I needed moral support. We both would need moral support in a big city with perfect strangers.

We wanted to visit Mother before we left for the big city. I needed her inspiration and her caring way from time to time. You'll remember when I lived with my grandmother years earlier, I would do anything just to be in the same town with Mother. It would take a lot more than Charlie Tanner to keep me away from her.

In the meantime, Mother had moved out of Aunt Grace's house and through a friend had found a little house with two rooms, only about a mile from Aunt Grace's home. Mother and Aunt Grace had gotten along just fine, but Mother was anxious to have her own place.

A few days later Marion and I put our few clothes in an old suitcase, I grabbed my little thirteen-dollar guitar, and we said good-bye to Nina and Ritchie. We hitchhiked to Brooklyn to see Mother. She was totally surprised but overjoyed to see us. Charlie had not come home yet. When he did come in, he never even acknowledged we were there. Mother wanted us to stay for a few days, but since there was only Mother's bedroom and a cot in the kitchen, I went to stay with Aunt Grace and Marion stayed with Mother. We knew it was time to move on when we saw the anger burning in Charlie's black eyes.

We said our good-byes to Mother around three o'clock in the afternoon and walked along the highway to Liverpool. I had a plan that had been rolling around in my mind for several days, but I didn't say a word about it to anyone. I still had money from the $32.50 that I'd made working on the ship. I had spent a few dollars for a pair of pants, a shirt, and a cheap pair of shoes.

We stopped in Liverpool and went directly to Woolworth's dime store. I purchased about twelve dollars' worth of such things as bobby pins, toothbrushes, toothpaste, soap, shaving cream, pencils, thread, safety pins, ladies' hair curlers, and a few other small items. My plan was to hitchhike the ninety-seven miles to Halifax and along the highway stop at houses to sell these items for a profit. That way I'd have more money when I got to Halifax than I had when we left. I took my guitar with me, and I'd offer to sing a song to the people in the household, thinking that this might entice them to buy some of my goods.

It was a beautiful summer afternoon as we walked along the highway. The birds were singing and the flowers were blooming along the side of the road. We carried our old beat-up suitcase, our articles for sale, and my guitar. We kept walking and looking back to see if a car or truck was coming, hoping that we could get a lift and enjoy some rest. We were pretty lucky. We caught a few short rides until we arrived in the little settlement of Chester Basin, which was at least one-third of the way to Halifax. We stopped at a house here and there to peddle my merchandise, but we didn't have much luck doing that.

At about 7:00 P.M. we knocked at a little white cottage, and a pleasant, middle-aged woman came to the door and invited us in. After we told her our mission and my plan to get on the radio, she gave us something to eat. After supper, when her husband came home, they had me sing several songs, which of course were Jimmie Rodgers songs. Their eyes lit up as they praised my talent over and over again, which sure made me feel good. The nice lady put us up for the night. The next morning she gave us a good breakfast, bought a few items, and wished us well. We thanked her for her hospitality, and we were on our way again.

After we had walked several miles, a big truck picked us up. It only took us about ten miles, and we were walking again. I made several more tries to sell my wares, with no luck. People wanted to hear me sing but didn't want to buy anything. I guess they had no money, like most of us. This got discouraging, and I didn't try too hard after that. A few more hitched rides, and we were at the edge of Halifax.

We had been given directions on how to get to the Prudhomme family, who lived in Fairview, which was northwest of Halifax about four miles. Leone Prudhomme was the daughter of Mrs. Herman, the elderly lady who was very special to me. Mrs. Herman had made me promise that if I ever got back to Halifax, I'd visit her daughter and family in Fairview. Accordingly, Mrs. Herman had written a letter to her daughter that we were on our way to visit them.

The family welcomed Marion and me with open arms. Leone had married Joseph Prudhomme, and they had two sons, Frank and Victor, and a daughter named Gloria. They were undoubtedly the nicest people I had ever met in my life. After Charlie and Wilbert it was hard to believe that people could be this decent and kind. They insisted that we stay with them just as long as we wanted to, and we were treated like royalty—as if we were part of their family. And every meal was a feast.

They wanted me to play and sing every song I knew and praised me without end. Their encouragement sure helped me feel confident in myself. They said I'd have no trouble getting on the radio station, and I'd have fans galore who would love my music just as much as they did. Because of their strong support, I was ready in less than a week to take the big step that was to determine my future.

I made a phone call to the station and the secretary said for me to stop by the next day at two o'clock. The next afternoon I put on my best clothes, picked up my faithful thirteen-dollar guitar, and started the four-mile walk into Halifax. Mr. Prudhomme had told me how to get to the Lord Nelson Hotel, where the office and studios were located. When I got there, I stood in front of the tall, beautiful hotel, but I almost didn't go in. I was getting cold feet. I had second thoughts about this, and I was very, very nervous.

My persistence got the better of me. I'd been through too much to turn around and give up. I straightened up my shoulders, walked inside the hotel, and took the elevator to the fifth floor. When I got off the elevator, I saw a sign: Offices of CHNS. I walked around the corner and saw a couple of ladies typing in an office. Miss Nickerson asked if she could help me. With a trembling voice, I said I had an appointment. She directed me to an upper floor and phoned the studio to let them know I was on my way.

I had to walk up a set of stairs that curled around where the door was, and I entered the small waiting room right off the one and only studio. I could see the microphones, music stands, a piano, and other instruments. Then I started shaking more than ever. In a short time, a pleasant face greeted me. The man shook my hand and said, "I'm Cecil Landry, chief engineer and announcer. Major Borrett informed me that you were coming in." Then he spoke these exact words: "Just a minute, Clarence, and I'll hear your stuff."

I was to get my audition after all. By then I was so nervous that I didn't know for sure if I could even sing, because my throat got so dry. Mr. Landry disappeared for a few minutes, then came back and took me into the studio. He sat me down on a straight-back chair in front of a long counter-type desk with a microphone sitting on it.

All of this looked scary, and when I took my guitar out of the canvas case, it was literally shaking in my hands. I settled down a little when Mr. Landry went into the control room and closed the door. I saw him through the big window, and he waved to me to go ahead with my song. First I sang a cowboy song entitled "A Letter from Home Sweet Home," and then I sang a Jimmie Rodgers song and yodeled with it. When I finished, Mr. Landry came back into the studio with a big smile on his face and said, "That was pretty good. You have a good voice and you play your guitar pretty well, too." Then he said something that almost scared me to death. "Clarence, think up something for a theme song and come on back here tonight, and we'll put you on the air at seven o'clock. You'll do a fifteen-minute show."

I almost fainted! My stomach felt like it was turning round and round. Go on the radio? Tonight? Me—alone? This was happening so fast, I was almost speechless. But this was the moment I had been dreaming of. Oh, this precious moment!

Now, folks, pardon my ignorance, but I didn't know what "theme song" meant. But I wasn't about to let Mr. Landry know, in case he changed his mind. I waited until I got back to the Prudhommes' and asked them. They were very excited for me. They explained that a theme song was a special song that would identify me in the future and that I would sing it whenever I came on and went off the air. I sat down and thought about it. Suddenly I knew my theme song had to be the Jimmie Rodgers tune entitled "The Yodeling Cowboy." After all, I had copied Jimmie's style, and I could yodel a bit. Of course, I couldn't yodel like Jimmie Rodgers or Wilf Carter.

Here are the lyrics to my theme song:

> At the set of the sun when my work is done
> On my pony I take a ride
> Where the varmints prowl and the coyotes howl,
> With my .44 by my side.

At the end of my show I would do the rest of that verse:

> I go down that lonesome trail,
> Just galloping along.
> I love to sing this yodeling
> Cowboy song.

Then I'd break into a yodel.

Mr. Landry did the announcing for me and introduced the songs that I'd sing. He saw I was very nervous, and he did everything he could to make it easy for me. You can't imagine how excited I was when he announced the second song, "My Blue-Eyed Jane." Remember the picture I drew on the scribbler cover and the title of the song I penciled in on the make-believe record? It was that song, "My Blue-Eyed Jane," that I most wanted to sing on the radio. I made it through the fifteen-minute live radio program with the professional help of Mr. Landry. One of my dreams had come true!

I couldn't wait to get back to the Prudhommes' house, and it seemed like I was there in no time. That four miles seemed like one mile because I was floating on clouds. When I stepped into the Prudhommes' big living room, I received a big surprise! The Prudhommes had invited several neighbors in to hear my first broadcast, and I received a standing ovation. The folks complimented me so much that I was embarrassed. But I'll never forget my feelings that night. The people at Prudhommes' were convinced that I was really going places.

And for a brief moment I believed it!

9

Radio Station CHNS

Let me go, let me go, let me go, lover,
Let me be, set me free from your spell.
You made me weep, cut me deep, I can't sleep, lover,
I was cursed from the first day I fell.

"Let Me Go, Lover,"
by Jenny Lou Carson and Al Hill

✦

ON TOP OF ALL THIS EXCITEMENT, about four days later I got a message to call the radio station. The Prudhommes didn't have a telephone, so I had given the phone number of a nearby grocery store, in the unlikely event that someone wanted to contact me. Pete Praught owned the store, and he had bought the remainder of my wares that I didn't sell during the trip to Halifax. He received the call from CHNS and had the message relayed to me.

I phoned the station and talked to Miss Nickerson, Major Borrett's secretary. In a pleasant voice she informed me I had a lot of fan mail at the station. Dumb me. What was fan mail? I didn't ask her but went back to the house and asked my friends. Someone said, "Fan mail is mail from listeners who are impressed with your talent and who enjoy the artist's work. It's a compliment—a letter of appreciation."

I could hardly sleep that night. I got up bright and early the next morning and made the long walk to CHNS. About ninety letters were waiting for me from various parts of Nova Scotia. Miss Nickerson was enthusiastic, too. "Clarence, the amount of mail you received from just one broadcast is amazing. This is highly unusual for a new artist. Consider also that perhaps only one listener in a hundred might actually take the time to write."

Radio station CHNS had 1,000 watts of power, I believe, and the signal reached out to a radius of about two hundred fifty miles. The station scheduled me for a fifteen-minute program every Saturday night. In a few days I saw an advertisement in the daily paper, the *Halifax Herald,* listing the programs of CHNS. In the 7:00 P.M. slot, it read "Clarence Snow and his Guitar." Boy, everything was falling into place and really looking good for me.

Cecil Landry was the chief engineer and chief announcer for the station, and I give him much credit for my success that was to follow. Everybody loved him. He was kind and unselfish—a real gentleman—and he became a friend I admired very much. He gave me tremendous encouragement and taught me much about pronunciation and how to handle lyrics effectively. He helped me with my diction, style, and the way I presented myself in front of a microphone.

Mr. Landry was the first person to record my voice and to play it back. The station had purchased one of the first disc-cutter machines, which recorded on aluminum discs. The records were played back on a regular Victrola with a wooden needle. I still have the two records he made for me. They're about the size of today's 45 rpm records, but they're not very good quality. The first song was "Old Faithful," and I thought it sounded great! On the other side he recorded me singing "The Old Rugged Cross."

He and I sometimes did harmony together. He had a deep voice, and at that time I was singing at least two full tones higher than I do today. I sang tenor with him, and we had a lot of fun. Later on, when I got involved with a band, Mr. Landry would sometimes play the Jew's harp with us. The Jew's harp is a small metal instrument placed between the teeth as it's played.

I enjoyed my weekly radio program, even though it was on a sustaining basis, which meant I wasn't paid anything by CHNS. Radio performers had to have a sponsor in order to be paid, and I didn't have one. But I was glad to have the privilege of getting radio experience, which was another step toward becoming a true professional.

I didn't mind the four-mile walk to the station, even during the hard winter months when I had rain, snow storms, and ice to contend with. I never had the fifteen cents to take the bus, which left Fairview and stopped just a couple of blocks from the radio station, on Spring Garden Road. But I never missed a performance. Sometimes the three Davidson brothers, who had a nice car, would give me a ride. They made periodic trips to Bedford, about ten miles from Halifax, and drove through Fairview where I was living.

Since I had no income, I was totally dependent on the Prudhommes and lived with them for several months. Marion stayed a few weeks with them in the beginning, but she soon found a job doing light housework in the ritzy part of Halifax. She wasn't paid much money, but she received free room and board. I felt relieved that she was in good hands with the people she was working for, and this also lightened the burden on the Prudhommes.

After a few months, when I became more acquainted with Mr. Landry, I asked him if I could try a new radio name. Since my idol was Jimmie Rodgers, who was known as "America's Blue Yodeler," I wanted to use the title "The Cowboy Blue Yodeler." He said it was okay to try it for a while until we could come up with something else that we both liked. The daily paper listed me as "The Cowboy Blue Yodeler at 7:00 P.M. every Saturday night."

I worked diligently on improving my delivery techniques, and I gradually became more confident and professional on my weekly program. My popularity continued to grow, and the fan mail kept pouring in.

During the early part of the summer of 1934, Frank, one of the Prudhomme boys, brought Jack Faulkner to meet me. Jack lived up on the hill from the Prudhommes' home, on Lightning Hill. He played the guitar quite well and began coming to the Prudhomme house often. We'd show each other our style of guitar playing, and this helped us both to become better guitarists. He was also an excellent tap and ballroom dancer. He was never without a date with some pretty girl, because they all loved to dance with him.

Jack and I were discussing music one day and he said, "Since you've been getting so much fan mail and gaining a lot of popularity, we ought to take advantage of this. I'll bet we can make a little money by touring the country villages and playing schoolhouses and lodge halls." I was anxious to play for an audience, and we followed a simple plan. We went into the town or village, rented a place to play, put up our handmade crayon-printed posters, waited about three days, and had the show. On our cardboard posters we printed "The Cowboy Blue Yodeler and his side pal, Rambling Jack."

Jack's dad bought him a new pair of shoes and a few clothes so he could go on the road. I had no money to buy anything until the mounted police drove up to the house and brought me a twelve-dollar check! It was my reward for snitching on the bootlegger in Bluerocks. I don't know how they found me, but it was a pleasant surprise. I spent it all on much-needed clothes and a pair of shoes.

Without a penny in our pockets, Jack and I hitchhiked along the highway and landed in the tiny village of Hubbard's Cove, about thirty miles from Halifax. We rented the Masonic Lodge Hall, which would hold about fifty people. It cost us $2.50, payable after the show. After putting up our posters, we looked for a place to eat and sleep. We saw a sign out in front of a little white cottage that read "Room and Board—$1 a day." We took a chance and rented the room anyway, hoping we would make enough money to pay the lady.

We practiced our guitars every day before the show until about 9:00 P.M. We were encouraged because several of the boarders heard us practicing and paid us compliments. They assured us that the audience would love our performance. In a way, the few days we stayed at the little cottage was like a vacation. The lady treated us like big entertainers because she knew I was a "star" on radio, or at least she thought so. The food was delicious, and we anxiously awaited the call to breakfast, dinner, and supper. But the more we ate, the more guilty we felt, thinking we might not be able to pay the rent. Naturally I worried. What will happen if nobody comes to the show? And will people come if we have a rainstorm?

As it turned out, I didn't need to worry, because the Masonic Hall was packed, and some people had to stand. Since we had no public-address systems, we had to play loud and project our voices so the audience could hear the lyrics. You could hear a pin drop in the hall. Everything went as planned, and our show lasted over an hour. We played guitar duets. I sang my songs, and Jack tap danced while I played the only three chords I knew on the old piano in the corner of the hall. We told jokes, and the audience had a great time, or at least they seemed to. Maybe they were taking pity on us, but I hope not.

We charged fifteen cents for children and twenty-five cents for adults. After we paid for the use of the Masonic Hall and for our room and board, we had money left over.

We continued our eight- to ten-day tour—if you can call it a tour. Of course, we had no bus, no car, no equipment, nothing except our guitars and our desire to entertain. Since there weren't too many cars traveling the dusty graveled roads, we did a lot of walking between hitchhiked rides. We'd pick blueberries along the roadside, walk a little, rest a little, and hope for a ride.

Our next show was in another pretty tourist village, called Chester Basin, and luck was with us. While we were there, a gentleman by the name of Phil Moore heard us practicing in the country hotel where we had rented a room, and he set it up for us to do our act at the nearby yacht club. It was a gorgeous place, and we enjoyed watching the members swimming and boating and having a good time. They seemed to like our show, and this gave our morale a boost.

When we finished, Phil said, "I'm on the board of directors at Lake

Williams, and I'll be driving there tomorrow to the Guides Meet to compete in outdoor sports. If you'll be ready by 8:00 A.M., you can ride with me. You boys can put on some shows during the three-day event and pick up some extra money." We did, and we had a great time. Lake Williams, located near Bridgewater, was one of the most beautiful places I've ever seen. The big lake sat right in the middle of all kinds of beautiful trees: pine, hemlock, spruce, fir, maple, and birch. We watched all the outdoor activities at the Guides Meet, which included swimming contests, diving, trap shooting, log rolling, and canoe racing.

Here's a description of our two-man show. We opened with an old song entitled "Side by Side." Then we did an instrumental called "The Cowboy March." Next I sang a Jimmie Rodgers song. Wouldn't you know my first song on the show would be "My Blue-Eyed Jane"? I sang "Lonesome for You," followed by a Rodgers blues number called "She Left Me This Morning." Next Jack and I did two instrumentals, "Beautiful Ohio" and "Mr. Gallagher." Following those, I sang another Jimmie Rodgers song, "The Lullaby Yodel." Then another instrumental, "The Mockingbird," followed by another Rodgers tune, "The Cowboy's Meditation." Next another instrumental called "It's a Long Way to Tipperary."

Interspersed between our playing and singing, Jack performed his tap dancing. Our show continued with two songs entitled "Twilight on the Prairie" and "Goodnight, Little Buckaroo." Another tune, "The Lonely Hobo," was followed by a Jimmie Rodgers song, "The Land of My Boyhood Dreams." Then came two instrumentals, "Grandfather's Clock" and "Calgary Stampede March." After that I sang a real old song that was very popular, "When It's Berry Pickin' Time at Old Aunt Mary's." Following was an instrumental of "Blackbird." And we closed our show with the same song we opened with, "Side by Side." We used this old song because some of the lyrics were appropriate for us.

Jack and I had the feeling that sometimes we were a little boring or the people didn't like us, since they didn't clap a lot. However, after the show many of them came up and shook our hands and told us how great our show was. We made ten dollars each and had enough money to pay for our room and board—and still had some left over.

For our last appearance we were scheduled to play for a dance in a small hall at Hunt's Point, about five miles from Liverpool. My Uncle Carl and Aunt Hannah lived at Western Head, about nine miles from Hunt's Point, and they planned to attend the dance. I was anxious for Jack to meet these wonderful people, and I had it worked out for us to stay with them a few days. Uncle Carl had been a soldier in World

War I, the "Great War," as it was referred to before World War II. The Canadian government gave him a job in Western Head, located right on the Atlantic Coast line. His job was to operate a power-driven foghorn and a revolving beacon light, which were used to give direction to all types of vessels, steamers, and ships in clear or foggy weather. Several years later the government installed wireless equipment, and since he had the expertise of a trained wireless operator, Uncle Carl was put in charge of it, too. The government also built a nice home next to the work station for Uncle Carl and his family.

When Jack and I arrived at the dance hall in Western Head, at least fifty people were waiting for us. They seemed to enjoy the show immensely. They had no trouble dancing to our instrumental guitar music or to the songs I sang.

During the dance I met Margaret Matthews, a very pretty girl. I had Jack ride back home with Uncle Carl and Aunt Hannah, and I hired a taxi to drive Margaret and me to her door. I remember feeling like a big shot in that beautiful new car with a pretty girl by my side. I bid Margaret goodnight, and the taxi drove me down to Brooklyn to Mother's home.

Charlie was in bed asleep, thank God, and Mother was happy to see me. We talked for a long time. I told her about my date with Margaret Matthews, and I was surprised when she said that Margaret's mother had been a friend of hers for a long time. I discussed my radio program and my tour with Jack. I complimented Jack as a fine boy, and Mother was pleased that I was associated with such a nice person. I slept on the tiny couch in the small kitchen for the night, and Charlie must have left real early that morning, because he was gone when I woke up. I told Mother good-bye, then hitchhiked to Uncle Carl's place, six miles away.

I wanted to see Margaret again before we left Liverpool, so I called her from Uncle Carl's and made a date for the next night. She said she'd bring a friend along to keep Jack company. Margaret was a wonderful and perfect young lady. I loved her very much, and I know she felt the same toward me. That night she gave me a little pearl heart with gold lines across the front, and she made me promise that if our communication ever ended and we drifted apart, I'd return it. I promised. However, I never saw her again and we never wrote. I still have the tiny heart among my most prized possessions, and I've often wondered what happened to her.

The night before we left Uncle Carl's to go back to Halifax, something funny happened. Uncle Carl said, "I've got a five-gallon keg of grape wine in the cellar, which has been sitting there for almost six weeks, and it should be ripe. I've been waiting for you before I opened it. I'll go down and tap it off, and we'll celebrate your success." He went down to the cellar and pulled the plug. As he was trying to ease the cork out, it flew out with a bang and the wine squirted with great force. He couldn't stop it. He tried to get the plug back in, but no luck. The wine went all over his face, his clothes, the ceiling, and everywhere. He came back up from the cellar laughing as hard as he could. With that sticky wine in his eyes, he could hardly see. He was literally drenched with five gallons of wine! And there wasn't enough left in the keg to fill a drinking glass. That's the kind of person Uncle Carl was. All the wine was gone, and he just laughed about it.

The following day Jack and I hitchhiked back to Halifax. We had a taste of show business for a little less than two weeks, and it made me want more. Jack wasn't interested in a music career, but he sure enjoyed our tour.

I continued my weekly radio shows. Several months later Mr. Landry started a country music show called "Down on the Farm." It was composed of a group of boys who played several instruments, such as guitars and fiddles. They were not great, but they were good. Mr. Landry asked me to do a number or two each Saturday night with them. He said it would give me more exposure to the listeners of CHNS. I certainly agreed.

At this time I changed my name again. This will answer many questions about how I got the name "Hank." Mr. Landry suggested I use Hank because it was a good western name, and I was singing a lot of cowboy songs. Since I wanted to follow the career of my idol, Jimmie Rodgers, I added "The Yodeling Ranger."

I also changed my theme song. I'd begin my programs with these lyrics taken from one of Jimmie's songs:

> They call me the yodeling ranger,
> My badge is solid gold.
> I've rode the land by the old Rio Grande
> And belong to that old ranger fold.

To conclude each program I'd sing the rest of the song, which went like this:

> There's no place where I am a stranger,
> And I'm never lonely long.
> Wherever we are I have my old guitar
> And yodel this old ranger song.

At the end of these lyrics I'd burst out with a yodel. I continued to use "Hank, the Yodeling Ranger" for several years. Later on, I'll tell you how I finally became "Hank, the Singing Ranger," which is still with me.

In the meantime, I had met a pretty girl by the name of Winnie Shrum. She worked as a nurse in one of the hospitals in Halifax, and if my memory serves me correctly, it was the Salvation Army hospital. She was a special person, and we dated until Halloween.

On Halloween, I went to a party with Jack at the home of Harvey and Nora Aalders. They lived in a comfortable home on the other side of the street and a few houses up the hill from the Prudhommes. At the party, several folks were gathered in the living room, and I noticed a beautiful girl just as soon as I entered. I immediately went across the room and sat down right next to her. She was friendly, and the way her eyes glistened, I knew she was something special. She had the prettiest smile I had ever seen, and it was so easy and natural for us to talk to each other.

Her name was Minnie Blanche Aalders.

I absolutely fell in love with Min that night. This very special lady became my bride, my partner for life, my inspiration, and my strength—the one who deserves the most credit for any and all accomplishments that lay ahead for me in music. Now, some six decades later, I still love her. I love her even more today.

I discovered that she and I had a lot of things in common. She was used to hard work, like myself, and she loved music, too. She and her sister, Leta, were taking guitar lessons when we met. Min was fascinated with my radio show and my talent, which pleased me to no end. I learned a lot about her that first night. She and Leta worked at Moirs chocolate factory in Halifax six days a week and half days on Saturday. Both were working as chocolate dippers, and they had also worked as timekeepers. Since there was no bus service between Fairview and Halifax, they had to walk four miles each way. Often during the winter it was raining or snowing, or there was ice on the ground. During the summer they had to contend with the summer heat. Before working at Moirs, they had worked at a dime store in Halifax, so they were used to a lot of walking. To walk that much showed a lot of spunk.

By the time I left the Halloween party at the Aalders home, I felt I knew Min pretty well. I thought she was the prettiest and nicest person I had ever met. Both Mr. and Mrs. Aalders made a point of telling me to come again, and they said I was welcome in their home anytime. This started a romance that continues to this day. I began visiting Min nearly every night. We had so many things to talk about. She even gave me a few lessons on how to read notes of music, as my guitar playing was strictly by ear.

One night Mr. and Mrs. Aalders invited me to stay in their home and said they would find a place for me to sleep. I was reluctant to do this because I had no job and the radio station paid me no money. Besides, I didn't want to be a financial burden on their family. I could have stayed on with the Prudhommes, but I thought it wise to live someplace else to ease their burden a little. So I accepted the nice offer from the Aalders, and I vowed to find a job if there was a job to be found anywhere in Halifax. At the Aalders home I slept on a couch in the living room. This time it was a warm and comfortable davenport, and I felt like a king.

The Aalders had ten children, eight boys and two girls. Mr. Aalders was the only Protestant working at a prominent Catholic college in Rockingham, located about a mile and a half from the family's home. The Aalders's sons—those who were big enough to work—had jobs. Some of them worked on the railway tracks by the station in Fairview. They kept the switches and tracks clear of snow and ice.

After I moved into the Aalders home, I went to the railway yard in Fairview and hoped to get a job shoveling snow. About six inches of snow was on the ground, and I was wearing shoes with holes in the soles. My clothes were not suitable for cold weather, and the wind cut right to my bones as I stood in the long line of men hoping to get a job. I kept going back, but I never did get hired. I searched all over for work, but the outlook was very bleak. Whenever I did have income, I'd give Min's parents money to help out. That was a small price to pay for their warm hospitality.

Min and I spent a lot of time together. Friends dropped by to play cards or to chat, and sometimes Min took me to visit her friends. But I was always embarrassed about my old clothes. One night we visited a Hyland family in northern Halifax, and one of the boys in the family had just bought a new winter overcoat. I guess they took pity on me. Mrs. Hyland said, "Why don't you wear this coat home, since it's so cold, and there's no hurry in returning it." As I think about it now, I never did return the overcoat.

Near the end of 1934 I heard about the Fuller Brush company in Halifax needing salesmen. I checked on it, and I was signed up for a two-week training period. I was given pamphlets to read, and I read each one several times. One of the sales representatives also helped me in learning how to make a sales pitch. The district manager complimented me. "You have really been studying, haven't you? We'll assign you to a section of the city, and I'll send a trained salesman with you for a few times to guide you as you make your presentations." He gave me a sample case of the household products, which included brushes, brooms, whisks, dustpans, furniture wax, toothbrushes, and a few other items. I liked the Fuller Brush products. It seemed like their brushes would never wear out.

I followed the Fuller policy. I'd stick the sales pamphlets on doors, with the date on which I would return to show my wares. When I returned to the neighborhood, I'd ask to see the lady of the house, and I'd give her my spiel. "Good morning (or Good afternoon). I'm with the Fuller Brush company, and this is your free brush, compliments of the company." Usually the lady's eyes would light up and she'd thank me. Then I'd say, "I have some new products I'd like to show you. Would you allow me to take ten minutes of your time?" Usually the lady would let me in, and I had a good line to go with each article I displayed. If the lady bought something, I wrote the sale on a duplicate ticket that had the date I would return to deliver the article.

I thought I'd be able to make some money with these fine products, except the company gave me one of the worst routes in the city. It was a slum district. I got depressed because I was trying so hard to sell, and very few ladies could afford to buy even one item.

Good luck again! Someone from CHNS called Praught's grocery store and sent word for me to call them. I couldn't get to the phone fast enough. It was Miss Nickerson. She said, "The Crazy Water Crystals Company from Texas wants to organize a small musical combo to represent them on the air. The job will pay you ten dollars a week. Are you interested?" You bet I was! This was heaven sent.

The next morning I went to the station to discuss the complete plan with Mr. Landry, and he told me the names of the other players who would be part of the show. The sound wasn't exactly what one could call country. Well, my part was, but overall it was a mixture of different kinds of music. The combo was composed of Richard Frye, CHNS's staff piano and pipe organ player; Andy McMannis, an accomplished violinist; Frank Blair, who doubled on clarinet and xylophone; Tommy Haire, on upright bass; and Clyde Connors, a really fine professional tenor singer. Naturally, I sang the country-and-western cowboy songs and played guitar.

Crazy Water Crystals was similar to the Hadacol mixture that later became popular in the United States. It had a laxative effect on those who drank it, and the company sold a huge amount of it.

Our combo was on the air each day at noon for fifteen minutes except Saturday, and the ten dollars a week seemed like a lot of money to me. Now I had a real paying job on the radio, and it made me feel like a big radio star, but I also kept my job with the Fuller Brush company for several weeks. I'd try to sell each morning, then get to the radio station by noon to join the combo for our daily program. After the radio show I'd go back to the slums again and try to sell more brushes.

My shoes were wearing out, and I wasn't selling much of anything. I told the district manager I'd found another job, but I appreciated the chance he gave me. He understood and said, "Well, it would have taken several months of hard work to move you up the ladder to a better district. I didn't expect you to sell much in your assigned district."

I turned in my suitcase of samples and prepared to settle my account. Then the manager said something that nearly floored me. "Of course, you owe the company some money." "How is that?" I asked. He explained, "You've been giving away our free brushes, and they cost the company three cents each. You owe us a little over nineteen dollars." I had no idea that I had to pay for those "free" brushes. No one had mentioned this before. I thought it was just goodwill and advertisement for the company. If I had known this, I certainly would not have been so liberal in giving them away. I gave brushes not only to the lady of the household, but to the sisters, aunts, cousins, just anybody at all. I eventually paid the company, but it took several months to save the nineteen dollars.

More good luck! Shortly after we got the Crazy Water Crystals show, I was asked by the Canadian Broadcasting Company to do an occasional program on the Maritime Broadcasting Network, along with Dick Frye, the organ and piano player. It was called the "Farm Hour." The announcer would give weather reports and farm news about crops and make market reports on livestock prices. It paid twenty-six dollars each time I did the show, which was about once every two months. The physical structure of these programs was very unusual. Dick played the huge pipe organ located on the first floor of the big Nova Scotian Hotel. I sang and broadcast from the studio on the seventh floor. We both wore earphones, since we had to hear each other's music in order to coordinate our playing. This show was a lot of fun, and we were well received throughout the Maritime Provinces.

All this radio exposure was bringing me more publicity and bundles of fan mail. During these radio days I received a telephone call from the manager of the Gaiety Theatre in downtown Halifax. I went to see him at his office on lower Barrington, and he offered me a job for a three-day run at the theater. It would pay twelve dollars. I'd do a twenty-minute show before the matinee and another twenty-minute show before the evening movie. Of course I took the job.

This program was just me and my thirteen-dollar guitar. My first scheduled performance was before the showing of a movie starring George Raft, and I was scared to death to sing for three hundred people in one place. There were no microphones or amplification. The matinee audiences were mostly children, and I was concerned if I could keep the attention of so many restless kids. If I'd had a band, it would have been much easier for me.

This was another important opportunity to become known to more people, and I wanted to sound and look the best I could. Mother had made my beautiful white satin shirt with full sleeves. It had a big wide collar with a red star on each collar tip and a big red star on each breast. The collar had a black border. The shirt had black silk laces that laced up in the front just like I'd seen in the Gene Autry Westerns. I bought a pair of black dungarees for around $2.75, and Min sewed a narrow white cotton stripe down the side of each leg and made me a neckerchief out of orange and red cloth. I still have the neckerchief among my souvenirs. I thought, when I walked out on the stage that afternoon, I was real important in my new cowboy clothes. And the show went extremely well.

I made a promise to myself that day—that whenever I would appear in public to sing, I would wear the most decorative outfits I could find. Throughout my life, I've kept that promise. I've always tried to go first class.

I valued the experiences I was receiving. I benefitted from working with those talented musicians on the Crazy Water Crystals program. Mr. Landry was the announcer on the show, and I treasure the time I spent with him. I think of him often, and whenever I look back, I realize how much he helped me as an artist and how he was like a father to me.

After one of my programs Mr. Landry said, "Why don't you write a letter to RCA Victor in Montreal and see if you can get an audition. I think there's a good chance they will add you to their roster of artists. I feel the headway you've made here at the station, and all the popularity you've established, gives you a mighty good chance with RCA. You can count on me and anyone here at the station to give you a good recommendation and help you in any way we can."

Through Mr. Landry's encouragement, I sent a handwritten letter to A. H. Joseph, who was the A&R (artists-and-repertoire) man in Montreal, Canada. Here is the letter I received back from Mr. Joseph, just a couple of weeks later:

RCA VICTOR
April 18, 1935

Dear Sir:

We have received yours of April 9th inquiring as to the possibility of your recording for RCA Victor Records. While, at the moment, we have a large amount of talent under contract to record the type of music in which you specialize, we are always interested, however, in trying out new artists. Though to do this, it is, of course, necessary to be present in our studio in this city, which is the only place in Canada where we record.

If you happen to be in Montreal, we will certainly be pleased to make a test record, though we could hardly recommend that you come here solely on the possibility of your being engaged. As even if your test did prove satisfactory, we could not give you any guarantee that we would be able to use you in the near future.

You do not state whether you write your own compositions such as the late Jimmie Rodgers and Wilf Carter, and unless you have original numbers it is very unlikely that we would be interested as our present catalog includes so many of the standard, old time tunes at the present time.

Very truly yours,

A. H. Joseph,
Manager, Repertoire and
Recording Department

Like when I received the letter from Major Borrett at CHNS, I was impressed and thrilled beyond words that such an important man would personally answer my crude handwritten letter. Even though Mr. Joseph's letter was not encouraging, I was by no means discouraged. I filed his letter away in my mind, fully intending to go to Montreal at some future date.

10

Minnie Blanche Aalders

With this ring I thee wed, my angel here beside me,
A moment more and heaven will be mine.
With this ring I thee wed, and every dream inside me
Comes true each time I hear the church bells chime.

"With This Ring I Thee Wed," by Steve Nelson,
Ed Nelson, Jr., and Jack Rollins

❦

MIN AND I WERE SO MUCH IN LOVE that we were determined to get married. Of course, that wasn't the logical thing to do, because I could barely support myself, and I never knew how long the paying radio program would last. If it ended, I would have no income at all.

I wanted to ask Mr. Aalders for his permission to marry his daughter, but I just couldn't get up the nerve. I tried several times but got cold feet. When I caught Mrs. Aalders in a real good mood I did ask her. She replied, "Both Harvey and I have become very fond of you since you've been staying here. You're a fine and talented young man, and you're making an earnest effort to accomplish your goals. However, we cannot agree to a marriage at this time." I guess I knew what she would say, but I was disappointed. Mrs. Aalders continued, "The music business is too unstable, and you'd be dependent on the small salary Min makes at Moirs factory. Even Min's steady job could end at any time, and if she should become pregnant, where would you be without work and a baby? How could you survive?"

Mrs. Aalders was absolutely right. But as you know, people in love are not always too sensible. So in spite of these poor circumstances, Min and I went strictly against her parent's wishes, and we planned our wedding. Soon I noticed a little loss of warmth from her parents, but when they learned that we were definitely planning on getting married anyway, they reluctantly agreed, and most of all they wanted us to have a good wedding.

Min's friends were excited for us, and several of her co-workers at Moirs gave her a shower. They were extremely generous with their gifts, and we received two barrels of pots, pans, and dishes, plus tablecloths, bedclothing, pillowcases, bedspreads, and many other household items. Fortunately, Min and I had saved up $150 from our jobs. That amount might compare with $2,000 today.

Min's mother, with help from some of the neighbors, went all out and arranged a beautiful wedding. We were married on September 2, 1935, in the English Church in Fairview by Reverend Cross, who presided over a very touching ceremony. The church was packed with Min's family and friends from everywhere, and I had never seen so many beautiful flowers in my life. Clyde Connors, the tenor singer and good friend, loaned me his tuxedo and it fit perfectly. I also spent $2.50 for a tuxedo shirt and fifty cents for a black bow tie, which I still have in my souvenir case. Min bought a beautiful wedding dress on a charge account, so we were both dressed in style for the biggest day of our lives.

Mother wasn't able to attend the wedding because of illness. But I was real anxious for her to meet Min, so right after we were married, we decided to go down to Lunenburg and visit her. I also wanted to take Min's mother with us. But the problem was that we had no way to travel.

The Cokely family lived right across the street from Min's house, and Mr. Cokely offered to drive us in his old beat-up car. It was a square thing that looked like a boxcar. He said, "I won't guarantee anything, but I believe my old car can get us to Lunenburg and back. My tires aren't so good, but we'll give it a try if you're game. You pay for my gas, and I won't charge you anything for the drive. The gas will cost about two dollars."

We piled in the car. I sat in the front seat with Mr. Cokely, and Min and her mother sat in the back seat. Mr. Cokely cranked up his old car and we were off. What a trip that turned out to be!

He drove down Dutch Village Road and pulled onto the gravel highway, and after about ten miles, bang! We had a flat on a rear tire. Mr. Cokely apologized. "I'm sorry folks, I don't even have a spare tire with me, and I'm going to have to find a way to get us back home." He came up with an ingenious plan. He walked down the highway until he found some tall elder bushes growing. He cut off a bunch of switch-like branches with his jackknife, squeezed them together, and put them in the flat tire like you would an inner tube. Then he pried the tire back on the rim.

We hadn't gone but a few miles until bang! The other rear tire blew out. "I should never have tried to drive on these old tires," Mr. Cokely said, as he packed the tire with branches. "Even the front tires are about worn out." He cranked the car up, and we were rolling again. He stopped every mile or so to add more elder branches.

Mrs. Aalders was thoroughly enjoying this ride and kept us laughing all the way home. She wasn't what you would call a fat woman, but she was hefty. When she laughed, she didn't laugh out loud, she kind of laughed to herself. It was like a snicker, and her whole body shook. The car was shaking and shimmering, and Mrs. Aalders was trying to conceal her laugh, and she was shaking like a bowl of jelly.

After a couple of hours we got to the paved streets outside of Halifax, and we were riding on bare rims. We drove through Dutch Village, just outside of Fairview, about five o'clock on a Sunday afternoon. Imagine us, making all that noise on bare rims, clanking through the streets with everybody stopping to watch us as we barely crept through.

Mrs. Aalders was trying not to laugh at Mr. Cokely, since he was trying so hard to get us home, but she just couldn't stop. And Min and I couldn't stop laughing at Mrs. Aalders. We finally got back home. It was worth the disappointment just to listen to Min's mother having such a jolly time.

Shortly we received a postcard from Mother. She was feeling much better and said she'd love to visit us. I wrote back and told her to come as soon as she could. In a few days a taxi pulled up and it was Mother. What a happy time it turned out to be! Mother, Min, and the whole family hit it off, as if they had known each other for years. Mother stayed with us for about two weeks and had a wonderful time. Then she returned home.

Min and I were anxious to move from the Aalders home into our own place. I was feeling the responsibility of being a married man, and I wanted to prove to everybody that we could make it on our own. Min still had her job at Moirs factory, and I still had my radio shows, so we were doing fairly well financially. Min and I gave part of our earnings to her mother and dad to help out while we were still living there. Mr. and Mrs. Aalders wanted us to stay in their home until we got on our feet, but we just didn't feel right about it, because they had done so much for us already. We looked for a couple of rooms in the city, as close to our work as possible, with reasonable rent.

Before we could rent a place, though, we had to have some furniture. Min and I pooled our money and went on a shopping spree. We walked into a secondhand furniture store in Halifax and bought an old iron bed, the kind with the curlicues on the head and the foot of the frame. It cost us exactly two dollars. When we got it up, it was so shaky we didn't think we were going to be able to lie in it. In addition we bought two chairs at fifty cents each, a table for a dollar, and a used mattress for one dollar.

Soon we found our first place to live. It was on Barrington Street, right across from the Halifax naval station. We rented two small rooms upstairs. They were dingy and cold. When people rented rooms in flats back then, it was common for everyone to use the same bathroom. The location was convenient for us, though, because the streetcar ran past our place and took us both within a few blocks of our work. We also had a view of the water, and we would watch the ferry going back and forth between Halifax and Dartmouth. It was a pretty sight all lit up.

We were able to open a charge account at Simpson's department store with a credit limit of fifty dollars. We charged on our account a small coal stove and linoleum for the bedroom and the kitchen. With our new purchases, along with the numerous gifts from the wedding and the shower that Min's friends had given her, we set up housekeeping.

Min became pregnant right away. Our budget was tight already, so we had to plan and save to be able to provide for the baby.

In the early spring we moved to another place more central in the city. As soon as we moved in, we wrote a letter to Mother and invited her to visit. In a few weeks she came by train. Our place was quite small, so Min borrowed an old army cot, and I slept on the cot in the kitchen while Mother and Min slept in the bedroom. It was a pleasure having Mother with us because she kept us laughing all the time. She was always in a good humor.

It was during Mother's visit that we decided to move again. Anticipating the birth of our baby, we moved next door into a place that was a little larger. Mother helped us carry our small belongings, and someone helped me move the stove, the table, and the heavier things. Unfortunately the kitchen was filthy. About six o'clock that first night Mother and Min began to scrape dirt off the moldings around the bottom of the wall. Everything was a complete mess. The boxes filled with pots, pans, and bedclothes were stacked right in the middle of the kitchen floor.

I went to the station for my program at seven o'clock, so I left them to continue cleaning. I figured when I returned, the kitchen would be clean and the boxes unpacked. When I returned home, both Min and

Mother were sitting on the boxes in the middle of the floor. Nothing had been unpacked. Nothing. "What in heaven's sakes happened?" I asked. "Why are you sitting on the pile of boxes?" Well, they started laughing so hard, for a while they couldn't even answer. Min explained, "It was very cold, and since we had no hot water to finish cleaning, we had to wait until the men hooked up the coal stove to heat water. Then, as soon as the stove was hooked up and a fire started, something bad happened. The heat hit the kitchen, and cockroaches started coming out of every crack in the woodwork and from everyplace else! Those roaches were an inch long and as fat as wooden pencils. You could see them on the ceiling even. They would drop off the ceiling and hit the floor with a thump."

There they were—Min and Mother sitting on the boxes—afraid of all the cockroaches that were all over the floor. We kept the coal stove fired up, and all three of us stayed awake until morning because we were afraid those monster roaches would crawl all over us. I was determined that before the next night we'd be sleeping somewhere else.

Early the next morning I went looking for a suitable place that we could afford. I had remembered looking at an apartment earlier, but I thought it would be too cold and drafty for a newborn baby. I looked at it again and decided to take it. I figured if it didn't work out, we could move again before the baby was born. Moving to me was no big deal. I had been doing that all my life anyway.

It was a two-room upstairs apartment on Artz Street. Artz Street was only about a block long and was located between Barrington and Brunswick streets in the slum district of Halifax. To get to our two cold, shabby rooms we had to walk up narrow, creaky wooden steps while holding on to a shaky wooden rail. At the top of the steps, to the left, was our kitchen, and at the extreme end of a long hallway was our bedroom. It wasn't much, but it was home. Min was like my mother in that she could make a home out of any old place. She made curtains and colorful little decorations and put them throughout the two rooms.

Not long after this move, Dick Frye, the musical director for the station, made a good suggestion to me. "Hank, you should develop your knowledge in reading music. It would certainly be an asset to your career. Publishing companies send me a lot of sheet music, and among this free material are some of the latest in western songs. Since I don't need the western sheet music, I'll be glad to give them to you."

I had always wanted to learn to read music, and after Dick gave me a bunch of sheet music, I decided I would. Min and her sister, Leta, had taken guitar lessons from Steve Heckendorf, a fine young musician. After Min showed me a few things on note reading, I began taking weekly music lessons from Steve for fifty cents each. I felt good about learning real music—note style—and not some easy course in the number style. Steve taught the M. M. Cole system (Spanish guitar) course. I practiced every day and every night. I was so fascinated by what I was learning that I sometimes practiced until the wee hours in the morning, or until the landlady started to raise hell.

The more I learned about music, the more my optimism increased. I started to give more serious thought to a trip to Montreal to see Mr. Joseph at RCA Victor.

Min worked at Moirs chocolate factory as long as she could before the pregnancy became too noticeable. But one day she fainted on the job and nearly fell down a flight of stairs, so I had her quit. She suffered a lot of discomfort and pain during her pregnancy, and I was concerned about her. It was not unusual then for women to have their babies at home, and Min's doctor, Dr. McClain, said there should be no problem with the birth if we had a warm house.

I kept the house warm and was thankful we had a good doctor, but the night Min's water broke I got real scared. I wasn't familiar with birth procedures, but I knew Min was in severe pain. I called downstairs for Mrs. Simms, the landlady, and she came up and reassured me that everything was probably normal, but she advised me to call the doctor anyway. I ran to a phone, a few doors down the street, and called Dr. McClain's residence. I was informed that he was sick with the flu and had arranged with another doctor to take his patients. That's all I needed. My wife was in pain, I was a nervous wreck, and the doctor I trusted was in bed with the flu! Anyway, I tried to call the replacement doctor after midnight, but I couldn't make contact. Again the landlady assured me that Min would be all right until I could reach the doctor later that morning.

When the doctor arrived and checked Min out, he said, "Mrs. Snow is too sick to have this baby delivered here at home. I'll have to get her to the hospital right away." I explained that it would have to be the Salvation Army Hospital because we had no money. The doctor made arrangements, and it wasn't long before the ambulance came. It was an old rickety, shaky thing, and the personnel had an old-looking canvas stretcher that was caved in like a hammock. I'll never forget them trying to get Min down those narrow, creaky stairs.

It was a cold and bitter day in February as I watched the ambulance pull away. Complications had already set in, and Min was unconscious. I didn't know if she would live or die. I was worried sick. I walked the floor and sobbed. I called the hospital every little bit to ask about Min and drove the people there nearly crazy. Throughout all of this I became so exhausted that I fell asleep.

I was startled when someone knocked at the door around noon and said I was wanted on the phone. I thought something terrible had happened, and I was trembling like a leaf. I hurried to the phone and a lady's voice said, "Mr. Snow, congratulations, you are the father of a six-and-a-half-pound baby boy. Your wife had a Caesarian delivery, but she and the baby are both doing fine."

Those were the most beautiful words I've ever heard!

I was walking on cloud nine. I was still doing a lot of praying, and I'll forever be indebted to the Salvation Army for their kindness, care, and great concern for the human race. I have always been close to them and always will be. Our only child was born in a charity ward of the Salvation Army Hospital. Thank God for their goodness.

We named our baby Jimmie Rodgers Snow, a tribute to my idol, and we even spelled Jimmie Rodgers the same way. When we brought Jimmie home, I borrowed a small heater and put it in our bedroom. Min had quilted a mattress, which fit right into one of the drawers of an old bureau. This was the only place we had for our baby to sleep. With the heater in the small room, little Jimmie, Min, and I were quite comfortable.

I don't know what it was, but we couldn't stop Jimmie from crying. He cried morning, noon, and night. Min was up with him almost constantly. We thought it might be gas, but nothing helped. Finally he outgrew it.

It took Min a long time to recover from the ordeal. The doctor warned her to never have any more babies, and that's the reason she never did.

Now that Min couldn't work, we sure missed that six dollars each week, but I still had ten dollars coming in each week with the Crazy Water Crystals program. It was hard to pay the bills and buy the special food we were supposed to get for the baby, but we managed.

I thought as soon as we could get financially ahead and the baby was doing fine, I would go to Montreal. It was not a matter of *if* I would record for RCA Victor, it was a matter of *when*. RCA Records would be my bread-and-butter ticket for the future. I just had to be patient.

As I got deeper into the mysteries of music, I wrote my first song. It was the only funny song I ever wrote in about one hundred fifty that I eventually composed. I don't know how to explain it, but amid all the bad times we were having, the words just came out and I wrote it in a few minutes. Here are the lyrics to "The Night I Stole Ole Sammy Morgan's Gin":

Listen, folks, and I will tell a funny story.
You may think it sad but I was in my glory.
'Twas a cellar I crept in,
Cobwebs brushing by my chin,
On the night I stole ole Sammy Morgan's gin.

As my hand fell on the jug I had to snicker,
But when I started for the door I went much quicker.
For just up above my head,
Someone jumped right out of bed,
On the night I stole ole Sammy Morgan's gin.

As I left that cellar, believe me, I was liftin',
And the hops from one arm to the other shiftin'.
Then I stopped and pulled the plug,
Sat there till I drained the jug,
Had my mind all set, no spare drops I was missin'.

On my feet I thought I was but I wasn't,
And for roads, I guess I saw about a dozen
When I reached the old porch door
I went smack-o on the floor,
On the night I stole ole Sammy Morgan's gin.

I just made one step and landed in the coal-box,
Then from off the mantle came a Big-Ben 'larm clock.
But I finally got upstairs
After passing seven bears,
'Twas the night I stole ole Sammy Morgan's gin.

By my bedroom door an owl stood taking tickets,
And a monkey stood before me baking biscuits.
But the funniest sight of all
Was two roosters playing ball,
On the night I stole ole Sammy Morgan's gin.

I saw mice as big as horses washing dishes,
As an ape came through the door dressed up in breeches.
Then the floor fell on my head
As I tried to get in bed,
'Twas the night I stole ole Sammy Morgan's gin.

Well, I woke next morning, guess 'twas closer evening,
And my room 'twas certainly in an awful shape.
Someone else had took my head,
Left an elephant's there instead,
On the morning after drinking Sammy's gin.

Min and I learned to maintain a sense of humor in the face of adversity. We had faith in the Great Almighty and the belief that there's a little sunshine behind all those big, black clouds. I'll always be grateful to Min, who helped me see the humor all around us.

Things went along fairly well for the next few months. I got a few one-night engagements through friends in the music business who would put on a show in Halifax now and then. They'd give me a few dollars to do the shows because of my ever-growing popularity on CHNS. Two theaters called on me every once in a while to participate in what was called a gala review. One was the Family Theatre on Barrington Street, and the other was the Community Theatre on Gottingen Street. I appeared on programs with other entertainment acts and was paid five dollars for each performance.

One New Year's eve I was asked to appear at the new, exclusive Capital Theatre. The manager was Len Bishop, a sedate man and a proper gentleman. I was to be part of a sophisticated show with several other artists, but all I had to wear were my neckerchief, dungarees, and the shirt Mother had made. When I went into the dressing room, Mr. Bishop saw me in my western outfit and said, "You can't go on the stage wearing that!" Immediately I was afraid I wouldn't be able to perform and get paid. But he said, "We advertised you to be a part of this show, so you have to go on, but definitely not looking like that. We've got an usher here who is just about your size. I would like for you to change into his suit."

I'm sure you know what an usher's suit looks like—with the gray pants with the yellow or blue satin stripes. It reminded me of what a waiter would wear in an exclusive restaurant. I had to wear this horrible outfit, and I was embarrassed. I don't know why it mattered what anybody wore, because throughout the performances you could hear nothing but damn whistles blowing and people yelling, screeching, and clapping. Against all that noise, I just went through the motions. I hardly even raised my voice. I barely made my mouth go and got the much-needed five bucks.

One day when I went to do the Crazy Water Crystals program, I was informed that the program was going off the air. I came home from CHNS and broke the bad news to Min. We sat down and just looked at each other and wondered how in heaven's name we were going to pay our bills. With a new baby to provide for, we were really worried. We knew her family would have been more than glad to help us, but we had too much pride to ask for a handout. I would have felt like a failure if I couldn't provide for my own family.

Something happened that same day that made me furious. Just before Min had to quit her job, I had bought a brand new L-4 model Gibson guitar on credit from a local music and jewelry store owned by Julius Silverman. I had been paying a dollar a week on the instrument, and that was not a problem while Min and I were working. Burt, the bill collector, would come to the house once a week to collect. I knew Mr. Silverman expected to be paid, but this time I didn't have the money. On that bad day I heard someone coming up the old rickety stairs. It was Burt. But the way he approached me, especially in the mood I was in, really got under my skin. He stood outside the door and demanded that I pay the one dollar. I replied, "Burt, today I don't have the money." He started yelling and I yelled back. "Listen," I said, "our program just went off the air, and my wife is not in good health. You'll have to give me a little time to get back on my feet."

His reply really riled me. "Well, you know what we do with fellows like you, don't you?" Then he tried to push the door open. When I tried to push it shut, he stuck his foot in the crack of the door and kept pushing. That was the straw that broke the camel's back! I threw open the door and grabbed hold of the stair railing. He had started down the stairs but stopped on the second step, and I put my two feet in his back and literally pushed him down the stairs. I picked up his hat and threw it after him and yelled, "Don't you ever come back here in a demanding mood like that again. The next time you might get your nose turned up so the rain will drip in it." I went back in and slammed the door.

Regardless of the humor that Min and I always shared, this time we were in a difficult position. And it wasn't funny. We simply had no food to eat. On that same afternoon, we received a letter from Mother with twenty-five cents in it! Mother often included a quarter whenever she wrote. It was perfect timing. I bought some bread, milk, and coal, and we were okay for a couple of days.

I knew I had to do something and do it fast, because we were not even able to buy milk for Jimmie. I had always made myself a promise that regardless of how bad things might get, I would never go on city relief. I'm sure a lot of people thought I was raking in the money because I was regarded as a pretty important guy with the radio show. How wrong they were! I went back on my promise for the sake of Min and the baby.

City relief worked this way in Halifax. For working one full day on the city streets, you were given $2.50 worth of food tickets each week, and tickets for a small paper sack of coal and a quart of milk were given out daily. I went to the building to get city relief and stood in line with at least one hundred fifty other people who were waiting to be registered and given their tickets. I was hoping no one would recognize me—a big radio star seeking a handout. It was freezing cold, and I almost froze to death while standing in line for about an hour and a half, with blacks, whites, Chinese, Frenchmen, Irishmen, people from all walks of life. Some of those poor souls looked like death warmed over. The cruel depression was reflected in the faces of those unfortunate people, and I felt sad for them.

These tickets were heaven sent. I knew we could at least keep from starving, and the baby would have fresh milk. Back then bread was five cents a loaf, milk was six cents a quart, and coal was ten cents for a twenty-pound bag. As soon as I got the relief tickets, I went immediately to the store and bought the things we needed. On the spur of the moment, I grabbed a small bag containing six cupcakes covered with white frosting. I just couldn't resist them. I came home all smiles, and I spread the groceries out on the kitchen table so Min and I could admire them before we put them away in the cupboard.

I opened the package of cupcakes and put them on a plate, and as I did this, we heard footsteps coming up the stairs. I grabbed the plate and stuck it in the bottom of a small cabinet, which had two tiny doors that opened out. It was our landlady, Mrs. Simms, coming to visit, as she often did. But what a time to visit! The Simmses were very good to us. Whenever Mrs. Simms baked a cake or pie, she'd run upstairs and bring Min and me a piece of it. So naturally I felt guilty about hiding the cupcakes from her, since she had shared treats with us so often. But then I thought, "Mr. Simms has a good steady job, and they're doing pretty well during these hard times. I guess we need these cupcakes a lot more than they do."

Mrs. Simms came in and sat on a chair facing the cabinet. You'll never believe what happened. As we were talking, the little cupboard door opened up, and one of those cupcakes rolled right out of the top shelf into the middle of the floor. Now, talk about being embarrassed! Min looked at me and I looked at Min, and neither of us looked at Mrs. Simms. I just went over and picked the cupcake up like nothing had happened, put it back on the plate, and shut the door. Nobody said a word. After Mrs. Simms left, Min and I had a good laugh over it. And I'm sure when Mr. Simms came home from work, his wife told him about it and they no doubt had a good laugh over it, too.

The day of the week came when I had to do my stint on the city streets. Friends, guess what location they had picked out for me in the city? You're right. I was assigned to work right in front of the Lord Nelson Hotel, which housed station CHNS on the seventh floor! My job was picking ice off the street and loading it on city trucks with a shovel. I could see the radio announcers I had worked with going in and out of the hotel. So I pulled my old worn-out hat down over my eyes, turned my collar up around my neck, and hoped no one would recognize me. If I was recognized, I never knew it.

When I got back home that afternoon around six o'clock, I told Min to go get me a mirror. She asked, "What are you going to do with a mirror?" I said, "Well, you and I are going to sit right here in front of it and watch ourselves starve to death, because I am never going back on city relief ever again." And I never did.

Around this time, Min was feeling well, and she wanted to go back to work. She loved her job at Moirs, and after all the years of working she hated to be idle. She made a deal with her sister-in-law, Geraldine, to take care of Jimmie during the day for the five days a week when she would be at the factory. We didn't anticipate any problems with little Jimmie, because he was doing real well healthwise.

Before Min went back to work, she showed me how to make my all-time favorite dessert—egg custard. Whenever we had any money to spare, we always bought the ingredients needed to make it. One day I had my mind set to make some custard. I had the right amount of everything I needed, and I followed Min's recipe closely. I broke six eggs and beat them well, added milk, sugar, and vanilla, and poured it into a good-sized aluminum pan. Then I sprinkled some nutmeg on top. I made real sure that the coal-stove oven was good and hot, and I put the pan of custard in the oven to let it bake for the desired time.

Min had told me what signs to look for when it was done. It looked perfect. I opened the kitchen door leading to the hallway, so I could take the hot custard and set it on the hall floor to cool. I took two cloth pan holders so I wouldn't burn myself and removed my custard from the oven. It was golden brown and it smelled so good. When I picked it up, it shook a little like a bowl of jelly, and I knew it was cooked just right. I carried the pan of custard out into the hallway, and would you believe this, it slipped out of my hands and went all over the hallway floor! I said to myself, "Oh my God, how could something like this happen to me, as hard as I've worked to make it?"

I was so damn mad, I kicked that pan all the way down to the end of the long hall, and I kicked it all the way back again. When I noticed a little pile of custard still on the floor, I took a spoon and scooped some of it up without touching the floor and put it in the beaten-up pan. At least I was going to taste it. As soon as I put a few spoonfuls in the pan, I dropped the damn thing again. I thought to myself, "Why am I being punished like this?" I started kicking the damn pan again. I kicked it clear down to the end of the hall. But when I turned around and made another kick at it, my feet flew out from under me, and I landed right on my butt.

By this time, Mrs. Simms came rushing up the stairs to see what was going on. I was getting up off the floor when she got to the top of the stairs. I was so embarrassed I didn't even try to explain what had happened. The pan by then was about half its size and full of dents.

That night, when Min came home from work and saw that beat-up pan, I thought she would die laughing. I didn't laugh at the time it happened, because I thought I was being punished for hiding the cupcakes from Mrs. Simms.

I continued taking guitar lessons from Steve, and after I felt confident in what I was learning, I wanted to give lessons myself and charge fifty cents for each one. I could use the M. M. Cole instruction book that Steve was using in teaching me. My first student was a Miss Grady, a tiny lady. I guess one could say a dwarf. Her hands were so small, her little fingers could barely span the fingerboard of the guitar. But after the first lesson she seemed impressed with the patience I took with her, and she wanted to continue. She lived across the harbor from Halifax in Dartmouth, and I went to her house for her regular lessons.

We lived at Artz Street for several months, until we got way behind in our rent. As you know, that never makes a person popular with the landlord. In the meantime, Mr. Simms's work had been cut back, and he was only working a few days each week. He got pretty mean with us, so I knew it was time to find another place.

Fortunately, Gordon Wright, a good friend, came to our rescue. I had met him after I started my first radio show. He loved country music and liked my singing, and when Min and I visited his home on several occasions, I'd play my guitar and sing for him and his family. Gordon was manager of Charman and Greene, a big grocery store in Halifax. I thought he was rich because he was making twenty-five dollars a week. He lived in Dartmouth, and he drove the store's panel truck back and forth on the ferry every day. Gordon mentioned that a friend had a garage for rent. The owner agreed to partition the garage into three rooms right away, and we agreed to rent it for three dollars a month.

About nine o'clock one night, Gordon drove his panel truck to Artz Street and helped us load up our few belongings. When the Simmses saw us moving, they did just about everything they could to stop us and made threats about lawsuits, because they figured they'd never get their rent after we had moved. There was no way they could stop us, and we proceeded across on the ferry to Dartmouth. The place had a concrete floor, which was damp, but it was clean. We had to leave Jimmie's bed, the little bureau drawer, that belonged to the bedroom on Artz Street, so Min, Jimmie, and I slept in our old iron bed. By this time it had gotten so rickety that one night it just folded up and we landed on the floor. After that, wherever we moved we had to drive two huge board nails in the wall and tie the bed to the nails with heavy cord.

With help from Gordon and the neighbors we put the stove up, and Min had the place looking pretty good, under the circumstances. To make a table I unloaded the pots and pans from the barrel, turned it upside down, and put a tablecloth on top. We didn't have a table lamp, so we put a few trinkets on top, and it looked fine to us.

I'll never forget the first heavy rain we had. The roof leaked, and the rain came down on the bed in big drops. Min and I moved the bed around the room and finally found a spot to keep Jimmie dry. I grabbed pots and pans, big and small, and stuck them on the floor wherever the drops were falling. There were so many leaks that I used every pot and pan we had. Friends, if you've ever heard real Chinese music, that's exactly what it sounded like to me, as the drops fell into the pans. With the different-size pots and pans we heard a ping, a pong, a ting, a tong, and so on, nonstop. Again, we found humor and made jokes about our misfortune.

Later on the landlord fixed the roof and roughly partitioned the garage into three spaces with some old lumber. They were makeshift, temporary walls with no doors.

I mentioned that Dick Frye and I had a show, which originated from the Nova Scotian Hotel and was carried on the Maritime Network. It happened that Bert Anstice had heard one of these shows, and he called me and asked if I'd like to make a tour of the Maritime Provinces—New Brunswick, Nova Scotia, Cape Breton, and Prince Edward Island. He had organized a traveling western swing dance band, like the kind that Spade Cooley had. Bert's group consisted of trumpets, trombones, clarinets, saxophones, drums, piano, and violins. Some of the musicians sang pop songs. Bert wanted me to play the guitar and sing the western songs. The format was to be a one-hour show, followed by dance music. The job paid fifteen dollars per week, plus food and lodging on the road. As soon as I received all the details, I called Bert collect in Sussex, New Brunswick, as he had instructed me to do. Naturally, I took the job.

Min had quit her job again, and I was concerned about leaving her and Jimmie, because we couldn't lock the only door in our garage apartment. But we worked it out so that while I was away, one of Min's brothers stayed with her.

Bert was a tall, robust, good-looking Englishman who had moved from England to Montreal. He was a good banjo player. We traveled in two large cars, and a steel trailer carried the instruments. We played every night, Monday through Saturday, in various towns and cities. The band played regular pop music, except my country-and-western songs. There were no public-address systems or microphones back in those days, and it was hard for the singers to be heard. However, we did have a megaphone, which was like a big horn that we aimed at the crowd and yelled through. There was no way we could put feeling into a song, believe me.

During the stage show the other band members wore country outfits, including bib overalls, but I wore my western garb. Bert supplied the suits for all the band members to wear during the dance portion of the show. We wore gray flannel pants, a dark blue jacket with gold braid trim, and the gold-braided letters M.B. on one breast pocket. The M.B. stood for Mountain Boys because the band was called Bert Anstice and the Mountain Boys.

Everyone read music. I could read a little from my lessons, but not well enough to play with the group. Bert told me, however, to play along on any of the songs that I knew because the guitar would sound good with the rest of the band. I was always given the sheets of music, along with the other members, so I sat on the stage with my Gibson guitar, playing what I could, then faking the rest just to make the people think I was reading the music.

Some of those people who came to the bandstands to watch us play must have thought I was some great guitar player. Sometimes it looked like they were trying to study my technique, and I'd get embarrassed. I said to myself, "What if one of them is a good guitar player? They'll know I'm faking it." Sometimes I felt like saying, "Look, fellow, I'm just sitting here because the boss wants me to, and I'm getting paid for it. But don't pay any mind to what I'm playing, because I'm not playing nothing."

I did pick out a few melodies that I knew. The one I played best was an old song called "My Buddy," and each night during the dance when the band played this number, I was asked to take the lead in a chorus. I felt real important whenever I played a guitar lead with such a professional band.

Bert had it arranged with the Canadian Broadcasting Company (CBC) that his band would schedule each Saturday night show where there were facilities for broadcasting a half-hour segment on the CBC Network. We might be in Halifax, Charlottetown, Sydney, or St. John, New Brunswick, for the broadcast, which would be sent coast to coast across Canada.

I used to sing an old western song on my radio program at CHNS entitled "Out on the Texas Plains," which was always popular with the radio audience. I started singing it on the Bert Anstice show, and after one of the network programs on CBC, Bert received a call from Vancouver, British Columbia, saying the song by Hank, the Yodeling Ranger was great. Knowing that I was being heard all across Canada gave me a lot of encouragement.

I had learned this song off the radio, when XERA, in Mexico, played it often on their late-night country-and-western music program. Actually, I copied many of my songs from the radio. I had a small secondhand radio, and I was always listening for songs that I wanted to learn and sing. I'd copy the lyrics and study how the artists phrased them, and this helped me further develop my own singing style.

At this stage in my musical development the most important thing to me was getting feedback from anyone, anywhere. I needed to convince myself whether or not my work was good and if it was commercial. I seriously considered all constructive comments and was constantly trying to improve my guitar playing and my singing.

I worked for Bert for about three months, and this tour was a step forward in my music career. However, it ended on a sad note. When the tour was finished, Bert owed me seventy-five dollars. He hadn't drawn the crowds he had anticipated when he started the tour, and he didn't have enough money to pay the band members all he'd promised them. He owed money for salaries, transportation expenses, and costs for room and board. When I'd ask Bert for the money, he would become angry. We became enemies, and I never did get my money.

11

First Recordings

This old train is speeding southbound,
And her whistle moans the blues;
And my heart's as cold as the ice and snow
That fills these walkin' shoes.

"The Restless One,"
by Hank Snow

WHEN OUR TOUR ENDED, I CAME BACK to our garage apartment, but something happened in a few days that caused us to move again. Mr. Harrison, our landlord, lived in front of us. One night I was going to his house to use the telephone as I often did, and I heard an awful racket going on inside. Naturally, I didn't go in. A neighbor told me later that Mr. Harrison had had a quarrel with his wife and had taken an axe and smashed up every piece of furniture they owned. I had been in his house several times before and had often admired their beautiful furniture. According to the story, strong liquor would drive him crazy, and he'd lose complete control of himself.

Friends, do you know who he reminded me of? That's right—Charlie Tanner. I didn't want to be around anyone who reminded me of him, especially for the sake of Min and the baby. We wanted to get the hell out of there.

Again Gordon Wright came to my rescue. He helped us find a place in Halifax, and he moved us again in the panel truck. We relocated into a big old house at 192 Agrigola Street, in the north part of Halifax, owned by the Levey family. We had two small rooms, a kitchen and a bedroom. Two other families lived there besides us. All three families shared the same bathroom on the second floor, and there was no shower. Of course we never had a place with a shower anyway, but there was a big old-fashioned bathtub that we all used. We lived on the first floor, and the Wheeler family lived in the apartment on the other side, separated only by a thin partition, so we could hear everything going on.

The first thing we did after we moved in was to drive our two big board nails into the wall to tie our old iron bed up with. Soon, though, the beaten-up bed wouldn't hold the three of us, so we set it aside and put the mattress on the floor. I remember at bedtime I'd say to Min, "Well, it's time to go to floor." It was important for us to keep the humor going, or it would have been a depressing life.

While living there, I was given another program on CHNS, another sustaining one—which meant no money. But it gave me a chance to plug my guitar teaching, and whenever I had upcoming personal appearances, I'd announce them on my radio show. Mr. and Mrs. Levey, our landlord and landlady, let me use their telephone, since I needed to give a phone number on my radio program in case I received calls for lessons.

At the time, I only had one student, Miss Grady. To give her a lesson each week in Dartmouth, I either took the car and passenger ferry for a dime each way or took a motorboat from a different location for five cents each way. One day, when I was supposed to give her a lesson, I had no money to get over there. I'd make fifty cents for her lesson, but I couldn't even scrape up the five cents to take the motorboat across. I used the Leveys' phone and told Miss Grady I'd be over the next afternoon. I was hoping something would turn up and I'd be able to get the fare. Min's family would have been more than glad to help us out, but Min and I had too much pride to ask.

Finally I came up with a complicated scheme that involved Min and her father's credit. Since Min's father had a steady job and was well respected, he had a weekly charge account at the J. C. Harris grocery store, not far from where we lived. When I explained my plan to Min, she reluctantly agreed to help me carry it out. I sent her over to the grocery store and told her to buy me two ten-cent packages of Oxydol and to put it on her father's charge account. That was no problem, as Min had on other occasions been sent to the store by Mrs. Aalders to purchase goods on the charge account, so the clerks all knew her well.

When Min brought me the two packages of Oxydol, she said, "Now, what do you want me to do? Are you going to send me door to door selling them?" I told her to take the two packs of Oxydol over to another grocery store and to tell one of the clerks that she had sent her son there earlier for two cakes of Surprise washing soap (a popular laundry soap that cost five cents a cake), and the clerk made a mistake and gave him two packs of Oxydol soap powder instead (which sold for ten cents a pack). Again Min reluctantly agreed. The clerk was apologetic. He gave her the two cakes of Surprise soap and the ten cents in change for the difference in the prices.

Now I had my ten cents for the fare over and back from Dartmouth to teach Miss Grady her lesson. She paid me my usual fifty cents, and from this deal I paid my ferry fare and had two cakes of soap and fifty cents. We never mentioned this to Mr. and Mrs. Aalders, but I'm sure they would have appreciated and laughed about my scheme anyhow.

By October, 1936, I made definite plans to go to Montreal to audition for an RCA Victor recording contract on the strength of Mr. Joseph's letter, dated April 18, 1935. I wrote Mr. Joseph and told him the date I'd be in Montreal, and if it was okay with him to please let me know. I received the answer in about ten days. He said to call him on a certain time and date, and he would set up an appointment for the audition.

Since our landlady lived right next door to us and Min would have access to their telephone if an emergency came up, I left with a free mind, knowing that Min and the baby would be safe and that they could get help from the neighbors if needed. In case something serious came up, Min could call me in Montreal.

Through advertising on my radio show I had picked up a few guitar students and saved every penny I could. By this time, I had scraped up enough money to buy a coach ticket, round trip, on the old Ocean Limited, one of the passenger trains that went to Montreal daily. I was finally taking the trip I had been dreaming of. After I paid for my train ticket, I had about thirteen dollars left to pay for food and a room for a couple of nights.

The train left at eight o'clock one morning, and it was a long, hard ride for the six hundred or so miles from Halifax to Montreal. We made many stops on the way. The porter came around the first night, taking orders for the people who wanted a berth for sleeping, and I wished I could have afforded one. I was riding the economy section of the train. It had hard wooden seats, but I was so tired that I just curled up on one of them and slept like a log.

The train arrived in Montreal around 6:00 P.M. on the second day, and I grabbed my old beat-up suitcase in one hand and my guitar in the other. I was somewhat ashamed of my suitcase. It had a rope tied around it to keep it closed, since the catch was broken. But I was proud of my Regal Zonophone guitar. I had bought it when I played on the

Bert Anstice tour. Although it was a dobro, a guitar with a big nickel resonator on the top, I tuned it Spanish style and played it like a Spanish guitar.

Here I was in the big city at last, and part of my dream had already come true—I was there. But I was so lonely. I knew absolutely no one. I knew the name Mr. Joseph, but that was all. I didn't know what kind of person he was or whether anyone at RCA Victor would even be friendly toward me or give me the brush-off. I was thinking that if I were not successful on this trip, this would be the end of the world for me.

As I stood in front of the train station, I didn't know which way to turn. I didn't even know how to get to the RCA Victor studio. A light snow was falling and it was really cold. I was exhausted after the long ride on the hard bench, but I picked up my new guitar and my old suitcase and headed for what I thought was the center of the city. I walked up steep hills and passed several streets until I came to what looked like one of the main streets. A sign read Saint Catherine Street. (I learned later that it is one of the longest streets in the world. It's about thirty-two miles long—not blocks, I mean miles.) There was a street leading off of Saint Catherine Street called McGill College Avenue. I spotted a sign that read Lotus Hotel, and I walked up the small winding steps and knocked at the door. A lady opened the door and began speaking French. I waved my hands and shook my head to let her know I didn't understand. Then she spoke some broken English. She understood me when I told her I wanted to rent the cheapest room in the hotel for a few nights.

My room had only enough space for a small cot and one chair. I hardly had a place for my guitar and suitcase. It was located on the first floor, and everybody used the same bathroom. I paid the first night's rent in advance—two dollars—and I had eleven dollars left.

I strummed the guitar for a little while because I was so lonesome. Then I walked down to the restaurant on the corner and bought a sandwich and a five-cent bottle of orange drink. Before I went to my room, I asked the lady at the desk to please awaken me in the morning because I was supposed to call Mr. Joseph around 9:00 A.M.

The next morning someone knocked and told me it was 8:00 A.M. I sat up in bed and looked out the window and saw a few people with heavy coats on rushing around. It was obviously very cold and windy. This was October, and winter had already set in with a vengeance.

I thought about Min and Jimmie and wondered how they were doing, and I reminded myself that I would not let them down. I would do my very best to have a successful audition. I got dressed, went back to the restaurant on the corner, and ordered a fried egg and toast for fifteen cents. After I finished eating, I went to a phone booth and looked through the large phone book to find the RCA Victor company listing. I dialed the number, and wouldn't you know it, another French-speaking lady came on the phone. I immediately said, "I no speak French," and then she spoke in broken English. I asked to be connected to Mr. Joseph, and she put me through after asking me several questions.

Mr. Joseph was very pleasant. He asked about my train ride and if I had a good rest the previous night. Then he offered to see me at two o'clock that afternoon. He told me which streetcar to take from McGill and Saint Catherine streets and where I had to transfer to another streetcar to get to his office.

I wanted to be on time. Throughout my life, I've kept my appointments on the minute. I didn't want to take a chance on getting fouled up on the transfer and possibly missing the other streetcar and being late, so I left my hotel room in loads of time, and I walked the entire seven or more miles to the RCA Victor studio.

I was in his office by 2:00 P.M. sharp—clean shaven, wearing the best clothes I had, and feeling thrilled that I would actually be talking to Mr. Joseph, who was such a powerful man in the recording business. He was in charge of the artists and repertoire service for RCA Victor throughout Canada. This meant he was the person who signed new talent and made major decisions about songs to be recorded.

Mr. Joseph was warm and pleasant to me, but his office was a disappointment until he explained what was going on. "Welcome, Clarence," he said, as he shook my hand. "It's nice meeting you. Pardon my makeshift office, but we're completely remodeling our studio, which is right next to my regular office on the second floor, and we're not recording here until the studio is completed. We're striving for better and greater acoustics."

I didn't know what that meant, so I just nodded my head and said, "I see." But when he said they were not recording there now, I thought to myself, "I came at the wrong time. Why didn't he tell me this before I spent my hard-earned money to come all the way from Halifax?" But I sure perked up when he said, "We're still recording, though. We're using an old vacant church, and the acoustics there are very good."

He asked me to sit down, and we talked about music, songs, and in particular one of my inspirations, Wilf Carter (known in the United States as Montana Slim). Wilf was a popular artist in Canada and has only recently retired, but he's still selling records. He wrote and recorded some great cowboy songs. Later on I met Wilf, and we became close friends and did tours in Canada together. He gave me his old bronc-riding saddle, which I still have. To think that Wilf would part with that saddle that he had used in many roundups out west gave me a great feeling. It told me what a fine friend he was to part with such a treasure. Wilf and I talk on the telephone at times and bring each other up to date on our latest country news and what we both are doing.

Anyway, Mr. Joseph asked me if I had my own original songs, because he indicated that RCA Victor was only interested in new material. Otherwise he would not be able to use me. This was the same thing he had written in his letter to me a year and a half earlier. Friends, I told him a little white lie. I said, "Yes, I have two good songs that I have just recently written." I'm sure glad he didn't ask me the titles. The only song I had ever written was "Sammy Morgan's Gin," and I'm sure that was not the type of song he had in mind for me to record.

"Clarence," he said, "we'll record you tomorrow at 2:00 P.M. He gave me directions to the old church at 1001 Lenoir Street and added, "If your audition proves satisfactory and your original songs are worth recording, we may be interested in you as an artist and songwriter for the future."

These were exactly the words I wanted to hear, and I was so happy that cold chills were running all over me. Big goose bumps broke out all over my body!

But I was in a mess. What was I going to use for songs? I was scared just thinking about it. I had to do something—and quick. I went back to my hotel room, and believe it or not, I wrote the two songs that I would record the next day. One was a copy of a Jimmie Rodgers blues song entitled "Lonesome Blue Yodel," and the other was a story song called "The Prisoned Cowboy." All of this was frightening. If I failed this great opportunity, I might never get a chance again. Perhaps my entire future depended on the next day's recording session.

At noon, October 29, 1936, I picked up my guitar and began the long, fateful walk to the old church, with the cold wind blowing in my face. I arrived early and walked through the big double doors into the church. With the exception of a bit of light coming through the top of a small glass window in the entry doors, it was pitch black and spooky. In a few minutes Mr. Joseph and his recording engineer, Mr. Delmont, came into the room from upstairs, and I was made acquainted with Mr. Delmont. They explained it was dark because the church hadn't been used for years, and only a few electrical lines were still working.

Mr. Delmont discussed the audition procedures. I would be recorded on the main floor, and he and Mr. Joseph would be up on the second floor, listening through the speakers so they could hear everything I was singing and playing. I would sit on the stool, and I was to sing and play into the microphone they had set up in the middle of the room. Next to the microphone was a stand with a red and a green light connected. Whenever the red light flashed, I was supposed to start singing and not to make any noise after the song was finished until the green light came on.

I sat on the stool in the lonely, dark room, and I was really nervous while waiting for the red light to come on. There were no two ways about it, I was nervous, really nervous. Just as bad as that first broadcast on CHNS.

I sang "The Prisoned Cowboy" twice, and then Mr. Delmont came downstairs and said that was good. I was shocked to know that we made it in two "takes" (a present-day term for tries). But I had been so nervous that my throat was real dry. If any of you have a copy of that first record on the RCA Victor Bluebird label, play "The Prisoned Cowboy," and you'll hear the hoarseness as I sang the first words: "Kind folks, you have heard the story . . ."

Mr. Delmont told me to prepare for the next song and again to wait for the red light. He said to relax until he could get another wax disc set up. We recorded the second song, "Lonesome Blue Yodel," and I wasn't quite as nervous as I was on the first one. I was relieved when we were finished, and I sure was hoping they sounded good. However, we didn't get to hear the songs, because they were recorded on thick wax discs and had to be transferred to aluminum discs for a reference copy before they could be played.

Before I left the makeshift studio, Mr. Joseph said, "We'll study the recordings of both songs, and if they're suitable, we might release the songs on the RCA Bluebird label. We'll be in touch, Clarence, and have a nice trip back home." I left with some apprehension. I simply didn't know whether to be happy or sad about my one big chance. Whether or not the songs would be released was highly speculative, and at any rate it would be several months before I'd even be able to hear them played back.

I still have my old dobro guitar that I made my first RCA Victor record with. It hangs on the wall in my museum at Opryland.

When I boarded the train to head back to Halifax, I met a man by the name of Howard Grace. He was a well-educated, humorous, happy-go-lucky person. He told me he was a writer and was working on a screenplay entitled *Dark Waters*. He took a liking to me and said that if it was made into a motion picture, he would contact me to possibly take a part in the movie. But I never heard anything more about the movie. It did, however, give me an idea for a song that I later wrote entitled "Down Where the Dark Waters Flow," which I intended to record for RCA Victor in the future—if I ever got to do another recording session.

Back in Halifax, I picked up a new guitar student off and on. I announced on my radio programs that I'd even go to homes at night if anyone wanted to take lessons and couldn't take them during the day. One student, Jim Pratt, was real nice to me. He was a tall, good-looking gentleman who also was a sergeant in the army reserve. Jim had a pretty wife named Rose. She was a tiny, dark-haired lady, with beautiful black eyes. I'd teach Jim at his home every Thursday evening at eight o'clock, and after we finished his lesson, Rose would always serve me delicious date and pineapple squares. This was a rare treat to me, and I always looked forward to our weekly session.

After giving Jim lessons for a couple of months, I told Min I wanted to ask the Pratts to our place for a meal sometime, whenever we could get enough money ahead to buy something special for them to eat.

I'll never forget one Sunday afternoon around 3:30, I heard a knock at the door. It was Jim and his two boys, who were around four and six years old. Rose's mother lived just a short distance from us, and the Pratts would usually visit her folks each Sunday afternoon. But on this day Jim decided, while his wife was visiting with her family, that he and his two boys would visit us.

We had a nice visit until around 4:30, when Jim said, "Well, I guess I'd better get the kids' coats and scarves and get back, because Rose will begin to worry about the kids." I wanted to time this thing exactly right. I waited until the boys were dressed with their coats and scarves and Jim had his big parka coat on, and they were about halfway out of the door. Then I said the words that Min and I will never forget. "Jim, why don't you stay for supper?" Min nearly had cardiac arrest! He thought for a few seconds and then said, "Well, maybe we will," as he took off his coat.

Min excused herself and went to the bathroom. Then she called for me, and she was furious. "Do you know that we have nothing in this house to eat? How can you do this to me? All we have is a little sugar, a half loaf of bread, some tea on the stove, and that's it."

Min didn't know I had thirty cents in my pocket, and she was somewhat relieved when I told her. I walked down to the corner store and bought a quart bottle of milk for six cents, a loaf of bread for five cents, a small jelly roll for five cents, a can of pork and beans for eight cents, and a half pound of butter for four cents. I'm sure you've heard the Bible story about the Good Lord serving the five thousand with two fish and five loaves of bread. Well, Min fixed a good meal for five of us, and we had jelly roll for dessert, but there were no second helpings.

For weeks after my recording session in Montreal I'd check the mail in great anticipation, hoping I'd hear good news from Mr. Joseph and RCA Victor. It finally came. Mr. Joseph said they had decided to release my record. But when I heard the record, I was disappointed. I figured I'd never record again. I was surprised that Mr. Joseph would release a record that I personally felt no one would buy. But, I reasoned, there was an outside chance that Mr. Joseph might have heard something in my voice that I didn't. In about three months, I received my first royalty check—for $1.96.

I still had my guitar students, and the teaching brought in just enough income for us to barely get by. One day a sailor phoned and inquired about taking lessons. He was with the Canadian navy, and his name was Danny Reardon. He was a clean-cut guy who had a good sense of humor, and we became good friends. I gave Danny a few lessons, and we began having a beer together every once in a while. He never coaxed me to drink with him, but the more people I met in the music business, the more I felt like joining them for a few beers. It seemed to be a real relaxer, and it helped me forget my worries and the hard times we were going through.

Unfortunately, I never once gave thought to the fact that Min was also having it just as rough as I was. Even more so, because she was caring for the baby twenty-four hours a day.

Also, I began going out at night for jam sessions. Since I was a radio performer, I was becoming quite popular and was always dragging my guitar wherever I went. I was having a good time and not properly handling the responsibilities of a married man.

After I came in late several times pretty well looped, Min put her foot down and told me she was not going to continue to make a home if I wasn't going to do my part. She had every reason to be mad, but you never think of these things when you're having a good time. It did, however, sink in, and I became more aware of it, at least for a while. But in a couple of the homes where I'd go to give lessons each week, some of the people would have beer, and I'd join them. However, I did try to keep it to a minimum, because I certainly didn't want to upset Min.

The rough times were a plus for me in some respects, as I was getting inspiration to write songs. It was natural to write about life as I saw it. I guess that explains why many of my songs were of a sad nature and about the hardships of life. While I lived at the Levey residence, my writing began to blossom, and some of my best songs were written in Canada before I came to the United States.

Art and his mother were nosey people. I think Mrs. Levey had a scheme to see how poor the Snows were. I mentioned earlier that our bed would no longer stay up by our driving nails in the wall and tying it up. The tenant in the next room must have heard one of us say something that caused him to believe we were sleeping on the floor, and he probably told the neighbors. After all, the walls were so paper thin you could hear a person breathing through them.

Mrs. Levey told Art to ask when it would be convenient for him to come in and paint the floor where the linoleum didn't cover in our bedroom, as she was having some fix-up chores done to the apartments. This was just an excuse, I'm sure, to see if we were really sleeping on the floor. You know how gossip gets around. They were going to prove that the Snows didn't have a bed, and the gossipers could then tell everybody that the big radio personality wouldn't, or couldn't, buy his family a bed.

I've always tried to keep a step or two ahead of people like this. So I told Art it would be a few days until I'd have any time for him to do the painting. I had a few dollars saved up from my teaching, and I told Min that I'd have a big surprise for Art. She laughed when I told her my plan. Back then, you could buy about anything for a dollar down and a dollar a week, without even having a personal reference for your honesty, because the competition was so great among the merchants.

I went to Glubies furniture store and said I wanted to open a charge account and buy a new bed and mattress. As soon as I mentioned my name, I was an instant hit, as they had heard me on CHNS. I picked out a stylish brown bed with a pretty flowered design on the closed-in headboard, and it had a nice mattress. The price was twenty dollars. I made it perfectly clear, however, that the bed was not to be delivered until seven o'clock that night. Since it would be dark at seven, the neighbors wouldn't be any the wiser—if my timing was right.

Right on the dot the truck pulled up to the front door. I held the doors open and told the two delivery men to hurry and not let the cold in because of sickness in the house. Everything had to be done quickly for my scheme to work. In a matter of minutes the new bed and mattress were brought in, and the old bed and mattress were taken out.

But I still had a problem. The new bed was wrapped in excelsior, a straw-like substance, and it was covered in heavy brown wrapping paper. I knew that unwrapping the paper would make a loud noise, and the tenants would hear it through the wall and be suspicious. This would spoil the surprise that Art would get when he came to paint. If the neighbors knew I had sneaked in a bed, I would be the laughingstock of the neighborhood. Also, I was wondering what I could do with all the wrapping paper and the excelsior. If Art saw that, he would know my secret.

I coughed real hard and loud at the same time I ripped portions of the paper off the bed, and I continued coughing until all the paper was removed. So far so good. But when I stuffed the paper and the excelsior into our coal stove, it created such a fire that the whole stove and the chimney got red hot. I was afraid the whole place might burn down. Min and I were almost at a panicking stage, but the stove cooled off, thanks to the Good Lord.

Art came over a few days later with his can of paint and a brush, and Min and I were anxious to see the look on his face when he discovered that we did indeed have a bed. Friends, I wish you could have seen his eyes. He looked so startled! It was really funny, and I'll never forget that look on his face. My scheme got us a paint job and a new bed, and we put an end to the gossip.

Now I want to display a little of my bravery. Our two-room apartment was on the ground floor, and since it was cold weather, mice would sometimes come into the house from outdoors. We didn't have any money to buy mousetraps, and besides, I didn't want to kill a little mouse. One night Min and I saw a mouse running across the kitchen floor, and I told Min how we could catch it in her cookie jar, which was a small glass jar with a glass cover. I said, "I'll get the broom and chase it around the kitchen. Since a mouse usually follows the molding on the bottom of the floor looking for a place to escape, you can have the cookie jar ready at the baseboard for the mouse to run into. When it does, you can put the cover on real fast."

Just about that time, the mouse ran over my foot, and it damn near scared me to death! I jumped up on a chair—me and the broom—and I thought Min would die laughing. Well, I figured I could chase the mouse from up there. So there was big ole me, standing on that chair with a broom to scare a wee mouse. I was giving Min the honor of the brave work by letting her catch it in the jar. I swung the broom, and the mouse was running around the kitchen, and when it was cornered, it ran right into the cookie jar. Min quickly put the cover on the jar, handed it to me, and asked, "What are you going to do with it?" I took it outside and let it go.

With a surprised look Min said, "Now, what was the use of me going to all the bother of catching that mouse and you turning it loose again? It'll run right back in the house." She no sooner had the words out of her mouth, when we looked around and there was a mouse! I don't know whether it was the same one, but I bet it was. Anyhow, same procedure. I jumped up on the chair, grabbed the broom, and steered the little mouse around so it went into the cookie jar. Then I took the jar outside and let the mouse go.

Another move was in store for us. Since I was giving some guitar lessons at night, the noise through our thin walls disturbed some neighbors. So the Leveys asked us to move upstairs above them in their house. Their residence was next door to the apartment we were already renting from them. I'd told myself I would never live above or next to a landlady or landlord, but I went back on my word, and that was a mistake.

After we moved, all went pretty well for two or three months. Then Min and I felt them cooling toward us. The Leveys would have to come to the bottom of the stairs and yell for me whenever I had a phone call, and occasionally I'd have to go downstairs to make calls. When I came in late from teaching at night, this bothered them. It reached the point where they threw insulting hints at us, trying to get us to move out, and we finally did.

Moving again was a good idea, because I needed another room for my teaching. In the Leveys' upstairs apartment, I had run a curtain across to divide our bedroom. I taught on one side, and Min and Jimmie would be behind the curtain. We all needed more privacy.

This time, if my memory is correct, our upstairs apartment was at 62 Agrigola Street and was owned by Mrs. Lou Dyer. This was her home, and we had three rooms just like I wanted. It was located not far from the Levey place, and it was on the streetcar line. Whenever I could afford it, I bought a weekly pass on the streetcar, which made it convenient for me, going to and from the radio station.

I had a tiny room off the kitchen where I could teach my students. With this good arrangement, I made my own sign and even had a flashing bulb inside to attract students. I took a cardboard box about eighteen inches long, ten inches high, and four inches thick and drew the words "Hank's Spanish Guitar Studio." I cut these letters out with a razor blade and glued some red cellophane paper across the letters on the inside of the box, mounted a light socket in the box with a twenty-five-watt bulb, put a flasher in the socket, and set it in the window facing the street. Then I walked across the street and looked up at the window, admiring my invention.

While at this apartment I wrote several real good songs. I don't know just why the inspiration came during those several months in 1937, but I was pleased. I had enough songs prepared for my next recording sessions in Montreal—if Mr. Joseph were still interested in me.

I wrote to Mr. Joseph and asked if he might consider recording me again, and if so, would he set aside some time in the near future for the sessions. He wrote right back and confirmed the recording dates. It was evident that he had confidence in my ability, and I couldn't ask for anything better. This time, however, I wanted to use a real good steel guitar player on my recordings. Several months prior I had received a mail catalog from the Peate music store, one of the largest wholesale music companies in Canada, listing musical instruments and accessories. On my upcoming trip I planned to check the store out and hoped the people there could steer me to a good steel guitar player.

By this time, Min and Jimmie were doing very well. I had saved a little money, and my songs were ready to be recorded. Again I took the Ocean Limited west to Montreal. When I arrived in the city, I went straight to the Lotus Hotel, where I had stayed on my first trip, and took the same tiny room at the same price. And like the year before, the weather was cold and snow was on the ground.

The next morning I visited the Peate music store on Mansfield Street and introduced myself to Joe Peate. In turn he made me acquainted with his son, Albert. They treated me with every respect, and I liked them both. Since I taught guitar, Mr. Peate said he'd sell music supplies and instruments to me on a wholesale basis. Some of my students either had no instrument and needed to buy one, or their instrument was old and hard to play. I figured I could get them a new guitar inexpensively from Peate's that would be easy to play and would have a good tone. With me buying wholesale, we could all benefit.

Before I left, Mr. Peate suggested a steel guitar player, a French gentleman by the name of Eugene Beaudoin. His friends called him "Johnny." I got Johnny's phone number and called him right away. He was interested, and he came to my room after supper and brought his guitar.

Johnny was a pleasant fellow, and he spoke excellent English. In my tiny hotel room we barely had enough space for his steel guitar and amplifier and my guitar, and for both of us to sit down. We got into our cramped positions, and I sang a couple of the songs that I planned to record. He fell right into my style and played exactly the type of steel I wanted behind my singing. He was a natural.

RCA Victor had completed their remodeling of the studio. It was absolutely beautiful, and the acoustics were excellent. This was the main RCA Victor plant in Canada, and I was impressed.

Johnny and I rehearsed at night, and each day at 2:00 P.M., we went to the studio and recorded. Wire or tape recorders were unheard of at that time. "Cutting a record" meant recording on thick wax discs. If you made a mistake while cutting the song, the top of the wax disc had to be shaved so that the previous grooves were removed. Repeated mistakes could be shaved until the wax disc was too thin to use. Then the engineer would have to put on a new disc. If you made an error, you had to do the whole song over from the beginning. It was not possible to overdub or "punch in" over mistakes like they do today in modern studios. If a power failure occurred, the recording equipment was run by a weight, the same way as the old grandfather clocks are powered.

Mr. Joseph must have had a lot of faith in me and my recording future, because I recorded eight songs for RCA Victor in a period of four days from November 6 to 9, 1937. Unfortunately, as before, the engineer couldn't play the wax discs back, because it would ruin them for being master discs. Even though I couldn't hear the finished product, I felt good about the sessions, and Johnny did some beautiful backup work with every song I recorded.

In about two months I received copies of the session on aluminum discs, which were well packed in wooden boxes. I could hardly wait to get them open. After we heard all eight songs, Min and I agreed that I'd done a good job and that Johnny was a great asset to the recordings.

Little did I know that one of these songs would become a smash hit all across Canada.

12

Return to Montreal

Darling, I received your last long letter,
And enclosed I found a petal from the rose
That I picked and placed within your hair, dear,
When we courted 'neath the moonbeams long ago.

"Just a Faded Petal from a Beautiful Bouquet," by Hank Snow

❧

"THE BLUE VELVET BAND" WAS ONE of the eight songs that I recorded in Montreal in November, 1937, and this song became just as big in Canada as my song "I'm Movin' On" later did around the world. The title was taken from an old song called "The Girl in the Blue Velvet Band." I changed the story and the melody and wrote a brand new song.

I had felt very good about the recordings on my second trip to Montreal, but physically I was not feeling well when I got back home. On my way to Montreal on the train I'd had a strange feeling, like water bubbling up and down my whole left side. Because I was so concerned about my recording, I ignored the symptoms. On my first night home I developed a high fever and night sweats and woke up with my underclothes and bed completely soaked.

Min insisted I go to the doctor right away, so I took the streetcar partway and walked the rest of the way to the hospital. In the waiting room a nurse asked who I needed to see, and when I told her my problem, she said, "You should see Dr. Allan Mortin. He has an office here in the hospital." In a few minutes I was talking to the doctor, who was a handsome and most pleasant person. After he gave me a chest examination, he said, "Clarence, I'm going to put you in the hospital. Over a period of time, you've developed wet pleurisy, and I need to remove the fluid that has collected between the outside lung tissue and the lung. Unless we act promptly, you could develop tuberculosis."

I told him it was impossible for me to stay in the hospital that night because I had to make arrangements at my home to be away. He was against me leaving, and he sternly warned me about the danger of neglecting the problem. I promised I'd be in his office next morning.

I was there bright and early, and right away the doctor took me into a tiny room to fluoroscope my chest. He put on a pair of thick rubber gloves, turned the bright light out and a red light on, and ran the big fluoroscope machine across my lung to determine where to insert the hollow needle to drain the fluid.

Then the doctor took me to another room and had me lie on my side on a high hospital table. He worked the hollow needle between my ribs to where the fluid was located. I saw the dark fluid running into a large glass bottle hanging on a stand that looked like a coat rack. When the bottle was over half full, he disconnected the tube from the needle, and leaving the needle in my side, he connected another small tube onto the needle and inserted air, which went between the tissue of the lung and the lung. This put pressure on the lung and collapsed it so I'd have no use of this lung whatsoever. Shortly, he withdrew the needle and stuck a gumlike substance over the hole to keep the air inside. Afterwards he drove me home.

Dr. Mortin said I should go to bed and be as still as possible for several days, and he'd drop by and see me again. On the third day I became very sick with a high fever, so Min called Dr. Mortin, and he came immediately and examined me. By putting his left index finger on my back over the lung and tapping it with his right index finger, he determined that more fluid had built up over the three days. It had to be drained. But I was too sick to be moved, so the doctor telephoned the hospital and had the interns bring the apparatus to the house. Soon I heard the men struggling to bring the heavy equipment upstairs. In no time the apparatus was in place, and the doctor was repeating the hospital procedures. He drained the fluid, pumped the area full of air again, which collapsed my lung, and stuck the gum over the hole.

Several times thereafter, I had to go to the hospital for what I referred to as "being pumped up again." After each treatment the doctor drove me home and told Min, "Mrs. Snow, keep him in bed and keep him warm. I'll be back in a week or so, but if you need me, please call."

Through all of this, I was concerned about losing my guitar students if I couldn't continue my teaching. This meant no job, no money, and no food. How long could this go on? We had to eat, and we had a baby to care for. I'd worked hard to get my students, so I felt I had to keep the lessons going. Min made me a comfortable bed on the cot in the kitchen and put a music stand next to it. I stayed there day and night, and when my students came, they'd sit on the side of the cot, put their instruction book on the stand, and I'd give them their lesson.

But I got caught in the act. Dr. Mortin dropped by unexpectedly. When Min opened the door, I was in the middle of a lesson. He shook his head and gave me a reprimand. "Clarence, you are not obeying the doctor's orders, and unless you do, I cannot bring you back to good health again. You are a real sick boy."

Another time when Dr. Mortin came by, I had recently received copies of the recordings I'd done in Montreal. Min played him "Blue for Old Hawaii," one of the songs I'd written and recorded. The doctor smiled and remarked, "Huh, doesn't sound like too much pleurisy was there when you recorded that song." He checked me over and said I was improving rapidly but to take good care of myself.

I felt I had to keep my music going, and I sang at CHNS for over a year with my lung fully collapsed.

Dr. Mortin was a wonderful person. I believe he saved my life. Without his care, most likely I would have developed tuberculosis. He prescribed lots of cod-liver oil and a thick chocolate-colored medicine called Neo Chemical Food, which was a mixture of several vitamins and minerals. They sure did speed up my recovery, and I've followed Dr. Mortin's advice throughout my life. I still take about thirty vitamins every day. Years before I developed pleurisy, I often got bad colds and coughs, and I still have spells of bronchial trouble, but I've not even had the slightest cold in many years.

Then Jimmie became ill, too. Big yellow blisters broke out on his cheeks, and he cried constantly. Min carried him around with his little head laid over her shoulder until she was exhausted, and he continued to get worse. We were fortunate enough to have the money to hire a taxi to take Jimmie to see a doctor at the emergency room. The doctor said he had to go into the hospital immediately. He had a disease called erysipelas, an acute disease of the skin, marked by spreading inflammation, which was caused by bacteria. Since it was so contagious, the doctor said we should leave Jimmie and go home, and he would keep us informed. We didn't know just how bad Jimmie was or what to expect. We went through two or three agonizing days and nights, and we were in constant touch with the hospital.

About three o'clock one morning we got a call to come to the hospital as soon as we could. We took it for granted they were saying, "If you want to see your son alive again, you better get here quickly."

When we arrived, Jimmie was in a tiny room surrounded by glass, and we were not allowed to go near him. We could only see him by looking through the glass window, and the hospital people had the side of his face painted with some kind of dark substance that made him look awful. When Jimmie saw us, he waved his little hands as if he were reaching for his mother. He was crying and we felt completely helpless. Min and I were heartbroken.

The doctor said, "There's a new serum on the market, and to my knowledge, only one drugstore in the city has it. I'll get in touch with the druggist right away, that is, if I can get him out of bed at this hour of the morning. This is the only hope I can see to save the baby's life." God was with Min and me that morning as the druggist rushed to the drugstore, picked up the serum, and got it to the hospital. The nurse called us at around 7:00 A.M. and told us that the baby's fever had broken and things looked very favorable for our baby Jimmie. We were, to say the least, two of the happiest people in Halifax.

In a few days we took Jimmie home. The doctor said that Jimmie could have been exposed to the bacteria in many ways, even from kindling wood. When Min and I thought about this, we realized we'd bought small bundles of kindling wood quite often, and sometimes Jimmie played with the sticks on the floor. We never knew for sure how he got erysipelas, but thank God he was back to normal health again.

My lessons were going well. I was picking up more new students, and some of my regular students began to call for additional lessons. Guy Stretch was one of those. He wanted to trade his acoustic guitar in on an electric guitar. Buying wholesale through Mr. Peate and taking his guitar in on the electric one, I made around eighty dollars. We sure needed it, and Guy was well pleased with his new instrument. With my agreement with Peate's Music, I was set up to almost double my money on instruments, strings, picks, songbooks, instruction books, anything in the music line.

Not too long after returning from my recording sessions in Montreal, Min and I moved to Lawrence Street, which was more central in the city, and we had a little more space. The house was owned by a Mrs. Graves. We were on the main floor. We had a living room, a bedroom, and a nice kitchen with hot and cold running water. A coal furnace in the basement provided heat during the winter. The backyard was big enough for Jimmie to play in. Friends, it's hard to believe that we actually lived at this location for about two years. In some ways Lawrence Street was lucky for us, because life became a little easier. We had our own telephone installed. I bought the guitar of my dreams, and I bought a car.

During my early days in Halifax I listened to the Sons of the Pioneers on CHNS. They were the finest group I had ever heard. Without a doubt they were the Rolls Royce of the western bands. In particular I was fascinated with their excellent guitar player, Karl Farr. He had the most beautiful-sounding Spanish acoustic guitar I'd ever heard. He played a D-28 Martin guitar, and I swore to myself that someday I'd have one just like it.

One time in Montreal, while I was visiting the Peate music company, Mr. Peate informed me he had repossessed a D-28 Martin guitar. It had a beautiful sound. He sold it to me for $125, and he let me pay for it on terms. I would use this fantastic guitar on my recordings for many years to come.

Min was anxious to get back to work, and we again hired her sister-in-law, Geraldine, to babysit with Jimmie. Min returned to her job at Moirs, and not only did we have her six dollars a week coming in again, but CHNS called me and wanted me to do a morning show—just me and my guitar to open the station each morning. It paid ten dollars a week. We had money rolling in!

Since I was always a night person, I'd stay up until the wee hours of the morning writing songs, planning my schedule, and taking care of financial matters. I used to tell Mother when she came to visit, "Gosh, I've done well this month, and after paying my bills, I'm going to have some left over." She would laugh and say, "Jack, what are you going to do with what's left over?" Every now and then I still think of Mother's expression and laugh to myself.

I was checking prices of used cars one day, and I found the car of my dreams—a dark blue Chevrolet coupe. Now, I didn't have that much left over, but I talked the owner, Mr. Tingley, into letting me have the car for $300. I agreed to pay him twenty dollars a month until it was paid in full. I thought having a car was the greatest thing in the world.

In addition to all this, I got my very first pair of cowboy boots, something I had wanted ever since I sang my first song in public. The Barnum and Bailey circus came to Halifax, and the star of the show was Hoot Gibson, one of the all-time greats in silent western pictures. I rescheduled my students that afternoon, went to the matinee, and got as close to the main events as I could. I asked one of the cowboys if he knew of anyone who might have a secondhand pair of boots to sell. He said he'd check, and if I'd come back the next day, he'd let me know.

The next day, I was there at the appointed time, and he said he had a pair of boots he'd let me have for twenty-six dollars. I looked them over, and I thought to myself, "Hell, they're not worth three dollars. They're ragged and scuffed and the heels are worn unevenly. Well, maybe I'd better take them anyway, as heaven knows when I may ever see a pair of real cowboy boots again." I took his word for the size, and I bought them without even trying them on. I paid him the cash and carried them home feeling just as proud as if they were brand new. But when I tried them on, they were way too small, and I had to struggle to get them on. Anyway, I polished them, and I wore them even though they hurt my feet. At least I had authentic cowboy boots.

Hoot Gibson's show was terrific, as were the rest of the acts. I especially enjoyed the trick riding by Hoot and the other cowboys. I wanted Min and Jimmie to see the show, too, but that seemed impossible, since Min was working every day. But the circus moved to Bridgewater, approximately sixty miles away, and they had a Saturday show.

On Saturday I made arrangements with my students to change their guitar lessons from the afternoon to 7:00 P.M. and after. I drove Min and Jimmie to see the show, and I waited outside until the show was over. They loved it, too. I didn't mind driving them the long distance in my Chevy coupe, even though the roads were dusty and bumpy. But we were late getting back, and three students were sitting on the front porch waiting for their guitar lessons.

I was glad I had Sunday to rest, since I had to get up every morning, Monday through Friday, and drive to CHNS for my early show at 8:00 A.M. Min and I would get up at 6:30 A.M., and after Min got ready and left for work, I'd sing and yodel at the top of my voice, trying to get my lungs opened. But I heard several complaints from the neighbors. One of them said, "What the hell is he, some kind of a damn rooster or something?" So I stopped practicing until I got into my Chevy coupe, and I'd sing all the way to CHNS.

I'd always park in the back of the hotel, take the freight elevator to the fifth floor, and walk to the CHNS studio on the sixth floor. I'd like to tell a story about one of the elevator operators. When I played Halifax on July 1, 1986, for a much-appreciated tribute that the premier of Nova Scotia was paying me, someone delivered a handwritten letter to me after the show. It said, "You probably won't remember me, but I was one of the elevator operators who used to take you up to CHNS each morning. You gave me a dime every morning to help me and my family. You might have thought it wasn't much, but it was a gold mine to us. I just wanted you to know, after all these years, just how much we appreciated it." That really made me feel good to know I'd helped someone else.

This reminds me of another story, but with a different outcome. Across the street from our house was a large grocerteria. I believe the name of the store was Manuel's Market. At that time, we had regular money coming in, so we opened a charge account at the store, and we'd pay our bill each weekend. One afternoon a lady with a small child came to the door. We invited her in and she gave us a sad hard-luck story. She said she had no money to feed her little child, who looked about five years old. She touched a soft spot, and I went to the phone, called one of the clerks at the store, and told him to give the lady about ten dollars' worth of groceries and put the charges on my bill. The lady's face really lit up when I told her to pick up the groceries, and I'd pay for them. I felt good about that, too. That is, until two days later. She came back so intoxicated that she didn't even know where she was, and this disappointed me to no end.

We were so thankful at this time in our lives. Life was much easier and more pleasant for us since we had money coming in on a regular basis. Min and I felt good that we could buy Jimmie nice clothes and even toys for Christmas.

Soon after I bought the car, I wanted to take it to show Mother, so the three of us climbed in my one-seated Chevy, with Jimmie on Min's lap, and we rode in style to Stonehurst. We had a good visit and persuaded Mother to come back to Halifax with us. As usual, she kept us laughing all the time.

When Mother had to go back home, I drove her to the train station. I no sooner got in the house when Min said, "Your mother just called. The train left early, and she missed it." I knew the train was heading south to Lunenburg, and it would come by Fairview to fill the engine with water, where the nearest big water tank was located. If I could pick Mother up at the Halifax station and drive her to Fairview on time, she could board the train there.

I jumped in my coupe and foolishly went through stop signs and red lights and weaved in and out of traffic, driving Lord knows how fast. I turned on South Street, which would take me to the station about six blocks away, and I headed up the hill. At the crest was an intersection, and I saw a big Graham Page automobile coming at a high speed on my left. I knew the driver couldn't stop at the intersection, and he was headed straight for the driver's side of my Chevy! If he hit me, no doubt I would have been killed instantly. Across the intersection on the far right corner was an old gentleman sweeping off the front porch of his house. I cut my car to the right, hoping the Graham Page car would miss me, but when I did this, I lost control of my car. It careened across the street, jumped the curb, and knocked about half the porch off the house, pinning the old gentleman between my bumper and the steps.

Immediately I jumped out, and God must have given me extra strength, because somehow I lifted, pushed, and tugged at the front of the car until I freed the man's legs. I helped him into the house, and quickly explained to the old gentleman about picking Mother up and that I'd be back. I ran out to my car to see if I could still drive it, as I knew Mother would be wondering where I was, and she'd be worried that something bad must have happened. The radiator was steaming and the steering was messed up, but I did manage to drive it to the station. However, the car would hardly turn to the right, as it was steering very hard. It turned out that I had to leave the car and have it towed to a service station, and Mother and I had to take a taxi back to Lawrence Street.

Mother was pretty shook up about my accident, and she stayed another couple of days. I found out that the man I hit was Mr. Cater. He recovered, and as I expected, he sued me for damages and his doctor's bills. I had just enough liability insurance to satisfy the legal requirement. The insurance company paid for my liability, but I had no coverage on my car, and it was going to be expensive to fix it up. I think I had to pay around 50 percent of the charges before the garage would work on it. After it was repaired, the car never drove well. The frame was bent and the steering gear was damaged. Since I had it paid for in full, I traded it on a 1934 Ford in excellent condition.

I loved my little Chevy, but I liked my Ford even better. It was bigger and had more interior room. I had never been in a car with so much power. I could barely touch the accelerator, and the car would almost fly out from underneath me. I kept the Ford polished and clean, inside and outside, and I had just as much pride in it as I had in my Chevy. To make the instrument lights look pretty at night, I covered them with different-colored cellophane paper under the dash and in front of the light bulbs. I also had a heater installed, and I thought I had everything an automobile could have. I loved it.

I started driving at night to the houses of other musicians, and we'd play music, sing, and have a big time until very late at night. Along with jamming came a few beers. Sometimes there was whiskey, but mostly we drank beer. I'd drive home after these get-togethers, and even if I only had one drink, I was concerned. I have always been a firm believer that your wits are not with you as they should be, even if you have just one drink. I have proven that over and over again by some of the foolish mistakes I've made.

My good friend Danny Reardon and I drank together. Often he'd come to the house, and we'd talk and drink beer. One Sunday night, when it was impossible to get more beer, we decided to drive out to St. Margaret's Bay Road, about thirty miles away, where an old black gentleman made home brew that we had heard so much about.

We drove up to the little shack, knocked on the door around 8:00 P.M., and were invited in. Several black men and women were sitting around in a dimly lit room on an old sofa and broken-down chairs, and they were all friendly to us. The old man brought out a couple of pitchers of his home brew. I guess it was home brew. I was afraid to ask. It looked like dirty milk, and the taste was horrible. Boy, did it have a kick to it! Most drinks don't give you a headache until the next morning, but this stuff would give you a headache while you were drinking it. I named it "moose milk." The old gentleman put it in fruit jars with screw-on lids, and we bought two jars for fifty cents each. It was terrible stuff, but I would be going back for more.

By the end of 1939 Canada had joined the war effort and along with other allies declared war on Germany. World War II was raging in Europe. Canadian troops had not yet been sent overseas to join the fighting, but Canada was preparing a convoy of ships to take food and supplies to Britain. There had been sightings of German submarines near the entrance of Halifax Harbor, which extends back into the inlands and forms what is called Bedford Basin. This basin was like a long lake that ran perhaps six or seven miles to the little town of Bedford.

My friend Danny belonged to the Canadian navy. He told me the navy had heavy steel nets placed at the entrance of Halifax Harbor to keep German submarines from getting into Bedford Basin, and that security was tight. On the Halifax side of the basin, and right in the middle of the city of Halifax, was the Citadel, a huge hill that overlooks the harbor. This Citadel was an ammunition dump, loaded with the explosive TNT. On the Dartmouth side of the basin was an even larger ammunition dump, and I presume the German intelligence was aware of this. Several military barriers were placed on all the highways leading into the city from about thirty miles out. Big sawhorses had to be moved for a car to get by. The purpose of these barriers was so military personnel could stop all vehicles coming in and going out of Halifax and search them.

One night Danny and I went again to the old shack for moose milk, and we sat around and drank until after midnight. On the way back I drove my car at an angle to try to avoid the barriers. But after the military police yelled "Halt!" twice, we decided right quick that we'd better stop. An MP said, "Boys, you could have been shot. This security business is serious, and if you ever try to pull this stunt again, we'll have to turn you over to the local police."

Danny and I were almost shot another time. We were going to his navy ship to get cigarettes. Danny was dressed in his navy uniform, and as we were making our entrance into the darkened navy yard, we heard a voice say "Halt!" We kept on walking, but I wondered why Danny didn't stop when the MP called out for us. Immediately we heard a second "Halt!" and at the same time we heard the click of the bolt action of a rifle. Brother, we both stopped dead in our tracks! I was concerned, too, because I was using a false card to enter the navy yard. But as soon as Danny identified himself, we were okay and boarded the ship.

As my records were being released, I looked around for good musicians to try my luck with road shows. While doing my daily radio show, I met several musicians to use on personal appearances. Ken Doyle, who lived directly across the street from me, was a piano accordion player. There were several fiddle players—Bill Davidson, Morris Jollymore, Gordon Wilkie, Scotty Fitzgerald, and George Chappell. Jimmy Reid played the acoustic Hawaiian guitar. Eugene McCabe was a drummer. Art "Bob" Hickey played piano accordion. Ross Parker, Lawrence Kelly, and Roy Curry played guitar. Estwood Davidson played guitar and fiddle. Naturally, I couldn't use all of these musicians at the same time, but it gave me a pool of talent to call on whenever I had a show. In case any of the boys couldn't get away, or if we had to leave in the afternoon and they couldn't get off work, I wouldn't be stuck. I planned to hire four or five of them for any one show.

With an abundance of good musicians and a good car with a roomy trunk, I figured we were all set to take our show on the road. I started booking some of the little dance halls and schools within a one-hundred-fifty-mile radius around Halifax. Since all these boys had steady jobs, we had to be back as early in the mornings as possible, so they could get some sleep before going to work.

I remember the first show I booked. I drove about thirty miles from Halifax to a little wide spot in the road called Lantz Siding, and I stopped at a hall owned by the Odd Fellows organization, which is similar to other service clubs such as the Kiwanis, Masons, and Lions clubs. The hall had around three hundred chairs for seats. I rented it for three dollars for one Saturday night. I had twelve-by-fourteen-inch posters printed up, and I drove around the countryside and put a dozen or so in stores and on telephone poles, and I advertised it on my radio shows.

My first show consisted of Bill Davidson, fiddle; Ken Doyle, piano accordion; Jimmy Reid, acoustic Hawaiian guitar; and myself on guitar and vocals. I also hired two black entertainers by the name of Merle Bruce and George Adams. They were outstanding tap dancers and comedians and were perfect gentlemen in every respect.

On the night of the show we were running behind schedule because some of my students had come late for their lessons, and I didn't want to turn them away. All of us, including Min, piled into my car, and with all our instruments we were packed so tight it was difficult for me to drive. The show was supposed to begin at 8:30, and we arrived about 8:15. Since we were a little late, the hall attendant had let the people go inside and sit down. I was amazed to find the hall full, and about a hundred people were standing outside. We slowly made our way through the crowd to the backstage area.

With people already sitting down, and since we had no tickets to sell, I was wondering how we could collect the twenty-five cents from adults and fifteen cents from children. While we were tuning our instruments backstage, I had one of the boys go on stage and make an announcement that a couple of people would be coming through the crowd to pick up the admission charges. That was the most honest bunch of people I have ever heard tell of. The people who were hard to reach were honest enough to squeeze through the crowd and pay. Even after the show a few of them who didn't want to get squeezed came to us and paid. I would bet my right arm that we never lost one admission charge.

We left the doors open, and the people who couldn't get inside stayed outside the door in the cold and listened. That was a real compliment to all of us. That night our music could not have been better. I sang my heart out, the musicians gave their best effort, and Merle Bruce and George Adams did a great job with their tap dancing and comedy routines. We gave the audience a much longer show than we had planned, and the people loved it.

I made an announcement that we'd be back soon. We did go back some months later, and the place was packed again. These were honest, downhome country people who loved good wholesome country music, and they treated us like we were heroes.

After this first show, and after the boys were paid their wages, I had about thirty dollars left. It was morning before Min and I got to bed, because I had to drive the boys to their homes. I was so pleased with the response on that first show that I told Min, "I'm going to book more shows. I believe now the people will accept me as a professional entertainer and we're on our way. All of our work and sacrifice is finally paying off." I was highly optimistic. I wanted to buy a public-address system, have big posters printed, and do everything in my power to have a first-class show. I was more convinced than ever before that I was on the right track.

13

Paying My Dues

Oh, the road of love is rocky, and it's lonely and so blue
When the one you dream of walks on ahead of you.
Well, I laughed the day she left me, said she'd come back in a while,
But for every inch I've laughed, I've cried a mile.

"(For Every Inch I've Laughed) I've Cried a Mile,"
by Tompall Glaser and Harlan Howard

I MADE PLANS FOR MORE ROAD SHOWS, but I still had a lot to learn about the business side of music. I checked with a couple of printing shops and found out that posters with pictures on them cost a lot of money, so I bought a hundred without pictures, twelve by eighteen inches in size. I had the headlines printed in red ink and the rest in black letters, and all I had to do was print the place, date, and time for the upcoming shows.

I bought a small public-address system and two small speakers. I only had one microphone, but it was a good one made by the Shure company. A representative of Manning Equipment in Halifax instructed me on how to operate my PA system, and he said my fifteen-watt amplifier was powerful enough for the halls that held three to four hundred people.

From a map I picked out several places where I wanted to take our show, and I wrote letters to the hall and school auditorium managers in these towns and villages. I asked if I could rent their facility for a one-night performance, and if so, what were the rental charges. Most of these contacts immediately wrote back, and I set up a file on their names and addresses and the cost for each.

I was learning the business side of the entertainment world slowly, but often the hard way. I didn't know I was supposed to have an entertainment license, and I didn't know I was required to sell tax tickets from the Nova Scotia tax office in Halifax with our admissions tickets.

Luckily, we had no problem with our show at Lantz Siding. I guess the tax people never found out about our program. But the tax and license business caught up with us in Lockeport at our second show. I had rented the hall from Charlie Bellish, a Syrian gentleman who had a wonderful family and the most beautiful girls I'd ever seen. He ran a general store in Lockeport, and he sold just about everything from a darning needle to an anchor. The hall was upstairs in the building and seated between two hundred and two hundred fifty people. When we arrived for the show, a lot of people were standing outside waiting for us.

Somebody else was waiting for us, too—one of the Royal Canadian Mounted Police. He asked to see our license and tax tickets. This was the first time I'd heard about this. I was informed that I was supposed have a square, galvanized ticket box with a big padlock on it, issued by the tax office. Whenever we sold an admission ticket, we were required to drop a tax ticket into the tax-box slot, and the locked box would have to be returned to the tax office. The tax was three cents for an adult and two cents for children on the twenty-five- and fifteen-cent tickets we were selling.

The policeman wouldn't allow us to put on the show, even though we had driven around a hundred and forty miles from Halifax. Charlie advised me to try to contact the tax man at his Halifax residence by telephone. Perhaps I could have the tax man call the Mounted Police, at my expense, and tell him it was okay to go ahead with the show. Naturally I'd agree to pick up my license and tax tickets on Monday morning. I got the tax man on the phone, and he was the rudest man I've ever talked to. "No, the show cannot go on. You should have applied for and received your license prior to booking your show. You should have known you're required to have tax tickets. The government has to live, too."

I went back and explained to the audience what had happened and said we would be back the next Saturday night if they still wanted us. Everybody started yelling, "Yes, yes, we want you, come on back." We did return, and the place was packed. The Mounties were there also, to make sure everything went "according to Mr. Hoyle." The folks loved our show and encouraged us to return soon.

I learned a real good lesson through this experience: Always ask questions when you're not sure, and by all means, always stay on the right side of the law. It pays.

After making this second trip, with all of us jammed into my little

Ford, I told the boys we had to find a more convenient way to carry our instruments. Eugene, our drummer, said his dad had a little trailer that he might lend us. He checked, and his dad not only let us borrow the trailer, he gave it to us. He wouldn't take any money for it. God bless him. It was a two-wheel, open trailer, and it was like brand new. Gordon Wilkie, one of the musicians, built a top for it to keep the rain out and to protect the instruments from getting damaged.

On some weekends I doubled up our schedule, and we played for dances, too. This enabled us to charge for both our regular show and dances that followed.

You folks, especially in Nova Scotia, might remember some of the tiny halls we played in, such as Lockeport, Shelburne, Riverport, Hubbards Cove, Chester, Truro, Canso, Sheet Harbour, Sherbrooke, and others. Oh yes, one other little wide spot in the road called Ecum Secum. I used to joke about Ecum Secum on stage and called it "You hide 'em and I find 'em." Once we played another wide spot in the road called Garden Lots. We put on a program for about twenty appreciative people crammed into a small garage owned by the Conrad family. We had great times at our shows. It didn't matter how many people came, we'd give them the best show we were capable of doing. As a developing artist with big dreams, I wanted all the practice and experience I could get.

Around about this time, I received a call from CHNS saying they had another sponsor for me, and I could use the musicians on the radio that I was using on my road show. The name of our sponsor was the Lambert Cough Medicine Company, and this program would be recorded in the studio at CHNS. By this time recording had become more practical and had better sound, and CHNS had acquired this new and more modern recording equipment. These would be thirty-minute transcriptions, and we'd be paid so much per recorded program. It wasn't much money, but it was more publicity for our personal appearances. I thought I was on a roll. The show was a lot of fun, and it was easy to do. Our theme song was "Lamplighting Time in the Valley," an old song, and we named our band the "Lambert Lamplighters."

I was still doing the morning show at 8:00 A.M., just me and my guitar. Since my band was making public appearances, I worked it out with the station that if I couldn't get back for my morning program, the station would play one of the open-end transcriptions that I'd record from time to time for such an occasion.

As the boys and I performed over the weeks and months, we improved our sound with every performance, and I added more color and flash to our stage outfits. I ordered every band member a western shirt and a neckerchief from Stockmann and Farmer, a huge western store in Denver, Colorado, which I had seen advertised in a magazine. I also bought each of the boys a straw hat from a store in Halifax. These were painted black, and the boys' wives sewed a narrow white cloth border around the rim. I wore a regular western hat and the white satin shirt Mother had made for me, with the red felt stars on the breast and on both collar tips. With the different-colored shirts, neckerchiefs, and hats, everyone looked real sharp. We had a picture taken of the band, and we offered a copy to the fans if they would write to us at CHNS.

In addition to advertising our personal appearances on my radio shows, I announced that I was available to teach guitar in the areas where we were scheduled to play, and anyone interested should drop me a line at the station. When we played a show, I'd mention that I wanted to rent a room in a listener's home to teach my students. I had lots of offers. Usually, the people wouldn't take money, but if they were interested, I'd teach them or their child free of charge. I didn't get too many students in these places, maybe two or three in each location.

The only problem with teaching was the loss of interest among some of the kids. If they were not ready to play in an orchestra after a few lessons, they'd drop out. Learning to play a guitar is like any other skill—it takes a lot of daily practice. The kids who did well were those who wanted to take lessons in the first place and who were willing to practice several times each and every day. The percentage of students who actually stuck to serious learning was very small, but I did have some fine students who did extremely well. Usually the adults were sincerely interested, and many of them turned out to be good musicians.

While I was involved with so much teaching, my eyes got a little weak, and an optometrist said I should wear colored prescription lenses until my eyes got strengthened again. He said I should give particular care to driving at night.

One bitter cold night in February I had taught three students in Lantz Siding, and I left the last home about 10:30 to drive the thirty miles back to Halifax. I was tired and anxious to get home. After driving about ten miles, I approached a blind hill with about a forty-five-degree incline and about the same angle of a decline on the other side. A light snow covered the pavement and the railroad tracks that ran across the highway. I was going around forty-five miles an hour when I crossed the crest of the hill and spied the big red pendulum swinging back and forth. The long wooden arm extended across the railroad tracks, and unfortunately, a freight train was crossing the highway. There was absolutely no way I could stop my car. A collision was coming, and I had only seconds to make a decision. I could either keep going and drive into the side of the freight train, or I could run into the big high steel post on the right side of the track holding the arm that dropped down with the red pendulum.

The choices weren't good! I knew if I hit the train, the front of my car would run under the boxcar, the train would drag me along the side of the track, and no doubt I'd be killed. So in a split-second decision I decided to hit the steel post. I pushed both the clutch and brake pedals to the floor and braced myself, holding a stern grip on the steering wheel with my arms stretched straight out from my body. I hit the post dead center on the front of my car, right between the headlights. I hit it so hard that it bent the steering wheel into the shape of a pretzel. The radiator was spewing water and steam. The bumper was broken in two, and both fenders and the radiator were bent out of shape. In other words, my car was a complete mess. Thank God I didn't have a scratch on me, but my glasses had flown off, and I was surprised that my eyes were not cut out of my head.

The engine on the freight train was so far around the curve, the engineer was not even aware of the accident. It was amazing that my car started up again, and I was determined to try to drive the twenty miles back to Halifax. I drove about two city blocks, when the headlights suddenly went out, and the engine stopped dead. My car rolled over a two-foot embankment on its side, and I just sat there, wondering what to do. There I was in the middle of the night, no phone, no heat, zero-degree weather, and I was freezing. I stayed with the car, all doubled up in the front seat until daylight, but I didn't sleep a wink. I was so cold that my limbs became numb, so I got out of the car a few times and ran up and down the highway to keep my feet from freezing. When daylight came, I found my broken glasses that had flown out onto the road. You readers are no doubt saying to yourselves that if I had left the beer alone, I wouldn't have had the accident. Well, I had not been drinking, not even one beer. If I had been drinking, maybe it wouldn't have happened.

By this time in my life I'd had a number of close calls, and any one of them could have been tragic for me. But each near tragedy reinforced in my mind that the Good Lord was looking after me.

The next morning I walked to a phone and called a mechanic I'd met at one of my shows, and he came and towed my car, free of charge, to a garage in Halifax. The owner of the garage said it would probably take a month before he'd have it put back together—if he could find the needed parts. It took even longer, and I had to travel by bus in the country and by streetcar in the city.

There's a funny story about one of my bus trips. It wasn't funny to me at the time, but as I think about this story now, I'm laughing to myself. One afternoon I had finished teaching my three students in Truro, and I was tired. I went to the liquor store and bought a couple of quarts—not pints—of beer. It was almost time to go to the station and get on the bus, so I drank the beer pretty fast. Now, folks, most of you know what beer does to your kidneys. You have to run to the toilet every fifteen minutes or so. I should have thought about this as I gulped those beers down, because I knew the bus had no restroom facilities.

This was near the end of February. We had zero-degree weather, with lots of snow and ice on the ground, when I boarded the bus for Halifax. About five miles down the highway I had to go to the toilet. I thought if I could sleep, then I wouldn't think about having to go to the restroom. So I curled up in my almost-new chinchilla overcoat, but there was no way I could go to sleep. I just had to go to a restroom—and pretty darn quick. I was ready to burst. Bad pains shot all across my stomach. To make matters worse, a talkative old man sat next to me, and he was constantly asking me silly questions.

Being a bashful and shy person, I was embarrassed to ask the bus driver to stop and let me off to run behind the bus in the darkness and relieve myself. But I came up with a perfect scheme to get the driver to stop. The small village of Stewiacke was about three miles down the highway, and there was a small grocery store on the side of the road, which stayed open till 9:00 P.M. I went up to the front of the bus and asked the bus driver if he'd stop at that particular store for just one minute so I could buy some cigarettes. I assured him I'd make it fast. Since it would only take a minute, I was sure he'd say okay.

He didn't say okay. "I'm sorry, but we're running late and we have very bad roads ahead, so I can't stop, but I'll let you have enough cigarettes to last you until we get to Halifax." I was crushed. He gave me a few cigarettes. I thanked him and went back to my seat and sat down. I didn't know what to do next.

I presume by now it's obvious to you what happened. When the next tornado hit me, so to speak, it did what tornadoes usually do, it started a flood! Man, what a relief this was! I then started talking up a storm to the old gentleman. When the bus pulled into Halifax and I got off in that freezing cold weather, it was, to make a comparison, just like jumping into a swimming pool filled with ice. My clothes were frozen stiff. My overcoat was so hard on the bottom that I could hardly get my legs to move so I could walk. I learned a good lesson about drinking beer and going on a bus.

One night Blanchard Ashley, a student at Lantz Siding, said he wanted to buy an electric guitar and asked me about prices. I told him about a fine guitar I could get for him at Peate music company. The next week I took my Peate's catalog with me to show him the guitar, and Blanchard wanted to buy it. The retail price was $175. He had a charge account at the big Simpson's store in Halifax, and I said that if he'd get us some furniture on his account, I'd deduct the price of the furniture from the price of his guitar. So we made the agreement.

Min and I went to the store and picked out a davenport, desk, lamps, and other knickknacks, which came to exactly $50. Blanchard had the furniture delivered to our home on Lawrence Street. This is how it all worked out. The guitar cost me $179.50 including shipping charges. Taking off the cost of the furniture, Blanchard paid me $129.50 in cash. I paid Mr. Peate $75. So in addition to the furniture that Mr. Ashley got for me at Simpson's, I had $54.50 to the good. Everybody benefited and nobody got gypped.

Bill Davidson was a big, husky, strong, and nice-looking guy. He was good to have around if somebody started to give you trouble. The boys and I liked taking him on our shows because he was a good friend and one of the funniest guys in the world. One night we were playing a wide spot in the road called Cole's Harbour. The area had only about three or four scattered houses. I had booked the hall, which would seat thirty people at most. There was no electricity and only one oil lamp on a stand on each side of the little dim-lit hall. On the tiny stage there was one oil lamp behind the two green cotton curtains, tied on a wire.

While the boys and I were getting dressed for the show, I wondered aloud if we had anybody in the audience, because I didn't hear a sound. Suddenly it got real dark behind the stage, and I discovered that Bill had taken the oil lamp, gone out on stage, parted the curtains, and stood in a bent-over position, holding the lamp above his head and trying to see if anybody had come to hear us play. I was peeved at him because he had been drinking beer before the show, and I was afraid he would drive the audience away. But they all stayed, about twenty-five of them, and we had a fine show.

My Ford and our two-wheeled trailer took us to a lot of show dates. Most of the roads were terrible, but most of the time we got through to all those backwoods areas. Many were not paved, and if the roads were muddy, I'd put the car in low gear and give it the gas, so I wouldn't get stuck in a mud hole. If we stopped and got mired, nothing could be done except have someone drag us out. Many times my car sank down to the axles, and several times we had to be pulled out by a horse and chain or by a farmer's tractor. Snow, ice, and mud were common obstacles. But almost all of our shows went on as scheduled.

On our way to put on a show in a backwoods area one night, a rear spring on the driver's side broke and was dragging on the road. Then the left rear wheel got stuck in a mud hole, and we couldn't get out. We had driven about forty miles and were about halfway to our destination, and we didn't know how to get help in this isolated area. One of the boys said, "If we could shift the weight of the car on the driver's side to the passenger's side, it would raise the broken spring off the ground, and you might be able to get out." Remember, too, we were pulling our trailer loaded with the instruments. We tried it. Three of the band members stood on the running board as far to the front as they could, and as I gave it the throttle, they bent backward, holding onto the inside of the door. It worked. We got out of the hole, and although the end of the spring touched the ground every so often, we took it slow and easy and made the other forty miles. We were late, but the crowd was still waiting. The boys' clothes were filthy from where the muddy water had splashed all over them, but after all, "the show must go on."

Another time I rented a small dance hall in a tiny town called Tancook. After we loaded our instruments and ourselves into the trailer and my car, I noticed that Bill had already had a few beers. The other boys had not been drinking, because they rarely ever took as much as a beer when we had shows to play. The same applied to myself, with the exception of a few times I'll tell you about later. As usual, Bill kept us laughing all the way to Tancook with all his original sayings and clever comments. We arrived early, parked, and went backstage and started taking out our instruments to tune up for the show.

When Bill opened his fiddle case, there was no fiddle, just the empty case. "Where is my fiddle?" he yelled. "I put it in the case before we left, and it's not here!" He was completely dumbfounded. He was looking at the case as if his fiddle was hiding from him. Some local kid, who had helped us carry in our instruments, spoke up. "I know a farm boy nearby who has a fiddle, and I'll bet he'll loan it to you." So Bill headed to the farmhouse to borrow the fiddle, but he stayed and stayed, and we became worried, as it was past time for the show to start. Finally he showed up with the fiddle, and do you know where he had been so long? The lady of the house had some homemade soup, which Bill loved, so he just made himself at home and enjoyed the lady's hospitality in dishing out a huge bowl of soup for him. The old fiddle wasn't much, but it served the purpose for the show. Bill was not the greatest fiddler, anyway, but he would play some jigs and reels. Frankly, his greatest value was his humor, and we all enjoyed being around him.

One night the fellows and I were at one of their houses, playing music and having a beer or two until the early morning. The boys all went home except Danny Reardon and me. He and I stayed until we ran out of beer. We wanted more, but there was no way we could get a drink in Halifax at that hour. Guess what? We got in my Ford, and away we went to the black bootlegger's place. We got the usual warm welcome and more of that dark-colored moose milk. Those folks didn't mind getting up any hour of the night to make a few bucks. We sat around and drank that horrible stuff for at least an hour.

I had to be at CHNS to put on my regular program with just my guitar at 8:00 A.M. I kept thinking about it and constantly checking the time. It was around 6:30 A.M. when Danny and I arrived back home on Lawrence Street. I tried to shave and clean up a little bit, as Min was getting ready to go to Moirs to work, and her sister-in-law, Geraldine, was already there to babysit with Jimmie. Min wasn't really the nicest person in the world right at that moment, I can assure you. But I assured her that I was perfectly okay, and I would be doing one of the best shows I'd ever done. I took one for the road, and I left for CHNS with my moral support, Danny Reardon.

We made it to the parking lot and took the freight elevator to CHNS. Danny went into the studio with me and sat down. When I was standing at the microphone, he was sitting on the bench facing me. I took my guitar from its case and proceeded to hang it over my shoulder to be ready to start when I got the cue from the engineer. The engineer was not Mr. Landry, and I'm sure glad it wasn't. I don't recall who the announcer was, but I do remember his cold looks as I peered through the window into the control room at him. He came into the studio, adjusted my microphone stand a few moments before air time, and he didn't say the first word—not a word. I would have actually felt more at ease if he had cussed me out than to leave me in suspense.

My throat was awfully dry. I tried to clear it. My tongue was thick, and my mouth actually felt like it had cotton in it. About a minute before the broadcast was to start, I realized the situation, and I panicked! It got real hot in the studio, and big beads of sweat popped out on my forehead and rolled down my face. I wondered, "How the hell can I get through the next thirty minutes? I can hardly talk, much less sing." I looked over at Danny who was all blurry-eyed and about half passed out from the heat. He was trying his best to sit up straight without falling on the floor. I thought to myself, "Danny, ole buddy, you sure ain't giving me much moral support."

Suddenly I was on the air. I coughed, cleared my throat, slurred a few words, missed a few beats on the guitar, but otherwise I managed to get through the program somehow. When I finished, the program announcer didn't say one word to me. Danny and I helped each other down to the elevator and into the parking lot, and it was sure good to get some fresh air again. I drove slowly home, and when we got there, Danny took a cab to the naval base, and I flopped on the couch and went fast asleep.

When Min came home, she was furious! "The girls at work heard your program today, and they said that it was pretty bad. They thought you had a bad cold. I'm sure that will end your job at CHNS. Now, why did you go to the station like that in the first place?" Min always bragged about me to the girls at work. She would give them frequent updates about my recordings and shows. She was unusually proud of me and sympathetic for all the hard work I'd done to get my music career going. Unfortunately, I had embarrassed her and me. When I got sobered up, I really felt bad for putting her in such a situation. I was truly ashamed of myself, and it took me a long time to get over that episode.

I made up my mind, right then, that I'd never embarrass Min again by drinking before any of my shows to the extent that my performance could be impaired. I owed that much to her, as well as to myself and to my career. Since I had worked so hard to have things go my way, I didn't want to blow it, and I needed Min's full support.

And things were looking up. Min was still working regularly at Moirs chocolate factory. I still had my one-man thirty-minute show at eight every morning on CHNS, and our Lambert Lamplighters half-hour show continued each week. In addition I was steadily building my student clientele, and our weekend personal appearances were getting to be a regular part of my schedule. I had a car, a trailer, musical instruments, a PA system, a pretty fair apartment with some new furniture, a good loyal bunch of musicians, and the support of Min. The Snow family was even eating like middle-class families should.

As my career progressed, and after about two years living on Lawrence Street, we could afford a little better apartment. This time we moved upstairs over a grocery store on Oxford Street. The rooms were much smaller and much easier to furnish than the big rooms we had moved from. Because of the furniture we got from Simpson's furniture store, we were able to furnish each room completely. The place had a convenient floor plan, well-maintained hardwood floors, a nice kitchen, and good closet space.

This was the best place we had ever lived. There were two apartments upstairs, and our next-door neighbors were Reg and Phoebie Hutchings. They were young, maybe a little older than Min and me, and we all became good friends. Reg worked at the power company as a lineman, and he drove a real nice car. He and I would get together occasionally and have a few drinks. Usually we drank apple jack.

Apple jack was a very popular drink in those days. It was produced in Kentville in the Annapolis Valley (where, incidentally, Min was born). It was stored in kegs and sold in the liquor stores for one dollar a gallon. Because it was priced so reasonably, it was a big seller, but you had to drink a lot of it to feel its effects, and it would have you running to the bathroom constantly.

Besides apple jack I usually drank beer, especially with Ken Doyle, the piano accordion player who worked with me and who lived across the street from us when we were on Lawrence Street. Ken and I had a few friends who worked at Keith's brewery in Halifax. Their job was to stand by the conveyor belt to check the quarts of beer as they slowly came by. They'd look through a large magnifying glass to make sure there was no dirt or specks in the bottles. Ken and I would visit the plant, and we'd stand by the conveyor belt with our friends and talk. They'd pass us several quart bottles to take with us, and we'd tuck these big bottles inside our belts, pull our jackets down over them, and walk out the door loaded down with beer.

A gentleman was stationed by the door to check everyone out as they left the plant to see if they were stealing beer. Ken and I would go in and out, over and over again, and we never understood why we were never checked. We must have looked like fat people with all that beer in our belts—either that, or he thought we were deformed.

Earlier I mentioned how I first got involved in entertaining at Lake Williams at the Guides Meets. The following year I was invited back and was paid about double what I was paid the first time. On the strength of my success there, the next year I was invited to perform at the Molega Lake Guides Meet. The setting around this lake was gorgeous, and there were a lot of beautiful women who attended this yearly event.

Friends, I have to make a confession to you before we go any further. I don't want all my wonderful friends and fans to believe I was a saint. I did my share of drinking, as I've mentioned, and I also had a very bad weakness for beautiful women. Our show certainly seemed to attract a lot of them over the years.

14

Adventures on the Road

Human, why can't you see I'm only human,
And that I'll always be just human?
Yes, that's my only alibi.

"Human," by Gary Usher

SINCE I HAD CUT EIGHT SONGS in 1937 and RCA Victor was releasing them periodically, there was no need for me to record in 1938. In 1939, though, I returned to Montreal and cut six more songs, including "Bluer than Blue," "Yodeling Back to You," and "The Texas Cowboy." On all my Canadian records in the 1930s, I continued to be known as Hank, the Yodeling Ranger.

My records were selling pretty well by the beginning of 1940. I had recorded, and RCA Victor had released on the Bluebird label, sixteen of my Canadian records. I was receiving some hefty royalty checks, too. The statements and royalty checks from RCA Victor came in four times a year, and they were usually between $85 and $150. Life was easier and I was enjoying it all.

When I played Molega Lake Park for the Guides Meet, I met a young man who was a maintenance worker there. I won't mention his correct name because I don't want to embarrass him or his family. Like me and the boys he enjoyed a brew. He'd drop by our apartment every once in a while, and we'd have a few beers together. This boy's mother was strictly against drinking. I mean strictly against drinking.

I had never met my friend's father, but I knew he worked for the government and the family was considered high up in society. One night about a week before Christmas the doorbell rang, and I went downstairs to see who it was. I didn't recognize the gentleman, but he said he had brought me a drink and asked if he could talk with me. I invited him upstairs and into our living room. He explained that his son had become a friend of mine at Molega Lake Park, and then I knew who the gentleman was. I'll call him "Mr. Allen." He had already had quite a few drinks, and I guess he was afraid to go home to his wife since she was so against drinking. Scotty Fitzgerald, my fiddle player, was with me that night, and we were playing music and having a few drinks ourselves. Mr. Allen was pretty witty, and we all laughed and joked and kept on having "another one or two." The old man was getting more intoxicated, and about eleven o'clock I thought it was time for him to go home. But he wouldn't leave.

Min and Jimmie were already in bed asleep. Scotty had to go to work on the waterfront the next day, and I had to be ready to do my 8:00 A.M. broadcast at CHNS. No way did I want to mess up again. I wanted to be completely sober whenever I walked into the studio. I had made a promise.

Scotty and I tried for about an hour to get rid of the gentleman, but no luck. Finally, he dropped off to sleep on the couch. He lived with his wife and son just a short distance away, so Scotty and I had to carry him home. I took hold of him under his arms and Scotty had him by the feet, and we carried him down the hallway to the top of the steps, but I couldn't carry him any further without resting. Because Scotty was bigger than me, he said, "Let's swap places. You take his feet, and I'll take him under the arms. It should be much easier for you that way."

We traded ends, and I took the man's feet, and we bumped him down the stairs, bumpety, bumpety, bump, bump, bump! One step at a time. Then I found out why Scotty really wanted to swap places. I smelled that terrible odor! It was bad—very bad. I told Scotty that something was wrong, and he couldn't stop laughing.

We got the man out on the sidewalk and stopped a few minutes to rest, and when I went to pick him up again, my hands slipped off of his feet. Folks, I'm sure if you use your imagination just a little bit, you'll know exactly what happened to our guest. Anyway, it was too cold to leave him on the sidewalk, so we carried him down the block to his residence. We took him up the big wide walkway to his big beautiful home as quietly as we could and sat him up against the front door. We knocked real loud and ran like hell. We didn't want to be anywhere near when his wife came to the door. It certainly was not the right thing for us to do, but I'll never forget it.

Bill Davidson's sister, Stella, was also dead set against drinking. If she detected just a faint smell of liquor on Bill's breath, he was in for a good lecture. Stella ran a big boardinghouse on Barrington Street, and sometimes Bill stayed there. When her rooms were filled with guests, she'd put a cot down in the cellar by the big furnace, and that's where Bill would sleep. During the winter months he'd tend the big coal furnace like a fireman would, and he called these quarters the "engine room." It was quite comfortable, and he even had an extension phone.

To get to the cellar you had to go through the door to the living room, make a sharp right, open the cellar door, and walk down the steps. As you went down the cellar steps, on the left-hand side was a huge wide ledge where Stella kept her pots and pans. She also hung kettles, pails, and other trinkets along the wall below the ledge.

One night Bill and I had been to a party, and I drove him home. I had only had a few drinks, and I insisted on going in with him to be sure he got to the cellar steps safely and didn't break his neck trying to find his way in the dark. If he fell, he'd wake up the whole place, and Stella would be upset if she saw that Bill was drunk.

I told Bill that as soon as we got to the cellar door, I'd slip out quietly and drive home. Even though he was high, he was quiet as a mouse as we sneaked into the house. The living room was dark except for a night light, and as Bill made his way, I could see his shadow moving as he tiptoed. You could hear a pin drop. As soon as I heard a squeak from the cellar door opening, I started to leave.

Then all hell broke loose! Bill stumbled and fell, and as he was sliding down the steps, I think he took every pot and pan with him to the bottom of the stairs. I never heard such a damn racket in my life! I didn't care if Stella bawled me out or not, I had to check on Bill. I figured if he hadn't killed himself, at least he probably had broken his back or arm or leg with such a terrible fall. I ran in to the top of the cellar steps and turned the light on. To my amazement Bill was sitting up on the floor at the bottom of the steps smiling at me. And above his head he was holding a half quart of beer that he'd brought from the party. Well, his beer was safe, and I asked him if he was hurt. He laughed and said he wasn't. And I got the hell out of there.

Bill was a people watcher. He studied people's actions and their speech, and he could make anyone laugh. In a crowd he'd suddenly imitate a person by walking and talking like the person he was mocking. He was a real good actor. Sometimes he'd lean over the back of a chair and pretend he was preaching at a religious camp meeting. He'd run to the other side of the room and pretend he was part of the congregation and yell "Hallelujah!" Then he'd run back to the chair and start preaching again.

A few situations I still feel ashamed of and wish I could undo. One involved a Chinaman's restaurant that was located next door to Stella's boardinghouse. From the back door of Bill's "engine room," you could see the rear of the Chinese restaurant. One night when a friend and I were visiting Bill, we got the idea to play a practical joke on the Chinaman. Bill picked up the phone and called the restaurant. "I would like you to make me one hundred and fifty sandwiches and give me a variety of all the kinds that you make. We're having a party, and I'll pick them up as soon as possible." The Chinaman's reply was, "No can do without you give deposit first." This made us about half mad, so we went over to the back door of the restaurant and slipped inside. We took out a huge tub of white rice and scattered it all around his backyard. It looked like a one-inch snow had fallen. Then we took a bunch of dishcloths and towels and threw them on top of his roof. We thought that was funny.

When I look back, as I have many times, that was not being funny. It caused the poor man a lot of grief. However, I'm proud to say that most of our trickery and the funny things we did were not intended to hurt anyone.

I had met a fellow while we were playing a show in New Germany, Nova Scotia, and he invited me to come back during deer season and go deer hunting with him and some friends. I accepted his invitation, although I knew I could never shoot an innocent animal. But I thought it would be fun going on the trip and getting away for a few days.

Several of us met at the man's house, and he drove us into the woods, and we began our hunt. We were walking along a logging road and saw a couple of does and a big buck deer crossing the road ahead of us. We fired. I fired over the top of them deliberately, and I was hoping the hunters would miss also. But one of the boys downed the big buck. I didn't let on, but it hurt me to see this deer killed. We loaded it into the truck and drove back to my friend's house, and they skinned the deer and cut it into quarters. They gave me two of the hindquarters, the skin, and the head, which had a real nice set of antlers on it. I didn't want to hurt anybody's feelings, so I took them. They put them in a large tub and stuck the tub in the trunk of my car. They all suggested I take the head to a taxidermist and have it mounted. I didn't tell them I wouldn't, but I had no intention of doing that.

When I got back home, I carried the meat upstairs and told Min I'd shot the deer. She knew better, because I was never very convincing when I tried to lie to her. Since we had no place to store the skin and the head, I kept them in my car trunk until I could find a place to leave them the next day.

You know how we all have a tendency to procrastinate. Well, I kept putting off finding a place to get rid of the unwanted cargo. It just so happened that we had a warm-weather spell for a couple of days, and a week after the hunt, I still had the stuff in my trunk. On the weekend some of us drove out to the black bootlegger's place and got more moose milk. I was thinking, too, that I might find a place along the highway to dump my cargo in the woods.

On the way we were stopped at a barricade stretched across the highway. The guard on duty asked us to open the trunk for inspection, and when he peered into the trunk, he smelled that awful odor. He yelled, "What in God's name is that?" I explained and asked if someone might possibly throw it back into the woods for me. No problem, he said, and he called one of the soldiers to come and get it. When the young private got a whiff of it, he jumped back and said, "My God, what is that smell, and how long has it been in the trunk? It's rotten." The private lugged it away, but it was over a month before the smell left my car.

One night my accordion player, Ken Doyle, and I drove down to Mahone Bay, about sixty miles from Halifax, to attend a party. When we were ready to leave about midnight, I was feeling pretty good and was sleepy. Ken hadn't had a drop to drink, and he insisted on driving. That was fine with me, because I'd be closer to the heater, which I had installed on the passenger's side under the dash. I had no idea how the heater worked, but I was told it was run by some sort of gas.

As we started for home, I scooted down on the floor and got as close to the heater as I could, with my knees up under my chin and my hands clasped on my knees in front. I was warm and comfortable and about half asleep, when suddenly I felt the car driving over a lot of bumps. Ken had fallen asleep, and the car had gone over a rough shoulder of the highway. It rolled down over a twenty-foot bank into a pasture and turned over on my side.

Ken woke up and cranked his window open, and I was yelling that something was dripping on my head. I was afraid it was acid from the battery, and I was also scared that the car would catch on fire, and it seemed like it took Ken forever to help me through the window. When we got free, we climbed up the bank and just sat there for a while wondering how much damage it did to the car. I had sobered up from the scare, and we were thankful we didn't get hurt. Ken walked down the highway to the house of a friend who had a small garage and a tow truck. He was soon back with the garage man, but the man said he'd have to come back the next morning with some special equipment to turn the car upright before he could lift it out of the pasture.

I had traveled that road countless times before while going to Brooklyn, Lunenburg, Bluerocks, and Liverpool, and I knew the Mason family who lived not too far from where we had the accident. It was around about 3:00 A.M. when we knocked on Mrs. Mason's door. The Masons got up immediately and welcomed us in their house and served us hot tea. I called my neighbor, Reg Hutchings, on the old crank telephone. He got out of bed and drove the thirty miles to pick us up and drove us back into the city.

The next day the tow truck towed my car to Ken's friend's garage, and since the spill didn't interfere with the driving of the car, I drove it back home to Halifax. I made a decision to get rid of this 1934 Ford. It had been a good one in pulling our trailer to many show dates, but the frame was bent, and I knew it would give me trouble sooner or later. I traded it in on an almost-new 1938 Plymouth with low mileage, financed the balance, and paid sixty dollars per month. I was surprised the dealer sold it to me on credit, because my credit was not the best, believe me.

Soon after I bought the Plymouth, Estwood Davidson, a brother to Bill, wanted Scotty Fitzgerald and me to take a trip with him to Chipman, New Brunswick, about three hundred miles from Halifax. Estwood planned to visit his mother and family for a few days. I'd been working extra hard for the previous couple of months, and it would be restful to take a trip to the country. Besides, I was anxious to drive my new Plymouth on a long trip to check it out.

We had a good trip to Chipman, and Estwood's mother and sister treated us royally, as did Fred, another brother to Bill and Estwood. Helen, one of the sisters, lived about sixteen miles from Chipman in a small town called Minto. We drove between the two towns frequently to visit and to play music for both families and their friends. We always had a blast, and in the few days we were there, we consumed a lot of beer.

We kept on the go so much that I got real tired and run-down. About 3:00 A.M., after we had played ourselves out with music, I wanted to drive back to Fred's mother's place, to catch up on my sleep. No one else wanted to leave the party, so I drove alone, which was a foolish thing to do. The sixteen miles was through a dense forest—and not a house anywhere. The forest harbored a lot of wild life, moose, deer, wildcats, and bears. If I'd had car trouble I would have been in danger. Hungry bears can tear into your car, break windows, and kill you.

The temperature was at least fifteen below zero. A lot of snow was on the ground, even though the snowplows had pushed most of it to the sides of the highway. The plows always tried to keep the roads clear so doctors could get through in case of emergencies. On the sides of the highway, in some places, the snow had been piled six or seven feet high. It was a beautiful moonlight night and the stars were brilliant. I was freezing even though my heater was going full blast, and I could hardly see through the windshield because my defrosters couldn't keep it clear. I was rubbing my hand on the inside glass and only had a small space to see through. All of a sudden I hit a bad patch of ice, and my car spun around on the highway like a top, round and round, three or four times. Luckily I never left the road. When my car finally stopped I was headed in the wrong direction, so I turned around again and proceeded toward Chipman.

The spin wasn't bad, but it's what came after that that puzzled me, and it still bugs me. You may not believe this, friends, but I'm speaking the truth. After the spin I glanced at my radio aerial, which was mounted on the left side of the car next to the windshield, and I saw three little green men climbing up and down my radio antenna! They were two or three inches high, wearing green suits and looking at me. As they clung to the aerial, which was swinging back and forth, they kept staring in through the small, clear space of my windshield. They were laughing at me. That's right, they were literally laughing at me!

I can't explain this. Maybe it was my imagination, but take my word for it, it was as real as anything could possibly be. I can still visualize them today, just as I saw them that morning going from Minto to Chipman. I've told this story countless times over the years, and it has become a big joke. When I told a lady friend of my family, she went out and bought a miniature Stutz Blackhawk car and attached three tiny men wearing green suits to the hood. I have them among my souvenirs.

Another story associated with my Plymouth was the case of the disappearing black entertainers. I'd been drinking with some of the fellows one afternoon, not thinking about the show we were to play that night in Riverport, eighty or ninety miles from Halifax. The three young black men I used on my stage shows were excellent tap dancers and did a great comedy routine. I mentioned two of them earlier, Merle Bruce and George Adams. Dave Upshaw was the other one. I kept the three of them on my list for the same reason I kept the names of many musicians. If one of them couldn't make a show date, I'd have others to fall back on.

I don't know why, but this night I took all three of them. Our trailer was under repairs at the time, and we had to pack our instruments in the car. Min was going, too, so seven of us were crammed into the car, plus a couple of the instruments that wouldn't go in the trunk. We pulled out from Oxford Street with three in the front and four in the back. I hadn't driven six blocks when my car picked up a baby carriage wheel that was lying in the street. It got caught under the car and was dragging on the street, and sparks were flying everywhere. The noise was awfully loud, and people were staring at us from every direction. I pulled into a nearby service station, and the attendant raised the car on the rack, got the wheel loose, and we were on our way again.

I drove another two blocks along Quinpool Road and saw a big hole in the middle of the street where men had been working on sewer pipes. The hole looked like a grave. It was about the same size. The workmen had hung red lanterns on each side of the hole, indicating to drivers to go around it. Instead of going around it as any normal person would do, I picked up speed and straddled it, and the car didn't touch the lights on either side. Everyone was yelling for me to look out, and Min was telling me to stop, because the police would soon be after us. I drove on for a few more blocks and got lost. Then I saw a sign that read "Dead-end Street Ahead." Just beyond the sign was a huge bank about fifty feet high that sloped on an incline at about a forty-five-degree angle. I was going fast enough that the car ran up the bank about twenty-five feet, stopped, and rolled back down again.

The moment the car stopped, both back doors flew open and the three black fellows piled out on top of each other. I have never seen the likes! They were running as fast as they could, and they never looked back. Bill grabbed the ignition keys and gave them to Min. She locked the car up, and we all had to walk back to our homes. That was one of the very few shows I ever missed during my whole career in music, and I learned a good lesson. Those black friends learned a lesson, too. They would never go anywhere with me again if I'd had as much as one beer.

In my planning, the idea hit me to buy a house trailer. Rather than having to drive back home each night after a show, I could take my musicians with me, those that didn't have a regular job in the city, and we could stay out on tour indefinitely. If I could line up enough show dates to give my musicians a steady job, I could put them on salary.

When someone told me about a twenty-foot house trailer for sale in Lunenburg, a friend and I drove to see it. It was exactly what I wanted. It wasn't made of aluminum like today's modern trailers. Instead it was covered with heavy metal and was very sturdy. An oil stove provided heat to the two rooms, and the bunks would sleep five people comfortably. In the kitchen was a table on hinges, which pulled up on the floor when needed, and it had bench seats built around the sides so there was plenty of seating space. It was wired for electricity with a male plug on the end of the cord to be plugged into an AC receptacle, wherever electricity was provided. An oil lamp hung down from the ceiling to be used when electricity wasn't available. A regular trailer hitch was attached to hitch to my car.

I happened to have the $150 to buy it. I paid the man, and we towed the homemade trailer back to Halifax. That was my first experience in towing a house trailer, and I discovered that if I gave it too much wheel too quickly, it would easily jackknife. So I was very careful with it until I learned all the tricks in driving it.

One thing leads to another, as you know. We only had a small yard on Oxford Street and no room to park the trailer. Besides, it was against the law to park a trailer for any length of time on the streets. Fortunately, Min's friends, Mr. and Mrs. Wilford Walker, rented us a two-room apartment on Dutch Village Road, and it had a big backyard to park the trailer.

Meanwhile, Min had quit Moirs chocolate factory again, but when Jimmie was about five years old and could play outside in the yard, Min decided to go back to work, and her mother offered to take care of little Jimmie. Our place on Dutch Village Road was only a few blocks from Min's family home. This closeness made me feel better, because Min could visit her parents whenever she felt alone while I was on the road. By working, Min could contribute to our income and pay her mother for taking care of Jimmie.

As soon as we got settled in our new place, I got in touch with Ross Parker. I had met him one night on the road while we were playing somewhere close to his home in Port Greville. We needed someone to collect tickets, and Ross volunteered. After the show he said he played the guitar and sang. I took a liking to him and said if he ever came to Halifax, I might be able to use him in some of our road shows. Later on Ross did move to Halifax, partly because of my offer.

Min and I took a lot of pride in our trailer. She fixed it up real nice by making curtains for the windows and giving the interior her personal touch. We had mattresses for the bunks. I had our show names painted on the outside of the trailer, and we were ready for the big time. This venture would be a challenge for me. Could I make enough money to pay our bills and to pay the musicians a steady salary? Only time would tell.

I got a map of the provinces of New Brunswick and Nova Scotia, including Prince Edward Island and Cape Breton, and mapped out areas of six or seven towns that were fairly close together. I sent handwritten letters to the managers or caretakers of the local dance and lodge halls. Since these were all small towns and villages, the halls were usually available to rent for a fee of between two and four dollars a night. Whenever possible I tried to schedule the shows in a row, so we wouldn't have to double back and waste our fuel and time. It usually took between two to three weeks for me to send my letter and get a response back, and afterwards I'd write or send a postcard confirming the date. In a rush, I'd make arrangements and confirmations by telephone. Sometimes I'd make a phone call anyway just to add a special, personal touch. Throughout my career the personal touch has paid off for me time and time again.

And I was beginning to understand that one has to spend money to make money. Consequently, I purchased better sound equipment and ordered top-quality posters to advertise our shows. I even bought western outfits for the band members. We wore contrasting western shirts, neckerchiefs, and western trousers. With my trailer, the 1938 Plymouth, new sound equipment, and snazzy outfits, we were set up for a first-class operation.

The tour usually worked this way. We'd leave Halifax, follow a certain route to the show places, and come back to Halifax in one to three weeks. While we were playing these shows, I located more potential show places and made my contacts in the usual way. I soon discovered that I could keep us as busy as we wanted to be, especially in the spring and summer weather. One of the nice things about this touring was the fact that none of the boys had to worry about getting back for a Monday morning job.

Most of our shows would last around an hour, or an hour and a half at the most. We didn't make them too long, because the people wanted to dance after the show until about midnight. The folks loved our entertainment, and as you know, there wasn't a whole lot of music in those smaller places back in those days. Radio and live shows were among the most popular means of entertainment.

After our show, we'd sit around in the trailer and tell stories. Maybe have a beer, rehearse new songs, or just listen to the radio. We'd sleep late because we didn't go to bed until all hours of the morning. Eugene McCabe, an excellent drummer, also did our cooking. His dad was a good cook and worked as a chef in various restaurants, and I presume he had taught Eugene. Eugene would go to the grocery store and come back with an armload of goodies, and we'd live high on the hog.

The musicians were full-time entertainers, and they loved it. They did pretty well financially, too. Usually we'd take in between $75 and

$150 a night on the show and the dance. That was a lot of money in the early 1940s. We all had a comfortable place to stay, and when we could plug into electrical outlets in the halls, we had electric lights, and we could listen to the radio.

We didn't do that much drinking during these times. Oh, we'd have a beer once in a while, but we had a policy of not taking any alcohol before going on the stage. Rarely would any of us do a show while having even one drink, because we were all dead serious about our work, and we were aware of how drinking could impair our professionalism.

There was always an exception, of course, and usually it would involve Bill Davidson. I remember one such night in particular. We were scheduled to play Guysborough, Nova Scotia. We pulled into this little town in the afternoon and were unloading our instruments, putting up the sound equipment, and getting things ready for the 8:00 P.M. show, when I noticed that Bill was feeling pretty good. He never staggered when he was drinking, but you could tell when he'd had a few drinks, because his disposition would change drastically, and he would talk funny. I was afraid if the people saw him drinking, they might think we were all drinking, and some might not stay for the show. So I was concerned.

Around 7:00 P.M. the people filed in, and the place was quickly filled with about three hundred people. We were in the tiny dressing room offstage, tuning our instruments, when Bill broke a string while trying to tune his fiddle. He was struggling to put on a new one, and because the lighting was poor, he said, "I'm going out on the stage where I can see." This was not a good idea. In the first place, there was no curtain, so he was exposed to the audience as soon as he walked on stage. When I looked for Bill, he was sitting on a chair in the middle of the stage, weaving back and forth trying to get the end of the string through the tiny hole in the fiddle peg. This lasted for about five minutes, and then I heard voices come from the crowd yelling, "They're all drunk. Let's go home."

On this note, everyone in the hall followed suit and they emptied the hall. Everyone left. I was so damn mad at Bill I could have fired him on the spot, but the damage had been done, and we lost around seventy dollars. This was one of the biggest crowds we'd had. As the people were leaving we could hear the negative comments, and I thought, "Boy, this will be really nice if the news gets around, or the newspaper prints it."

As we were packing our instruments away, a Royal Canadian Mountie came into the hall. He introduced himself as Spike Donaldson, and he told us that some of the fellows outside were angry and might do damage to the trailer. But he said he would keep watch over it until we were ready to leave, and he even offered to let us tow it to his place and put it in his driveway, which was only a few blocks away.

I guess you folks are beginning to think we were drinking beer or some kind of alcohol all the time. But this is incorrect. These stories I've been telling took place over a period of several years, and we only drank occasionally and hardly enough that anyone could even tell it. There were times when I'd go for a year or more and never take one drink of alcohol. However, there were certain times along the way that the boys and I overdid the drinking. In hindsight, I wonder how we survived some of these misadventures.

15

The Theater Circuit

The band, it was playing "The Star-Spangled Waltz,"
The lights in the ballroom were low;
Though 'twas sweet to my ears, I fought back my tears,
For that waltz broke my heart long ago.

"The Star-Spangled Waltz,"
by Hank Snow

THE BOYS AND I CONTINUED TO PLAY towns and villages in Nova Scotia, Cape Breton, and Prince Edward Island. Throughout the years in which I traveled for these shows, I covered just about every nook and corner, village, and town in Nova Scotia. Some of the most dramatic scenery in all of Canada lies in this province.

If you travel east through beautiful Cape Breton, you can go down the breathtaking Cabot Trail alongside the Atlantic Ocean. Forty years ago the trail was dangerous because it was narrow and unpaved, and it ran along the very edge of huge mountains much of the way. These mountains were right on the seacoast, and if a car went over the edge, it would fall straight down over a thousand feet into the Atlantic Ocean. I've never had the pleasure of driving down the entire Cabot Trail, but I understand that the road has since been widened and many tourists travel it every spring and summer.

Inland you'll find the beautiful Annapolis Valley, the apple hub of Canada, and the home of Evangeline in the famous narrative poem by Longfellow. I've often played show dates through the valley in apple-blossom season in the spring, and I've always marveled at the apple orchards when the trees were in full bloom. I've seen miles and miles of pretty white and pink apple blossoms, and this must be one of the most beautiful valleys in the whole world.

We made extended tours in eastern Quebec, and I was well pleased with the popularity we gained and the crowds we had at our shows. This area had beautiful scenery, too. One of the most scenic routes we traveled was the Gaspé Coast, which had the most majestic Catholic churches I've ever seen. The great domes of many of those big churches were painted gold, and the insides were breathtaking, in their holy beauty.

Most of our shows were conducted through agreements with priests in the various parishes, and most of the agreements were on a percentage basis—50 percent of the income to them and 50 percent to us. Splitting the income was worth it to us, because we couldn't go against the priests and make an agreement with independent sources. We were furnished the big halls, which were owned by the parish and used for their church functions. The priests would announce the upcoming event at mass on Sunday morning, and strongly encourage the church members to attend. They would make it plain that the show was to make money for the church, and I was told that almost all the church members attended. We had full houses at every location. When the father told you to be at one of the shows, you should be there!

It was understood that we would present a family show, and that was no problem. From the beginning and throughout my long career of making personal appearances, I was known for presenting a clean show for adults and children.

The priests treated my boys and me with every respect, and we had the same admiration for them. Even though I'm a Protestant, I think we all believe in the Great Almighty, and as a nondenominational believer, I've always tried not to judge other people's religion.

On one occasion, though, I did have a conflict with a priest. I forgot his name. This happened in a small town near Moncton, New Brunswick. It was to be an outdoor show, and I was pleased that the grandstand was filled with three to four hundred adults with their children. Right before the eight o'clock show was to begin, the father of that parish walked up to me and said, "Mr. Snow, no children are allowed at this show. You must tell the parents with children to leave!"

Unfortunately, this show was not a percentage deal with the church. I was paid a flat rate for the night. I tried to explain that most of the adults had children, and if I had to tell the parents with children to leave, then most of the audience would be gone. "I just can't do this and disappoint these people," I argued. "Well," he continued, "since it's our policy to have an 8:00 P.M. curfew for the children in this community, I must stand by my commitment. I insist that you tell the parents with children to leave, and they must leave now." I responded coldly, "This show will go on. I will call the law before I will cancel our program." The priest replied, "Mr. Snow, I am the fatherly law!" It turned into a heated argument, and unfortunately, we had no show that night.

In the fall of 1941 I planned a big move that I hoped might lead me to bigger things. I wanted to try my talent in Montreal. Several friends said it was foolish to give up our income and move to a large city without first having a job. But something was driving me to try an entirely new territory, and if I did fail, at least I'd know I had tried.

Eventually, I had my sights set on going to the United States to become a major entertainer, but I'd take one step at a time. I'd listened to powerful radio stations from Old Mexico, like XERA and XERF. I also listened to American stations such as WWVA in Wheeling, West Virginia, and WLS from Chicago, among others. I had dreams of my songs being played on these stations like those of Jimmie Rodgers, the Sons of the Pioneers, Bill Boyd and the Cowboy Ramblers, Jesse Rodgers, and other popular artists.

I had been encouraged by band members from the Bert Anstice show, who said I should be able to find work in some of the nightspots in Montreal. One member suggested I learn to play bass, as this would increase my chances of finding nightclub work. I didn't give much thought to that, because I wanted to make it on my singing and guitar work.

By going to Montreal, I was giving up some pretty good money I'd been making from personal appearances, especially since I'd been using my trailer for extended tours. Min would also be giving up her job at Moirs chocolate factory, where she was getting a steady income every week. In spite of this Min and I agreed we should give the big city a try.

I parked our trailer and stored our household goods and personal things. I sold the 1938 Plymouth, which had just about seen its last days anyway. All the traveling and pulling the heavy trailer had taken its toll on it. I hoped I might strike it lucky and make enough money in Montreal to put a down payment on another secondhand car.

Min, little Jimmie, and I took the long train ride on the old Ocean Limited to Montreal, in the province of Quebec, to an unknown future. When we arrived, a taxi took us directly to Johnny Beaudoin's place. You'll remember that Johnny was the steel guitar player who played on all my Canadian records. Johnny, his wife, Claire, and their two little boys were glad to see us and treated us with every courtesy.

Johnny was French, but he could also speak English very well. Claire could only speak French, and Min and I spoke English only. It was fun trying to communicate while Johnny was at work, using motions and signs, and we all got a big kick out of it. Usually, though, we would have to wait until Johnny came home after work, so Claire could tell him what she was trying to tell us.

After several weeks at the Beaudoins' home we found a cheap one-room place to rent in east Montreal. It was small and we were cramped, but we had to be careful with the money we'd saved, so the small room had to do us.

Montreal was a big disappointment to us. I went job hunting every day, and I found absolutely nothing. Most people in the French province spoke French only, and it was extremely difficult for us to get along without being able to speak French. Min and I felt very uncomfortable there, even though everyone was nice to us. I made only one appearance, and this was a guest shot with another entertainer who invited me onstage to sing one song. I died the death of a rat. I don't think the audience understood any of my lyrics.

Some good did come out of our move to the big city. I learned of a place that sold theatrical vaudeville supplies and equipment for the stage, and that's where I met Johnny Brown, a costume designer. I asked him to order me a pair of fancy cowboy boots. The old ones that I'd bought at the Hoot Gibson show were on their last legs (no pun intended). After wearing boots that were too small, it would be great to have a new pair that actually fit. Johnny ordered them from a company in Texas, and when they arrived, I was walking on cloud nine. They were beautiful from the tops to the soles and had pretty flower designs carved on them. I tucked my pants inside them, even though this was not the proper way to wear these boots, unless you're wearing riding britches. I wanted people to see the beautiful tops. To make them even flashier I added rows of rhinestones all along the tops and around the flowers. With the customs duty they cost me about a hundred dollars, but I would have paid even more if I'd had to.

I had purchased a portable disc-recording machine in New Brunswick and had plenty of time to use it in Montreal since I had no job. This kind of recorder existed long before wire and tape recorders were made. Here's how my machine worked. A sapphire needle would cut the grooves in the blank acetate disc and make the recording. A microphone came with the machine, and of course it had to be used to produce the audio. But I had an electronic technician rig it so I could also record off the radio without using the mike, by plugging in a special cord from the recorder to the radio. This permitted me to record songs by my favorite artists directly from the radio. It was a good source for me to listen, study, and improve my vocal delivery. Recording was not new to me. You'll remember that Mr. Landry, at CHNS, had used a professional recorder to cut transcriptions to play when I was out on tour.

On my disc cutter I'd also record interesting programs from American radio stations. On December 7, 1941, I taped a historic message. I was listening to the radio on this particular Sunday morning when suddenly the music stopped and a voice broke in: "This is a special bulletin." I immediately started my disc recorder. In a stern and somewhat angry tone, President Franklin D. Roosevelt was announcing the surprise attack on Pearl Harbor by the Japanese forces.

Min and I were totally discouraged with my lack of opportunities in Montreal, and we decided to leave after I received a letter from Stan Chapman in Campbellton, New Brunswick. Earlier I'd written managers of several radio stations about a job, and his was one of the first replies. He offered to put me on the air as a one-man entertainer at CKNB, a 1,000-watt station owned by Dr. Houd, a dentist, who also owned a 1,000-watt station in New Carlisle, Quebec. I had sent Mr. Chapman a list of my RCA Bluebird recordings, and I was happy when he said they were being played. Folks were familiar with Hank, the Yodeling Ranger, and I accepted his offer. In addition to my radio program, I wanted to do personal appearances in areas covered by the two sister stations.

In February, 1942, Min, Jimmie, and I boarded the train. I got off in Campbellton, New Brunswick, and they continued on to stay a while with Min's family in Fairview, where I knew they'd be safe and in good care.

Mr. Chapman was like Mr. Landry at CHNS. He was a wonderful man who offered to help me in any way he could. Mr. and Mrs. Chapman and the two announcers at the station, Jimmy Wood and Dick Dickerson, were like family to me. Mr. Chapman suggested that I print a book of my songs and advertise it over the station, and I did. I also listed my RCA Victor Bluebird records and included a photograph of myself and my recording musicians. I sold a whole bunch of these booklets for fifteen cents each.

Folks, I got favorable mail from places I didn't know existed. I never dreamed that a 1,000-watt radio station would reach that far. I received letters from border towns in the States and even some places in Massachusetts.

Before leaving Montreal, I had purchased a single-neck, six-string, electric Hawaiian guitar and a small speaker from Peate's music company. I found it relaxing to play the Hawaiian guitar, but I could only play what Mother had taught me years earlier. One day after my radio broadcast I was fooling around with my Hawaiian guitar in the studio, and Mr. Chapman heard me. "That's very good," he said. "Why don't you play soft Hawaiian music as background for the show I do of narrations?" I was flattered. He did wonderful narrations of poems every Sunday night on his program called "Fireside Verse." He knew how to inject just the right feeling into every narration he did.

On the first couple of Sunday night shows, I was nervous because I had to play continually for the full fifteen minutes, and I was afraid I might run out of tunes. But it was no problem. I knew how to ad-lib, which means you make the tune up as you go along. Mr. Chapman liked my music and said the slow Hawaiian sound inspired him to put even more feeling into his readings.

I only knew how to tune a single neck one way, and that was the old "A tuning," which did have a nice, mellow sound. The listeners liked it, too, and I continued to play the background for him for as long as I remained at CKNB. Listening to his delivery helped me years later when I did narrations on my records, stage shows, and the radio. My album *Tales of the Yukon* consists entirely of narrations of Yukon days and the Gold Rush period. It's one of my favorites.

After one of my shows at the station someone suggested that I put on a show and dance at the Northshore Pavilion, located about three miles from Campbellton. I went to see Doc Roy, the owner, who ran dances there every Saturday night. He was helpful, and we set my dance for Thursday night. Since I didn't have a band, Doc said not to worry, that I could use the drummer who played for him on Saturday nights. I called my friend and fiddle player Eugene Beaulieau in New Carlisle, Quebec, and asked him if he would play the dances with me. He came right away.

When Thursday came, I wondered if anybody would show up, since this would be my first appearance in the area. The dance was scheduled from 8:00 P.M. until 1:00 A.M., and I planned to sing a few songs every forty-five minutes. That's how I advertised it on CKNB. That night I had never seen so many people in such a small space. I don't believe the place held over three hundred people, but I swear there had to be at least five hundred, including those on the outside who couldn't get in. If anyone fainted, there was no room to fall down! One crowd would go outside to get air, and another crowd would pay to get in, making a constant flow of people in and out of the pavilion. And with only a drummer, a fiddler, and my guitar, the music was quite good.

My radio program at CKNB was very popular, and since I was drawing heavy mail, Mr. Chapman scheduled me for another half hour in the afternoon, which gave me more advertising to sell my songbooks and plug my records.

My association with Stan Chapman was super nice. It was through his efforts that I got a job from Gordon Gaisley, the manager of the Capitol Theatre in Campbellton. Mr. Gaisley said, "Hank, I'd like to try you on a weekend. I'll give you a twenty-minute spot Friday night between our two feature pictures. On Saturday you can take twenty minutes between our newsreel and matinee feature picture, and twenty minutes between the two feature pictures at night. I have a feeling, with the popularity you've gained at CKNB, you'll do real well. Are you interested?"

You bet I was! The Capitol Theatre was one of a chain of twelve to fourteen first-class theaters in New Brunswick, Nova Scotia, Prince Edward Island, and Cape Breton, owned by F. G. Spencer, whose head office was in Saint John, New Brunswick. I knew this job would be difficult, being a one-man show, but I wanted the challenge. The pay was twenty-five dollars for a two-day run, and if I did three days, I'd be paid thirty-five dollars. I advertised my upcoming theater appearances every day on both my programs at CKNB, and Mr. Gaisley ran big double-column advertisements in the Campbellton newspaper, as well as the daily newspapers in the surrounding villages.

Needless to say, I was nervous about facing an audience alone. But the nervousness left me when I received a standing ovation as soon as I walked out on the stage. Would you believe it? Friday night the theater was jam-packed. I sang a couple of songs, told a few jokes, and sang a few more. I received tremendous applause after each song, and as a matter of fact, the applause would break into the middle of my songs. After each show I'd have to do an encore. Moreover, my jokes must have been extra good, because years later I heard the same jokes on network TV shows by popular comedians. Every show was sold out several days before, and people waited in long lines to get into the theater. Imagine what this did to my ego!

After the last show Mr. Gaisley sent word that he wanted to see me. When I went into his office, he said, "I've never heard such a response from an audience in my life, and I've had some big shows here over the years. This is far beyond my wildest expectations. On the strength of your success here, Mr. Spencer may be interested in having you play in all of our houses."

It was customary for the theater managers of the Spencer chain to report to the head office in Saint John each weekend as to the amount of business done for the week. Naturally Mr. Gaisley told Mr. Spencer of the success the theater had with my act, and Mr. Spencer wanted to try me in more theaters. If I continued to do well, he said he would use me throughout the complete chain.

I specifically wanted to schedule some shows at the Spencer Theatre in Dalhousie, just sixteen miles away. This was a large town, with a huge paper mill sitting just a stone's throw away from the Saint John River, and it employed hundreds of men, so the economics were excellent. The people loved country music, and I had a lot of fans there because of my program at CKNB. Mr. Gaisley called Willard Beaudreau, manager of the Capitol Theatre in Dalhousie, and I was booked there, too.

I was interested in playing as many areas as possible, so I'd written Fred Lynds, manager of CKCW in Moncton, New Brunswick, inquiring about doing a regular show on his station. I received his immediate reply. "Hank, we're playing your records here at the station and getting lots of requests for them. We've heard about your success at CKNB, and whenever you're ready to come to Moncton, just let me know. We'll work out something beneficial to both of us."

My plan was to leave CKNB in the spring of 1942 and do personal appearances during the warm spring and summer weather. Ideally, I wanted to play the Spencer theater circuit, but I hadn't received an offer yet. However, I did contact Mr. Spencer and told him I'd come to see him about this possibility at a later date. I hoped to get a job with station CKCW during the fall of 1942, but if I didn't get the theater job, I was pretty sure I could start with CKCW earlier than the fall. I enjoyed my stay at CKNB as much as any place in my music career, thanks to the people at CKNB and the great audiences everywhere I played.

Before checking on the theater work and the radio job, I took a trip to Fairview and spent some time with Min and Jimmie. My plan was to get established in a new area and then have my family join me. After my stay with Min and Jimmie, I took the train west again to Moncton, New Brunswick, about two hundred thirty miles away. When the train arrived, I took a cab to the Barker boardinghouse. It was not a fancy place, but it was only a few blocks from the radio station.

I unpacked my things, got cleaned up, and dressed to go see Fred Lynds. His office and the studios were on the second floor, and a pretty young lady at the front desk ushered me into his office. Mr. Lynds was young, with a slight resemblance to Clark Gable, and he was just as nice as his appearance. "Hank, your reputation has preceded you. We'd love to have you for a daily show. We'll pay you twenty-five dollars a week, and we might be able to locate a sponsor for you, too. If so, that would be additional pay. You could also line up a few musicians and play some towns around this area. Does this meet with your expectations?"

Everything about the job was excellent, but I couldn't commit myself at that time because I had a meeting scheduled with Mr. Spencer in Saint John in regard to playing his theater chain in the summer. I asked Mr. Lynds if the same offer would stand in the early fall. "It certainly will. Just let us know a few weeks ahead when you can start with us."

I took the bus to Saint John, about ninety miles from Moncton. When I met Mr. Spencer, I was pleasantly surprised to learn that he wanted me to play all the theaters on his circuit. The entire circuit! However, he noted that if, perchance, my drawing power became insufficient, he'd have to cancel any remaining appearances. I fully understood, because I knew this arrangement had to be strictly a business deal, and I was glad to be given the opportunity to try it. Thanks to the Good Lord, everything worked out just fine, and I got rave reviews in the newspapers.

After I started working the Spencer chain, I received calls from the other two major theater chains, asking if I'd consider working their houses, too, if it didn't conflict with the Spencer chain. I took this up with Mr. Spencer. "No problem, Hank, none of those theaters are in the Spencer territory, so you go right ahead." The other two chains were B&L Theatres, owned by Bernstein and Lieberman, and Independent Exhibitors, owned by Arthur Fielding.

Throughout the summer of 1942 I performed in all of the theaters of the three chains. I'm not sure of the exact number, but I think there were about twenty-five all totaled. My pay was the same in most of them: twenty-five dollars for a two-day run, and thirty-five dollars for a three-day run. But a couple of theaters in the large cities paid fifty dollars when I did three days. In addition to playing these three circuits, I worked six or seven independent theaters, and received the same pay. I didn't have much expense except for lodging, and as soon as I got a little money ahead, I bought a new suit and overcoat from Bond Clothes. Otherwise I was very careful with my money. I was hoping to save enough to make a down payment on another car in the near future.

The theater tour gave me a lot of valuable experience, especially about how to handle an audience, and helpful ideas about the business side of music. It's so different when you have musicians with you than when you're the single act on stage. When you're alone, your mistakes stand out more, and it makes you work harder to keep the show going at an entertaining pace. If there's a dead spot during a routine, you can easily lose the attention of the audience. Many times that happened to me, and I had to work like the devil to get the audience back in the palm of my hand again. "Don't ever let your audience see you sweat" is a saying that artists try to follow. In the entertainment field the performer has to be careful about time, but I had to be especially careful to finish my show and be offstage by the time the motion picture was scheduled to begin.

Along with the regular featured movie, newsreels of the war effort were shown. I never understood the reasons, but the audiences wanted to hear war, patriotic, and sad songs, in addition to the current hits of the day. I sang a variety and tried to give the folks what I thought they would enjoy the most. This kept me on my toes to learn new material, but it also gave me a chance to write new songs to try out onstage and to consider for future recording.

The only real hitch with doing these theaters was not having a car. I was tired of loading and unloading my show equipment—amplifier, speakers, guitar, mike stand, mike amplifier, and my wardrobe—on and off buses and trains. But during the early part of the tour a friend made a helpful offer. "I'll get my friend up here this afternoon, Hank, and if you'll set your equipment side by side, he'll measure around each piece and construct a sturdy box with appropriate divisions for everything you carry."

The carpenter made it right away, and it was perfect. I put a padlock and several "fragile" stickers on it. When I moved to another location, I'd send the big box by train, and my equipment was delivered to the theater. Usually it was waiting for me when I got there. Once in a while there was a mix-up, and I'd have to have the box picked up after I arrived at the theater, but I never missed a performance because of a foul-up in delivery.

Throughout these shows I met many people who were extremely nice to me. One situation, though, was very unpleasant, but I won't mention any names. One Saturday afternoon when the newsreel finished and before the feature movie was to begin, it was time for me to go on stage. The lights came on, but the curtains had not been drawn completely apart. They were separated just enough to give me room to stand between them for my act. I would only have a small space, and the curtains would almost touch me. I asked the boy who helped around the theater what was going on. He said, "I have to do exactly what the boss tells me to do." I replied, "Well, you just march yourself up to the office and tell the boss that I want to see him right now, or there will be no show."

The house was full, and as he was going to tell the boss, the audience started clapping and stomping their feet. They were anxious for me to start. The boss came running backstage and yelled at me, "What's your problem?" I said, "It's not me who has the problem, but you're going to have one hell of a problem in just a few minutes if you don't open those curtains all the way!" He answered. "Hey, we have a lot of miners and roughnecks who come to these matinees, and we have experienced in the past that if they didn't like the performer, they'd throw tomatoes, eggs, or anything else at him. We just installed a brand new movie screen, and I'm not going to take a chance on getting it damaged." "Okay," I replied, "why don't you just open the curtains and start the movie, because I think just as much of my guitar as you care about your damn screen."

The man looked at me with a stare that would knock your eyes out, but he didn't say another word. He had the curtains opened all the way, and I played to one of the nicest bunch of people I've ever played for. Those old and young miners were whooping and hollering, and they had a great time. When I left the stage, they demanded an encore. Believe me, they got one. The picture show started a little late, but I didn't care. Several came up to me after the show and congratulated me on a fine program and promised to come back again that night.

There was a possibility that I might lose my job in all the theaters because of this confrontation, but I did what I thought was right, and I didn't let the audience down. I've had a fault all my life, or maybe it's a good point. Some say it's been a great asset to me in my long career. Regardless of the circumstances, I've never let people push me around. I've always held my ground and stood up to the biggest man who ever walked. Boys in my band would vouch for this. They've seen it. But on the other hand, if I feel I'm in the wrong, I'll be the first to admit it.

16

Wheeling, West Virginia

Pardon me if I'm sentimental when we say good-bye,
Don't be angry with me should I cry.
When you're gone, yet I'll dream a little dream as years go by,
Now and then there's a fool such as I.

"(Now and Then, There's) A Fool Such as I," by Bill Trader

WHEN THE THEATER TOUR WAS OVER, I went back to see Mr. Lynds and told him I could start the radio show anytime, and he scheduled me for a half-hour program at seven o'clock each night, Monday through Saturday. That was perfect. I started at CKCW in the late fall of 1942, and I worked through the entire winter of 1942–43.

By this time, my name was pretty well established in New Brunswick, and I wanted to play show dates in the nearby towns. The station manager agreed that I could make transcriptions, and the station would play them when I was away on personal appearances.

Therefore, I got a few good musicians together, including a drummer from Moncton and a French fiddle player, not Eugene, but another good artist. I also used Morris Boulieau, from Edmundston, New Brunswick, whom I'd met while playing the theater circuit. He played several instruments extremely well, doubling on piano, banjo, acoustic guitar, fiddle, and steel. He was a very important part of my show. With this new band, I booked several small halls around the country, and we had great shows and a fine time. To me, live performances were still the most satisfying of all the aspects of entertainment.

In April, 1943, I took the bus and went back to Saint John, New Brunswick, to meet with each owner of the three theater chains again. Their letters of appreciation had invited me back, and they were all pleased when I told them I was free to play the circuits again. They would work out the schedules and contact me.

During the theater tour I met Curtis Rogers and his wife, Addie. Curtis was musically inclined, and he became interested in my work as an artist. He did a little bit of everything—and did everything well. He had his own jewelry store in Moncton. He sold musical instruments, bought and sold cars, and dealt in real estate. He also took care of the clocks in train depots throughout Nova Scotia and New Brunswick, to keep them set on the correct time and to repair them when necessary. During the last few years he's served as mayor of the town of Petitcodiac, New Brunswick.

Curt knew I needed a car in the worst way, and he said that his uncle, Zeddie Rogers, wanted to sell his 1941 Buick Roadmaster and buy a new one. He drove me to his uncle's dairy farm to look it over, and it was a real beauty. The car was like new, with very low mileage, and Uncle Zeddie, as we called him, offered it for $2,200. I wanted that car from the minute I laid eyes on it, but I didn't have that kind of money. I did have an account at the Bank of Nova Scotia, and I went to see the manager about financing it. Because of so much red tape, he said he would make me a loan rather than finance the car. I certainly appreciated their service, and that's one of the good reasons I'm still doing business at the same bank.

With my loan I bought the beautiful Buick. Now I had comfortable transportation, and I could load all of my equipment in the roomy trunk. The personal appearances continued, and we had responsive and appreciative crowds.

My records were playing throughout Canada, and I soon had another hit record. "Wandering On," a fast song that I had written and recorded, became a smash hit in Canada, just as "The Blue Velvet Band" had earlier.

Usually once each year Mr. Joseph set up a recording session for me in Montreal to record more songs, and I felt good that I was an established artist on the RCA Victor roster. I kept my dream alive to someday record in the United States and become just as popular there as in Canada.

But something had happened in 1942 that threatened to interrupt my recording. I was worried that the momentum I had established through a lot of hard work might be lost. The American Federation of Musicians union (AF of M) was having a contract problem with the recording industry, and the union refused to let any recording take place. This of course affected all the major companies, which were RCA Victor, Decca, Capitol, and Columbia. Mercury didn't exist during this time.

Thank God for Mr. Joseph. He took a chance during this contractual dispute, and in May, 1943, he sneaked me and my musicians into the studio, and I recorded sixteen songs for future release. He figured the feud could last for years, and he wanted to have songs ready for periodic release. In the four-day session the songs I recorded included "We'll Never Say Good-bye, Just Say So Long," "When My Blue Moon Turns to Gold Again," "Heartsick and Lonely," "Rose of the Rio," and "Goodnight, Little Buckaroo." Before I left for home, Mr. Joseph had the engineer dub copies on regular aluminum discs, so I didn't have to wait until the records were released to hear my efforts. By this time the studio had more modern equipment and could transfer these recordings to discs fairly easily.

My second theater tour was coordinated with the three circuits, and I traveled in style in my Buick Roadmaster to the many theaters in the provinces of New Brunswick and Nova Scotia. After this successful tour I was invited again to play all three circuits the following summer.

In 1944 a lot of luck and valuable experiences came my way. My name had traveled across the border into parts of the United States. One day I received a letter postmarked Browder, Kentucky, from a young lady by the name of Willidean Stephenson. She had heard some of my records on a station in Canada, and she made me an honorary member of her country music fan club. I thought I had the world in my hands when somebody from the United States—the country I'd read about and watched in movies so many times—would honor me.

Not long after that, I got a letter from Jack Howard, a young man from Philadelphia, Pennsylvania. Apparently the young lady in Kentucky had told Jack about me and my Canadian records. Jack was a promoter in Philadelphia and ran a music-publishing company, and we began corresponding on a regular basis. After he had heard some of my records, he invited me to spend a couple of weeks with him in his home, and he said he could get me on some American shows. Jack had sent me an eight-by-ten picture of himself in which he was wearing a beautiful tailored cowboy suit. He said it was made by Globe Western Tailors, and if I'd come to visit him, he would take me there to get measured for a suit like his.

I had also been corresponding with Big Slim, the Lone Cowboy, for about a year. He was a popular singer on the Wheeling Jamboree over station WWVA in Wheeling, West Virginia. I listened almost every night to Slim, as the powerful 50,000-watt station beamed signals into Canada and was received in our apartment as clear as a local station. I used to record WWVA programs on my home recorder and learned a lot of new songs from Slim. He was on the air from one until two every morning, and I especially loved one portion of Slim's program called "The Little White Church." He had sound effects played behind his beautiful religious narrations and songs, and I loved his voice and his unique delivery. It was most touching and inspirational. Through our correspondence Slim invited me to come to Wheeling to see him. When I mentioned this in a letter to Jack Howard, he said he'd be glad to accompany me there.

While I was thinking about my next move, something was disturbing me. I hadn't yet received my call from the Canadian army, and I was wondering why, since many of my friends had already been drafted. I knew if I were drafted, I could forget about my plans in music until the war was over. I wasn't looking forward to serving in the army, not because I was a coward, but because I thought I was on the verge of a major breakthrough, and any interruptions might upset all my well-laid plans.

Just as I expected, here came a letter with OHMS on the outside of the envelope. I knew it meant "On Her Majesty's Service." It had been sent first to Halifax and then forwarded to Moncton. I was to report in Fredericton, New Brunswick, on March 15, 1944, to be examined for service. I wanted to do what I was supposed to do and get it over with. Then I could go on with my career.

I left Moncton on March 13, about 8:00 A.M. on a cold, rainy day. Since I only had about a seventy-five-mile drive, I got there in plenty of time to rest up. At the hotel restaurant on March 14 I ran into some old buddies of mine who were scheduled to have their physicals, too. I invited them to my hotel room, and somebody brought beer, and we began to celebrate our induction into the army. We partied until about 3:00 A.M. on March 15, and I was supposed to be at the barracks by eight o'clock for my examination.

I was there on time, but I wasn't sober. I checked in and was directed to go to a waiting room and take off all my clothes and wait with about a dozen other guys. As you would expect, I had a hell of a hangover and was feeling silly. Everything was funny to me. I looked at the stark naked boys, and I couldn't keep from laughing at all those odd-shaped figures. I was full of funny sayings and had everyone laughing so loud you could hear them a block away.

I was the first one called in. A doctor in a white coat with a stethoscope around his neck motioned for me to come stand in front of him to check me over. I made a lot of wisecracks as I stood there weaving back and forth, but he didn't say a word and he didn't smile. He kept putting that stethoscope all around my chest and I knew my breath was terrible in his face. He said, "I want you to jump up and down like you're jogging until I tell you to stop." When he told me to stop, he listened to my heart. Then he gave up. "There's no way I can examine you and be accurate. You shouldn't have come in here intoxicated. I want you back here tomorrow at 8:00 A.M. sharp, and be sober!"

I felt really bad about it and apologized to the doctor. No more beer for me. I returned the next morning feeling much better. But there was a different doctor. He looked at my chart, asked me a lot of questions, had me jog in place, checked my lungs and heart several times, and had someone X-ray my chest. "Come back tomorrow afternoon, and we'll have a full report for you."

The next day the doctor told me the top of one of my lungs was disfigured, and the X-ray showed I'd had some serious lung problem. When I mentioned my terrible bout with wet pleurisy, he said, "You should have told me about it yesterday. You're not qualified for active army duty, because it's likely you'll have more problems with your lung. The army is careful not to take men with serious health problems. However, I see on your chart that you're a recording artist, so the army might enlist you for the Entertainment Division, Special Services. How would that strike you, young man?"

Well, I knew if the army wanted me they had the authority to draft me, so I said that I'd be most happy to serve in any way I could. Actually, that sounded very good to me. At least I could make a contribution to help boost morale in the military, and it would be another experience in entertainment that could benefit my career. The more I thought about it, the more I looked forward to serving. The doctor said if I didn't hear from the army within six weeks, I'd likely be turned down for service. In about three weeks, I received my certificate of rejection, and I was never asked to serve in Special Services. Now I could move ahead with my career plans.

I was fortunate to play the three theater circuits, for the third time, during the summer of 1944. During this tour I dropped the word "yodeling" from my stage title. I was playing a theater in Amherst, Nova Scotia, and the manager asked, "Hank, why do you call yourself 'The Yodeling Ranger'? I've never heard you yodel." I explained that I'd used that title for years and I used to yodel, but my voice had deepened and I didn't yodel much anymore.

So I changed my name to "The Singing Ranger" and I've used that name ever since.

The theaters still showed newsreels of World War II, and the audience always requested war and patriotic songs. This gave me a chance to sing some of the war songs I'd written and recorded. "Your Little

Band of Gold" was one of these, which seemed to be a strong favorite with the many audiences. Here are the lyrics and the narration:

On the raging field of battle in a dugout dark and cold
Lay a soldier boy in tears and wracked with pain.
We gathered close beside him as our captain said a prayer,
We knew his chance to live was all in vain.
He opened up his big blue eyes and smiled through flowing tears,
These last few words then to our Captain told.
"In this pocket by my heart, sir, is a message, send it, please,
And with it send this little band of gold.

Chorus:
"I promised you, sweetheart, someday I'd meet you,
Your tender form close to my heart I would hold.
But I'll never keep that promise, I have trod the last long mile,
So I'm sending you your little band of gold."

Narration:
He didn't know when he left you there that day
To sail to that land far across the blue way
That soon he'd be called to the Master's great fold,
To tread with the angels on the bright streets of gold.

Or he'd never have told you as he held you that night
And kissed away the tears in your big blue eyes so bright
That some day he'd return and your hand again hold
And place on your finger that little band of gold.

But we knew when we picked up the paper today
That your true soldier sweetheart had fell in the fray,
And with hearts that were heavy, and filled with despair,
We bowed down in sorrow and whispered a prayer.

And we looked up to Heaven and asked as we prayed
That our boys be protected and our freedom be saved.
And though he never returned with your little band of gold,
But he died a brave hero, for the freedom we hold.

We laid him down in silence, 'twas so hard to leave him there,
Our hearts were heavy as we walked away.
But we know tonight in Heaven there's another soldier boy
Who'll be marked a hero on that judgment day.
We wrote his dear old mother, sent his love to folks back home,
And told her God had called him to the fold.
And the message to his darling we so carefully mailed away
With his picture and her little band of gold.

Chorus:
"I promised you, sweetheart, someday I'd meet you,
Your tender form close to my heart I would hold.
But I'll never keep that promise, I have trod the last long mile,
So I'm sending you your little band of gold."

In addition to my patriotic and other original songs, I'd sing some of the current hits, such as Ernest Tubb's "Walking the Floor over You" and "There's a Star-Spangled Banner Waving Somewhere," which was a smash hit for Elton Britt at that time.

Big Slim wrote me more encouraging letters. "Hank, I'm sure I can get you some work here, and I'll talk to Mr. George Smith, the manager of the station, and there's a slight chance I can get you on the big WWVA Wheeling Jamboree. You can visit Jack Howard on your way down, and you can stay with me when you get to West Virginia."

Through my correspondence with Slim I learned that he was a real, honest-to-goodness cowboy, not the drugstore type. He and his wife, Hazel Holly, each had a horse on which they did trick riding in their road shows. Slim talked a lot about his famed horse, Golden Flash. Since I loved animals so much, I was anxious to see them perform.

I wrote to Jack and Slim that I'd take two weeks off from my theater tour and visit them. We all agreed that the summer would be suitable for all concerned, and I got permission from the owners of the theater chains to take this time off during my 1944 tour.

In the middle of July I boarded a train in Moncton and headed to Philadelphia, where Jack met me at the station. We had coffee at the depot and got better acquainted before we took a taxi to his place on Kensington Avenue. I liked Jack right away. He was truly a fine person, as I would find out. I also learned that he was an excellent promoter. He could sell ice cream to the Eskimos. When big acts like Gene Autry and Roy Rogers came to Philadelphia, Jack would immediately contact them and help promote their shows. If they gave him a few dollars for doing so, it was much appreciated. If he got nothing at all, that was okay, too. Jack sincerely enjoyed helping any person in the entertainment world, even unknown performers. Unfortunately, he was not too well off. He lived in the poor part of the city with his elderly mother, but he'd give you the shirt off his back if you needed it. It was sad that some of the people he helped never gave him a penny for his hard work.

Jack was so efficient in promoting talent, he already had arranged for me to do several personal appearances. My first show was at the famous Labor Plaza in downtown Philadelphia, where I performed before five thousand servicemen. I wore a big red cross on my sleeve and sold war bonds during the afternoon. Then Jack took me to radio station WFIL in Philadelphia, where Uncle Phil, the announcer, interviewed me on the air. On Sunday afternoon Jack had me scheduled in Wilmington, Delaware, where I performed at Cousin Lee's Radio Park. I was a guest, along with other entertainers, including the two nationally known Cackle Sisters, at this outdoor family park.

I appreciated Jack's help very much. Everywhere I performed I received a warm welcome and a lot of praise. I felt I was heading in the right direction to become a part of American entertainment. It was just a matter of time.

After the Sunday show Jack and I took the train to Wheeling to visit Big Slim and arrived about seven o'clock the next morning. We cleaned up in the lavatory at the depot, changed clothes, and walked the short distance to WWVA, on the top floor of the Hawley Building. While waiting for Slim, we were told that he and other artists came in each morning to check their mail in regard to the products they were selling over the air. The letters were counted, and they received ten or fifteen cents per letter from the station. The more letters an artist received, of course, the more money he'd make. Big Slim received the most mail of all the radio entertainers.

When Slim and Hazel came in around 10:00 A.M., I knew Slim immediately from the eight-by-ten picture he'd sent me earlier, and he recognized me from pictures I'd sent him. We all hit it off right away. We sat around the table, talking and drinking coffee. I never drank coffee before. It was always tea in Canada for me, but Jack got me started. I became well adapted to coffee, and since that time I believe I've kept Maxwell House in business.

After Slim and Hazel finished checking their mail, Slim drove us to their apartment on the outskirts of Wheeling. Their place was located on a short street with a dead end, and that's where Slim's stables were located. Slim's and Hazel's trick horses were kept there, along with a couple of mules used on his road show for comedy, and a coach dog.

Slim drove us out to a huge green field where their horses were kept for grazing during the summer. Those horses were beautiful, especially Big Slim's horse, Golden Flash, who wasn't actually golden at all. He was jet black and pure snow white. Slim and Hazel went through many of their show acts for us, and it was very exciting to me, as I had never seen anything like it before. Here was a real cowboy doing authentic trick riding, and I was impressed. Jack took several photographs with a professional camera that he'd borrowed. He got some great shots that I took back to Min. All this activity was planting a seed in the back of my mind that someday I might have a trained horse.

Before we left, Slim said, "If you come back late this fall and stay for a while, I'll do whatever I can to get you a spot on WWVA. Even if you can't get on at the station, you can probably find a good entertainment job to give you a livelihood for the winter."

We took an overnight train back to Philadelphia. After we rested up Jack took me to Globe Western Tailors, and I was measured for a western suit. I paid the tailor, and Mr. Globe promised to send the suit by airmail as soon as it was made. Afterwards Jack and I took the taxi to the train station, and he encouraged me to return in the fall.

On the way back I wrote a song, and I did a lot of thinking. Before the train pulled into Moncton, I had fully decided that Min, Jimmie, and I would return to Wheeling as Slim and Jack had suggested. I had a gut feeling that before long I'd be singing on radio station WWVA. Min was all for it, too, and she continued to support me in all of my calculated moves. Without her encouragement I don't think I would have taken on so many challenges.

I went back to the theater tour, and in the meantime Mr. Lynds had invited me back to resume my radio show on CKCW as soon as the tour ended. About five weeks before finishing the theaters I hadn't received my western suit from Globe, and I was worried. Come to find out, it was held up at the customs office in Halifax, and they didn't know how to reach me. But finally it was delivered to me at the theater in New Glasgow, and I couldn't open the box fast enough. I quickly tried the suit on, and I had the thrill of a lifetime. The western shirt and trousers were a beautiful blue with gold trim. The suit had absolutely no flaws. That night I wore it onstage at the Roseland Theater in New Glasgow.

A situation occurred in Edmundston, New Brunswick, that helped me learn an important lesson. I was staying in a big hotel around the corner from the theater. Since I was so close, I'd change into my stage clothes at the hotel and walk over to do my program.

My new street outfit consisted of a pair of white flannel slacks, a fawn sportcoat, a matching-colored flowered sport shirt, and brown-and-white oxfords. After a matinee I met a fellow from Nova Scotia. He said he enjoyed my show and asked if I'd like to join him and get something to eat. He wanted to find out more about show business. I felt sorry for him because he was poorly dressed, and I figured he was out of work and had no money. I told him I would, but first I went to my room to change out of my stage clothes, and he waited in the lobby.

We went to the restaurant and had an early supper, then returned to the lobby of the hotel and talked until it was almost time for my first evening performance. I invited him to see the next show, but he said he was not feeling well and was going to rest. He didn't say where he was staying, but he said he'd see me after the show. I went upstairs and changed into my stage clothes, walked over to the theater, and did my two programs.

When I returned to my hotel room, my door was open and all of my new summer clothes and my new camera were gone! But here's the funniest part. The guy left his old shirt, pants, shoes, and everything lying in the middle of the room on the floor. He had undressed where he stood. He put on my new clothes and was gone. I realized then why he didn't go back to the theater with me. He had planned to rob me.

I asked the desk manager if he had given the guy a passkey. He assured me he hadn't. I called the Royal Canadian Mounted Police, and they came to the hotel. After I explained what happened, they said they'd drive along the highway, out of the city, and perhaps they might find him hitchhiking in the clothes I'd described. They returned to the hotel later and reported they hadn't found the thief, but they had issued a bulletin to have officers check along the Canadian and American borders.

You know, the desk manager bawled me out. "What do you mean, bringing the RCMP around here, causing a disturbance and scaring our customers away?" I replied, "My friend, I couldn't give a damn about your hotel. Tonight I've had valuable clothes and a brand-new camera stolen from my room. Since you don't have a sign up saying you'll not be responsible for stolen goods, I might just sue the hell out of the hotel for the whole thing." I didn't sue the hotel, and neither did I hear of the thief again.

It was another experience down the road of life for me, and I learned a good lesson: Don't trust anybody.

I finished my theater tour and almost immediately began my work at CKCW. During my stay at the station I planned my trip to the United States for late fall. Three weeks before Christmas I left CKCW and prepared for my next recording session, which was scheduled to begin on December 20, 1944. The conflict between the musicians' union and the record companies was still on, but Mr. Joseph sneaked me and my musicians into the studio again. During the four-day session I recorded eighteen songs. Nobody knew when the recording feud would end, so again Mr. Joseph wanted to have new songs available for periodic release. The long list included "Your Little Band of Gold," "Soldier's Last Letter," "Blue Ranger," "You Broke the Chain That Held Our

Hearts," and "You Played Love on the Strings of My Heart." This last song became one of my biggest sellers in Canada.

After the session we loaded up our few things in the Buick and Min, Jimmie, and I took off for the U.S.A. One thing concerned Min and me about making this change. Jimmie was only eight years old, and we were taking him to a strange place. We weren't sure how he'd adjust. Every year Min and I made sure he had a good Christmas, even during our most impoverished early years. Sometimes we had to go without food so we could buy him toys, but it was always well worth it. Seeing the glow on his little face as he opened the gifts made our hearts feel good. We stopped on our way to Wheeling and bought some of the things Jimmie had mentioned he wanted for Christmas. We were hoping that Slim and Hazel would have a Christmas tree to put his gifts under.

As expected, Slim and Hazel gave us a warm welcome. They didn't have much room for guests, but they fixed us a sofa bed in the living room and set up a little bed for Jimmie. They had a tree, so we put Jimmie's presents under it and hung his Christmas stocking. We celebrated our Christmas the same way we had been used to in Canada.

Right after Christmas we moved out. Slim and Hazel had been extra good to us, but we didn't want to impose on their good nature any longer. Besides, I was anxious to have our own place and to be closer in towards town. Slim mentioned the Wheeling Hotel, which had a homey atmosphere, where a lot of the entertainers from the Jamboree often stayed. Their weekly rate was reasonable, so we rented one big room. It was clean and comfortable, and we cooked on our two-burner hot plate.

As we gradually got settled in, I became concerned about the tryout for the job at the radio station. Even though I felt I would be hired at WWVA, it didn't lessen my worries. I've always been a worrier, even when everything was going my way, because I always expected surprises waiting around the corner.

A few days after Christmas, Slim arranged for me to meet George W. Smith, manager of WWVA, and to read for him concerning a job at the station. It was strange how the interview was conducted. I was sent into the studio and given something to read, and farther down the hall Mr. Smith was in his office, listening to me on his speakers. I read a few short commercials, and I must have done it right, because Mr. Smith had me come into his office. "Hank, you have a pretty nice voice for announcing," he said. "And we'll arrange some time slots for you. I've heard some of your Canadian recordings, and I think you'll create a good following here. When would you like to start?"

I told him I was honored by his kind comments, and I was ready to start whenever he gave the word. My hair felt like it was crawling all over my head. I was so hyped up, I couldn't wait to break the good news to Min, and she was just as happy as I was.

This was one of my big chances! I was going to be on a powerful 50,000-watt radio station that was heard in parts of Canada and in many states in the U.S.A. I was hoping with all my heart that the American people would like my singing as well as my wonderful Canadian friends did.

So I started 1945 with a bang. I was given two shows from the beginning. I went on the air at 2:30 in the afternoon for a half hour, and again at 11:30 at night. Then Slim came on at midnight for a one-hour program. On Saturday nights I was on the famous WWVA Midnight Jamboree. The Jamboree used to be held at the Capitol Theater, and it was operated along the same lines as the Grand Ole Opry. All of the entertainers performed for a live audience. During the war years, for some reason, it was cancelled at the theater, and the entertainers did the show from the studio.

I was billed as "Hank, the Singing Ranger," and it was just me and my guitar. Slim also worked alone, except sometimes he had Johnny Hill, an outstanding guitarist, play behind his work. I became a regular part of the WWVA family on the Saturday night show and began receiving a lot of mail, which pleased me to no end. Of course Big Slim was the star of the Jamboree, and he continued to draw the most mail.

My income was quite good at the station from the two products I handled over the air. I sold statuettes, as well as tulip bulbs from a well-known nursery. Statuettes were my biggest seller. I'd ask the listeners to send in small snapshots of themselves, and these would be passed along to the company. The makers would cut out forms designed from the pictures and mold them into small, rounded statues. They could be placed on a mantelpiece or wherever, and they were very attractive.

I was getting great exposure through the station, especially with my late-night show, but as yet I didn't have any record releases in the States. I wanted the listeners to hear me sing on the radio and like me well enough to buy my records. Realistically, I didn't think RCA Victor would release any of my records in the States until I could build a following strong enough to warrant it.

Besides my radio work, I felt I needed exposure from personal appearances. I'd heard the artists around the station talking about playing dates within a hundred miles or so of Wheeling, but they had to make sure they made it back for the Saturday night Jamboree. Most of them traveled in their cars and had luggage trailers to carry their instruments.

Living in the Wheeling Hotel was getting to Min and me, and we wanted more breathing room. Many of the performers had a house trailer, and we thought it would be nice if we had one, too. We could fix it up and rent a spot at the trailer park adjacent to the Hawley Building, which housed WWVA. We were advised to go to Detroit, Michigan, in order to get a real good buy, so we took off.

If we found a trailer we liked, I didn't have enough American money to buy it or to make a down payment. I had some money in the bank at Moncton, but the law only allowed Canadians to bring the amount of 150 American dollars across the border into the United States. Even to bring that amount, you had to go to the bank and get a certain form, called form H. How far would $150 go?

Here was my plan. I wired my bank in Moncton and told them to transfer $2,000, which just about wiped out my savings, to a certain bank in Windsor, Ontario, just across the bridge from Detroit. They transfered the money pronto, and Min and I were there to pick it up. I knew it was risky to bring that much Canadian money across the border, and if I got caught, I'd be in real trouble.

How could I get my life's savings through Customs and Immigration without having it confiscated? I stuck the $2,000, all in $100 bills, in the outside breast pocket of my jacket. Then I bought a newspaper, and I planned to nonchalantly read it and pretend I had nothing to hide when the agent started asking me questions. I was hoping I could go right on through with no problems.

Now, friends, I'm the kind of guy who can be as innocent as a person can be, and I'll have a guilty look on my face. If I were in a room with a thousand people and something got stolen, I believe everyone would look at me and think I was the thief. It's a feeling I've always had.

There I was in a long line to go through Customs and Immigration. When it came my turn to show my green card, which a noncitizen had to have to come into the United States, I looked up from my newspaper and handed the man my card. He asked me a few questions, like "Where are you from, and where are you going?" I was trying to keep my composure as best I could, but I was beginning to sweat. Well, I must have had that guilty look because the agent said, "You'd better step inside the office with me."

I thought, "Oh, brother, they'll take all my money now." Inside, the agent asked me more questions in front of two more immigration officers, and I used an old psychology stunt I'd used before. I wanted to sway his mind from my problem, so I asked him questions like "How did the hockey team do in their last game? Where do the Toronto Maple Leaves stand in the play-offs with the American teams this year?" I talked about the weather, politics, and American ball clubs. When I mentioned American ball clubs, those Americans' eyes lit up, and we talked baseball, which at the time I knew very little about. I just answered yes and no to the things he asked me about the game. The agent got excited and told me the names of several players that he knew personally. Then I finally heard the welcome words, "All right, Mr. Snow, you're free to go. Have a nice trip back to Wheeling."

I had Canadian money, which was no good in the United States, especially as far south as Wheeling. Therefore we had to go into a bank in Detroit and get it exchanged into American currency. I coached Min on what to say and sent her into the bank. I was shocked when she returned and said the bank would not exchange the money for under 20 percent of the total, which would only leave us with $1,600 in American currency. I usually look at the bad side first. I was afraid the bank might become suspicious and call the law and have us arrested for having that much Canadian money with us. I told Min to do it, so we could get out of there. She showed the bank the necessary identification, and the exchange was made.

We looked all over the city of Detroit for a trailer with no success. We finally found a small trailer we liked, with a sign reading "For Sale—$900." We inquired at the office, but it had been sold a few hours earlier. My heart was broken. After all that time to get the money and losing part of it on the exchange, I was upset. We had made a foolish trip to Detroit and spent a lot of money on gas and wasted a lot of time. We drove back to Wheeling to be there in time for my next radio program.

We began looking for an apartment, and we saw an ad in the Wheeling paper for one with three rooms on Wheeling Island. This island is directly across the bridge from Wheeling on the Ohio side. There's just a bridge between West Virginia and Ohio, and it was within walking distance from the bridge to the apartment. It was furnished, and we rented it for $60 per month.

One day when I was at the station, the Ohio River went on a rampage, and it was the biggest flood people had seen there in several years. I couldn't get back home to Min and Jimmie, so we kept in touch by phone. And to make things worse, Jimmie came down with the measles. Min knew that anyone with the measles should be kept in a dark room, so she kept him away from the window. Besides, she didn't want him to be frightened by the flood waters.

The station stayed on the air all night to give bulletins on the flood and its status, and the entertainers did extra shows. Many people were flooded out of their homes and isolated from each other, and the phones were constantly in use because many relatives were calling about the safety of their kin. Min said the flood waters were up so high that she could reach out the upstairs window of our apartment and put her hand in the water. She saw logs floating by with cats and dogs on them, and people in boats were trying to rescue their pets. But in a few days the flood waters decreased, and things slowly got back to normal.

Discussing his horse one day, Slim said, "Hank, since you like animals so much, you should buy a trained horse. You can keep him at my stables." It didn't take too much urging to get me interested. He said, "I know a Mr. Daniels, out in the country, who has a beautiful horse that's trained for show business. But I'm a little afraid that he might be too much for you to handle, because he can be very rough at times." Well, I wanted to go look at him anyhow, and Slim and I took a trip to check it out. The horse was definitely too big for me. I would have looked out of place on a horse that big, as small as I was.

A little later Slim heard about a smaller horse for sale at Sleepy Hollow Ranch, outside of Philadelphia. When he told me, I immediately wrote a letter to Elmer Newman, the owner, and asked several questions. A letter was back in less than a week with a picture enclosed. The horse had been in show business for several years, so he was not young. He had traveled to South America with the Pan American Rodeos and had played in movies with Charles Starrett and the Sons of the Pioneers. I also received a typewritten list of the many tricks in his act, as well as their cues. I was highly impressed.

Elmer stated that he had turned down a dozen chances to sell him, because he wanted to be sure the new owner would be faithful and good to the horse. I guess my letter had impressed Elmer, and he said if I were interested to let him know. He'd send the horse to Wheeling by a van, and I could pay the driver when he was delivered. Absolutely I wanted him, sight unseen!

In just a few days Shawnee arrived at Slim's stables, and I fell in love with him the exact moment I laid eyes on him. He was born in Shawnee, Oklahoma, which is where he got his name. He was not a huge horse like Trigger, but just the right size for me. Shawnee was beautiful. He was chestnut brown and snow white, and he had the most beautiful and expressive eyes I have ever seen. They looked almost human, as many people would say to me later.

Buying Shawnee was one of the best things I've ever done.

17

Making Big Plans

The world's a stage, they say,
And we're all part of the play,
And you were only acting when we met.
You played the lover well,
So how could I foretell
That you would find another and forget.

"Act 1, Act 2, Act 3," by Charles Tebbetts

SHAWNEE WAS VERY TIRED AFTER the long ride from Pennsylvania, so I made him a warm bed in a box stall that Slim had let me use. I fed him a good meal and left him to rest for the night.

The next day I couldn't wait to get out there and become better acquainted with Shawnee. I took Slim's curry comb and a big brush and gave him a real honest-to-goodness cleaning. He loved it. Then I had to see if he would respond to my cues and do any of his tricks. He reacted to every one the first time I tried them. He looked at me with those kind and approving eyes, and I knew we would be friends forever.

Slim said he'd teach me trick riding, but I'd need a special saddle for that. He directed me to a saddle shop in Ohio, seven miles from Wheeling. I drove there and bought a beautiful new saddle for $150. This was my first one, and I was proud of it. I painted the hand-tooled roses pretty shades of red and yellow and the leaves green, and it was even more beautiful. Min kidded me about loving that saddle so much.

I stayed at WWVA all winter, and I'd go see Shawnee nearly every day. I'd ride him and practice his trick routine. Sometimes I'd just clean him up, pet him, and give him candy or a piece of sugar, which he dearly loved.

Slim told me about working in Toronto at the exhibition one year, and he said he'd love to go on tour with me to Nova Scotia, New Brunswick, and eastern Quebec. If I wanted a big road show, he would be glad to bring Golden Flash and Hazel's horse and his two trained mules that he used for comedy. If I learned trick riding and we added Shawnee to the show, we'd have something real special.

Slim got me interested in this idea, and Min and I thought it would be a plus for me. A lot of the eastern Canadian people were familiar with Big Slim from his radio shows. "You'll need about everything I use for my show," he said. "That's a lot of equipment, and it will be very expensive. It might take you a year to get everything together. If you want to try it, why don't we plan to do the tour next summer?" I pretended to Slim that finances would be no problem, and I assured him I could easily get the money. Of course I had no earthly idea where it would come from, but I had always been a dreamer, and since things were going pretty well for me at that time, my dreams simply got bigger.

Min and I drove out to Slim's place one evening, and we discussed what I'd need for our extravaganza. Slim went down a long list. "You'll need a rectangular-shaped area for trick riding. Rather than buy a tent, which would be extremely expensive, I'd advise you to buy a canvas sidewall to encircle the area. The canvas should be about six feet high so people can't look over it, and it should be made in sections. Buy enough to go around showgrounds of 200 by 75 feet. You'll also need wooden posts to put up every six feet to hook the canvas onto."

As Slim talked, I wrote all of this down, including the dimensions of his portable ticket booth and his portable stage. "Hank, you'll also need a marquee to hang over the entrance to the showgrounds, and of course all these things need hooks and hinges so they can be easily assembled and disassembled. The grandstand should seat at least five hundred people, so for two shows you can accommodate a thousand people. Oh yes, you've either got to buy a semitrailer rig or rent one. It might be easier at first to rent one or to hire a truck driver with a semi."

I was squirming as Slim was talking. I could see that all this was going to be real expensive, but I wrote it down anyway. "You'll either have to hire a crew to put the equipment up or have your band members handle it," he said. "Remember that you have to have it inspected by the safety officals. You'll also need a portable power plant, because a lot of places will not be close enough to hook up to the electric power lines. Your stage will need a canvas roof over it, and to be really effective, you'll need a 2,000-watt colored spotlight with a colored wheel that you can turn to make it change to different colors. In order to keep Shawnee healthy and comfortable, you'll need a sturdy van to carry him in and to haul his food." The list went on and on.

When Slim finished, I had mixed feelings. The show convoy would certainly be noticed. It would practically advertise itself. I had confidence in putting together a first-class show that would cater to the entire family, just like a circus would. On the other hand, I'd be heavily in debt for all this equipment, and it would certainly be a burden to transport it from place to place and put it up and down, not to mention store it each winter. When Min and I left Slim's place, we gave his ideas serious consideration.

Slim had promised he could make a trick rider out of me, but that was yet to be seen. He indicated, because I was small and lightweight, I'd be a natural for trick riding. I loved being around horses. I had ridden them and taken care of them—but a trick rider in a show? I didn't know, but I'd soon find out.

Anyway, I told Slim I'd do my best to learn everything he wanted to teach me. To encourage me Hazel said that when Slim and she first got married, she was scared to death to even go near a horse. But folks, if you had seen her do her daring rides, you'd never believe it. One of her tricks scared me to death. As her horse went at a gallop, she'd lean down over the side of the horse with her feet still in the stirrups and pick up a handkerchief with her mouth.

Slim said to never wear cowboy boots when learning to ride, so I bought a pair of sneakers. I was enthusiastic and went to Slim's place whenever he had time to teach me, which was usually a couple of times a week. But I'd go there almost every day to practice. Slim was a great teacher and as patient as anyone could be. After a few lessons he said I was light on my feet and had excellent coordination. He praised me as a fast learner, and this encouraged me to work even harder.

One of the tricks was a single and double vault. I had converted my regular saddle horn into a round steel post about six inches high to use as a hand grip. As Shawnee was going at a steady gallop, I'd hold onto the grip with both hands, go down on each side, and touch my feet on the ground. Using my sense of rhythm and coordinating my movements with Shawnee's speed, I would touch the ground with my toes. Then I would again wait for Shawnee's natural rhythm to toss me up and over him so that my toes would touch the ground on the other side. I'd do this back and forth a few times and then land back in the saddle. You've probably seen this same stunt in western movies made back in the 1940s and 1950s.

Another trick was the tail crouper. I used one of Slim's saddles to practice this until I got my saddle converted, as I had to have two hand grips attached to the back of the saddle. As Shawnee galloped, I'd hold onto both hand grips and slide down over Shawnee's rump. As soon as my toes touched the ground behind him, I'd coordinate my rhythm with the rhythm of his gallop and my lift with his lift, and he would throw me up over his rump and into the saddle. The success of this trick depended on perfect timing. When he went up, I had to go up with him, and when he went down, I had to go down with him to touch my toes on the ground. It took a lot of practice, but I finally mastered it. I also learned how to lower myself on one side of Shawnee, go around his neck, go back up on the other side, and get back in the saddle as he was galloping. This was tough and somewhat dangerous.

Before my family left for Canada, I was a fairly good trick rider. I could do many of the things that Hoot Gibson had done when I saw him in the Barnum and Bailey show.

When I finished my stint at WWVA, I made plans to ship Shawnee to Moncton, New Brunswick. And I made arrangements with Zeddie Rogers, the man who had sold me my Buick, to have Shawnee stay at his dairy farm in Moncton. As I prepared for Shawnee's long ride, Slim said, "The first thing you have to do, Hank, is get Shawnee vaccinated. I've been through all this before when I took my animals to Canada. You can't use a regular licensed veterinarian, you have to have him vaccinated by an appointed government-licensed vet. They want to insure there's no distemper or any other kind of disease that can be taken into Canada by an animal." This had to be done thirty days prior to crossing the border. Someone told me where I could find a government-licensed veterinarian, so I took Shawnee and had him vaccinated, along with Mickey, my little Boston terrier dog.

Next I built a portable stall to have Shawnee shipped in on the train. I made sure it was sturdy, because if it wasn't, the train personnel wouldn't ship him. Naturally, one end had to be left open so Shawnee could walk in and back out. I hired a big truck to take Shawnee to the station. When it came, we loaded the portable stall on the truck, the driver backed the truck up to a small bank, and Shawnee walked right into the stall. I followed the truck to help transfer Shawnee to the train. At the station Shawnee was led from the portable stall. The stall was lifted onto the boxcar, and he walked into the stall with no trouble at all.

We bid Slim and Hazel so long. We were anxious to get back home to Moncton, as we had been gone all winter. I had already made arrangements to do my theater tour for the circuits again and to return to Wheeling in the fall.

We would beat Shawnee to the border, but I intended to wait for him at Calais, Maine, which joined Canada by a long bridge at Saint Stephen, New Brunswick, where he would be crossing. I wanted to make sure he was put on the right train to take him on to Moncton.

The next morning, on a hunch, I told Min I was going to call customs to see how Shawnee was getting along and where he was at that point. It's a good thing I did, because the man who answered at the customs office said that my horse was being held in Troy, New York. "He's fine, but we're holding him because the veterinarian who vaccinated him was not a licensed government vet, which is our requirement before we can let any animal enter Canada." We turned around and drove several hundred miles back to Troy, New York. We had no other choice. I'd have to look up another government vet to vaccinate my horse and dog. I was really upset about the vet giving me the wrong information, and I was worried sick about Shawnee, wondering if he was being properly fed and watered.

When we got to Troy, Shawnee looked very tired, but bless his heart, he was glad to see me. I immediately took him outside and walked him, and the exercise perked him up. With the help of the people at customs, the animals were soon vaccinated and the proper papers completed.

We left Shawnee again and went on our merry way to Moncton. Before we left customs, though, the people said it was not necessary for us to wait for Shawnee at the border, as he would be well taken care of with food and water. I was told they had several animals, including expensive racehorses, going back and forth every year. So Min and I decided we'd drive straight through to Moncton. We pulled into Moncton late at night and had a good rest. The next morning I called customs on each side of the border, at Calais, Maine, and Saint Stephen. They said Shawnee had just arrived, and he was fine and would be shipped directly to Moncton.

Shawnee was at the station at seven the following night, and I was never so glad to see anything in my whole life. I was surprised at how good he looked. Zeddie was waiting there also. We loaded Shawnee in his truck, and Zeddie drove him to his dairy farm and put him in a nice clean box stall covered with straw. He was given his regular meal of bran, oats, and hay, and he had plenty of fresh water from the automatic watering device in his stall.

I returned to the hotel, and in a few days I went to see Walter Colpit, who owned and operated a large business in all kinds of building and carpentry work. They made truck bodies, trailers, self-haul equipment, you name it, and they did it well. I said, "I might have a pile of work for you soon. Some afternoon I'd like to sit down and have us go over what I'll need for a big traveling show and have you give me a ballpark figure of the cost, so I can see if I can swing the deal." Mr. Colpit assured me he could build anything I needed and would be happy to work with me.

"But first," I explained, "I need you to make me a sturdy horse trailer. I plan to pull it with my Buick, so I can take my trained horse with me on my theater tour this summer. Can you do it?" "Hank, my boy," he said, "you've come to the right place. Get me the dimensions, and we'll get right on it. I've got the best work crew you'll find in these parts, and we'll make sure everything is done exactly the way you want it."

I took the dimensions and several good ideas that people had given me, as well as pictures of Slim's horse trailer, and gave them to Mr. Colpit. We talked about it, and the foreman, who was a very skilled craftsman, also came up with helpful suggestions. He made it clear that I must have a safe and sturdy trailer hitch on my Buick to hitch my trailer. He insisted that the front of my trailer have a safe connection and a safe trailer bar with a locknut, so that it would be impossible for the trailer to come loose from the car under severe pressure or on bad roads. I agreed because I was especially concerned with safety. I didn't want to take any chances whatsoever.

The horse trailer was ready in just over three weeks. It was beautiful, compact, and comfortable. The small windows could be opened so Shawnee could have plenty of fresh air when needed, and if we were on dusty roads the windows could be shut.

Before I could deal with the show projects, I had to get everything ready to do my theater shows for the summer. For this tour I took along my friend Ross Parker, who had worked with me before. He would help me with Shawnee. Of course, we couldn't take Shawnee inside the theaters, but usually we'd find a good spot nearby, like an open field, and I'd put him through his routine. I advertised on the radio as "Hank Snow and his famous trick horse, Shawnee." He had to kneel for some of his tricks, so I had a 35 by 35–foot canvas-like mattress made and stuffed it full of straw. I didn't want him kneeling on any hard surfaces, and I made sure he was comfortable in every way.

Many people came outside after my theater performances to watch Shawnee perform, and they loved it. He was the star attraction. His popularity began to spread across the country through newspapers and radio.

When we were playing a theater in New Brunswick, I saw a beautiful German police dog, whose name was Pal. I was admiring the dog when the owner said, "I'll be glad to give him to you, if you'll give him a good home. I don't know where he came from. Someone must have put him out of a car, and he stayed here. He's a fine dog. You'll notice that he likes to bluff a lot, but he's as kind as a kitten." He sure wasn't friendly when I tried to walk up to him! But the owner assured me that once I got to know him well, he would be a faithful, one-man dog. But I wanted to think about it overnight.

I decided I wanted the dog, and Ross went with me to get him. We put Pal in the back of the Buick. Ross sat with me in the front seat, and I leaned forward, huddling over the steering wheel as I drove. The big dog put his front paws on the back of my seat, and I felt him breathing on my neck, puffing and panting. He was really nervous, and so was I! It was laughable, though, as I glanced over to find Ross halfway under the dash.

When we reached the trailer, both Ross and I were afraid to take him out of the car. When we finally got brave enough, we led him out and tied him to the horse trailer, and I fed him a good meal. It didn't take long for me to get adjusted to him, and vice versa. I had a purpose in mind when I took the dog. If I ever got my big traveling show going, I wanted him to help guard my horse and to patrol the outside of the canvas sidewall, so nobody would slash the canvas.

In a few days I went to see Mr. Colpit, and we spent an afternoon going over my complete show list. I gave him the dimensions of everything I'd need, just as Big Slim had told me. I was trying to be optimistic, but I had no idea how much this whole thing would cost or as yet where the money would come from. But thinking, planning, and dreaming didn't cost one penny.

We went over the estimate for the grandstand, nine-piece stage, posts for the canvas sidewall, lighting plant, ticket booth, and everything else we needed for such an outdoor show. Mr. Colpit gave me a ballpark figure, adding or taking away here and there, of around six thousand dollars. At today's prices, that would be at least thirty thousand dollars. He assured me that his crew could have everything completed in time for the big show in the summer of 1946. He gave a word of caution, however. "If you're able to get the finances to begin these projects, I want you to come back and sit down with the foreman and me, so we understand exactly what you want. We want to be positive that all the dimensions are correct."

Friends, I've always been very careful with my money, because there have been too many poverty days. I had managed to save around twelve hundred dollars, but that would not even be sufficient for a down payment for Mr. Colpit.

I took a bold step that was completely out of character for me. I had always heard that you have to spend money to make money, and by now I believed it. My goal was still to become a major artist and sell records throughout the world. In a reckless moment I got up enough nerve to write a thoughtful and lengthy letter to Mr. Joseph at RCA Victor. I told him exactly what my plans were for the coming year. "Now that my records are selling pretty good across Canada, I hope you might have enough faith in me to do what I consider a favor of all favors. My plans are to bring Big Slim, the Lone Cowboy, and Hazel Holly, and their trick horses into Canada next year. I was wondering if you could discuss this with your Board of Directors, and see if it is at all possible for you to loan me $4,000." After I dropped the letter in the mail, I realized I had done a foolish thing. Why should my record company loan me that much money when my royalty checks were only between two hundred fifty and three hundred dollars every three months?

What a surprise! In about five days Mr. Joseph wrote back. "I've taken this up with our executives, and they have agreed that we will advance you the money to start your road show." RCA Victor, and Mr. Joseph in particular, had given me a vote of confidence, and I intended to do everything in my power to justify their faith in me.

With a little over five thousand dollars in the bank, I was ready to go ahead with the big projects. I went to A. G. English, who owned a Cadillac, Buick, and Oldsmobile dealership in Moncton. I told him I wanted to buy a new truck in which I was going to have a van body built on for my horse. And I wanted to buy another truck with a semi-flatbed, with regular side racks, to carry all of my show equipment. The flatbed trailer would have to be open, and the side racks would have to come on and off for easy loading and unloading all of our equipment.

I ordered both trucks and the flatbed trailer from Mr. English, and he ordered the trucks and trailer from a firm in Oshawa, Ontario, Canada. I also informed Mr. English that in the fall I planned to trade my 1941 Buick in for a brand-new 1946 Buick Roadmaster. You should've seen the expression on his face! With these big plans of mine I'm sure he must have thought I was losing my marbles. Of course, orders like these don't knock on your door every day. I said I could make a good down payment and pay the remainder so much each month. He was very kind to me, and he worked out the satisfactory finances.

Afterwards I went back to see Mr. Colpit at his shop to make sure he knew exactly what I wanted and to arrange a schedule for paying him. He was pleased to work with me and insisted that I come by his place often to get a progress report—which I was happy to do.

Next I flew to Toronto and ordered canvas for the sidewall and canvas to cover the stage from the Ontario Tent and Awning Company. I gave them all the dimensions and told them that I needed the finished product just as soon as they could deliver it to me at Moncton. They said they would ship it to me on a certain date. I gave them cash, because I couldn't get credit there, since I wasn't from that part of the country.

Things were moving fast. The canvas sidewall was shipped on time. Soon I got in touch with a friend, Johnny Brown, who had the theatrical supply company in Montreal. I told him I needed a powerful spotlight with a color wheel that would change colors. He recommended a 2,000-watt spotlight, and it cost me somewhere between one hundred fifty and one hundred seventy-five dollars.

For my portable power plant I contacted Harold Reid, a friend in Moncton, and he recommended a 10,000-watt plant. He said that was sufficient power to handle everything: lights, PA system, electric razors, hot plates, air conditioners, toasters, spotlight, just anything we would have on the show, including our electric instruments. I wanted more power than we needed, in case we added something else to the show that would require more voltage. The power plant I ordered was automatic. For example, you could turn on an electric bulb or any appliance in the show and the plant would automatically start. It would also quit when the power was turned off, and this became a great convenience.

I've always believed in the saying "If you can afford it, always buy the best. If you can't afford it, don't buy it at all until you can afford it." I believe this saying, too: "Everything that is worth doing is worth doing well."

Man, I was having a ball, getting all these things together. I was learning so much as we went along, such as how to run the power plant, how the sidewall should be put up, and a dozen other things. It was awful nice not to be stingy with every penny, and I was beginning to feel like a successful businessman, although it was almost a year away before I would start getting a return on my investments. My theater shows were doing great, and I continued to meet all of my monthly obligations.

When I inquired about an electrician, I told Mr. Colpit I wanted a first-class man to do this work. He replied, "Don't you worry about a thing, Hank. We're familiar with the codes of all the provinces across Canada. John Beaudreau is a licensed electrician. He's a great old guy, and he'll make sure you have a very safe wiring system to run all of your equipment. He'll wire right along with us as we're building your projects." I knew the codes were different in some places, and the electrical set-ups always had to be inspected by the fire chief at any location in which we'd play. This could be a hassle if we didn't meet the code requirements.

I had been following Big Slim's instructions almost to the letter in getting the equipment built. I upgraded a few things and made adjustments here and there. I had a lot of faith in the people I was doing business with. They were proud of their work. Whenever I dropped by to see see how things were coming along, Mr. Colpit or his foreman would give me suggestions for modifications. This pleased me, because they were beneficial things I hadn't thought about.

During my theater tour I had a burst of creativity and wrote a number of songs that I thought were very strong in preparation for my next recording session. My plan was to record in December and leave immediately for Wheeling.

Toward the end of the summer I finished my fourth and final theater tour. I had been constantly traveling around the country in my car and pulling the trailer with Shawnee. I was exhausted. Therefore, as planned, the Snow family prepared to go back to West Virginia, even though I didn't have a definite job. I was much more confident in my future than ever before. As you can tell by now, friends, I'm not quite the pessimist I once was. A little bit of success can certainly work wonders for a person's point of view.

Before we could leave for Wheeling, I had to find a place to board Shawnee for the winter, since we couldn't take him with us. Zeddie couldn't keep him again, because he was planning on selling his dairy farm. But Zeddie said his brother, Tom, had a farm about twenty-six miles from Moncton, and he might be able to keep Shawnee, since he loved horses so much. This farm was located in the small town of Petitcodiac. I contacted Tom, who was glad to take care of my horse, and I paid him for his board and care. Tom fell in love with Shawnee, too. He had a special stall for him in a warm, comfortable barn, and I knew Shawnee would be well taken care of.

During the fall of 1945 I got a phone call from Mr. English at the dealership, informing me that he had just received two brand-new Buicks, and one was a big Buick Roadmaster. I was tickled to death to trade my 1941 Buick in on the 1946 Roadmaster. Of course I had to finance the car, but the payments each month were not too high. Since I was investing a lot of money in my Canadian show for the next year, I wanted to put on a real good front.

Nevertheless, I was getting a little uptight about going so far in debt. What if the tour with Slim and Hazel didn't work out? Suppose it rained all summer? Furthermore, I had no guarantee of a job back in Wheeling. I might have all expenses and no income. A few years earlier I would have been too scared to take on so much responsibility. At this time in my life, everything was a challenge to me. I had been in tight spots before, and I told myself this would all work out.

During December, 1945, Min, Jimmie, and I drove to Montreal to do the two-day studio session. I recorded some of the finest songs I'd ever written, such as "My Mother," a special tribute to my own mother. This song turned out to be a standard in country music. I also recorded "Just a Faded Petal from a Beautiful Bouquet" and "Brand on My Heart." These songs sold a lot of records. I was pleased with my efforts and the combination of musicians I was using. Bass, steel guitar, violin, and my guitar were excellent tracks and were complementary to my singing and guitar work.

This was the first time my family had been with me when I recorded, and Mr. Joseph let them sit in the small control room to watch and hear everything I did. As I recorded, Min was alert and listening for any mistakes that I might make that no one else would hear. After my songs were recorded, they made a disc of Jimmie singing a little kids' song, entitled "Playmates."

We finished the session on time. We went back to the hotel, got our things, and left that night, December 18, around nine o'clock, for Wheeling.

After crossing the border into the United States, I mentioned to Min that we should stop in Philadelphia and see Jack Howard and perhaps stay until after Christmas. We were always very concerned about having a good Christmas for our son, no matter where we were. When we arrived in Philadelphia, we rested up for about twenty-four hours, and I called Jack to come to the hotel. He went Christmas shopping with Min so she could pick up a few presents for Jimmie.

Jack was the most obliging person you'd ever meet. On Christmas Eve he and I drove out of town and down a side road until we saw a bunch of trees. Jack took the handsaw, climbed up a tree, and sawed the top off. It was a pretty fir tree. We took it to the hotel, trimmed it after midnight, and filled Jimmie's stocking. Along with his gifts, Jimmie had a great Christmas.

In a couple of days we left for West Virginia and again took a room at the Wheeling Hotel. The next day we went to see Big Slim, and I brought him up to date on everything I was putting together for our upcoming tour in 1946. Slim was well pleased.

I was disappointed when station WWVA couldn't use me again, but they said there might be an opening later on. However, Big Slim mentioned a station in Washington, Pennsylvania, twenty-six miles from Wheeling, where he had been on the radio at one time. He suggested I go see the manager, and maybe he could use me until something opened up at WWVA.

We heard that Toby Stroud, an artist on WWVA, had his twenty-eight-foot house trailer for sale for $1,500. We went to Toby's place, and Min and I fell in love with the beautiful trailer. It was in perfect shape. It had heat and everything one needed, from cooking arrangements to bedding, the whole works. I gave Toby a 50 percent down payment and promised him the balance as soon as I could arrange the financing.

In a couple of days we hitched up our new home on the back of the Buick and headed for Washington, Pennsylvania. We drove right through the little town, hoping to find a trailer park, but no luck. We did find a clean service station with a sign "Trailer Parking for Rent." The owner gave us permission to stay there, and he hooked up the water to our trailer for household activities. He said we could use the private restroom, which was entered from the outside of the station, and we'd have the only key. Also, there was an outside pay phone for night use when the station was closed, and we could use the station phone at no cost during the day. Electricity would be at our disposal, with an AC outlet on the outside of the station that we could hook up with our heavy-duty extension cord. We hooked up our extension cord and went to bed for a much needed rest.

18

Hollywood, Here I Am

Stolen moments are all we have together,
Two hearts that must find love on borrowed time;
Stolen moments, the seconds that we treasure,
Must this forbidden pleasure be a crime?

"Stolen Moments," by Joe Sherman
and Sid Wayne

IN THE AFTERNOON I WENT TO SEE Bob Clemente, manager of WJPA. "Hank, we've heard about your good work on WWVA," he said. "I'd be happy for you to join us. How about starting out with a guest shot on our show in the morning?"

I sang a couple of songs on the show, and I was impressed with the fine radio musicians. Pete Palcic played piano accordion and doubled on piano. Earl Langley played guitar and sang. Lew Wade played bass, sang a little, and did comedy. There were two girls on the show, Terri Frameli and Mary (I don't recall Mary's last name). They did pretty harmony together and sang a lot of the old as well as the new country songs.

When the program ended, Mr. Clemente offered me a job as the headliner for the entire winter. But I didn't want to commit myself for such a long period, because something might still open up at WWVA. The Wheeling station had 50,000 watts and WJPA had only 1,000 watts, so to get the most exposure in the States WWVA was my obvious choice.

Moreover, I'd be taking over the job of the young man who was the headliner on the regular program, and I told Mr. Clemente I didn't want to edge him out. But he assured me the young man was leaving voluntarily to take a job elsewhere. So I accepted the job to be the headliner on a short-term basis, with the understanding that I could leave at my discretion. I was also thinking that if the band turned out to fill the bill as backup musicians for me, I might ask them to join the Canadian tour with Slim, Hazel, and me.

I took over the radio band. The three boys, the two girls, and I had the 7:00 A.M. slot for a half hour every morning, Monday through Friday. We played instrumentals. I sang, and the girls sang together. I did commercials during the show and offered various products to the listeners. We got a lot of fan mail, and it was a good experience.

The band members encouraged me to set up personal appearances, within about a hundred-and-fifty-mile radius, and I booked several small theaters that would seat between three hundred and three hundred fifty people, in small coal-mining towns. We didn't get rich, but we were well received by the audiences.

The boys and the girls in the band were clean-cut and good people. They didn't drink or take drugs. So I asked if they would be interested in working with me during the next summer in eastern Canada. When I explained my show plans with Big Slim, Hazel, and our trained horses, they got excited and started talking about traveling arrangements. Lew and Pete already had nice house trailers. Earl planned to get a tent, since he enjoyed camping so much, and the girls said they would work out their transportation.

In the meantime, I drove back and forth to Wheeling every so often to meet with Slim to discuss our plans. I appreciated his suggestions. He had been in show business a long time, and it would have been foolish for me not to learn from his experiences.

After a little while I got itchy feet and I decided to make a drastic move. I would go to Hollywood! I had this wild dream of being a singing cowboy, like Gene Autry and Roy Rogers. Actually, I'd thought about this trip for a long time, but I'd planned to wait until the big tour with Slim and Hazel was finished. However, I had this driving need to make things happen, instead of waiting for things to happen. Min and I discussed it and she said okay, as soon as she knew I'd made up my mind to go anyway.

I had been corresponding with Allen Erwin. He was a Canadian who had spent a good deal of time in Hollywood, trying to make it in western pictures himself. He was a good-looking guy, a real cowboy and a good rider, and had done a lot of bit parts in westerns. Allen's professional name was the Calgary Kid, based on where he was born in western Canada. He was well known around movie sets, and he knew just about everyone in western pictures. So I had at least one contact in Hollywood.

One important thing I had to do before leaving. I would not, under any circumstances, leave Min and Jimmie alone, parked on the outskirts of the city, with no one around during the night. I asked the musicians if they knew of any trailer park close by. Earl said, "Hank, we have lots of room in our front yard where you can park it, and you can run an extension from our house to the trailer for electricity. Min and Jimmie can use our bathroom, and we have a telephone, so they can call you whenever they need to." Plus, Earl said he wouldn't think of taking any money.

I left for Hollywood in my new Buick, loaded down with big dreams. This was before freeways, and the highway had only two lanes. Driving day and night, just sitting and looking at miles and miles of pavement through the desert on rural highway 66 was very tiresome. I drove through Amarillo, in the northern part of Texas, through Albuquerque, New Mexico, and Needles, California. My car had no air conditioning, and when I hit the warm weather in California, it was uncomfortable.

In spite of the tiresome ride, I enjoyed the trip. I was seeing the West I had heard of and seen in western movies. I loved the western outdoor wildlife, the cactus, prairie, desert flowers, and tumbleweeds. To help break the monotony, I bought a fifth of wine to sip on, and it lasted me for hours. Usually I'd drive about five hundred miles each day, spend the night in a cheap motel, and start out real early the next morning.

Late one afternoon, driving through the northern part of Arizona, I saw Flagstaff Mountain. On a clear day you can see the mountain from a hundred miles away. I drove and drove, and it seemed like the mountain was getting farther away instead of closer. I was extremely tired and hungry, as I had been up early, so I wanted to stop, get something to eat, and have a good night's rest.

Finally, I got to the mountain and over the top. I came to a wide spot in the road called Hyde Park, Arizona, and stopped at a service station. I saw a sign: "Post Office, Groceries, and Cold Beer." There was a large motel and small cabins, and it was a bus stop. It was around dusk when I pulled up to one of the pumps, and a hefty young guy came out to the car. I found out later his name was Galyn Vandyke. He seemed like a happy-go-lucky person and was quite witty. As he was filling up my tank, he said he was the son-in-law of the couple who owned the place. I parked my car, and Galyn took me inside to meet his sweet wife, Helen, and the owners.

The owners were two of the nicest and most charming people I've ever met in my entire life. The gentleman was Dennis Arnett, and his wife was Jean. Dennis called her "the wart." They treated me like family and gave me a wonderful dinner. We talked for a long time, and they seemed genuinely interested in me. I told them all about my family, the entertainment world, my profession, and my dreams. I gave them a couple of my 78 rpm records, and they were excited for me and my potential. Dennis passed drinks around, and I got my guitar and sang for them until real late, even though I had planned to leave early the next morning.

Friends, would you believe this? I stayed for two solid weeks, and I had the time of my life. Galyn even took me antelope hunting one day, and we had a ball. I was having such a great time that I hated to leave such wonderful people, and I sensed they hated to see me go, too. Dennis and Jean insisted that anytime I was near Hyde Park, they would be deeply hurt if I didn't visit with them. As I pulled out they said, "Now, you promise to keep in touch, and if there's any way that we can help you, just let us know." Indeed, people like that are hard to find.

I had no earthly idea just how important these people were going to be to my career and to my family. Later on Dennis became our sponsor for our family to become American citizens. An immigrant has to have a sponsor who is financially stable and of good moral character, and he must assume all responsibility for the immigrants. It sure takes special friends to lay their faith on the line like they did for us, and I shall never forget it.

After leaving my new-found friends, I continued on my trip to Hollywood. I stopped at another wide spot in the road, Amboy, California, for gasoline, and I met another fine couple, Conn and Lillian Pulis, who were especially nice to me. It was a bus stop, post office, motel, and cabins, exactly like the Arnetts' place, with the exception of their restaurant.

Conn was a Greek gentleman. He and his wife invited me in and made me feel right at home. He was an excellent cook and fixed me a big juicy steak. After dinner Conn and I had several drinks, and as we sat around in the living room, I poured out my life's story to him and Lillian. They wanted me to stay with them a few days, and I enjoyed their hospitality for over a week. Would I ever get to Hollywood? Not if I kept meeting these kinds of people. I left them a couple of records and finally was on my way again.

When I arrived in Hollywood, I took a run-down room in a hotel on Western Avenue that rented by the week. I shared a bathroom down the hall with other tenants. But it was comfortable, and it had the necessities. I parked my car in the parking lot across the street for fifty cents a day, and I was ready for Hollywood.

The next day I called my friend Allen Erwin, the Calgary Kid. He wasn't in, so I left a message for him to call me. He called around 10:30 that night, and we arranged to meet in the lobby of my hotel the next morning at nine. He offered to show me around Hollywood and Los Angeles and help me in any way he could. Allen hoped he could stir up interest in getting me some parts in movies, and perhaps I could become a singing cowboy. If the movies didn't work out, he thought he could help me find a few singing jobs in nightclubs.

Becoming a singing cowboy in the movies sure fascinated me, but Allen warned me not to expect too much too soon. He mainly wanted to take me around so I could meet people who might be able to help me somewhere down the line.

First we went to Republic Picture Studios to meet a Mr. Scott, one of the officials there. Allen thought that since I was with RCA Victor in Canada, the gentleman might be able to get me some small parts in movies for a start. Mr. Scott said he could possibly help me, but I'd have to locate in Hollywood indefinitely.

Then Allen took me to meet a lady who was responsible for getting several cowboys and western actors to star in western pictures. I was told she was a lot of help to Jimmy Wakely, who did a lot of western pictures, as well as other cowboy stars. This lady took a look at me and said, "Well, you're not the tallest person to be inquiring about making western movies, but then, two of the all-time greats were just about your size. Both Bob Steele and Tom Mix were short. Hank, you'd make a good character actor in westerns, and I'll see what I can do for you. I'll get in touch with you if something comes up."

Allen also hired a professional photographer to make pictures of me with celebrities.

One night Allen and I drove out to Santa Monica to a huge ballroom that was built right on the shores of the Pacific Ocean. If I remember correctly, a small portion of it extended out over the ocean, and this ballroom was so big, it could dance eighteen thousand people—nine thousand couples! This was a choice spot, and the sunset each night as you looked out over the Pacific Ocean was the most beautiful you could ever imagine. Spade Cooley had the leading western swing band in the nation at that time, and he played for a dance there every Saturday night. He was an excellent violin player. He was charming and the people loved him.

Allen wanted to acquaint me with as many important people as possible. He introduced me to Spade that night, and Spade let me do a number before all those people and gave me a wonderful introduction. That was my first experience singing in front of such a great man and such a large audience. And I was nervous. I sang an old standard entitled "Molly Darling." Unfortunately, the band played it too slow for the way I was used to singing it, but it still went over quite well. Spade was a considerate fellow. He called me into his office during the intermission and said he'd help me in any way he could. He became a special friend, and I have an important story to tell about him later on.

Allen took me to another western nightclub called the Painted Post on Ventura Boulevard. In the entrance to this western nightclub Tex Cooper, a colorful old gentleman, acted as doorman and took tickets. Tex was eighty-five years old and at least six feet, six inches tall. He was very slim, with a white moustache and a long white beard that reached almost down to his waist. He wore a big black Stetson hat. He was dressed in black tails and wore a big gold watch chain across the front part of his vest. You talk about someone being well dressed in the western style, it was Tex. He had been in countless Westerns with big western stars like Tom Mix, Ken Maynard, and Buck Jones. Allen said Tex had married a dwarf. He was sure a fascinating gentleman.

"Happy" Perryman was a fine singer and the leader of a six- or seven-piece band at the nightclub. He was the brother of Lloyd Perryman, who was a member of the Sons of the Pioneers. Allen introduced me to Happy during the evening, and he invited me on stage to sing a couple of songs. He introduced me as an RCA Victor recording artist from Canada, and I was pleased with my reception.

While in Hollywood, we visited the Painted Post several times, and one night I met Jane Powell. She was trying to break into the movies, too. She was with her manager, who was taking her around to all the famous nightspots on a public-relations campaign. *Life* magazine was doing a story on her when I was there.

One day Allen drove me out to the country to meet Al Jennings, an old gentleman who was well over eighty years old. He told us one story after another, and I sure wish I'd had a week just to listen to him talk about his past. Some of you older folks might remember reading about the famous Al Jennings. He had worked with the Dalton brothers, robbing banks and holding up trains. He had also worked with the Ford brothers, and he told us he knew Jesse James well but never did work with him. Al said one of Jesse's good points was that he'd rob the rich and give the money to the poor. Al had met Ma Barker and her family. He also knew Clyde Barrow of Bonnie and Clyde fame.

At Republic Studios I met Randolph Scott, Lassis White, Roy Rogers, Gabby Hayes, and the Sons of the Pioneers, who at that time were Lloyd Perryman, Bob Nolan, Tim Spencer, Pat Brady, Ken Curtis, and the Farr brothers, Karl and Hugh. In later years Karl turned out to be a special friend of mine. I loved his playing on the acoustic Spanish guitar. My style of playing comes from listening to his records and his work with the Sons of the Pioneers. Ken Curtis, who played Festus in "Gunsmoke" for many years, was affiliated with the Sons of the Pioneers for a time.

I met Dick Foran and saw his home. He was an actor in the movies who played about the same type of characters as did Errol Flynn and Clark Gable. I met Rod Cameron at his home. I met Mason Wynn, who also was a movie actor in westerns but not well known. I bought a .38-40 Frontier pistol from Mason, which I keep among my memorabilia.

One day Allen took me out to the Will Rogers ranch to see the old horse named Soapsuds that Will always rode in all his movies. Soapsuds was about thirty-two years old at that time, but he still had lots of life in him. I was introduced to Foy Willing and the Riders of the Purple Sage. I also met Sunset Carson, who was real popular. He showed me his horse van, and I took mental notes. It was partitioned with an office in the front, and that's what I had in mind for the van I was having built.

A great songwriter I met was Ernie Brewer. He wrote a smash hit years ago entitled "Does the Spearmint Lose Its Flavor on the Bedpost Overnight." Later on I recorded one of his songs in Canada entitled "I Knew We'd Meet Again Someday," and later in Nashville I recorded his composition "Chattin' with a Chick in Chattanooga."

Other folks I met in Hollywood included Carolina Cotton, Ray Whitley, Lon Chaney, Jr., Lucky Hayden, Kermit Maynard (brother to Ken Maynard), Cottonseed Clark (a popular disc jockey), Jimmy Wakely, Gene Autry, and Smiley Burnette.

Allen asked me who made my stage suits, and I said Globe Tailors in Philadelphia. He replied, "Globe is a good tailor, but out here Nathan Turke does all the western wardrobes for people in country music and for most of the actors in movie studios. He's located on Ventura Boulevard." I went to see Mr. Turke, who took my measurements, and I ordered two suits from him. Since he had my measurements, anytime I needed a new suit he could send me samples of fabrics, and he'd make the suits from the fabrics I'd chosen and forward them to me.

Allen also took me to see Edward H. Bohlin. Mr. Bohlin was well known for original designing and making silver-mounted saddles. He was the originator of silver saddles for the cowboys as far back as Tom Mix, Ken Maynard, Hoot Gibson, Roy Rogers, and Gene Autry.

Allen knew about Shawnee and suggested I have Mr. Bohlin make a saddle for him. But I had no job yet and no assurances of movie work, and I was already spending thousands of dollars on equipment being made for the upcoming tour. So I said no at first, but when I saw Mr. Bohlin's work, I couldn't resist it. I ordered a saddle, silver spurs, and a silver-studded gun belt for my .38-40 Frontier pistol that I'd bought from Mason Wynn. I made a small down payment and arranged to pay so much each month. It was a great thrill knowing I had ordered these beautiful things to go with Shawnee and my new wardrobe. I was confident the Good Lord would take care of me.

After my stay in Hollywood it was time to head back to Washington, Pennsylvania, as I was anxious to see Min and Jimmie again. Nothing big happened to me, but I met a lot of people who would become good friends and some who would help me in the future. In addition to Allen Erwin, several people gave me a lot of encouragement.

Before I left, Allen said, "Hank, this has been your first trip out here, and remember, you need to come back and spend several months if you can see your way clear to do that. I'm sure you can make headway in pictures and in the music business, but it will take time." I thanked Allen for his tremendous help during the weeks I was in California, and I assured him I would be back.

I was so excited to tell Min and Jimmie all about my trip, I drove two thousand miles and never once stopped in a motel. But I did pull over to the side of the road and slept a little in the car and occasionally stopped for a bite to eat. I stopped briefly in Amboy, California, to visit with Conn and Lillian Pulis, and I made a brief stop to see Dennis and Jean Arnett again and to rest for a short time. They wanted me to spend the night, but I was just too excited about so many things. I remember Dennis saying it looked like my eyes would pop out of my head, and it wasn't safe to drive when I was so tired.

It was silly to push myself, and I knew it was dangerous to drive if I wasn't fully alert. But we all do dumb things sometimes. Anyway, I got home safe and sound, thanks to the Good Lord.

Around the first of March in 1946 we hooked up our trailer and my family and animals took off for Canada. I was anxious to see how all my equipment was coming along. The weather was quite chilly going through Pennsylvania, New Jersey, and New York, and when we got to the border at Calais, Maine, around nine o'clock that night, the weather was terrible. From the beautiful California sunshine, here I was in the middle of a severe snowstorm.

There was not even one track broken from Saint Stephen to Saint John, about seventy miles. With our big trailer in tow, I was nervous. From Saint John to Moncton, about ninety miles, there were a few tracks. Actually, the whole drive was dangerous, since it was hard to tell where the shoulder of the road was. The snowplows were out when we got close to Moncton, but when we arrived downtown, the snow had all the driveways blocked, and we had to park our trailer right in the middle of the street.

The place looked like a ghost town. Not a soul was stirring anywhere. It was way after midnight and we had the street to ourselves, and I was happy to park. The three of us managed to get out of the car, wade through the snow, and get into our trailer. We slept the rest of the night until the snowplow started about seven o'clock the next morning. Then I had to get up to move the trailer off the street. The weather started to clear. The snow began melting, and it was a slushy mess. The driving was still very hazardous.

Luckily, Mr. Lynds at CKCW gave me permission to park our trailer in a big field beside the station's transmitter on the outskirts of town, and the crew there made us feel right at home. They helped me run a long extension cable to an outlet on the outside of the building, so we would have electricity.

We were settled in, and I went to Mr. Colpit's place every day to keep an eye on the work and to make sure everything was progressing on schedule. I discussed a few ideas about the van that I learned from Sunset Carson in Hollywood, and Mr. Colpit made sure the changes were made.

In April I was notified that my power plant was in, and I had it installed in the trunk of my car. With overload springs, which I had put in my Buick, it would be no problem pulling my trailer with the extra weight.

The big truck to pull the flatbed was already at Mr. English's dealership in Moncton, but the flatbed trailer was being built in Oshawa, Ontario. I sent the guy I'd hired to drive the semi–tractor-trailer rig to pick it up at Oshawa and to drive it to Moncton. He was back in time to have the folks at Mr. Colpit's go over it and add some things to make it easier to load and unload the equipment.

I was busy doing many important tasks. I got our posters ready to put up in the towns where we were scheduled to play. I wanted our advertising to precede our show dates by at least three weeks. On our posters I had pictures of Big Slim and Hazel, as well as the rest of the band members. I had souvenir programs printed with pictures of our show people, the lyrics to several of the songs I had written, some of the songs that Big Slim had written, and a list of several of my recordings. In addition I prepared the radio advertisements.

I sent the road manager ahead of our show dates to make sure we'd have a solid foundation to erect our grandstand. This was his top priority. Our grandstand would be built and tested by authorities for safety, according to the safety rules for its capacity load. But any grandstand, regardless of how strong and sturdy it might be, is dangerous if it's put up on soft, muddy, or swampy ground.

Not long before our first show was scheduled, I hired Art Rhyno, a friend of mine who I mentioned earlier. He was handicapped from being stricken with polio at an early age, and he had to walk with crutches, but he did a fine job on the steel guitar. Terri and Mary, the girl singers, had arrived early and were at the motel resting. They had come from the little town of Bentleyville, Pennsylvania. Pete, Earl, and Lew arrived in their house trailer, and with Art, we had all of our band members together.

Just before the big tour, my saddle, spurs, and gun belt arrived in Moncton. I was away when Min received a call from the customs office saying they had arrived. The officials generally opened packages for inspection, and she was told that everybody around the office was admiring the silver saddle. I could hardly wait to see it.

When I first saw it, I was in seventh heaven. I put it on Shawnee, and he was as striking as any horse I'd ever seen. His chestnut-brown and glistening snow-white colors sparkled with his silver saddle. Nothing, but nothing, could be more beautiful!

A few days later Big Slim and Hazel telephoned from Calais, which was about three and a half hours' drive to Moncton. When I met them at a designated place, they parked their car and the van driver parked the van. After a brief visit I led them to their motel, where I'd already made reservations for them. I knew they were tired from the long trip, and I knew the van driver was exhausted after driving the big van with two horses, two mules, and a coach dog. After they got settled, I helped take care of the animals.

The next day Big Slim and I sat down together and figured out the best way to line up the show—who would do what and when. We wanted to keep the complete program to a maximum of two and a half hours, and this could become a problem unless the acts were well coordinated. Then we got everyone together and worked out the complete show routine. After the first run-through, I knew we had an unusual show with a lot of variety, and I was sure the public would enjoy it.

Everything was in place. It had taken nearly a year to get prepared and ready for the big tour. I was deeply in debt. Would the tour be successful? Would people come to see this kind of show? We would soon find out.

19

Canadian Road Show

The next voice you hear will be your conscience
As you lie awake and try so hard to sleep,
And your unfaithful heart will have to listen
To those shabby little secrets that you keep.

"The Next Voice You Hear,"
by Cindy Walker

I HAD PURPOSELY SCHEDULED OUR first show in a ballpark in the city of Moncton, which was our home base. The park bleachers would be used for the audience, and we wouldn't have to transport the grandstand. I had been somewhat afraid the semitrailer wouldn't be ready in time, so having the permanent bleachers was a plus for us. As it turned out, the semi was ready on time, and everything else was completed a few days before the Moncton show, which was scheduled in the middle of May.

My concern then turned to the matter of having a good show. Would everything go off as scheduled? Planning the routines on paper was not the same as doing a brand-new show in person in which livestock would be used. Being a natural worrier, I was uptight about surprises waiting "around the corner." I didn't need to worry. The first show was an absolute financial and artistic success! Everything worked as smooth as silk, and the capacity crowd seemed genuinely overjoyed.

It would have been nice if we could have always played in ballparks and I wouldn't have had to buy a portable grandstand, but ballparks were rarely available, especially during the summertime. So for most of the tour we had to go through the entire routine of erecting and breaking down all of the equipment. The three band members and Big Slim assembled and disassembled the huge sidewall, the grandstand, the portable stage, and the canvas covering that went over the stage.

We all often pitched in to set up the two big backdrops that I had especially painted for the stage background. Usually we'd roll into the town in the afternoon, and after getting the equipment set up, we'd rest so we would be ready for an energetic show by curtain time.

I'll describe our usual show routines. To open the program, the band would sing and play for about fifteen minutes. I'd be seated on Shawnee and on standby just outside the entrance to the tent, waiting for Earl, one of the band members, to introduce us.

Sitting in my silver saddle, I thought I looked like a real cowboy. I wore my silver spurs and gun belt made by Mr. Bohlin. For my gun belt, I had my .38-40 Frontier pistol I'd bought from Mr. Wynn. I wore my embroidered quilted shirt and my riding britches, both made by Mr. Turke. Wide elastic bands across the bottoms of my feet held my britches in place on the inside of my boots.

When we were introduced, Shawnee would spring into a fast gallop and stop in front of the grandstand. I'd rear him up on his hind legs, and when he came down, I'd dismount. I'd have him kneel on one knee with his head bowed, and I'd take off my white Stetson hat and wave to the crowd. My horse groom would then lead Shawnee out of sight, and I'd rush onstage to sing and play with the band for about a half hour.

I sang a few current hits and several of my original songs, in particular the western ones, and I used a backdrop of an appropriate western setting that covered the entire back of the stage. With our colored spotlight it provided an appealing atmosphere for my songs and my trick riding. Little Jimmie took a great part in our show, too. I had him dressed in a little outfit to match mine, along with a cowboy hat and a pair of cowboy boots, and he upstaged everybody when he sang two or three songs.

In the meantime, my horse groom would remove the silver saddle, breast strap, and bridle from Shawnee and wait for the cue to saddle him again, this time changing to my trick-riding saddle.

After I finished my music segment, I'd introduce Terri and Mary to the audience. The girls would sing for about fifteen minutes, and when they did their Hawaiian songs, we switched to another backdrop that had a pretty moonlight Hawaiian scene painted on it, with palm trees and the moon shining across the water. The girls dressed in black skirts and white blouses, with colored Hawaiian leis around their necks and a big white rose in their hair, plus a wide red sash around their waists. Their harmony was excellent, and they sang such songs as "Down Where the Tradewinds Blow" and "Beyond the Reef." It was a fine act, and it made for good variety on the program.

By the time they finished their part of the show, Shawnee and I were ready for the trick-riding routines and his funny tricks. For my trick riding I performed the single and double vault and the tail crouper. Those were certainly crowd pleasers. After performing these somewhat dangerous acts, I'd have Shawnee maintain a steady trot, while I stood up on his rump and waved my hat to the audience.

After the trick riding, Shawnee did the comedy routines on cue. First I'd show the audience how a lazy cowboy got off his horse. Shawnee would immediately lie down on his side until I got off, and then he'd get up again. Next I'd have him show what he'd do if someone came up behind him to interfere with our show. He'd kick his hind heels high in the air. And pity anyone standing behind him! Then I'd have a Coca-Cola bottle filled with water and pretend I was intoxicated. I'd stagger a bit, and he'd get behind me with his nose against my back. Each time I'd try to take a drink from the Coke bottle, he'd butt me in the back with his head and shove me a little bit further, and I'd spill the water from the bottle all over me. Sometimes Shawnee would get careless and bite at my back, and it would hurt a little.

Then he did what was called the camel crawl. He did this on straw that was spread over a square on the ground, about twenty feet by twenty feet, so he wouldn't hurt his knees. He'd get down on his front knees and crawl along, sort of like a camel. He also did a trick in which he'd untie a handkerchief off of his forward ankle, reach to the back, and while balancing himself, untie a hankie from his rear ankle.

Next he did an act that was always good for a lot of applause. I'd put a small lasso in his mouth. The loop was about five or six feet in circumference, with a swivel on the end, so when he'd swing his head to start the lasso spinning, it wouldn't tangle up. On top of the swivel, about two inches down from the top, I tied a lump of sugar, which he loved, in a clean white cloth. This was his cue to start twirling the lasso. While he was spinning his rope, I'd climb on his back, and while standing, I'd swing a sixty-foot loop that circled around his whole body. After I had a good rhythm on the loop, one of the girls, carrying a guitar, was helped up on Shawnee, and she stood beside me. While I twirled the loop, she strummed the guitar as I made the chords, and she sang and yodeled the song "I Want to Be a Cowboy's Sweetheart." In the meantime, Shawnee was spinning his little rope. Doing all of this together was difficult, but it was a real crowd pleaser.

Then Shawnee and I did a balancing act. I'd take him by his two front hoofs. This would be his cue to rear up in the air, and when he did, I'd keep one hand under each hoof and balance him in the air.

This looked like I was lifting the horse, but he was holding his entire weight. The audience loved this one, too.

A funny thing about Shawnee—the more applause he got, the better he'd work for me! If the applause was light, he'd be stubborn, and I really had to raise my voice to him to make him work harder. It seemed like he could understand what the applause meant.

Again on cue, Shawnee would put his nose to my ear as if he was whispering to me, and I'd look at him and say, "Can't you wait until after the show?" This always got a laugh. After that I'd give him arithmetic problems, and he'd count and subtract by pawing his front hoof.

During the shows at night the big colored spotlight would shine a pale blue color, representing the moonlight, on Shawnee and me. Under the spotlight, and with the moonlight color on us, we would lie down in the straw. I'd crawl up between his front legs and toss a blanket over both of us. However, I'd leave Shawnee's part of the blanket covering only part of him. Then he'd reach back, take the blanket in his mouth, and pull it all the way up over both of us again.

Sometimes I'd have him lie on his side while I sat on his side and played my guitar and sang to him, as if I were singing him to sleep. Believe it or not, he would squint those big brown eyes and then squeeze them tight shut as if he were sound asleep. Then I'd say, "Come on, Shawnee, time to get up." And up he'd come. While doing the latter two acts, my boys would be off in the darkness, singing softly the old western song "Roll On, Little Dogies, Roll On." It was really a striking act.

Here was another popular one. I used a small table that my horse groom would bring to the middle of the show area, and I'd put a coffeepot and two cups on the table. I'd bring Shawnee to a sitting position on one side of the table, and I'd sit on the other side, and we'd pretend we were having coffee together.

Then Shawnee and I would do our finale. I had drilled a hole in each end of a stick that was about the size of a chair rung and about two feet long. I mounted a small American flag on one end and a Canadian flag on the other. I'd have Shawnee kneel, holding the flag stick in his mouth. I'd be standing beside him, and I'd bow, holding my Stetson in the air. We usually received a standing ovation on our closing.

When we concluded this segment, Lew Wade was introduced and did his comedy act. He dressed up in comedy attire and an old hat and had his face all speckled up with a black pencil. He blackened his two front teeth, which made him look like he had two teeth out. He'd do tricks with one of Slim's mules for about eight minutes, and it tore the house down. Lew rode the mule frontwards, backwards, and sideways and bounced all over it. Even though he had never worked with animals before, he was a daredevil. He'd do anything for a laugh.

When Lew first began to practice his comedy routine, Big Slim warned him to be very careful. If he were to fall off, he should get away from the mule in a hurry, because the mule might accidentally step on him. One night Lew did get too careless. He fell off the mule and the mule stepped on his chest. We rushed him to the doctor, and he suffered quite a bit of pain and distress for a while. He never did the routine again. We all felt the act wasn't worth the health risk to continue it.

Before introducing our main act, we'd take about a fifteen-minute intermission, during which we'd use the same old carnival approach of selling pictures and books.

For the main act I'd give a big buildup and announce, "Direct from the big WWVA Wheeling Jamboree, from Wheeling, West Virginia, here is Big Slim, the Lone Cowboy." Then Slim would ride in on that beautiful black-and-white horse, Golden Flash. He would rear his horse up in front of the audience. Then he'd introduce Hazel as she rode her horse into the center of the show area.

They both would dismount, and Slim would do his whip act with Hazel. Hazel put a cigarette in her mouth, and Slim took his long black whip and snapped it several times until he cut off all the cigarette except the part between her lips. You could hear the "oohs" and "oh mys" from the audience as they observed this dangerous routine. Next Hazel would stand about eighteen feet from him, and Slim would crack that big long whip, and the lash would wrap around and around her waist. You'd think he was going to cut her in two.

Following the whip acts, Slim and Hazel performed their trick riding. Slim was an expert rider on Golden Flash, but to show you how unselfish he was, he didn't do the same tricks that I did with Shawnee in the show. He insisted that we not duplicate the tricks. He let me do mine, and he did those that I didn't do. Slim and Hazel did outstanding stunts on both horses, and this is when Hazel would do the death drag.

After Hazel had performed and Slim had done his trick-riding stunts, the band would play a few medleys, while Slim prepared to go onstage. Big Slim would sing his songs in the final segment of the show. For the finale little Jimmie would stand up on a chair and join me in singing the last song.

Usually the shows ran between two and a quarter and two and a half hours. It was a clean variety and family show, which appealed to the adults and to the children. I'd love to take such a show on the road again. Road shows these days are all pretty much alike. You'll hear everything the artist has recorded, or as many songs as he or she has time to sing. There's no variety, except every once in a while an instrumental will be featured, such as a Spanish guitar or a steel guitar.

Our show even looked good traveling down the highway. We used a convoy pattern. Big Slim and Hazel would lead with their car, followed by Slim's horse van and my horse van. Then came the three cars pulling our house trailers, plus two or three other cars. The big tractor trailer with the load of show equipment followed. Besides looking like a really big show, it was good advertising.

Sometimes Big Slim, Hazel, and I would lead a parade with our three spotted horses, if the area was celebrating an event. I'd have Shawnee do side passing, like I did sometimes in our show. This means he'd walk sideways to keep people from stepping off the curb and getting in the way of the parade vehicles and other horses. He'd strut proudly when leading a parade, especially when the band was playing. With our colorful outfits and with Hazel's golden hair flying in the breeze, we looked high class in any parade.

My custom-made van was painted cream with medium blue, with lettering on the sides. Shawnee's stall was in the rear of the van, and I had my office in the front. A partition between the two had a twelve-by-twelve-inch shutter that slid open so I could check on Shawnee and give him a treat. And just about every day he would slide the shutter open with his nose and stick his nose in for a piece of sugar, candy, or whatever I had. I kept my silver-mounted saddle in the office on a saddle stand that Mr. Colpit had made for it. I had a three-quarter-size bunk bed built over the cab as sleeping quarters. The van had knotty pine paneling throughout, and even Shawnee's part was varnished to a high luster.

Shawnee's stall was built with two sides that could be lifted out so he could lie down in the thick straw anytime he wanted to. The sides of the stall were used just for driving, so he wouldn't rock back and forth in the van. I had the van built with windows on the sides and in the back, so as to give him proper ventilation and to keep him cool when we were driving in hot weather. When it was warm, I'd let Shawnee sleep outside at night and graze on the fresh green grass, and he loved it. When the weather was bad, I'd keep him inside and make sure he had lots of clean straw in his stall.

I had two galvanized feed bins made to fit in the two corners of Shawnee's section, one in the left front corner and one in the right front corner. These were kept full of the best oats and bran. I gave Shawnee a tablespoon or two of molasses in his oats or bran every time I fed him. This made his coat glisten like silver with a real pretty gloss.

We needed straw for Shawnee's stall and hay for him to eat, in addition to his bran and oats. If there was a feed store in town, we'd buy a bale of each to take with us. On the road we'd stop along the highway at some farmer's home and buy a bale of straw and hay, or bags of each, whatever was available.

We either backed Shawnee out of his stall to drink or we took his water bucket to him. Rest assured, he got the very best of care. I even had a special kind of leather shoe made for him, with rubber soles that slipped on over his hoofs and buckled around his ankles with straps. We used these whenever Shawnee walked on the pavement or in a parade. The pavement is very hard on a horse's feet, so he was well protected.

Min shampooed Shawnee with the same shampoo that people use. Not only did he look beautiful with his snow-white coat, mixed with chestnut brown, he smelled so good from the shampoo. Min loved shampooing Shawnee, and he loved it, too. He was just a big baby. I hired a horse groom to curry and brush Shawnee and to keep him spotless at all times. The groom was careful to feed him at the same time every day. The gentleman also kept the van spotless and used disinfectant on it daily.

Friends, you're no doubt wondering how we could stay in the front of the van with Shawnee in the back. Wasn't there an odor? My builders thought of everything. They had that van so insulated that you could not smell the slightest odor even during the hottest days of summer.

One day Min had our house trailer door open while she was sweeping, and Shawnee put his two front hoofs right in the door of the trailer, looking for a treat. Min happened to have a piece of bread, already spread with butter, and she laid it on the floor for him. But Shawnee didn't like butter. He turned the slice of bread over with his nose and slid the slice of bread back and forth over the floor of the trailer until the butter was wiped off the bread, and then he ate it. To me, Shawnee was almost human.

Sometimes we would drive through the streets and advertise the show, but we had to pay for a city license (usually five dollars) to do that. I had my own power plant, which produced 110 volts, and I had a public-address system rigged up on the van. There was a large speaker installed in the middle of the van, in front just below the top. On each corner in the back, just below the top, a small one was installed. In my office section I had a turntable to play records and a microphone to make my announcements as we drove through the streets. I advertised our shows to start at 8:00 P.M. sharp.

In getting all my equipment built for the tour, I had made one big mistake. If I had it to do over again, instead of buying the six-foot sidewall with no top, I would have splurged a little more and bought a regular show tent. Of course this would have cost a whole lot more money, but as the old saying goes, "If you're going to be a bear, be a grizzly," and that's what I wanted to be. The tent would have been easier to put up and take down, and we wouldn't have had to worry about rainy nights. There was no way people were going to turn out to see a show if the weather was rainy, windy, or cold.

Unfortunately, in the Maritime Provinces during the summer of 1946 we had a lot of rain and cold, dismal fog. Sometimes the fog would blow in from the Atlantic Ocean over the mainland, and our audience would be small. But for the first three or four weeks of the tour the weather stayed good, and we had fine crowds. I checked to see what rain insurance would cost for the show, but it was very expensive, so I forgot about that.

I could accept the rainy days that we were certain to get, but I was not prepared for the serious problem I was about to face.

One day Big Slim decided he had to go back to Wheeling. I didn't know whether he didn't like Canada or what was wrong, and he didn't give me a good reason. Along with Slim, Hazel would go. And to make matters worse, Mary, one of the girl singers, and her boyfriend decided they wanted to leave, too. This was a terrible blow. After planning for over a year and going into debt up to my neck, my show, along with my dreams, was crippled.

Big Slim, my main drawing card, would be gone. I had five thousand songbooks printed for the tour, including pictures and information on Slim and Hazel, the trick horses, the mules, and many of Slim's songs. Plus, I had placed newspaper ads and radio spots to advertise the coming shows, as well as the material our road manager had for advance advertising.

It did leave us in one hell of a mess. When I asked Slim for a reason, he just said, "Well, I have some very serious matters that were completely unexpected, and I'll have to go home for a few weeks. Rather than come all the way back, let's just call it quits right now. Hank, I hate to do this to you, but I have to leave tonight right after the show. I surely hope it doesn't upset our friendship."

The show that night didn't have much spark, I can assure you. Everybody seemed down, and I couldn't shake off my depression. After the show we all said good-bye, and Slim, Hazel, and Mary headed back to the States.

I found out later, when I returned to the United States, what the problem was. Big Slim was in love with a woman in Wheeling who was a part of the WWVA Jamboree. I knew he had worried a lot about getting mail in several towns, and he did an awful lot of long-distance calling, but that's all I knew.

Lew, Pete, and Earl all expressed how bad they felt about the situation. They wanted to regroup and continue on. They were fine people, and I was grateful for their support. But still I wasn't sure what to do. We had to make a choice—either throw my plans through the window and quit, or reorganize the show with new advertising, new souvenir programs, the whole ball of yarn. I was definitely not a quitter. The old saying stands, "The show must go on."

This became one of the biggest challenges of my life. I could come out of this smelling like a rose, or I could die the death of a rat. I chose the rose.

The show did go on. The boys were fine musicians, and the girl was a pretty fair singer and sang harmony with me. I called radio stations and changed the information on our radio spots. We had all new posters made and a thousand new souvenir programs printed. The new programs included pictures of Earl Langley, Pete Palcic, Lew Wade, Art Rhyno, Terri Frameli, little Jimmie, and Shawnee doing some of his tricks. We included pictures of the horse van and tractor trailer, plus the words to many of my recorded songs. It made an attractive book, and we sold them all during the rest of the tour.

We were on our way again. New show, new everything. Believe it or not, hardly anyone during the rest of the trip asked what happened to Big Slim and Hazel. We had won the last round. My show went over extremely well, thanks to my band and everyone else involved, but mainly to the folks in Canada.

My son, Jimmie, added a lot to the show, too. He had been a part of show business from the time he was only five years old. His vacation from school coincided with my summer tours, so I let him perform on stage. He always went over great, and he really knew how to talk to an audience. The people got a kick out of seeing him climb up on the little box we had for him so he could reach the microphone.

Of course, in show business everyone has ups and downs, that's just part of it. You have the good and you have the bad, and in spite of our successful shows, we had some bad experiences.

We were playing in a little mining town in Cape Breton called New

Waterford. Earl laid his fiddle on the back of the stage while he shifted to his guitar, and someone stole his fiddle. A couple of weeks later the police in New Waterford found it, and Earl was overjoyed, as this fiddle was special to him.

That same night Min was selling tickets in our portable booth, and we were a little late in getting started due to a problem with our AC generator. Four or five boys picked up the ticket booth with Min inside, carried it about fifteen feet, and set it down again. Good thing it had a floor in it, or they would have been dragging her and probably causing her severe harm. Some of the crowd, including a policeman who happened to be at the show, ran to her rescue. The boys were drinking beer and having a good time and said they didn't mean any harm. They said they knew the booth had a floor in it and were being very careful. Min was shaken up a bit but not hurt, and we went on with the show.

One of the towns I was most looking forward to playing was Liverpool, since I was born in Brooklyn, just two miles from there. Mother, my three sisters, and several close friends and relatives lived in Liverpool, and I wanted everything to come off without a hitch. When the day rolled around, I was real excited. I wanted to show Mother just how far I'd come as an entertainer since I'd first played her mail-order guitar. I knew she was proud of me, and I fully intended to put on the best show we had ever played.

We pulled into the show area that afternoon, and it was a beautiful day. The boys started to set up the canvas sidewall, grandstand, stage, and other equipment, when one of them came to me and said that the spot where they were going to put up the grandstand was slightly sloped. However, they thought it would be okay, and they went ahead and erected the grandstand.

The program was supposed to begin at 8:00 P.M. Around six o'clock we were getting dressed for the show, when there was a knock on the door. Someone had come to tell us about a tiny bird lying outside in the show area. It was hurt. Possibly its wing had been broken. That's all I needed to hear. Though I'm not superstitious, I've always heard, and I can remember my mother saying this time and time again, "It's very bad luck if a bird should fly in your house." It didn't fly in, but I went outside and got the little bird and brought it inside. I carefully placed it in a cardboard box with cotton in the bottom, and I was hoping to nurse it back to health again, but unfortunately the little bird died. This upset me and put me in a very sad mood.

I looked out the window about 7:00 P.M., and droves of people were headed to the grandstand. I'd never seen so many people coming at one time to a show. Then roughly twenty-five minutes later, my sister Nina knocked on my trailer door. She was shaking all over and could hardly talk. She said there had been a bad accident. The grandstand had been jam-packed and had fallen down with all those people on it. Immediately I realized it had been a mistake to have loaded the grandstand to capacity, knowing there was a slight slant on the ground where it was erected. I ran out there as quickly as I could. People were yelling and screaming. The grandstand had fallen, pinning people's arms and legs under the seats. In a short time I heard the sirens from police cars and ambulances coming. I didn't know how many had been hurt, and I was really worried.

Zeddie Rogers, our advance man, had always made it a top priority to insure that the ground for the grandstand was perfectly level. This spot was so little on the downside, it was hard to detect the slight angle. When we examined the ground more carefully, we discovered the ground was a bit swampy just below the surface. That was the main reason for the collapse. The slant to the ground was very slight, but the weight of the capacity crowd had made the difference. The equipment was usually inspected at the locations and was always found to be safe.

Being concerned about safety, I did carry insurance to cover the public as well as my employees in such situations. I've made that a priority throughout my career. After things had settled down, I noticed that people were still crowded around. It seemed like nobody had left, and several people asked us to go on with the show. Mother, my sisters, and several relatives came to the trailer to tell me the same thing, but I told them I didn't think, after that scare, that I was in the mood to sing, especially the sad songs. At this time, one of the local policemen came to me and said, "Mr. Snow, I just wanted you to know that no one was seriously hurt. Scared and shook up, yes, but nothing serious. People want you to go on with the show, and as far as we're concerned, you have our permission to do so."

To make matters worse, a heavy fog moved over the city from the Atlantic Ocean, and a cold, light rain came. But surprisingly the crowd stayed. The people had to sit on the ground or stand up, but they loved the show, and we put on one of our best programs ever.

I was proud that it was such a good show for Mother and my sisters to see, but I was quite embarrassed that the grandstand collapsed, especially since *Billboard* magazine and other trade papers carried the story. After that incident I became more superstitious because of the little bird. I expected more bad luck, and sure enough, it came.

A few days after the grandstand collapsed, the driver of my big semi-tractor trailer backed into a water hydrant in Yarmouth and broke it all to pieces. It was like a flood running over the street. Luckily, the fire department came right away and shut the water off. But I had to go down to the courthouse and pay the bill for the damages, and that accident cost me an arm and a leg.

Not too long after that, we were on our way to another show, and I stopped my horse van to let Mickey, our little terrier, go to the bathroom. I took his leash off because I never expected him to run out in the highway. But just as a big semitruck topped the hill, Mickey started to cross the highway and ran right underneath the semitrailer. I said to Min as we watched, "This is the end of Mickey, I'm sure."

I saw him underneath the big semi, bouncing around every which way, but the big wheels never did touch him. When the semi passed, Mickey was just sitting there, like he had no control of his back end. He was in a daze. I thought his back was broken, so I gently picked him up and took him to a veterinarian not far away. I carried him into the office, and the vet immediately put him upon the table to examine him. But as soon as the vet turned around to get something from a shelf, Mickey jumped down on the floor and started exploring everything in the office! We were shocked to realize that he had come through without a scratch. The vet assured us there was nothing wrong with our dog. We thanked him and went on our way.

In spite of the hard luck, we had a pretty good summer in 1946. We had appreciative and enthusiastic crowds just about everywhere we played. Since we were having such good crowds, we added a few more weeks to our tour. Our last scheduled show was played in New Brunswick. Thereafter the band broke up. Art left for his home in Dartmouth, Nova Scotia. Pete, Earl, Lew, and Terri left to go back to the United States. The drivers drove my van and the big semi-tractor trailer back to Moncton, and Min, Jimmie, and I followed in my car. We parked my horse van and our house trailer by the CKCW tower transmitter.

We stayed around the area long enough for me to take care of a lot of business. Bills had to be paid, my big semitruck had to be winterized, and all the show equipment had to be stored in a huge warehouse. Plans had to be made for someone to occasionally check on all of it to see that it was being well taken care of. I had a pile of money tied up in this equipment, and I wanted to be sure that everything was in good shape for the summer of 1947, as again I had big plans in mind.

I was fortunate that Tom Rogers agreed to keep Shawnee for me. This was a great relief, as Tom and Mrs. Rogers had fallen in love with Shawnee, and I knew he would receive the best of care. I was also fortunate to find a good home for Pal, our German shepherd dog, until we would return to Canada the following spring. Pal sure deserved a good home. He had been so faithful on the road, helping to guard the outside of our show arena.

In a few weeks we began to plan our trip back to Washington, Pennsylvania.

20

On the Road Again

Every day I listen to the surgin' tide,
And I always wonder why the sea's so wide;
Miles of salty water, endless skies above
Stretch out far between me and the one I love.

"Rocking, Rolling Ocean,"
by Ted Daffan and Theda Roush

WHEN WE ARRIVED BACK IN WASHINGTON, we parked our trailer at the Earl Langley home again. My plans were to leave Min and Jimmie there, and I'd go visit Jack Howard in Philadelphia. I wanted to see if he could help me line up a good western band for the summer of 1947. The band from the 1946 tour didn't want to tackle Canada again. The work was hard, putting up the equipment, performing in the show, then taking the equipment down.

I drove to Philadelphia and took a hotel room and stayed for a couple of weeks. Exciting things for me happened through Jack, like they had happened through Allen Erwin in Hollywood. Jack had a lot of valuable contacts in the area. Since I had always been a great fan of the famous Mills Brothers, he took me to meet them when they were appearing at the Earl Theater. It was an honor to have my picture taken with them.

One night Jack took me to meet Jesse Rodgers at his home. His father and Jimmie Rodgers's father were brothers. That's one reason I wanted to meet Jesse, plus I liked his singing. I used to listen to him over the Mexican radio stations, and he also did some recording for RCA Victor. We had a long conversation about his career, his dad, his days in Old Mexico, and of course Jimmie Rodgers. Jesse had his own radio program over station WFIL in Philadelphia, and his beautiful wife, Sally, had a popular daily kids' show on the same station. They were down-to-earth people, and I liked them both. Before I left the city, Jesse had me as a guest on his radio program, and I sang a song or two. I also remember buying a beautiful embroidered shirt from Jesse that was too small for him.

Next Jack took me back to Globe, the western tailor, and I ordered some more stylish clothes.

Jack's word was as good as gold when he said he'd help me any way he could. He put me in contact with one of the finest western trios I'd ever heard, which he thought I might want to hire for my next summer tour in Canada. I won't mention their names, because the story is not going to turn out so well in their favor. I had a long conversation with them individually, and they were enthusiastic about signing on for the 1947 road show. In a couple of days we had contracts drawn up by a lawyer, and I was looking forward to working with them.

I left Philadelphia pleased and drove back to Washington. I didn't do much the rest of that winter except chum around with Earl, Lew, and Pete, and play a few shows with them around the area. During that winter, though, I worked out my plans for my second Canadian tour, and I kept in touch with the boys in Philadelphia. I had a lot of confidence in the upcoming summer tour, in spite of Big Slim and Hazel leaving the show a few weeks after our opening night on the first tour.

In early spring we drove back to Moncton, and I went to see Mr. English, who I'd bought my two trucks and Buick from. I asked him to order me a 1947 brand-spanking-new canary-yellow Cadillac convertible after my upcoming summer tour. His eyes almost popped out of his head. He laughed and said, "Boy, you sure are looking forward to a good summer's work, or maybe you've struck gold somewhere." I specifically told him I wanted an automatic shift and power steering in the car. He said, "No problem, you've been real faithful in your financial dealings with us. We'll have your car here when you're ready for it, and we'll take your present car as a trade-in."

Back in Moncton I had the trucks and all the equipment serviced and any repairs done that needed to be done. In late spring of 1947 I got all our advertising ready to send to the places where we'd be touring. I even had another program booklet made, with several pictures and the lyrics to all the songs I'd recorded for RCA Victor.

The trio from Philadelphia had asked me to meet them at Saint Stephen, New Brunswick, just across the border from Calais, Maine. I didn't know why, but I drove the one hundred and fifty miles to Saint Stephen and met them as planned. When I saw them, I was disappointed and embarrassed. They looked like a bunch of tramps. At least they could have gone into the restroom and cleaned up. They didn't have a dime among them, and I don't know how they got food and gasoline to travel that far. But I was still enthused about the tour, and I did have cash on hand to finance unexpected situations. I loaned them about eight hundred dollars, and we all went back to Moncton, and I put them up in a motel.

The next day I drove to their motel to rehearse and plan our show together. I was pleased with the rehearsal, especially their professionalism as musicians and as a great trio of vocalists. But I was not impressed with their personalities. I hadn't remembered them being difficult when I first met them in the States. However, I could live with that. Having a good show was most important. We got together one other time, and I thought we had our routines worked out. Everyone knew his part, I thought. Certainly I knew mine.

I had scheduled us to play in the new territories of Ontario and upper Quebec, where I'd never played before. I was concerned as to how well I'd be received, not being on the radio in these provinces, with the exception of the occasional network show that I did and the commercials that went national. Did the people remember my network appearances with Bert Anstice and the Mountain Boys a few years ago? And above all, did they like and buy my RCA Victor records? Up until this time, I'd only played the Maritime Provinces and a few places up the Gaspé Coast of Quebec. But I had hired a good advance man to schedule and advertise our shows in the various towns. Everything was set, and I was looking forward to this new venture.

On a negative note, I found out that these three boys had been partying somewhere each night before we were to leave. On the night before we left Moncton, I was informed that they were partying in a crummy restaurant until the wee hours of the morning. I could hardly believe what I heard. I'd been working hard to get a good show organized, and I was upset that they might not be taking the tour seriously.

The morning we were supposed to leave for Montreal, we waited and waited for the trio. They didn't show. I drove to their motel, and the clerk said they had checked out that morning around six. We were supposed to travel together in case of car trouble, but I figured that for some reason they had gone on ahead and would meet us at the RCA Victor building in Montreal.

We left on our five-hundred-mile journey, and I followed the rest of the caravan in case of an accident. We had one small problem along the way. I noticed a deep crease in the black asphalt pavement, and after about five miles I saw that our big tractor-trailer rig had pulled over to the side of the road. The right rear of the trailer was sagging nearly to the ground. One of the big dual wheels had worked loose on the wheel hub and had dropped completely off the trailer and rolled off the highway into a big field. The hub of the wheel had been cutting into the asphalt, leaving the line. I couldn't understand why the driver of the rig couldn't feel the trailer dragging the engine down as it pulled the trailer along on the hub rim. When we finally found the big dual wheel and tire assembly, we had a wrecking truck lift it and pull it back to the trailer. We couldn't have done it without help. In a few hours we were on the road again.

I stopped at the next town and made two phone calls, one to the immigration service at the border, and another to RCA Victor, to see if there was any word from the trio. The immigration office phoned along the border to other places they might have crossed over, but there was no word as to their crossing, and no word at the RCA Victor company. We drove through the eastern part of Montreal and found a level open field. We pulled in and all went to sleep, except the drivers, who were put up in a motel.

At two the next afternoon our caravan drove into west Montreal at RCA Victor's studios. Mr. Joseph came outside, and we made a few pictures of him beside the equipment and with Shawnee. Mr. Joseph was always camera shy, but he was a good sport, and he even let us take a picture of him with my big white Stetson on. We enjoyed our brief stay, but I was worried sick, not knowing where the boys were. I was afraid they had had a serious wreck and were in a hospital somewhere.

We left Montreal and stopped in Ottawa, where Min phoned the immigration office at the border. She gave us the disappointing news. The immigration office had word from another border crossing that the trio did cross the border into the United States the same morning we left Moncton. How could people be that low! And this is not the end of the story.

With this trio's pictures printed on our posters and in my souvenir book, it sure left me in a mess again. I hired a couple of musicians from down east, and our show was just as good. I did my routine with Shawnee, who actually upstaged us all. He was the star of the show. And again, little Jimmie won the hearts of the audiences.

Only occasionally did we have a problem with the equipment. I had been extremely careful, when the equipment was being built, to make sure it would meet all safety requirements. But after we set up the equipment and grandstand in a suburb of Ottawa, the fire inspector checked our wiring and said it didn't meet the code standards for the province. We were prohibited from having our evening show until the problem was corrected. Actually, it didn't matter, because around 6:00 P.M. a terrible rainstorm hit, and we would have had no show anyway.

Throughout our tour in Quebec and Ontario we had less than great crowds. I wasn't known there like I was in the provinces of eastern Canada, but since I hadn't traveled in these provinces, I wasn't too discouraged. I knew it would take more time to establish myself. Nevertheless, I made enough money on the shows to pay the overhead and salaries. Eventually I was able to draw capacity crowds across the complete dominion of Canada. People from all over Canada, from Newfoundland to Vancouver and Victoria, have all been wonderful to my family and me.

When our tour ended, I decided to go back to my old stomping ground and give upper Canada more time to learn about me. We did exceptionally well in New Brunswick, Nova Scotia, Prince Edward Island, and Cape Breton, where I had been so successful before, and I had a pretty good roll of money saved up when the last show was concluded.

After our lengthy summer tour of 1947, we drove back home to Moncton, New Brunswick. This time we parked my van and tractor trailer rig at the Colpit firm. I put my horse at Tom Rogers's farm again, and I found a good home for Pal, my big German shepherd dog. My next plan was to go back to Hollywood and take Shawnee, my horse van, the new canary-yellow Cadillac convertible I had ordered, and my new silver-mounted saddle, and try my luck there again.

I parked our house trailer on the outskirts of Moncton, in a little settlement called Sunnybrae. Something happened here that makes me cringe when it comes to mind. Every morning I'd take our little dog, Mickey, out on his leash to go to the bathroom. And if the weather was fine, I'd tie his long leash to the rear bumper of the Buick and let him enjoy the fresh air. One day I was running late for a broadcast at CKCW, and I ran out of the trailer, jumped in the car, and took off down the highway. All of a sudden people started yelling and waving, and I thought, "What's wrong? Do I have a flat, or what?" Then it struck me. Mickey was still tied to the back bumper and I was driving about thirty-five mph! I slowed down to a stop, because if I had tried to stop short, it would have driven him up under the back of the car.

I jumped out, and he was just standing there, trembling, and lifting his little paws, one after the other. "My God," I thought, "what have I done?" It took at least three weeks for the cushions on the bottom of his little paws to heal before he could comfortably walk again. I felt terrible about it. People who witnessed this told me that Mickey was in sort of a sitting-down position, as if he was trying to brace his feet and hold the car back. Thanks to the Good Lord for coming to the rescue and taking care of Mickey.

After the completion of the 1947 tour and the hassle of having to store a million things, I made a hasty decision. I decided to sell the semi, grandstand, portable stage, generating plant, ticket booth, the whole kit and caboodle. I'd unload everything but my van, saddle, Shawnee, two dogs, and our personal belongings. For my second trip to Hollywood I'd need all the money I could get my hands on. It took a while to sell everything, but as soon as I did, I paid Mr. Colpit and Mr. English what I owed them. It was a good feeling to have these big bills paid up, and I had a little money left.

I had been corresponding with Buck Ritchey, a disc jockey in Tacoma, Washington. He was playing the devil out of my records, and I'd been encouraged by his comments that he liked my work as an artist. In one of Buck's letters he said he thought I would do well in personal appearances throughout his area. Min was in full agreement about me returning to the West Coast and giving the Pacific Northwest a try. She was always supportive of anything that would advance my career. The plan was for Min and Jimmie to stay in Moncton, and I'd send for them after I was firmly established out west.

One day I was having some work done on my van as it was parked beside Mr. Colpit's place of business, and I happened to see a big flatbed trailer go by, hauling a canary-yellow Cadillac convertible. I just knew it had to be mine. Who else in Moncton would have ordered a 1947 canary-yellow Cadillac convertible?

Only Hank Snow, of course.

It was mine, and I was flying high when I went to look it over. But I was disappointed when I saw it. It had a stick shift and not the automatic shift I had specifically ordered, and it had no power steering.

And there was a problem with my Buick trade-in. About four weeks prior to the time my new Cadillac came in, I made the two-hundred-mile trip to Campbellton, New Brunswick, to visit close friends before heading west. After spending four days in Campbellton, I was anxious to get back home, so I decided to leave at night and take the shortcut. By taking the shortcut, I was told, it was only about one hundred fifty miles back to Moncton, and there would be very little traffic on the road. But I'd have to travel through a dense forest that harbored bears and wildcats, and bears had been known to attack stranded cars.

One foolish thing leads to another. I called Hubert Smith, the taxi driver I had always used when I worked at CKNB, to buy me a bottle of vodka. I'd sip on it as I made the long, boring trip back home. But when Hubert returned, he had a quart of 100-proof geneva gin, not vodka, and I truly despised gin. To me, gin smells like perfume and tastes worse, and he brought the worst brand of all. It was better than nothing, I thought, and would be good company while driving.

It was a beautiful moonlit night in the early fall, and I was having a few nips and feeling in high spirits as I was driving. I was in a thinking mood and wondering about what the future held for me in California.

My thoughts were interrupted about fifty miles from Moncton, when my left rear tire blew out. I had just gotten through the forest, so I felt halfway safe. I took a swig of that terrible perfume, jacked the car up, and changed the tire, but I got filthy dirty and real irritated. My spare was a recapped tire, and I'd never had good luck with recaps. Well, I hadn't gone another twenty miles until I heard a funny noise that sounded like something hitting the back fender. By my odometer, I wasn't too far from civilization, so I kept on driving, hoping to come to a house that would have a telephone to call a garage for help. However, it was Sunday, and it was unlikely I could get help before businesses opened on Monday.

The engine got hot and was steaming so bad I could hardly see the road, and soon the engine stopped completely. I made a major mistake by not stopping the car. A long strip of rubber that came loose from the recapped tire had knocked part of the oil line loose, and every drop of oil was lost. I had burned up the engine in my car!

As soon as the car stopped, I hid the horrible gin in a gutter under some tall grass. If the Royal Canadian Mounted Police came by and caught me with the bottle, I would have been in trouble. I picked out certain landmarks to show me exactly where I hid it, then walked toward a farmhouse in the distance, about a mile away. I used the farmer's telephone, but I was unable to reach anyone at that hour. I walked back to the car and went down to the gutter to get the gin and have a swig to settle my nerves. You know, I couldn't find it anywhere! I looked and looked, but no bottle. While I was gone, someone must have been watching me and took my gin. My only moral support was gone.

I'd been looking forward to trading in my car on the new Cadillac, and needless to say, I was heartbroken. On that lonely road with a burned-up car, I was wondering what to do. Would you believe this? Two good friends of mine, Ovilo Cormier and his wife, Teresa, who I used to chum around with, drove up and stopped. She was a fine singer, and we used to do harmony together. They were on their way to a place nearby where we used to get the best home brew I'd ever tasted. They asked me to go with them, and since I was so depressed, I said, "What the hell. But what will I do about the car?" They suggested we push it into a nearby field, and I could ride back to Moncton with them. On Monday morning I could get a wrecker to handle the problem. I said, "People celebrate everything else, why not celebrate my bad luck?" So we went to the bootlegger's place. Since both of my friends sang and played guitar, we had a ball all day Sunday, and I forgot about my worries. Late that night we drove back to Moncton.

The next morning I broke the news to Mr. English at the garage as to what had happened to my Buick. He sent a wrecker and towed it in, and naturally this altered the trade-in price of my car. Nevertheless, he took it in on trade for my new Cadillac, and I financed the rest.

Shortly before leaving for Hollywood, I received a letter from the head office of the American Federation of Musicians in New York. The trio I'd hired for the 1947 tour, who never even appeared for the first show date, had filed a lawsuit against me through the union. They claimed I didn't uphold my part of the contract that I'd signed with them. The boys had simply lied to the union in hopes of getting more money from me. This was a severe blow. These good-for-nothing parasites had taken my eight hundred dollars, and without giving the first inkling of their plans, left me in a mess. In my wildest dreams, I couldn't imagine the union even considering that I was wrong in any way.

I made a huge blunder. Instead of immediately taking this up with the AF of M in Halifax, Local 571, to which I belonged, I thought I could handle it myself. Since I'd never had trouble of any kind with the musicians' union, how could I make a mistake? Everything was obvious. I had abundant proof that the trio was completely in the wrong. I typed a two-page letter to the union office in New York, and I poured out my complete story to them. I mentioned the trio's drinking at the restaurant in Moncton, their carrying on all hours of the night, the money I had advanced them, and their failure to notify me of their intentions to go back to the States.

Actually, I should have gotten a lawyer, or at least made my letter brief, stating only the facts in about three or four paragraphs. The way I had written the letter, the union took it as a personal squabble between us rather than a violation of a business contract. So I cut my own throat. The AF of M answered my letter, requesting more information, and the problem dragged on for months. I knew if the case went against me, the union would take my card, which was my bread and butter. I couldn't operate without my union card. There will be more about this story later.

While crossing the border at Saint Stephen one day, I met a clean-cut, religious young man, and I told him about my plans to go to Hollywood. He said if I needed a driver, he was free to travel. He showed me his chauffeur's license and references, and he seemed qualified to drive my van with Shawnee and two dogs. As soon as I decided when I'd be leaving for the West Coast, I telephoned the young man and said I'd pay him for driving and pay his way back home. He said he'd come right away.

Before going west, I went to Montreal for another recording session. During December 2–5, 1947, I recorded twelve more songs, including "Wasted Love," "Somewhere along Life's Highway," "Journey My Baby Back Home," "My Two-Timin' Woman," and my one and only comedy song, "The Night I Stole Ole Sammy Morgan's Gin."

Min and Jimmie were settled in Moncton with our close friends Curt and Addie Rogers. A few days after I returned from Montreal, the van driver arrived. The two dogs, Mickey and Pal, were put in the van with the horse, so they would have lots of room to move around, and we left Moncton for the long drive to Hollywood. We took our time driving, and I followed behind in case something went wrong. When we got tired, I got the driver a motel room close by, where there was space to exercise Shawnee and the dogs. I slept in the bed over the cab of the van.

It was only natural when we reached Hyde Park, Arizona, that we'd stop and visit with Dennis and Jean Arnett and their daughter and son-in-law, Helen and Galyn. They put us up in two comfortable cabins, and they wouldn't let us leave for three days and nights. When we got to Amboy, California, we also stopped for a brief visit with my friends Conn and Lillian Pulis. They made us feel right at home as they had done before, and Conn made us a big thick juicy steak. Again we had a wonderful rest before leaving on the final leg of our journey.

We arrived in Hollywood during the evening around eight, and I couldn't help but wonder if my second visit would pay off. What did I have for Hollywood, and what did Hollywood have for me?

21

Hollywood Again

In the misty moonlight
By the flickering firelight,
Any place is all right
As long as I'm with you.

"In the Misty Moonlight,"
by Cindy Walker

WE DROVE THE HORSE VAN AND MY CAR out Ventura Boulevard, which then was just a two-lane highway. I spotted a small field, and we parked side by side for the night. After I fed and watered Shawnee and the two dogs, I drove the van driver to a motel, then returned to sleep in the bed in my van. I didn't want to stay in a motel and leave the van with my horse and dogs, my silver saddle, and the other things of value.

The next morning I was up bright and early and drove back to the motel to pick up my driver. After breakfast we began looking for a permanent place to park. The van was going to be my home while in California. I had a two-burner hot plate in my office in the van, and I could save a lot of money by making my own meals. After an extensive search out Ventura Boulevard and asking a dozen questions at several places, we finally came to a small white wooden-frame house, sitting next to a wide vacant lot, with several big willow trees. It looked to be shady and cool, and I hoped I could rent the lot. The name of this little wide spot in the road was Calabasas. It was about thirty miles from downtown Hollywood.

I talked to the old gentleman who owned the vacant lot. He told me he worked in movies and owned a mule train. Whenever his mules were needed for movies, mostly Westerns, the studios would hire him and his team. He was a stern man. I doubt if he ever smiled one time in his whole life. He said, "I'll let you park there, as long as you don't tear anything up." I thought, "What would we tear up? Would I dig a tunnel through the lot or just dig it up like groundhogs or gophers or something?" "As long as you're a good tenant," he continued, "I won't charge you nothing, because the property isn't being used."

The old man helped me hook up the electricity to my van from an outlet on a huge post close by, and he showed me where I could get water. There was a toilet back of his house that I could use, and he offered me the use of his shower. I told him I certainly didn't want all this for nothing, but he wouldn't have it. He said, "We'll drink a beer together now and then." He seemed nice, and I kept looking for him to smile at least once, but it never came.

I put Shawnee on a long rope and tied it to the back of the van, so he could exercise and walk around the area, and I could run him around in a big circle every day. I got him hay, oats, bran, and fresh clean water and made him comfortable. I found a small restaurant where I got scraps of meat and bones to feed my two dogs, and I bought myself a few groceries from a nearby store. After my driver had a good rest in the motel, I drove him to the train, and he was on his way back home.

I could see Betty Grable's ranch right across the huge, prairie-like field. The property where I was parked bordered her property. I would see someone out riding every so often, and I presumed it was her or her husband, Harry James.

During the next few days I made several visits to the old gentleman's home. He told me many stories about the work he had done in movies, and I began to feel more at ease with him. However, he did say, "If you ever come home and see that big German police dog laying dead, you'll know I shot him. I never allow no dogs near me. If one ever shows a sign that he's going to come after me, I'll kill him right on the spot." That worried me every time I was away, because I believe the man meant exactly what he said.

Some people I met suggested I go to the Music Corporation of America to inquire about opportunities with MCA in the country music field. The MCA offices were in Beverly Hills, and I talked to the manager, Rhuel Freeman. I showed him my album of pictures of me and Shawnee and the tricks he could do. I played him several of my RCA Victor Bluebird records, and I believe I made a good impression on him, but he didn't seem interested in Shawnee or his trick routine. He did say, "Being with RCA Victor and trying so hard to build a career in the country music field, I compliment you for your spunk and persistence. But I do think the film capital of the world is the last place you'd want to come to build a career in country music."

I explained that I was thinking about organizing a band and trying my luck through Washington and Oregon and possibly some other states. He responded, "I'll be glad to put you under contract with MCA. That might give you a little prestige, although I can't promise you anything. But if any clients ask for your type of act, we'll certainly be glad to promote you." That was a start. I went back to see Mr. Freeman, off and on, for about three weeks, but nothing came of this contact. Nevertheless, I appreciated the fact that he wanted to help me.

One day I was walking along Hollywood Boulevard and noticed a sign that read "Frank Foster, Booking Agency." I went inside to check it out, and I apologized to Mr. Foster for not making an appointment first. Frank and his wife, Betty, impressed me, and I talked at length with them and told them what I had been doing. Frank said, "Come in again the first of the week, and bring some publicity from your past work. We've handled country acts before, and I believe we can help you. I don't know about using your horse, though, unless it would be appearing in a parade or in a rodeo, but we'll keep flexible on it. But first, get a band. Then have a bunch of publicity pictures made of you with them, and I'll start a file on you, your band, and your horse act."

I was thrilled with all these possibilities and was confident Frank could help me, and I wanted to follow his suggestions completely. The next day I drove downtown to the musicians' union and checked their book listing all the musicians in that particular locale. I made some phone calls, and I lined up a fine fiddle player, who had played with one of the big western bands. He recommended other musicians, and I soon had a really good swing band put together. It was bigger than I should have had, but I wanted to do everything up right. Swing music was very popular at that time in California, the Pacific Northwest, and especially Texas.

Friends, I'm sure you've heard it said many times, "Ain't it funny how time slips away." In my case it was "Ain't it funny how fast money slips away." Every day I checked my bankroll; it was disappearing, even though I was living just about as cheaply as I possibly could. When I first arrived in Hollywood, I had around twenty-one hundred dollars, and it was almost gone when Frank Foster said, "Hank, it's going to cost you more to do things properly. For your publicity you should take out a couple of full-page advertisements in *Billboard,* a major trade magazine, and you'll need money for other ads, as well as money in reserve for unseen expenses."

Boy, I had to get something going—and fast. I decided to take a trip to Amboy, California, about two hundred miles away, to see my friend Conn Pulis. Conn seemed to be interested in helping my career, especially in the United States. The old gentleman I was living next door to agreed to keep an eye on my van and my animals. So I drove to Amboy and talked to Conn. He said, "You can stay here as long as you want to, and I'll help you financially as best I can. If you do good, you can pay me back, but if you don't, then you don't owe me anything. I'll take the chance because I believe in you." He loaned me some money, as he had off and on—not to any great extent, and certainly not the amount I needed, according to Frank Foster, but it was a big help. And Conn gave me a room or a cabin, whichever was available, whenever I needed a place to stay.

I went back to Calabasas and for a low fee rented a room in the basement of a hotel in downtown Los Angeles that had been a nightspot. My band members rehearsed in the big room in anticipation of getting a good show ready for the road, and I was excited about the future.

I phoned my old friend Lew Wade, from Maryland, to join my group. He had been part of my 1946 Canadian tour as a comedian, and he played an upright bass. I persuaded him to join me, and I paid his expenses to California and his hotel bill. Next I needed someone with experience to drive my van, because I wanted to have Shawnee with me, in case I could use him in any of the shows. Besides, I couldn't leave my two dogs and Shawnee and the van while I was away.

I did have a driver in mind. Earlier when I was driving through Santa Rosa, New Mexico, on my way to the West Coast, I stopped at a service station, parked my van there, and got a few days of rest. I met this odd character who said he'd like to travel with my show and he wouldn't charge me much to drive the van. He claimed he was a safe driver and had driven all kinds of rigs. I inquired about him through references he had given me, and as far as they knew, he was okay. I phoned him and he came right away.

The boys in the band loved the songs I had written, as well as the old country standards that I sang. I don't remember all the names of the band members. We only worked together for a short time, but I remember Andy Folaro, a young Italian boy, who played drums well. He said he had formerly worked with Spike Jones and the City Slickers.

The band and I had spent a good deal of time rehearsing, but we didn't have any jobs scheduled as yet. I kept checking daily with the Frank Foster agency, but no offers were coming in. I began to realize that perhaps I had gone too far and had jumped too quickly in organizing a big band. I was afraid I was taking on too many obligations. According to the union, I still had to pay the band members for the rehearsal time and pay the cost of bringing their instruments to and from the place to practice. Thank goodness the boys didn't charge me much for rehearsal time, but it got to the point that I had to put the band members on a weekly salary. And for that I needed more capital.

Just in time, Frank Foster booked us for five or six days in Washington and Oregon. However, these engagements were mostly for dances in big ballrooms. Although the seven-member band and I put together some real good dance music, my main interest was to put on shows. Since these were paying jobs, I couldn't turn them down. We would receive flat rates to play the dates on the tour, but most of the money would go to pay the salaries of the band members, with barely enough money left over for gas, motels, and other necessary expenses. Again I needed more money.

As much as I loved Dennis and Jean Arnett, I hated to approach them for a handout or to even let them know how desperate I had become. But sometimes a person has to do some embarrassing things and forget about pride. I finally got up enough courage to call Dennis one night. I was telling him what I had accomplished thus far and that the future looked good, but it was going to take time and cost a lot more money. Before I had a chance to say another word, he asked, "Do you need money right now?" I was spellbound, because as little as Dennis knew me, he was offering to help me. I told him about having to put the band on salary and that I had to pay the Frank Foster agency $500 right away to run a full-page ad in *Billboard* magazine. Dennis said, "No problem, where can I wire it? And if I can help you later on, don't you be afraid to holler." I gave him the Foster agency address, and through a connection with a bank in Los Angeles the money arrived the next morning.

Frank ran the full-page ad in *Billboard* before we left to play the tour. He gave us a small two-wheel luggage trailer, which fastened to the bumper of my car. Without it, it would have been difficult for us to carry all the luggage, instruments, equipment, and clothing we had to take with us. But one day on the tour the trailer hitch snapped completely off the bumper, and a wheel came off the trailer. Since we were running late for our date, and we were out in the wide open spaces, there was nothing we could do. We took everything out of the trailer and put it in our cars. Then, as much as we hated to, we rolled the trailer down over the bank and went on our way.

We had a pleasant tour. As it turned out, we did a mixture of music. We played for the dances until about 10:00 P.M., and after a forty-five-minute stage show, we again played for the dancing until around 1:00 A.M. But when the tour ended, I had very little money left, and buying another trailer was out of the question. Moreover, another bill was facing me. I had engaged Nathan Turke in Hollywood to make each of the boys two new suits for these few days on the road. At his prices, I was looking at another thirty-five hundred dollars.

In addition to these money problems, something happened that reminded me of the Swede during my days at sea and how he had tried to kill me. This event took place at one of the dance halls where we played, and it scared the hell out of me. My van was parked about seventy-five feet from the back door of the nightclub. It was a hot, muggy summer night, and it was very dark. I went out to the van during the intermission to see if everything was okay. When I opened the side-door entrance to the van to look in, a voice came out of the dark, "Halt!" And I heard the click of a pistol, followed by "Don't you move, or I'll kill you!" Like the other time when I told myself, "Feet, don't fail me now!" I took about three jumps toward the back door of the club and was inside in a flash! I was trembling all over. The manager of the club called the police, who came in a few minutes, and they arrested this guy and took him to jail.

It was my weird van driver from New Mexico! I had to go down to the station to file charges against this character. He was in his cell, lying in his bunk, and he was as cool as a cucumber. He didn't say anything, as he couldn't care less. The police said if I pressed charges, I'd have to appear at the trial. I said I wasn't in a position to do that, and I'd drop any charges if they would get him out of town right away. I found out later, in a statement he gave the police, the reason he got mad. He said it was a hot night and I made him stay with the van instead of going inside the dance hall. Some excuse! I believe he would have shot me, had I not gotten away in a hurry. The police seized his pistol and sent him out of town, and I've never heard tell of him since.

Now I was broke and owed money, and I was worried sick. The day after returning from our tour, I went in to see Mr. Foster, and he said, "We're going to need more publicity. You've made a good start in building your career in the States, but we need to do much more, and it's going to cost you a lot more money."

Well, I realized that, but I said, "Just run another full page in *Billboard.*" He responded, "Yes, I'll do that, but there are other trade papers just as important as *Billboard.* We should take full-page ads in *Variety, Cash Box,* and *Record World.*" Frank was talking about possibly another two or three thousand dollars. One thing I did appreciate. Frank kept only half of the commission I owed him on the Pacific

Northwest tour, so I knew he was trying to help me. He said I should try to come up with the money as quickly as I could, so that we wouldn't lose the publicity momentum we had started.

I began racking my brain. How in the world could I come up with a plan that would get me another loan? I didn't want to ask Conn or Dennis again, even though I was sure they would help me. I remembered that the Gordon V. Thompson Publishing Company in Toronto, Canada, had published my first songbook, and Bill and Sinclair Low, who owned Canadian Music Sales, had published the next one. They were connected in some way with Southern Music in New York. Therefore I went to Southern Music's office on Hollywood Boulevard and met Nat Vincent, the man who was handling the office on the West Coast. He listened to my sad story, everything I'd done and wanted to do, and how I was broke. I explained that many good opportunities were looking me right in the face if I could come up with some cash at this time. I said I had a good booking agency with Frank Foster, and I told him of my RCA Victor Bluebird records in Canada, which had a good chance of being released in the United States before too long.

I even offered to sign all my future songs with Southern Music. Mr. Vincent replied, "Hank, my boy, as much as I'd love to help you, I'm not authorized to make any kind of advance payments. If I could, I wouldn't hesitate a minute. I don't believe, even if I got in touch with our New York office, they would be interested, since you're not established in the States, and your records are only released in Canada at this time."

Friends, I'm going to tell you right now how people can miss out on an exceptionally good deal. I left the office of Nat Vincent and Southern Music and walked only a few blocks to the offices of Hill and Range Songs, Inc. This publishing company was owned and operated by two brothers, Julian and Jean Aberbach. I went through the same story with Julian that I had related to Mr. Vincent. I said I was in a financial bind and hated to have to quit now, as I thought good things were about to happen for me.

To my great surprise Julian asked, "How much do you need?" I didn't want to press my luck, so I said, "If you could let me have $300, it would be a big help." Again I was shocked. I almost fell out of my chair when he said, "How about $1,000 for now, and we'll see how you get along."

Julian had not asked me to sign any kind of contract, as a songwriter or as a performer. But he said, "Keep in touch with us. We'll be anxious to know how things are going, and later we'll sit down and talk about your future needs with our firm. We believe you'll be happy with what we can do for you." Julian did not say, "Sign here, and we'll give you $1,000." He sincerely seemed to be more concerned about my welfare than the money. Before I left, he added, "Hank, any songs that come through our office that we think will make you a hit, we'll send them along to you. We'll help you in any way we can."

I really did appreciate Julian's kindness and generosity. I walked into his office completely broke, and walked out forty-five minutes later with $1,000!

In a few weeks I went back to the Hill and Range office, and Julian discussed their business offer in detail. I signed with them in 1948 as an exclusive writer with their publishing company. Moreover, the Aberbachs were able to get all of my Canadian material signed over to them.

My dreams were coming true—at least on paper. But I knew I had to work hard to make all the pieces fall into place, and I wanted desperately to prove to those who believed in me that they had made a wise investment. My confidence had reached the peak of the mountain, and I was anxious to see exactly what was on the other side. Would I finally take a giant step in Hollywood? I would soon find out. But every place I turned, I needed more money, one more ad in a trade paper, and a dozen other things. I was sure I was on the right track, and I believed in Frank Foster, but I needed more operating capital. Besides, I still had to support my family back home. So, unfortunately, the $1,000 Julian gave me didn't last long. Again I was nearly broke.

I continued to rack my brain for possibly one more way to raise cash without having to go back to my good friends, Dennis and Jean Arnett. Through my disappointments in several people along the way, I had become a pretty good judge of character. Although my friend Conn Pulis was always good to me, I thought he had dollar signs in his eyes. He began to be overly nice to me and was calling me "Son." Then one day, while we were sharing a beer together in the living room of his home, he said, "I think now you and I should come up with a contract to protect me. I've already loaned you a couple hundred dollars, and I've given you free motel rooms. So in all fairness, Hank, we should have a contract."

Conn was talking about 15 to 25 percent of everything I would make in the next ten years, and of course I knew the union wouldn't sanction a contract like that nohow. By this time, I had a lot of confidence in myself because of what other people had told me, and I didn't want to be tied to something that big. I certainly would have been glad to sign a short-term agreement with Conn and guarantee him his money if I ever got income on a regular basis, but he wanted to tie me down to a long-term contract. I figured he would have to take his chance along with me, so I kind of shied away from him after that.

The ole brain was still working, and as much as I hated to do this, I decided to borrow money on my horse van, silver saddle, gun belt, and silver spurs. No way could I get a loan on the new Cadillac—it was not yet paid for.

I was completely committed to go all out for promotion, and Frank told me about possibly getting a loan from the Vine and Sunset loan company. I went to see the head honcho and told him my story. It took me about an hour and a half, explaining everything in detail and what my plans were in achieving my goals. He responded, "Well, sir, I think we may be able to help you, but first we'll have to see a bill of sale on the equipment you want to borrow on, and then we can talk more powerfully." In a few days a man from the loan office came to examine my equipment. Then I gathered all of my receipts and the title on my van, went back to the loan company, and told the man I needed $3,000. He kind of raised his eyebrows, but since I had good collateral, he made me the $3,000 loan after I filled out and signed about a million papers. They set up the loan with an exorbitant percentage rate and high monthly payments, but I took the loan because I was desperate.

A few blocks away I opened an account at a bank on Hollywood Boulevard. Next I sent some money to Min and Jimmie and then sent money to my creditors in Canada. I still had several obligations to meet, and I wanted to get square with the world. I still owed Mr. Turke money on the boys' and my wardrobe, and I had to make a payment. I also had to give Frank Foster a good amount of money for publicity, more pictures, and other necessities for his aggressive and first-prize effort. But I was wondering if all this effort with Frank was finally going to pay off. It was the kind of situation where you don't know whether it's money well spent or money down the drain. Anyway, I intended to continue my assault on the West Coast, even though it was a typical Las Vegas gamble.

In the meantime, Frank got us a few more show dates, including appearing with Shawnee at a rodeo in San Diego. I loved shows where I could show him off, with his pretty silver saddle, and put him through his trick routines. However, these kinds of events were hard to get because many cowboys were trying to do the same thing, including Tex Ritter, Sunset Carson, Rex Allen, and others who were well known through their movies.

About this time, I met a gentleman who was managing people who were doing extremely well in movies, and he had excellent credentials. "Hank," he said, "I believe I can get you started on a good career, but this will cost you money." That's all I kept hearing, wherever I went. From him, Mr. Foster, Mr. Whoever. "It's going to cost you money." "Check me out, my reputation is excellent, but you have to pay for good service." "You'll have to put quite a bit of money up front, because that's the name of the game." How many times have I heard these words over and over and over again!

I didn't have the money, and I was already two or three months behind with my monthly payments to the loan company. It was taking an unbelievable amount of hard cash to get things going, and before I knew who could or could not help me, my $3,000 was gone. It didn't take long before the loan company was knocking at my door, and I believe they desperately wanted that silver saddle and horse van. That's the old Hollywood game. I got the official letter from the Vine and Sunset loan lompany giving me exactly fifteen days to bring my account up to date, or they would foreclose.

What should I do? I could run, but where? I could leave Hollywood in the night and go somewhere, maybe to my dream city, Dallas, Texas. Yes, maybe Dallas!

It would not be a spur-of-the-moment decision, because several events had preceded this possibility. I had been corresponding with Bea Terry for about a year before going to California for the second time. Bea lived in Greenville, Texas, about fifty miles east of Dallas, and she had been encouraging me to try my luck in Texas. While I was in Hollywood, I got a letter from her insisting I call her on the phone. I did, and she said, "I don't know who has been sending your Canadian records to KRLD, but they have two or three of them, and they're being played on a nightly popularity poll by a disc jockey named Pappy Hal Horton." KRLD was a 10,000-watt AM station, and I was delighted that a powerful station was playing my songs. She told me more encouraging news. "Your song 'Brand on My Heart' has been number one for sixteen consecutive weeks. Unless things are happening for you on the coast, why don't you give Dallas a try?"

I knew from her letters that she promoted several artists throughout her area, and I was getting good vibes out of the situation. A number-one record in the States! Well, not really, but number one on a powerful radio station in Texas, that sounded great to me, too.

The timing could not have been better. Bea's reasons for me to go to Dallas were good, but the best damn reason was the fact the loan company was breathing down my neck. I mentioned to my band members that going to Texas had been a dream of mine and that I would be leaving for Dallas soon. One of them said his wife was there and she needed him to come home. He offered to drive my van, just for the free transportation, so I jumped at the chance. Of course, I didn't tell the loan company I was leaving, nor did I mention it to Frank Foster. I had paid the commission I owed him, and he and I were square.

I didn't know what to expect from Texas, and I was taking another gamble. But I had some things in my favor. A radio station had been playing the devil out of my Canadian records, and I knew Bea Terry was a terrific promoter. If I lingered in Hollywood any longer, I could see my van, saddle, and everything else disappear. So I said, "To hell with it, I'm going to Dallas."

As I was making the long drive, I thought about the fine young lady who had done me such a giant favor by sending my Canadian records to KRLD. Her name was Betty Goudie. She lived in Victoria, British Columbia, and we had corresponded frequently after she became a big fan of mine through my fan club, which I had started back in Moncton.

This fan club had been another brainwave of mine to try to raise money by charging one dollar for membership. Min and I published a full page of information in the club's journal every three months to bring the members up to date on what I was doing and to inform them of my new record releases. Min was my editor, and she wrote under the name of "Queenie Dalhardt." I would advertise my fan club on the radio stations everywhere I went, and a lot of folks sent in dollar membership dues. At one time I believe we had as many as three hundred members in the club.

My mind wandered as I drove, and I wondered why RCA Victor thought I couldn't sell records in the States when I had been selling quite well in Canada. I was feeling anger toward Frank Walker, chief of the RCA Victor office in New York. I thought about my unsuccessful attempt to meet him when I first came to the States and met my good friend Jack Howard in Philadelphia. I had told Jack I wanted to personally meet with Mr. Walker and try to convince him to release some of my Canadian records in the States. Jack, being the great person he was, arranged a meeting.

I remember the incident well. Jack and I had taken a train to New York and went directly to the RCA Victor building for my 2:30 appointment. We got off the elevator, right into the reception room, and Jack introduced us to the receptionist. She said, "Mr. Walker's busy at this moment, but I'll let him know you're here." I heard her phone him and announce that I was on time for our appointment. We waited for him from 2:30 that afternoon until 4:30—two solid hours. All of a sudden, four or five men came out, talking and laughing. They glanced at Jack and me and proceeded to get on the elevator. We just sat there, as I'd never met Walker before, and neither had Jack, but if he had been one of the men who left, I was sure the receptionist would have told us. She finally awoke from her dream and said, "Oh, you were waiting for Mr. Walker. He just left." You see, friends, little ole Hank Snow didn't mean a damn thing to the big-shot Frank Walker.

Walker also lost another artist. He had recorded four songs with Ernest Tubb, when Ernest first began recording. And Walker, in his great wisdom, released Ernest from RCA Victor. He missed the boat on that one, too, because Ernest was a tremendous seller on Decca Records in those days.

My mind shifted back to Texas, and I was wondering what would become of me in Dallas. I was so disappointed about my luck on the West Coast and all the money I'd spent in vain. Oh sure, it was good experience, but when would all of this experience pay off? I was flat broke, and I presumed the loan company would soon be following me, and I was disgusted with it all. I had good reasons to forget about my dreams. But give up? No, sir!

My life's philosophy came to my rescue again. I reminded myself that the bad luck would make me appreciate the good luck more. In other words, I was a firm believer in the sayings "There's a silver lining behind each dark cloud" and "It's better to have tried and failed than never to have tried at all." I had come too far to turn back now. My mind was set like steel, and I've never been easily discouraged. This has paid off for me many times. I would always tell myself, "Just don't get discouraged or let anything sway you from your beliefs. Keep going." Most people give up in the face of adversity, but if you give up, you'll definitely not be successful, so hang in there. Some people get so close to success, and just before they reach it, they quit. I have never been one to do that.

From the early days of Charlie Tanner to this time, I had changed from a pessimist to an optimist, and I was certain that Dallas would be the beginning of something really big in my career. When we pulled into the outskirts of the big city late one night, something about being in Dallas, Texas, gave me a strong, positive feeling. Somewhere along life's highway was a pot of gold.

Maybe it was Dallas.

22

Dallas

My troubled old heart, dear, is beating with pain,
You've gone and I know I'm the one who's to blame.
You've gone in the world, dear, to make a new start
And left as a mem'ry your brand on my heart.

"Brand on My Heart," by Hank Snow

WE STOPPED AT A PLACE CALLED Five Points, about ten miles from downtown Dallas, and parked beside a tavern that had a wide spot in the back. The van driver called to have his wife pick him up, and I immediately walked my horse and two dogs. After I fed and watered them, I went to bed, wondering what the next day would bring.

Right around the corner, the next day, I found a huge field, and the friendly folks said I could park there as long as I wanted to. Shawnee had a great big space to roam around in, and my dogs had a long rope, so they could run to and fro. I was all set, except I had only eleven dollars to my name.

Next day I drove to Greenville, Texas, to see Bea Terry, and while I was driving, I was pleased to hear my records being played on two different radio stations. I was glad for the opportunity to meet Bea and her family, and they gave me a warm welcome. Bea said, "Hank, I want to take you to our local radio station to be interviewed, and maybe you could sing a song, so please bring your guitar with you." I took my guitar, and naturally I sang "Brand on My Heart."

Now, listen to how this unwinds. I was just off the air when I received a telephone call from Steve Stephens, manager and owner of a well-known nightspot in Dallas, the Roundup Club, located on South Ervay Street. He said, "If you're available, I'll pay you $250 to play at my club for a two-week period. The house band will back you up, so you don't have to worry about getting your own band together. If you want the job, come to my office tomorrow and we'll work out the details." That was a fortune to me, and I went to see Steve the next day. He was a rather old, rough-and-tough, colorful-looking Texan, but he was kind and gentle. He wanted me to play Monday through Sunday, seven days a week, for two shows, one at 9:00 P.M. and the other at 11:00 P.M.

My wardrobe was in excellent shape, and I was ready for the big time. Steve had a good house band, led by Cecil Luna, who was quick in learning and playing my songs. My music went over so well that Steve held me over for two more weeks, and the additional $250 couldn't have come at a better time. I'd put on my flashy gold suit, get behind the wheel of my big Cadillac convertible, and drive through downtown Dallas on my way to the club. With my records being played on the radio, I'd pull up in front of the club, and I thought I was John D. Rockefeller!

Soon I was getting a lot of requests and inquiries, people asking me where they could buy my records in the city. I always hated to say none were available, but I quickly added that I had high hopes they would be in the near future. One night at the club someone said they had seen one of my records in a music store downtown. I couldn't believe this, and I called the record store. Sure enough, he was right. Steve Sholes had replaced Frank Walker as head of RCA Victor in New York, and Mr. Joseph had persuaded Steve to release my first record. About two days later a letter came from Mr. Sholes, but the release had reached Dallas before the letter. I guess Steve had already heard about my success in Dallas through the RCA Victor distributor in Dallas, the Adleda company. I was making an important mark in Dallas, and I could shove Hollywood out of my mind.

Unfortunately, though, other acts were scheduled after me at the Roundup Club, so I was not able to play there on a regular basis, but I still had hopes of selling a lot of records throughout the area. Don Snellings was one of the salesmen at the Adleda company, and he certainly knew how to push records and how to promote an artist. He drove me for interviews to all the surrounding radio stations, within forty miles or so, and he arranged to have my records stocked and on display at all the record stores, including the big department stores, such as Sears, Roebuck.

Don scheduled me to appear in Sears one Saturday afternoon to sign autographs, and when Don and I arrived, a whole bunch of people were waiting for me. Somebody asked if I would sing a couple of songs for the crowd, but I didn't have my guitar with me, as I wasn't expecting this request. However, in a few minutes one of the employees brought a cheap guitar to me that sounded horrible. I stood up on one of the big counters at Sears, and I sang my heart out for twenty minutes with that cheap little guitar that wouldn't stay in tune. In the music business you have to do away with pride. I don't believe I've ever sung before a more appreciative audience than I did on that day. I autographed records for the buyers. Sears sold every record of mine in stock and promised the folks they would order more, come Monday morning.

Don was especially helpful. He took me wherever records were sold, and after the Sears incident, I always took my guitar with me. I'd sing anyplace, anytime. One day he took me to a record shop way out in the country, where there wasn't a house around for at least a mile. They put a microphone and speaker out on the front porch of this little old building, which housed the record store. I sang out there just the same as if I had been at the Hollywood Bowl.

In the meantime, Steve, the owner of the Roundup Club, let me park my horse van in a big fenced-in lot that was part of the club. This made it much easier for me to get around without having to drive in and out of Dallas. I began spending more time at the radio stations during the days and nights. Both Don and Bea went with me to meet several radio personalities, and I loved it.

Through these interviews I had a chance to meet a lot of top country artists, such as Floyd Tillman, Jimmy Wakely, Bob Wills, and Al Dexter. Usually there were parties at the hotels for those artists after their shows, and I was always invited to come along and be with these big-name stars I had often listened to on the radio. I was in country music heaven, and the folks at these get-togethers made me feel very much at home.

I hadn't yet received any royalties while I was in Texas. It would take more time to build up a following, but I had confidence that I would. I was taking small jobs, singing here and there, and saving every cent I could because I was planning on bringing Min and Jimmie to Dallas.

I had quite a bit of free time on my hands, so in the evenings I'd go to the Roundup Club and sit around and have a beer with many of the artists and friends I had met, even though I was not playing there any longer.

About a half block from the Roundup Club, on the same street, was another club known as the Silver Spur. Some friends took me there one night, and I met the owner, Jack Ruby. Jack was in stiff competition with Steve, but I would visit Jack's place, sing a song, drink a beer with some of the boys, then go back to the van and go to sleep.

I'm sure you folks are familiar with the story about how Jack Ruby shot Lee Harvey Oswald after Oswald allegedly assassinated President John F. Kennedy. Well, Jack had always seemed like a fine man to me. I had never found anything wrong with him, except he was high-strung and had a quick temper. I've seen guys come into the club, give Jack a little lip, and the first thing I knew, that guy was on the floor. I got to know Jack quite well. Often, after he closed the Silver Spur at night, he would take some of us to other all-night spots that he owned. These were swank speakeasy places with gambling, and the customers received the red-carpet treatment.

In Dallas a huge country show called the Big D Jamboree was held every Saturday night in the Sportatorium. The Sportatorium could seat about seven thousand people. They booked big-name stars like Hank Thompson, Floyd Tillman, Cowboy Copas, and Ernest Tubb. Because I was an entertainer, the manager of the auditorium, Ed McLamore, would let me in free and let me visit with the artists in their dressing rooms.

During my stay in Dallas, Bea Terry made arrangements for me to lead a parade in Greenville, her hometown. Can you imagine me, a Canadian, leading a parade in a Texas town? This was a parade in which Governor Alan Shivers of Texas participated. Bea thought Governor Shivers was one of the finest governors the state had had in many years, and the parade was in his honor. I felt real proud riding Shawnee as I led the big procession, with the governor close behind me in a convertible. The parade was at night, and I knew the light shining on my bright, shiny silver saddle and on Shawnee, with his silver-white fur mixed with the chestnut brown, was a dramatic and flashy sight. After the parade a reception was held in a large auditorium, and I had the privilege of meeting the governor. Bea never missed the chance of getting me in the limelight, bless her heart.

Early on December 18 Steve Stephens brought Min and Jimmie over to my van as I was sleeping. What a pleasant surprise! I didn't think they would come until a day or two before Christmas, but they wanted to surprise me. Min had thought I would be on tour, so she contacted Steve by phone and had gone directly to his place. I was so glad to see Min and Jimmie after such a long absence on the West Coast, and I always felt better when I had them with me.

The first thing we did was buy groceries. Then we began to look for an apartment suitable for a family of three, with two dogs, and a place to keep Shawnee. By this time, though, my money had dwindled again, and I didn't know whether we could afford even the first month's rent, since I was out of a job. And we needed to get Jimmie started in school, come January, 1949.

Through a friend I was referred to Ola Wendal, who owned a big home in a part of Dallas known as Oak Cliff. She rented us a big room, which was comfortably furnished, and gave us the use of her kitchen, but I had to keep my van parked in Dallas. This was a poor setup, having to drive down to Dallas two or three times a day to look after my animals. I kept my silver saddle and all my other valuables at Mrs. Wendal's place, but I was still taking a big risk of getting my van stolen. In spite of our hardships, we again had a good Christmas for Jimmie.

In early 1949 I called Don Snellings, who knew the city better than I did, and asked him to help me find an apartment with reasonable rent in a more convenient location. He took Min and me to a brand-new duplex, way out in south Dallas on Lovett Street. The apartment had three rooms, with hardwood floors and all of the modern conveniences. This furnished apartment was sixty dollars a month, but the landlord wanted the sixty dollars in advance, just as I expected.

How were we going to arrange this? I had to swallow my pride again and ask a friend for a loan of thirty dollars. I had the other thirty dollars, and so we paid the first month's rent, with no earthly idea where the next month's rent would come from. Besides the rent money, we had to scrape together another five dollars to have the electricity turned on. We could do without a telephone until we got on our feet, since we could use the pay phone right up the street on the corner.

We were broke, and can you imagine this? I'm driving around in a big Cadillac convertible, without money enough to even change the oil, still putting on my big front. I just hoped I had enough gasoline in the tank to keep us going until a new job turned up. I had built up a friendship with the owner of the station where I bought my gas, and of course with my big Cadillac he was sure I was in good financial shape, so he let me open a charge account.

I couldn't get any shows at this time, and the Roundup Club was fully booked with various acts. So for the next couple of weeks Min, Jimmie, and I almost starved to death—and this is no exaggeration. If you have never had hunger pains in your stomach, feeling like it's tied in knots, you haven't missed anything, I assure you. This was like those hungry and poverty days back in Canada. The Snow family went three days with just bread and water. We did have a little sugar, which we put on our bread to give it some kind of flavor.

We were so desperate, we searched everywhere to find even fifty cents, anything to buy a loaf of bread. One afternoon Min was going through her purse and found a Canadian five-dollar bill. Believe me, that looked like $5,000. The Good Lord had stepped in again and helped us through another severe problem. With this new-found money, I kidded Min that I wasn't sure I had enough strength to walk to the store to buy something for us to eat. And I do mean walk, because the gas tank on the car was completely empty. I had promised the station owner I'd pay my gas bill every week, and it was way past the deadline. We lost a bit on the exchange because it was Canadian money, but we had a little food again.

Another thought came to mind on how to raise money. The next morning I took the bus to downtown Dallas, and I was able to pawn my 16-mm Bell and Howell movie camera and my diamond ring for $500. I had bought the diamond ring from my friend Curtis Rogers in Moncton a few years prior to this, when I was doing well with my road shows. When I was in Hollywood earlier and needed money so bad, I had gone to a pawnshop and gotten a loan on the ring for $300. The jeweler said the ring had a small black spot on the very edge of the ring, which he called carbon. He said the spot could be taken out for about a hundred dollars and it would greatly increase the ring's value. I remember telling him if I had a hundred dollars to spend I wouldn't be asking for a loan. A few years later, I did have the spot removed and was shocked at the value of the ring when I had it appraised. That same ring has been in and out of hock many times since I bought it, but it's still on my finger today—at a much higher value.

Anyway, with the $500 I was in the money again. I paid the servce-station bill, and I apologized for being late, explaining that I had been out of town for a few days. But just as soon as I came up with something to tide us over, another problem appeared on the horizon: The Vine and Sunset loan company in Hollywood had tracked me down in Dallas and was ready to repossess my horse van and silver saddle. I talked this over with some friends, and they came up with a good suggestion. They said to seek out a reputable loan company in Dallas and refinance the loan, which I did. The Dallas loan company paid off the West Coast loan company, and I was to pay the Dallas loan company instead. It cost me a higher fee to make this change, but I thought the Dallas loan company would be more lenient with me—at least for a while—and temporarily the pressure was off.

I stayed in touch with Ernest Tubb. I wrote him from Canada, Hollywood, and Dallas. I considered him a real good friend, even though I hadn't yet met him. Our love for the music of the late Jimmie Rodgers and the strong influence that his music had on us was a special bond between Ernest and me. I had mailed Ernest a couple of my Canadian records, and he was impressed with my singing. He said if he could ever help me in any way, he would.

One day someone contacted me from Fort Worth and said they were having a big country show called the Cowtown Jamboree. This was to be held at the Northside Coliseum. Ernest Tubb was the headliner of the big package show, and most of the artists were from Nashville's Grand Ole Opry. I was offered twenty-five dollars to be on the show, and I jumped at this opportunity, knowing that I could sing my local hit, "Brand on My Heart," and I could meet Ernest in person.

On the night of the big show I dressed up in one of the new suits Mr. Turke had made for me, and I drove my Cadillac convertible over to the big coliseum, which was packed with about six thousand people. I introduced myself and went back to the dressing room. As soon as Ernest came into the room, he smiled and shook hands with me. It was truly a thrill to meet him. The weather was a little on the cool side, and I remember Ernest was wearing a western-style topcoat and of course his customary big white Stetson hat. He showed me the original Jimmie Rodgers guitar and asked if I'd like to try it. I first said, "Gosh, Ernest, I'm afraid I might drop it." "Go ahead and try it," he said, as he carefully handed it to me. I strummed a few chords, but I was extremely nervous while I had it in my possession. It really did give me a funny feeling to hold the same guitar that my idol had used on most of his recordings. I immediately heard the special tone the guitar had. Maybe I was getting vibrations from the master as I played it. I've always believed that an artist leaves his certain touch on his instrument.

During our conversation Ernest said, "Hank, it's all happening in Nashville. Nashville is the home of country music. If you want to advance your career, you should be there. I promise you I'll do my best to get you on the Opry, but there's one problem. The Opry will not sign any new artist unless the artist has a hit record. However, I'm on my way to the West Coast, and I've taken a leave of absence from the Opry for a few months. Maybe they will accept you as a stand-in for me while I'm away."

I knew Ernest was telling it like it was. He laid it all out for me, and I already knew the odds against getting on the Opry were staggering. I was still struggling with regional success in the States, mainly around Texas and a wee bit in the South. And I would not have had this small success, had Mr. Joseph not been able to convince RCA Victor to release a few of my records in the States. Realistically, I realized there were hundreds of artists in the United States who were planning the same thing I was. Moreover, I was still a Canadian citizen, and I didn't know if this would hinder my career in some way.

Ernest had promised he would call me as soon as he talked to the officials of the Opry. In a few days I got the call. "Hank, I talked to Jim Denny, manager of the Opry, and Jack Stapp, the program director, and they both said they couldn't handle it at this time. I'll keep trying when I get back to Nashville, so keep your fingers crossed." And so for the time being I filed away in the back of my mind what Ernest had said, and I returned to the reality of trying to make ends meet in Dallas.

One night while I was visiting at the Roundup Club, I met Lucky Moeller. I had just finished doing a couple of numbers and was talking to friends, when Lucky came up and introduced himself. "You have a lot of talent, Hank, and I like your unique style of singing. Would you be interested in working with the band and me on a ten-day tour around Oklahoma and Texas? I can pay you twenty-five dollars a night and your motel rooms." Indeed I was interested! Immediately $250 flashed in my mind, and that was mighty good money in 1949.

Lucky was the leader of a first-class western swing band, and he held a dance every Saturday night at the Trianon Ballroom in Oklahoma City. He didn't play himself, but he'd sing a few songs during the dance. I remember one of the songs was an Eddie Kirk hit entitled "The Gods Were Angry with Me." Lucky had excellent twin violins in his band. Bob White and Keith Coleman were the players. His band was as good as any western swing band I've ever heard.

I loved working with Lucky and his band, and I was never treated better in my life. I played guitar and sang a song or two every now and then. Lucky was pleased with the reception I received from the audiences, and he gave me a lot of encouragement to continue on with my career.

Lucky and his family lived in Oklahoma City. Later I met his wife, Bernice, his son, Larry, his daughter, Dixie, and their son-in-law, Jack Andrews. It didn't take me long to discover I was getting to know one of the finest families I had ever met.

While I was hanging around the Roundup Club, someone told me about the Louisiana Hayride in Shreveport, Louisiana. This successful country music show was run somewhat like the Opry, and it drew a large crowd every Saturday night. A powerful 50,000-watt AM radio station broadcast the Hayride. It had a 50,000-watt sister station in Little Rock, Arkansas, which also promoted good country music.

Frank Page was in charge of booking the talent for the Hayride. I called him from a phone booth and discussed my success in Dallas and Fort Worth and asked if he could use me on some Saturday night. I offered to bring Shawnee with me and put him through his trick routine on the stage, if they had facilities to handle it. Mr. Page said to send him some of my records to play over the station to see what the response would be to my music, and he'd look over the roster to see what was available during the next couple of months. He apologized that he couldn't pay me much money, but I assured him that was no problem. I'd get national exposure, and that was worth gold to me. He added, "Hank, when we schedule your appearance, bring your horse, and since you're from Canada, this will lend curiosity to your stage act. Give me your phone number and I'll call you back in two weeks."

I told Mr. Page a little fib. I didn't want him to know we couldn't afford a telephone, so I said we hadn't had a chance to get it hooked up as yet, and I'd call him back in a couple of weeks. In exactly two weeks, I was on the phone again. He scheduled me for two weeks from that day, and I was quite surprised when he said the job for me and Shawnee would pay $125. That was big money for an unknown. And the facility had a huge freight elevator that could bring Shawnee right to the stage.

A friend drove Shawnee in the van, and away Min, Jimmie, and I went to Shreveport. The audience gave me a fine reception and much applause at the end of my act, but to be honest, Shawnee stole the show. He performed his act better than ever before. That night I met several other country acts, including Curly Fox and Texas Ruby. Hank Williams, Sr., was not on the program that night, and I was disappointed that I didn't have the chance to meet him. He had been a member of the Hayride only a short time, but he was becoming very popular.

After the successful Hayride appearance, I told Min and Jimmie I had a feeling something big was about to happen for me and my music, and when it did, we would live like human beings again. Feeling so positive, I went to Sears, Roebuck and opened an account. I put ten dollars down on a television set, so Min and Jimmie would have some entertainment while I was out gallivanting around, trying to get myself established. Television sets had not been on the market very long in early 1949, and people were fascinated by this new medium. I went hog-wild by buying the big console and having to fork out five dollars each month. We were so used to living on credit that it seemed like we were back home again.

I had been writing Steve Sholes every so often in regard to doing a session for RCA Victor in the States, because I was confident I could sell records and not be a liability to the company in any way. I updated him on what I was doing in Dallas with the radio stations and said that Ernest Tubb was trying to get me placed on the Grand Ole Opry. My song "Brand on My Heart" was so successful on the KRLD Hit Parade that I sent him a copy of the KRLD charts, showing it to be in the number-one position on this giant station.

In the meantime, on his frequent trips to New York, Mr. Joseph had been trying to persuade Steve to set up an American session and to produce new songs with me. The Canadian songs released in the States were selling quite well, especially in the Dallas–Fort Worth area. So in my heart I was confident that I would soon be recording brand new songs in the good ole U.S.A.

23

First American Recordings

Do you take this woman to be your dear wife?
Do you vow to love her the rest of your life?
And will you protect her and honor her name?
Oh, don't cause her heartaches and don't bring her pain.

"Marriage Vow," by Jenny Lou Carson

IT HAPPENED! AROUND THE FIRST of March, 1949, here came a letter from Steve Sholes with the word I'd been waiting for. He wanted me to come to Chicago to record four songs! I had been optimistic that the label would eventually record me in the States, but the usual procedure was to cut only two songs and then test them in the marketplace to determine the degree of commercial appeal.

However, Steve said he would have me record a total of four songs, and he added that if the songs I had written were strong enough, two of the four could be mine. To me this was a vote of confidence in my writing ability. He sent me several songs to listen to, ones he thought would suit my style, and he made it clear that I should plan on recording at least two of those he sent. I got a kick out of one of the titles. It was "Grandma Got to California 'fore She Died." He sent "Marriage Vow" by Jenny Lou Carson, who is well known for writing great songs over the years. I was not crazy about the song, as far as its suiting my voice, but it did carry a real good message.

Since Steve left the door open to possibly recording some of my material, I was concerned because I didn't have enough good songs ready for the studio. Naturally, I couldn't record the same songs again that I had written and released in Canada. He wanted original material. However, I did have one special song I'd been working on for over a year. It was as good as anything I'd ever written, and I wanted to record it most of all. I had sung it to many people, in many places, who said it would be a hit record.

The song was "I'm Movin' On."

A few days before the recording session Min, Jimmie, and I took off for Chicago in my Cadillac. I was feeling somewhat desperate as I drove. I had a few songs ready, but I needed more in case Steve didn't like some of them. Maybe he wouldn't like any of them, and I was thinking that if this first American session didn't come off well, there might not be another one. I brought paper along for Min to write down the lyrics of songs that I'd try to write in the car. Believe it or not, I wrote three songs before we got to Chicago. How I managed to do this, I'll never know, and if I do say so myself, they weren't bad at all.

We arrived in Chicago in the afternoon and checked into a crummy hotel in a poor part of the city, and a bellhop showed us to our room. As we were unpacking, I said to Min, "Where is the bed?" We looked in every corner, and no bed. We thought perhaps there was an adjoining room. We checked that out, no adjoining room. I called down to the desk and said, "Sir, there's no bed in this room." In a few minutes the bellhop came back up and reached up over his head and pulled a full-sized bed out of the wall. I'd never seen or heard of this before, and I felt embarrassed.

I was supposed to meet with Steve that same night, tired as we were, to decide what to record the next afternoon. So Min, Jimmie, and I drove to the big Edgewater Beach Hotel and knocked on his door. When we entered the room and made ourselves acquainted with Steve, he in turn introduced us to two other men. One was a bass player by the name of Charlie Greon, and the other fellow was Al Gallico, who was just starting a music company. In the following years Al gave me much credit for recording hits that got his publishing company off to a good start. Today he has one of the most powerful and best-known music companies in the United States.

Steve said, "Let's go over the songs you've prepared to record." Nervously I took my guitar from the case, sat on the side of one of the beds, and sang my heart out. Four of the songs he liked, and then I played "I'm Movin' On." When I finished, Steve looked around at Charlie Greon, and they decided it was not a song we should record. Needless to say, I was thoroughly disappointed, because I had a lot of faith in the song, but I had no choice in the matter.

The next day, March 8, 1949, we went into the studio and cut four sides during a three-hour session, including "Marriage Vow" and "(I Wished upon) My Little Golden Horseshoe." We used a steel guitar, violin, bass, and rhythm guitar. I played rhythm guitar with my singing and played lead in some parts of the songs, as I had done on my Canadian records. The musicians were all exceptionally good, including bassman Charlie Greon. But I always thought Charlie was the cause of "I'm Movin' On" being turned down. I believe Steve had Charlie there primarily to hear my songs and to be an advisor.

When we finished the session, Steve thanked me and said, "I thought you did well on all the songs. You'll hear from me about a release." I was pleased that I had finally done a recording session in the States and that two of the songs we cut were ones I had written. Min, Jimmie, and I checked out of the hotel and had a pleasant trip back to Dallas.

In less than two weeks I received a letter from Steve saying RCA Victor was planning an immediate release of "Marriage Vow," coupled with "Star-Spangled Waltz," which I had written. I was happy, but as a worrier, I wondered if the record would sell. Only time would tell.

At the Roundup Club one night Steve Stephens informed me he was going to open up Roundup Club Number Two in West Dallas, and he asked me to bring Shawnee there on opening night. He said he'd have lots of clean straw outside in front of the club, with proper lighting, where I could put Shawnee through his routine. I was glad to do it, because Steve had done me several favors. On the afternoon prior to his opening night I followed Steve through the streets in downtown Dallas with my horse van, and I advertised the opening of his new club through my loudspeakers. On the night of the opening, my horse was spotless as usual. The stableman where Shawnee was being boarded kept all of the horses curried, brushed, and cleaned as part of his job. Shawnee did a super routine, and people said he was the smartest horse they had ever heard tell of.

After the show it was still hot and humid, and since it was the wee hours of the morning, I told the driver to take Shawnee to my apartment and park the van out on the street. We would take Shawnee back to the stables later in the day. At the apartment I led Shawnee out of the van and into our garage. Because it was so sultry, I left the door up. To prevent him from wandering off, I parked my Cadillac convertible across the big garage door. He would at least have some air blowing on him.

Early the next morning Min came into the bedroom and said, "Are you in a good mood this morning?" I replied, "Well, why do you ask me that?" She said, "Because Shawnee chewed and tore up half of your convertible top. It's in riddles." I got so damn mad, I said, "I'm going out there and kill that horse!" I went outside and Shawnee was standing back of the car. I stood there for a minute and just looked at him. He looked so sad. Those big brown eyes won me over right then, and I didn't say one harsh word to him. Instead I went up and patted him on the neck, and all was forgiven. It wasn't his fault. Horses, like all animals, have to have a certain amount of salt in their diet, and I always kept a brick of salt in his feed trough so he could lick it whenever he needed it. The canvas top had some salt in the material, in the way it had been treated at the factory. That was the reason Shawnee chewed the canvas.

Even though spring in Dallas was generally beautiful, quite often during the afternoon thunderclouds would suddenly appear and it would downpour a heavy rain. Then it would be beautiful weather again. I'd drive downtown, and no sooner would I get there when a downpour would come, and away I'd go back to the house. I often got wet through the tattered canvas, and this went on until I raised enough money to buy a new top for my convertible.

I knew it would be several months before I'd get a royalty check from New York—even if my record sales were good. So when we were almost broke again, I determined that the Snow family should pull up stakes and go back up to Canada. I wanted to begin a tour in British Columbia, then work our way to eastern Canada. Since my name was well known across the Dominion, I thought I'd be able to get our finances in better shape.

Around the middle of May, 1949, I hired the same driver I had used earlier to drive the van and take care of the animals. Min, Jimmie, and I followed in the Cadillac, and it was a long, tiresome drive to New Westminster, a good three thousand miles or more. New Westminster was a nice-sized town and is only about twelve miles east of Vancouver. Before I made definite tour plans, I wanted to have a talk with the people at station CKNW. We got permission to park near the residence of a family in the horse-training and racing business, and they gave us a good clean place to keep Shawnee for a small fee per week.

The day after we arrived in New Westminster, I ventured into town to see Bill Ray, the owner of radio station CKNW. Bill had an excellent knowledge of country music, and his station played some of the old artists like Jimmie Rodgers and the newer ones like Red Foley and Ernest Tubb. The station had a top-notch western trio, the Rhythm Pals, and a small but good CKNW staff band. The Rhythm Pals in later years joined the Tommy Hunter radio show in Toronto, and they stayed with him for many years on his popular television program.

Bill gave me a job singing with the staff band, and Min and I decided to make the area our home until we could get a foothold and determine the next move for my career. We enrolled Jimmie in school for the brief time left before school closed for the summer.

My career was in limbo again, and we were basically broke. I was still concerned that my records might not be accepted by the public as a whole. Sure, I had some success in good old Texas, but maybe that was just a fluke. I didn't think so, but my success still had to be proven to RCA Victor. I had the feeling I was on the verge of a major breakthrough in my career—but how many times had I had that feeling in the past? If my RCA Victor records were successful in the States, I was sure Steve would record me again. On the negative side, if my records didn't sell, they would drop me anyhow.

My biggest hope and dream was that Ernest Tubb would get me placed on the Grand Ole Opry. I knew Ernest was like me, he was persistent and never gave up. I also knew he was a man of his word, and he'd do anything he could to help others reach stardom. Somewhere down the line I just knew I'd be walking on stage at the Opry to thunderous applause from a jam-packed house of appreciative country fans. But there were always unknown factors that were hard to plan for. I would have to be at the right place at the right time. To make it big, though, I had to be different. Yes, I was different because of my Canadian accent, but I had to be fundamentally different. Maybe my songs would catch the public's fancy, or maybe I'd capture a certain musical style that would catch on.

I continued to do my best every day in writing better songs, improving my music, promoting myself more effectively, meeting more people, and just working harder. I believed I was doing everything I could, and I had great faith in the Good Lord. At the right moment He would reach down with His powerful hand and touch me and let me have the success I constantly dreamed about and worked for. But when?

After I'd been on the station with Bill Ray's band for about a month, he suggested I use his staff band and play a few shows during the week over on Vancouver Island. That sounded good to me. I still had to make a living until my big break came, and I sure liked working with the musicians. This was the time when Min made her debut as an advance agent. She had helped me before in planning shows and selling tickets, doing whatever needed to be done whenever she was on the road with me. Even Jimmie helped out by selling pictures. We were developing a Snow show all the way. Min took complete responsibility for booking me and doing all the advertising. The first place she booked me to play on Vancouver Island was called Nanaimo. She rode the ferry over to the island, went around by bus, and put posters up in the best spots in town. After Nanaimo we scheduled several towns around the island. We'd play an hour or so and run a dance afterwards until about 1:00 A.M., and we did well in those small towns.

One day Bill came up with a wild idea that would sure enough blow your hat in the creek. He said, "Hank, I'm going to rent the Vancouver Gardens, which will hold over seven thousand people, and we're going to put on the biggest country-and-western show the people in this part of the country have ever seen. I'll hire local talent in addition to you and the staff band. I want you to take your horse on stage and give the audience a real treat. We'll plug the heck out of this show a dozen times over the station, every day."

On the day of the country spectacular, Min and Jimmie gave Shawnee his regular show shampoo, dried him off, and brushed him down. He glistened. I loaded him in the van and took him to the Gardens early to check to see if I could get him on stage without a big hassle. The Gardens had a huge freight elevator, even bigger than the one in Shreveport, to bring Shawnee up to the back of the stage, where he could walk on stage without any trouble.

The place that night was jammed to capacity. I was billed as the headlining act, Hank, the Singing Ranger, and his trained horse, Shawnee. When it came time for my part of the show, I proudly rode Shawnee out on the stage, on the beautiful shiny silver-mounted saddle. I had Shawnee take a bow, and we received a tremendous standing ovation. Shawnee was truly a professional in every sense of the word, and he did a tremendous act for the capacity crowd. After our successful show I signed autographs until around 3:00 A.M.

We did several more shows around Vancouver, and while in that part of the country I visited two Indian tuberculosis hospitals and put on shows for the folks. These hospitals, I was told, were set up and financed by the Canadian government to take care of any of the Indians who needed hospital care. One hospital was in a town about sixty miles northeast of New Westminister called Chilliwack. I'll never forget the wonderful people I met there. The staff, the patients, and especially the little children appreciated my visits and my show. I can still see the gleam in the kids' eyes as I sat by their beds and sang to them. I felt so sorry for them, but they were receiving excellent care. Many of the Indian patients created special gifts for us. They gave Min the most beautiful necklaces and rings I've ever seen, made out of different-colored beads. They made me a beautiful beaded belt with my name in beaded work. All of these items are still in my souvenir case, among my collection from around the world.

During our stay in New Westminster, I got more threatening letters from the American Federation of Musicians. I showed one of them to Bill Ray. He said, "Hank, you need a good lawyer to get these people off your back. They're treacherous and mean. They can take your membership card and stop you from working. They don't give a damn about your livelihood." I called the lawyer in Vancouver who Bill recommended. Thanks to the Good Lord for sending him. He knew the music business and how the union operates. He worked it out so I didn't have to begin making payments for thirty days, and he cleared me for the time being, so I could go ahead with my shows.

But this problem would hound me for a long time yet. Remember, friends, this whole thing stemmed from the trio that I had signed in Philadelphia to work with me during the Canadian tour of 1947. I'm sure they had had troubles before, because they knew the ropes as far as dealing with the union was concerned. They violated our contract, and they were suing me! So I was fighting the AF of M, and I couldn't understand what this suit was all about.

Even when I was in Hollywood, striving to make something good happen, I had to hire a lawyer because the AF of M was about to take my card away, and I wouldn't have been allowed to work. The lawyer got the union off my back for a little while, but then it started all over again. I couldn't keep my payments to the union current with all my other expenses when I was making very little money anyway. I was worried to death. Even when I was recording in Chicago, I was holding my breath. It was a constant concern as to what might happen next, and it seemed unfair to me that the union had so much power.

After a while in New Westminster, I hired a few additional musicians, apart from station CKNW. The staff band couldn't venture too far from the town because they had to be back at the station for their radio shows. I would use the staff musicians to play the dates when it wouldn't interfere with their jobs, but I wanted to extend my appearances to areas where I had never played before, with the goal of spreading the name Hank Snow as far as possible.

I telephoned Billy King, an old friend from my early days in Lunenburg, Nova Scotia. He was a professional juggler and a master of the art. Billy couldn't believe it was me, as we hadn't talked to each other for many years. "As soon as you get your band together," he said, "let me know. I'd love to travel with your show again." Soon thereafter I hired a small band and Billy joined us. I booked dates within a hundred miles of Vancouver, and we had a fine lineup of talent. Billy liked my son, Jimmie, and taught him juggling, and he used him as his juggling partner in certain parts of his show.

A problem developed right away. The bandleader was late on our first two shows. That bugged me. I had to constantly keep after him, and a few times he was even an hour late. One day I sat down with him, and we had a long discussion. I explained that being on time was one of the most important things in life and that starting a show late was a good way to make a bad impression with an audience. He said he understood, and I thought this would settle the problem, but it didn't make a damn bit of difference.

This was one time my judgment of character proved to be wrong. I was about to get into another bad situation, like the trouble with the trio in Philadelphia. But as I was feeling down in the dumps about this, something happened that cheered me up again. Someone from the radio station called and said my publisher, Julian Aberbach of Hill and Range Songs, wanted me to phone him. I called Julian, and he told me that Ernest Tubb had just recorded "My Filipino Rose." I was on cloud nine! Ernest was a major star. He had already sold over a million of his song "Walking the Floor over You."

I had written and recorded "My Filipino Rose" in 1947, and RCA Victor released the song, but with only about thirteen million people in Canada at that time, it didn't bring me much in royalties. I went around telling everybody, "The great Ernest Tubb has recorded my song." That really gave me a completely new outlook on life. I wasn't thinking about the royalties I'd get as writer, I was thinking about how Ernest was a true friend to me. He didn't have to record my song. There were hundreds of good songs being written, and because of his popularity he was being pitched songs by the best writers and publishing companies in the country. Besides, Ernest was a real good writer himself, and he could make more money by recording his own songs. It was a great feeling to know that such an unselfish person was working in my behalf, and I was confident that, if it was in the stars for me to get on the Grand Ole Opry, Ernest would be the one to make it happen.

British Columbia was beautiful country, and we loved it. We did well in that part of Canada, and Min and I managed to save a little money. However, as the old saying goes, "We were ready to strike out for lands afar."

I had been hearing about a popular dance place in Winnipeg, Manitoba, which was at least fifteen hundred miles east of British Columbia. I got the name of Andy Patterson, who operated Patterson's Barn, and called him on the phone. After a few minutes I could tell he was really a character. He talked and laughed at the same time, and I liked him right away. He said, "Hank, you're pretty popular around Winnipeg. They're playing your records on all the radio stations. If you come here, I can pay you a few dollars each week to play for the dances, and you can play small towns around Winnipeg if you want to. You can even use the boys in my band. They only play for me on Saturday nights." I told him I appreciated the offer, but I had my own band. He laughed and said, "The more the merrier, so bring them along."

To get to Winnipeg via the Canadian Rockies was a treacherous drive. Many of the roads hadn't been paved yet, and some of the mountains were very steep. We were strongly advised to go to Winnipeg from the American side, down through Montana and up into Winnipeg. The mountains on the American side were not so steep, and it would be safer for us, the van, and the horse. Certainly I took their word for it. I hired an experienced young fellow from Vancouver to drive my van.

The day came to leave, and we bid all of our friends around New Westminster and Vancouver a fond farewell. My van and Cadillac were both in tip-top condition, and we made the trip with no major problems. Before getting to Winnipeg, though, I stopped and called Andy Patterson. He had planned on me being there that night to play for the dance, but we were running late. "Andy, we're down here at the Customs and Immigration, which is fifty or sixty miles from Winnipeg, and it's now around 5:00 P.M. We're very tired and won't be able to work tonight." "Well, that's too bad," he said. "I was depending on you." His answer surprised me, and I said, "Okay, Andy, I'll do my very best to make it." He laughed and said, "I'll hold things until you get here."

We pulled into Patterson's Barn after all the hard driving, and we hadn't had a bath in two or three days, and we looked terrible. Andy said, "Well, do you think you can handle the job tonight?" Then he laughed, with that big old hearty laugh he had, and that's when I realized he had been kidding me all along. But I joined in with his band anyway, and I played until about 1:00 A.M. I've always done my best if somebody treats me half decently. I don't care how bad the circumstances are, I'll do everything I can to please that person. On the other hand, if they are mean or cross me, I'll do everything against them.

Patterson's Barn was a neat building in the shape of a barn. The dance part was upstairs, and it could hold or dance approximately two hundred fifty people, possibly three hundred. It had no air-conditioning, and the only ventilation came from a small window in the back of the stage and small windows on each side to help keep the air circulating. Can you imagine playing upstairs in a place that reminds you of a hayloft, with the temperature outside ninety degrees? You could hardly breathe. Every chance I'd get between songs, I'd go to the tiny window and stick my head out, and even though it might be ninety degrees outside, it felt like twenty below in comparison to the oven we played in. I'd fill my lungs with fresh air, and I'd breathe in and out as hard as I could. But after a few minutes I could wring my clothes out, and sweat would roll down my face again. Well, at least I had a paying job.

Two or three days later, here came my bandleader and the other musicians. We began playing at Andy's place as agreed, but not only was the bandleader often late to the dances, the other musicians had become lax, too. Andy's helpers ran a small restaurant downstairs, and they were fussy when the band didn't start on time. I didn't blame them, because they relied on the people at the dances to work up a sweat and buy sandwiches, cold drinks, and beer.

Since Patterson's Barn had a dance only on Saturday nights, I had the time to schedule several appearances around the Winnipeg area. While I was playing at one of these shows, the man in charge jumped all over me. "Look," he said, "the show was supposed to start at eight and here it is almost nine. People are getting restless. They'll ask for their money back and go home. You'd better get something going real fast." I didn't like getting criticized, and I didn't want to get a bad reputation. The band finally came, and I was fit to be tied. I told the guys I couldn't put up with it any longer, and I sent them home.

They went back to Vancouver, and as I expected, it wasn't long before here came a letter again from the famous American Federation of Musicians. Those cats claimed I had fired them without justification, and I was right back in the same old hot water. I was beginning to wonder if I would ever get the union off my back.

Not having a band to make personal appearances, I had more free time than what I was used to, so we spent a good deal of time with the Pattersons. There were several boys and several very pretty daughters in the Patterson family, and they were among the nicest people we had ever met. We began calling Andy "Pop" and Mrs. Patterson "Mom." Min liked Mom so much she almost lived at their house, and Pop and I had more fun than a barrel of monkeys. He and I would have a few nips during the day, and the more he drank, the funnier he got—and he was funny to begin with.

One day Pop asked me to go with him to Portage-la-Prairie, located about sixty miles west of Winnipeg. He told me about the mental hospital located there and said it would do us both good to pay a visit. "They have about a hundred fifty patients, and I'm sure those poor souls never get to see or hear any live entertainment. Why don't you bring your guitar and sing for the folks? They'll appreciate it, even if they don't understand it." We enjoyed the scenic beauty that afternoon as we drove to the hospital. The folks in charge of the institution made us feel welcome, and they had everything set up for the show in the small auditorium.

Some people seemed tired, judging by the expressions on their faces, and some of the audience looked depressed and sad. Some smiled constantly, and others showed no emotion at all. I felt sorry for these people, and I thought how thankful I should be that I had my good health.

I sang for about a half hour, and they did seem to enjoy it. Then all of a sudden someone came running in and said, "There's smoke coming from inside your car." That shook me up and I ran outside. I had parked my Cadillac close to the building, and I remembered smoking a cigarette before I went inside. The cigarette lighter had stuck and gotten hot, and the rubber on some of the wires under the dash had burned off. I took my handkerchief and pulled the lighter out as quickly as I could. If someone hadn't noticed the smoke, my car might have burned up.

After this excitement I went back into the institution, and the people in charge asked if I'd shake hands with the people I entertained. Pop suggested, "Since it's a beautiful day, why don't you let the folks go outside and form a line, and then Hank can shake hands with all of them as they come down the line?" It just happened that I had a bunch of eight-by-ten pictures of me in the car. So when they were all in line outside, I shook hands with each patient and signed a picture for each person. It was sad and very touching, but nevertheless, there is a little humor that goes with this story. One fellow, about twenty-five years old, came to me with a big smile on his face and shook my hand for the longest time. He was a happy guy and we started talking. He wasn't making much sense, but I shook my head and went along with his conversation. I signed his picture, and he walked away. I continued to autograph pictures and said something pleasant to each person. After I'd talked to about eight people, that same fellow came up to me and showed me the picture I had signed a few minutes earlier, and he shook my hand again. I smiled and he walked on. When he got to the end of the line, he came back again, and again—five or six times. Each time I smiled and shook his hand.

I was pleased to help bring a little joy into the lives of those poor souls, and events like these have never escaped my mind. But you would never believe the funny stories Pop told from his observations at the institution. He had me constantly laughing all the way back to Winnipeg. No harm was intended. After all, he was the one who insisted on going there in the first place. Pop was a big lovable Irishman who had a big tender heart. When we got back home, we told Min and his family about our trip and said we all should count our blessings.

We stayed in Winnipeg, and I worked at Patterson's Barn until way into the summer. Billy King was still with me, and he did a floor show with his juggling act wherever I played. Even though I had dismissed my musicians, I still sang with Pop's band and all the dances he put on.

The time with the Pattersons that summer was one of the most pleasant periods of my life. I kept in touch with them over the years, and every time I returned to play the auditorium in Winnipeg, I made a point to see them. Seeing their family was the first order of business. I'd call ahead and let them know I was on my way, and I would run by and spend a few minutes with them. Whenever they were able to attend my concerts, I made sure they had choice seats, and I'd always mention their names during the show. I sang and dedicated my song "My Mother" to Mom Patterson at each concert. Mom and Pop have passed away, and I know both are in heaven. I'll always have the fondest of memories in my heart for the Patterson family. God bless them.

By the end of the summer of 1949 it was time to move on again. I made the decision to go east and maybe play a few show dates in eastern Quebec, New Brunswick, and Nova Scotia. But most of all I had the urge to go to Newfoundland. I had never been there except when I was at sea and our vessels went into various ports for fresh bait. If I could make it to Newfoundland, then I would have traveled clear across the Dominion of Canada, from British Columbia to Newfoundland, from the most western part to the most eastern part. So I had to do it.

There was a radio station in St. John's, Newfoundland, I believe it was CJON. The disc jockey was Mengie Schulman. Mengie was from some part of New England, and how he happened to wind up in St. John's, I don't know. But I heard he was playing a lot of my Canadian records on the station. So in going there I wouldn't be completely unknown.

Before leaving, I tried to find a driver for my horse van, but I couldn't. Luckily, I had saved enough money to ship my Cadillac to

New Brunswick by rail. I had never driven the big horse van, but I had to try to drive it myself. We bid the Pattersons a fond farewell, and Min, Jimmie, Billy King, and I jumped in the van and headed east.

I drove real slow for the first hundred miles, trying to get the feel of the gears, but I constantly clashed them. I knew if I didn't do better than that, I'd tear the rear end out, and we would be stranded out on the highway. But I was learning to synchronize the clutch with the speed of the vehicle, and it wasn't long before I was driving as if I had driven it all my life. My biggest worry was going through towns, because when I pulled up to a traffic light, I had to be careful to not stop short, because it might harm the horse.

As we were driving along, we came to a small town where I had to follow a detour sign, and I had to drive on a narrow but paved country road. I came to an underpass, and this put some fear in me. Was it high enough to let my high van pass underneath? Some of the underpasses back then had no signs telling the height and width. I got out and looked at the underpass and then the van. It appeared as if the van would go under the bridge without any trouble. I got in and drove almost up to the underpass, and again I got out to look things over. I was still convinced I was well in the clear. What I didn't check was if the pavement had rises in it. I got the van halfway through, and would you believe it, we were stuck under the underpass. We couldn't move forward and we couldn't back up. Either way would severely damage the top of the van. I was baffled.

Luckily, no cars were held up during this episode, so I just stood there beside the van and tried to figure something out. There had to be a solution. I presumed I needed an inch or two to make the clearance. "Ah," I thought, "I know just what to do. I'll let some air out of all the tires." I did, and that lowered the van just barely enough to get it through without even scraping the top. Fortunately, there was a service station close by, and I had the tires blown back up to where they should be. Then we were on our merry way.

After about another fifty miles down the highway, I did something I should not have done. I was exhausted because of the problem at the underpass, so I mentioned to Billy that I felt like having a cold beer, and Billy was all for it. But Min spoke up, "You should not be bothering with drinking beer while you're driving the van. You're not that familiar with it yet." Anyway, we stopped at a roadside store, and Billy went in and got us a six-pack. I drank a beer as we were cruising down the highway. Soon we came up on this big open field, right at the side of the road, and I pulled over to let the dogs out for a while and to exercise Shawnee. Besides, I needed a rest. Billy and I drank another beer, and then I backed Shawnee out of the van.

It's funny how Shawnee could always tell if I'd had a drink. When he smelled alcohol, he would get as stubborn as a mule. He would do just the opposite of what he was supposed to do. I would never work Shawnee at any show if I had taken the first drink, because I couldn't get him to do a half-decent act. So when I took him out of the van to exercise him that night, he was difficult. I'm sure he didn't mean to do it, but he was feeling good, being out in the good clear fresh night air, and he kicked his hind feet out behind him. The shoe on one of his hind feet struck me right in the ankle, and I thought my whole leg had dropped off. This was the worst pain I'd ever had, and I thought I would go berserk.

For the next three or four days I could hardly straighten my leg out all the way. Every time I tried, it would throb and pain something terrible. Moreover, this was the foot I used for braking. The brake pedal, of course, was on the right side, and I had to shift my left foot over to the brake pedal in order to slow down or stop. I did manage, but it was a slow process. I had a limp for quite some time, and when I was limping around, I swear I could see Shawnee *smiling* as if he was saying, "That'll teach you to drink and drive!" It took a long time for my ankle to heal, and it still gives me a problem, especially in damp weather.

We made it to Campbellton in early morning and stopped at Doyle's Cabins, about three miles from town, and rented two cabins. This place was close to Doc Roy's Pavilion, where I'd played a dance a long time earlier. The next day I called my old friend Hubert Smith, the taxi driver, and he drove me to the railroad station, where my car was parked in a big freight shed. I drove to the radio station to see my good friend Stan Chapman. It was nice seeing him again and the other folks I had worked with several months before. I asked Mr. Chapman if he could give me a radio spot. I explained that my plans were to book a few show dates up the Gaspé coast in Quebec and around the areas surrounding Campbellton.

Mr. Chapman responded, "Well, Hank, you can have a half hour either in the afternoon or in the evening, or you can have them both, whatever suits you the best. We want to please you. I know you'll have a fine program. You always did, and I know our listeners will be real pleased to know you're back with us again." I thanked him and asked for the 2:30 P.M. slot, as well as the one at 7:30. But I told him I would give up the evening radio show as soon as I got my band organized to make personal appearances, and that was fine with him.

I called Eugene Beaulieau, my old friend in New Carlisle, Quebec, who had worked for me before. He was a heavy-set, healthy-looking man, and a fine old-time fiddle player. I told him my plans. He said he'd get his work caught up, and he'd be glad to drive the van and would love to play the shows in eastern Quebec and up the Gaspé coast—provided we could play close enough to New Carlisle to return at night.

I lined up a few other musicians and booked many of the same towns where we'd had shows earlier, when I had my old homemade trailer. Of course, I would always announce to my radio audiences where and when we'd be making personal appearances. We played Richmond, Bonaventure, Carlton, and New Carlisle, among other places. I didn't use Shawnee on these shows, but I always parked my horse van in Eugene's yard, and Min, Jimmie, and I would sleep in the van rather than be an extra burden to Eugene and his family.

The folks all up the coast were friendly. Most of them were Roman Catholic. Many of them spoke French but understood both French and English. As I mentioned earlier, in most of my shows up the coast I had to make arrangements with the priest in each parish, and we split the proceeds on a 50-50 basis. I enjoyed working with the priests, and that's one of the reasons I wanted to play the Gaspé coast again.

I was surprised at one place where we were scheduled to play, when the priest sent a message he'd like to see me. So before I got dressed for the show, I went over to his office. The priest and I shook hands. He said, "I thought you might like to have a drink with me before your program." I was startled for a minute. I didn't know whether he meant a drink of ginger ale, Coke, or what. However, he got two glasses from a nearby closet and poured out two drinks of rum, and I mean it tasted like it could be 100 proof. Then he poured out the second drink for us, and certainly I wasn't going to refuse the kindness of the priest, so we drank them together. That night I was extremely relaxed onstage, and we had a real good show.

I have nothing but praise for the Catholic people and how nice they treated us all the times we were in Quebec. They were true Hank Snow fans and loved country music. And many of them turned out to be steady record buyers of mine.

After we completed our tour of the Gaspé coast and New Brunswick, we continued on east to my home province of Nova Scotia. The band members returned to their homes, and Eugene drove my van to Halifax. Then Eugene had to get back to his regular work. I understood and thanked him for working with me all those weeks and for driving the van.

We stayed with Min's family, and I started laying out my plans for our trip to Newfoundland. I had heard about Gus Winter in St. John's, who ran a big record store and had a bunch of jukeboxes throughout the area. After my initial contact by letter I phoned him, and he said, "Yes, come on over here, Hank. Your records are being played on CJON, and I believe we can work out some good things together. I'm sure you'll pack the houses here, wherever you play." He seemed so confident that I could hardly wait.

I was feeling pretty confident, too. I had been hearing reports that "Marriage Vow" was selling real well in the States, and I felt I was over one more hurdle in my music career.

24

Grand Ole Opry

That big eight-wheeler rollin' down the track
Means your true-lovin' daddy ain't comin' back.
I'm movin' on, I'll soon be gone.
You were flyin' too high for my little old sky,
So I'm movin' on.

"I'm Movin' On," by Hank Snow

NOW IT WAS JUST BILLY KING, JIMMIE, and me. Billy was a great entertainer with his juggling act, and the folks loved Jimmie when I put him on the stage dressed in his cowboy suit. But I needed to hire some musicians and find a place to board Shawnee before we could go to Newfoundland.

Through my good friend Angus Allen I located a gentleman who maintained regular racehorse stables in Sydney, the town where we were to take the boat to Port-aux-Basques in Newfoundland. He said he'd be glad to keep Shawnee and my dog Pal, and he wouldn't charge me a penny. It was hard to believe that someone I'd never met before could be that good to me. I'm sure it was because of Angus, who was a super-nice guy.

I hired Bernie O'Connell, a fair steel player, and Roy Curry, a former guitar student of mine. Roy was a satisfactory rhythm-guitar player and a pretty good singer, and he agreed to drive my truck to Sydney to the stables where Shawnee and Pal would stay. I planned to park the horse van and my car in Sydney, at a safe place near the docks. Mickey, our little terrier, was to go with us to Newfoundland. He would be company for Jimmie while we were on the island.

We were ready to leave for Sydney, when we suddenly discovered that Mickey was nowhere to be found. We all became very upset over this, especially Jimmie. We searched and searched, and we drove around the streets within about a twenty-block area. No luck. Then we had to leave, or we would have missed our reservations on the boat, since it was a good two hundred fifty miles from Halifax to Sydney, Cape Breton. You'll never know how bad we hated to leave without our little dog. Several people told us they would keep inquiring in the vicinity, and if Mickey turned up, they would keep him until we returned. We were all so sad, we hardly talked as we drove to Sydney.

When the boat landed at Port-aux-Basques, Gus Winter had someone meet us and drive us to a cheap hotel, where we checked in, cleaned up, and had a good night's rest. We left the next morning for the long train ride to St. John's, and all the way we were worried sick about little Mickey.

My first impression of Newfoundland, from years earlier, was how cold it was for the end of summer. The temperature was about thirty-five degrees, and it was damp and foggy.

Since Gus was so enthusiastic about me bringing my band to St. John's, I thought he would effectively promote our shows, and I had expected us to have full houses wherever we played. Apparently he didn't believe in advertising very much. He thought all he had to do was send someone into those small towns and villages, spread the word by mouth in the streets that Hank Snow and his show would be appearing, and we'd pack every hall. He soon found out it didn't work that way. Audiences at many of our shows were small until I got on the radio station with Mengie Schulman, the disc jockey, and announced where we would be playing in the next three or four days. I cut several radio spots to be used on Mengie's program. Then we started having good crowds, but the biggest hall wouldn't hold over three hundred to three hundred fifty people. We were only charging fifteen cents for children under twelve years of age and twenty-five cents for adults, so we didn't make much money. Nevertheless we met a lot of fine people, saw great scenery, and enjoyed our leisure time. This last was unusual for me. During most of my career I was going full blast, trying desperately to make something happen, so I didn't have much time for taking life in a relaxed sort of way.

Since we didn't have our own transportation, I hired Charlie Windsor, a taxi owner, to drive us to the halls where we played. Bill Grant worked for Gus Winter, and he traveled with us to help set up the public-address system and do just about anything we needed done. Bill loved pulling jokes, and he was a real funny guy. One afternoon, at one of the villages where we were to play that night, I asked Bill if he'd drop by Gus's record store and pick up a sound-effects record of a huge crowd laughing and carrying on. I told him about my idea for us to have some extra fun on the evening show.

He found one and brought it with him before showtime. It was perfect. It sounded like ten thousand people all bursting into laughter. Backstage, behind the back curtain, I had a record player hooked into the speakers out front that projected to the audience, so we had what we needed to play a practical joke on the people in the hall. I said, "Bill, somewhere in the middle of my show, I'll tell the most unfunny joke I can think of. It will make no sense at all. At the end of the joke, or what is to be the punchline, start the record of this laughing, clapping, and yelling. We'll see how many people will turn to each other to see who's laughing, and they'll be wondering why." Bill thoroughly understood that about the middle of the show I'd sing a song to alert him that I would tell my joke after that song was over.

That night after I finished the song, I said to the audience, "Friends, before I do another song, I have got to tell you the funniest joke I've ever heard." Well, this put the audience on the edge of their seats. I told this joke that didn't make a damn bit of sense, and the people just sat there motionless. There was no laughing. No yelling. No clapping. And nothing came through the speakers, as it should have at that moment. Bill had missed his cue! He couldn't find the switch to start the turntable, and I just stood there with the cold sweat pouring off me in bucketsful. Then, as everything got deathly still again, Bill started the record, and here came the sound like thousands of people laughing, applauding, and yelling—but there was a dead silence in the hall.

I was on center stage and had just laid the biggest egg in my entire life. But you know the old saying, "Never let them see you sweat." Well, it didn't work that night, believe me. After I wiped my brow and gained my composure, I told the crowd how it was supposed to have worked. Then we got a big laugh from the audience, as we would have if it had worked the way it was planned. Bill and I have laughed about that incident many times since.

After three weeks of shows in Newfoundland we boarded the boat back to Sydney with a lot of good memories. I had satisfied my ambitions for a music tour across Canada, from Vancouver, British Columbia, to the island of Newfoundland.

At Sydney we took the van from where it was parked and picked up Shawnee and Pal, who were very glad to see us. I offered to pay the man, but he wouldn't take a penny. "I enjoy your records," he said, "and that's pay enough." After we picked up my car, we headed back to Halifax.

As we drove along the highway, we talked about little Mickey and wondered if we'd ever see him again. As soon as we got settled in Halifax, I called the radio station, CHNS, gave a description of the dog, and offered a reward to anyone who found him. In a couple of days someone called and reported him found. Mickey was as happy to see us as we were to see him. Thanks to the Good Lord, our prayers had been answered. Later on some neighbors told us the sad story. They had seen Mickey several times sitting on this particular corner where the streetcar stopped, and he'd sit there, hour after hour, waiting for one of us to get off. Our van was about the same color as the streetcar, and the corner where the streetcar stopped was close to where our van was parked before we left for Newfoundland. Mickey must have thought we had deserted him.

When I picked up my mail in Halifax, I had a letter from Bea Terry. She wanted me to contact her as soon as I could. I phoned right away, and she said Ed McLamore, of the Dallas Sportatorium, had been inquiring as to my whereabouts. As she was talking, I had visions that maybe, just maybe, this was the big break I'd been waiting for. Whatever was happening, I thought we should go to Dallas and check it out. I thanked Bea for the information and told her I would call her the minute I got there.

We stayed a few days in Halifax with Min's family, and I took care of business matters. I made arrangements with a friend to drive the van. He was an experienced truck driver and had driven livestock many times before, so I had an easy mind about my horse and dogs being well taken care of. As always, I followed the van a mile or two behind, in case of any trouble. We arrived at the border in Calais, Maine, and had no trouble clearing the animals, as they had been previously vaccinated by a government-licensed veterinarian. We stopped several times at night to get the van driver a motel room so he could rest up. We always slept in the bed over the cab of the van and used the driver's motel room each morning to shower and clean up.

In Dallas we parked the van a few miles from downtown, where I could take Shawnee out every day and exercise him. We planned to live in the van while I looked for a small apartment. As soon as the driver got rested up, I paid his way and he returned to Halifax.

I called Bea Terry. It was not Ed McLamore who wanted to see me, but Fred Edwards, who had been a disc jockey at KRLD when "Brand on My Heart" had made it on KRLD's big hit parade. Bea gave me Fred's phone number, and I called him. He told me he had been contacted by a club owner around Fort Worth who was running a big show in Corpus Christi, Texas, with Hank Williams as the headliner. He asked if I'd be interested in doing a spot on the show. If so, it would pay me $200. Naturally I grabbed the chance.

I liked Hank Williams right off the bat. I had heard rumors that he was a heavy drinker, but he certainly wasn't drinking at that time. It was a fine show. Hank received a lot of applause, and I could see he was a fine entertainer because of the feeling he projected in each of his songs. I felt I was a part of the success of the show, because many people applauded me, too.

Between shows Hank and I had a long talk, and I soon discovered we had a lot in common. We were both very poor as we grew up. We both wrote many sad songs, and we had lived many of the songs we sang. We were both beginning to see our careers take off—even though I wasn't sure about mine at that time. Hank had just released on MGM Records his number-one hit, the old song "Lovesick Blues," which was being played across the country. He knew I had appeared on the Louisiana Hayride previous to our meeting, and he invited me to come on back again as a guest. I knew this kind of exposure would do me a world of good.

Min and Jimmie stayed in Dallas, and I drove to Shreveport to be on the Saturday night show. I was happy about my reception on the Hayride, because I received a big buildup when I was introduced. When I finished singing, the applause was tremendous, and I thought about how much I enjoyed the appreciative American audience.

After the show Hank and I talked some more, and he invited me to his house for a visit the next day. He knew how hard I was trying to get a hit in the United States, and he was unusually kind to me. The next day, Sunday afternoon, I drove to his wood-frame house. It was small but cozy. I remember at that time he was driving a big car to his show dates, and he towed a big black luggage trailer, which was parked in the yard. "Hank Williams and the Drifting Cowboys" was painted in gold on the side of the trailer.

Hank's wife, Audrey, was in her bedroom when I visited. She was pregnant at the time with Hank, Jr. After we visited for a while, he invited me to drive downtown with him to a jewelry store and pick up a ring he'd bought for Audrey and to pick up some colored pictures he was having enlarged. He showed me the pictures of him and Audrey, and they were impressive, but I didn't see the diamond ring.

We went back to the house. Audrey never did come out of the bedroom. Being pregnant, she might have been in a bad mood, so I understood. But Hank went into the bedroom and came back out suddenly. At the time I didn't know what was taking place, but he told me later he was having problems with Audrey. When he gave the ring to her, she looked at it and then threw it across the floor. She said, "If you can't do any better than that for me, then just forget it." I felt sorry for Hank that day. He was good to me and I never forgot it. I felt I'd made a fine friend.

After our visit I drove to the hotel, checked out, and headed back to Dallas. Driving always gave me a chance to clear my mind and set things straight, and believe me, I've done a heck of a lot of driving in my days.

Time passed by, and no word from Ernest. I became somewhat depressed. Maybe I'd never get on the Opry.

In the meantime my friend Don Snellings was taking me to many radio stations where disc jockeys would interview me. He also took me to record stores to meet people and to autograph records. All this attention pulled me out of the dumps about not hearing from Ernest. Then, because of a sudden burst in sales of my RCA Victor records in Dallas, as well as throughout Texas, Don was walking on air. He was a top-notch salesman for the record department of the Adleda company, and he was happy for me, too.

About this time I began attending all of the Saturday night shows at the Dallas auditorium, known as the Big D Jamboree. I was permitted to visit the dressing rooms of the artists, and I had a chance to meet many of the big country artists of that era. One Saturday night I met Cowboy Copas for the first time. He had a big hit called "Breeze," and I liked his singing. I remember that same night, while carrying a huge box of souvenir books, he had a bad accident. He slipped on one of the ramps and fell and broke his ankle. A few months later he and I did a few record-store autograph sessions together.

Through Cowboy Copas I met a gentleman who was one of the great promoters of country music. His name was Oscar Davis, and all the performers knew and respected him highly. I asked Oscar one night, after the Big D Jamboree, if he would promote me. I showed him pictures of Shawnee doing his tricks with me, my Canadian songbooks, a few records, and an eight-by-ten picture. Oscar advised me to continue doing what I was doing. "You've got plenty of time, Hank. Get a little more seasoning in the States with your act, and I'll get in touch with you when the time is right." Oscar was a multi-talented person. He created a lot of original radio advertising, sayings, and methods that promoters would later copy. The commercials he invented contained dramatic sayings that held one's attention to the last word. Often he would say, "And don't you dare miss it," in his New England accent. Friends, if you've paid attention to radio stations plugging a country show coming to your town, I'll bet you've heard those words many times.

It seemed like Oscar was poor most of the time. He didn't put one bit of value on money. It burnt holes in his pockets. He used to flash a big diamond ring, maybe a five-carat stone, and if he didn't have that ring on his finger, you knew he was broke and his ring was hocked. When you saw him again and he had the ring on, you knew he had money. I remember he'd tip bellboys, taxi drivers, and others twenty dollars, maybe fifty dollars, just for taking his suitcase upstairs or riding a few blocks in a cab.

Later on, during the 1950s and 1960s, Oscar did promote many shows in which I was the headline act, and none was a failure. We were always assured of a full house whenever he promoted, even in places like the Denver Coliseum, with twelve thousand capacity; in Miami, Florida, with fifteen thousand; in Fort Worth, Texas, with seven thousand. His passing a few years ago was a blow to the music world. They don't make promoters like him anymore.

Anyway, about this time, I went to see a Cadillac dealer in downtown Dallas to look at the new 1949 Cadillacs. I wanted to trade my convertible in for one. Mine was still in good shape, but I was determined to have a four-door Cadillac, and mainly I wanted the automatic shift and the power steering. I found the perfect car in a pretty shade of blue, and since blue has always been my favorite color, I made a deal on the trade-in and bought it. Later I had the lower half of the car painted canary yellow, so it would be a contrast in colors. The colors were loud and flashy, just the way I wanted it.

Between my new Cadillac and my colorful stage wardrobe, you could certainly see me coming! "Keep that big front, always"—that was still my motto. That's the way I thought I should do it. I wore expensive, custom-made western suits, which I still owed for, and I drove a big Cadillac that wasn't paid for.

Some people already thought I was a big-time performer. I was still getting many requests for radio interviews and record-store appearances, just like the big stars of the day. However, the most important thing to me was to hear from Ernest Tubb about getting on the Grand Ole Opry. I had been waiting and waiting and waiting.

Finally, the big moment came!

I got a phone call from Ernest. "Hank, I had a talk with Mr. Denny yesterday, and he told me to bring you in to see him. He thinks he'll be able to place you on the Opry, so come to Nashville right away if at all possible. I'm really happy for you, so give me a call just as soon as you get to the city." Again, I was walking on cloud nine. I could hardly wait to tell Min the good news.

My plan was to leave Min and Jimmie in Dallas until I could work everything out with the Opry. I would have to find a place to live and locate a place to board Shawnee. Then I'd send for my family.

Bright and early the next morning I was on my way to Nashville in my brand-new Cadillac. On the way I was wondering how Ernest ever convinced Mr. Denny to put me on the Opry. Earlier, when Ernest had taken my records to WSM, they told him I sounded too much like him. Now, I sound as much like Ernest Tubb as I do Dolly Parton. This of course had been a brush-off. Naturally, I wondered if Mr. Denny would put me on the Opry on a trial basis, or whether I was being hired sight unseen. I reminded myself that no one had been hired before unless they had a hit record. This was reality, and it brought me down from cloud nine as I thought about it. After all, I didn't have a hit record in the U.S.A., I had a hit record around the Dallas area. If it didn't work out with the Opry, I'd be on my way back to Dallas. But I was optimistic, and I was like a little kid waiting for Christmas.

When I arrived in Nashville, I checked into a motel out on Franklin Road. I called Ernest at once, and as luck would have it, he happened to be at his record shop on Commerce Street. I went immediately to the store. After we had a brief chat, he took me to see Mr. Denny, just a few blocks up the hill from the store, on Seventh Avenue.

As we walked up to the big building that housed the WSM studios and offices, I was anxious. Mr. Denny was an important man, and I wanted to make a good impression on him. In addition to being the manager of the Opry, he was in charge of the Opry Talent Agency, which booked the Opry acts. When I met Mr. Denny, I was highly impressed. He was a very pleasant man, and it was obvious he was a good friend of Ernest. I felt at ease with him right away.

Mr. Denny didn't say anything about a tryout, and I didn't ask. He said he wanted me to start on the Opry on January 7, 1950, and I'd be paid seventy-five dollars per week. My dream had come true! A steady job at seventy-five dollars a week! And I would be a part of the world's biggest country music show! Everyone wanted to be on the Grand Ole Opry. This was the pinnacle of success, and it would bring a performer instant recognition.

WSM's 50,000-watt, clear-channel signal covered much of the United States. In addition to carrying the Opry live, the station had a half-hour show, sponsored by the Prince Albert Smoking Tobacco Company, that carried a half hour of the Opry on the national network across America.

Mr. Denny said, "Hank, we'll set up a publicity campaign and make up a press kit on you to send to the radio stations and to the promoters and buyers. We'll place ads in *Cashbox, Billboard, Variety,* and other trade papers. You'll need a few current eight-by-ten pictures of three different poses." He sent me to Henry Schoffield, a professional photographer, and his staff did the pictures right away. All the wheels were put in motion to promote Hank Snow.

Since I had over a month to get my family moved from Dallas, I took a room at the Clarkston Hotel, located right next to the station, and I began to plan my next moves.

One day I had breakfast with Hugh Cherry, a disc jockey, and the next morning he did an interview with me on his program, which was downstairs in the Maxwell House Hotel. I was thrilled when Eddy Arnold joined us. In our conversation I told Eddy I was looking for a place for my family to live, and he mentioned the name of a friend of his, Clarence E. Chance. He was in the real-estate business and lived in Madison, roughly six miles from Nashville. Eddy said he was honest and had a good reputation.

I contacted Mr. Chance and told him I wanted to bring my family to Nashville in a few weeks, and if things went well for me at the Opry, I might be in the market for a new home. He recommended I rent a small house on Sarver Avenue in Madison. I looked it over, and it was just the right size. It had plenty of yard space for Jimmie to play in and for the dogs to romp around in. The house was quaint and comfortable. It looked like a palace compared to some of the places we had lived in over the past years.

Mr. Chance even offered to take care of Shawnee. He had a clean barn and had just the right box stall for him. I was pleased and took him up on his offer. He said, "When you're ready to buy, I'm sure I can find just what you need. I hope things do work out for you in Nashville, and good luck at the Grand Ole Opry."

With a place for Shawnee to live and a nice home for the Snow family, I was ready to return to Dallas and share my excitement with Min at being hired on the Opry. I was never so happy in all my life, and I drove straight through to Dallas, over seven hundred miles.

Again one of my friends offered to drive my horse van, and as soon as I got everything squared away, we bid our close friends good-bye, and we were ready for Nashville. You'll remember the van had a partition between where Shawnee lived and my office in the front. We put Min's big console TV set in the office, as well as my silver saddle, clothing, and other personal items. We didn't have any furniture to fool with. What little we had was being stored in Moncton, New Brunswick.

So we headed out to the country music capital of the world—Nashville, Tennessee. We had a safe trip, and the whole world looked good to us. Why not? After all, I was going to be a regular on the famous Grand Ole Opry, a job that any country entertainer would give anything to have. We drove through the city of Nashville in late afternoon and out to Madison to see Mr. Chance at his home, where his stables were located. We got Shawnee settled in his new home, and after he was fed and watered, I took the driver of the van to a motel for the night. Then I drove the Snow family to our rented home for a much-needed rest.

The next day I drove my driver friend to the airport and paid his way back to Dallas. Then we made arrangements to get Jimmie started in school. It didn't take long for us to get settled in our small home and for Min to have everything cozy and comfortable and looking like a home should look.

Everything was gradually falling in place. I did a few guest spots around Nashville, which were mainly interviews with disc jockeys, and I continued to write songs.

But my main thoughts were centered on my upcoming first night on the Opry, and I had a lot of time left to worry about it. Listeners from many parts of the country would be listening to me sing for the first time. My future would be in their hands, and their hands alone. If the public didn't like what I was doing, that could easily be the end of my career, as far as the big time was concerned. They could end my dream. I had been paying my dues for many years. I was thirty-five years old, and I felt I had one big opportunity remaining.

Since I didn't have a band at the time, Ernest said I could use his Texas Troubadours on the Opry stage until I could afford to hire my own musicians. I was all set when January 7, 1950, finally arrived. To put it mildly, I was horribly nervous. In a way, I was most concerned with not letting Ernest down. I wanted to prove to him that his faith in me was not misguided. I didn't want to lay an egg.

I remember that night so well. I put on my beautiful custom-made gold suit, and I did something that I have done very few times since. I wore my big white Stetson hat. Back then hats were not so important to country singers. Most artists on the Opry didn't wear them. Only a few did, like Ernest Tubb. He was known for his white Stetson.

Believe me, I say this in all honesty: I said many prayers during the few weeks before my Opry debut that I would be a success. God has His plan worked out for all of us, even a little weakling from Nova Scotia, Canada.

Ernest introduced me, "From up Canada way, here's the newest member of the Grand Ole Opry, the Singing Ranger, Hank Snow!" My whole body was trembling as I went out on that stage, and I sang the song that had done so much for me in Dallas, "Brand on My Heart." When I finished, I got only mild applause, not anything near what I was getting in Dallas or back in Canada. I felt sort of embarrassed, and I couldn't leave the stage fast enough. All of the artists received a great deal of applause—except me. I had been looking forward to this moment for many years, and now I was completely discouraged. Apparently no one had ever heard of Hank Snow in the States, at least not outside of the Texas area.

After the show Min and I got into our new Cadillac and went back to our rented home in Madison. I told her how disappointed I was. "Min, I am never, never going back to the Opry. The Grand Ole Opry is not for me. I'll go back to Canada, where people know and appreciate me. I'll carry on in Canada as I have for so many years. It's better to be a big toad in a small puddle than a small toad in a big puddle."

Min sure set me straight and pronto, thank God. She said, "Now, you can't expect everything to happen in just one night. People will become more familiar with you as time goes on. You're lucky you've been given this chance. I think you'd be crazy, after all you've been through, to get discouraged over one night, and above all, to let Ernest down after he fought big odds to get you here."

I listened to Min, and I continued on the Opry. I gave it the best I had, but I was still getting only mild applause. The audience seemed to look at me curiously, as if studying me. Let me give you an idea of what I'm talking about. I'm sure most of you are familiar with the way the little RCA Victor dog, Nipper, is posed with his head cocked to the one side, like he's listening in the big horn on the gramophone to his master's voice. Well, that's the way those people looked at me, at least those I could see beyond the footlights on the stage. In other words, I thought they were thinking, "What in the hell is he trying to prove?" Nevertheless, with my hard-headed stubbornness, I said to Min, "You're right. I'll be damned if I'll quit, as long as they will let me stay."

Trying to be optimistic, I decided to get some good musicians together in case RCA Victor wanted to record me again. Somebody told me that Joe Talbot played a good commercial steel guitar, so I got in touch with him and invited him to our rented home. Joe and I had a nice visit. I played a few of my Canadian records. Then I played and sang several songs, and he started playing backup behind me. After a short time he said, "I really do like your style of singing, and with a real good fiddle player, I believe we can create an original sound for you, Hank. I know an excellent fiddle player who would do your music and singing justice. His name is Tommy Vaden."

I got in touch with Tommy and invited him and Joe over together one Sunday afternoon, and we played several of my songs. As soon as I heard the rich tone of Tommy's fiddle, I knew immediately I wanted him to work with me. Tommy's music and Joe's music were made for each other. Together they created exactly what I wanted for the Hank Snow sound.

I knew I had a unique singing style, but I had never been able to establish a definite music style. Because I had used so many musicians over the years, it had been difficult to create any certain and long-lasting sound. Friends, I'll say this now, as I've said a million times before, Tommy Vaden and Joe Talbot set the style of music that has stayed with me for the rest of my career. I sure hit the jackpot when I met them. Many of our top musicians in Nashville have come to me time and time again and said, "Hank, Tommy and Joe are part of you and your music. They have created a definite and rich sound that every musician searches for." They were so right.

After I'd been several weeks at the Opry, producer Steve Sholes called RCA Victor in Nashville and said he was preparing to come to Nashville and record some of the RCA Victor artists. I was one of them, and he left word for me to call him. When I got Steve on the phone, he asked if I had some strong songs ready to record. I said I did, and it wasn't a white lie like I had told Mr. Joseph before my first session in Montreal. This time I did have what I considered excellent material. I had songs I'd written and songs that had been sent to me from Hill and Range publishers by the Aberbach brothers.

I also told Steve I'd like to use Joe and Tommy, and he said, "No problem, just call RCA in Nashville, and they'll set up what they need at the studio for our session. Work out the arrangements on several songs, so I can decide which four would be the most commercial for you to record, and I'll see you soon."

RCA scheduled the recording date for one night only, at Brown's studio, which was a small upstairs studio in downtown Nashville. It was barely big enough for four or five people with their musical instruments, and it had a tiny control room. RCA was using it temporarily until they could make arrangments for a larger studio.

Since I was not pleased with the way I was being received at the Opry, I certainly didn't want to be a flop in my second recording session. The first session in Chicago had gone so well, but I wanted this session to be even better. I desperately needed a hit record! I rehearsed the songs alone that I hoped to record. Then I had Tommy and Joe out to our house, and together we practiced them many times over. Like me, they were enthused that we would be recording together for RCA Victor.

The song I wanted most to record was "I'm Movin' On." I told Min, before we left to go to the session, "I'll bet you money that Steve won't remember the song or remember turning it down in Chicago, because he's a busy man and listens to dozens of songs every day."

Our scheduled night for recording was March 28, 1950, at seven o'clock. We gathered into the little two-by-four studio to go over the songs so Steve, the producer, could decide which ones we would record. As we finished tuning our instruments, he said, "Okay, Hank, let's see what you've come up with." Naturally the first number I chose was "I'm Movin' On." I was going to be extremely disappointed if Steve turned it down again. After we played the song the way Tommy, Joe, and I had rehearsed it, Steve liked the drive and rhythm behind my singing. To my astonishment he said, "Okay, someone come up with a good, lively introduction." Friends, if you're familiar with the original record of "I'm Movin' On," you'll hear the excellent fiddle introduction that Tommy played. The introduction by Tommy and Joe, along with the combination of instruments and the driving rhythm we created, made the success of this record.

Steve never did say, nor did I ever ask, whether or not he remembered the Chicago session when he turned down "I'm Movin' On."

I'd like to point something out, but don't hold me to this. We recorded on one track only. This session was even before two-track machines came along, so all my work back then was done on one track. When I took the guitar lead on the chorus, I had to leave the singing and jump right to my position on the guitar to do the guitar break and then back to the singing again. Recording was very difficult then, compared to how it's done these days.

Steve agreed with my four selections, and we recorded these songs: "With This Ring, I Thee Wed," by Jack Rollins, Steve Nelson, and Ed Nelson, Jr.; "Paving the Highway with Tears," written by Steve Nelson and Ed Nelson, Jr.; "I Cried but My Tears Were Too Late" and "I'm Movin' On," two songs I had written. We captured a good sound and feeling on all of them. Steve was pleased, as were the musicians.

Besides me on these recordings, we had Velma Williams on rhythm; Ernie Newton, a fine bass man; Tommy on fiddle; and Joe, on steel guitar, who did those lonesome train whistles.

Velma was one of the first of the outstanding rhythm players when country music in Nashville was in its infancy. In addition to country, she played rhythm and blues, rock and roll, and any other style. She was busy all the time in the various studios. To get her to do a session, you had to make arrangements weeks in advance. She was also a perfect lady and a wonderful human being. Velma went by the name Williams, but she was Hal Smith's wife. Hal was an excellent fiddle player and a fine gentleman. He went into the publishing business and bought out the rights to some big publishing catalogs in Nashville. Later on he played with me when Tommy wasn't available, but it was a rare occasion when Tommy had to miss a play date with me. I believe Hal and Velma eventually bought a successful park in Kentucky, known as Renfro Valley.

While I was anxiously awaiting my first single record to be released out of this session, I stood in front of a Grand Ole Opry audience every Saturday night. My acceptance was still only lukewarm. Maybe I was expecting too much for a beginner on the Opry. However, I was getting more heartsick with every appearance I made, and it got to the point where I wasn't even looking forward to Monday coming around, as I knew I would have to go back there at the end of the week. This was an awful feeling to have, and Min would keep on saying, "Give it more time." Of course, she was right.

This may sound foolish, but during February, 1950, I wanted to buy a home. With the hard time I was having at the Opry, it was silly to even have such thoughts, because I couldn't afford it anyway, at seventy-five dollars a week. Since I had no contract with Mr. Denny, I didn't know if I could stay on with the Opry. However, I was never one to let the uncertain future stand in my way. If my records were successful in the States, I could buy a home for a small down payment and so much a month. After all those years of sacrificing for the hope of better days, I thought Min and Jimmie deserved better than the tiny, run-down apartments we had lived in throughout the years. We seriously wanted to have a home of our own.

One night at the Opry I told Mr. Denny I was looking to buy a house. He responded, "Don't do it, Hank, not now. If you want me to, I'll tell you when I think you should buy a house." This man was very careful. I guess he knew if I didn't come up with a hit real soon, the Opry might drop me from their roster. It wouldn't be his decision, but Jack Stapp, the program director, and Harry Stone, the manager of the entire operation, would act on sound business judgment. If I was not helping business, they would let me go. Nothing personal. That's the way business works.

Then in April, 1950, it finally happened.

After years and years of hard work and sacrifice, traveling from one end of Canada to the other, playing in numerous towns and villages, singing my heart out on so many radio stations, and paying my dues in a hundred other ways, I had a hit song. All these years of frustration came together with just one song—"I'm Movin' On."

Mr. Denny confirmed my earlier fears. He said, "A few weeks ago, Harry Stone was at the Opry and heard you sing for the first time. As he stood in the wings and watched you on stage, he said, 'Who in the hell is that out there trying to sing?' So I can tell you now, Hank, 'I'm Movin' On' was a miracle if I ever saw one. The management was just about ready to drop you from the Opry." The Good Lord was with me again. He answered my prayers in greater measure than I had ever dreamed of.

Through the years, when I've been interviewed by the news media, they often ask how I managed to stay on the Opry, the few months I did, without a hit song. Here's my response: "Just as the Opry was about to let me go, the Good Lord stepped in and guided my pen as I wrote the song 'I'm Movin' On.'" Actually, this song was written over two years earlier, but when I was in the most desperate need of a hit, the Good Lord also guided me to record it.

Several weeks after the single had been released, Mr. Denny gave me a vote of confidence. "Hank, now you can buy a house. Your song has been in the number-one spot for weeks, and it looks like it's going to remain there much longer. I think you're on your way."

"I'm Movin' On" stayed on the national charts in the number-one position for twenty-nine weeks, and altogether it was on the charts for fourteen months. These days it's rare for a song to remain number one for more than a week or two, and most songs drop completely off the charts after a few more weeks. *Cashbox, Billboard, Variety,* and a dozen other trade papers have said that this song holds the record for the most-played country record of all time.

Many people have branded me with the title "I'm Movin' On," and I hear it often. Sometimes when I'm in public, somebody will yell out to me, "Movin' On."

After "I'm Movin' On" was released, many positive things happened to me. I continued on with the Opry, and the audiences changed overnight. It was like magic. They were completely indifferent one week, and the next week they were wildly enthusiastic. I received one encore after another. It seemed like they just couldn't get enough of Hank Snow. Not only was "I'm Movin' On" a smash hit, so was the backside of the record, "With This Ring I Thee Wed."

Needless to say, I was happy with the success of my double-hit record, and I was confident about future releases. In particular I was overjoyed because I wanted to prove my success to Ernest Tubb. He always believed in me, and he was just as happy about my success as I was.

Feeling optimistic about the future, I went to see Mr. Chance about buying a house. He said he had a three-acre place that he felt would suit our needs. It was located in Madison, but the house was only about half finished. We looked at it and bought it right away. Since our home was in the process of being built, we had the opportunity to make a few custom changes. In the meantime, we continued to live on Sarver Avenue, and Mr. Chance continued to board Shawnee and take good care of him.

25

Memories

I don't hurt anymore, all my teardrops are dried.
No more walking the floor with that burning inside.
Just to think it could be, time has opened the door,
And at last I am free, I don't hurt anymore.

"I Don't Hurt Anymore," by Don Robertson and Jack Rollins

❖

ABOUT THE SAME TIME THAT I became part of the Opry family, Hank Williams did, too, and I was pleased when Mr. Denny booked him and me on a six-day tour in southern Texas. We were to play Corpus Christi, Harlingen, and a few other towns not far from the Mexican border. This was before I got my own band, but Mr. Denny worked it out with Hank for me to use his band when I was making appearances with him.

Part of Mr. Denny's job at station WSM, aside from running the Opry, was to book artists who were under contract with the Grand Ole Opry Artists Bureau. When he called me into his office, I almost fainted when he said I'd be paid $500 a day. That's right, $500 a day! If he had said $500 for six days, I would have been happy. I could hardly wait to get home and tell Min this fantastic news. I told her we were going to be millionaires. This was a far cry from two years earlier, when I made $25 a show.

We had capacity crowds in south Texas. I was singing to the music of Hank's band, the original Drifting Cowboys, and everything was working out just fine until the last day. On the afternoon of our last show, in Harlingen, Hank suggested we all go over to Matamoros, Mexico, which was just across the bridge from Brownsville, Texas. We went over and ate good Mexican food, had a beer, and bought a few souvenirs, and I remember buying a western jacket with long fringe on it.

On the way back to Brownsville, naturally, we had to stop at the U.S. Customs and Immigration office to be checked in and to pay duty on goods we had bought. An agent asked the standard question, "Where were you born?" One of Hank's musicians, who was substituting on fiddle, had to go into the office because he was Italian and answer more questions about his background. But he got it all straightened out, no problem. Then one of the agents asked me, "Where were you born?" "Canada," I proudly answered. "Are you carrying a validated American green card to show you're legally in the United States?" "Yes, sir," I said, as I pulled out my green card from my billfold. Oh God, wouldn't you know it—the card had expired a few weeks earlier! I was still a Canadian citizen and had not taken citizenship with the United States yet. Back then, until a person became a citizen the United States government would issue a green card. This was part of your identification if you wanted to cross in or out of the country. These cards were temporary and had to be renewed every six months.

This set off a chain of events that you'd never believe. I had to go inside the immigration office, and the agents grilled me through and through. They asked a million questions, and I knew I was in serious trouble. Hank Williams, bless his heart, talked to the agents and said, "I can vouch for Mr. Snow. He's been a regular on the Grand Ole Opry for quite some time now. We have a show tonight in Harlingen, and if you can clear him to be on the program, I'll see that he comes back here if it's necessary. I know the sponsors and promoters would greatly appreciate your cooperation, too."

Hank somehow impressed them, and they made several phone calls. The officer in charge said, "We feel we can handle it this way. We'll bond you through our Houston office, but you must return to Brownsville in exactly three weeks. Then you'll have to go over to Old Mexico and have a Mexican doctor give you a thorough examination, and you'll have to get new visa pictures taken before you can get a new permanent visa. As of now, Mr. Snow, you're a foreigner with no home country."

When he said I was without a home country, that scared the hell out of me. However, I appreciated the efforts made by Hank and the immigration office for working out this temporary solution. I felt bad that I held everybody else up, since it had taken two hours before I was cleared to leave. I signed a bunch of papers and we left.

That night, before our Harlingen show, I became deathly sick. It may have been because of all the hassle at the immigration office playing on my nerves, or maybe it was the food in Mexico. It certainly was not from drinking. I had only two small glasses of Mexican beer, and that was in the early afternoon. I managed to get out on stage somehow that night, but I was as weak as a rag and shook like a leaf. I did sing a couple of songs, but I felt like I'd fall down any minute, and big beads of sweat popped out all over my face and forehead. I didn't want to let the promoter and the audience down, and somehow I made it through.

After our show our group was supposed to go down to a nightclub and present a short program, but I was getting sicker with every minute. Actually, I didn't think I could stand up, much less sing. I was beginning to think I was a jinx to the others. Our promoter was Dave Lebby, and to show you what a fine fellow he was, he said, "Hank, I appreciate you going on stage tonight, because I know you're very sick. You're as pale as a ghost. I'll take you back to the motel so you can get to bed, and I think you'll be better by tomorrow. We'll take care of everything, and I certainly won't hold anything from your check." I felt better by morning, and we hit the road back to Nashville.

Yes, friends, that was the way it happened, but the worst was yet to come. I had to carry that immigration burden on my back, and I wasn't looking forward to returning to Brownsville, which was about eleven hundred miles from Nashville. I would have felt better about going back to Mexico if I could speak Spanish, but I couldn't speak a word.

I've always hated to be late for anything, so I allowed three days to drive to Brownsville. I arrived there in time to get a motel room. The next morning I walked across the bridge to Matamoros. I didn't drive because I'd heard that the kids would steal anything they could get from your car. First I wanted to find a professional photographer, and through hand motions I tried to tell the people at several businesses what I wanted. Finally, I found a woman who understood the word "photograph," and she steered me in the right direction. It took more than an hour to take five small black-and-white pictures, and I was told to pick them up later after they were developed.

Next I tried to find the American consulate, but no one understood the word "consul," so I walked up and down the streets until I saw the American flag flying on a building. What a relief to find people who could understand me. I should have gone there first, and they could have guided me to the places I needed to contact. An official said, "Mr. Snow, you must have a valid health certificate from a Mexican doctor before we can issue you a visa. To save you time, and because we feel it was just a lapse of memory that caused your green card to expire, we'll begin filling out your papers. You can sign them when you return from the doctor's office."

By that time, it was the middle of the afternoon, and for an hour I answered questions and told them my whole life's story. Afterwards they gave me the name and address of the doctor, and I got there around 5:30 P.M. The doctor gave me a clean bill of health and signed my papers. Then I picked up my pictures and returned to the immigration office. After I signed all the papers, I headed back for the good old U.S.A. I had a home again! It was 9:00 P.M. when I crossed over the bridge to the United States. I had been in Mexico for twelve hours, and I was unusually tired. From that day on, I made damn sure my immigration green card was always valid.

I arrived back in Nashville all dragged out. I had hoped to rest up before hitting the road again, but I knew Mr. Denny would keep me extremely busy because "I'm Movin' On" was still number one on the charts. It was being played across the country on all the stations, on all the jukeboxes in cafes, pool rooms, wherever country music was being listened to. Mr. Denny immediately scheduled me for three shows in Louisiana with Whitey Ford, professionally known as the Duke of Paducah. For each show I used a local band. Whitey was one of the funniest men I had ever seen on the stage, and he was a real gentleman.

I truly appreciated Mr. Denny and the WSM agency. The agency took care of all advertising, all radio spots, and all the necessary details of promotion. What a relief that was for me, not to have to worry about those things like I had to do in Canada.

About this time, our house was completed and we moved into it. It's the first home we could truthfully call our own, with the exception of our trailer home and our quarters in the horse van. Our place has a spacious front yard, a long driveway to the back of the house, a big backyard, and a three-acre field in the back. We intended this to be our first and last home, and it has been.

I had a nice little barn built for Shawnee. Then I retired him. He had been an important part of many of my shows, and he always did a remarkable job. He deserved to be treated special and to have the best of care. With a barn and three acres of clover to graze on every day, he was well fixed for the rest of his life. I loved to sit and watch him enjoy his new home and run and gallop around the field. He was certainly a part of the family.

As soon as we moved in, I named our home and three acres "Rainbow Ranch," and I named my band the "Rainbow Ranch Boys." I still use the title "Hank Snow, the Singing Ranger, and his Rainbow Ranch Boys."

We're proud of our home place, and Min knows just how to keep it homey and comfortable. We've always lived humbly. Min never did want a maid to help her with housework. After a few hit songs, we certainly could afford to hire help, but Min enjoyed taking care of the house herself. Even though she's been in bad health over the last several years, Min still enjoys cooking, but she now has a full-time housekeeper.

While our home was being completed, one of the carpenters' helpers was Willie Fred Carter, who went by the nickname "Squirlie." I often visited the carpenters while they were working, and I noticed that Squirlie was the life of the party. He kept the workmen laughing with his humor. When our home was completed, I asked Squirlie if he'd like to come to work for us. His reply was, "Doing what?" I said just about everything. "Well, what would you pay me for doing just about everything?" When I told him what I'd pay, he said, "Yes, I'll give it a try for a while."

Squirlie did just about everything, and he did it for twenty-six years. He was a gardener, ran all the errands, and was an all-around handyman. But his most important job was to take great care of Shawnee by keeping him clean, well groomed, and well fed, and he also took good care of my dogs, Mickey and Pal. Both Min and I really appreciated that, and it was worth his salary just to keep him around for his clever wit. I didn't know what a bargain I was getting. He became one of the family.

The few times when Min, Jimmie, and I went on a vacation, we gave Squirlie the keys to the place, and when we came back, everything was exactly the way we left it. He was an honest man. If he saw that someone was trying to rip me off, he'd protect my interests twenty-four hours a day. He was one of the most faithful people I've ever been associated with. We had a lot of good times together.

With everything going so well, it was like living in a different world. However, whenever it appeared I had smooth sailing ahead, a storm would pop up. This time a legal problem surfaced. My good friend Joe Talbot had gone through college studying to be an attorney. He passed the bar and began to practice law in Nashville. He called me one day and said, "Hank, I don't want to worry you, but I don't want to see you get into any kind of a legal hassle either. Somebody is trying to railroad you." Joe was referring to Conn Pulis. I mentioned earlier that Conn and his wife, Lillian, had been nice to me in Amboy, California, but a few things happened that caused me to become somewhat suspicious of him. Joe explained, "Conn has contacted the district attorney in Nashville and is demanding $2,600 from you immediately, plus a good percentage of everything you make for the next ten years."

That hit me like a ton of bricks! Conn was trying to charge me for the few times I stayed at his motel for free—with his approval—and for the money he had loaned me. That would add up to $500 at the most. Min and I were just beginning to get money ahead after paying off most of our bills, but my potential for making good money was evident. My sources of income were the Opry, personal appearances, record sales, Hill and Range Songs, and BMI. I guess Conn thought I was rolling in the money by this time, and I would have gladly paid him what I felt I owed him, but I didn't like being ripped off.

Joe said, "I'm not trying to tell you how to run your business, but as your friend, I'd advise you, if it's at all possible, to pay the $2,600 to get him off your back. Otherwise, he'll no doubt file a lawsuit to claim a percentage of your future earnings."

When I cooled off, we raised the money, and he was paid off in full. Of course, I knew Conn had no basis for any percentage whatsoever on my future earnings. I had never signed any agreement or even made a verbal promise to him. Even though a lawsuit was not justified, I didn't want the publicity it would bring, so the situation was settled and I never heard any more about it. I phoned him a few times to tell him it was all water under the bridge, and I was holding no grudge against him whatsoever. I did get a Christmas card from Conn each year, up until he passed away a few years ago.

Otherwise things continued to go along smoothly for my family and me, with an occasional setback. Mr. Denny was a good organizer, and he was superb at putting the right entertainers together for the road shows. Sometimes I was part of a big package show, and sometimes I was the headliner. And the audiences were big and responsive. I truly felt I was appreciated and always tried to do my level best to give the people a good performance.

Mr. Denny booked me on a show with several other performers at the Hippodrome Theater in Baltimore, Maryland, for six days. I was to be paid $900 for my part. Little Jimmy Dickens was the headliner, and he was paid considerably more. Even though "I'm Movin' On" was still on the charts, I wasn't known to the extent that Jimmy was. He was hot in those days, and he was like a ball of fire with his energy. He's still a popular performer, whom entertainers have named "Mr. Showman." Jamup and Honey were funny blackface comedians who were also on those shows. They were members of the Opry when I first joined.

After the theater engagements were finished, I stayed over to fly back to Nashville on Sunday morning. When I boarded the American Airlines flight, Eddy Arnold and Tom Parker were on board, and we had a nice visit. They had a car waiting for them at the airport, and they drove me home. After I got into the house, I discovered that my wallet was gone. I was devastated. Nine hundred dollars down the drain! I immediately called the hotel where I had stayed, the Baltimore police, and the airline, but I never found it. I had barely scraped up the money to pay Conn Pulis the $2,600, so we really needed the money.

About this time Pop Patterson called from Canada. "Hank, we've had a serious flood in Winnipeg, and the local officials are sponsoring flood-relief shows to raise money to help these poor souls. We'll be forever grateful to you if you can come up here and help us out. We can't pay you anything, but we'll take care of your expenses." Throughout my career, I've never minded giving my free time for a good cause, like many other artists do from time to time. You bet I'd help Pop Patterson. I would have done almost anything for him. I flew to Winnipeg, and it was sad to see so many beautiful homes and farms flooded, but I felt good about having a small part in helping. I played with several local bands, and a considerable amount of money was raised for the flood victims.

Back in Nashville Mr. Denny lined up one tour after the other. Since "I'm Movin' On" was still the most popular country song, I was getting standing ovations everywhere I appeared. The moment I started singing, the applause would drown out my singing for at least a minute. That was a most pleasant experience, I can assure you!

The agency booked me on a tour through the Pacific Northwest, into British Columbia—one place I'll never forget. I still hadn't hired my own band, so I was working as a single but using the local bands in the various shows. Playing with unknown musicians can make you sweat, but I didn't know what sweat was until this particular date.

I was scheduled to play a small town, almost to the Alaskan border, named Prince Rupert. I flew part of the way by regular commercial airline and the rest of the way by seaplane. By air that was the only way I could get there. That old seaplane was the most shaky, rattling piece of equipment I've ever traveled in. When it took off over the water, the pontoons shook and the whole plane quivered, and I thought it would fall apart. Nevertheless, we made it safely to the town and taxied into the wharf. I got out in one piece, but I felt like the whole town was moving. I soon found a small, pitiful, third-class hotel. My tiny room had curtains that looked like cheesecloth. An old beat-up dresser stood in one corner, and on top sat a huge, old-fashioned basin and a pitcher to carry water from downstairs to clean up in. I was three thousand or more miles from home, and I felt I was on the frontier.

After I recuperated from my disappointment, I called the auditorium to see what time the show was supposed to start that night. The man who answered the phone said, "What show? There's no show here tonight, but two shows are scheduled here tomorrow night. The whole Grand Ole Opry's coming with Hank Snow. One show is at seven o'clock and the other at nine. This place seats about two thousand people, and we've been sold out for a week. Sorry, mister, you can't buy a ticket anywhere."

Immediately I got a sinking, shaking, nervous feeling in my stomach. I had left a fancy hotel room in Vancouver, and here I was in this little junky room. I certainly wasn't looking forward to staying there by myself for another whole day and night. I was worried, too, because I knew nothing about the other Opry entertainers being on the show. My contract plainly said two shows on that date, and it mentioned no one else, period. If other Opry entertainers were scheduled, surely they would have been on the same flight with me. Well, I had seen mix-ups before, so what the hell—that's just part of the job. So what if I'm a day early, I would survive. I always did.

The next afternoon I got a taxi, no doubt the only one in town, to take me to the auditorium real early to make sure everything was set up properly. I had hoped they would have a decent sound system, but with the foul-up, I couldn't be sure of anything. When I arrived, a gentleman came up to me and said, "Where's the rest of your show?"

"The rest of my show? What do you mean, the rest of my show? My contract specifies only Hank Snow, one person, and I have a union contract that states just that. So here I am." The gentleman was as shook up as I was. "We were supposed to have Cousin Minnie Pearl, Rod Brasfield, Cowboy Copas, Red Foley, and Hank Williams. Where are they?" When my head stopped spinning and I got my composure, I said, "Where in the name of God did you get that? Who gave you all this information? This is all completely wrong. Look at your contract. Your contract specifies Hank Snow, and according to my contract, you are supposed to supply me with regular country union musicians."

This was the worst predicament I had been in thus far in my music career. On very few occasions have I ever done solo performances in front of two thousand or more people. I could do it, but with this false advertising the people were likely to be greatly disappointed and demand their money back. After all, they would expect to see all the Grand Ole Opry performers as advertised. This whole episode put a lot of pressure on me. I was being paid a pretty fair salary, and I had a responsibility to honor my contract. In order to meet my obligation, I could go on stage and entertain the audiences for each of the two shows. I had worked many times during the early stages of my career with just myself and my guitar, but I'd be handicapped without the rhythm backup like I got on the Opry. However, the old saying is "The show must go on."

And it did. Here is what happened. I told the people in charge to get me five country musicians, including fiddle and guitar, or there would be no show. In addition I said they would be obliged to give the people back every cent of their money. (I was really bluffing.) Someone explained that since it was fishing season, many of the men were out on their boats and wouldn't be back for several days. Apparently there were no country musicians around. They asked me what they could do.

I said, "I don't know what you're going to do, but I know what I'm going to do. I'm going to put on two half-hour shows, just me and my guitar, and that's it. I don't even have to do that because of the foul-up in my contract, but I don't want to let the audience down."

Then one of the men came up with an idea. "We could get a local marching band together." I thought to myself, "Oh, no. But what can I say?" In about an hour here came eight or nine men carrying trumpets, bassoons, trombones, drums—you name it, they had it. I listened as they began warming up before going on stage. I never ever heard such god-awful sounds in my life! I wished they'd had a soundproof dressing room, so I could have gotten away from all that noise. These poor guys were probably tired from working all day, and music was not their profession. It was just a sideline.

They did their best, though, and with their help, they did make it possible for me to put on the two shows. I'll have to give them a lot of credit. Most likely they had not picked up an instrument in a long time, and to be called at the last minute was a burden on them. They played a lot of the old-time marches and pieces like the "Blue Danube." When they finished, I went on stage and explained about the mix-up in the advertising, and everything was fine. I never played for a more appreciative audience in my life. Believe it or not, I got standing ovations on both shows. All in all, I felt good about my evening.

The next morning I boarded that rickety old seaplane and made it safely back to Vancouver. I finished my tour and went back to Nashville.

The pressure of the hectic life I was living sometimes got to me. Being on the road so much, rushing around from place to place, dealing with problems, trying to be pleasant when you didn't feel well, playing in hot, stuffy halls where there was no air-conditioning would zap your energy real fast and make you less than cheerful.

After one hectic tour through the Carolinas and Virginia, I returned home in August, 1951, around suppertime. I was completely exhausted, and Min met me with a problem. She said Pal, my big German shepherd, was not able to get out of his doghouse. "He's really sick. You should go check on him as soon as you finish supper." I didn't wait. I bolted down to the barn and saw Pal lying about halfway out of his doghouse, and he appeared to be in a lot of pain. I took him by his collar and sort of helped him out of his house, as he yelped. He couldn't use his hind quarters. As big and heavy as he was, I picked him up in my arms and carried him into the house and laid him on one of the twin beds in our spare bedroom.

Then I called Dr. Mobley, who came right over. He checked Pal carefully and then gave me the bad news. "Hank, he is very old and almost every part of his body is about gone. I strongly advise that you let me put him to sleep." That hit me hard. Pal had been with me for a long time, and I'm sure you all know how you can get attached to an animal. It tore me up so much that I left the house even before the doctor did. I had to get away. It was very wrong, leaving the dog lying on the bed, and having Min deal with the problem, but I couldn't bear to see Pal put away. I couldn't deal with it. It was like a part of me dying.

I got into my car and flew to the motel where I'd dropped off a female companion earlier. I picked her up to take her with me to Printer's Alley and to the Carousel that night, to have a few drinks and, I hoped, erase some of the pain from my mind. The tiredness I felt from the long road trip, the sadness from losing my faithful old dog, and the few beers I'd had earlier all hit me like a ton of bricks. We didn't make it to the club.

On the way downtown, onlookers told me later, I was almost flying when I reached the Jefferson Street bridge. From the bottom of the bridge, there's an incline of about fifteen degrees to the top and a decline of about twenty degrees down to the other end. We drove over that bridge going about ninety miles an hour, or more, if that was possible. When I came to the intersection on the other side of the bridge—there was sort of a rise at the intersection—my car went so high up in the air that witnesses said a person could have easily walked under the car. It literally left the ground, and it came back down on the two wheels on the driver's side. At that time my arm must have hit the door handle, and my door flew open. I went out the door, and my lady companion went out over the top of me, onto the concrete. The lady's back was broken, and I got a fractured skull, along with bruises and bumps on many parts of my body. It was one of God's miracles that we were not killed instantly.

The accident was near a ballpark, and several people came running out to see what had happened. Then someone ran back inside the ballpark and asked if there was a doctor in the crowd. Friends, can you imagine this? My doctor, Cleo Miller, was present at the ballgame, and he beat the ambulance to the hospital. I had a severe cut across my head and forehead, which Dr. Miller said took forty-two stitches to sew up.

My fans were the greatest. During the next several weeks I received approximately twenty-two thousand get-well cards and letters from all parts of the world, wishing me a speedy recovery. I was told that WSM had a special line going into Connie B. Gay's station in Washington, D.C., giving bulletins on a seven-station network every so often about my progress. Connie B. Gay booked a lot of country talent out of Nashville and ran a cruise ship down the Delaware River each Sunday, which carried around two thousand people. I did a stint on this cruise occasionally. Connie was a fine gentleman who gave country entertainers a lot of help in selling their records through his radio stations. His concern meant a great deal to me.

While I was in the hospital, Steve Sholes, RCA Victor's top recording producer, sent me a telegram wishing me well. He also stated that he was having RCA Victor give me a substantial increase in record royalties to cheer me up after the accident. That was the kind of man Steve was, and I appreciated him very much.

The lady recovered, and in about four weeks, believe it or not, I was back on the road playing personal appearances again. The first show I did was in Washington, D.C., with Ernest Tubb. My head had been shaved in the hospital, and Ernest kidded me about wearing a hat on stage because of my bald head. The only other time I wore a hat on stage was the first night I appeared as a new member on the Opry.

Back in the early years in Nashville, whenever we played on the road, I had to return to appear on the Opry on Saturday night. After the Opry show I'd go home, catch a few hours' sleep, and be at the airport around 5:30 A.M. to go to the show date. The boys would always leave right after the Opry and drive to wherever we were playing the next day. Then they would meet me at the airport. We did this year in and year out.

Let me explain the policies the boys and I had. We agreed that none of us would ever take even one sip of any drink that contained alcohol before any show, and I wouldn't hire anyone to become a Rainbow Ranch Boy unless he agreed to this policy. Also, if a band member drank the night before a show and he looked like hell the next day because of a hangover, this was completely unacceptable to me, too. But if the boys wanted to have a few drinks and party a little after the show, that was all right, and sometimes I'd join them. Another policy was that after we finished our shows at night, we agreed that none of us would go out to a nightclub and play free for the club. We all felt that this wouldn't be fair to the people who had hired us.

I was the first to break the no-drinking-before-a-show policy. I was scheduled to play Gulfport, Mississippi, on a Sunday for a matinee and a night show. After the Opry, as usual, the boys drove ahead. I went to bed around two Sunday morning and was unusually tired when I got up in about four hours. I called a taxi to take me to the airport, and on the way I asked the driver if he could get me a pint of Smirnoff vodka, and I insisted he buy only the Smirnoff brand. Even though the liquor stores were closed on Sundays, he said, "No problem. Since we'll get to the airport plenty early, it'll give me time to pick up your vodka and get back before your plane leaves. Wait until I return to pay me. If for some reason I don't get back before your plane leaves, then you won't be out any money."

I felt I really needed a picker-upper that morning. I repeated, "Now remember, nothing but Smirnoff!" The taxi driver returned, but the bottle was not Smirnoff. Instead it was some cheap old brand. I had drunk it before and knew it tasted like perfume. That was the only thing he could get, especially that early in the morning, so I bought it anyway.

At the time, there was a strict rule that no one was allowed to drink strong liquor on any airplane. So on the flight to Gulfport I made periodic trips to the restroom to take swigs of that horrible stuff. And after my face got back in shape again, I'd return to my seat. That stuff was about as bad as the moose milk I used to buy from the old black bootlegger, but I continued to sip from the bottle. In Gulfport I took a cab to my motel, and by the time I got checked in, that stuff had crept up on me, and I was floating around in my room. I moved around in slow motion like a ballet dancer while I showered, shaved, and cleaned up—and continued to sip that potent stuff. The only thing worrying me about drinking this mess was that I was afraid my face might get drawn out of shape from the awful taste and never get back to normal again.

I called a cab about 1:00 P.M. to take me to the auditorium for our matinee show at 2:30. On the way I talked the ear off the cab driver, and I just knew I was going to do the best show that afternoon that I had ever done in my whole life. That's the feeling I had.

In the meantime, the local band, which was playing as a warm-up part of the show, had brought a washtub full of ice, with a collection of whiskey, beer, and wine. The musicians told the Rainbow Ranch Boys to help themselves to the drinks. But Tommy said he spoke up, "We appreciate the offer, but Hank has a policy that none of us, including him, will take a drink of alcohol before a show. But after the show tonight we sure would appreciate a drink." Right about then, with perfect timing, I burst into the dressing room like gangbusters. "How're y'all doin'?" I was a nonstop talker, and the boys couldn't believe what they were seeing. They looked at me and their jaws dropped, but not a word came out.

Now, this was one of the rare times that I ever went onstage drinking. My boys told me later I sang "The Golden Rocket" about five minutes straight, and I repeated the same verses over and over again. The musicians continued playing as if the unending song was planned. They said Buford Gentry, our steel guitar player, was so embarrassed that he bent down and pretended he was trying to fix something behind his amplifier. I don't believe anyone noticed that I'd been drinking, because I didn't stagger. My tongue was quite thick and I'd talk funny. So I didn't talk much, I just sang. We've had a lot of laughs about this situation over the years.

Don't get me wrong, folks, we weren't habitual drunkards, but there were times when we would have a drink. There were times, too, when I would go a full year and never taste a drop of any alcohol.

On March 31, 1970, I took my last drink, and I've never touched so much as even a beer to this day. I've never craved any kind of alcoholic drink since. I said, "That's it, I never want to taste alcohol again as long as I live." Thanks to the Good Lord, I haven't.

One of my favorite stories took place in the early 1950s when Joe Talbot, Tommy Vaden, and Norm Riley, my manager, were traveling with me on a few show dates in the Carolinas. Some small towns in the southern states sometimes set up "speed traps," but I don't know if they had a speed trap in this incident or not. Anyway, I was driving my Fleetwood Cadillac faster than I should have been, and when I saw those famous blue lights flashing, I knew a North Carolina highway patrol car was after me. The patrolman pulled me over, walked up to the car, and asked, "Where's the fire, buddy?" As he was looking at me, I was biting my lips and squirming back and forth in my seat. I said, "Officer, I'll tell you, I've got to find a restroom just as quick as I possibly can." He said, "Well, I've heard it all now. Go ahead. Get out of the car—every minute counts."

It just so happened there was an old shabby gas station with old-fashioned pumps out front. It looked as if it had been closed for a long time. I ran up the hill behind the service station, and sure enough, there was an old outhouse. I stayed up there about five minutes, then I came back down, got in the car, thanked the officer for not giving me a ticket, and drove away. As we were driving, Joe Talbot said, "I'm going to tell you something, Hank. You're wasting your time in country music. You should be in Hollywood, because that's the best job of acting I've seen in my entire life!"

The Rainbow Ranch Boys and I were playing a date in Des Moines, Iowa, at the KRNT Theater, where my friend Smokey Smith booked numerous talent from the Opry and many other places. Immediately after our night show we returned to our motel to go to bed, so we could leave early the next morning for another show. I woke up early and could not for the life of me get back to sleep. So I lit a cigarette, turned on the TV, and began watching the news. I planned to call the boys after the news was over, and we would all go to the restaurant for breakfast before hitting the road. I watched television for only a few minutes, and I fell fast asleep. While I was sleeping, the bedclothes and the mattress caught on fire, and I woke up gasping for breath in the smoke-filled room. I rushed to open the door before I smothered to death, and I was able to put out the fire.

I knew I had to report this to the desk clerk and suffer the embarrassment of being so dumb as to smoke in bed. I called the clerk and humbly reported the accident. The gentleman replied, "Were you hurt in any way?" "No," I replied. "I just wanted to report it so I can pay the damages. You have my address in your guest register, and when you have the chance to get it checked out, send me the bill and I'll send you a check to cover it." He told me not to worry about the damage, because they had insurance to cover the loss. I thanked him for his consideration.

But that is not the end of the story. We packed up and placed our things in the trunk and on the top rack of my Cadillac, and we were on our way. About seventy-five miles down the highway, I realized I didn't have my briefcase. I said to whoever was driving, "My God, find me a telephone quick so I can call the manager of the motel. I left my briefcase under the bed, and it has $5,000 in cash and several valuable papers in it." We found a roadside phone booth and I made the long-distance phone call to the manager. I said, "Sir, I hate to trouble you again, but this is just not my day. I've got a bad streak of luck going. When I checked out a little while ago, I left my briefcase under the bed, and it has got a lot of money in it." He said, "Don't worry about it, Mr. Snow. The maid has already brought your briefcase to the office. We didn't open it, but we knew it had to be yours, because you had called us about the bed. We were expecting your call. It's here now, safe and sound." A couple of the boys drove back to the motel, while the rest of us stopped at a restaurant for doughnuts and coffee. They made the one-hundred-fifty-mile return trip and brought back my briefcase with the $5,000—just as I left it.

Friends, now suppose I had checked out and not mentioned the bed being burned. The manager, I'm sure, would have been very perturbed, and he might have made me wait and worry a while before returning the briefcase to me. Or maybe he would have turned it over to the police. There are two morals to this story: "Don't smoke in bed" and "Honesty is the best policy."

I smoked cigarettes for many years and occasionally smoked a pipe. During my medical checkup in 1979, I remember the exact words of my doctor. "Hank, if you don't quit those damn cigarettes, you're going to be awfully sorry in about another year that you didn't." That was all I needed. I quit that day and have never smoked since. I'm so glad I had the will power to throw those hazardous things away, with the help of the Almighty. But for about a year I nearly went out of my mind.

A couple of bad habits I never got into, thank God—gambling and taking dope. I was the unluckiest guy in the world and a bad loser, so I never gambled. I never wanted to give my hard-earned money away, and the road to gambling looked like the road to poverty to me.

But there was one situation with the dope. We were playing an outdoor theater in St. Louis, Missouri. As usual, my boys and I played the Opry on Saturday nights, and afterwards they drove ahead. I went to bed for a few hours' sleep and got up early to catch the early flight to St. Louis. When I met the boys at the airport terminal that afternoon, it was at least a hundred degrees in the sun, and I was so exhausted I wasn't sure I could make it through the afternoon show. Tommy spoke up, "Hank, I have something that will get you through this tiredness without any trouble at all." He had two sizes of brown and yellow capsules, which were full of what looked like tiny buckshot. "Take the big one. It won't harm you in any way." I was somewhat hesitant. "I don't know," I said. "I'm not one to take something unless I know what it's for and how I'll react to it." But I took the big capsule anyway.

That afternoon I played things on the guitar I had never played before and have never played since. I had never even practiced the tune "St. Louis Blues" before. Never. But I played it that afternoon! I thought I sang and played better than ever before. Actually, if someone had recorded the program and played it back to me, it would have sounded terrible, and I would have been deeply embarrassed. My boys said later it was awful. After the show I was a nervous wreck. I didn't sleep for three days and three nights, and I ate nothing during that time. Plus, I was constipated for a week. That was the first and last time I took any kind of narcotics unless it was medication the doctor prescribed. It was a rare occasion when the doctor would even give me medication to relax. I don't like to take any kind of pill, except vitamins.

26

Entertaining in Korea

Well, come all you children, give a listen to me,
Let me tell you 'bout a new boogie beat;
There's no hesitation, it's sweeping the nation,
It's the "Rhumba Boogie" done the South American way.

"The Rhumba Boogie," by Hank Snow

❧

THE KOREAN WAR BEGAN IN JUNE, 1950, and it was still going strong in March of 1953, when I volunteered to go to South Korea to help entertain the troops. Hollywood stars and entertainers had gone to South Korea on several occasions to bring a little bit of home to a lot of homesick boys in this far-off land. The war lasted a lot longer than most people expected, and the troops needed all the moral support they could get.

Like some of the other entertainers, I contacted the appropriate office in Washington, D.C., and volunteered the services of the Rainbow Ranch Boys and myself. Many of the entertainers had gone through the United Services Organization (USO) office in Washington, but I didn't want to be paid. I wanted to donate my time free of any compensation whatsoever. Many of the country entertainers felt that in this way we could contribute to the war effort. It seemed the right thing to do.

After we signed up, I was pleased when Ernest Tubb wanted to join me and take his Texas Troubadors along, too. Others who volunteered included Annie Lou and Danny Dill, Lou "Doc" Childre, and Bill McDaniel. There were fourteen of us altogether. Annie and Danny were a married vocal team, and Danny was a real good emcee for the show. Doc was an Opry member and a real funny comedian. He sang and played the Hawaiian guitar, and he did a dance to add to his humorous routine. Bill was publicity director for WSM at the time, and he went along to do write-ups for the press.

Tennessee governor Frank Clement and a host of other people came to the airport to see us off. The news media took pictures, and we left with a lot of publicity and good wishes. Both Ernest and I took our 16-mm movie cameras along, and I filmed the whole round trip from the Nashville airport back to the Nashville airport. This footage is precious to me, and it brings back many strong memories.

We refueled in Hawaii on our way over and stopped at Wake Island, then flew directly to Tokyo, Japan, before going to Korea. All along the way some of us had a few drinks, and some of us had more than a few. We sang and played all night long, as the crew of the Pan American flight let us enjoy ourselves.

Something funny happened in Tokyo, and I don't believe Billy Byrd will mind me telling this. Billy was a fine lead guitar player with Ernest's band. On the morning we were supposed to leave Tokyo for Korea, he had been having a little too much moose milk the night before, and he overslept. The rest of us met in the lobby of the Dai-Ichi Hotel at 5:00 A.M. to take the bus to the C-124 army aircraft. If we missed that plane, we would have had to wait at least eight hours for the next one. We all boarded the bus, but still no Billy. A couple of the boys made a few trips to his room to get him up and ready to go, and finally Billy came on the bus in a really bad mood. Somebody said something to him like, "How are you feeling?" Or something polite, anyhow. Billy looked at him and said, "Don't you fool around with me this morning or I'll catch the bus and go home." Can you imagine catching a bus in Tokyo and driving across the Pacific Ocean to get home!

The entertainers were in South Korea, of course, to entertain the troops, and to do that we had to go into areas where fighting was taking place. Because of the nature of guerrilla warfare, it was sometimes hard to tell where the enemy was. This was unlike World War II, in which battle lines were clearly defined. Often the North Korean guerrilla fighters would show up in surprising places, attack, and then disappear into the countryside.

Several nations, including Canada, had combat troops in Korea as part of a United Nations Combat Force, but most of the soldiers came from the United States. The goal of the United Nations Combat Force was to prohibit the North Korean Communists from taking control of South Korea, which was non-Communist. Korea had been divided by the thirty-eighth parallel of latitude, and American foreign policy during that time was to contain Communist forces and prohibit them from taking over the territory below the Thirty-eighth Parallel.

When our group arrived in March, the weather was still extremely cold, and it snowed part of the three weeks we were there. However, we all dressed in warm army fatigues, even though they didn't fit some of us too well. On our first night in Korea we were assigned to tents, which were located on the side of a mountain, and we were issued sleeping bags. Each tent had an oil stove, and in addition we could light the aluminum feet- or hand-warmers, so we were quite comfortable zipped up in those sleeping bags.

From this location we were flown to a number of places, and we entertained one group after another. We played to several hundred troops on a makeshift stage, and as you would expect, the GIs loved hearing country music from home. During our shows and at night we often heard gunfire and mortar fire in the background. It was a dangerous and dismal atmosphere, and I had sympathy for the poor guys who were sacrificing so much for their country.

We even played close to the Thirty-eighth Parallel, which was as far north as we could go without butting heads with the enemy. The army kept us on the move to entertain as many troops as we possibly could, and it was a hectic pace. The only protection the entertainers had was Captain Spicer. His assignment was to travel with us twenty-four hours a day, as sort of a road manager and guide. He carried a pistol, and his was the only weapon we had among the fourteen of us.

I remember distinctly a frightening situation one night. After one of our shows we had been invited to have a few drinks with the officers. Shortly thereafter a sergeant came hurrying inside the tent and ordered us out on the double. He told the officers, "We've got trouble, prepare yourselves for attack." That scared the hell out of me, and we all got out of there and ran into our tents in a hurry. The next day we were told that approximately three hundred fifty of the enemy had almost broken through our defense line, within an eighth of a mile from where all fourteen of us were laced in sleeping bags. I don't know how many of the enemy were killed to stop the attack. If they had broken through the line, you can imagine what would have happened to us, since we had virtually no protection. It would have been a massacre, I'm sure. As I'm telling you this story, it gives me the shivers.

The next night we were camped at the same location, and we played for the noncommissioned officers' club. Anytime we played for the NCOs, the drinks were lined up for us, and if we didn't drink with them, they would have been insulted by us not being sociable. But under the circumstances they didn't have to coax us too much.

After the show Ernest and I went to our tent, which we were sharing, and he went to bed. But I went to Danny's tent to have a nightcap with him before turning in. His tent was about the fifth tent down the hill from where I was sleeping. It was a cold, dreary, dark night, with snow on the ground. Remember, too, that our tents were pitched right on the edge of this mountain. If we stepped off the edge or slipped, we would have had a long way to fall.

Danny and I had one drink, and then another, and another and another. We were laughing and having a ball. The alcohol seemed to keep us warm. Or, the more drinks we took, the less we minded the cold. After a while I told Danny, "I'd better be getting on back, because we've got an early call to take a plane to our next location." Danny replied, "Hank, I'd better walk up to your tent with you to make sure you get home okay and don't slip and fall down the mountain." Well, that was like the blind leading the blind. I replied, "No, you don't need to do that. I'll find my way, I'll be all right." He insisted, and we took our time slowly strolling up the mountainside, which was at about a forty-five-degree angle. When we finally made it up to my tent, I said, "Danny, ole boy, it's an awful long way down to your tent. If you happen to make a wrong move, you'll fall off the side of the mountain, and it's good-bye, Joe, so let me walk down with you." We were really in a silly mood by then. I think we walked each other up and down that mountain at least four or five times.

Then Danny said, "Man, I'm freezing, let's go talk to Ernest for a while." We went in and ole Ernest was lying there snoring and sleeping like a baby. The oil stove was red hot, so I took off my clothes and stood next to the stove in my long-handled underwear, and the heat felt so good. Danny and I were still laughing and goofing around, and we woke Ernest up. "What the hell are you all doing up this hour of the morning? Knock it off and go to bed. I want to get some sleep." The next thing I knew, my long johns were on fire, and I yelled "Fire! Fire!" and ran outside the tent. Danny grabbed a blanket and chased me in the dark. When he caught me, he wrapped the blanket around me to put out the flames, but there was no fire. It had just scorched my underwear real brown. I had only yelled fire to see what Danny would do.

The next day a plane took us to another area, and we put on several shows. I remember the troops were flown in from the combat zones to see our entertainment, then flown back out to engage the enemy again.

I was told that throughout this conflict, whenever the troops had to retreat from an impossible enemy situation, the soldiers used the code "Let's pull a Hank Snow." This prevented the North Koreans from knowing what the Americans were doing, as they didn't know what this meant, even if they understood English.

One day we played in what was known as a "neutral zone." This area was shaped like a horseshoe, with huge mountains all around in a semicircle. About five thousand GIs were there that afternoon to see us entertain. The army personnel told us before we went onstage that the enemy was on top of the mountain watching our show, and if they thought they could pull it off, they'd open fire while there was a large group together. This was part of the tactics of the guerrilla fighting, and it was a nerve-racking situation for us to be in, not knowing what to expect. That afternoon was about the fastest I ever went through a show, but the GIs sure did enjoy it, and they didn't seem distracted at all by the sound of shells exploding in the distance.

We also played in a building called the Rice Bowl, and we heard gunfire in the background. The next morning we were flown to another area to entertain, and we received a report that the Rice Bowl was blown to bits the night after we played there.

We were transported by helicopter and cargo plane to the various places in the field where we entertained. I didn't care for helicopter flying all that much. I didn't mind the aircraft, except I didn't like the giant three-decker C-124 cargo planes. When they started down the runway, you wouldn't think they would ever get airborne. Their cargo area was so large that several Jeeps could drive right up the ramp into the plane for transporting. In addition, tons of baggage could be stored in the cargo area. The personnel assigned to these three-decker planes had to communicate with the other decks by way of microphones, through a regular communications system. These prop planes were truly workhorses for the military, but they were just too darn big, as far as I was concerned.

We usually hopped back and forth over the mountains to the many camps by helicopter. These choppers were practical for carrying medicine and supplies to the wounded in hospitals across the mountains. The choppers could take us to places where planes couldn't land because there were no runways. These rides were interesting. The pilots would sometimes fly real low and point out areas of interest and tell us about some of the Korean customs.

One time we were walking by a place where a Korean funeral was underway. The mourners were dressed in white paper suits, and they carried the remains in a wooden box, loaded on a small hay-wagon-like cart. The wagon and the canvas top were decorated in all colors of paper strips.

There were two hospital ships, the *Constellation* and the *Haven*, anchored offshore in the Yellow Sea. One day we were flown to Inchon and then took a boat out to the *Haven* to entertain. Choppers had what looked like glass cages, about the size of a regular pontoon on a seaplane, where the wounded were strapped in and then flown from the fighting zones to the hospital ship. The ship had a pad on the aft deck where the choppers could land, and doctors and nurses were standing by to administer emergency treatment. The wounded were often treated in less than thirty minutes from the time they were injured.

We had just climbed up the ladder on the side of the ship from our motorboat and were being introduced to some of the ship's personnel when someone yelled that a chopper was approaching. We watched it come down toward the stern of the big ship, and as it was about seventy-five feet off the deck and over the landing pad, the engine cut out and the chopper hit the deck with a bad crash. Parts of the chopper were smashed, crippling it from taking off again. The wounded were quickly unloaded and rushed by stretcher to the emergency quarters. Thirty seconds earlier the chopper would have fallen into the Yellow Sea, and God knows what would have happened to those in the chopper. We finished our one hour of entertaining the wounded and bedridden, and we were on our way back to Inchon.

I remember another incident, in a lighter vein. Tommy and I dressed up in our bad-fitting army fatigues. He had drawn crossbones and a skull on the front of the army cap he was wearing. We certainly weren't ready for a military inspection, the way we looked. As we were going to lunch, a colonel passed by. He looked at us and yelled back in a stern voice, "Don't you ever salute an officer?" I almost busted out laughing. Now, who would believe that either Tommy or I could be soldiers in those baggy clothes? We explained to him that we were not in the army. We were here entertaining the troops. The officer was embarrassed, and he apologized and wished us well.

One day we were at a small airport waiting for our plane to come and pick us up, and I noticed a little brown dog sitting way out on the side of one of the runways. He seemed to be lost or waiting for someone. It got to me, and I asked one of the GIs, "What is that little dog doing on the runway? He's been sitting there the whole time we've been waiting for our plane, and that's well over an hour." I'm sorry I asked, because the GI told me a sad story. He explained that one of the combat pilots had found the stray dog, and he and the little fellow became friends. It was a two-way love affair. The dog loved his new master and followed him everywhere he went. The little fellow would always wait at the end of the runway for his master's plane to land. Whenever the pilot returned from a mission, he would take his friend to camp to feed and care for him. Somehow the tiny dog seemed to know which was his master's plane, and he'd get real excited when it landed. But one day the pilot took off for another bombing mission, and he never returned. He was shot down over enemy territory. The little dog, I was told, would sit at the end of the runway all day, every day, waiting for his master's return. That really upset me. I'm so darn sentimental anyhow.

On our trip to the Far East, we entertained thousands of GIs and talked to hundreds of them. They thoroughly enjoyed us bringing them a small bit of America. It was an emotional experience for us to see the soldiers brought in from the fighting, dirty, unshaven, and tired, just to see our show and then fly back to the combat zone. They were given a cold beer, and they sat out on the cold ground and enjoyed every minute of our show.

After being in Korea for about three weeks, we were getting pretty weary and were looking forward to going back home. Rumors were we'd be leaving via Pan American airlines in a couple more days, but then the disappointing news came that we would be flying to north Japan to entertain the troops up around Hokkaido. However, we all agreed we should entertain as many GIs as possible, since we were already there. So away we went for another seven days to north Japan.

Our last show in the Far East was in the Ernie Pyle Theater in Tokyo. The theater was named after the popular American journalist who lost his life during World War II. The theater was beautiful. It had the best sound and lighting systems in the world. This facility had been taken over after World War II by American occupation forces, but soon after we played there, I heard it was given back to the Japanese. After the show some high-ranking officers of the American army and a few top Japanese officials came backstage to compliment the performers. The American officers thanked us for our contribution and invited us to a dinner the following night to honor us.

Also, someone brought two Japanese movie actresses backstage to meet us, but they couldn't talk to us, since they didn't speak a word of English, and we couldn't speak Japanese. This episode turned out to be truly funny. Ernest Tubb always called any lady he talked to "honey." So when someone introduced the two movie stars to Ernest, he softly and politely shook hands with the first one and said, "Hello, honey, I'm so glad to meet you." That did it! I want you to know this brought roaring laughter from the two girls and all the other Japanese folks who were gathered around us. Ernest didn't know that human waste, in both Korean and Japanese, is called "honey."

On Sunday, the night before we were to leave for home, an army bus took us out to one of the bases where high-ranking army officials were waiting for us at a long and beautifully decorated table. Man, that table was filled with just about any kind of food and drink one could imagine. We began having a few drinks, and Billy Byrd and I got in a happy, laughing mood. Some of us were asked to give a short talk about our tour and experiences in the Far East, as well as to toast each other. I think Billy and I must have made about five speeches each. They couldn't keep us sitting down. Somebody would say something, and we'd jump up and make another speech saying how great it was being over here and all so forth. The combination of happiness to be going home and the many drinks we had put us in a celebrating mood.

The next morning we boarded the Pan American flight and were on our way back to the U.S.A. The month we were in Korea and Japan was like being in a different world. It was a great experience, and I wouldn't trade it for anything, but as the old saying goes, "There's no place like home."

During these shows in Korea and Japan, "My Mother" was the most frequently requested song I sang to the troops. I had written it back in the 1940s, especially for my mother, whom I dearly loved. The song had a special meaning to the soldiers in that distant land. Every show I played, it was requested, and sometimes I was asked to sing it a second time on the same show. It was very touching when I saw tears flowing down the cheeks of many of the GIs. After I sang this song, I announced, "If you'll give me your mother's name and address after the show, I'll write your mother a personal letter and tell her I've seen you and you said hello." I was forbidden to ask for the soldiers' addresses or locations, as this was strictly against regulations at the time. Even though I couldn't pass on specific information about the boys, I could write a general letter to their mothers. I figured I'd get perhaps three to four hundred addresses, but I received over seven thousand. They were written on chewing-gum wrappers, toilet paper, paper towels, cigarette packages, and anything else that could be written on.

After all our shows many of the boys came by and shook hands with us and thanked us for coming to see them. One GI asked me a special favor. He said his wife lived in Goodlettsville, Tennessee, and would I send her a dozen roses. I kept my promise to him, but I was sure glad everyone didn't ask this favor. I would have gone bankrupt.

When I got back to the States, I hired one of the secretaries from WSM to type the envelopes, and I had a form letter printed. The secretary typed the name of the GI's mother on the letter, and it started like this: "Dear Mrs. ______, I met your son in Korea/Japan and shook his hand. He is doing fine but he misses you, and he sends his love." I told about a few things we had seen in the Far East. Then I signed the letter with love. It was sent with tender care and a lot of love in my heart, I can assure you. I don't believe anything ever gave me more pleasure than doing this. To this day I run into people on personal appearances, or wherever I go, who tell me their mother received my most-appreciated letter. A lot of them carried the original letter in their wallet and proudly showed it to me.

I've learned that little things mean a lot in this world of conflict and confusion.

27

Jimmie Rodgers Memorial

Oh, the gold rush is over, so honey, bye-bye.
Stake out your claim now on some other guy.
I've wined you and dined you till my money is gone,
But the gold rush is over and the bum's rush is on.

"The Gold Rush Is Over," by Cindy Walker

As YOU KNOW BY NOW, I HAD GREAT respect and admiration for Ernest Tubb. He was responsible for getting me on the Opry and enabling me to achieve my wildest dreams in music. He was undoubtedly one of the most unselfish people I'd ever met. When I came to Nashville, I saw him help many other artists, too. I can't remember them all, but they include Jack Greene, Cal Smith, Stonewall Jackson, Carl Smith, and Charlie Walker, and the list goes on and on.

Among my fondest memories was getting involved with Ernest to promote the appreciation of America's Blue Yodeler. I'm speaking, of course, about the late and great Jimmie Rodgers. Both Ernest and I considered him to be our idol and inspiration, and we wanted to keep his memory alive and his great music before the public. So I wasn't a bit surprised when he asked me to help him establish a memorial to Jimmie Rodgers.

Earlier I told you how I'd sit for hours and listen to Jimmie's records. I'd try to imitate him note for note and word for word, and I'd even try to pronounce the lyrics exactly as he did. A great many country artists were influenced by Rodgers, and he even influenced some of the pop singers during the 1930s and 1940s. Ernest was right on target when he wrote in the liner notes to my album *The Jimmie Rodgers Story,* "Not only was Jimmie a great inspiration to Hank and me, but his singing inspired countless others throughout the world. The great contributions this man made to what we now refer to as country and western music has directly or indirectly affected more performers in this field than anyone I can think of. Jimmie Rodgers had more impact than any other single individual, past or present."

Jimmie wrote many of his songs, and their themes were about real situations and problems people face. Traditional country music has the same theme today. It deals with universal problems, the kind that all of us experience at one time or another. Jimmie was a stylist, and something about his delivery would keep you listening to his songs over and over again.

And I loved his famous blue yodels! Jimmie's blue yodels were vastly different from the well-known Swiss yodels. Wilf Carter, known to Americans as Montana Slim, did various Swiss yodels on his great RCA Victor records such as "My Swiss Moonlight Lullaby" and "Going to Ride to Heaven on a Streamline Train," among others, and he did them well.

Anyway, Ernest first mentioned his idea about the Rodgers memorial to me in 1951, and our plan was to celebrate the twentieth anniversary of Jimmie's death, which would be May 26, 1953. We wanted to have a marble statue carved in Italy and shipped to Atlanta, Georgia, for inscribing, and then have it erected in Meridian, Mississippi, Jimmie's birthplace. We agreed to split the $5,000 cost of the statue. We also wanted to have a big celebration with a huge country music show and invite a lot of celebrities, so we could draw a big crowd and get lots of media attention. It was our sincere hope to make the memorial celebration so spectacular that it would become an annual event.

Of course, those were big plans, and we didn't even know if we could sell the idea to the city officials in Meridian. Even if we could, we knew it would take much work to do this project correctly. And Ernest and I were so busy making personal appearances that we filed the idea away in our minds for the time being.

In early 1952 Ernest and I set a date to go to Meridian to discuss our proposed plans with the city officials, but he developed a bad case of the flu and wasn't able to go. So I drove the three hundred fifty miles to Meridian from Nashville and met with Nathan Williamson, a brother to Mrs. Jimmie Rodgers. He was a prominent attorney in Meridian and was known affectionately as "Mr. Nate." I explained in detail what Ernest and I wanted to do and hoped the city would agree to let us have the statue erected on the courthouse lawn. Mr. Nate said he would talk to the city council about the project and try to convince them that Jimmie was truly an international figure. He said he would contact me after he had met with the city council.

In a few weeks Mr. Nate called. "Hank, I've talked to the city officials and they are definitely interested in the project, but they do not want the statue placed on the courthouse lawn. Two statues are already there, and they would rather find a different location for yours. I've made an appointment for you and me to go see them, and you can discuss it with them in more detail."

I drove back to Meridian, and Mr. Nate and I met with the officials. I thought perhaps I could change their minds about the location, but I couldn't. The council members recommended a place on Tom Bailey Drive, one of the major highways on the outer edge of the city. Right after the meeting I went out to their suggested location, and it was not exactly what I would recommend. It didn't please me because it was an industrial part of Meridian. I returned to Nashville and told Ernest about my disappointment. He wasn't too thrilled either. "Surely they can do better than that, Hank. But now that you've broken the ice, I'll go down with you, and perhaps we can get it worked out to suit us all."

In a few weeks we drove down to look over the location. To my surprise Ernest said, "Well, this place isn't all that bad. It would be an ideal spot to make a nice rest area or roadside park for the people passing Meridian, going east or west. It's a pleasant setting, with all these beautiful pine trees around, and when tourists stop they'll see the statue. So if the city can't do any better and we can't pressure them, I believe we should settle for this." When Ernest and I talked with the officials, they were still quite insistent, so we agreed to their recommended area. We wanted to cooperate completely with them, because we needed their full support. We all knew this project would take a lot of planning and hard work.

On one of my early trips to Meridian I wanted to place a permanent wreath on the grave of Jimmie Rodgers. I didn't have any earthly idea where his grave was located, and I got the shock of my life when I stopped at a classy up-to-date service station and asked where Jimmie Rodgers was buried. The attendant said, "Who?" I repeated, "Jimmie Rodgers." He went inside, and I heard him yell to someone else, "Where is Jim Rodgers buried?" He didn't say Jimmie, he said Jim. Well, this irritated me to no end. I thought, "My God, here is a famous man known around the world, and people who live in the town where Jimmie was born never heard tell of him."

But they would, if Mr. Nate, Ernest, and I had anything to do with it. This made me more determined than ever to make Jimmie Rodgers a household name.

After asking several more people at a number of places, someone said he thought the grave was in the Oak Grove Cemetery. I finally found the grave site. I hadn't been there more than five minutes, when out of the clear blue sky here came a photographer and a newspaper writer. News sure traveled fast! I was glad to see them. I told Mr. Phillips, the newspaper man, what we were trying to do. He made several notes and said if he could be of any assistance to let him know. Indeed I would, he could count on that. I placed the wreath on Jimmie's grave, and the photographer took several pictures. This event led me to meet more officials of the city government, news people, and disc jockeys. In a few days the story broke in the Meridian daily paper, and I knew we were on our way.

The city council established some committees and got the ball rolling. Mr. Nate worked with Ernest and me, and I talked to Mr. Nate frequently on the phone. We had papers to sign, and we needed to discuss dozens of issues in which we had to get the council's approval. I made many trips down to Meridian by myself, as Ernest stayed busy on the road almost constantly, and sometimes I made the round trip of about seven hundred miles twice a week. Without Mr. Nate I wouldn't have gotten anywhere. As a fine attorney who was well loved by the folks in Meridian, he was able to overcome many obstacles during the long months of working on this project.

Whenever I returned from Meridian, I always went to see Ernest to bring him up to date about our progress. Since we were in close contact, we could keep on top of any problems that might arise. I was concerned that something might go wrong and the whole project might fizzle out. I wanted everything to be exactly right. Being a worrier, I had a lot to be concerned about. I worried if the statue would be finished and arrive in Meridian in time for the opening. I worried that some of the big country stars would not show up. I worried that the celebration might not be considered newsworthy beyond local interest. After all, if some people living in Meridian didn't know where Jimmie was buried or even care, would people from other states care? Would they come to the celebration? Mrs. Jimmie Rodgers was still living, but would she attend the ceremonies and be given proper respect for Jimmie's widespread influence? Maybe Mrs. Rodgers would be disappointed at the results of our efforts. Even if our efforts were successful, would the celebration be noteworthy enough to become an annual event? Yes, I worried, but Ernest and I believed in what we were doing, and we had faith in the good country people.

Toward the end of 1952 and in early 1953 we had meeting after meeting. Many of the people who were working on the project got together and made reports to the committees as to the progress and problems encountered. I continued to make many trips myself, and once in a while Ernest would be available and we would drive down together. Sometimes our mutual friend Henry Cannon would fly us in his private plane. Henry had been a flier during World War II, and he was an excellent pilot. Most of the time he would fly his wife, Sarah Cannon, the famous Minnie Pearl, to her concerts.

When we were notified that the statue was completed, we had it flown from Italy directly to Atlanta, Georgia, for inscribing, and it was delivered to Meridian in plenty of time for the celebration. It seemed like everything was falling into place as Ernest and I worked on the project off and on until we went to Korea to entertain the troops. After we returned from our tour in Korea, we took care of the final details. And we announced the upcoming event frequently on radio station WSM and the Grand Ole Opry.

The big day, May 26, 1953, finally arrived. Some local people earlier had made arrangements to lay a temporary railroad track from the train yards in Meridian out to Tom Bailey Drive. The Bigsby Railroad donated an old locomotive that they had retired, and this was exactly like the old steam locomotive in which Jimmie worked as a brakeman, conductor, and baggagemaster in the 1920s and 1930s. Two local passenger cars were hooked to it, and an engineer was provided. Passengers were loaded at the depot downtown, just before the big celebration was to take place that afternoon for the unveiling of the monument. Right on schedule, the train pulled up and stopped directly behind the monument. This made an ideal setting for our dedication.

The celebration was bigger than we had ever imagined in our wildest dreams!

Unfortunately, Ernest was very sick on that day, too. But Justin came in his dad's place to help us out and to unveil the monument. At the unveiling there were speeches by several dignitaries, such as Governor Hugh L. White of Mississippi. Many of them talked about the musical contributions of Jimmie Rodgers and named him the "Father of Country Music." The statue was a beautiful, life-size, Italian marble likeness of Jimmie with his guitar. The inscription, on a large bronze plaque, had been placed on the front of the base of the statue. It reads as follows:

> He is the music of America;
> He sang the songs of the people he loved,

Of a young nation growing strong.
His was an America of glistening rails,
Thundering boxcars and rainswept nights,
Of lonesome prairies, great mountains,
And a high blue sky.
He sang of the bayous and the cotton fields,
The wheated plains, of the little towns,
The cities and of the winding rivers of America.
We listened. We understood.

Country music took a giant step on that day, promoted by people who had known Jimmie and had been influenced by him. A huge flagpole was given by Ralph Peer of Peer International and Southern Music. It was set on a huge concrete base and had a big bronze plaque on the front with a beautiful inscription. We were happy that Mr. and Mrs. Peer had such a big part in our celebration. Ralph Peer had discovered Jimmie. He had recorded him for the first time in Bristol, Tennessee, and promoted his career.

Celebrities came from everywhere. Frank Clement, governor of Tennessee, was one of our honored guests. Country music's friend George D. Hay, founder of the Grand Ole Opry, was on hand, as were a lot of the Opry stars who donated their services, including Roy Acuff, Bill Monroe, Lefty Frizzell, and Minnie Pearl. J. B. Elliott, a vice president from RCA Victor in New York, came down to be with us and made an excellent speech.

People from all walks of life joined in the festivities, but Mrs. Jimmie Rodgers was the main celebrity, of course, and she was treated like royalty. I remember so well her touching speech. She was very humble and thanked everyone for the great work they were doing around the world and for buying Jimmie's records and keeping his name alive. She thanked the people for the hospitality she was receiving at that spectacular event.

Meridian was overflowing with people, and everybody was in a great mood. Folks came from all over the U.S.A., Canada, England, Australia, and several other foreign countries. Ian Lee from England was only twenty-one years old, but he was a follower of Jimmie's music. Dizzy Dean, the great baseball player, came to be with us, as did country music fans from California, New York, Chicago, West Virginia, wherever there was a country music station and people heard about the event. So you see, friends, the Father of Country Music had followers throughout the United States and from all around the world.

Reporters from radio, TV, and newspapers from across the country and abroad came to interview the many celebrities. The event was reported on the daily news and on national television and radio shows. I have a film clip of Mrs. Rodgers doing an interview on CBS, coast to coast.

We were thrilled and surprised with the success we had. In the previous months, while lining up the events for the celebration, we had gotten together with the merchants in Meridian and planned an outstanding parade, which, with all of the floats, was approximately two miles long. Little Johnny from the Philip Morris Company was on hand to yell his famous slogan, "Call for Philip Morris."

On the night of May 26, we had four hours of great country entertainment. Luckily we had rented the big stadium, which held about thirty thousand people, and it was packed. We charged an admission, and the proceeds went into a fund that started the Jimmie Rodgers Memorial Foundation, through which anyone in country music who was ailing with tuberculosis could receive financial help. Since tuberculosis was the dreaded disease that took Jimmie's life, it was appropriate that the money should go toward helping those with that illness.

Besides the well-established artists that Ernest and I had invited, entertainers were there I'd never heard tell of. Everyone wanted to be part of the show. It was just like one big giant jam session. The celebration continued throughout the week, with more shows and good family fun for everyone.

And as Ernest and I had hoped, the Jimmie Rodgers Celebration did become an annual event. I'd like to mention a few of the many celebrities I met over the years during these celebrations. Governor Frank Clement was a fan of country music, and he came to Meridian every year to help us. One year we had presidential candidate Adlai Stevenson. I remember he let someone put a big Stetson hat on his head and a guitar strap around his neck with a Gibson guitar, and he let us take movies and photographs of him. Jimmie Davis, former governor of Louisiana and a great country artist himself, always attended. He had several hits, including "Be Nobody's Darling but Mine" and "You Are My Sunshine." I also met Ross Barnett, the governor of Mississippi.

Mrs. Casey Jones came to the first memorial. She was a dear lady, ninety-four years old at the time. We talked about her husband, the late Casey Jones, and the train wreck that is the subject of a great train song, known as "Casey Jones." She told about the train leaving the rails and the death of Casey. Sim Webb, who escaped the wreck, was there, and he told us about Casey's final words just before the fatal crash. Casey looked at Sim, his black fireman, and said, "You'd better jump." In those last few seconds Sim said he begged Casey to jump with him, but it just seemed that fate intended a tragic end for Casey.

Ernest and I continued our Meridian memorials for several years until a station in Shreveport moved in and began commercializing the Jimmie Rodgers name. That year Ernest and I kept a low profile. This unfortunate turn of events hurt Mrs. Rodgers very much. She was totally disappointed with the exploitation, as were many people who had worked so hard to establish the project. It was no fault of little Johnny, but the Philip Morris company was one of the culprits who used the celebration to do their advertising. They took a free ride on what we had worked so hard to build. To me that was very cheap. Did they do anything to help Ernest and me in getting the event established? No. Not one thing!

We held the celebration for several years before Mrs. Rodgers passed away, and I'm glad Ernest and I did it non-commercially. I can speak for Ernest, who is no longer with us. When Mrs. Rodgers passed away, he and I both thought it was not in our best interest to continue with the project. We had accomplished what we set out to do. We established the memorial for two reasons: to keep the name of Jimmie Rodgers alive, and to pay tribute to Mrs. Rodgers and Jimmie from the entire music community.

In recent years the statue was moved from the Tom Bailey location and placed in a beautiful city park about two miles from downtown Meridian. The monument is still protected by a steel wire fence to keep tourists from breaking pieces off. The old steam locomotive is placed behind the statue, as it was at the original location, and it's painted and well maintained. A regular life-size railroad depot, exactly like the old depots back in Jimmie's time, has been added. It gives you a nostalgic feeling to see the depot and the engine in this beautiful setting. They remind you of a little country town back in the days when life was simpler.

Also located there is the Jimmie Rodgers Museum, where you'll find the very things Jimmie used: his travel trunk, stage clothes, and interesting miscellaneous items. The Jimmie Rodgers Hall of Fame is part of this complex, too. It's the same as you'll find in Nashville through the Country Music Association. I'm pleased and honored to say that both Ernest and I were entered into this Hall of Fame not too long after the depot was built.

Before I get away from the story, I want to tell you how I happened to get one of Jimmie Rodgers's original guitars. Bill Bruner, from Meridian, sang so much like Jimmie you couldn't tell the difference between them if you played their records one after the other. When I heard Bill sing two Jimmie Rodgers songs at one of the memorial celebrations, I couldn't believe what I was hearing. I was truly amazed! The story goes that when Jimmie was too ill to make some of his engagements, Bill filled in for him. They played the guitar exactly alike, yodeled alike, and sang alike in every way.

Jimmie gave Bill one of his guitars, and during the first celebration Bill made a gift of this prized guitar to my son, Jimmie Rodgers Snow. At the time, my son was beginning his singing career, and Bill gave him the guitar to use in his performances. This was a kind and unselfish gesture on Bill's part, and both Jimmie and I appreciated this treasured gift. Jimmie lets me keep it among my souvenirs, and it's now in my museum at Opryland.

Friends, when you listen to true country music, remember that it was this gentleman, Jimmie Rodgers, who influenced and still influences much of what you hear today. I'm proud to have been a part of this enduring project to honor the man who is known as the Father of Country Music and the man who in many ways dominated much of my life. I thank you, Jimmie, for your great inspiration. I know you will never be forgotten.

Many things happened to me in 1953. In addition to working with Ernest to establish and officially open the Jimmie Rodgers Memorial Celebration, I helped entertain our troops in the war zones of Korea. I continued to record, and in June, "Spanish Fire Ball" hit the charts, giving me twelve bona fide hits to that date.

But 1953 was also a sad year. It's the year my dear mother passed away in Liverpool, Nova Scotia. You know how much I loved her. My sisters and I dreaded the day when we would have to lay her to rest.

Mother had two strokes by 1953. The first was slight, but the second was severe, and it came shortly after the first one. A great portion of her brain was affected and her speech was impaired, making it hard to understand her, and her mind wandered in and out. After Mother suffered the second and massive stroke, the doctors told us she could go on for years in that state or she could pass away at any time. During the months that followed Min and I made several trips to see her in the Liverpool hospital, and we frequently made long-distance calls to the hospital and to her doctor to inquire about her status. My sisters were living quite close to Mother, so Min and I checked with them often to get first-hand reports. By keeping in close contact, Min and I could be ready to leave Nashville at a moment's notice, and by plane we could be in Halifax in a short time.

During the summer of 1953 Mother took a turn for the worse, just as I was about to leave on a twenty-day tour of the Pacific Northwest and western Canada. I had signed all the contracts and was preparing to leave Nashville the next day, when we got the shocking news of the seriousness of her illness. I called the doctor immediately, told him about the proposed tour, and asked his professional opinion as to whether I should cancel my shows and return to Canada. The doctor said, "Mr. Snow, even though your mother is gravely ill, she could rally and even live several more months. I would strongly advise that you keep your plans and honor your contract, but keep in touch every day."

In September the doctor thought I should come to see Mother, so Min, Jimmie, and I jumped in the car and drove the approximate two thousand miles to Liverpool. When we got there, Mother's mind faded in and out, and she was extremely thin. It was really sad to see her in that condition. But Mother and I had some wonderful conversations. At times her mind was as sharp as ever, and we talked about some good ole times we had together. Even in her condition she had a quick wit, but then her mind would drift away and she didn't remember anything.

As I mentioned earlier, Mother always called me "Jack," as did my sisters and my schoolmates. When I sat close to Mother on her bed, she would say, "Oh Jack, dear, I'm so glad you're here." But when I'd move away from the side of her bed for only a few minutes, she would say to Min, "I don't know where Jack is or why he doesn't come to see me." And she would say, "It's awfully dark in here. Why don't you turn on the lights," even though the lights were bright in the room.

While I was sitting with Mother one day, I did something completely unknown to her. I set my tape recorder on a chair near her bed and put the microphone on her pillow, close to her head. I taped a whole hour's conversation with her. Mother was always a very humorous person and the life of the party. She came out with some of the wittiest sayings I had ever heard from her, and even in her state of mind she kept Min and me laughing constantly. When I brought up funny things in the past, she would add more humor to them. We had a ball! I have all of this on tape, and it is my most prized possession.

We stayed for a few days, then we had to return to Nashville. Friends, one of the hardest things I've ever tried to do was to say goodbye to Mother on that last day. I felt deep in my heart I was seeing her alive for the last time, and I didn't know what to say as I held her feeble hand. I thought about the many sacrifices she had made for me, her toleration of Charlie Tanner to try to keep her family together, and her undying support of everything I set out to do in life. I remembered all these things, and I wanted to tell her how much I appreciated her and how much I loved her, but I didn't know how to say good-bye. What do you say, and how do you say it? It tore me apart trying to get the courage to leave her.

I didn't say good-bye. I couldn't.

I didn't know what my parting words should be, so I gave Mother a big hug and she held me for the longest time, which made me believe she knew what I was feeling and trying to say. With tears running down my cheeks, I walked away.

Back in Nashville, I was booked for a twenty-day tour by A. V. Bamford, one of the top agents who booked talent from the Grand Ole Opry. These twenty days would take the Rainbow Ranch Boys and me through Louisiana, Texas, Arizona, and up through the Pacific Northwest and into British Columbia, Canada. But before I left on the tour, I called Mother's doctor and told him I didn't want to leave until I found out Mother's condition and got an update on her failing health. "There have been no drastic changes since you were here," he said. Consequently, Min and I decided I should go on with my road tour. Min would be in constant touch with my sister Nina, and I would call Min every day to check Mother's status instead of bothering the doctor.

My boys left Nashville and drove to Vancouver, British Columbia, where we were to open our tour. That weekend I stayed to do the regular network portion of the Opry, which was sponsored by Prince Albert Smoking Tobacco, since it was my turn to be the emcee and the featured performer. I made plane reservations to fly out the next day, and the boys were to meet me at the airport in Vancouver. Before I took the long flight, I called Nina to see if Mother's condition had changed. I was prepared for the worst, but I was still totally shocked when Nina said that Mother had taken a turn for the worse and she might not make it through the night.

My flight would take me to Chicago and then to Minneapolis before going on to Vancouver. The minute we landed in Minneapolis, I hurried to the terminal and called Min, who had just arrived in Liverpool and was at the hospital. She said there had been no change in Mother's condition and for me to call again as soon as I arrived in Vancouver. I was feeling pretty low and so alone during the long nonstop ride, and I did a lot of praying.

When I stepped off the plane at Vancouver, my boys rushed up to get my luggage, and they said there was a message at the ticket counter telling me to call Min as soon as I could. When Min came on the phone, she said, "As much as I hate to tell you this, your mother passed away just a few hours ago." Although I heard her words clearly, I still said, "What did you say?" Again she said, "Your mother passed away a few hours ago," and she began to cry.

And so did I. I doubt if anyone is ever prepared to accept death. I wasn't. But I'll never forget the reaction of my band members. They carried my burden, too. I hadn't thought about that until Mother died, but I shall never forget the love and sympathy that Tommy Vaden, Hillous Butrum, Buford Gentry, and Sleepy McDaniel showed me. It's during crises that we become aware of who our true friends are. My boys showed me a real friendship—every one of them.

We drove to the hotel, where prior arrangements had been made, and I went to my room and sat down and stared at the wall. The Rainbow Ranch Boys came in and invited me to join them in their room for a while. I thanked them but said I'd rather be alone at that time, and I wanted to call Min and my sister again. I called and talked to Min and Nina. They had talked to the doctor, and he said the undertaker would have to bury Mother within thirty-six hours. She had also contracted cancer, and it broke out on parts of her body, and that had contributed to the graveness of her illness.

I checked with the airlines to see if I could get a flight out to Halifax, which would put me about ninety miles from Liverpool. From there I could take a taxi to Liverpool. However, at the time there was no way I could possibly travel the nearly four thousand miles across Canada and be there before the funeral. I called Min back and explained this impossibility. She said, "You can't do anything about that. I know your mother would want you to go on with your shows. It will be one of the hardest things you've ever done, but try to carry on with your obligations."

I stayed awake the best part of the night, wishing I was in Liverpool with Min and my family during this crisis. Finally, I was so tired I fell asleep and slept for several hours. When I woke up, I lay there and wondered what I should do about the show. My thinking was fuzzy, to say the least. But I thought to myself, "Mr. Bamford has a lot of money tied up in advertising in all the cities and towns where we are to play, and I can't get back home for the funeral, so I'm going to try to go on with the shows."

I spent much of the day alone in my room at the Vancouver Hotel, except Bill Ray came to see me. Bill owned the radio station, CKNW, at New Westminster. He had bought the show from Mr. Bamford for that night in Vancouver. When Bill knocked on the door, I was lying on the bed crying my eyes out, and he tried to console me. He also thought I was doing the right thing in going on with the show.

But going on stage that night was the hardest thing I've ever tried to do in all the years I'd been in show business. When the master of ceremonies introduced me, he told the audience that I had lost my dear mother the previous night. Naturally, I got a standing ovation. I announced when I entered the stage that I would do the show as a loving tribute to Mother, and I'd do the best I was capable of doing under the circumstances.

I struggled through the show somehow. In closing, which I had to do since I was the headliner, I told the audience I didn't want to end on a sad note, but I had to do the special song I had written earlier for my mother. I sang and cried through the song, and it seemed like it lasted forever. I was so glad when I finished it. Needless to say, I got another standing ovation, and it went on for several minutes.

Here are the lyrics to "My Mother":

There are friends who will want you, but just for a day,
There are pals you think true, but they'll cast you away.
But there's one lovin' soul, boys, I'll sure recommend.
Through this old world of sorrow, she'll be true to the end.

Mother, though her hands are all wrinkled and old,
Mother, silver hair that has lost all the gold,
You left her alone, went to roam through the years,
But all that you left her were heartaches and tears.
So kiss her old brow, whisper softly and true,
"Mother, you're just an angel, and I love you."

Narration:
On the door of a cottage a wreath sadly hung,
And a hearse stood there waitin' as the choir softly sung;
There were flowers in their beauty and the old parson, he prayed.
This was the last tribute as we left for her grave.

She won't meet you tonight, son, when you crave her caress,
She has reared you to manhood, and now you've laid her to rest;
Those flowers in their beauty, to her they're unknown,
'Cause tonight she's with the angels up around God's great throne.

So don't wait that late, son, to try and repay,
Give those flowers and give those treasures, but give them today;
Let her know that you love her, and kinda show her that you care,
Cause she's your mother, God love her, she's as true as a prayer.

So kiss her old brow, whisper softly and true,
"Mother, you're just an angel, and I love you."

I saw a lot of tears on many faces that night. The song communicated to the crowd my feelings of grief, and I thought the whole audience, in a way, was expressing their sympathy to me. I walked offstage, helped by a local police officer, and I sat down and again cried my heart out. When I got back to the hotel, I called Min. She said the arrangements had been taken care of, and that Mother would have a real nice funeral. It was such a relief to me to know that Min was there to properly take care of things.

I was relieved when the twenty-day tour ended and I got back to Nashville. I knew those shows were not as good as usual, but I thought it was better to give the best performance I could under trying circumstances rather than disappoint the people and not show up.

It was ironic how my dad's situation was so much like my mother's. A few years after Mother's passing, Dad died in the same hospital complex. Again I was constantly in touch with the doctor and the hospital personnel. It happened almost the same way.

I was taking another twenty-day tour with the same promoter, A. V. Bamford, and this tour took us to many of the same places where we had played before when Mother was so ill. We started this tour in Arizona and continued on to the West Coast and into Canada. My boys left early, and they were to meet me at the airport in Phoenix. Again I thought I'd better check with the nurse, Mrs. Ray. When I asked her how my father was doing, she said, "I have very sad news for you. Your father has just passed away." I had to go onstage that same night, and it was very difficult to do. I did the show as a tribute to my father, and I closed by singing the touching song "That Silver-Haired Daddy of Mine."

I was exhausted when I finally got through with the show. It was also a rough twenty-day tour, but I made it.

28

The Golden Period

From old Montana down to Alabam'
I've been before and I'll travel again.
You triflin' women can't keep a good man down,
You dealt the cards, but you missed a play.
Now hit the road and be on your way,
I'm gonna board the Golden Rocket and leave this town.

"The Golden Rocket," by Hank Snow

I KNEW IT WAS RISKY to have RCA Victor release another train song when "I'm Movin' On" was still riding the charts, but I did. In August, 1950, I recorded "The Golden Rocket" as a follow-up to my smash hit. My career as a major artist might have ended if my gamble had failed. But my instincts said to do it, and I was right. As soon as "The Golden Rocket" was released, it climbed to the number-one position, and it stayed on the charts for twenty-three weeks.

Trains have fascinated people since the very first one, and like my idol Jimmie Rodgers, I wondered why the big iron horses had so much appeal. I guess it's the freedom we feel as a train takes us away from something unhappy, or the warm feeling we get from the expectation of something exciting waiting for us beyond the horizon. To me there was nothing more touching than to hear one of their lonesome whistles at dawn or late at night. During my career I recorded many train songs, just as Jimmie Rodgers had done.

RCA Victor continued to release my records systematically, sometimes one, two, or three a year, depending on what the sales were. They wanted to give each record ample time to reach the top, or as far to the top as it was going to go, before releasing the next one. I had songs on all the trade charts during most of the decade. At one time, and this was when the trade papers listed only the top ten each week, I had three songs in the top ten. On a special list that RCA Victor issued on its own artists and distributed to the trade, I had six songs listed out of the ten. Pee Wee King, who was also a number-one seller on RCA Victor, kidded me about hogging the charts: "Doggone it, Hank, if you had four more, you'd have your own chart."

Not long ago I received a clipping in the mail from Billy Deaton. I don't remember which magazine the clipping was from, but it said that Eddy Arnold, Hank Thompson, Patti Page, and Hank Snow were the only four country entertainers in the business who had songs on the charts each decade for five decades. I'm proud of that accomplishment.

For about fifteen years in the 1950s and into the 1960s, anything RCA released on me climbed the charts. In my opinion, the 1950s was the heyday of good down-to-earth country music. My timing was perfect. The Good Lord was good to me, because I had a stream of top-ten hits, as well as several number-one songs such as "I'm Movin' On," "I Don't Hurt Anymore," "The Rhumba Boogie," "The Golden Rocket," "I've Been Everywhere," and "Let Me Go, Lover." These all held the number-one spot in the trade papers for a considerable length of time.

Then something very unusual happened. After 1962, when I had one of my biggest hits with "I've Been Everywhere," I didn't have a number-one song until 1974, when "Hello, Love" became a smash hit. I still hold the record for the longest period of time between number-one hits on *Billboard* magazine. The twenty-four years from "I'm Movin' On" in 1950 to "Hello, Love" in 1974 edge out Elvis Presley's twenty-one years.

From 1950 on, I was billed as a star, and during many of these fabulous years, I'd travel a quarter of a million miles annually on tours. The prices for my personal appearances increased, but so did our traveling expenses and commissions to the agents. Here are some examples of how my drawing power was boosted in a short time. When I played in the Northside Coliseum at the Cowtown Jamboree in Fort Worth with Ernest Tubb in 1949, I received twenty-five dollars. Two years later and after several big records, I returned to Texas, making a whole lot more money, and I was told that I broke all attendance records there—my crowd was over seven thousand. When I returned to the Big D Jamboree in Dallas for a show, I had the largest crowd ever had at the Sportatorium. And I still hold the attendance record as of this writing.

In 1950 I had played the Hippodrome Theater in Baltimore, Maryland, when Little Jimmy Dickens was the headline act. But in 1953, when I returned for a six-day run as the featured performer, with many hit records to my credit, I was paid at least four times the money that I was paid before. I was also credited for breaking the house attendance record at this theater. It was fascinating to me, and flattering, how an artist can suddenly become a big star. It was a great feeling to be in the limelight and make good money after all those poverty years.

From the early 1950s I began to receive awards, and those voted on by country music fans were very much appreciated. In 1951 Bea Terry, who was then a writer for *Southern Farmer,* called me to say the national magazine had named me America's favorite country and folk singer. It conducted a contest every year, and I had been chosen by over a million subscribers. I was especially pleased with this honor because it was voted on by subscribers rather than by peers. Frankly, I wish the awards to entertainers today were chosen by the listeners and readers rather than by people in the trade, since there's a conflict of interest in the ways honorees are chosen. Both jealousy and favoritism could be a part of some of these elections. *Music City News* still has its regular subscribers vote on the honors it bestows on its entertainers. In my opinion, that's the most fair way to do it.

The outstanding country-and-western magazine, *Country Song Roundup,* ran its annual poll and let the readers make their choices. The readers and listeners are the ones who buy the records and turn out to see the shows, so why deny them this privilege? Bert Levey was the founder of *Country Song Roundup.* He was an honest man, assisted by Norman Silver, and both were good friends of everyone in the country-and-western field. Each year their magazine honored top artists chosen by the public. I was fortunate that in 1950, 1951, and 1953, I was voted by its readers across America as the top country singer.

During the 1950s there were no labels like "middle-of-the-road country," "hard-rock country," "crossover," "pop country," and other such things. Our disc jockeys understood the music they were playing, and most of them knew each artist on a first-name basis. The artists loved and respected the deejays. Our deejay friends played a big part in our careers and in promoting our music. It was common practice back then that disc jockeys on the country music stations across the U.S.A. and Canada interviewed artists whenever they were in their town. Unfortunately deejays seldom do that anymore.

I was also fortunate in having a good deal of success with my songwriting, which gave me a lot of personal satisfaction. Songs I wrote that brought me world-wide recognition include "Brand on My Heart," "I'm Moving On," "The Golden Rocket," "The Rhumba Boogie," "Music-Makin' Mama from Memphis," "Just a Faded Petal from a Beautiful Bouquet," and "Bluebird Island," to name just a few. Inspiration for a song came to me in many different ways, from both expected and unexpected sources. Sometimes the story would unravel before I got the melody, and other times the music would come first.

I wrote several songs while driving. "Bluebird Island" came to me when I was driving between Oklahoma City and Tulsa. Fiddlin' Arthur Smith, a big name on the Opry when I joined, was on the same tour, and he was riding with me in my canary-yellow Cadillac. We were on our way to Tulsa and about halfway from Oklahoma City when he said, "I've got a friend who has a farm about forty miles back off the main highway, and he makes the best moonshine you'll ever taste. He's real nice to me, because he thinks I'm going to marry his daughter one of these days. I ain't interested in his daughter, but I haven't told him that. I feed him a line, and he gives me a jug of moonshine. We've got plenty of time, Hank, so let's go see him." We drove on this narrow dirt road, and it seemed like we would never get there. It was more or less a wagon trail, and it reminded me of the backwoods in Canada, which I was so familiar with. It had ruts full of water from a recent rain, and I wasn't sure if we'd make it.

When we finally pulled up to this old, broken-down house in my big Cadillac, the man looked like he'd never seen such a car, and he probably hadn't. His was the first real moonshine still I'd ever seen. The old gentleman was a nice fellow. His name was Sam. The girl that Sam wanted Arthur to marry was extremely pretty. Actually, she reminded me of Daisy Mae in the Li'l Abner comic strip. She flirted with Arthur as we took a few swigs from the moonshine jug. Arthur sort of sweet-talked to her, and the old man was all smiles. Sam tried to persuade us to stay all night, but we told him we had a show to do in Tulsa at 8:30 and had to get going.

We bid them good-bye, and we left with our jug of moonshine—and the inspiration for a song. As I was driving and talking to Arthur, I don't know why, but a picture of a sailing ship on an ocean flashed in my mind. Now, this was odd. Most of the time when I wrote songs, I'd have to be in the right mood, and usually I had seen or heard something to spark the idea. Then I'd let my imagination run wild and work the idea over and over, to see which way the song would be best.

My mind drifted, and I pictured a silver sea and an island in the South Pacific. Tradewinds, I thought. Thousands of pretty bluebirds were all around this island, enjoying their haven together. Then came "Bluebird Island," and then "The tradewinds there on Bluebird Island." Soon I had the beginning of a song, "My ship set sail to Bluebird Island, and slowly drifted out to sea." With those serene words came a melody that seemed tailored to fit the lyrics. The words kept coming, and I almost had the song finished when we got to the motel. As soon as I went into my room, I wrote the lyrics and the melody down. I didn't have any way to record the melody, but even before I learned to read music, I had my own way of putting a melody down on paper so I wouldn't forget it.

After the show I finished the lyrics and phoned Min to tell her I had written another song. I read the words to her, and she said, "They are beautiful. Do you have a pretty melody?" I answered, "Yes, and it suits the words extremely well. I won't sing it over the phone, but I know you'll love it."

In a few days I got back to Nashville and played the song for Min. She thought I had a hit and should record it in my next session. Min has always been my best critic. If she didn't like a song, she would tell me in no uncertain terms, and I'd find out later she was right. I did record "Bluebird Island" on January 26, 1951, with Anita Carter, and it went to number four on the national charts. I thought this particular song needed a female voice, and Anita Carter was the right one.

"Bluebird Island" is a song I love to sing. Like "I'm Movin' On," "I've Been Everywhere," "A Fool Such as I," and some others, it has never lost its popularity. People still request all these songs frequently. "Bluebird Island" was easy to write. Other songs took months to complete, and "I'm Movin' On" took about a year to finish.

I wondered where the inspiration came to write "Bluebird Island." Perhaps it was "Daisy Mae" and her lonely expression as we left the backwoods that put me in this melancholy mood to write these lyrics and the music. Mood is certainly important in writing songs. If you're composing a sad song, you have to be in a sad mood. If you're going to write a funny song, you have to be in a funny or a lighthearted mood. At least that's the way it is with me. The mood gives you the inspiration to write whatever comes into your mind, and the inspiration can lead you to write about any subject. Of course, getting into a certain mood is not that easy, as the mood must be real or it won't work. You can't just snap your fingers and jump into the mood you want. No matter where or how the song comes to you, I do know that all the ingredients have to be just right in order to have a hit song.

It was very unusual the way I got the inspiration to write another South Sea island song, entitled "A Message from the Tradewinds." The Rainbow Ranch Boys and I were doing a few show dates around New York and a guest spot on the Perry Como television show. We were staying at the Victoria Hotel, where we always stayed when we were in that area. In my room was a sixteen-by-twenty picture of a Hawaiian girl. I spotted it the minute I walked in. It was hanging over the head of the bed, and I was fascinated by it. This Hawaiian girl had several leis hanging around her neck, and she wore a bright rose in her hair. The sadness in her face as she was looking out over the Pacific was haunting. I wondered who would paint a picture of a South Sea island girl and give her such a lonely expression. Every time I looked at the picture, I felt the girl's sadness. It was strange.

This picture was a copy of a painting, and I'm sure it wasn't worth very much. If I had called the hotel manager and offered him money for it, he might have said, "Take the picture if it means that much to you. You and your group have been good visitors here on many occasions, so take it as a souvenir of our hotel." But I didn't have the courage to do that. Yes, I'd "borrow" it, but I had a problem. The picture was too large to fit in my suitcase. So the next morning, as was customary when checking out of a hotel, the Rainbow Ranch Boys packed up their garment bags and put them outside their doors to be picked up by the bellhops. Then they went to the restaurant to have breakfast. Before I joined them, I took the picture off the wall and put it in one of the boys' garment bags and zipped it up again. We checked out of the hotel, and when the bellhops brought our things down to the front door, the garment bags were loaded on the rack on top of the car.

As we were driving out of New York City on our way to the New Jersey Turnpike, I said to whoever was driving, "Pull over the first chance you get, because Hillous, you have something that belongs to me in your garment bag, and I want to get it out." "Hank, how in the hell could I have something that belongs to you in my garment bag?" "It's there," I said, "I'll prove it to you."

We stopped the car and went through the inconvenience of unlacing the canvas on top of the car to get the garment bag down. As Hillous laid it on the ground, he complained. "This is a hell of a lot of work for nothing." He unzipped the garment bag, which exposed the belongings, and there, as big as life, was the picture. Hillous was about half mad, or at least he acted like it. "Boy, that beats all," he said. "You were too chicken to bring the picture out yourself. You stole it, and you were going to blame it on me. What would you have done if I'd got caught? Would you have denied it?" After Hillous calmed down, we all laughed about it. That picture gave me the inspiration to write "A Message from the Tradewinds," from the girl who was looking so sad across the Pacific Ocean. It was a hit record, and the picture is now in my museum at Opryland.

In addition to the hits I wrote and recorded, I cut many other songs that were written by some of the best and best-known writers in the business. The titles included "A Fool Such as I," "These Hands," "I Don't Hurt Anymore," "With This Ring I Thee Wed," and "I've Been Everywhere."

Occasionally, though, I would get a song from an unknown writer that turned into a hit. Jack Toombs was a good example of this. He was working as a cab driver in Nashville, and he wrote a beautiful song entitled "That's When He Dropped the World in My Hands." I have been singing it on the Opry for many years now.

Sometimes another artist would pitch a song to me, hoping I'd record it. Hank Williams did this during the early part of our career at the Opry. The Rainbow Ranch Boys and I were scheduled for two shows on a Sunday in Indianapolis, Indiana. After the matinee I went to my dressing room in the basement and was surprised to find Hank Williams waiting for me. "How you doing, Hank? I had a friend drive me all the way from Nashville so I could see your show and tell you about a song I'm writing for you. I've still got a few more lines left to write, but I'd like to play it for you. I think you'll like it, and you can make it a hit if you record it." Hank was having a serious back problem at the time, and he had hired a guy to drive him around in his Cadillac convertible to his scheduled shows.

Tommy Vaden and I listened as Hank sang the song. However, to be honest about it, the song didn't impress me very much. It didn't match my voice or my style, but I knew it could be a smash hit for him. Usually I could hear just a few lines and I'd know immediately if the song could be a potential hit for me. Occasionally, though, a song would grow on me after hearing it a few times, especially if I liked the subject.

After Hank finished, he said, "If you like it, you can record it. It's yours." Trying to be diplomatic, I answered, "I'd like to have the completed song when you're through with it, so I can try it out, to see whether or not I can do it justice." Hank replied, "I may make a few lyric changes before I give it to you. Audrey and I aren't getting along right now, so I'm not staying at home. Call me tomorrow at the Hermitage Hotel in Nashville, and I'll have the song ready, and you can drop by and pick it up."

I did try to reach him the next day at the hotel, but he wasn't there. Actually, Hank didn't show up in Nashville for about eight days, for whatever reasons. Later on he recorded the song himself. The title was "Jambalaya." Tommy and I were the first to hear it, and Hank wanted me to record it. The rest is history. "Jambalaya" was a smash hit. Hank Williams had the voice and the rhythm for the song, and his band, the Drifting Cowboys, put together great music tracks to make an excellent record. It stayed number one on the charts for a long time. It's a classic.

I had another opportunity to record a song of Hank's. One Sunday morning around nine o'clock Hank called on the phone. "I've written you a song that I think you'll like. My boys and I are going to the WSM studio, and the engineer will put our demo on tape. Come on down and hear it to see if you want to record it." When I arrived at the studio, the Drifting Cowboys were set up to record and were waiting for Hank, who came in a few minutes after I arrived. The engineer checked the instrument and voice level, and Hank and his boys ran through the song before recording it. The title was "You Better Keep It on Your Mind." Hank said to me, "You've got a good deep voice, so why don't you join in on the chorus with the other boys," which I did.

I took the tape home and listened to it several times, but it wasn't my style either. It was tailor written for Hank. After he passed away, the song was released on MGM records. They kept my vocal part and dubbed it into the master tape. My name is not listed on the record, but you can certainly hear my voice as I joined in with the other boys on part of the lines. Hank sang, "Better keep it on your mind all the time," and his boys and I came in and sang, "All the time."

In interviews that Hank Williams did with the trade papers and radio deejays, they would often ask, "What is your biggest disappointment?" He would say, "I wrote two songs for Hank Snow, and he didn't record either one of them." I had my chances, but I let them slip away. I regret that I didn't record at least one of his songs before he died, but I did add one in an album many years ago. It's a beautiful song called "Mansion on the Hill." Hank Williams passed away January 1, 1953. I lost a great friend, and the world lost a great talent.

Friends, when I talk with pride about my hit songs, I don't mean to brag, and please be aware that I give much of the credit for my success to the musicians, background singers, producers, and songwriters.

Tommy Vaden, Joe Talbot, Ernie Newton, Velma Williams, Pete Wade, and Lloyd Green were among the finest musicians on many of my records. When I used background singers and quartets, I had the best—sometimes the Jordanaires and sometimes the Anita Kerr Singers. On my religious songs the Blackwood Brothers or Mother Maybelle Carter and the Carter Sisters were usually the background singers. I also used the Glaser Brothers for backup vocals. They were the cream of the crop in the U.S.A.

Mother Maybelle Carter, bless her heart, what a fine country talent she was. Her guitar playing was unique, and her grand style was copied by nearly every guitar player in the business through the years. I used to listen to her with the original Carter family on RCA Victor records way back when I was a teenager. The original Carter Family consisted of Mother Maybelle, A. P. Carter, and Sarah Carter, so it was always an honor to have Mother Maybelle and the Carter Sisters be a part of my records.

In 1955 I recorded two duets with Anita Carter entitled "Keep Your Promise, Willie Thomas" and "It's You, Only You, That I Love." Then in 1962 we recorded the album *Together Again,* which was one of my most popular and best-selling albums. Mother Maybelle and the Carter Sisters supplied the background voices on these tracks. Anita and I had planned to do another album together because the demand was so strong, but unfortunately, every time I was ready to do it, we were on separate labels. Recording companies back then didn't usually permit their artists to record on other labels with other artists.

Anita and I are both free from any labels at this writing, and I've talked with her about recording together again. But she's been in poor health for some time now, so I can't make any promises. If it ever does happen, I'll let my son, Jimmie, produce the album. Jimmie is a fine producer and has an outstanding studio in Nashville, where they're doing video and audio work for many of the top names in the country music and gospel fields.

Back then the record companies were not so downright competitive as they are today, and they would usually let the artists pick what they wanted to record. After my session in Chicago I always insisted that I find my own material. I wanted suitable songs, whether I wrote them myself or they came from other writers. I would record songs from RCA Victor if I thought they warranted recording, but I'd never record a song I didn't like, especially drinking songs, or suggestive songs, or songs about dope.

Likewise, my shows on the road have always carried the reputation of being clean family shows. The fans always knew that when they came to see a Hank Snow show, they could bring their small children, or their minister, or their priest, if they wanted to.

It seemed to me that through the 1950s country music was more fun. Many times after a show, if we didn't have to leave right away for our next appearance, the entertainers would get together in one of our motel or hotel rooms and have a few beers. We'd get the instruments out and jam, rehearse, or maybe just sit and tell stories until bedtime. Friends of the entertainers would often drop by unexpectedly and join the party. When we were not on the road, we would often get together in one another's homes in Nashville.

One time when Min was in Florida with Mother Maybelle and the Carters at their summer cottage, I invited Moon Mullican and the Rainbow Ranch Boys to the house. I was anxious to hear Moon's outstanding piano playing. Tommy Vaden was sick, and Don Sleyman, a fine fiddle player, took Tommy's place that night. We had a few beers and tuned up our instruments to play music. I was in the process of setting up a tape recorder to record our party and discovered that the microphone cord wouldn't reach the piano, which was three rooms away. We soon remedied that problem. The boys went in and picked the piano up in the living room, carried it out to the den, and set it down in the middle of the den floor.

Moon was at his best that night. He sang and played for about two hours nonstop, and we all joined in with our different instruments. We had a ball, singing and playing until the wee hours of the morning. Nobody got real tight and nobody got out of the way. I have a whole tape of some of the finest honky-tonk piano you could ever hear.

Moon was the king of the honky-tonk piano players, and since then others have copied his style, including Jerry Lee Lewis and Mickey Gilley. Moon was not only a piano player, he was a good singer, too, and he spent many years on the Grand Ole Opry. He did quite a bit of recording for King Records in Cincinnati, and he had several hit records, including "I'll Sail My Ship Alone."

Speaking of Moon Mullican coming to the house reminds me of something Marty Robbins did that I'll never forget. I called Marty at his home and asked him to come by sometime to look over a few songs with me. We had already planned that he would record an album of my songs, and I would record an album of his songs. So Marty said he would drop by that afternoon.

When Marty came in, I told him about Min being ill and in bed, and he asked if he could see her. "Hank, If you'll let me use one of your guitars, I'll sing her a few songs." I handed him my guitar and we went into the bedroom. He sat on the floor, leaned up against the wall, and sang song after song to Min for about an hour and a half. Both Min and I thought that was one of the nicest things anyone could ever do. She has never forgotten it, and neither have I. Min was personally serenaded by one of the giants in the business. Marty was a precious person, and I'm sure he's playing beautiful music in heaven right at this minute.

Many times I've heard people say that I was a favorite of Marty Robbins. Now, wasn't that funny, because I thought the same thing about him. He put more feeling into a song than anyone I've ever heard, and he could stir every emotion by the treatment he gave the lyrics of any song he sang. I was always flattered when people said that Marty did imitations of me during his road shows.

Min's illness reminds me of another story. Our family doctor, Cleo Miller, visited our home on several occasions. It was the good doctor who attended me when I had the serious automobile accident in 1951. Back then Dr. Miller would make a house call if time permitted. He was also a friend of country music. On one of these house calls he said, "Hank, sometimes I'll pick up my guitar and fool around with it, and it gives me relaxation, but doggone it, I've got a little ole guitar that makes my fingers so sore on the ends that I can't play it very long."

I said, "Doctor, it's because the guitar strings are too high off the fingerboard. I don't mean to put your guitar down, but some of the inexpensive guitars are built that way. Let me find you a good instrument." Back then I owned a music store and we took trade-ins. I picked out a fine-sounding guitar, one that was easy to chord, and I delivered it to Dr. Miller. He tried it and was tickled to death. "Gosh, Hank, it almost plays by itself. I love this guitar. How much do I owe you." "Doctor, since you've made several house calls to check on Min, I make house calls, too. The guitar is yours. A little gift from me." He was so appreciative, and it thrilled me to be able to give him something that meant so much to him. Throughout the years I gave him many albums of my songs. He was more than a doctor. He was a friend in the truest sense of the word.

I'd like to tell you about my little bear and how Ernest Tubb and Red Foley became involved with him. I bought a stuffed cub bear, along with several other items, from a taxidermist in Livingston, Montana. For the life of me, I can't understand why anybody would shoot an innocent cub, but someone did. I named him Bruno. He's about three feet high and stands on a platform with his two paws outstretched, and he's holding an ashtray.

I was at the Plantation Club with Red Foley and his second wife, Sally Sweet, before they were married. Dub Albritten, who used to manage both Ernest and me, was there, but Ernest wasn't with us that night. We were sitting around having a few drinks and telling stories, and when the place closed up, I invited them out to my house to continue the party. This was around five o'clock in the morning, and of course Min was sleeping. I always wanted Min with me anytime we entertained guests, and even though she never took a drink in her life, sometimes her clever wit stole the show. But I seldom brought guests home at that ungodly hour. This time I did, and bless her heart, she got out of bed as she always did and joined us. She looked as fresh as a daisy and was as cheerful as could be.

We were having a good time, and Min continued to put up with us. After Red had a few more drinks, he took a liking to Bruno. All of a sudden Red said, "I'm going to call Ernest and tell him there's a bear in your den. Hank, dial the number for me." Red and Ernest had a feud going on between them. It was a made-up thing, of course, not a real feud. But anytime Ernest got on the radio and Red wasn't there, he would run Red down and vice versa. Each always tried to outdo the other with a joke or practical trick. It was funny the way they did it, and many of the country entertainers, as well as the public, got a big kick out of it. No matter what was said, however, Red and Ernest were the best of friends.

Red called Ernest and woke him up out of a sound sleep, as Ernest told us later. He yelled in the phone, "What in the hell do you want, calling me at this hour?" Red responded, "Hey, Ernest, Hank's got a bear here in his den, and we're having a conversation. Have you ever heard a bear talk? Would you like to talk to him?" "Hell no, what's going on? I can't understand you, you're polluted." Red's tongue was so thick he was slurring every word, and this hilarious conversation lasted at least thirty minutes. That was one funny conversation. I had my tape machine running throughout this humor, and it's one of my most prized tapes in my collection.

Here's how I first met Mickey Mantle. I had just come home off a tour in Georgia one afternoon, and the Yankees were playing in Nashville. Min said, "The press has been desperately trying to get in touch with you. Mickey Mantle is a big fan of yours, and they want you to come down to the stadium to meet him and have your pictures taken together." Well, I was a big fan of his, too, and I was anxious to meet him. You've never seen anyone take a shower, shave, and dress as quickly as I did. I drove down, and it took me forever to convince security that I'd been invited by Mickey. I finally did, and a gentleman took me on the field and introduced me to Mickey. What a thrill for me! Nobody was a bigger baseball star than Mickey Mantle. We had pictures taken together for the Nashville press, and Mickey autographed a baseball for me, after hitting a home run. Thereafter Mickey and I corresponded, and I sent him practically every album I ever recorded. I met him another time in Baltimore, Maryland, and through him I had the pleasure of meeting Whitey Ford and Yogi Berra. They were all good country fans.

In Canada, the United States, and several foreign countries a number of good people throughout my career have organized fan clubs to further my music. One was as far away as Ceylon.

In 1953 I received a letter from Eugene Gooneratne, a gentleman from the island of Ceylon. (Since that time the island has been renamed Sri Lanka.) From Nashville, this is about halfway around the world. He was employed at radio Sri Lanka. His letter stated, "Mr. Snow, with your permission I would like to establish a Hank Snow Fan Club. I can give you an abundance of advertising over Radio Sri Lanka, and because it's carried on two shortwave beams, it goes just about around the world." Through our correspondence I sent Eugene pictures and he got an international fan club started. As time went on, I began making tapes for him to play over the radio station.

One year I made a half-hour Christmas show. I transferred several of my records on tape, and between songs I'd talk to the listeners as if I were a disc jockey. The Christmas show was so popular that it became an annual event. I would play and dedicate several songs to the boys and girls who were confined to a hospital or were sick in their homes. My songs included "Rudolph, the Red-Nosed Reindeer," "Santa Claus Is Coming to Town," and "Frosty, the Snow Man." On each program I always played "Christmas Roses" for all the folks who were in a foreign country who couldn't be with their sweethearts, wives, mothers, or other family members during the yuletide season. Here are some of the lyrics, which were written by N. A. Catsos and Paula Frances Ianello:

> Christmas roses to you I'm sending,
> May they bring you Christmas joy though we're apart.
> Christmas roses will say I love you
> As their tender message echoes from my heart.
> Though I can't be with you on this Christmas day,
> Remember that I'll always love you though I'm far away.
> Christmas roses to you I'm sending,
> May they bring you Christmas joy though we're apart.

I also did the same type of show at Eastertime, in which I played mostly Easter songs and hymns. This helped me get better acquainted in many foreign countries. Children from all over the world began writing me letters and calling me "Uncle Hank," so I used this when talking with them on the show: "All right, kiddies, this is your Uncle Hank. Here's a special song just for you." I did these shows for many years, maybe thirty years in all, and I still get foreign mail as a result of these programs.

One day I received a disturbing letter from Eugene, stating that he had had a serious motorcycle accident. The doctor said his leg would have to be amputated because gangrene had set in. Eugene had gone to one of the free clinics, which was a godsend, because he was only making twenty-five dollars a month. There was a lot of poverty in Sri Lanka. The hospitals were run by the government and medical facilities were crowded, especially the free clinics.

I immediately cabled Eugene and told him to send me the microfilm of his leg X rays and to not have any operation until I showed the X-ray pictures to my doctor. When I received the microfilm, I took it to Dr. Miller. As soon as he saw the X rays, he said, "Hank, cable the man right back and tell him not to even think about letting them amputate his leg. It isn't necessary. With proper care, it will heal within four or five months. It's easy to take a leg off, but it's not that easy to put one back on." After Eugene's doctors got my message, they changed their minds and treated Eugene with medication, and he was back driving his motorcycle again in no time.

I never got to meet Eugene, but we continued to correspond. He was still walking fine, with just a slight limp, when he passed away several years later.

After Eugene, Jayaratne Perera, who I had been corresponding with, took over the club, and he did a good job, too. Because of some trouble between him and Livy Wijemanne, who took over the duties as top executive of the radio station, the last Christmas show was never played, so I stopped sending tapes. There are two different stories why the show was never put on the air, and since both of these gentlemen are my friends, I'll not comment further.

Livy visited me at my home during 1959. He was sent to Washington, D.C., as a goodwill ambassador from Sri Lanka, and he said the reason he accepted the free offer by his country was that he wanted to come to Tennessee to see Hank Snow! I didn't know Livy was coming until I got a telephone call one night from the old Sam Davis Hotel in downtown Nashville. After I picked up the phone, a strange voice answered back. "Mr. Snow, this is Livy. I'm in Nashville and no one here will rent me a room. I've been going from hotel to hotel, and I don't know what to do."

I told Livy to stay right there, and I'd be down to help him. I drove to the hotel, and sure enough, it was Livy. I remembered him by his picture. At that time, blacks and whites were separated throughout the South. Hotels, schools, buses, restaurants, and even restrooms were segregated. When I explained to the manager of the hotel that Livy was a goodwill ambassador from Sri Lanka and that he had just come from Washington, D.C., where he had been a guest for the past two days with top officials, the scene quickly changed. Livy got his room, and during the next few days we had several visits. We took pictures, and I taped greetings for him to take back to the people of Sri Lanka.

In this way I suppose I was a goodwill ambassador, too.

29

Elvis and Parker

You put your heart upon an auction block and sold it,
Selfish greed and envy were the auctioneers;
The highest bidder won your heart but he can't hold it,
Love that's bought with gold can only end in tears.

"The Highest Bidder," by Hank Snow,
Mary Shurtz, and Boudleaux Bryant

I'VE HAD SEVERAL MANAGERS throughout my career, and I can say good things about every one, except Tom Parker. I once was a business partner to the man, and after I tell this story, you'll know why I lost all respect for him.

Many people have heard of Tom Parker, manager of Elvis Presley, and refer to him as "Colonel." But a book about Parker stated that he actually was born Andreas Van Kuijk in Holland and took this honorary title unto himself. It said that he was not born an American or born on the southern carnival circuit, as he had claimed, but that he was an illegal Dutch immigrant without papers or a passport. I personally feel this is the truth, and I refuse to call him "Colonel."

A lot of people from newspapers, trade papers, television, and radio have approached me over the years to hear my side of the story about my conflict with Parker over the Elvis Presley–Tom Parker association. Many have criticized me for not speaking out on the matter. Some years ago I even had a call from Louella Parsons, a famous gossip columnist, who was quite upset with me because I would not divulge to her any information on this subject. Over the years I've read many books and many articles in a number of newspapers from many parts of the world about Elvis and Parker. Some of them were highly distorted or completely untrue, and some accused me of being a poor businessman and a man of short foresight for letting my part of the Presley contract slip through my hands.

Since the passing of Elvis I've been flooded with phone calls from all parts of the nation eager to get my comments. One book called me an angry man and said that I had sold my story to a national magazine. The truth is that I have never even considered selling my story to anyone, anytime, for any price. I always felt the time was not right until now. So in the next few pages I shall set the record straight as to how I felt literally conned and cheated out of my part of what I thought was a firm contract with Elvis Presley.

In the early fall of 1954, years after I had been established around the world as one of RCA Victor's best-selling recording artists, and at a time when I was seeking a new agent, I started to negotiate with various booking agencies. I was trying to locate a reputable agency to handle my affairs in every aspect of the entertainment business. This would include booking my personal appearances, making television and radio commitments, and renegotiating or revising any contracts necessary.

Knowing that Parker had once managed country singer Eddy Arnold, and on the advice of several people, I arranged an appointment with Parker. He and Eddy had dissolved their relationship quite some time prior to our meeting. I neglected, however, to question their sudden split—a mistake I would regret later on.

Parker lived on Gallatin Road in Madison, Tennessee, only a few blocks from my house. His office was in a small corner of his garage, in the back of his residence, which was not very impressive. When I entered his office and addressed him as Tom, I was quickly informed, "At all times from here on out, you refer to me as Colonel Parker." (This is the last time I will use the false title "Colonel.")

The meeting with Parker lasted approximately two hours. The biggest portion of this time was taken up with stories of the great things he had done for Eddy Arnold. He told me he would make me a star and put my name in lights in every corner of the globe—this at a time when my RCA Victor records were already selling in every part of the world and my services for personal appearances were highly in demand! He also mentioned he had formed his own agency, Jamboree Attractions, and was booking such artists as Whitey Ford (known as the Duke of Paducah), Cousin Minnie Pearl, Cowboy Copas, Tommy Sands, and others. He also said he had formed a music company under the name of Jamboree Music.

After several meetings we finally agreed that he would represent me and would act as my exclusive manager. A crude contract was drawn up to serve as a temporary one until the finished contract could be prepared. It was understood that I would pay $2,500 for the few remaining months of 1954, for what he called "special services rendered to start handling Hank Snow's personal management," and that the new contract would go into effect on January 1, 1955.

A few months later, during another meeting, Parker said he felt it would be a good idea if we formed a fifty-fifty partnership to be known as Hank Snow Enterprises–Jamboree Attractions. He said we needed a good headline act such as myself to headline the agency. He thought that I should be a part of Jamboree Music and that we would continue to book good talent, not only from the Grand Ole Opry, but from any part of the United states. He believed I would be very valuable in heading up and working closely with the music company. He considered the value of Jamboree Attractions and Jamboree Music to be $5,000. This included all equipment and music material on hand at that time. He mentioned that one of his employees, Tom Diskin, owned 25 percent of the companies. The following is an exact quote from our agreement:

> It is understood that before any agreement can be made to merge Hank Snow Enterprises and its connection into this company, $1225.00 must be repaid to Mr. Tom Diskin as its legal share in the company. The remainder, $3750.00, will have to be divided into two parts, 50% to Col. Tom Parker and 50% to Hank Snow. This will make the company a fifty-fifty partnership deal. The company will be written up as a start of $3750.00, owned by Hank Snow and Col. Tom Parker. Hank Snow is to pay into Col. Tom Parker the sum of $1,775.00, to become a 50% owner of this agency and music company. The above agreement will in no way be a part of the exclusive management agreement.

I was now a 50-percent partner with our new agency, Hank Snow Enterprises–Jamboree Attractions. Throughout 1955 we continued to book acts on different package shows, and Parker set up several tours for me under our personal management agreement. I was excited about the agency and our new working agreement, and there was no doubt in my mind that this venture could work into a truly successful agency.

During 1955, when Bill Haley and his Comets were the hottest rock-and-roll group in the country, we decided that we should do a tour with Haley and myself sharing the billing. We did this more or less on a trial basis to see if Haley's type of music would mix with country music and prove a good box-office draw. Therefore we arranged a tour of six or eight major cities throughout the Midwest, and it turned out to be a huge success, playing to sell-out houses in every location.

In order to book this tour, it was agreed that both Parker and I would put up a certain amount of money, which would go into a designated fund at a local bank for promotional expenses, plus the cost of the talent and general operation expenses. I distinctly remember contributing my share to promote the Bill Haley–Hank Snow Tour, in the amount of $15,000. Back in those days the promotion and expenses involved in any tour were far less than they are now. I shall always believe that it was my money alone that financed this tour and that Parker never did contribute his share. When he presented the financial results of this tour to me in a crude typewritten statement he had prepared, I was completely shocked and discouraged. I still have these papers in my files.

Other tours worked out about the same. These jumbled-up statements that Parker gave me from time to time were the only things I had to go by concerning the state of our finances. At that time I was working under a heavy schedule, doing around two hundred fifty personal appearances a year, the Grand Ole Opry, and my RCA Victor recordings, in addition to being involved in the ownership of two radio stations. I simply did not have the time to get too involved with the activities of the agency, and I had to trust in Parker's honesty and accept these statement as the actual figures.

In early 1955 Elvis Presley entered the picture. During one of our conversations Parker mentioned a young artist who seemed to be creating quite a disturbance in certain parts of the Midsouth and especially Texas. He strongly suggested that we try to arrange a guest appearance on one of my Grand Ole Opry performances, in which I was the headline act and master of ceremonies. At this particular time Bob Neal of Memphis, Tennessee, was managing Elvis. We arranged a spot on the Grand Ole Opry, and I introduced Elvis Presley for the first time to the Opry audience.

One of the stories I've read claimed that I had to ask Elvis his name before introducing him. Like countless other statements this was completely untrue, because Elvis had been to my home several times before he made his Opry appearance. Elvis sang one of the first songs he recorded for the Sun label, "Blue Moon of Kentucky," but the reaction of the Grand Ole Opry audience was far less enthusiastic than that of the audiences he was playing to in the South. I learned later that he was disappointed and fully discouraged with his debut on the Opry. However, if the Grand Ole Opry did nothing for Elvis, it did a special favor for me. I met one of the finest and most polite gentlemen I had ever known, and he soon became a very close friend to my family and me.

In the months that followed, Elvis made periodic visits to my home and often would sit and play the piano and sing for us. It made me happy to learn from him that he had been a fan of mine since he was a young boy, and I was delighted to hear him sing many of the songs I had written and recorded years before. Elvis and my son, Jimmie, being about the same age, had a lot in common. At that time, Jimmie was also trying to break into the musical world as a country entertainer, and they became very close friends. I can remember times in the backyard when they had knife-throwing contests to see who could make the best score at sticking the knife in a tree.

Throughout 1955 our agency set up several tours, one of which headlined Andy Griffith and included my son, Jimmie, as well as other country acts. Although I did not travel with this particular tour, Parker and I worked out an agreement whereby my band, the Rainbow Ranch Boys, would travel with this tour, along with other musicians. We continued to use Elvis as an added attraction on the different shows, for which we paid him $250 per week. It is interesting to me now to look at an old picture of the huge banner stretched along the outside of the auditorium in Tampa, Florida, displaying the names of the acts on this show. The name Elvis Presley appears in small letters.

I'll never forget the opening night of our first tour together. I was truly amazed at the reaction Elvis received after his first performance on stage. The crowd went wild. For a completely unknown artist to capture an audience in this manner was unbelievable. Since I was the headline act of the show, it was customary for me to close each performance. Since Elvis preceded me on stage, I soon found I was walking out on his applause. This can be a little embarrassing to any performer, and I mentioned this to Parker and told him of the difficulty I was having. We both agreed, on the strength of this, we should have Elvis close the shows. This would relieve me of the pressure of following Elvis, and it would prove his strength as a performer in doing his act on an already lengthy show. In addition we could test his popularity in competing with other well-established artists. It was on this first show that I sensed that this young man had a tremendous future.

As the tour continued through a number of cities, we noticed the audience would start to leave after my portion, thinking this was the end of the show. I would immediately make an announcement that the act to follow was well worth the price of admission, and I suggested they stay. Then most of the folks took their seats, and many of them came to me after the show, saying they thoroughly enjoyed Elvis's act and were glad they had stayed.

During these tours in which I headlined the package, Elvis was still advertised as an "extra-special, added attraction." He continued to have a tremendous impact on the audiences, and as we discussed the situation, Parker strongly suggested on several occasions that we should get Elvis signed to our agency. Parker was now aware that Elvis and I had become close friends and that Elvis had faith in me, not only respecting me as an artist, but liking me as a person. Parker informed me that I should "baby-sit" Elvis and try to convince him that he should sign with our agency.

I would talk with Elvis at every opportunity in the dressing rooms, in the car, or backstage, and sometimes we would talk for hours at a time. I didn't try to force him to sign with us, but I told him from time to time that I thought he had a great future under the proper guidance. Also, I mentioned that Eddy Arnold had enjoyed much success under the guidance of Tom Parker, and I firmly believed if he signed with our agency, we could be a great asset to his future. I talked about the things we had in mind for him, such as television, radio, and movies.

Although I felt the Sun Recording Company in Memphis, Tennessee, had done a good job in launching Elvis on records, I did not believe they could properly exploit him internationally. Regardless of whether or not he signed with our agency, as a special friend I hoped to get RCA Victor interested in him. Elvis had faith in my ability to try to steer him in the right direction. His answer was, "Thank you, sir. From your lengthy experience, your personal guidance means a lot to me." He told me that anything that was worked out with his parents would certainly be fine with him.

In the meetings that followed between Parker and Elvis's parents, I gathered from certain people close to the Presleys that they did not care for Parker. It looked doubtful, at that time, that we could convince them to place Elvis under our guidance and sign him with Hank Snow Enterprises–Jamboree Attractions.

Thinking about the wonderful reception Elvis had gotten on previous tours with me, I felt the time was right to speak to Steve Sholes about him. Steve was top executive and A&R chief for RCA Victor throughout the United States. He made periodic trips to Nashville from New York to supervise recording sessions for the various artists, and it was on one of these trips that I first approached him about signing Elvis to RCA Victor.

I remember this first meeting well. Linebaugh's restaurant, located on Broadway Street, was just around the corner from the old Ryman Auditorium, the home of the Grand Ole Opry at that time. Opry artists would often go there for a coffee break between shows. It was there, over a cup of coffee, that I first mentioned Elvis to Steve. I told him of the tremendous success Elvis had enjoyed on our tours and said I believed this boy had a bright future. I said that I thought Elvis's present recording contract with Sun Records could be purchased for $10,000. Steve's reply was, "Hank, we aren't interested in signing any new artists at this time, as we're up to our ears with beginners and unknowns, but maybe later on."

About this time, I headlined a promotional tour with a huge package of Grand Ole Opry entertainers, financed and promoted by RCA Victor. We played fourteen major cities in the United States. I mentioned and promoted Elvis everywhere I went. I constantly gave him a tremendous build-up during all of my personal appearances, as well as on my radio and television interviews. I was always trying to familiarize people with our new protégé, Elvis Presley.

Several times during this tour I made telephone calls to Steve, hoping he would change his mind about Elvis. After one of our shows I called Steve at his home in Tenafly, New Jersey, and he showed much more interest in considering a contract with Elvis. Soon thereafter, hearing more accounts of the effects Elvis was having on his audiences, RCA Victor decided to sign him—provided an agreement could be worked out with Sun Records.

The offer that was made to all concerned was presented during a conference call between Parker, Bob Neal, Tom Diskin, and me. I have in my possession a typed memorandum of this call, dated July 22, 1955, which reads as follows:

> SUBJECT: Elvis Presley (Package Deal Proposition)
>
> Tentative propositions submitted to Bob Neal regarding Elvis Presley: 26 television guest shots on the Hank Snow TV series. 26 radio and television guest appearances on 26 Saturday nights. One hundred personal appearances to be made by Elvis Presley at locations designated by Col. Parker. $10,000 in cash to be paid by Hank Snow/Col. Parker towards obtaining full and absolute release of Elvis Presley artist service from the Sun Recording Company and signing to a label-recording company selected by Col. Tom Parker for a period of three years with two, one-year options and with record royalties on the following terms: 3% royalties to Elvis Presley. 2% royalties to

> Hank Snow/Col. Parker. Total package price for the above: $40,000. The acceptance of this tentative proposition would be contingent upon a complete and absolute break with the Sun Recording Company, leaving Elvis Presley free and clear of all recording commitments and enabling Col. Tom Parker to negotiate a contract with another company.
>
> Copies of the above to Bob Neal, Col. Tom Parker, Hank Snow and Tom Diskin.

The contract on the fifty-fifty partnership for Hank Snow Enterprises–Jamboree Attractions was completed and signed by all parties. It stated that any talent booked by the agency would be charged its regular commission, which would go into a designated bank account set up for the agency.

There was also a separate contract drawn up whereby Parker would continue to act as my personal and exclusive manager. While this agreement was in effect, my current contract with RCA Victor was due to expire. Parker started to negotiate with Steve Sholes for a new five-year contract. This was during the period of my recording career when I was one of the top record sellers for the company. Actually, anything I recorded through the fifties and early sixties, even religious material, was good for a sale of between six and eight hundred thousand records. The new contract finalized for me was for five years with a royalty rate of 3 percent and a guarantee to apply against royalties for the period. (When this contract terminated, I negotiated the next one myself, for the same time period—and for a far greater royalty rate and three times the guarantee. I feel I could have made the same deal with RCA Victor on the previous contract, which Parker negotiated.)

One day in the early spring of 1956 Parker informed me that he had prepared a contract and was leaving for Memphis to talk with Mr. and Mrs. Presley about signing Elvis to our agency. He also said that if his meeting with the Presleys looked in any way shaky, he would call me to come to Memphis. He was aware of the closeness between my son and Elvis and of the confidence Elvis had placed in me. He felt that my influence with the Presleys would be highly valuable. At approximately ten o'clock that same night, I received a phone call from Parker advising me to fly to Memphis the next morning. I gathered from the tone of his conversation that there were serious problems. Seconds after our conversation ended, I made my reservations.

I arrived late in the morning and was met at the airport by representatives from RCA Victor, Hill and Range Songs, and others, who drove me directly to the Peabody Hotel, where a luncheon had been prepared for the fifteen or so people involved. These were press and television personnel, disc jockeys, and so on. Bob Neal, who was managing Elvis at that time, was present, and if my memory serves me correctly, Sam Phillips, who recorded Elvis for the first time, was also on hand.

During this hour-and-a-half luncheon I seemed to be the center of attraction, at least in terms of speaking. My main topic was to impress everyone present with the greatness of Tom Parker. Mr. and Mrs. Presley listened intently to each and every word I had to say, and I sensed from their facial expressions they were becoming more interested in signing Elvis to our agency. Following the luncheon, we met with radio and television reporters, interviewers from newspapers and trade papers, and photographers, who took pictures of Elvis and me.

There were three contracts signed. Steve Sholes of RCA Victor had decided to sign Elvis. It cost RCA Victor $40,000 instead of the $10,000 that they could have bought the contract for from the Sun Recording Company if they had signed him when I first approached Steve some months earlier.

The Aberbach Brothers, Julian and Jean, were the owners of Hill and Range Songs, Inc., a successful New York publishing firm that enjoyed an international reputation. At that time they were turning out many of the top songs in the country field, several of which I had recorded and which rose to number one on the charts. Since I had become a good friend of the Aberbach brothers, it was only natural that Steve work closely with them, and they signed Elvis to Hill and Range Songs.

During the afternoon, and as the many conversations between these people continued, I became anxious and was looking forward to the main event—the signing of Elvis to our agency, Hank Snow Enterprises–Jamboree Attractions. As the afternoon passed, I became quite concerned, and at five o'clock, I still had heard nothing in regard to the signing. Around six o'clock that evening Parker informed me he was getting ready to drive back to Nashville and asked if I'd like to drive back with him instead of staying over and flying back the following morning. He said this would give us a few hours to discuss the happenings from the day's events. I agreed, and after shaking hands with all the people, we left for home.

En route to Nashville, Parker mentioned he had prepared two contracts. One had been in his left coat pocket and the other in his right coat pocket. If the Presleys had shown any signs of refusal on the first contract, which I presumed was pretty strong, he had another contract ready. Which one he produced, he said, would depend on their reaction during the negotiations. Parker said they signed the first contract, and there was no doubt in his mind that someday we could retire on the setup with Elvis.

However, he never did mention the terms of the agreement, and to ask Parker any questions or show any signs of mistrust could be a very touchy situation. He was a temperamental person and would fly off the handle in a split second and would always come back with his famous saying, "What, don't you trust the Colonel?" When we arrived back in Nashville, I didn't know any more about the transaction than I had before I left Nashville.

A short time later I made an appointment with my attorney, Cecil Simms, who had a reputation of being one of the finest attorneys in the South. I reported to him, in detail, everything that had taken place during my association with Parker. Also, I showed him several statements of settlement from some of the shows I had done with Elvis, Bill Haley, and others, which Parker had always given to me in a rough typewritten format.

After a study of these documents Mr. Simms asked me if the company had formed a corporation in accordance with the laws of the State of Tennessee. He seemed quite disturbed when I told him no. He then advised that this be done immediately and that the books of the corporation be available at all times for the inspection of a CPA, myself, and the IRS. He seemd to focus on the Jacksonville, Florida, show and strongly suggested that an extensive investigation be made into Parker's activities, starting in Jacksonville.

This was a touchy situation for me. However, I agreed, and within a few weeks certain affidavits were obtained (copies of which I have in my files) from the people in Jacksonville who helped promote the tour, including disc jockeys and record-store personnel who were selling advance tickets. These documents proved that the gross ticket sales had been altered and were not included in the final gate receipts. On the strength of these documents and others, and since there was no corporation, Mr. Simms advised me to inform Parker immediately of our meetings and tell him that a corporation must be formed. His words to me were, "Parker is a dangerous man, and you could be heading for serious trouble with the IRS, since you are a 50-percent partner of this agency."

I telephoned Parker and asked him to come to my house, explaining that I needed to talk with him briefly about something of extreme importance. He arrived in about fifteen minutes, and I informed him of the lengthy discussion that I had just had with my attorney, who had advised that a corporation be formed at once and the books of the agency be open at all times for inspection by my CPA.

Parker immediately flew into a rage. Pacing up and down my office floor, he told me he thought we should dissolve our relationship in every aspect of our business. He said, "I have things that I want to do, and I'm sure you have things you want to do. Since we do not think the same way, we should dissolve our association." I thought for several minutes and then asked him, "If we do, what happens to our contract with Elvis Presley?" He twirled his big cigar back and forth in his mouth, pointed his finger at his chest, and said, "You don't have any contract with Elvis Presley, Elvis is signed exclusively to the colonel."

With that statement my thoughts raced back to the conversation I'd had with Parker while driving from Memphis to Nashville and to his statement about the two contracts he had prepared—if the Presleys didn't sign the first one, he had another one ready. It was then that I realized, and I'll always believe, that the only difference in the two contracts was that one involved Hank Snow Enterprises–Jamboree Attractions and the other was Parker's own personal contract.

With my experience from the beginning of our association and the haphazard way in which things had been handled, I was actually prepared for this. But it still cut me deep. I felt it was my influence with Elvis and his parents, and with Steve Sholes of RCA Victor, that brought about the signing of the recording contract, as well as signing him to what I thought was our agency. By then the pieces had fallen together in my mind, and I wondered how one human being could undermine, con, and rob another in such a conniving scheme from the start. It is plain to me that this man has no conscience, but I do hope he has enjoyed his fame and fortune and the praise that has been dished out—so unjustly deserved, in my opinion.

In the months that followed, my attorney advised against filing a lawsuit. He felt that Parker would go to extremes in fighting me and that it could be a long-drawn-out process. Being determined to go forward with this, after Mr. Simms's death, I approached other attorneys. Their advice was the same. On the strength of this, and faced with the likelihood of years of court battles, I decided not to pursue the matter. Fortunately, I was financially stable, and I felt my time was too valuable to go through the hassle.

During my association with Parker, which lasted about a year and a half, my impression of him as a person dwindled day by day. I will not go into detail about the many embarrassing times I spent in his presence before other people. He would never let anyone forget how great he was.

Since the untimely passing of Elvis, this global giant in the entertainment world, I've watched many television shows about him and have read every book or anything else I could find pertaining to his life. It was heartbreaking to my family and me, as I'm sure it has been to the countless millions around the world who loved him, to see such ridiculous stories appear. Many of these stories were completely distorted, and it makes my blood run cold to read the praise that went to Tom Parker—the most egotistical, obnoxious human I have ever had dealings with.

Regardless of all that was said and all that happened, I have two things in my possession that all the wealth in the world could never buy. I have a huge picture personally signed by Elvis: "To Hank, my best to you and thanks for all the fun and good times—Your friend, Elvis Presley." The other is the album in which he recorded my song "I'm Movin' On." I'll always remember Elvis as I knew him years ago—a perfect gentleman, who left an unremovable mark on civilization, and a true example of a great American.

I have a video tape in which Vernon Presley made a short comment after the death of Elvis, thanking the public for their kindness during his sadness. His words carried a lot of emotion, and I thought they were well spoken—until he said, "Tom Parker was an honest man."

With that, I got cold chills.

30

A Helping Hand

Would you mind if I tell you that I go for you?
Would you mind if my heart is beating so for you?
Yes, if you should find I'm the lovin' kind,
Would you mind, would you mind, would you mind?

"Would You Mind," by Cy Coben

NEAR THE END OF 1959, I RECEIVED a letter from a young lady in Australia who told me her brother, Stan Tyrie, was a big fan of mine and loved my music. She wrote, "Hank, Stan is slowly dying with cancer. He's written to you on several occasions, and you've always been kind enough to answer his letters. He hasn't much longer to live, maybe a few days, maybe a few weeks, we're not sure, but he would love to have a certain album of yours, which is not available here in Australia."

For some reason Stan wanted the album *Songs of Tragedy.* It has all sad songs in it. Immediately upon receiving the letter, I put a phone call through to Australia and talked to the lady. I told her I wouldn't take the chance of mailing the album, as it might get broken. Instead, I would make a reel-to-reel tape from the album and send it on the morning flight to Australia. I had the necessary equipment in my den to do a good-quality taping, so I immediately transferred the complete album on a tape at a speed of 7½ ips and sent it special air mail to Australia.

A few weeks later I received a letter from Stan's sister. Below are parts of it.

Dear Hank,

I am Stan Tyrie's sister, Aileen, and I am writing this letter on behalf of our family in appreciation of what you did for Stan. We lost him on the 17th of January, 1960, Hank, and God help him. No one would wish him back seeing him suffer like he did.

We all feel we owe you a lot for what you did for Stan. I only wish you had been at his bedside when he played that tape recording you sent him. Hank, he was propped up in bed with all the nurses, sisters, visitors and the patients who could gather around his bed. We had hired a tape recorder and he had it on a chair beside him. When he switched it on, you could have heard a pin drop in that ward, and he laid with such a proud look on his face and when it finished he looked up and said, "How about that! That's what I call a friend to do that for someone he has never met. Hank Snow is a wonderful guy." There wasn't a dry eye in that ward.

I've been a fan of yours for 16 years now and we all shared Stan's love for western music, but now it is not just your singing we love. We feel as Stan did that there must be a truly wonderful and sincere guy behind that voice.

I am enclosing a clipping from the paper. I hope it helps to convey to you, your interest in Stan was justified as he was a very popular boy and just loved life. I think he was the most courageous person I've known—the way he took his fate lying there dying, yet knowing he had so much to live for. His one ambition when he got married (he was to have married about February) was to get his home, then go to America to meet you, Hank. I have his little fiancee down with me now. God help her. She's been a little Rock of Gibraltar to him.

May God watch over you for being the kind of person you are.

Heartfelt thanks.
Yours in appreciation
(Mrs.) Aileen Hodge

Over the years I've not only learned, but I've proven it time and time again, that it's the little things in life that really count. These are the kinds of heartwarming stories that I've never forgotten, nor will I ever forget.

As I look back over my life, a lot of unusual things happened to me. Some were humorous, some were exciting, some were heartwarming, and some were sad and tested my faith in the goodness of people. I certainly have met every kind of person and many, many fine people along the way. People have always intrigued me, and I feel like I can figure most people out. But not always.

I started getting letters from a young man at the state penitentiary, located in West Nashville. His name was Robert (I won't mention his last name), and he was from Knoxville, Tennessee. Robert sent me handwritten letters quite often, and they appeared to be sincere. He explained that he'd been drinking with some friends about ten years earlier and was caught and charged with armed robbery. He was sentenced to ten years in prison and had already served his time, but he had been completely forgotten by the prison officials. He stated that unless someone did something to help him, he was afraid he'd spend the rest of his life behind bars. He claimed the officials wouldn't listen to him and didn't care if he rotted in prison, and it would take someone who was well known and in the public's eye to get him out. He wanted me to write a letter on his behalf to the governor of Tennessee, who at that time was Buford Ellington.

Soon after I heard his story, I received a hand-tooled leather wallet from him, which was extremely fine quality. I had seen Nudie's leather goods in Hollywood, and his was every bit as good. Del Wood of the Grand Ole Opry could vouch for his precise work, and she, too, was trying to help him, as he had written to her before he began writing to me.

I wrote Robert a nice letter and thanked him for the beautiful wallet and commended him for his fine workmanship. After that he started sending me all kinds of leather items. He made me two huge scrapbooks, with my likeness hand-tooled on the front and a train on the back, along with the names of some of my hit songs. In addition he made Min several gifts, including a hand-tooled leather portrait of herself, like the one he did on the scrapbook, and it was almost like a photograph. He made us a coffee table and a serving cart for my office. The tops were hand tooled in leather, and they were beautiful.

At this point I started sending him checks to cover his work. I had offered before to pay him, but he wouldn't accept any money. Then all of a sudden he asked me if I could get him a picture of the governor's daughter, Ann. He said he'd like to do a leather portrait of her and have me send or take it to the governor. When I received this finished hand-tooled masterpiece, it was unbelievably beautiful and almost lifelike. He continued to write and pour his heart and soul out to me, and if he wasn't sincere, he sure had me fooled.

I thought Robert had made the portrait of the governor's daughter for a reason, and if he did, it worked. I wrote him another letter and said I'd talk with Governor Ellington and do everything in my power to convince the governor that he had served his time. Either he was being taken for someone else, or he was being completely overlooked, and I hoped the governor would be able to work out a parole for him as soon as possible. I made an appointment with Governor Ellington, whom I knew pretty well, because I had been in his company several times before he became governor. After he became governor, I had been to the state mansion, entertaining on a few special occasions. He was a kind and considerate man, so I knew he would listen to my request.

As always, I was on time for my appointment, and the governor didn't make me wait. He told his staff to hold all his phone calls, and he took me right in his office. I remember I was wearing one of Nudie's western dress suits with silver buckles on it. The governor was a big man in comparison to my five feet, five and a half inches. After we shook hands, he said, "Hank, I'll toss you for that suit. What can I do for you, friend?" That broke the ice, and I told him the story about Robert. He listened carefully and thought for a minute, then said, "Fortunately, we have a gentleman here who has a lot to do with the corrections system and especially things like this. He no doubt will be familiar with Robert."

The governor called the gentleman into his office, and he joined in the conversation, "Yes, I'm familiar with that name, and there's no way we could release him. The crimes this fellow has committed would not warrant a release or pardon at this particular time. He's too much of a threat to society to put back on the streets."

I was devastated! Robert had lied to me. A lot he hadn't told me, and I was very angry about it. I had been made a fool of. I told the gentleman about the beautiful hand-tooled leather work I'd been receiving, and this rang a bell, because he spoke up and said, "Now, Mr. Snow, I know who you're talking about. We have two inmates with the same name, and I was thinking of the other prisoner. I had them confused. If I'm correct in my thinking, the one you're speaking of has been serving ten years, and I'll check to see if he has served all his time. I'll get back to the governor in a few days with the information." I felt relieved, thinking that Robert was on the level after all.

Within the next few days the gentleman got in touch with Governor Ellington and said Robert had served his time, and he was checking further into his parole. In another few days he called the governor again and said he could release the inmate under certain conditions. He would not be allowed to stay in the state of Tennessee, and he must have a legitimate job outside of the state with confirmation that his employer was running an honest business.

Due to the outstanding work that Robert had done with leather, the first thing that popped into my mind was Nudie, the famous rodeo tailor in Hollywood, who made all my western stage suits after I left Nathan Turke and Globe. Nudie made stage costumes for just about everyone, not only in country music but for western movies, too. His place of business also made hand-tooled western saddles, belts, and boots, and they were all beautiful. I phoned Nudie and told him the story. "Yes sir, Hank, we're running shorthanded with leather people at this time. We had our top man just leave for his home in Old Mexico." We talked some more, and Nudie said to send Robert out and he'd put him to work.

I immediately called Governor Ellington and said I had Robert a job with Nudie. The governor was already familiar with Nudie, as he made many trips to Nashville to take orders for suits. The governor knew that Nudie had a legitimate and reputable business and that he could go ahead and confirm this with the corrections department. The governor called me back and said he could release Robert as early as the next day. But I said, "As much as I appreciate everything you've done, unfortunately, I'm leaving tomorrow for a two-week tour. Could you please make arrangements to keep Robert until I return? I'd like to be here in Nashville to pick him up at the penitentiary to make sure he gets on the plane to Hollywood, where Nudie will be waiting for him at the airport." The governor said it would be no problem. This would give them more time to take care of the paperwork.

When I arrived back home after my tour, I made arrangements to pick Robert up. I went to the prison on the appointed day, and I was taken through several locked prison gates to a waiting room where I found Robert. He was clean shaven and was well dressed in a black-and-white, small-checked business suit. I shook his hand and began a conversation with him. He was not very talkative, and I noticed he had jet-black eyes that pierced right through me. I immediately associated him with Charlie Tanner, my cruel stepfather, and that gave me an uncomfortable feeling. He signed his way out of prison and was given his few personal belongings, and we walked to my car.

I drove straight to our home in Madison, where Min had prepared a big southern-fried chicken dinner with all the trimmings. He talked a little over the dinner table. He told us about two gifts he was making for Min and me but hadn't had time to finish. He said he'd send them to us as soon as they were completed. After supper we sat and talked for a while, and then we left for the airport in lots of time before his flight.

We never did see the unfinished leather work, and we never saw Robert again. But here's where the story gets really interesting. Earlier I had made a reservation for him on an American Airlines flight to Los Angeles, where Nudie would be waiting for him at the airport, as I had given Nudie his arrival time and flight number. I paid for the ticket myself, and it made me feel good to know I had helped Robert that much, anyway. The next day Nudie called and told me Robert had arrived and everything was fine. Nudie got him a small apartment, paid his first month's rent, and put him to work at the store.

About three weeks later Nudie called again. He said, and I quote, "This bastard couldn't hand tool a letter in the top of a pound of butter, and he stayed drunk day and night." He added that Robert had stolen from him, but to what extent he wouldn't know until he checked closer. When Nudie confronted him, he acted dumb to it all. Nudie said he would not be responsible for Robert any longer, and he never wanted to see him near his place again. Friends, believe it or not, Robert wired me to send him $200. Can you imagine that kind of nerve?

I found out later it was Robert's cellmate who had done the handtooling all along, and he and Robert had been selling the goods and were splitting the money. I also heard that Robert was back in the penitentiary again, but I've never heard anything since. I don't know what happened to him. The only thing I feel hurt about was putting Nudie in that position like I did. Nudie was a close friend, and I had great admiration for both him and his wife, Bobbie. He said later, "Hank, you didn't know what the guy was really like, so don't feel bad. You were just trying to lend a helping hand. We'll charge the whole thing to profit and loss, but I'm glad we both got him out of our lives." Riffraff like Robert cause people to not trust others, and it's not fair to those who really need help.

The Rainbow Ranch Boys and I were playing in a club in Boise, Idaho, and during this time I heard one of T. Texas Tyler's records on the jukebox. He was without a doubt a gifted artist, and he had long been a favorite of mine. He did fabulous narrations. One he was well known for was "The Deck of Cards." I also loved to hear him sing. He reminded me a lot of Jimmie Rodgers in much of his work. Another of his great records was "Remember Me When the Candle Lights Are Glowing." Because of the growl he put in this song, people started referring to T. Texas Tyler as "the man with the growl in his voice." So he began putting the growl in his other songs, thereby making good use of this gimmick.

The sad story is that both T. Texas and his sweet wife, Claudia, became alcoholics and were addicted to narcotics in a bad way. They sank as low in the gutter as anybody could possibly go. I had met them a few years earlier when we were on a show together. They were devoted to each other, and I truly liked them.

Hearing Tex's songs on the jukebox one night brought him back into my mind, and I felt sad when I heard he was still on drugs. I talked to Bill Crowe, the club owner, and told him I wish there was something I could do to help Tex. Bill said, "Hank, if you could help him out of this rut, it would be the greatest thing in this world. I wanted to book him in here, but I can't because he stays hopped up all the time, and he messes up his shows completely. I like the man as much as you do, and I wish there was something that could be done for him and his wife, but what can we do?"

I answered that it would be great if we could get Tex free of drugs. "Well, he's playing in a club about a hundred fifty miles from here," Bill said. "If you're willing to talk to him, I'll drive up there after we close tonight, and I'll have him back here by breakfast time in the morning." When the club closed at 2:00 A.M., Bill was on his way. I remember the night so well. It was one of the worst rainstorms I had seen in a long time, and I was worried about Bill driving in such terrible weather, but it showed me his concern and honesty were real.

I lay awake half the night thinking about what I could do for Tex—if I could help get him straightened up again. Perhaps I could get him on the Grand Ole Opry and arrange a recording contract with RCA Victor. I could certainly book him on tours with my show. I was willing to try to help him if he was willing to accept the help. And not only him, I wanted to help Claudia also. After all, everyone needs a helping hand every now and then. We all make mistakes, and I'll never forget the many times people came to my rescue.

I slept off and on during the night, and around 10:00 A.M. I was awakened by a knock on my door. Bill had sent someone to tell me the Tylers were next door in the motel and were anxious to talk to me. I dressed quickly and went to see them. I had never seen two people who looked so down and so terrible in my entire life. It was pitiful. I wanted to break down and cry, and I had a hard time keeping my composure. Tex was shaking so bad, he even had a tremble in his voice. He was trying to tell me, "You don't know how much we appreciate this." I said, "Tex, I'm willing to take this big chance on you, if you will make me a promise that you will get off of alcohol and drugs." Tex got down on his knees before me, and with tears flowing, he made me a solemn promise. "Hank, I'll do anything you ask me. Both Claudia and I will thank you for the rest of our lives—if you will only help us."

By then I was convinced they were ready for help, which is the first step to improvement. I told them what I thought should be done. "First, go on back to the town where you're playing and finish your engagement. I'll get you a cab to the bus station and get your bus tickets. When I'm back in Nashville, I'll rent an apartment for you, and I'll call you in a week." But in a week they called me collect before I had a chance to call them, saying they were finished at the club and were ready to come to Nashville if I could wire them some money. I did.

The next day I went to see Mr. Denny, the manager of the Opry. I discussed Tex's situation and said I wanted to help him. "Oh yes, Hank, I'm familiar with the talents of T. Texas Tyler, and I'm also familiar with the fact that he has a serious drug problem. I can appreciate your wanting to help him, but we can't take a chance on him while he's involved with drugs." It appeared that Mr. Denny wasn't interested until he said, "I'm willing to help you, since you're sticking your neck out for him, but here's what Tex has to do first. To prove that he's off both drugs and alcohol, he'll have to stay in Nashville for sixty days without drinking any alcoholic beverage of any kind, and without taking absolutely any drugs of any kind. If he'll prove to us that he's straight, I'll put him on the Opry on a trial basis."

Mr. Denny's offer was certainly fair, and I appreciated his willingness to help. Tex would now have the opportunity to get his life back together and get another big chance at show business. I got Tex and Claudia a real nice apartment in West Nashville, paid the first month's rent in advance, had a telephone put in, and gave them money to stock up on groceries. I said I'd check on them often, unannounced, and I warned him about the seriousness of the situation if they got back into drugs and alcohol. I emphasized to Tex over and over again that he had to keep his promise to me—down to the last letter. "If you come off the wagon, all opportunities are off." He thanked me again and again.

I agreed to advance them money for food, pay their rent when due, and pay their electric bills. I called Nudie in Hollywood, who knew Tyler perhaps better than anyone, since he had made wardrobes for him in his earlier years on the West Coast. "Nudie, I want you to make two western suits for Tyler and ship them to me. Make them both in white gabardine. On the back of one suit I'd like to have the map of Texas embroidered in various colors. On the other white suit please put a deck of playing cards in the form of a fanned-out pack showing the ace, jack, king, and queen in the shape of a fan, and make them in colors, too. Send me a big white Stetson to go with these suits." Nudie already had Tex's measurements for the suits and his hat size, so that was no problem. In about six weeks I received the custom order, and Nudie as always did a beautiful job.

As far as I knew, both Tex and Claudia were staying off the alcohol and drugs. After sixty days I told Mr. Denny that Tex was ready for the Opry. As promised, Mr. Denny hired Tex, and he was popular right from the beginning. Usually he was on my portion of the Opry, and he would always get as much applause as any other artist onstage, as he was well remembered by his records from a few years back. His talent was not to be forgotten quickly.

Around about the same time, I called Steve Sholes in New York. He, like everyone else in the business, was familiar with Tyler and his popular recordings of past years. I asked Steve about the possibility of signing Tex to a contract, even though Tex was under contract with a small label owned by Bill McCall in Los Angeles. Steve answered, "If we can buy his contract fairly reasonably, we'd like to have him. Find out and let me know. He has lots of talent, unless he's lost it since his last recordings." Naturally, Steve had reservations, too. "But Hank, you'll have to vouch for his being sober, and you must keep him under your wing."

I called Bill, and he gave me the runaround until I mentioned that Mr. Sholes might be interested in buying Tex's contract. Bill knew Steve personally, so I suggested we set up a conference phone call in which we all could talk from our three different locations. Over the phone the general provisions were worked out. Steve told Bill he would send the contract to Los Angeles as soon as he and I straightened out a few incidental matters.

I was happy for Tex. He was on the verge of being signed with a major label as a recording artist, and I had already placed him on the Opry. Moreover, the Rainbow Ranch Boys and I, along with several other artists, were preparing to go on a twenty-day tour, and I planned to take Tex with us.

I told Steve to hold off on the contract until we got back from the Florida-to-Texas tour. This would give me a chance to see how well Tex would keep his word to me. If he did anything out of the way, it would show up while we were on the road together. My son, Jimmie, was on the show, and he would room with Tex. I fixed it that way purposely. Nevertheless, I felt completely confident that Tex was off alcohol and drugs and that he would make a solid comeback.

In the meantime, Tex had been calling me a little more often for money than I thought he should. "Hank, could you let me have fifty dollars, or could you let me have seventy-five dollars?" Or "I need sixty dollars for this, forty dollars for that." Min and I talked about this, and we wondered what Tex was doing to ask for money two or three times a week. We didn't think he was buying drugs or alcohol, because when he was on the Opry, he never showed any signs of drug abuse. Some of his old buddies in country music who were part of the Opry had offered him drinks, and he did refuse them—at least around the

Opry. I was somewhat suspicious, but I reasoned that I was being distrustful for no good reason.

On the tour we took two cars. My boys and I drove the Cadillac limousine with the rack on top for the instruments, and Jimmie and Tex rode in the other car. On that entire trip the boys and Jimmie said they never saw Tex take the first drink of anything, beer or whiskey, or take any kind of pills. I was proud of Tex. He had gained weight, and he was looking healthier. It seemed like his complete disposition had changed for the better.

Tyler was about six teet two and weighed around a hundred seventy pounds. He had black curly hair and was a handsome and stylish man. He was most impressive on stage in his white suit and white hat. He was famous for his poem called "The Deck of Cards." This is a touching story in which he mentions each card in the deck, and he tells how each is associated with the Bible. But before beginning his narration, Tex would take off his big white Stetson hat and hold it across his heart. The spotlight would keep a tight blue circle around his person from his waist up to his head. It was something you'd never forget, and the audience loved it.

San Antonio was the last city on this twenty-day tour. Because of this I had invited Mrs. Jimmie Rodgers to attend this final show, the matinee starting at 2:30 on a Sunday afternoon. I wanted to have an impressive show for her and to show Tex off.

Most of us got to the auditorium early to check out the sound and to tune up our instruments. But there was no Tex. Jimmie said when he left to drive to the auditorium with the Rainbow Ranch Boys, Tex was in his room. I was real worried when it was nearly time for him to be introduced for his thirty-minute spot on the show, and I began walking the floor. I didn't want my boys ever to be late. That was a set rule. Where was Tyler? Did he fall asleep, or what? I began to imagine the worst. Someone called his hotel room and let the phone ring and ring. No answer.

Brace your feet, folks. I saw a stranger in the dressing room, and I thought he was just some guy hanging around, which was common at these shows. That is, until the stranger spoke up and said, "If you're waiting for T. Texas Tyler, I can clear that situation up quickly, because I'm an undercover agent, and we have Tyler locked up downtown. We caught him at his hotel room with forty-five marijuana cigarettes." San Antonio is very close to the Mexican border, where there was, and is, a lot of dope coming across from Mexico into Texas, and the kids were peddling it on the streets.

This really hurt. I never got such a shock in my whole life. I was thinking if Tex could make it to the final show, he would have made it all the way from the start of the tour. The undercover agent added, "It's a good thing that the other gentleman wasn't in the room, or he would be in jail, too." My glory, to think Jimmie was rooming with him, and if he hadn't left with the boys when he did, he would have landed behind bars.

Tyler had such a great act, and I wanted so much for Mrs. Rodgers to see him perform. He was so colorful. Mrs. Rodgers was disappointed, as we all were. Everyone was sincere in wanting Tex to make it. After all this confusion and the great disappointment, I still had to go onstage to close the show. I tried to look real happy. Show business does involve acting.

As soon as I left the stage, I went to the phone and called the jail and asked if I could see him. "No sir, not under any circumstances until Wednesday." They didn't tell me why I'd have to wait, and I didn't ask. There was nothing we could do. We left around midnight to drive back to Nashville. Mrs. Rodgers happened to know one of the important and prominent judges in San Antonio, and unknown to me, she was able to have Tex released from jail. She also paid for his plane fare and he left for Nashville the next day. It took the rest of us a couple of days to make it back, and to our surprise Tyler beat us home.

As soon as I walked in the door at home, I called Tyler's apartment, but there was no answer. Then I called the apartment manager, and he said Tex and Claudia had left the apartment and taken the keys with them. I went over to the office, got a master key from the manager, and went into the apartment. Everything had been cleared out. That is, until I opened the doors to the walk-in closet. To my great surprise, there were beer cases piled clear to the ceiling and whiskey bottles piled high in the corner—and more on the shelves. Rolled up in a bundle were the two beautiful white suits I had bought Tex. They were filthy dirty. Tex and Claudia had left Nashville. I guess they were ashamed to face me after the drastic letdown. Again I could have bawled my eyes out, and I hated to have to tell Min about the tragedy.

We found out later that Tex had been using drugs and pills throughout the twenty-day tour. I felt sad for him and Claudia. He had a great opportunity, and he blew it. Of course, he was finished at the Grand Ole Opry, and RCA Victor was no longer interested in his talent as a recording artist. They couldn't afford to give him another chance, and in a way I felt betrayed. I often wondered how many chances Tex had had to make a better life. But I was afraid of what the answer might be.

Friends, this is a serious letdown story, but there's more to it, and it has a warm ending.

I kept a record of the finances involved in the whole affair. I needed them for the Internal Revenue Service, and if Tex had ever made it big again, I would have expected to be reimbursed. I spent a little over six thousand dollars, which would be like twenty thousand dollars these days. The money concerned me, but what concerned me most was the fact that I couldn't help Tex.

Claudia and Tex disappeared, and I had no idea where they had gone. However, about two or three years later I was surprised to receive this letter from him from the Pacific Northwest:

Dear Hank,

I have let you down so bad that I just could not face you again in Nashville, so Claudia and I thought it best that we get out of that city as soon as we could. I can write you now that I have given my soul to God because Claudia and I are trying to live a good life. I'm preaching, and I don't believe anything will ever change my love for God and the way I'm living now.

We plan to continue serving the Lord for the rest of our lives. You have done more for me than you can possibly realize. You gave me a chance. You believed in me, and I never forgot that. Enclosed is a money order in the amount of $25. Hank, I know this is not much but we don't make much money in the ministry. However, here is a promise that I will make to you right now. I'll send you money whenever I can, and I will pay you back—every penny in full.

God Bless You,

Your Buddy,
Tex

I wrote a letter back to him the same day I received his, and I returned the twenty-five-dollar money order. I said, "Tex, you'll never know how proud I am of you. You can forget the past. We all make mistakes, and I can assure you of one thing. As long as you continue to live your life for the Lord, as you are doing now, you don't owe me a dime. Consider the debt paid in full. But if you ever backslide and I find out about it, I'm going to chase you to the end of the earth till I get back every dime I spent on you" (which was a bluff). That was the only letter I received from Tex. I learned not much later that he had passed away. They discovered that his body was full of cancer. Claudia, bless her heart, didn't last too much longer after he was gone.

It was told to me that Tex preached and saved people all up and down the Pacific Northwest, and I'm thankful they turned their lives around. I feel I've been paid more than enough, and I'm not one bit sorry that I tried to help him. I'd like to think that maybe I had something to do with him turning back to the Bible. The Good Lord works in wondrous ways!

One of my favorite places to play was the KRNT Theater in Des Moines, Iowa, for my friend Smokey Smith. But it also represents one of my saddest memories. It involves Jerry Byers, a local piano player, whom I met at the KRNT Theater. Smokey told me before the show about Jerry. "Hank, the boy is dying of cancer, and the doctors gave him just three months to live, but he's already lived a year after that. He's a determined young man. Even though he's very weak, he wants to play with the local band and the other artists for the matinee and the night performance—if his strength holds up."

During the matinee I listened to Jerry play several numbers. He did an outstanding job, to the delight of the audience. When he left the stage, I saw him make a rush to the restroom, which was next to my dressing room. When he came out, he was as yellow as he could be, and the sweat was pouring from his face. But as sick as he was, he stopped and we had a short conversation before he went to lie down. He looked so frail, and he probably weighed no more than 110 pounds. It made me sad to see him struggle so hard to cover up his illness and then give such a splendid performance. I was proud of Jerry. God bless him. He sang and played on the night show, too. How he did it under that pressure, I'll never know, but he never missed a beat.

After the show Jerry's manager said, "Hank, this boy goes in and out. He might be pretty good for several days before going into a coma for three or four weeks. Then all of a sudden he snaps right out of it again. He's got more determination to live than anyone I've ever known, and I'm sure that has kept him alive this long. His lifetime goal has been to make an appearance on the Grand Ole Opry. He's talked about that for as long as I've known him. You know, being on the Opry would do him more good than anything else in this whole world, even if it's for one number only."

Immediately I replied, "Friend, I won't commit myself because I'm not the manager of the Opry, but I'll give you hundred-to-one odds that he'll make that appearance. I'll do everything I can—I mean everything I can—to make it happen." He said, "If you can arrange it, I'll take off from my regular job and we'll fly down, and I'll stay with him in a motel and bring him back home." This gentleman was more than a manager to Jerry, he was a true friend.

When I returned to Nashville, I went to see Ott Devine, the manager of the Opry at the time, since Mr. Denny, the prior manager, had passed away. Mr. Devine said, "I think I can take care of this request without even a little problem. We'll just go ahead and arrange it." And so it was. His manager flew with Jerry to Nashville on a Friday. I invited both of them to my house that afternoon, and we sat and talked and had an evening meal. I made arrangements for them to stay at a motel until Sunday morning, when they would be flying back home.

At the Opry on Saturday night I announced that Jerry Byers was my guest. He went out on the stage, and without any help or any coaxing from the audience, this young man received thunderous applause. I could feel the magic in the air that existed between him and the audience. Can you imagine what this did for him? It sure did a lot for me!

Jerry went into a coma about five or six weeks after his Opry performance, and he passed away in a few days. I was thankful I had the chance to lend a helping hand.

I mentioned earlier about me doing a song with Spade Cooley and his western swing band at the Santa Monica Ballroom in Santa Monica, California. Spade was an accomplished violinist and a super bandleader. He had more personality and more energy on stage than twenty other people put together. Unfortunately, his career was cut short when he was found guilty of murdering his wife many years ago. He was sentenced to serve his time in the penitentiary at Vacaville, in northern California. The murder was a severe shock to people in the entire country music industry and to those who knew Spade. I understood that Spade had domestic problems with his wife, and he was on a drinking spree when this tragedy happened.

During the 1960s when I was in the area, I made arrangements to visit Spade in prison. After our meeting he and I corresponded for several months. Then about a year later the boys and I were playing in northern California, and I made arrangements to visit him again and for my band and me to play a show for the inmates. It was so sad to see Spade dressed in a prison uniform and looking so pale and thin. He was trying to make the best of a bad situation, and I tried to be cheerful while I was there. The officials let us have some time by ourselves with only one guard, who was completely out of listening distance. Spade didn't elaborate much on the tragedy, but he did say that after seven years he would be ready to go out into society. However, he felt that he would never be released. I made Spade a solemn promise that day. I told him that I would do anything and everything in my power to try to get him paroled.

At Vacaville during that time there were about five hundred inmates, and some were doing life. They all seemed to enjoy the show, and I was called back several times to do encores. Afterwards the prison officials asked the boys and me to be their guests at a specially prepared meal, and Spade was permitted to eat with us. During our meal Spade said he wanted to give me a souvenir. The guards let me go back with Spade to his cell, where he had an old Martin guitar. "Hank," he said, "I want you to have this. There's no one else in the world that I'd rather give this to." This treasure is now in my museum at Opryland. As my boys and I were ready to say good-bye to Spade, he handed each of us a ring he had made while in prison.

When I got back to Nashville, I called the Martin guitar factory in Nazareth, Pennsylvania, and talked to Mr. Martin himself and asked him the age of the guitar Spade had given me. He said it had been made in the small factory in New York, and they were making only six guitars a month back then. As close as Mr. Martin could figure it, it was about ninety years old. Now it's well over a hundred and twenty.

I had promised Spade I would do my best to get him out of prison, and I kept my promise. I contacted the governor of California and two governor friends of mine in the South. I wrote letters and had a petition signed by over three hundred people in the country music field who either knew Spade or were familiar with his fine work as an entertainer and bandleader. I wrote letters to the warden and the correction officials in California, and I'd like to think I was partly responsible for getting him released from prison.

Yes, Spade was released from prison, but it turned into a tragedy. His release was handled badly and without any thought whatsoever. A booking agent around Nashville, one of those fly-by-night people we all try to stay away from, heard that Spade was going to be released on a certain date, and he booked him to do a show in a big auditorium in Oakland. As soon as Spade left prison, he was driven directly, that same Sunday afternoon, to Oakland, California, to perform during the matinee. The person who set up this appearance didn't have brains enough to give Spade at least a week to adjust to the outside world after being locked up in the penitentiary for years. I won't mention the promoter's name. It wouldn't help, but it was a stupid thing to do. The promoter was trying to cash in on a big-name artist, and he didn't consider what was best for Spade.

Jean Valli, a longtime friend of mine, was on the same show with Spade. She saw how this tragedy happened. Being on the stage for the first time in all these years, Spade naturally was under tremendous pressure. When he was introduced, he walked out on stage and started to play his specialty number on his violin. Almost immediately he fell backwards into someone's arms and was carried to the dressing room.

A doctor was called, but Spade died a short time later. At the time, I was playing at a matinee in the Queen Elizabeth Theatre in Vancouver, British Columbia. The news was telephoned to me via the radio station in Vancouver and was relayed to me at the theater.

This was a gigantic blow because of the close association I'd had with Spade in previous years. I had been looking forward to the day when he would be released because I firmly believed that he had been rehabilitated and was ready to go back into society. I'm sorry for what happened, and it hurts me to think of this turn of events.

31

How the Wind Is Blowing

Way down in the state of Georgia,
Through the swamps and everglades,
There's a hole in Tiger Mountain.
God help the man who gets lost in Miller's Cave.

"Miller's Cave," by Jack Clement

BACK IN THOSE EARLY YEARS IN THE United States I found it exciting to try new business ventures. If they paid off that was okay, and if they didn't, that was okay, too—provided that I didn't lose bundles of money. I had a pretty good income by the early 1950s, and I kept my eyes open for good business opportunities.

One of my earliest investments was in 1954 when Bill McDaniel, who was involved with promotions at WSM radio, and Ernest Tubb and I bought two radio stations. One was located in Whitesburg, Kentucky, and the other in Harriman, Tennessee. They were sold almost three years later, and I made a little money. Since I really didn't know the first thing about running a radio station, I thought I should stick to something that I knew more about.

In 1958 I had a chance to purchase a music store from Jack Kendall. I got my faithful CPA together with Mr. Kendall, and as we were figuring the inventory for the sale price, Jack said for a certain amount he would throw in his forty-one-foot Chris Craft cabin cruiser, which I liked so well. Before I knew it, I said yes! So I became the owner of a big beautiful cabin cruiser, which I kept on Old Hickory Lake, and I had me a music store in downtown Nashville on Church Street. I had the store completely remodeled and put a huge neon sign out in front that read "The Hank Snow Music Center, Inc. and School of Music." The School of Music was located in the newly remodeled upstairs section of the building, and I had two teachers to give instructions. I also formed two music companies and located them in the building. One was the Silver Star Music Company, and the other was East Star Music Company, both incorporated.

My music store did fairly well, and many of the fine musicians in Nashville patronized it. I had good managers and good teachers. Henry Farrell was managing the store when I bought it, and he stayed on in that capacity. He was also a great guitarist and a fine ukulele player. After Mr. Farrell left, my friend and great steel guitar player Joe Talbot became manager.

After Joe quit the business, Ted Daffan and his lovely wife, Bobbie, took over. They did a superb job, too. Ted also played steel guitar, and he did some of the teaching in the music school. He was an outstanding songwriter and wrote several big hits, such as "Born to Lose" and "Truck Driver's Blues." He wrote some of my hit songs, including "Tangled Mind" and "Rocking, Rolling Ocean." Ted was also constantly on the lookout for top songs from other writers for me to record. When he'd say he found a good song for me to consider for my next recording session, I knew I should listen, because Ted was usually right and it would be a hit.

I found it hard to get top-brand instruments during the years I owned the store, especially Martin, Gibson, and Fender instruments. They were in strong demand, and most of the time we could get only one of each, and they were usually sold the same day we received them. Pawnshops were not even in the music business, but they would get these top-brand instruments and sell them way below our prices, even though the main music stores, including ours, actually had the franchise for these instruments. We complained to the guitar wholesalers, but it did no good.

The money from the store wasn't that great, but there were additional benefits. We followed the same pattern that Ernest Tubb did with his record shop. We would broadcast a country music program from the store every Friday night at eleven over WSM radio, and with its powerful 50,000-watt clear channel, it reached about thirty-five states. The Grand Ole Opry brought people into Nashville on Thursday, Friday, and Saturday, every week of the year. Some of the tourists, hearing about my store over the radio, would drop by to visit and buy from us. They would tell others about our store, and we met a lot of nice people in this way. But after nine years I came to the conclusion that the profit from the store was not worth the amount of trouble in running it with all its responsibilities, and I sold it.

Friends, after my experience with Tom Parker, I swore I'd never again trust anyone to be a business partner, but I went strictly against my own promise, and here's how that situation developed.

On my first European tour I was booked by the German-American Agency, owned and operated by George Adamson. He had been a major in the American army, and after he retired he began to book American talent on the military bases in Europe. Big money was to be made in this field, especially if the agency knew the people on the bases who were in charge of the entertainment. So Adamson had an advantage on booking these shows.

During one of my tours in Europe Adamson said, "Hank, why don't we form an agency with Jolly Joyce, you, and me. You're well known and well respected, and with the expertise that Joyce and I have, we can make a lot of money. Many of the bookers are ripping off the entertainers and the clubs. They charge the clubs an arm and a leg, and they send over rock-and-roll shows and even classical outfits from England. The GIs don't want that. They want to hear good down-to-earth country music from America.

Adamson explained that the military clubs raised a lot of money to put into their entertainment funds, since entertainment was considered extremely important in the welfare of the GIs. So the military personnel were willing to pay the agents big money for the shows. This sounded like it would be a good business arrangement for me, and it seemed like a good opportunity to help country artists make more money. Besides, I was always interested in promoting the kind of music that I believe in.

Adamson continued, "If you're interested in this arrangement, you first need to go to Washington, D.C., and talk to the right people in the Pentagon. Tell them what we want to do. They can give us permission to set up frequent tours, and it will be a snap to schedule any country acts you want to send over here."

The other person in this business deal would be Jolly Joyce. I had met him before, when his agency had booked me on a couple of tours. His agency was well known and booked people like Mickey Rooney, the Harry James band, and several other big-name bands and actors. The plan was for Joyce to handle the business arrangements in New York before sending the performers overseas.

I told Adamson I was definitely interested, and a few days after returning from my European trip I made an appointment with Tennessee governor Buford Ellington. I told him my story and asked if he could advise me on who to see in Washington. He first paid me a nice compliment. "Hank, it's kind of you to want to help our armed forces in Europe. These boys crave a touch of home, and I think it's a mighty good gesture. Call me in a few days, and I'll see what I can come up with."

When I called Governor Ellington back, he had already set up an appointment for me with Robert Baker, who was the Secretary to the Senate Majority. "He's an important man in Washington, and he can direct you to the people you need to talk to. But I suggest you take your attorney with you, Hank. It will carry a lot more weight if you do."

I thanked the governor, and in less than a week my attorney and I were on our way to Washington. Mr. Baker kept two senators waiting out in the hallway for an appointment while he took my attorney and me into his office. We talked for about forty-five minutes, and he was sympathetic about me trying to send more country acts to Europe. He gave me several names of people to contact and told me how to go about it. He also said he was a fan of country music and my work, and he loved the guitar talent of Chet Atkins. He added, "Hank, I'm in the process of opening a big new nightclub in Ocean City, Maryland. When I get it under way, I want you and Chet to come up some weekend and entertain. Will you promise me that? When you get back to Nashville, please speak to your good buddy, Chet, about it."

It looked as if I would have no trouble getting federal support for the agency. But it wasn't possible to see all of the people I needed to see on that first trip, so I made an additional appointment. I returned to Washington two weeks later by myself, and I was pleased that all those I went to see took the time to hear my story and requests. I was also pleasantly surprised to learn they were all country music lovers.

But this thing didn't turn out the way I had hoped it would. One of the big wheels said, "As much as we all would love to help you, the government cannot get involved, because it would appear as if the government was acting as a booking agency overseas." That was the bottom line, so we decided to drop our efforts to work through the federal government. But we did go ahead with establishing the agency.

Jolly and I flew to Germany and took the train to George Adamson's home in Bamberg. We met with him that same evening and discussed the forming of the agency until way into the night. After we had come to a complete understanding, Adamson's secretary, who was on hand to do the typing, drew up the contract that same night. It was signed, sealed, witnessed, and sworn to in the presence of a notary. We were in business as an agency.

Adamson would schedule the shows on the military bases in Europe. I would contact the artists in Nashville and negotiate the best deal possible, then send them to Joyce in New York City. Joyce would arrange the entertainers' hotel reservations, meet their plane on arrival, brief them on the tour, and then put them on the plane to Frankfurt.

The first act I sent over was Lonzo and Oscar and their band, and the second tour was the Kitty Wells show. Even though the big moneymaker would be our agency, the artists were not cheated. They were paid what they had agreed to. According to our agency contract, we would split the income three ways after expenses. One fifteen-day tour could do perhaps seventy to one hundred thousand dollars, so I thought I was well on my way to making real good money.

However, by the time I was ready to line up the third show, I was becoming concerned because I hadn't yet received a penny from Adamson or Joyce for the first two tours, which had already been completed.

I found out how the wind was blowing. The truth came out! I received a phone call at home one afternoon from Lucky Moeller. Lucky owned the Moeller Talent Agency, and he booked my band and me. He was familiar with my booking partnership, and he said, "Hank, I have two people sitting in the outer office, so I'll have to talk low. They came to me to sign up country talent for the overseas military bases, and they're trying to go over your head and cut you out." I knew at once who he was talking about. It was Adamson and Joyce. I hit the ceiling. I asked myself how damn crooked can some people be. I had made two trips to Washington and had invested a lot of time and money on this partnership, and these characters were right under my nose in Nashville trying to bypass me. I guess they figured they didn't need Hank Snow anymore. They had come to Nashville themselves to do the booking. It was mighty nice of Lucky to tip me off. He could have worked out a deal for himself if he had wanted to be dishonest. But not good ole Lucky, bless his heart.

I made my mind up that these characters were not going to get away with their sleazy operation, and I certainly knew that Lucky wasn't going to deal with them. I thanked him for his call, and after I hung up, I quickly called my attorney, and he had warrants issued for their arrest. Under what circumstances, I don't know. I presume it was breach of contract. Somebody from the sheriff's office called and asked me if I had any idea where they might find these two men in order to serve the warrants.

At that time, WSM studios on Seventh Avenue broadcast the Friday Night Frolics, a country music show hosted by Opry members such as Ernest Tubb, Roy Acuff, and myself. I told the caller that Adamson and Joyce might go there, and I arranged to meet the deputies in the lobby of the radio station at 6:00 P.M., when the first program would begin. I met the deputies and told them to stay in the lobby until I came down from the upstairs studio after doing my radio show at 7:30. If Adamson and Joyce were up there, I would point them out when they got off the elevator.

Sure enough, a few minutes after I came downstairs after the end of my show, those schemers came walking off an elevator amidst a bunch of people. We were well out of their view, so Adamson and Joyce didn't see us. I told the deputies that Lucky had said these characters were staying in the motel that was just about a stone's throw from the WSM studios. We watched to see where they went, as the deputies wanted to spare them the embarassment of being served warrants in front of the other people who came down on the elevator with them.

As anticipated, Adamson and Joyce went to their motel room, and the deputies and I stood outside the doorway for a few minutes, listening to them talking up a storm about booking shows in Europe. There were more than two people talking, and I thought I recognized one of the other voices. When the deputy knocked on the door and we walked in, you could have knocked Adamson and Joyce over with a straw! I never saw two people any more surprised in my whole life. Their faces turned all colors, and they didn't say a word. But I was in for a big surprise, too. With these two cats were three Opry people who I thought were friends of mine. They were going to join these guys in their booking business. I won't mention their names, because I don't want to embarrass them.

When I talked to my attorney about pursuing this breach-of-contract case, we decided not to follow through on it. To get money out of Joyce and Adamson we'd have to go to New York and hire lawyers there, and then we would have to go to Germany and repeat the same thing. This would not only be a big hassle but would cost a bunch of money for plane fares, hotels, lawyers, and so on. I figured I had already lost almost eighty thousand dollars, and I chalked this one up to another great experience down life's highway. But I got a lot of personal satisfaction from having these characters caught. I was hell-bent that they not get away with something that was in every way morally wrong.

Friends, have you ever idolized big-name country stars or movie stars and prayed that someday you'd get to meet them? If so, were they like what you expected, or the opposite? Several times this happened to me, and most of the stars were like I wanted them to be. Only a few were conceited or were too busy to talk to me.

One of my dearest idols was Gene Austin. I remember Mrs. Jimmie Rodgers telling me that Gene and Jimmie played some show dates together. Gene was a great blues singer. When I lived in Halifax, I used to listen to him on the radio every time I could catch a station playing his records. I admired his talent. Among his many hits were "My Blue Heaven" and "Sleepy-Time Gal." He was an extraordinary singer and piano player, and the combination of Gene's piano work and his guitar player's "fills" was outstanding. When I was first on the air at CHNS in Halifax in the mid-1930s, the station had a bunch of Gene's transcriptions, and they let me play them and copy down the words to several that I really liked. Then I learned to sing them.

Many years later the Rainbow Ranch Boys and I were playing in Medford, Oregon, and we checked into a motel. The lady at the desk knew I was a fan of Gene's. She called my room and said, "Mr. Snow, I thought you might like to know that Gene Austin is staying here at our motel, and he's playing in a town about forty miles from here. He'll be back tonight, and if your show doesn't run too late, we'll arrange it so you can meet him."

I could hardly wait to get through our show to actually meet Gene Austin. One of my boys went with me over to Gene's motel room, and he welcomed us with open arms. He was a friendly and warm person, and as I shook hands with him I said, "Gosh, Mr. Austin, I've been a fan of yours for many years, but of course you hear this all the time." He replied, "Well, Hank, I never get tired of hearing it!" I told him that I sang several of his songs, and he was surprised. Then I sang one of his old ones, entitled "I'm Coming Home." He said, "I wouldn't have thought about that old song in a million years." We visited for a while, and he was exactly the person I wanted him to be—kind, courteous, and understanding. We had our picture taken together, and doggone it, of all the pictures I've had taken in my life, it's this picture that didn't turn out.

About seven years later I received a call from the Beverly Hills hospital saying that Gene was ill. I talked to him a couple of times at the hospital. He got more seriously ill and passed away a few hours after our last conversation. I'm thankful I got to meet him.

I've been fortunate enough to collect keepsakes from my fellow artists who are no longer with us. Some of these items are on display in my museum at Opryland. I have Patsy Cline's belt, with her name hand-tooled in the leather, and the guitar strap and belt that belonged to Hawkshaw Hawkins. These were items they had worn when they died in the tragic plane crash. Mary Reeves, widow of Jim Reeves, gave me a neck scarf and a pair of leather gloves that belonged to Jim. I have a pair of Hank Williams's boots, also a pair of his cuff links and a tie.

I would have given my right arm to have had something of Gene

Austin's, but I had no connections with any of the family. However, I discovered that my friend David Houston, a member of the Grand Ole Opry, did an album with Gene. David's dad and Gene Austin had been close friends over the years. I asked David one night at the Opry in 1987, "Would you happen to have something that belonged to Gene that you would consider giving me?" I said I've always tried to get a memento that belonged to artists I most admired who have passed away. "I'll dig up something one of these days and bring it to you," he said. Sometime later at the Opry David gave me an old picture of Gene's mother in an old-fashioned oval frame, a rare album Gene had recorded, and several other keepsakes. These items are very important to me, and I wouldn't sell them for a million dollars.

At one of our shows I wanted to play a Daredevil for excitement. The Rainbow Ranch Boys, Cousin Minnie Pearl, and I were playing the state fair in Tampa, Florida, and one of the main attractions before the audience in the grandstand was the Hollywood Daredevils. Wild Bill Reed was the driver in charge of the Daredevil team, as well as the whole entertainment program. The Daredevils drove open convertibles and did all kinds of wild stunts in building up to a climax, in which Wild Bill did the finale—the high jump. In the high jump Bill would come down the racetrack in his convertible doing about ninety or a hundred miles an hour. He would go up the one ramp, go through the air right in front of the people in the grandstand for about seventy-five feet, and about sixty feet high, and land on the ramp on the other side.

That afternoon I was out with Bill's advance man doing our show promotions on the various radio stations. I casually asked him if he thought Bill would let me take the evening jump with him. He was surprised and asked if I really wanted to do that. I assured him I did. He replied, "We've never had a volunteer to do this, only trained personnel have tried it. I don't know if Bill can let you ride with him on account of insurance, but I'll check on it and let you know." But nobody said anything more about it that afternoon, and it was forgotten.

After my boys and I finished our part of the grandstand show, it was time for the Hollywood Daredevils' stunts, and I settled down to watch the excitement. Their show was terrific. Their cars rolled on two wheels and crisscrossed in front of each other at extremely close distances while going at tremendous speeds. It was a precision act of split seconds. As I watched, I was a little disappointed that no one had reported back about me riding with Bill, but deep down I suppose I was glad. After all, why should I risk my life for such a foolish thing? It was scary just watching all the dangerous acts taking place.

But hold it! One of Wild Bill's boys came up to me and asked, "Are you ready?" I said, "Ready for what?" "To take the jump with Bill. He'll be preparing for it in just a minute." Well, I couldn't back out, and I didn't want to be called chicken. About that time someone put a pint of Smirnoff vodka in my shaky hand, and I took a couple of big swigs, and then I walked across the racetrack to the car.

Bill met me at the convertible. He gave me a big smile and said to get into the car, and he would prepare me for the jump. He gave me a big piece of foam rubber to hold against the side of the windshield so I wouldn't cut my hand. Hell, I wasn't thinking about cutting my hand, I was thinking about getting out of the car alive! I said to myself, "What if he misses the ramp altogether? What if his timing is off just a split second? Maybe Wild Bill will be distracted with me in the car. What will the extra pounds do to his timing?" I thought about all the bad things possible in those few seconds before we took off. To make matters worse, some of the other drivers were teasing me, asking what kind of flowers I liked, and who was my next of kin, as they were laughing their heads off.

After I was seated and strapped in and had my crash helmet on, Bill got in the car and checked to see if I had my seat belt properly fastened, and he gave me instructions. Down to the other end of the racetrack we went and turned around. Bill stepped on the gas, and it looked like we were headed straight toward a brick wall. That ramp looked straight up as I saw it coming closer and closer. However, Wild Bill hit that ramp about as perfect as he could hit it—right in the middle—and we went sailing through the air as high as the people in the top row of the grandstand. What a sensation I had while we were up in the sky! It seemed like we would never hit the ramp on the other side.

We did it! Bill made a perfect four-point landing that was beyond a doubt the biggest thrill of my whole life. When I got out of the car, one of my band members said, "Please don't do anything like that again. We like our jobs too well."

About six months later a tragedy occurred. I was told how Wild Bill lost his life while doing a different kind of stunt. The Daredevils were playing a fair in Mayfield, Kentucky. In this stunt Bill was coming down the racetrack at a very high speed, and when he got abreast of the grandstand, he was supposed to turn the convertible so it would head toward the nine-foot-high concrete wall under the grandstand. But when he made the sharp left turn, his convertible turned over and pinned him underneath. He died instantly. One of the saddest things about the accident was that his wife and son were sitting in the audience and saw the whole thing happen. Bill was wild when performing his fantastic stunts, but away from the show he was a kind and soft-spoken gentleman.

Not all the memorable people I've met during my country music career have been musicians or public performers. One Saturday night at the Opry, Stoney Cooper brought a gentleman back to the dressing room and introduced him as a priest. This was not unusual, because artists often bring friends and relatives backstage, where there's a friendly atmosphere among all the people milling about. I treated the priest with respect, and we had a brief chat.

On the following Monday morning I appeared on the Ralph Emery show. I took several items of memorabilia, including Patsy Cline's belt and Hawkshaw Hawkins's guitar strap. Ralph wanted me to show them to his audience. When I returned home after Ralph's show, I set the items outside my den door in my studio. Unfortunately, I forgot to put them back in the souvenir case. On Tuesday night I was all alone. Min was visiting in Florida with Mother Maybelle Carter, and I was practicing songs I planned to record. About 8:00 P.M., I was interrupted by a knock at the back door, and I peeked out through the venetian blinds to see who it was. To my surprise it was the priest that Stoney had introduced to me.

I wasn't in the habit of opening doors to strangers, but when I saw a priest standing there, I asked him in. After we talked for about thirty minutes, he said, "Would you have a beer with me?" I was surprised and replied, "No sir, but thank you anyhow." Then he asked, "Would you mind if I do?" I said, "Sure, it's all right with me, but I don't have any in the house." "That's okay," he said. "I have some out in the car." He excused himself and returned with a six-pack of beer. He tore open the carton and began drinking. In a few minutes he asked if I minded if he got more comfortable. I responded, "No, I guess it's all right. One has to have a little relaxation every now and then, so make yourself at home."

I was still believing this was an honest-to-goodness priest. He ripped off his backward white collar, ripped his black gown open, and rared back and finished the bottle of beer. Then he opened the second one. By this time, I was beginning to get suspicious and concerned. Something wasn't right, so I excused myself and went into my bedroom and called Stoney Cooper, who had introduced this man to me at the Opry. When I got Stoney on the phone, he said, "Hank, I just heard today that he is not a priest. He's a con artist and has already swindled money from Faron Young and Jim Reeves. He'll try to win your confidence, then steal you blind. Several people in the city would love to get their hands on him, and you'd best get him out of your house right away. I tried several times today to reach you, but your phone was busy."

As I hung up, I heard the "priest" banging on my guitar. It had been sitting in the corner of my den on a stand. I never let anyone handle my guitar. So that did it! I tried to conceal my anger, and I said as I took my guitar from him, "Sir, that is a no-no with me, and I would rather you leave now. I have to get up early in the morning." He left and I went to bed.

The next morning I remembered the memorabilia I had left outside my den door, and I went to put them away in the souvenir case. But everything was gone! While I had been talking to Stoney on the phone in the other part of the house, the so-called priest had set the items outside the back door, and when he left he took everything with him. I immediately called the police and reported what had happened. The detectives' office and the police station had already had several calls, and they were looking for the fake priest. The next day the police caught this guy in Memphis, when he tried to use a stolen credit card. The pleasant part of the story is that the police were so efficient they got back every item he had taken from me. The Memphis police forwarded the articles to our local police station, and I went down and picked them out from a bunch of other things he had stolen from other people. It makes me sad that a con artist would even think about posing as a minister or priest of the gospel.

32

Overseas

The postman dropped a letter in my door.
The address wasn't plain, but I could see
It had travelled far across the great Pacific
From my Filipino Rose across the sea.

"My Filipino Rose," by Hank Snow

I HAD THE GREAT PRIVILEGE AND pleasure throughout my profession as an entertainer to visit a lot of countries overseas, and I'd like to tell you some of the stories that are most vivid in my mind.

Lucky Moeller became my booking agent, and I told you earlier about the great help he was to me and my family when I met him at the Roundup Club in Dallas, Texas. After he moved to Nashville and formed his own agency, he looked me up, and I was glad to be associated with him again. One time someone asked Lucky if he had me under contract. He replied, "Hank is a very sensitive person. He's a good friend of mine and I want to keep it that way. The quickest way to break off our friendship and business dealings would be to ask him to sign a contract with our agency. We have a verbal agreement, and there's never any doubt in my mind that Hank would ever do anything against me or our agency as long as we treat him right. Hank Snow is a man of his word, and his word is all the contract that we ever needed."

We never had any problems—ever. Lucky did so well with his Moeller Talent Agency that he built a huge office building on Music Row in Nashville. He loved to talk, and he got a kick out of people. He once booked me and a cast of performers on a twenty-day tour of New Zealand, and he went with us on this particular trip. He also booked Rusty Greaves, a popular New Zealand country entertainer, and his band on this same tour. Rusty told a lot of jokes in his part of the show, and in his New Zealand brogue, he was really funny. Lucky stood in the wings every time Rusty was on stage, and I saw Lucky literally double up laughing at Rusty's jokes, regardless of how many times he had heard them. I got a big kick just watching Lucky.

The Rainbow Ranch Boys and I played many American military bases in Europe, and the servicemen were enthusiastic and appreciative audiences. I was taking a few drinks back in those days, and my favorite was Smirnoff vodka. When I'd go on stage to greet the servicemen, I would say, "Gentlemen, before we start our entertainment, I did want to mention to you that I don't drink," and after a short pause I would add, "only vodka." This would always get wild cheers from the GIs, and after the show there would be rows of glasses half full of vodka lined up on the front of the stage.

We always liked visiting the tables in the military clubs and having a drink with the GIs, and they enjoyed it, too. I wanted them to know we were human beings, too, and we enjoyed having fun. I shall never forget what some of the GIs did. Several took their chains from around their neck, which carried the crucifix, and gave them to me as a keepsake. And I didn't dare refuse, or they would have been highly insulted. They wanted to show their appreciation in this way. It was touching to me, and I treasure every one.

Usually we'd play two shows each night on the military bases. One was for the enlisted men, and one was for the noncommisioned officers' club. After the last show was completed, I'd always be invited by the custodian of the club to have a nightcap with him and some of his friends, but those nightcaps usually lasted far into the night. A lot of times I'd take my guitar, and I'd play and sing for them until two or three o'clock in the morning. To show their appreciation, many gave me a cap or some other souvenir to remember them by.

When we played in Germany, Frankfurt was our headquarters, and we were booked by either the German-American agency or by the Giesler Gunther Agency. From Frankfurt we would fly to other countries, which may seem like thousands of miles of flying, but it's like being in Tennessee and flying to other states, because the countries in Europe are so close together. It's just a few hours' flying time, say from Germany to Norway, or from Italy to France, Ireland, Scotland, or England.

On the first trip to Germany we stayed at the small but homelike Klee Hotel in Wiesbaden. We made friends with the owners, Mr. and Mrs. Wilhelm Mhyer, and they always went out of their way to please us every time we played in Germany. We loved to stay there so much that their hotel became our living quarters. The distance was only about twenty-six miles between Wiesbaden and Frankfurt, where the two agencies were located, and we traveled back and forth on the Autobahn.

During one of my European tours the Rainbow Ranch Boys and I played the famous London Palladium. Before show time one of the promoters said, "You have a big fan who'll be here tonight. He's already made reservations for box seats, and he wants to meet you, Hank. We'll bring him backstage after the show, if that's okay with you." When he said it was Ringo Starr of the Beatles, I almost fell through the floor! The Beatles were the hottest group in the world at that time. I thought, "Why would a rock star come to see a traditional country show, and why does he want to meet me?"

Anyway, Ringo came back to my dressing room after the show and brought his pretty companion. He was extremely nice and humble. He said, "Hank, we thoroughly enjoyed your show. I've loved your work for a long time, and I sing quite a bit of country myself. I'm thinking about recording some country songs in Nashville in the not-too-distant future." Well, it was a big surprise to learn that he was also into country music, and it was nice meeting and chatting with him. We had some pictures made before we said good-bye. Later on Ringo did come to Nashville and cut an album. He was kind enough to send me an autographed copy, and he did an extremely fine job on singing country songs.

While in London I wanted to meet Patrick McNee, an exceptionally fine English actor. He had a television series in the United States some years ago called "The Avengers," in which he always used a cane and wore a derby. The RCA Victor personnel in London arranged for me to meet him at a club at 4:00 P.M. But doggone it, there was a mix-up in the time our transportation was to pick us up to take us to our play date, and we had to leave at 1:30 P.M. I learned the next day that Patrick was there on time, and the RCA people explained the mix-up to him. He said he understood, because those things happen in show business. Since I missed the meeting, he said he'd write to me and maybe we could get together in the States. Unfortunately, we never got to meet, but I did receive his personal letter.

Another event I remember quite well during one of my tours of England was somewhat bizarre. The boys and I were playing the theater in Coventry, and I signed autographs out in a small booth in front of the theater. A gentleman and his wife came to the booth and handed me a letter. I didn't take time to open and read it then. I waited until I got back to the hotel. The letter read as follows:

Sunday, 18th November

Dear Mr. Snow,

Welcome to Coventry. We have waited for years to hear you in person, but alas, you came too late to be heard by your most devoted fan in our family, our beloved mother who, when she died six years ago, requested and had a picture of you placed in her coffin, in appreciation of the joy your voice brought over the years especially when you sang her favorite, "My Blue River Rose", a few bars of which would be much enjoyed by eight members of her family who will be in your audience tonight.

Good luck, sir, and thank you for including Coventry in your tour.

Sincerely yours,

The McClintock Family

When I read this letter, I got a strange feeling. This was morbid to know that my picture was lying in her coffin.

The Rainbow Ranch Boys and I made several trips to the Far East, and on our first tour we played one day in Manila, the Philippines, at Clark Air Force Base. It was one of America's largest bases, if not the largest. It was like a city, and we played to forty thousand servicemen and women. From there we played twenty days in Japan, performing for civilian Japanese audiences and also at a couple of military bases.

When we checked into a Japanese hotel on our first day, my room looked like a funeral home. I never saw so many flowers in my life, in one's bedroom, that is. There were flowers from the RCA Victor company in Japan and from many fans in the area. Plus, a big bowl of fresh fruit was waiting for me. They served the finest of food and the service was super good. I've often remarked that I think courtesy was born in Japan, because those people went all out to make us feel welcome and at home.

For this first tour I was under contract to a Japanese agency under the guidance of Toreo, a young Japanese gentleman. He was connected with RCA Victor in Japan, and he was a fine businessman. This tour was thoroughly advertised, and we performed before sell-out houses just about everywhere we played. And the Japanese people were the best audiences I've ever played to.

I was worried about the language barrier, and I asked Toreo for an interpreter for my stage show, because I didn't know if the people would understand me. His reply was, "You don't need an interpreter, Mr. Snow, because 90 percent of them understand the English language. But to make you feel more comfortable I'll get you one, and you can see for yourself that it's not needed."

When I went out on the stage for my first show, I said, "Good evening, ladies and gentlemen." Then I waited until the interpreter spoke in Japanese. I said something else and so on, and it was boring me to death. I don't have that much patience, but I went through with it for the first couple of nights. By then I knew Toreo was right. I didn't need an interpreter. Even though they couldn't speak English well, they understood English when they heard it.

The welcome and the applause I received were super. During the shows a pretty Japanese girl or several girls would bring a big bowl of roses onstage and make the presentation. This courtesy really warmed my heart. The Japanese had decorative auditoriums and the finest sound and lighting equipment money could buy. One of the most beautiful was the famous Copacabana in Tokyo.

We had quite an entourage as we toured from city to city. An attractive Japanese girl, Masaka Hara, joined me on stage. Toreo had told me she was popular in Japan and that she could speak and sing English quite well. So at each performance I introduced her and she sang a song in Japanese, and then we sang some songs together, including the song Anita Carter and I recorded for RCA Victor, "Down the Trail of Aching Hearts." Masaka imitated Anita's part. Her deep, rich voice blended nicely with mine, and she added something extra special to the show.

Sometimes we traveled on the beautiful Japanese trains, and we could hardly tell we were riding on them, they were so smooth. These were electric trains that traveled anywhere from 150 to 175 miles an hour. When they pulled into the platform for loading and unloading, you stepped right off the train onto the platform and vice versa. The Japanese believed in convenience for their passengers and above all, punctuality. If they said we would leave at 2:30, they meant 2:30, not 2:31, and I certainly admired them for this. But you had better be ready to hop on board, because as soon as the last passenger had boarded, away they went like a bullet. They always ran on split-second timing. If something happened to the engineer, like a fainting spell or heart attack, and his hand fell from the throttle, the train would immediately and automatically come to a stop.

Trains were painted many different colors, including bright green, blue, yellow, red, and orange. When the trains were being made up on the different tracks in the switchyard, it was a beautiful sight to see, with the interesting blend of bright colors. The Japanese followed that trend with the city lights, and I've never seen such huge neon signs in so many different colors. It makes the lights in New York City look pale by comparison. They had huge signs and figures doing everything you can imagine, such as a cowboy lassoing a bull, a speeding train, or a ship on the ocean. Some signs on the outside of tall buildings were several stories high. I saw neon signs of huge aircraft with four propellers spinning and gigantic birds with their wings flapping.

The cities were kept so clean you could eat off the sidewalks. One of the main streets in the downtown area of the city of Tokyo was called the Ginza. I think it was sixteen lanes wide. And they had some of the most beautiful department stores you would find anywhere in the world.

Japan is a progressive, modern, and fashionable country. The Japanese go in for beauty, accuracy, tidiness, and above all, politeness and courtesy. They used to copy a lot of things we make in America. For example, they come close in making guitars as fine as the famous Martin guitars. They also copy a lot of American talent. At one of the clubs I heard a girl singer who sounded exactly like Patti Page. They had their own Anita Carter, Patsy Cline, Ernest Tubb, Merle Haggard, and Hank Snow. They had imitators of American rock bands and our quartets, as well as our musicians who play steel, Spanish, and classical guitar. They even had the Tokyo Grand Ole Opry.

One Sunday afternoon when we had no show scheduled, I was asked to do a spot on the Tokyo Opry. I said if they could clear it with our tour manager, I'd be glad to do it. They apologized in saying they could only pay me $300, but I told them that was fine. I was more interested in repaying them for their courtesy and hospitality than anything else. So the Rainbow Ranch Boys and I went down to their Opry one afternoon and did about a half-hour show. A few days earlier I had learned about the Blind Child's Orphanage in Yokohama, located about twenty-six miles from downtown Tokyo. I asked the Japanese to donate the $300 they were going to pay me to the orphanage, and they did.

Seiji Wada, the young fellow in charge of the Tokyo Grand Ole Opry, asked if I'd consider driving to Yokohama some afternoon and putting on a half-hour show for the blind children. He said the children had their own little band, and some played guitars, some played banjos, and others played harmonicas. He said, "Mr. Snow, we would like to donate new guitars to the children who play them, and we would be most grateful to you if you would personally autograph the instruments and present them."

I was more than pleased to do this, especially with my love for unfortunate little children. Jimmy Widener, my rhythm guitar player, and

I went to the orphanage one afternoon. There were probably between one hundred and one hundred fifty children at the orphanage, ranging in ages from five to fifteen years old. They really enjoyed the songs I sang and the instrumentals that Jimmy and I played. Although they all were blind, they seemed to appreciate me signing the instruments. Several could speak a little English, and I carried on a conversation with them. Then the gentleman in charge had the children sing and play for us a couple of American songs, which they had learned in English. One was "Deep in the Heart of Texas." It was very touching, and I felt unusually blessed on that day.

A short time after we arrived back in the United States, I received a kind letter from the president of the orphanage, stating that I had been made honorary president of the Blind Child's Orphanage in Yokohama, Japan. It pleases me to know that I'm associated with that organization, which is helping little children.

While in Japan I met K. Uyeda, and he and his family became longtime friends. He's a businessman in Tokyo and has two large jewelry stores in the city, and he's also on the board of directors of the Olympics. He is one of the largest dealers in the world for cultured pearls, and on one of my trips to Tokyo, he made Min a beautiful ring. It has a big genuine pearl in the center and two rows of diamonds surrounding the pearl. Mr. Uyeda said he had made rings for several big names in Hollywood, including one for Frank Sinatra for $25,000, and rings for Bob Hope and Marilyn Monroe.

Several years later, while on his way to Montreal to serve on the international board for the Olympics, Mr. Uyeda and his daughter visited with us one afternoon during their layover. I showed Mr. Uyeda a medal I was given in Korea for entertaining the troops. When he looked at it he said, "Oh yes, I made these medals for everyone. If you have the box it came in, you'll find my name and the address of one of my stores on the inside cover." I went to get the box, and his name and address was there as big as life. A few years ago Mrs. Uyeda paid us a visit in Madison and spent several days with Min and me during her visit to the United States.

The Uyedas' son, Masemi, is a steward for Pan American airlines and flies from Tokyo to Los Angeles and back frequently. He's a singer and plays the guitar quite well. He sings a lot of my songs, and I was flattered when he said he had learned to sing and play by listening to my records. On one of his trips to Nashville, I had him as a guest on the Opry, not to sing, but to talk about country music for a few minutes, and the audience loved it. Later, when Masemi made a trip to Nashville, he got several of the best Nashville musicians together and recorded a country album. He and the musicians did a terrific job, and I'm proud of the album he autographed for me.

The Uyedas invited me to their home for dinner one afternoon. Rather than go by myself I asked Jimmy Widener to go along with me, and he accepted. When we got to the residence, we removed our shoes (cowboy boots in my case), which is an old Japanese custom, and we placed them inside the front door. The floors were all bamboo and so were the walls. In the center of the dining room was a huge square hole. The Japanese people sit on the floor, with their feet and legs down in this square hole, to eat their meals. If I'm correct, the Japanese people believe that if your feet are warm, you'll be warm all over.

During the time the dinner was being prepared, Jimmy and I were served several drinks of sake. Boy, I wasn't used to it. It sneaks up on you like tequila, and it sure gives you an appetite to eat a big dinner. After dinner the family got out their banjos and guitars and played and sang good country music. I continued to drink sake, and thank goodness Jimmy didn't. After we sang, the family began passing a microphone around the room, and we all had to make speeches. I still have a tape of those funny speeches in my tape collection, and I wouldn't part with it for love nor money. When it came time to leave, I walked to the door, holding on to Jimmy's arm, making all kinds of far-out comments. I had everyone laughing. When I tried to put my boots on, that was a circus, I can assure you! I couldn't do it. I was too unsteady. Jimmy came to my rescue, and we finally got them on. We made it back to the Okura Hotel and charged the whole thing up to a wonderful evening with our precious Japanese friends.

The Japanese have a tradition of presenting gifts. They might not be large or expensive, but it's not the price that really counts. It's always the thought. During the trips I made to Japan I always came back home loaded down with neatly wrapped and pretty gifts. I made sure every time to let the givers know I sincerely appreciated their thoughtfulness. One time, when our tour ended and we were ready to fly home, I had to purchase two large suitcases just to carry the gifts in.

When we were booked to play in any foreign country, the booker or promoter always took advantage of every day and every hour. They wanted to make as much money as they could, and therefore they had the artist follow a rigid schedule. On one of our tours to the Far East we were scheduled to play a date in Hiroshima, where the first atomic bomb was dropped in 1945, which helped to end the war. It just so happened that it was snowing quite heavily at the airport in Tokyo and our flight was grounded. Since our show had to be cancelled, our promoter asked me if I would consider taping a one-hour television film to be telecast at a later date. It wasn't in the contract, but since we had a day off and the folks had been so gracious to me, I agreed to do it, even though I don't like doing television work.

Friends, that almost turned out to be a disaster. Let's say that a lot more was involved than just a one-hour TV show. The folks wanted me to record twelve songs as an open-end program, where commercials would be inserted between songs. This program was to be sold and played on television. The Japanese are excellent business people, and they wanted to make this a good commercial program. No problem. But first I wanted something in writing to say that this program could only be televised to the public twice. After that they would be required to renegotiate for more viewing time, and they would be prohibited from chopping the program up to use songs in other shows. They signed an agreement to that effect. However, I knew there was no way I would ever know if the agreement was being followed, once I was so far away in Tennessee.

I was confident I could record the twelve songs in an hour and a half, or at tops two hours, since my boys and I had done these songs a million times. We were at the studio at 6:00 P.M. ready to record. The director said, "Mr. Snow, you please sing first song without you talk before song. After first song you talk and we record next song. Then you tell story about next song, then you sing song. Okay?"

Well, I wasn't expecting it to be this way, because I didn't think I was supposed to talk at all—just start and do twelve songs right through to the end. Anyway, I said the boys and I would do it. We started out and recorded three songs, then somebody said, "Stop, we have problem upstairs we must fix." The control room was upstairs, and the folks inside were looking down on us as we recorded in the regular television studio. The next time we got to the sixth song. "Stop, stop, new problem!" Then several of the people rushed around adjusting lights and moving microphones and then went back upstairs and did microphone checks again. Each time we stopped, we had to start at the first song again. They simply didn't pick up where we had left off.

I don't mean to criticize, but I don't believe, in the early 1960s, those poor souls knew anything in the world about editing or even recording television programs. After many attempts, about 10:30 or so, I was getting real tired, and my throat had just about had it. But we continued to try for all twelve songs without something going wrong. However, the same old problems came up. Finally they announced that all the bugs had been worked out. "Now, Mr. Snow, we are ready to record twelve songs, one after the other and do not much talk. Just tell name of song." By then it was around twelve o'clock. I felt relieved that all the problems had been corrected, so the boys and I could go right on through the twelve songs.

We were able to get to the eleventh number, "I Don't Hurt Anymore." Jimmy Crawford was our steel player at the time. I guess poor Jimmy was tired out like the rest of us, and he started the wrong introduction to the song. But instead of stopping, I jumped in with my guitar and did an introduction over his introduction, and I began singing. Even after the wrong introduction, "I Don't Hurt Anymore" sounded pretty good, and I was thinking about the fact that we had only one more song to go. I put everything I had into the last song, which was "The Golden Rocket."

I breathed a sigh of relief when we finished, and I started to put my guitar away in the case. Then at that moment someone yelled, "We have equipment trouble again. We solly, we very solly. We must do one more time 'The Golden Rocket.'" I stopped in my tracks and looked at the Rainbow Ranch Boys and said, "You know what, boys? They're trying to get back at us for winning the war." This relieved some of the tension in the air, and we all laughed.

Again the director said, "We need do 'The Golden Rocket' one more time. Not all songs—just last one. No talk, we splice in last song, okay?" Well, what a surprise! That's a new twist. If they tell me they can splice "The Golden Rocket" in with the other eleven, why in the hell couldn't they splice them all as we went along? "No," I said. "That's not okay. I quit. I'm not doing any more." I walked over and laid my guitar down inside the case and started to close the case. Then I thought for a moment, "We've been here from 6:00 P.M. until 1:30 A.M. Since I've gone this far, I think I'll go back and do one more for these people." So I sang "The Golden Rocket" again.

Finally we finished, and as we were going out the back to get into the van to take us to our hotel, I told my boys, "I wish I could get my hands on that little producer. I'd break his damn neck!" I was really perturbed and unusually tired. Do you know that when we started out the back door to leave, the first guy I saw was the show's producer! He was standing there with his hand out to shake mine. He only came up to my shoulder, and he had on a great big smile from ear to ear. He said, "You do good job, Mr. Snow, you do good job. Thank you." His big smile softened my anger. I smiled, too, and shook his hand.

One night one of the servicemen at a club where the boys and I had been having a few drinks mentioned it would be real nice to fly up to Okinawa and play for the servicemen at the air-force base. Well, that planted a seed of thought in my mind. It would only mean an extra couple of days on our tour, and the servicemen would appreciate that touch of home. It was only about fifteen hundred miles away and about a three-hour flight, so why not go?

When I got back to my hotel room, feeling tipsy, I decided to call Okinawa. Can you imagine calling at about three o'clock in the morning to get information on how to set up a show? Anyway, I got the overseas operator to call Okinawa. Nobody answered, and I got upset and blamed it on the operator. I thought she wasn't trying hard enough, and I'm ashamed to say I used some heavy language. In my anger and stupor, I slammed the receiver down on the telephone cradle so hard it broke the handset into two pieces. I thought to myself, "What am I going to do? Now that the receiver is broken, and without the receiver lying in the telephone cradle, the phone will continue ringing at the switchboard at the hotel desk." I sat there for a few minutes with my hand holding the cradle buttons down, trying to decide what to do. My boot was the closest thing I could see, so I put the heel of the boot on the telephone button that cut off ringing the night manager at the desk. Then I went to bed and fell asleep.

Later that morning there was a knock at the door. It was Jimmy Widener, who had come to my room to awaken me, and the first thing he eyed was my boot on top of the telephone. He stared at it. Then he stared at me for at least a minute. He didn't know what the hell was taking place. He seemed to be in a daze. He asked me what the cowboy boot was doing on top of the telephone, and when I told him, he laughed and got a big kick out of it.

I was feeling guilty because of what I had done, and I called the desk clerk. "Sir, I had a little accident. I dropped the receiver from the telephone, and it struck the bed and broke in two. If you will send up a bill to my room, I will gladly pay for the damage." "No problem, no problem," he said. I went out that afternoon, and when I returned to my room, the bill was lying on the dresser in an unsealed envelope. When I took the bill out, it looked like I was being charged $1,000, and I said to myself, "My God, it's a good thing I didn't break the whole damn telephone!" Then I came to my senses and realized that was only 1,000 yen, which, if my memory serves me correctly, was equivalent to about three American dollars.

I remember well my first trip to play for a Chinese audience. From one of our European tours the boys and I were scheduled to play shows in Hong Kong. We flew on Chinese airlines, and I've never seen an aircraft so beautifully decorated. There were large, brightly colored dragons painted on the inside and on the outside. This gave the plane an entirely different look than any other I had ever flown in.

Our flight took only a few hours, and we were scheduled for two shows that same night at the Grand Hotel. These performances were in two different locations in the hotel. The first would be for the hotel staff, and the second would be for the American servicemen who were on R&R from their ships. I felt confident that the servicemen would like our show, but I was somewhat apprehensive because I didn't know what to expect from the Chinese. Could they understand English? Would they know anything at all about country songs from America?

A big freight elevator carried us and all of our instruments to the top floor of the hotel, and when the elevator door opened, we walked right onto the stage. The hall was sort of dingy looking and could hold hundreds of people, and from the stage of this big concert hall to the floor must have been at least twelve feet down. I thought this was odd to be looking down so far to the audience.

We got set up for our one-hour show, and as usual we started right on time. I looked out at the audience and saw sixteen eyes staring at us. There were only eight Chinese people sitting way down there looking up at us as if they were trying to figure out where we were from. Were we from outer space or were we for real? I want you folks to know I sang every type of song I knew. I tried rhumbas, American love ballads, train songs, blues, cowboy songs, and Hawaiian songs, and I did not see their expression change one time. Nor did they applaud. Not once. Those people looked up at me as if to say, "What in the hell are you trying to prove?"

When we finished the show, we got the surprise of our lives. They applauded, and I didn't think they would ever stop. They gave us a standing ovation. One of the Chinese waiters told us after the show that the Chinese people are that way. They will never interrupt any type of entertainment with applause. They'll wait until after the complete performance before showing their appreciation. Boy, I sure wish we had known that in the beginning.

After we finished the first show, we went downstairs to the main ballroom, where there were about fifteen hundred servicemen waiting for us, and what a rousing welcome we received. The show went over great, and they didn't want to let us go, so we extended our show much longer than it was planned.

The next day we did some shopping, then flew back to Frankfurt, our home base, to continue our tour.

It was always interesting to me to see how people in other places lived. In a way these trips were like getting a college education, and I learned a lot about the culture of each country wherever we played.

During the Vietnam War, I wanted to entertain the troops, as I had done during the Korean War. Many other artists were going there from the United States, England, France, and several other countries. A number of countries were concerned about the spread of communism, and the United States had gradually sent a lot of troops to help the South Vietnamese to stop communism from spreading any further in the south. I felt I had an obligation to offer some morale boosting to the GIs, and I especially wanted to go during the Christmas holidays. I got in touch with the proper authorities at the Pentagon and told them of my desire. The Rainbow Ranch Boys and I went there on the same arrangements as we did in Korea, because we wanted to entertain without charging for our services. My son, Jimmie, and his wife made the trip also. They wanted to visit the sick and wounded in the hospitals.

We took off for Vietnam, which was a long and tiresome flight of around twelve thousand miles. We were pretty well beat up when we arrived, and I believe the temperature that day was over a hundred degrees. It was so humid we could actually wring the water out of our clothes. That was the filthiest country I was ever in, but the trip turned out to be one of my greatest experiences.

During our three weeks in Vietnam, we were offered one day off each week, but we told the people in charge of the entertainment that we would rather continue our shows with no time off. There was nothing to do, anyway. What could you do in that godforsaken country? In most places where we went, we had netting all around and over the top of our beds to keep these big helicopter-sized mosquitoes from eating us alive.

Anywhere in South Vietnam was dangerous. Driving along those narrow roads, we never knew when we might be hit by a mortar or when we might drive over a land mine. We entertained in the Mekong Delta, and the enemy was all around us. Guerrilla fighters would attack, and nobody knew when or where. The GIs endured the constant danger from the North Vietnamese and many jungle hardships. The entertainers had to be alert, too.

We requested to play in some of the remote areas, if possible, where the entertainment never got to go. The officer in charge said in a pleasing tone, "Why sure, we can take you to some very remote areas if you're willing, but we never send shows to some areas because of the extreme danger involved." The boys and I talked about it, and we all agreed to go anyplace the army asked us to go, regardless of any personal reservations. We were flown to a remote spot where the Green Berets were stationed. These servicemen really spread the welcome mat out for us, and I believe they would have applauded us if we had only opened our mouths and spoken. They were so anxious to see and hear anybody from the States.

During our travels I had a chance to meet a few of the other entertainers who were there for the same purpose. One very special lady was Martha Raye. She was humble and kind, and as you may know, she is a great comedienne. The people in charge of entertainment told us jokingly that half the time they had to run Martha off. She wanted to be there all the time entertaining the troops, and they all loved her. She was like a sister to them, the same as the great singer Gracie Fields was in World War II. Gracie was the toast of the military then, and Martha Raye was the toast of the military in Vietnam.

As we traveled to entertain, we were told not to be around large groups of South Vietnamese, as it was impossible to tell the North Vietnamese from the South Vietnamese. A North Vietnamese could easily be in the crowd. Little kids as young as five or six years old, not knowing what they were doing, were trained to pull a pin on a hand grenade and toss it into a crowd and blow people away. Moreover, we were advised to always walk in pairs but never more than two, three, or four people together. The Viet Cong were North Vietnamese who had infiltrated down through South Vietnam, and one never knew where they would be at any time.

One of the biggest scares I got was one foggy night while we were in the midst of doing a show. An American officer ran on the stage and made us stop right in the middle of a number we were playing. He told us the Viet Cong were spotted in the immediate area and that for our protection a personnel carrier was parked directly behind the stage. This carrier was about the same as an army tank, which could carry several men inside, and it was bulletproof. The officer said, "Now, if I give the word, don't wait a second. Throw those instruments down and run as quickly as you can off the back of the stage and into the personnel carrier. The crew will be ready for you if you should have to do this." That message was loud and clear, and believe me, it was hard to concentrate during the rest of the show, not knowing if we would make it through.

On another occasion we were playing in an area where the army had a makeshift hospital. From the back of the hospital, down a long concrete walkway, there was a canopy out to the helicopter pad. This was where the pilots flew the wounded in. We were in the middle of our show, standing out on the walkway and close to the pad, when the chopper came in. Naturally we had to quit, because it was too noisy to continue. As soon as the chopper landed, the wounded soldier was rushed into the hospital, and it was only seconds before four or five doctors were around the soldier, ready to treat him. Some were taking off his clothing, others were passing instruments around, and the nurses were hurrying and helping the doctors. I've never seen such accuracy and speedy work in my life. They all did a fine job, and I'm sure they saved many lives by their caring duty.

Also while we were there, some of the troops showed us this huge python snake they had captured in the jungle. They brought it out of the cage and let it crawl on the concrete walkway. The first thing it started to do was gradually crawl directly toward me. This snake, I was told, measured twenty-two feet long. It must have weighed a ton, and it was icy cold even in that hundred-degree weather. Supposedly it was harmless, but if you put a live chicken in its cage, the chicken would be gone in a matter of minutes if the snake was hungry. If the snake wasn't hungry, the chicken would be safe. On the other hand, there were many poisonous snakes in the jungles, and the servicemen were exposed to killer snakes and other dangerous animals.

When our tour was ended, we were mighty glad to board the Pan American jet and fly back to the good ole U.S.A., but we were happy that we had the opportunity to entertain the troops. I've often thought about the loneliness of the servicemen and the terrible conditions of war facing them in this far-off land. I admired those who fought with such courage and bravery.

I continued to do tours, both overseas and in the States, until 1985. I still may from time to time do a few dates on the road, but I've curtailed my traveling to spend more time at home with my wife. After all, back in the 1950s I traveled between two hundred and two hundred fifty days a year. And to this writing I've been going for around fifty-eight years.

Friends, I believe I've paid my dues, don't you?

33

Chubby and Vito

Listen to a story 'bout a gal I know,
She's my music-makin' mama, I'm her hillbilly beau,
She's sweeter than the music when she tickles the strings,
Sweeter than the flowers down in New Orleans.

"Music-Makin' Mama from Memphis,"
by Hank Snow

I BELIEVE THE TWO GENTLEMEN I had the most fun with during my career were Bill Davidson and Robert "Chubby" Wise, both fiddle players. I told you a lot of stories about Bill earlier in the book. Now I'd like to tell you about Chubby.

Anytime anything unusual happened to anybody in the band, it was Chubby. It seemed like trouble came looking for him. One night at the Grand Ole Opry, at the old Ryman Auditorium, an incident occurred involving him that I'll never forget. The Rainbow Ranch Boys and I were scheduled to do the Prince Albert national network radio portion of the Opry. Different artists took turns in hosting this popular radio show. We were always a little nervous on this particular program, because it went live across the whole United States, and at the same time, the show was played to a live Opry audience in the Ryman Auditorium.

That night was hot and humid. It was around ninety degrees outside, and with the heat from the footlights I'm sure it was at least 110 degrees inside. Furthermore, there was no air-conditioning in the old Ryman, just two big fans, one on each side of the stage. And making things worse, there were about three thousand people breathing toward the stage.

The big thick heavy stage curtain didn't part in the middle like most curtains do, where one half goes right and the other goes left. It rolled up on a heavy wooden rod by a motor. The curtain had to go up and down every time a segment of the Opry began and ended. About thirty-five minutes before our Prince Albert show was to go on the air, Chubby was already out on the stage with his fiddle, and he had on his regular stage outfit. I don't know why he was out there early, because a show was scheduled thirty minutes ahead of ours. Anyway, there was ole Chubby standing close to the big curtain talking to someone on stage.

Suddenly the curtain went up to begin the show, and somehow the end of the rod on the bottom of the curtain caught in the leg of Chubby's pants—and Chubby was going up with the curtain! His feet actually left the floor, and he was hanging on to his fiddle. If the rod hadn't torn the whole side out of the upper leg of his pants, it would have taken him all the way up to the top, and it might have hurt him seriously. Luckily it ripped the pants so bad that it cleared itself, and Chubby dropped back onto the stage.

Chubby's outfit was a mess. He didn't have another stage suit to change into, and he looked like a hobo. He was important to our show. He and our steel player had twin parts worked out for our songs, but he couldn't go on stage with the big rip in his trousers. Chubby was determined to do the show. A lot of people were scrambling around trying to find a pair of pants to fit him, but all we could find was an old mackinaw in one of the back rooms, which was actually a thick winter jacket.

There he was on stage with a three-quarter-length heavy winter coat in July, which fortunately covered the tear in his trousers. Unfortunately, during the show the sweat just rolled off poor ole Chubby in the severe heat on stage. I can imagine what the people thought, because we heard a lot of snickering in the audience. But Chubby was a good sport. Those who witnessed that "curtain-raising incident" said they would never forget poor Chubby hanging on to his fiddle with one hand and trying to shake himself clear with the other.

The boys and I used to kid Chubby about flying, because he was desperately scared to fly. Every time we had to take a plane to a show, Chubby would start drinking about six hours before flight time. He'd get stoned to help him deal with the stress of being in the air, and then he didn't get too concerned about flying. Sometimes I worried whether or not we'd get him through the check gate and onto the aircraft when he was so tipsy—and there were several times when we almost didn't make it. A tipsy Chubby was so funny, he would have everybody in the airport laughing. But it always turned out that about twenty minutes after we were in the air, he'd be almost sober again, and his fear of flying would come back.

Chubby made only one trip to the Far East with us, and I remember two funny incidents that happened on our way home from that tour. We were flying at around thirty-five thousand feet out over the Pacific Ocean, and he was sitting next to this kind of hefty lady who, we had learned, was an opera singer. She was on her way to Los Angeles to begin a United States tour. Of course Chubby had been drinking, because "no drink, no fly." He was everybody's friend, and he loved to talk to strangers. When he had something to drink, nobody was ever funnier. This opera singer (whatever nationality she was) couldn't understand anything Chubby was saying, but she was doing her best to comprehend whatever in the world he was talking about. But it didn't matter, because Chubby couldn't understand her, so he just kept right on talking anyway. He used dramatic hand motions, and this classy lady was talking back to him with her hands. It was a funny sight for sure!

During this circus the stewardess brought dinner to the passengers, which included a bowl of soup. I watched as the stewardess set the meal down on Chubby's tray. Minutes later he fell asleep. As he was moving his hands in his sleep, he hit the tray, and the whole meal, soup and everything, spilled all over Chubby's lap and legs, and he never even woke up. The stewardess came back and cleaned up the mess, and this distinguished opera singer was absorbing all of this in astonishment. She didn't know whether to laugh or to cry.

We landed in Honolulu, and after a brief stop to refuel we were on our way to L.A. We had only been in the air for about thirty minutes or so when the message came over the loudspeaker, "This is your captain. I'm sorry to interrupt your flight, but we have to go back to Honolulu. We have a little problem, but don't be alarmed." (When you hear those words, they should know you're going to get alarmed.) The captain explained, "We must dump four thousand gallons of fuel so we're lighter for landing. A small green light will not come on, indicating our landing gear is not down." However, we landed in Honolulu with no problem.

After a three-hour delay we took off again for Los Angeles, and we had fewer passengers after the bad scare. That's understandable, because many people don't feel like flying right after a scary incident like we had. Most of us need to pull ourselves together and get our minds straightened out before we ever fly again. After a few minutes in the air the stewardess came wheeling the cart down the aisle, and

Chubby started buying whiskey again. I don't know how much whiskey he drank, but I do know he was stoned when we landed in L.A., and he made funny speeches as we were lined up in the aisle to leave the plane.

Suddenly Chubby burst out laughing! He always laughed out real loud when he saw something funny. He pointed to this weak, frail little guy with a sharp chin. His chin was longer than the average chin, and he had sideburns that stuck out from the side of his face. He had sandy-colored hair and a little chinner that was gray or sand colored and tapered down to a sharp point on the end of his chin. Chubby turned around to us and said, "There's a goat on the plane!" Honestly, this little guy did remind me of a goat. Even the guy who looked like a goat was laughing! Whether he heard Chubby's remark or not, I don't know. By this time, everyone getting off the plane was laughing, and this continued right to the terminal and to the luggage claim department. Many people didn't know what they were laughing at, but Chubby kept pouring it on. Even Chubby's laugh was so funny that it seemed to be contagious. Then to make it funnier, Chubby kept tapping himself on the throat to make a sheep sound like "baaah, baaah, baaah."

On another occasion we were supposed to leave for Europe at 11:00 P.M. on a Pan American flight, and Chubby had gotten looped much earlier, so he was well prepared for the flight. But it so happened that when we called the airport to check the status of the flight, we were advised that an error in the seating arrangements had been made, and the flight we were scheduled on had been sold out. We couldn't leave for Frankfurt, Germany, until the next day. They offered their apologies, rescheduled us, and paid for our hotel for the night. Poor ole Chubby. He was already looped to the gills. He had wasted his money on getting drunk, and all he had to show for it was a bad hangover the next morning. The next day he had to go through the same process of drinking to prepare to fly again.

Kayton Roberts told me a story that involved Chubby, Willie Nelson, and himself. On one of our European tours Willie traveled as part of a package show, and he and the boys were together one night at a hotel, telling stories, but I wasn't present at the time. Chubby always called me the "Little Chief," and he called everyone else "Hoss." Kayton reported that after a few drinks Chubby said to Willie, "Hoss, you're supposed to be pretty smart and good at psychology. I want you to do something for me. For the next week, hang around the Little Chief as much as you can. Talk to him. Get to know him. See if you can figure him out. I've been playing fiddle for the Little Chief for many years, and I still ain't got him figured out." About a week later, sitting in one of the hotel rooms again, Chubby asked Willie, "Well Hoss, what did you find out about the Little Chief?" Kayton said Chubby started grinning and leaned back in his chair expecting a long discussion from Willie. Willie simply said, "There ain't nobody in this whole world that can figure that little bastard out!"

Chubby and I used to relax and have a beer together, whether it was in my home in Madison or on tours. That is, after a performance and almost never before. However, there were a few exceptions. On one of our tours we were scheduled to play in Halifax, Nova Scotia, and we were staying at the famous Lord Nelson Hotel. I wanted everything to go like clockwork in Halifax, because I had been on the air over CHNS for many years, and I knew so many people. So I was a little bit uptight and afraid that Chubby might have a beer before the show. But we put on an unusually fine performance, and Chubby never had one beer before, and I was so pleased.

But the next night we were supposed to play another town. I think it was Sherbrooke. Anyway, we had to get up and be ready to leave around 9:00 A.M. at the latest. Well, Chubby had gone out partying the night before, right after the show, and he was far from being sober the next morning. It was time to leave, and no Chubby. I sent someone to tell him we were running late, and we were all in the car waiting for him. The messenger came back and said, "Chubby is entertaining a lot of people in the hotel lobby. He's telling funny stories, and you can hear him all over the hotel. He's still about two-thirds tight. He's laughing and putting on a show, and he completely ignored me when I told him we had to go."

I sent the boy back a couple more times, but Chubby paid no attention to my message. Finally I said, "You go back in there and tell Chubby I'm giving him five minutes to get his butt out here and get in the car, or we're going to leave without him." So off he went again and delivered my ultimatum. Soon the boy came back again with a message from Chubby. "You tell the Little Chief if he fools around with me this morning, there's going to be some bear walking around this lobby. He better stay where he is. Tell the Little Chief I'll come when I'm good and ready."

Cowboy Copas was with us on this tour, and when he heard what Chubby had said, he nearly died laughing. This was completely out of character for Chubby. He wouldn't harm a fly, really. However, he came out in his own good time, and when he did, he wouldn't get in my car, where he always rode. Actually, he was one of the drivers, but instead he got in the other car with Copas. They told me that Copas stayed doubled up with laughter as he listened to Chubby all the way to our destination. That night, after about a gallon of black coffee, Chubby sobered up, and as usual he did a fine job.

I mentioned that on our first European tour my boys and I stayed at the Klee Hotel in Wiesbaden, owned by Mr. and Mrs. Mhyer. It's strange and kind of interesting how I became friendly with Mr. Mhyer.

In Wiesbaden one night when we didn't have a show scheduled, Chubby and I went out to a well-known club and had a few beers. We arrived back at the hotel by taxicab about 1:00 A.M. We were laughing and making a lot of noise, and we flopped down on the couch in the hotel lobby and decided we should have a nightcap before retiring to our rooms. The problem was, where could we get a drink?

It just so happened that Mr. Mhyer was working the all-night shift because the regular night clerk was out sick. Chubby was coming on strong with the funniest sayings I've ever heard, but by then anything made me laugh, and we were getting hard looks from Mr. Mhyer. Then I asked the question, "Mr. Mhyer, do you happen to have a drink around this place? We need a drink before we go to bed." "No," he said. And he emphasized the word "no." "You people are going to have to be quiet. We have guests from the United States and several European countries, and some of them stay with us for a month at a time. The last thing I want to happen is to have them disturbed. So gentlemen, I ask you to please be quiet and go to bed."

Well, it crossed me in the wrong way. I guess it was his tone of voice. I didn't think we were making that much noise, and this was one of those times I wanted to get even. There was a public telephone booth across the lobby, and only a short distance from where Mr. Mhyer was standing behind the desk. I purposely put through several overseas calls, knowing there would be nobody to answer on the other end of the line. I pretended they couldn't hear me, so I yelled into the phone, and after each of these make-believe calls I would again ask Mr. Mhyer, "You say you don't have a drink around somewhere? Just one little drink?"

Chubby knew my scheme, and he laughed so hard it nearly shook the hotel. Finally Mr. Mhyer got tired of this, so he broke down and brought out a fifth of the very best Scotch whiskey. "Now, if you promise to be reasonably quiet," he said, "I'll have a drink with you." He came over and joined us where we were sitting next to a coffee table. He set the fifth and some glasses on the table, and we talked softly and told stories until nearly dawn. Whenever Chubby talked or laughed a little loud, I'd say, "Shhhh, don't wake up the whole hotel full of guests." Mr. Mhyer was, I believe he said, either a major or a captain in Hitler's army, and he told us some fascinating stories. When he saw my American cigarette lighter, he became interested in it, so we traded lighters. That night began a strong friendship that continues today. Mr. Mhyer was an interesting and a delightful person, and Mrs. Mhyer was just as sweet as she could be. Whenever we returned to Europe, we always stayed at their hotel.

Chubby had one bad habit. In strange cities, regardless of what country we were in, he would go out at night and wander around the streets, sightseeing or window gazing, or go into in a cheap bar. Everybody was his friend and he was everyone's friend. Wherever he was, he treated people as if he had known them all his life. If you happened to pass by a bar, you just might see him sitting on a stool having a beer and perhaps talking to a sailor, soldier, salesman, or just about anybody.

The people at the Klee Hotel warned him to never wander around the streets or go to clubs by himself. They said it wasn't safe, but Chubby wouldn't listen. One night Chubby drifted off by himself, and by midnight there was no sign of him. The boys and I became worried. We wondered if he had drunk too much and had fallen asleep somewhere. Knowing Chubby, that was a reasonable explanation, but I was afraid someone might have robbed him and beaten him up. We had no earthly idea where to start looking for him. I checked the lobby every so often to see if he had come in and gone to his room.

About 7:00 A.M. one of the boys and I went to the lobby to check, but still no Chubby. The night clerk hadn't received any calls, and no one had seen him. About that time, I happened to look out the hotel's front door, and I saw a taxicab parked in front, and the cab driver was pulling Chubby out of the cab. He had his two hands under Chubby's arms, pulling him with his feet dragging on the ground. The driver got Chubby into the hotel, and several of us in the lobby carried him upstairs to his room. He wasn't hurt, but he was still pretty well stoned—and his wallet was missing.

That should have been a good lesson for him, but it wasn't. Later on in the tour, and after finishing our service-club show in Naples, Italy, Chubby went out roaming alone again. Some of the nice people in Italy had advised us to take every precaution if we went out after 9:00 P.M., and by all means not to travel alone. When Chubby came back to the hotel, he told his story. "As I was walking down the street, some young kids walked up to me and asked for a couple of cigarettes. As I reached for the package of cigarettes, they grabbed me from behind. They took my wallet, my cigarette lighter, the ring off of my finger. They even took my little shaker of false-teeth powder I use to hold my false teeth in!

Two of those little bastards yelled with delight when they saw this white stuff. They probably thought they had hit the jackpot and had found cocaine. I hope that powder glues their nostrils together!" Chubby wasn't hurt, and we were all thankful for that.

I could tell you many more funny stories about those good old days involving Chubby. He was a lot of fun to be around. He came up with the most original and funniest sayings I've ever heard. I love him like a brother.

After eighteen years playing with me, Chubby and his wife, Rossie, moved to Texas, where he had a smash hit on a fiddle tune called "The Maiden's Prayer." He started a new career for himself and was booked as a single on various shows, and he has done extremely well. Chubby and Rossie are now living in Florida. I see him every now and then, but he's more or less retired. However, he still plays a few bluegrass festivals around the country.

Another interesting and funny gentleman was Vito Pellettieri. Vito was an accomplished violinist, and at one time he had his own pop band in the South, but for some reason he gave up playing. His wife was an accomplished piano player, and she used to teach piano. Vito worked at the Grand Ole Opry and radio station WSM as their librarian. He was also stage manager each Saturday night at the Opry. But I didn't know anything about Vito when I first met him. One day I walked into the WSM office, and there were two men working on files. Vito looked up at me and said, "What in the hell do you want?" I was shocked! I didn't know what to say. My first thought was, "Is this man a complete idiot, or is this just his way of greeting strangers?" When he saw how surprised I looked, he smiled and said, "May I help you?" I soon discovered that he enjoyed playing practical jokes on people, and he enjoyed expressing himself in colorful language. When I called him on the telephone, he would always have some bad name for me right off the bat. "Okay, you bastard, what do you want now?" Or something else just as bad.

One day, before I had a chance to tell Min what his personality was like and how he loved to kid people, he phoned our home while I was out. When she answered, he said, "This is Vito down at WSM radio station. Where is that son of a bitch?" It nearly knocked Min off her feet, but in a polite way she answered, "He isn't here right now, but I expect him back any minute. I'll have him call you as soon as he gets home." When I walked into the house Min said, "I don't ever want to talk to anybody who calls here from WSM again. I was never talked to in such a crude manner in my whole life. Some man with a strange name that sounded Italian called you a 'so and so,' and I didn't like it."

However, after Min and I got to know Vito and his sweet wife, Catherine, they came to be very close friends. But he never stopped his humor and his practical jokes. He did a lot of little things to annoy you. Here's an example. One time I needed to have a music stand on the Opry stage to hold a song lyric that I hadn't memorized. As I was walking on stage to sing the song, he had turned the lyric sheet upside down to confuse me. He got a big kick out of doing things like that.

After taking this kind of thing on the chin, over and over again, I kept thinking of some way to get even with him. I wanted to give him a dose of his own medicine and catch him whenever he least expected it. A plan came to me when I was on tour in Canada during the mid-1960s.

During one of those July days, on a beautiful Sunday afternoon, we were in St. John's, Newfoundland, on the shores of the Atlantic Ocean. We were not playing a show that day, because back then shows of any kind were not allowed on Sundays. Min was with me on this tour, and she and I were taking a stroll on the beach and were having a lazy day, and I was taking color movies. We walked by a tiny inlet, which extended in from the ocean, and I saw a dead squid floating on top of the water. I wrapped the dead squid in a piece of newspaper and took it back to the hotel with me. With its tentacles it was about ten inches long. A squid reminds one of an octopus. In other words, this was an ugly-looking thing!

I wrapped the squid in tissue paper and put it in a cardboard box, with newspaper around it so it would stay steady in the box. I printed a message on a piece of cardboard that read "Mother's not dead, she's only a-sleeping." Then I sent this package to Vito via airmail. From Newfoundland to Nashville it would take three or four days, and by that time, with all the hot and humid weather in Nashville, the squid would be in the condition I wanted it to be in—good and rotten!

I found out later how this practical joke turned out. At the time, Vito was on vacation, and he was at home painting the outside of his house. My package went to the post office first, but it was addressed to Vito at the WSM offices. However, one of the postal clerks called WSM and said, "Please send someone here immediately to pick up a package addressed to Vito Pellettieri. It's stinking up the whole post office and we can hardly stand it any longer." The secretary at WSM told the postal clerk that Vito was on vacation and gave Vito's home address. Well, to get the stinking package out of the post office, they made a special delivery to Vito's home.

Vito told me later that when the postal clerk brought the package, he smelled it clear from the gate to where he was painting. He had to dip a rag in turpentine and hold it under his nose to receive the package from the delivery man! As bad as the smell was, Vito said he still was curious to know what the hell it was. But first he went behind the house and dug a hole, ready to bury whatever it was, and then he opened the package and read the message on the top. He said he buried that monster in a hurry, but the smell lingered around his house for a couple of weeks.

The word got around the Opry that Hank Snow had played a practical joke on Vito, who was the biggest practical joker in Nashville. Vito and all the rest of us got a big laugh out of it and still do to this day.

Another time I pulled a really neat one on him. I was playing a one-week engagement at the Casino Theatre in Toronto, Canada. During one of those days Sleepy McDaniel was passing a pawnshop and went inside to browse. He found a real bargain on watches, so he purchased three of them. When I saw these watches, I got an idea for another trick to play on Vito. I sent Sleepy to buy me one, and he came back with a top brand, probably a Hamilton or a Bulova. Then I asked him to take it to a jeweler located a few doors from the theater and see if he could possibly change the works inside and make the watch run backward.

Sleepy presented the jeweler with my request. He laughed and said, "Well, I've never had a request like this before, but I guess it's possible to make it run backward. I'll see what I can do, but it'll take me a long time since I can't work on it in the store. I'll have to work on it in my spare time at home. I'll insure it and mail it to you as soon as I finish it, and I'll include the bill. Is that okay?" Sleepy told the jeweler to go ahead with it. In about five weeks the watch arrived in Nashville at my post-office box. I could hardly wait to get it out of the box to wind it up and try it. It was an expensive project, but it would be well worth it—if I could pull this on Vito.

Vito lived in the eastern part of Nashville, about four miles from downtown, and since he didn't drive a car, he always traveled to and from his work by bus. He would leave his house at 6:40 A.M. and walk about six blocks to the bus stop at the corner of Stratford and Gallatin roads to catch the bus at seven o'clock. I made Vito a gift of the watch, and I hoped he wouldn't use it before he went to work the following morning. Fortunately that's how it worked out.

The next night, when he got home from WSM, he called me as soon as he walked in his door. The first thing he said was, "You bastard, I'll get you back one of these days." He was laughing so hard I could hardly understand him. Then he explained what happened. "I got up and fixed my breakfast, and while I was eating, I decided I'd wear my new watch to the office and show off your gift. I set it with the kitchen clock and headed for the bus stop, the same routine I do every morning. "While I was walking along, naturally I glanced at my watch. The first time I checked it, it was 6:35. I was baffled and thought to myself, 'That's funny, did I misjudge the time? I've never done that before.' So I hurried, thinking I had misjudged the time and I might miss the bus. Then I glanced at the watch again and this time it was 6:30! I was completely confused. I caught the bus, took a seat, and didn't say a word to anyone, because I didn't want to make an ass of myself. I figured I must have looked at the watch wrong. Anyway, I got off of the bus and walked up the hill to the radio station, took the elevator to the seventh floor, and again I looked at my watch. It was 6:00 A.M., and Hank, that's when I began to smell a rat. I yelled out, 'That bastard. Snow has done it again!'"

Vito told me that during lunchtime he took the watch to a jeweler to have it checked out. He asked the jeweler if he had ever seen a watch run backward. The jeweler laughed and took the back off. Then he looked straight at Vito and said, "Someone has performed a miracle on this baby. I've never seen anything like this before. The works in the watch are upside down. I certainly don't know how it was done, but it's a good trick if you can do it."

Friends, you couldn't have bought that watch from Vito for a million dollars. We had a good many laughs over it.

The next time I saw Vito, which was at the Opry the following Saturday, he said, "You son of a bitch, I don't know what's coming from you next, but I'll get you back. Just give me time. Hell, you're almost as bad as I am."

I truly appreciated and loved Vito very much, as everyone else did. He and Catherine used to send Min and me a pretty Christmas arrangement every year. She was a wonderful lady. When she passed away, it was a horrible loss to Vito. He idolized her, and they were so devoted to each other. After she passed away, it was Vito's wish to go to a nice quiet rest home where he could be with other people his age and where he would have good care. His rest home was only a three-minute drive from our house. I used to visit him quite often, and sometimes Min would go with me, as Vito thought Min was a wonderful woman. We'd sit and relive old memories. Reminiscing usually put him in a happy mood.

The year before he took ill, he had become quite feeble, and his friends drove him to the Opry every Saturday night. He'd sit in his wheelchair on the stage and make sure the right talent got on stage at the right time. Just something to occupy his mind, and let him know he was still important to the show. And every Saturday at the Opry he brought me a big red apple, and I was so pleased he thought enough of me to do that.

One night around eleven o'clock I went to visit Vito, and he was not responding to the efforts of the nurses. I held his hand and talked to him, and he softly squeezed my hand. I stayed with him for about an hour and went home. Then I got to thinking about how ill he was, and I decided to go back and sit with him. I had the feeling he wouldn't last much longer. I stayed for another hour or so, then I went home because Min was alone. I squeezed his hand again before I left, but this time there was no response. Not long after I left him, he passed away in his sleep. He was eighty-two. I had known and loved him for many years. He was a special friend with a good and kind heart.

I've collected a world of memories over the years. Some are sad and some are funny, but all are a part of me.

34

Rainbow Ranch and Squirlie

These hands ain't the hands of a gentleman,
These hands are calloused and old;
These hands raised a family, these hands built a home,
Now these hands raise to praise the lord.

"These Hands," by Eddie Noack

THEY SAY A MAN'S HOME IS HIS CASTLE. I believe it. Min and I never owned a home until we bought Rainbow Ranch in 1950, but we sure had lived in many towns and cities before that. We took a lot of pride in our new home from the first day we moved into it. We intended it to be our one and only home, and we're still living here. It's located in Madison, Tennessee, a suburb of Nashville.

My so-called ranch is three acres of property. Our home has a two-car garage, plus another garage we had built under the house when we first bought it. There's a huge cement platform in back of our home, where I park my big Silver Eagle touring bus. I had a neat little barn built for Shawnee, with an automatic watering device in his stall, so he could enjoy the later years in his life with lots of cool water and plenty of good food. Throughout the property we have loads of pretty shubbery, many kinds of flowers, and especially my favorite, the rose.

A lot of people over the years have asked me to describe our home. They often say, "Why doesn't Rainbow Ranch look like a ranch? How many horses do you have? Is it really a ranch with cattle?" Friends, Rainbow Ranch is not a ranch. It's only a name I gave our home in the early years. Just the same as Hank Snow is not a ranger.

We expanded the house whenever we needed more space. After the additions, over a period of time, we now have three bedrooms, a living room, dining room, two baths, den, trophy room, recording studio, control room, record room, workshop, and storeroom. Our home is modest, but it's everything we've needed through the years, and we love it just the way it is.

My trophy room is loaded with trophies and awards, which I've been fortunate enough to receive over the years. Many of my mementos are from all over the world, and each of these I dearly prize. I've mentioned several of these throughout this book. I also have a collection of animal heads: bear, fox, and mountain lion, among others. Many people have seen these heads and said, "Oh, did you kill the animals?" I reply, "No ma'am, or no sir. I wouldn't kill a mouse." I bought most of these in a store in Livingston, Montana, during the 1950s. My polar-bear rug came from the Arctic, and I have a leopard hide that came from Sri Lanka. In one corner of the trophy room I have my Jimmie Rodgers corner, where I keep my collection of train items and my Jimmie Rodgers souvenirs.

In my record room I have hundreds of albums that I've collected by various artists, in both the pop and the country fields, as well as a few thousand 45 rpm records and a huge collection of the old 78 rpm records. I have my collection of guitars there, too. My office is located next to my studio.

The reason I added my eight-track recording studio was to make it more convenient to record some of the tracks of my single and album releases. Sometimes the musicians and I would lay down the tracks in the RCA Victor studios in Nashville, and I'd bring the master tape home and play it back on my eight-track tape machine. This made it easier for me to record some of my guitar lead parts, and a few times I added voice to the master tracks.

I cut my last instrumental album, *Instrumentally Yours,* in my studio. I worked at the recording during the night hours when everything was quiet, with no phone ringing and no interruptions. It was a "multiple recording," where I dubbed in several parts such as vibes, ukulele, two and three guitar parts, and so forth. Then I had Mark Morris, a fine drummer, bring his drum set out to my studio and put the drums down on one of the tracks. After that, my long-time friend and producer Chet Atkins took my tape to his home, where he had a twenty-four-track studio, and he added bass. This was the finished product, with the exception of the mastering, which was done by experts in Nashville. Then the master tape was turned over to RCA for packaging and distribution. This album of twenty "standards" was released by RCA in 1979, and it's one of my favorites because I did most of it myself at home in my studio.

The accoustics in my small studio are not as good as RCA's, but they're good enough to meet their standards. I have all the necessary equipment it takes to do a major recording. Besides several tape recorders, I have microphones, mixing boards, a console that can enhance the sound in the recording process, an echo chamber, and other gadgets that are used in regular commercial studios.

While speaking of studio work, I must tell you about my big thrill as a steel guitar player. This came about when my son, Jimmie, had a contract with RCA Victor back in the 1950s, and I thought he would be making country music a career. Of course, this was years before he went into the ministry. Jimmie had cut several records, which RCA Victor released, and it was on a couple of these records that I played steel. I was not an accomplished steel or Hawaiian guitar player, but I used to dabble around on the steel guitar and thought it sounded pretty good. I used what was called "A tuning" and played on six strings only. These days most steel players have two and even three necks on the guitars, with a dozen strings on each neck. Before I went in the studio, I did a lot of practicing, and Jimmie and I recorded the songs in my little studio. When we went into the big RCA Victor studio facilities, we breezed through these songs, and they turned out pretty well.

People ask me frequently if I have all the records I've recorded throughout the years. My answer to this is yes. I have a copy of every record I made for RCA Victor. This includes all albums, as well as all 45 rpm and 78 rpm records. I also have lyric copies of every song I've recorded and a huge amount of sheet music of various songs. Altogether I have about five thousand songs, including the more than one hundred fifty that I've written.

Among my treasured collection are nearly five hundred one-hour tapes that I made over the years of special events. I have recordings that go back to my first wire recorder, which existed before tapes came on the market. I have prized recordings of my son, Jimmie, when he was only two years old. I have many tapes from the Grand Ole Opry network shows, as well as tapes of every show I did from the Hank Snow Music Center when I owned the music store. There are many interesting tapes of events in my career, too, such as those made at the Jimmie Rodgers Memorial show each year in Meridian, Mississippi.

That's Rainbow Ranch—our home, our castle. My house carries many sentimental stories and brings back wonderful memories. I can look around me and relive some great times of the past.

It's impossible to talk about our home without talking about Willie Fred Carter, known to everyone as "Squirlie." Even though he retired several years ago at the age of sixty-five, he's still a part of Rainbow Ranch.

During my married life Min and I have laughed about the Snow luck. If we send away for something to come by mail, there are 99.5 chances out of 100 that it will be broken, won't fit, will be the wrong color, won't work, or whatever. This happens time and time again. If I had a suit with one coat and two pairs of pants, I'd burn a hole in the coat. This actually happened. When we receive a package in the mail, I automatically say to Min, "I don't think I'll open this one. Let's send it back and have another one sent instead. It will save the trouble of opening and closing it again." Squirlie and my family have used this luck business as a joke, but we all realize that in fact I've been one of the luckiest guys in the world.

My first boat was a twenty-one-foot cabin cruiser, which I was able to take care of myself. However, when I bought the forty-one-foot Chris Craft cruiser (which I named the Golden Rocket), Squirlie was a big help in maintaining it, but he often resisted going to the lake just for his relaxation. "Oh no, I couldn't do that," he'd say. "I'll never get my work done around the place. The pasture needs mowing, and I've got painting to do. I'll never get caught up around here." He always thought that working around the place was more important, but I would keep on, and finally he'd go. When I wasn't on the road, it was relaxing for me to spend time on the boat and to get away from the phones ringing.

One day Squirlie and I were at the boat dock, and we were trying to straighten out a canopy rod. It had been bent when a drunk in his cabin cruiser ran into it while trying to dock his boat in the slip next to mine. We wanted to bend the rod back into its original shape so the canopy over the stern of my boat would be drawn tight again, to cover the back of the boat from the weather. We had a rope tied on the end of the rod, which went through the canopy, and we were both standing on the walkway that ran alongside the boat. Squirlie was in front of me, and we were both pulling as hard as we could, and the rope broke. I fell backwards off the walkway into the chilly water, and I was down in water over my head. As Squirlie looked back he saw me surface, hair all down in my eyes and huffing and puffing trying to get my breath. He said he never saw anyone move as fast in the water trying to scramble out as I did. And I never saw anyone laugh at me as much as he did.

Squirlie never did drink much and barely ever drank at work, except on a rare occasion—and then it took a lot of persuasion from me. Occasionally, I would get home about the same time that Squirlie came to work, around 6:00 A.M. I didn't make it a habit to come in at that hour of the morning, but sometimes I'd meet an old-time friend downtown, and I'd bring him home to have a few more drinks and play records. If I saw Squirlie doing his chores, I'd motion for him to come up to the house to meet my friend and have a few drinks with us. "It's too early in the morning for that," he would say. I'd coax him and he'd say no again. But about the third time he'd give in. "Just one little drink." That meant I had him in my power. I'd offer him another one and he'd say, "Well, I might have one little one and that's it." Then he'd have another and another. He was really funny anyhow, and with the drinks it was a real circus. I've laughed at him many times until the tears streamed down my face, and I'd double up from laughing at his sayings.

One morning I brought a featherweight boxer home, after a bunch of us had been out drinking all night. The boxer and I were having a few more drinks at my place, and when I saw Squirlie, I motioned for him to come to the house, and I made him acquainted with my new friend. Again I had to coax him several times, and he said the same thing. "Well, maybe one little drink." After a few more belts Squirlie was walking on air. Then, right out of the blue, he said, "No boxer scares me." He tapped the boxer on the chest with the back of his hand and again repeated, "No boxer scares me." The boxer was totally surprised, and we all three had a big laugh over it.

Squirlie was a lover of Jimmie Rodgers's music, too. He played the Hawaiian guitar, using the "A-string tuning," and he sang pretty well also. Occasionally he and I would sit around and play music together and relax. He'd slide that bar up and down the strings, and he'd sing old bluegrass and country songs. Sometimes I'd say, "Squirlie, we're going to pretend you're a disc jockey," and I'd turn on my tape machine and do a countdown. "Three . . . two . . . one . . . you're on the air!" He would announce, "Friends and neighbors, this is the Squirlie Carter show. For my first number I'm going to sing 'Salty Dog.'" After the song he'd say, "Don't forget to send in your cards and letters, and remember our sponsor, Carter's Little Liver Pills." Those times were among my best and most relaxing of all the days gone by. It was good clean fun, and we didn't have to worry about annoying people around us. We could just be ourselves. Let our hair down and say anything we wanted to. I still have several of these treasured programs on tape.

One morning in the heat of the summer, with the temperature around ninety degrees, Min said, "I haven't seen Squirlie in several hours, and it's beginning to worry me, because he never leaves the place without letting us know where he's going." I knew where he was, because this was one of those few mornings when Squirlie and I had been having a few drinks together right after he had come to work. After he and I had sipped a few, he excused himself and went outside to get fresh air, and he didn't come back. Later I walked down to the barn and saw Shawnee roaming around in the pasture and grazing, and soon I found Squirlie. He was lying in the straw in Shawnee's box stall. He was sound asleep. I woke him up and he said, "Oh, I'm so sleepy. Please let me sleep."

I let him go back to sleep, and he stayed down there until it was time for him to go home. I woke him up again and he said, "I don't dare go home. If my wife sees that I've been drinking, I'll be in deep trouble." His wife was dead set against any drinking, but I knew she would be worried, so I sent him on his way. He only lived a short distance from our home, and he was perfectly all right to drive. The next day he told me the rest of the story. "As soon as I got home, I grabbed a wrench and crawled under the house and started banging on one of the water pipes. We don't have a basement, and there's not much room from the ground to the floor of the house, but it was real cool under there. When my wife came out to see what was going on, I told her a pipe had broke loose and I was having a hard time fixing it. I said it might take me a few hours, so I laid there where it was cool and dozed off. Every now and then I'd wake up and bang on the pipe a few times. This way she thought I was working. After my wife went to bed, I came out from under the house feeling like a new person, and she had no idea I had even had one drink."

I was playing an outdoor park in Indiana in the 1950s, and this friendly guy came over and asked the boys and me if we'd like to have a cold bottle of home brew. It was at least a hundred degrees under the hot sun, and I told him we sure would, but we would have to wait until after the show. Since I always signed autographs after my shows, I didn't want the fans to smell any alcohol on my breath. After the night show and the autographing the boy came back and gave us each a pint of his home brew that he had made. It was cold as ice, and with its golden color it sure looked good. That turned out to be the finest beer I had ever tasted in my whole life. We thanked the young man, and I asked if he would give me his recipe. He said he would, so I left him my address, and in a few days here came the recipe. I showed it to Squirlie and he wanted to make a batch right away. So he went out and bought everything he would need: a five-gallon crock, a bunch of bottles and caps, and a bottle capper to put the tops on.

Well, Squirlie made it, and it fermented for about a month down in the barn. He tasted it every now and then to see how it was doing.

"It's coming along real good," he'd say. "It's starting to bubble, so it's almost ready." As that stuff was fermenting, it was as black as coal, and it still looked muddy when it was ready to drink. It reminded me of the moose milk I used to get in Canada.

Squirlie's moose milk would knock your head off. Man, it was strong. I brought a couple of quarts of it in the kitchen one day and set them on the sink, and in a matter of seconds, the tops literally flew off. They sounded like firecrackers, and that stuff went squirting all over the kitchen ceiling. What a mess! Squirlie had warned me, "Don't annoy it, handle it with care." By then it was apparent to me that Squirlie had messed up on the recipe.

Soon thereafter, the Rainbow Ranch Boys and I were ready to leave on tour, and I suggested that we take a few bottles of that stuff with us. One of them said, "Sure, we'd like to taste Squirlie's home brew. Is it as good as what we had in Indiana?" I replied, "Boys, I'll let you be the judge." I set six quart bottles on the floorboard of the Cadillac in the back, and before we even pulled out of the driveway, we heard pop! pop! pop! All the bottles exploded, and broken glass flew all around. There was no way we could take it in the car, it was much too fragile. We never figured out how Squirlie messed up such a great recipe, but he claimed he followed it to the letter.

Tompall Glaser, one of the Glaser Brothers, got involved with Squirlie's home brew, too. The Glaser Brothers are very talented musicians, singers, and songwriters, and their voices blend into the most beautiful harmony you could ever hear. The trio worked as backup singers on a lot of Marty Robbins records, and they sang backup on some of mine, too. I've also recorded several of their songs over the years such as "(For Every Inch I've Laughed) I've Cried a Mile," which is one of my all-time favorites, written by Tompall Glaser and Harlan Howard. Others include "I'm Not at All Sorry for You" and "I've Done at Least One Thing That Was Good in My Life."

Chuck Glaser opened a first-class recording studio in Nashville later in his career, and he became a fine record producer. He produced two of the last country albums I recorded before RCA and I dissolved our relationship. The other two brothers are Jim and Tompall. They're fine artists in their own right and have had several big records of their own.

Sometimes I'd invite friends over to the house, or they would drop by and we'd listen to records, jam a little bit, and have a few drinks. That was better for me than driving around town, being half tight, and probably having a wreck and killing somebody. On this particular night I was sitting alone in my den writing a song, and someone knocked on the door around midnight. It was Tompall. He had a bottle in his hand, and we sipped on his vodka until it was gone. Then I called a taxi-driver friend and asked him to bring us a bottle. He did and we drank some of it. Suddenly I remembered Squirlie's home brew, which was stored in the basement, and I wanted Tompall to try it. I went down to the basement and gently carried a few bottles up, and I very carefully set them down by the sink in the kitchen. Tompall pulled the tops off a couple of bottles and threw the caps into the garbage disposal in the sink. Then we went back in the den to play more music. He left around 3:00 A.M. and I went to bed.

At that time my office was in the basement. It was finished in knotty pine, and in the middle of the ceiling, I had an electrician install a pretty chandelier. Everything looked real nice. In the hot weather I didn't need to turn on the air conditioner because it was cool down there all summer. Squirlie came to work around six that same morning, and after he fed and took care of Shawnee and my dogs, he went inside to check on things, as was customary for him each morning. He walked into my basement office, and there was water at least an inch high. He ran into my bedroom and said, "Hank, get up. There's water running out of the chandelier!" I thought Squirlie had completely flipped out. The beer caps that Tompall had thrown in the garbage disposal had somehow caused one of the water pipes under the sink to burst open. After I'd gone to bed, the kitchen and the den upstairs had become flooded, and the water poured down into my office through the fixture in the ceiling and into the chandelier, which was hanging by chains. It took about two weeks for the carpets and the mess to dry up completely.

Another incident that took place shortly before Squirlie retired I think is a masterpiece. I had just hired a new rhythm guitar player, whose name was Curtis Gibson, "Curt" for short. Squirlie didn't know I'd hired Curt, and Curt didn't know the nickname that people had given Squirlie. One day Curt came over to get his amplifier off my bus, and Squirlie was out in the front where some men were fixing our electronic gate. Squirlie was friendly to people and would always introduce himself first. He'd walk up to the stranger, shake hands, and say, "I'm Squirlie," rather than use his proper name. When we refer to someone as "squirrelly," and I'm sure you folks will agree, it suggests the person is a little bit off his rocker—he's strange and appears real nervous. So when Curt pulled into the driveway and got out of his car, Squirlie walked up to Curt and said, "I'm Squirlie." Curt immediately replied, "Don't feel bad, I'm about half off myself!"

Squirlie was loyal, and he always had our interest at heart. If he went on an errand that might involve money, he would always speak up if he thought I was being overcharged. After he retired I knew I could never replace him. Squirlie was a lot of fun, and I sure miss having him around, just like I miss ole Chubby. However, he still drops around every now and then to pay us a visit, and he's just as funny today as he ever was. He was and is very special to Min and me. He's part of the family.

I had a sad experience back in 1961. It was on the coldest day in January and snow was on the ground. Soon after Squirlie came to work, he ran into the house and yelled through the door into the hall that adjoins my bedroom, "You'd better get up as quick as you can and come down to the barn. Shawnee is lying down on his side by the door and can't get up." I jumped out of bed and put a few clothes on and rushed to the barn. Poor Shawnee was partway out of his stall, and he was jammed in the doorway on his side. He was wringing wet with sweat, even though it was feezing cold. Evidently the poor thing had been trying to get up for a long time, and no telling how long through the night he had been lying there. He was obviously in pain. He was panting like it was hard to get his breath.

I ran up to the house, and I was fortunate to get in touch with our veterinarian, Dr. Mobley, at that hour. He had been our regular vet ever since we arrived in Nashville. He came right away and listened to Shawnee's heart and thoroughly checked him all over. Then he looked at me and said, "Hank, Shawnee has been a gallant animal, but his heart is in very bad shape, and his kidneys and lungs are about gone. He's in serious pain. We can perhaps get him back on his feet, and he may last a week or maybe two, but being past thirty years old, his age is against him. I know this is a hard decision for you to have to make, because from the years I've been attending him, I know you love him very much. But I have no other choice than to level with you, and my decision would be to let me put him to sleep. This is my honest judgment."

I didn't want to accept the facts. That was one of the hardest things I had faced since the death of my dear mother in 1953. I was never so hurt in my whole life about losing a treasured pet. To me it was like losing one of my own family. Shawnee had been part of my life for years. He had done his job well during those thousands of miles we traveled across Canada and the United States, doing shows and all the trick riding and stunts together. He was like a human being to Min, Jimmie, and me. We had been through a lot together during those early and difficult years in show business. It always seemed to me that Shawnee did his best to help me make it, and he always did what he was supposed to do.

Now, how could I agree to have him put to sleep? Well, I had no choice. I couldn't bear to see him suffer, so I told Dr. Mobley, reluctantly, to go ahead. Under those circumstances, it was better to not let Shawnee suffer any more than he had to. The doctor went back to the office to get the proper instruments. While he was gone, I stood there looking Shawnee right in the eye. Like I told you earlier, he had humanlike eyes. As I was looking into those big beautiful and sad eyes, he looked up at me as if to say (as the saying goes in the song "Old Shep"), "I hate to, but you understand." Then I turned and went back up to the house and cried my eyes out.

After Shawnee was dead, Dr. Mobley sent Squirlie into the house to see if I wanted him to arrange to have Shawnee taken away. I said, "Squirlie, that man can't be serious, can he? Dr. Mobley surely can't be serious. How can I have Shawnee taken away to some glue factory, and let him be ground up to make glue, fertilizer, or whatever?" About half mad, I said, "Definitely no! Shawnee is not leaving this property. This is his home. He was content here in this pasture, frolicking and enjoying life, and here is where he's going to stay! Please call the man we know in Hendersonville and ask him to bring his bulldozer as soon as possible to dig Shawnee's grave."

In less than two hours the bulldozer came, the grave was dug, and Shawnee was laid to rest. He had lived a long life, and we had taken good care of him. I have no regrets. He's buried in the pasture, along with six dogs, a mynah bird, and four cats. All the animals have graves, and their names and ages are carved in concrete squares.

I never bought another horse, but we always had animals around our home. Both Min and I love our animals. We now have four cats: Buttons, Mabel, Blackie, and Fluffy. The mother cat is a Himalayan, and she had the three kittens. When they were born, Min and I decided to keep them and take care of them ourselves. Otherwise they might get abused by someone when they're not wanted. We have had more joy from these cats than one could ever imagine.

I've always said if you can't take care of animals and love them, then you should never have them. Some people have dogs and cats, and once the novelty wears off, the animals become like little orphans because they never get any more attention. Most times the owners never bother to pet or talk to them. I am strictly against that, and I have always felt that anyone who would abuse an animal in any way is capable of abusing a child. There's too much abuse in this old world already.

35

The Hank Snow Foundation

Little children are the hope of the world,
So guard them day and night, be sure you teach them right.
You can teach them by the things you do and say,
The way you live today, the way you pray.

"Little Children (Hope of the World),"
by Paul Mitchell

❧

THREE EVENTS, TWO IN 1973 AND ONE IN 1976, had a strong impact on me and are branded on my memory.

My good friend Stringbean (the Kentucky Wonder) met an untimely death. The Rainbow Ranch Boys and I were on tour in England for about three weeks in the fall of 1973. Whenever I was on an extended tour in the States or overseas, I kept in frequent touch with my wife at home. On a Sunday afternoon I called Min and she said, "You will never believe what happened here last night. Both Stringbean and his wife were shot to death after the Opry at their home on Ridgetop. It was a cold-blooded murder, and the whole community is really raging about it."

I couldn't believe what I was hearing. Who would ever think about killing Stringbean? He was a comedy actor with the Opry, and you folks might have seen him on a personal appearance or a television show, especially the well-known "Hee Haw," where he was a regular member. He and his wife were loved by everyone. Stringbean was one of the finest people I've ever met. He was easygoing and friendly, and both he and his wife were honest and good Christian people.

A few guys who Stringbean and his wife thought were their friends and who were neighbors had broken into his house and were waiting for him when he returned from the Opry. They cornered him on the inside of his home, and while he was trying to protect himself, they shot him. When his wife ran for help outdoors in the dark, they shot her in the back of the head. Both died instantly.

After I got off the phone with Min, I immediately called Jimmy Widener in his upstairs hotel room, and he came down to hear the shocking news from home. When I told him about the double tragedy, I thought he was going to pass out. Both of us just stood and looked at each other in silence. We didn't know what to say or what to do.

The second shocking and tragic event was yet to come. After we finished our tour in England and returned to the U.S.A., we did one show in Tulsa, Oklahoma, and then we had three weeks off before our next scheduled tour. This was during the late fall of 1973, and gasoline and diesel fuel were rationed. Because of the energy crisis, it appeared that the show tour buses would get very little fuel, if any, and we entertainers would not be able to travel to and from our show dates. Naturally, we were all concerned because it would affect our business. Commercial buses like Trailways and Greyhound had the top priority over show-business buses.

A couple of weeks after our England tour and our show in Tulsa there was a scheduled meeting on a Tuesday morning in Nashville, in which bus and truck drivers could discuss possible solutions to the fuel problems. For some reason I couldn't go, and I asked Jimmy Widener to attend the meeting for me, because we needed to keep abreast of what was happening in this fuel crisis. Jimmy attended, and he called me afterwards and talked a few minutes about the meeting. Then he said he had to go to the airport and speak to someone about his guitar. His electric guitar had gotten messed up on the plane on the way back from England, which I had noticed when we played Tulsa, and he wanted to find out about collecting insurance for the damage. He said he would call me later.

He did call me later in the day and said the fuel conflict was going to be worked out, and that the entertainers would get enough diesel fuel to do our shows. They considered our usage as commercial since it was our livelihood. I tried to reach Jimmy again that night, but he wasn't home. Then I remembered that a lady from Los Angeles named Mildred Hazelwood was coming into town to plug some of her husband's songs. Her husband's name was Jimmy also. They had all been friends for many years, so I figured Jimmy Widener was out with her to help get some of her husband's songs placed with publishers or producers. Her husband had passed away some months previous to this, and she probably needed the money.

About 10:30 that night, when I was getting ready for bed, Min said to me. "I just heard on the ten o'clock news about another double murder downtown. The reporter said the names haven't been released as yet." The first thing that came to my mind was Stringbean and his wife and how they had been killed. I was thinking, "Why do we have so much violence in this country? Why do we have so many senseless killings? Why do we have so much child abuse?" It just doesn't make any sense to me at all. I went to bed, but it took me quite a while to go to sleep because I couldn't get Stringbean off of my mind.

Around five o'clock the next morning, I got a phone call from my son, who lived next door at the time, and it startled me at that hour. He said, "Dad, the police are here and they want to talk to you." Since I have an electronic gate for security reasons, they couldn't get into my place. I immediately opened the gate, which works remotely from anywhere in the house, and I slipped on my robe and went to the office. I invited the officers in, and one of them calmly asked, "Mr. Snow, do you know a James Phillip Widener?" I said, "Yes, he plays rhythm guitar in my band. He's been with me for around twelve years. What's the problem?" He replied, "Mr. Widener is deceased."

The words sounded so final. I couldn't speak! My legs didn't want to hold me up, and I quickly sat down. I got sick to my stomach.

The police wouldn't or couldn't tell me anything else, but they gave me a phone number and said to call and talk to a certain detective at the police station. As soon as I got my head together, I called the detective, and he told me that Jimmy and a lady had been robbed and murdered. He asked if I could come down about 7:00 A.M. and identify Jimmy's body. I just couldn't believe this tragedy, and when I told Min, she too almost passed out. We were in a daze. I couldn't get my mind straightened out. Finally, I made a phone call to Bobby Wright in Gallatin, Tennessee, who was my bass player. He was almost speechless. I said, "Bobby, would you go down with me? They want me to identify the body, and I don't think I can do this by myself."

We went to the police station, and a policemen drove us to General Hospital, and a nurse escorted us to the room where the bodies were. Mildred was lying on an elevated hospital bed at the end of the room, covered by a white sheet, and Jimmy was lying at the side of the room against the wall. Neither body had been cleaned up yet. Their hair was matted with blood, and the police pointed out where the bullets went in and penetrated the back of Jimmy's head and came out in the front. They remarked that Jimmy's face was so puffy and so swollen that the three men who killed him must have beaten him real bad. I presumed that Jimmy had been trying to protect Mildred and had fought the murderers. It was a horrible scene to walk into. I was devastated. I must have turned ghostly white, because one of the nurses quickly came and asked if she could give me something to steady me. She stayed with me for several minutes to make sure I was all right.

How ironic this whole thing was. Just three weeks earlier, almost to the day, Jimmy Widener had sat with me in the London hotel room, and we were feeling so terrible about the death of Stringbean and his wife. Then the same tragic end came to him and Mildred—almost identically the same. Some things in this world just don't make any sense at all.

The police put the situation together as they thought it had happened, which proved later to be correct. Jimmy and Mildred had been seen together around 9:00 P.M. in a coffee shop next to the Ramada Inn, which was located behind the Capitol Building in Nashville. Mildred was staying at the Holiday Inn. After they left the coffee shop, Jimmy took Mildred to her room to see that she got in okay. But when he drove his car into the parking lot behind the Holiday Inn and they got out, three black men forced them back into the car. They made Jimmy drive to a dark and secluded black section of the city. That's where they were shot and pushed out of the car. Their bodies fell into a little brook, and according to police, Mildred was lying face down across Jimmy, who was also face down in the tiny brook. The next day the detective took me and showed me where the tragedy happened.

I believe Mildred's body was flown back to California, where her family lives, and Jimmy was laid to rest with military honors in Forest Lawn Cemetery not too far from our home here in Madison.

The three murderers used Jimmy's car as the getaway car. They drove to Memphis, where they were soon arrested when they tried to use Jimmy's credit card at the airport to make reservations to San Francisco. One of them turned state's evidence. The second served I believe two years, and the third, the trigger man, got life and is still serving time in Nashville.

As I mentioned earlier, our last show together was in Tulsa, Oklahoma, and I have the guitar Jimmy played during his last show. It's hanging on the wall in my studio. I drilled two holes in the pick he used, ran a thin wire through it, and fastened it tightly to the guitar. The pick has not been moved. It's still in the same place he put it that night after the show in Tulsa.

This was a great personal loss and a very sad time for my boys, my family, and me. Jimmy Widener was a gentleman, a fine man, a brave man. He had served in the United States air force as a wireless operator during World War II, and it's ironic that he had gone through World War II, with all the dangers of flying in army planes, only to return home and get murdered in downtown Nashville.

If I had the power to choose just one thing in this world it would be to eliminate violence. I would wipe it from the earth entirely.

Friends, right here I'd like to tell you about my efforts to fight child abuse and child neglect. As you know I was the victim of child abuse, first from a grandmother who resented me and later from a cruel stepfather who physically and emotionally abused me. I never got over that treatment. No one ever does. It's a tragic thing to abuse helpless children, who don't understand why they are unwanted, and consequently carry more than physical scars for the rest of their lives.

I have seen children battered, bruised, and barely hanging onto life in the United States, Canada, and just about every country I've visited throughout my years. I have seen fear and hopelessness in the eyes of thousands of children, when I visited children's homes and hospitals. It is a sad thing to see a child literally starving for love.

In Vietnam, with my son and his wife, we visited many makeshift hospitals. Jimmie prayed for the sick and the wounded, and he had special prayers for the helpless little children. I saw kids only three or four years old who had been hit with shrapnel or wounded from shell fire or hand grenades, with their little arms outstretched from their body and strapped to boards so they couldn't move them.

These were terrible sights in Vietnam, but I don't think any child abuse ever touched me more than the murder of little Melisha Gibson in Cleveland, Tennessee, in 1976.

When I read about this case in the newspapers, I couldn't sleep for days. Melisha was a pretty little girl, five years old, who was brutally beaten by a cruel stepfather. He made Melisha take her clothes off and walk through the house continually, for almost three days and three nights. Each time she stopped walking, he repeatedly lashed her with his belt and buckle. All of this took place with the mother watching television part of the time, and apparently she did nothing to stop this cruel brutality. Melisha's whole body was covered with raw stripes from the continuous beatings, and she was refused food. When she begged for water, the stepfather gave her hot sauce to drink, and she was forced to take cold showers. When she finally collapsed, she was made to lie on a urine-soaked mattress on the dirty floor. After three days of constant torture, death relieved little Melisha from this terrible pain. She had made the supreme sacrifice.

It was alleged that this situation was a bad case of neglect by the Human Services Department and that the department had been warned that not only this child's life was in danger, but there were twenty-six other children in the same town who had been subject to abuse. I was told this by a doctor in the vicinity at the time. It was evident that more and better services were needed to deal with these situations. Not enough was being done for neglected and abused children throughout the United States.

Immediately upon reading about this case in the newspaper, I called the sheriff's department in Cleveland, Tennessee, and talked to Detective Sergeant Robert Lawson, who had investigated the case. I asked if there was anything I could do to help raise money for additional services in this East Tennessee town. He replied, "Hank, this town would welcome a benefit show if you can get a country music show together. Perhaps it can raise enough money to add to the small shelter we already have here to protect the children while the courts decide what to do." He explained that the present facilities were not big enough to accommodate the problems they were having.

I immediately got in touch with some of our fine artists at the Grand Ole Opry and started organizing a show. Believe me, this was no problem. Our folks at the Opry are always ready to help the helpless, and so are most people in country music. I've always found it easy to get country artists to donate free time for charity benefits. The benefit program was advertised and promoted, and we had a packed house for the December, 1976, show, and we took in around seventeen thousand dollars that night.

This got the ball rolling, and I became convinced that I should take the leadership in doing more for helpless children. The Associated Press and others from the news media were present for the special concert. Americans throughout the country read about our efforts and about my ideas for dealing with this increasing problem.

I received telephone calls and letters from just about everywhere, but the one telegram that meant the most to me was from Dr. Henry Kempe. Years earlier he had organized and founded the big child-abuse facility in Denver, Colorado. He was a top pediatrician and so was his wife. It was a training center for people to learn how to deal with situations when children were abused or suspected of being abused. Dr. Kempe congratulated me in his telegram on what I was trying to do, and he encouraged me not to stop. "Press on," he said, "and I'll give you whatever support I can. We need hundreds of centers in this country. This problem is an epidemic."

The more I read and talked to people, the more I was convinced that much more had to be done. I didn't want to walk away from this problem. Therefore, soon after the Cleveland show, I began to establish the Hank Snow Foundation for the Prevention of Child Abuse and

Neglect, International. That was the official name. But the important thing was the fact that we stirred up a lot of interest that led to some concrete results.

This became my number-one project. I wanted to have the center in Nashville and to provide care for abused children. I also wanted to have a training program in which counselors could work with parents as they were doing in Denver. To raise money I organized a gala country show once each year in August. We used the Grand Ole Opry house, and it was jam-packed to capacity every time. I asked the most popular stars each year to join us for the show, and they did, gladly. We had more volunteers than we could use, and we raised thousands of dollars each year.

In addition to these shows I gathered a cross-section of folks in the city of Nashville, business people, music people, people from all walks of life. Different businesses were represented on our board of directors. We rented a building, hired an executive director, and we were in business. Our foundation started a parenting program, teaching parents how to deal with their children. We had programs for unwed and teenaged mothers. We had a program where our workers would go into the prisons and teach inmates how to relate to and deal with their families and their children after they were released from prison. It was a people-oriented operation with some solid results.

However, we found it extremely difficult to raise sufficient money to operate a foundation. It was costing thousands of dollars each month. It got to the point where our overhead was between eight and ten thousand dollars per month, and we might only be taking in around seven hundred to a thousand dollars. We struggled along and tried to make ends meet, but it was impossible to keep operating and go further in the red every month. We had the annual Opry show for seven years, and occasionally I put on a benefit show outside of Nashville. We received sizable donations from the National Life and Accident Insurance Company. Also, we received money from other businesses and some from private donors. So we kept our heads above water for a few years.

My dream was to construct a huge complex of buildings where we could have recreation, counseling, live-in nurses, and cooking and kitchen facilities where parents could come for help, on both a short-term basis and a long-term basis. This would allow us sufficient facilities, so that we could keep kids while the judge in a court case deliberated on whether they should be sent back to their parents or sent to a foster home. Our aim would be in most cases to work with the abusive parents and try to help them, so they would not resort to abuse. Education was the key objective.

So much was needed and so little money to do it with. I had this all planned out in my mind, and it was going to be called the Hank Snow Rescue Mission. After I started looking into the cost, however, I discovered it would cost more than a million dollars to build and perhaps a half million dollars each year to operate it.

Then one day an executive from the Nashville branch of the Exchange Clubs of America came to talk to me about the foundation. He said he knew we were having financial troubles, and he wondered if I were interested in the Exchange Clubs of Middle Tennessee taking over the foundation. I knew the Exchange Clubs of America was a fine and reputable organization, and I was seriously interested. He said, "Hank, you would stay on as a member of the board of directors. You have been making a difference, and you have raised the nation's conscience about child abuse. People everywhere are being educated about child abuse. Hot lines have been established, and this problem is not being swept under the rug. We must maintain this momentum. It would be a shame if you had to close your doors."

I agreed, and we made plans to turn over the assets and established programs to the Exchange Clubs of Middle Tennessee. I would continue my support with the new organization, and I'd try to channel future donations to the Exchange Club. Also, I was told there were nine hundred people at three of the chapters in Middle Tennessee who would be active in trying to raise money for the programs. Pooling our resources made a lot of sense to me.

After seven years, instead of the Hank Snow Foundation, it is the Exchange Club Foundation for the Prevention of Child Abuse and Neglect. This organization has done an outstanding job, and I will continue to work on behalf of little children.

Min and I have become strongly involved with the Christian Children's Fund. I'm sure you've seen actress Sally Struthers on TV and in some of the national magazines talking about this program. Sally is the national celebrity spokesperson of the Christian Children's Fund, and she works closely with the head office and on an international basis. It is a reputable organization, and the cost of helping a child is only a few cents a day. We know our money goes to help feed, clothe, and give medical care to the children we have selected to help. One of the most satisfying aspects of this program is the personal contact we get by exchanging letters.

Min and I are sponsoring ten children, and nothing I've done in my life gives me more pleasure and more satisfaction. Here are the names and countries of our present adopted children: Gualter Rodriguez, from Guatemala; Mangeni Humphreys, from Uganda; Pathloth Lakshmiah, from India; Rajdaporn Kamguan, from Thailand; Maria Glauciane dos S Araujo, from Brazil; Maria Cuevas, from Mexico; Anusha Samaranayake and Upul Priyankara, from Sri Lanka; Bethelhem Lema, from Ethiopia; and Jhony Delada, from the Philippines. We have a file on each child and a picture of each one. They write a few words in their language, and then the person in charge of that certain complex translates it into English and types it on the bottom of their letter. Min and I write letters to them frequently. We also send them pictures of our kitties and of ourselves, and we send them money at Christmas time.

There are sponsors of the Christian Children's Fund from television and movies, such as Edward C. Newman, Sarah Purcell, Carol Lawrence, Paul Newman, and Gary Collins, among others. You may have seen some of these folks on television when they were visiting these starving children in foreign countries. You can join these caring people, so please do me a great favor. I urge you to contact the Christian Children's Fund. You will bless a child's life as well as your own.

36

Hard Traveling

I've been everywhere, man,
I've been everywhere, man,
'Cross the deserts bare, man,
I've breathed the mountain air, man,
Of travel I've had my share, man,
I've been everywhere.

"I've Been Everywhere,"
by Geoff Mack

SINCE COMING TO THE UNITED STATES, I've had several managers, including Norm Riley, Dub Albritten, Hubert Long, Lucky Moeller, and Billy Deaton. They sure sent me all over the world, and they all did a fine job.

Throughout the years people have said to me, "Boy, you all have it made, don't you? You go out on the road. You see beautiful scenery. You eat in fabulous restaurants. Then you go on stage, do an hour show, and make a fortune."

Folks, that is completely wrong! Hard traveling. That's what it is. People don't understand what entertainers have to go through while traveling on the road. I'll tell you some of the negatives.

Most performers didn't use buses until around the mid-1960s, and for me it was even later than that. Before buses, we rode in cars, and this didn't make for the most comfortable travel. I've mentioned my big Cadillac limousine in many of my stories during the 1950s and into the 1960s. It had a big rack with a tarpaulin on the top to carry our instruments and luggage. This car had jump seats. Those were seats between the front seat and the back seat that folded up behind the front seats during the daytime, so the boys in the back would not be so crowded and could stretch their legs out. At night we'd pull the jump seats back, and me being so short, I would use the jump seats for my bed.

We always had six people in the car, three in the front and three in the back, and often we'd drive a thousand miles without going to bed. Most of the time it would be anywhere from five to eight hundred miles from one show date to another. Some tours were between twenty and forty days straight, and often we would play every night, unless of course it was too far to make it driving overnight and the next day in time for the show. We've traveled up to twenty-six hundred miles without a single night's sleep in a bed. One time we drove non-stop from Nashville to Red Deer, Alberta, Canada, and arrived just in time to play our two shows. When I say non-stop, I mean the only time we stopped was to get something to eat or to refuel.

In hot weather we had to keep the windows closed because of the air conditioner. If it was cold, we had to keep the windows closed to keep the heat in and not freeze to death. In the winter months like December, January, and February, oddly enough, we would be booked somewhere in Western Canada, like Edmonton, Calgary, Winnipeg, and other places where I've seen temperatures reach thirty-seven below zero.

Can you imagine sitting straight up, three in a seat, for three days and three nights, breathing that same stale air? It was a very unhealthy condition. And when we got to our destination, we would be so tired we could hardly hold on to our instruments during the show. But we always kept that smile going. People didn't pay to see a bunch of haggard-looking entertainers with no smiles. We always put on a false front under these circumstances, which were often, I can tell you. Audiences don't like excuses, and we never gave them. I've gone on the stage many times when I've been sick with a cold and sometimes a high fever, and I always tried to do my very best.

Many times we would have to pack up right after the night's show and maybe drive another five hundred miles to be ready for the next day's show. We ate all kinds of food from some of the worst greasy spoons you could possibly imagine—truck stops, hamburger joints, bars—anywhere we could grab a quick bite to eat. Sometimes we couldn't even find places open after our shows to get food, especially in some of the small towns. Eating different kinds of food and hurrying our food down so we could make our shows on time was enough to tear one's stomach inside out. We were never without indigestion, gas, or heartburn. Losing sleep and the hectic pace made us feel dragged out most of the time.

I have over fifty-five years of driving on all kinds of roads, with the dangers of traveling on ice and snow and passing thousands of cars within inches. Sometimes mechanical problems would cause us to spend hour after hour waiting around until the car could be repaired. Sometimes we had to check into a motel or hotel and wait until a certain car part was flown in before the job could be completed. We've been in such cold weather that the car's gasoline lines froze up, and I've seen feet and ears so frozen they turned as white as chalk.

One time we were driving over the Colorado mountains, through a blinding snowstorm, and we could barely see the front of our car. The snow was falling so fast there wasn't a track to follow, and we couldn't tell if we were on the road or on the shoulder of the road. The guardrails on the side would not even hold a small car, and if we had slid and dropped off the edge of the mountain, we would have dropped a thousand or more feet straight down.

When I was towing Shawnee to our shows in a trailer, at the top of huge Percy Mountain in Canada one day the trailer broke loose from the car, and it could have dropped over a thousand feet straight down to the water. I stopped the car immediately and jumped out and was able to steer the front of the trailer in the opposite direction. It dug into the gravel road, and luckily it stopped.

Another time we were in a tornado alley somewhere between Wichita, Kansas, and Kansas City. The radio station said there were fourteen tornados all around us. The wind was blowing so fierce it was tearing down electrical power lines, and we could see the sparks flying all over the place as the wires made contact with each other. It even got worse. We turned our car around as fast as we could and went back to the town we'd just come through and parked behind a service station. The gale was so strong it could have turned our car over.

A million bad, inconvenient, and upsetting things that you have no control over can happen on the road, and they did. Like Murphy's Law, "If anything can go wrong, it will." When I think of these conditions, I'm amazed that we survived. I'm sure the Good Lord was looking out for us.

However, traveling did get easier when I acquired my first bus in the middle 1960s. It was made by the Flexible people in Ohio, and it had many modern conveniences. On it we had comfortable bunk beds to sleep in. We had hot and cold running water. We also had excellent air-conditioning. We had a refrigerator with AC and DC current to keep cold drinks and all kinds of food, and we could eat anytime we wanted to. When we got tired of sitting, we could get up and walk around. We had color television and the top brand of stereo equipment to play tapes, and we could listen to the radio. We had a mobile telephone so we could call anywhere while we were on the road, and we had a telephone intercom system within the bus.

My bus had a sophisticated burglar alarm, and no one could get in without setting it off. Doors, windows, every part of the bus was protected all the time. We had two lavatories, with hot and cold running water, one in the front of the bus for my boys, and another in the rear next to my office for myself. Thank God for buses.

After a while I decided I wanted a larger bus, so I bought the big Silver Eagle. The Silver Eagle is an eighteen-ton bus, like the ones that Trailways or Greyhound uses, and most have automatic transmissions. We had the same conveniences as on my first bus. This is the most popular size, and many of the artists use this kind today. Usually these luxury buses are remodeled to fit the specific needs of the show people. Many of these show buses look like hotels inside. I know just about all the entertainers would much rather travel to their shows by bus than fly. When it comes to flying, it seems like there's no courtesy left whatsoever. It's push and shove and everyone for himself.

Many entertainers have their own bus driver, someone who does all the driving and takes care of the maintenance of the bus, helps load and unload, and usually operates the sound system. In my case two of my boys did the driving. Usually each would drive about six hours, then stop and have the other take over. The one who completed his driving would go to bed. This way we always had a fresh, rested driver. However, if the driver started to get sleepy, even after three hours, it was our policy to pull the bus over and everyone would go to bed.

My room or office in the back of the bus was fixed up more like a bedroom, sitting room, and office all in one, with a wall intercom phone to talk to the driver whenever I wanted to. If we carried a girl singer, we had a special room that she would fix up to suit herself, and it always looked like a doll house.

Instruments, luggage, and any large items would go under the bus in what are known as bins, which had huge doors that lifted up and remained stationary while we loaded and unloaded the bus. Up overhead in the front part of the bus were small lockers with the names of the band members on them. We had three clothes closets, one for the boys, one in my quarters, and the girl singer had one in her room.

An AC generator of 10,000 watts took care of all the electrical gadgets, electric razors, television, coffeepots, sound equipment, reel-to-reel tape decks, cassette players, and so on. This generator could also operate the air-conditioning in case the regular bus system went out. I also had an extra diesel fuel tank installed, and this, along with our other two tanks, held about three hundred gallons of fuel. This would permit us to go about a thousand miles without refueling. Our water supply came from a large tank that held a hundred gallons. Our toilets were always kept sanitary by using the proper recommended chemicals.

The average air to handle the braking system on a bus is around one hundred twenty pounds, but anything over ninety pounds is okay. Our bus, like most buses, has automatic devices in case the air should go below sixty pounds so that the bus will automatically come to a very slow stop. This is an important safety feature.

I don't have any trouble with my boys taking any kind of alcohol or any kind of narcotics, and when I lie down to go to sleep at night, I know I have two good drivers who will take turns at the wheel.

But there are always dangers on the road. One time in Colorado we were going up this four-mile mountain in the snow, and the roads under this newly fallen snow were very slick, as there was ice under the snow all the way up the mountain. Dozens of cars ahead of us were sliding all over the road. My boys are good drivers in the snow or on ice, but some people who drive cars are not. This was scary, not to be able to control the situation. As soon as we got over the crest of the mountain, we saw a car that had slid to the edge, and there was about a fifteen-hundred-foot drop straight down. The car was resting on its undergear with the front end out over the edge of the mountain and the rear of the car back on the edge of the cliff. The car was slowly teetering back and forth. The driver had managed to get over the seat and into the back, and how he ever managed to get out of that car is a miracle. This is just one of many possible tragedies I've seen in my travels.

We always had a fear of the big semirigs coming toward us. They could jackknife, turn over on us, or even hit us head on. Friends, have you ever given a thought to the hundreds of thousands of cars and trucks that are on the road every day and every night? Many pass by within inches of you. It's frightening. We all should always drive as carefully as we can. At all times be completely alert, watch out for the other guy, and do not drink and drive or drive when you are the least bit sleepy or tired.

Throughout my career I've done a lot of flying, too. There was no way I could travel across the country and halfway around the world and avoid flying, so I accepted that fact many years ago. Nevertheless, I've had some pretty narrow escapes in airplanes, too. One was with Cowboy Copas. He and I had played a show in a small town in Iowa, and the next night we were to play another show for Smokey Smith at the KRNT Theater in Des Moines, Iowa. Copas and I were sitting in this tiny airport waiting room, watching our watches and listening for them to call our flight. After a while we began to get concerned, because we were afraid we would miss our show. So Copas went up to the desk and asked the person at the counter what was holding our plane up. Was it grounded somewhere? The answer was, "Your flight left thirty minutes ago." Copas hit the ceiling as only Copas could do, and we both swore that they did not call our flight. He was fuming when he told the airline agent, "We are going to hold you responsible if we don't make our date tonight. You'd better hope we don't miss our show."

We did find a way, however. We hired this pilot and his little puddle-jumper airplane, but the ride was far from relaxing. When we were about fifty miles from Des Moines, our plane was flying so low we were just barely missing the treetops. The pilot was looking around. He didn't know where the damn airport was! He didn't even have a map, and it was dusk. We were afraid to ask any questions, afraid that the answer would have been too alarming. It's a good thing we had been nipping on a bottle of whiskey, or we would have been shook up a lot more. However, we made a safe landing at the airport and took a taxi to the auditorium and arrived just barely in time to change clothes in the dressing room and get ready to start the show at 8:00 P.M. We had no time to wash or shave.

I was never too scared to fly, but I always felt somewhat uncomfortable in planes, especially in small aircraft. Besides the Des Moines incident, I had a couple of narrow escapes, one in a chartered small aircraft, and one in a commercial plane.

One time I was booked to play a fair somewhere in Pennsylvania on a July Fourth weekend. I had my plane reservation to Harrisburg, Pennsylvania, the closest airport to my show location. The boys were to meet me there. Then we'd drive to the fair, which was another hundred fifty miles or so, and we would still have lots of time to make our shows. I waited for the Nashville ticket-counter person to call the flight, which should have left forty-five minutes earlier. Then came the news over the loudspeakers that the flight would be delayed for an indefinite length of time. I went immediately to the ticket counter and asked how long they thought this delay would be, but they didn't know any more about this than I did. They said it could be an hour or so, or it could be grounded completely.

Since I was under contract to appear and my boys would be waiting at the airport, I had no other alternative except to hire a private plane. But after the Des Moines scare, I was leery of small planes.

Whenever I hired a one-engine plane, I always called on Henry Cannon, to see if he was available to take me. He was a very careful pilot. I called his office, and the person who answered the telephone said, "Henry is in bed with the flu, but I have a gentleman here who is a good flyer. He can fly Henry's plane and take you to your show and bring you back." That was a lucky break for me, because I always felt extremely strongly about meeting my obligations. I expected the managers and promoters of the shows to uphold their contract, and certainly I wanted to do the same.

It was a beautiful Sunday morning when we left Nashville. There was not a cloud in the sky. But when we got over the West Virginia mountains we ran into a dense fog. I began to feel uneasy because we couldn't see much further than the nose of the small aircraft. I kept my eyes on the control panel and specifically on three important instruments: the compass, the gas gauge, and the altimeter, which shows the altitude. The pilot got real quiet, and this bothered me because we were constantly in conversation up to that point. I got up the nerve to ask if he knew our location and was everything okay with the exception of the fog. He answered, "I think we're on course, and we should run out of the fog soon. Just hang in there with me."

Well, I didn't have any other choice! I did know there were mountains as high as six thousand feet or higher in parts of West Virginia, and I noticed we were flying much lower than that. But if the pilot was correct on his navigation and flight plan, there should be no worry. I tried to convince myself of that. But actually I thought we were going in circles. About the time I noticed our gas gauge was showing very low, the pilot said, "I'm going to shift over to our reserve tank now." That was all he said.

We flew around until the gauge on the reserve tank showed low, and then I was really worried. I was sitting up straight in my seat, and I began to sweat. I knew the pilot was confused, but I'll say this, he held his composure and tried not to let me become aware of how serious our problem was. But being on our reserve gas tank and still lost, I became scared to the point I was saying silent prayers.

About that time the clouds opened up, and there as big as life was the Charleston, West Virginia, airport—directly below us. Thank God! But then, all of a sudden, a severe thunderstorm hit that area with high winds and big hailstones, and I expected hailstones to come through the windshield of the plane. The pilot tried to contact the tower to request landing space, but his radio was knocked out by the storm. The small plane began to tremble from the high winds, and I thought we were gone. However, the crew at the tower was well aware of what was taking place, and they gave us the green flashing beacon to land.

When we walked into the airport, I was still shaking. The storm didn't last long, and I was surprised at what the pilot said to me. "I can still get you to the fair in time for your performance. The storm has passed over, and I'm sure I can get clearance now to take off." "No sir," I replied, "under no circumstances. No way will you get me off the ground tonight. Definitely not. I'm getting me a room for the night, but thanks anyway."

That was another one of God's miracles, and I thank Him for always being there for me in those dangerous times.

My contract read that I was to be paid a flat guarantee against 60 percent of the gross at the grandstand show, so I lost quite a bit of money. I called Harry Cook, the gentleman who had booked me for the fair, and he said it was a beautiful evening there, with not a cloud in the sky. But that was about the only place in six surrounding states that didn't have bad weather, according to the airport personnel. Mr. Cook understood my problem, and except for losing the money, everything was okay. But the episode was not over yet.

The next morning was beautiful. The skies were clear, and we left for Nashville. Can you believe this? Somewhere over East Tennessee, we were again plagued with dense fog and we were flying blind. It was as bad as it was over West Virginia. All aviation maps were clearly marked that any aircraft should never fly over Oak Ridge, Tennessee. This was where the atomic energy plant was located, and any plane entering that area was in great danger of being shot down. Planes avoided flying over this air space at all cost. Suddenly the fog lifted, and do you know where we were? Yes, right over Oak Ridge! I was holding onto my bottom, as I fully expected a bullet to come through the underside of the plane at any minute. Thank God we got out of there in a hurry, and we made it back to Nashville in one piece.

Another scare I got was on an American Airlines plane. We were returning from New York City when a problem occurred over Cincinnati, Ohio. Over the intercom the captain called one of the stewardesses to come to the cockpit. After several minutes she came back and made an announcement. "Ladies and gentlemen, there is no cause for alarm (hell, that would scare one to death to begin with), but the captain said there is a little problem. The landing-gear green light won't come on (little problem!). This means that our landing gear won't come down, or the light is not functioning properly. It probably has a malfunction, but we have to prepare you for a crash landing."

Everybody was deathly quiet as the stewardess showed the passengers how to prepare for such a landing. We went through the routine of putting our heads down between our knees, with a pillow on our lap, and all the rest of it. Then she said she needed two volunteers to help us know how to disembark after a crash landing, should this happen. I always made it a habit of trying to get a seat in the rear of the aircraft, as you never hear of a plane backing into a mountain. But being seated in the rear of the plane and close to the passenger door, I was called upon to be a volunteer, along with a gentleman who was sitting across the aisle from me in a rear seat.

The stewardess continued, "We are now going to demonstrate how to slide down this fireproof chute, in case the plane should catch on fire, should we crash. If this happens and the plane lands on its nose, it could be a long jump to the pavement, and you could break your legs or arms. The purpose of the chute is to permit you to slide to safety with ease. However, we don't anticipate any such landing." The other guy and I were supposed to help the passengers into the chute to slide to safety. I tried not to show how frightened I was, but I was scared to death, and the other guy looked pretty upset, too. I knew we'd be the last ones to leave the aircraft, and I was mentally preparing myself for the crash with silent prayer.

We circled the tower at the airport several times, and the flight controller radioed to the pilot that the landing gear was down. Then the stewardess made the report that we could all relax because the problem was just a malfunction in the green light.

I again thanked the Lord for His guiding hand, but I didn't relax until we were safely on the runway and heard the familiar words I was praying to hear, "Thank you for flying American Airlines."

37

RCA Victor

Old Father Time has seen a million, million hearts
Break with pain down the highway of years.
I never dreamed that the love I thought was true
Would deceive and just leave me these tears.

"The Only Rose," by Hank Snow

I HAVE OFTEN BEEN ASKED ABOUT how many singles and albums I've had released by RCA Victor Records. The number of albums is around one hundred forty. A few of these were EP (extended-play) albums and had either two or four songs on each side. Most of the albums were the regular kind, with six songs on each side during the 1950s. Later, when the record companies got more money-greedy, they began to put only ten songs on an album. My best estimate of single releases is about 675 songs in the U.S.A., plus the seventy-five Bluebird 78 rpm records released in Canada before I came to the States. Altogether, I probably recorded a few more than a thousand different songs.

In 1974, when my attorney and I were negotiating a new contract with the executives of RCA Victor, one of the reporters asked how many records I had sold up to that time. According to RCA, I had sold something in the vicinity of eighty-six million records from 1936 to 1974. I don't know the number of records I've sold since 1974, but I would estimate it to be several million.

I wrote and recorded several songs that became hits, including "I'm Movin' On," "The Rhumba Boogie," "The Golden Rocket," "Music-Makin' Mama from Memphis," "I Cried but My Tears Were Too Late," "My Filipino Rose," "Little Buddy," "Brand on My Heart," "Just a Faded Petal from a Beautiful Bouquet," "Bluebird Island," "My Mother," "I'm Gonna Bid My Blues Good-bye," and several more.

After I came to the United States, Hill and Range published all of the songs that I wrote. The owners, Julian and Jean Aberbach, sent me many songs from other writers throughout the years that became hits for me, including "With This Ring, I Thee Wed," "Let Me Go, Lover," "In the Misty Moonlight," "I Care No More," "I've Been Everywhere," "Ninety Miles an Hour Down a Deadend Street," "I Stepped over the Line," "The Gold Rush Is Over," "The Next Voice You Hear," "These Hands," "Down the Trail of Aching Hearts," "Yellow Roses," and many more.

Hill and Range was sold to Chappell Music, which later became Warner-Chappell Music, and I'm still associated with them. They are running my two music companies, Hank's Music and Hank Snow Music.

Julian and Jean Aberbach helped to make it all happen because they were not afraid to take a risk. In the years ahead, I would pay them back a hundred fold. They gambled $1,000, and I'm sure one of my songs alone—"I'm Movin' On"—made them a bundle, because it made me some mighty good money. I'm told it still holds the international record as being the all-time most-played country record by the disc jockeys. Like the late Hank Williams used to say, "It bought me a lot of biscuits." People are still buying my first songbook, which was released by the Gordon V. Thompson music-publishing company in Toronto, Canada, in 1938, and my other songbooks continue to sell. I had three songbooks released by Canadian Music Sales in Toronto. These were later transferred to Hill and Range Songs in New York, who took over international publishing. In later years Hill and Range also published four or five other books of material I had recorded.

Julian and Jean Aberbach also put me in touch with some of the top songwriters in the nation, such as Jennie Lou Carson, Cindy Walker, Jack Rollins, Don Robertson, Vaughn Horton, and Vic McAlpine. Others who wrote me some hit songs were Boudleaux and Felice Bryant, Fred Rose, Jean Chapel, Wayne Walker, and Cliffie Stone.

A big thrill for me was to do two instrumental guitar albums with Chet Atkins, *Reminiscing* and *By Special Request.* As you know, he is one of the world's greatest guitar players. We had a lot of fun recording together, and I was thrilled that Chet liked my guitar work. He thought I had a unique style of playing, and that my touch on the guitar was very sweet and what he called "tasty."

Having one hit record after another never brought any conceit with it. That was God's work, and I've always given many people credit in playing a big part in my musical success. Countless people have said, and many of them from the Opry, "Hank, one thing about you, you never did let success go to your head. It's never changed you. You're the same every-day guy you've always been, and people appreciate that."

I mentioned earlier what a great man Hugh Joseph was. He produced my first record in Montreal for RCA Victor on the Canadian Bluebird label in October of 1936. Under his guidance during the next twelve years I recorded about one hundred fifty songs, which I had written.

After I came to the United States, Steve Sholes took over the reins of producing me. He would travel to Nashville periodically to record the various RCA artists. In 1950 he came here to produce my first Nashville session. For the next several years Steve was the gentleman who guided my career, and we had a long stream of hit songs during the 1950s.

In 1956 Steve Sholes and the top executives at RCA Victor arranged to have Min, Jimmie, and me fly to New York for a special dinner to honor me for twenty faithful years with the company. It was attended by a host of important Victor people, plus Julian and Jean Aberbach, owners of Hill and Range Songs, who I was signed to as an exclusive writer. Several dignitaries from around the city attended and number one on my list was my sincere friend Jack Howard. I was presented with a bronze likeness of the Victor dog, Little Nipper, and he sits on my desk in my office as a treasured gift.

Unfortunately, toward the end of the 1950s, Steve met an untimely death. One afternoon I came in off the road, and Min told me the shocking news and the circumstances. Steve had a bad heart, and he always carried nitroglycerine pills with him. If he felt like his heart was acting up, he would place a pill under his tongue. Steve had flown to Nashville to conduct a recording session, and his friends on the plane with him said he seemed fine, because he was joking and laughing, and he hadn't mentioned the need to take any of his pills. At the airport Steve rented a car and was driving downtown, and as he crossed over the Cumberland River bridge, he had a serious heart attack. His car swerved from one side of the bridge to the other side, and he died instantly.

I had great respect for this wonderful man, and he was loved by everyone who knew him. I always appreciated the fact he worked so hard on my behalf throughout the years.

Chet Atkins had produced alongside Steve for several years, so it was natural that he would become the main producer for RCA Victor. Chet produced my records for the next eighteen years.

When Chet took over, I wasn't writing as many songs as in earlier years, so both he and I were constantly on the lookout for potential hits. If he had material sent to him that he thought would be good for me, he'd save it, and I would listen and consider songs sent to me from Hill and Range and other publishers and writers. Before any sessions, Chet and I would get together at the RCA Victor office, and we would carefully listen to all the material. From these we would pick out the songs we thought warranted recording. We both had good ideas, and we were always willing to try each other's suggestions. If they worked, fine, and if not, we threw the ideas out. We thought that pooling our ideas made for better selections. It did work, because we had a whole lot of hits during the 1960s and 1970s.

After the songs were selected, I would rehearse them in my home studio, and I'd have the arrangements worked out and ready to record before going into RCA's studio. This cut down on expensive studio time and overtime for the musicians. My agreement with RCA was for me to pay the studio musicians, and RCA took care of the other expenses.

I was fortunate to have had three top-notch gentlemen to work with who were professional in every way. Mr. Joseph taught me a lesson that I would never forget, and it served me well over the rest of my recording career. He said to always be prepared before going into the studio to record. I learned that lesson well, and after that first session, I always was ready. I appreciated what Chet once said about me: "We wish everybody in the business was as well prepared as Hank Snow is when he comes into the studio. He knows exactly what he's going to do, and he has a rough idea of the arrangement he wants. He has everything timed to the second, and this saves a lot of wasted time. With the cost of overtime in the studio, it really pays off." Chet added, "I've seen Hank come into the studio and do a complete album in less than five hours. No other artist has ever done this that I know of, and he does them well. He's a real professional."

During the mid-1970s and into the 1980s, country music became more pop oriented, and I became frustrated. Chet was my producer at that time, and he always did a great job. However, as country music changed, he wanted me to change and be more contemporary. And since some of my records toward the end of the 1970s were not setting any woods afire, Chet felt that to be fair to the company he had to follow the trend and go more into the pop-oriented songs, with arrangements aimed toward the younger generation. I certainly didn't blame him for that, but I told him if I couldn't continue recording in the same way that had made me successful, I didn't have the heart to record anymore. If some of the artists wanted to sing pop, with all the musical gimmicks, that was perfectly okay with me. But I was a country singer, and as long as I was appearing before the faithful public who had stood by me all these years, I was going to keep it that way. And I have.

When country changed, naturally Chet had to select songs and produce records in the way he thought would get an artist a hit. Of course, he was always under pressure from RCA to produce hits, as were other producers at other companies. Companies had to have hit records in order to make money. However, all this put Chet in a bind with artists like me, who were strong willed and determined as to what material they would agree to record.

Sometimes Chet would say, "Hank, with the proper arrangement, I believe we can take this song to the number-one spot. This is the type that the younger generation will like." I would take the song home and work on it, maybe arrange it differently, or change the beat, but it didn't matter, I couldn't let myself like the song. When it came time to record, I'd say, "Chet, truthfully speaking, I do not like the song. I cannot feel it, and I cannot sing it."

In all of my years of recording, I've never recorded a song that I didn't like, but Chet was trying to do his level best, because he had to keep the new generation of record buyers in mind at all times. He knew it was the young people who were buying most of the records. Nevertheless, I believe that the older, dyed-in-the-wool country fans didn't buy records partly because they couldn't find the kinds of records they liked in the stores anymore. Tape decks and compact-disc players were being installed in the young kids' cars, and the record companies wanted to make sure the kids had plenty of loud, fast-tempo music to play continuously.

If I had tried to change my style, changed musicians, added a lot of gimmicks, and mixed the music so loud that people couldn't hear my lyrics, maybe I could have continued the hit records. I don't know. I do know, in some cases, I would have preferred not to have had violin sections, or background voices, or some of the gimmicks, but we did use these on some of my records anyway. And I do concede that some of this, especially the voices on a few of the recordings, was quite effective.

However, I've always believed that the power of simplicity should not be distorted. My first recording of "I'm Movin' On" was a simple production, but it had a driving force in which the music created a train effect, and it was done with a minimum of music. Moreover, it was recorded on a one-track machine! Most artists today record on a twenty-four-track machine, but a few country artists still use simple arrangements to create beautiful feelings in their songs, and their sales have done extremely well.

After eighteen years, Chet and I decided to dissolve our recording relationship, but it was mutual and a pleasant parting of the ways. I still count Chet a great friend of mine, and I believe the feeling is mutual.

About two years later, though, Chuck Glaser persuaded me to do more recording. Chuck wanted to produce songs without me making any radical changes from what I'd been used to doing. I agreed to give it a try. As the saying goes, "It is better to have tried and failed than not to have tried at all." Chuck did a fine job producing both albums, *Still Movin' On* and *The Mysterious Lady*. Both were released by RCA, but they didn't sell like we expected. We had good songs and they had a different beat, but the feeling just wasn't there like the old-style Hank Snow records. My style of music, unfortunately, was being less and less played by radio stations across the United States and Canada.

But I'm glad to say that in recent years traditional country music is having a rebirth. Some of the newer artists have discovered what has made country music great and meaningful to the listeners over the years. A little later I'll talk more about these changes.

I've been asked many questions over the years about my association with RCA Victor. (Later the company was called just RCA Records, and now it's RCA/BMG.) I was assigned to them from 1936 until 1981, and I'm glad to say that RCA is the only company I've been associated with. After much research by RCA it was found that I hold the longest-running contract by any artist on any label. In other words, no one has ever had a contract with the same label exclusively for forty-five years. I'm proud of that record. My relationship with this company was cordial and cooperative during most of this long period. On the other hand, I was loyal to them, and I worked hard through the years to be completely professional and to record the best music I possibly could.

But in 1981 the big brass at RCA in Nashville decided to clean house and let many of its artists go, many of whom had been faithful to the company for many years. I won't mention his name, but the big wheel at RCA had a serious ego problem. The little guy was going to make country music what he thought it should be. Yes, he wanted to remake the company and make a big name for himself, so he dropped some of the biggest names from the label. He started with people like Porter Wagoner and with Jim Ed Brown, who had much success back when he was part of the Three Browns—Maxine, Bonnie, and Jim Ed.

They sold millions of records and were outstanding artists. Jim Ed and Porter are still great to this day and are both part of the world-famous Grand Ole Opry. Others who were dropped included Helen Cornelius, Dave and Sugar, and several more. But I couldn't believe my ears when I heard that Chet Atkins was no longer with the company. After all the great things that he did for RCA in producing records, which made the company millions of dollars, not to mention recording and selling his own records—this blew my mind.

As this housecleaning was going on, friends would call me and say, "Are you still with RCA?" I answered that I assumed I was because I hadn't received word about being dropped. I had signed a new contract with RCA a couple of years prior to that, for a period of ten years with five two-year options. Anytime you have a contract with options, you can rest assured that you only have a contract as good as the first option period. So after the first two years RCA had the option to keep my contract in force or to drop me from the label. But the contract also stated that if RCA didn't intend to pick up my option, I would be notified thirty days prior to its termination. I hadn't given my own situation much thought, because the company hadn't sent me a notice that they were dropping me.

My big dream, after forty-five years of hard work with the label, was to see if the Good Lord was willing to let me make a half century with them. Maybe He was, but the big shot at RCA wasn't. This character had other plans.

It just so happened that my attorney was in a meeting in Atlanta when some of the RCA people were there, and he heard a rumor circulating that I, too, was being dropped by the company. When my attorney heard this, he immediately asked, "Has Hank been notifed by letter? If he has, he never mentioned anything to me about it." He told the executives in the meeting that if they were dropping me, it would be common courtesy to notify me of their intentions. The letter I received three weeks later from Jerry Bradley gave me no reason for my release.

When I was released, I was still making money for the company. My royalty checks were sufficient to cover my advanced royalties, which I received each year. If my royalties were under the guarantee, the balance would be deducted from royalties in the future. My annual royalties are substantial, and even at this writing, they still would have covered my guarantees. So RCA had nothing to lose but a lot to gain by keeping me on.

Anybody with the least bit of brains would know that Mr. Ego's action was foolish from a business standpoint. In five years more, I would have completed fifty years of continuous service with RCA. In 1986 RCA could have produced a special album they could have advertised with some catchy title such as *Hank Snow's Half Century Album.* What a selling point that would have been, and they would have been able to promote such an album worldwide. That would have been prestigious, not only for me, but for the company, too.

It was obvious to me, in the first place, that Mr. Ego never liked me. In the second place and most important, it was obvious that he wanted to push everybody else out of the way and become the big cheese. Well, he did accomplish that, and I hope he's satisfied now, being the big cheese. What a way to have to accomplish something, by tramping over artists who had done so much and had been so loyal to the company for so many years.

But friends, I have the last laugh on RCA Records, and they will be paying me back royalties for several years. It happened like this. I had been advised by several artists in Nashville that it was good business to audit any record company every five years. But I had never placed an audit on RCA Records, which I have regretted many times. I trusted them. Who would have thought that the biggest and best-known recording company in the whole wide world would ever hold back money due their artists?

But I was encouraged to audit RCA by my good friend Marty Robbins, who had just recently audited his recording company. So in the late 1970s I hired two top law firms. The first was Barksdale, Whalley, Gilbert, and Frank. And Richard Frank of that firm lined up Prager and Fenton in New York City to conduct the audit. The results of the audit showed, according to Prager and Fenton, that RCA Records was in my debt for nearly half a million dollars. This audit took over a year and cost me around twenty-seven thousand dollars. We negotiated a complete settlement for a certain amount, and because of Uncle Sam, I made them stretch out the payments over fifteen years at the rate of 10 percent interest.

Because of the statute of limitations, my accountants could only go back five years. Therefore, this settlement did not cover my big hits of the 1950s, such as "I'm Movin' On," "Rhumba Boogie," "I Don't Hurt Anymore," "A Fool Such as I," and "Down the Trail of Aching Hearts." I had about forty songs in the top ten during this time, so how much do you think I lost during the 1950s? I estimate two million dollars.

I'm thankful that Hugh Joseph lived long enough for me to write him about how cheap my association with the company turned out. But I'm sorry that Steve Sholes didn't live long enough to hear about it, too. I will always believe the main reason I was dropped from the label was that I had RCA Records audited.

But as I look back now at my career with RCA, it has been fabulous. My wildest dreams have come true. I was one of the few country artists who recorded just about every kind of song. I recorded blues, ballads, cowboy songs, Hawaiian songs, love songs, story songs of everyday life, marriage and divorce songs, Latin American songs, religious songs, train songs, novelty songs, talking blues songs, and a lot of narrations. I recorded several instrumental singles and albums, and even two albums with "Mr. Guitar," Chet Atkins, plus a successful album with Anita Carter.

After dissolving my recording relationship with RCA, I had several calls from other studios to record, but most of them had no substance. When I went into the details of their offers, they turned out to be nothing I was interested in. Besides, I wasn't sure I wanted to record for any other company, because I still have strong positive feelings about my association with RCA Victor. I was respected by the people I met during the years with the company, so I don't want the image of that egotistical individual to change my feelings about the great people I was associated with during my long stay with the label.

I was discouraged from ever wanting to record again, but I kept hearing of Willie Nelson recording with so many artists. I decided to call him and mention doing an album with him. He was all for it, so my boys and I went to his home on the outskirts of Austin, Texas, and we cut an album together in September, 1984. I had planned on staying in Texas for three days. I thought it would take that long to record the ten-song album, but things went exceptionally well, and we finished early. We went into the studio around ten on a Monday night and were finished by four the next morning. We had a good time doing the songs, and I remembered just how much fun recording could be. Willie insisted we call the album *Brand on My Heart,* after the song I had written years ago. The album was released by Columbia Records in 1985.

RCA still releases my albums occasionally, mostly on CDs. The regular 33⅓ rpm albums and the old 45 rpm records are hard to find these days. Almost everything has gone to tapes and compact discs, but I will say that the sound of the old records put on compact discs is about as noise free as it can be. I'm amazed at the beautiful sound quality of the songs I recorded back in the 1950s, after they were put on compact discs.

Richard Weize, of Bear Family Records in Germany, has set out to release on compact discs everything I ever recorded, including transcriptions, army recruiting shows, and my early recordings that were never released. This pleases me to know there is still wide interest in my music.

38

Changes in Country Music

Well, look who's coming through the door,
I think we've met somewhere before.
Hello love, hello love.
Where in the world have you been so long?
I've missed you so since you've been gone.
Hello love, hello love.

"Hello, Love," by Betty Jean Robinson and Aileen Mnich

AFTER RCA AND I PARTED WAYS, I continued to make occasional personal appearances, but I've pretty much retired from the road after fifty-five years of hard traveling.

A lot of people have asked me why I don't appear more often on television. Well, I have appeared on many local and national television programs throughout the years, but I seldom accept an invitation to be on a TV show anymore. Frankly, I've never liked doing TV work. I was discouraged from going on television way back in the early 1960s.

Let me give you my reasons. On one of the network shows I sang my ballad "A Fool Such as I." The producer of the show thought it was too long and asked me to cut out the guitar break, which I play between verses on most of my songs. This guitar part ran exactly twenty seconds. Then a few minutes later in the show, they had some unfunny comedian come on the stage and do fifteen minutes of pure nothing.

On some television shows, not only would the officials cut out verses and the instrumental parts, they often wanted me to do something ridiculous. One producer wanted me to stand in one position and sing a verse, then walk up two flights of stairs and do another verse, plus have my band members scattered so damn far away I could barely hear them. To me this is nonsense for a country show. If the TV people would turn on a couple of cameras, leave the set, and go have coffee during the entire show, they would have a natural and excellent presentation from the artist, not some chopped-up program that makes no sense at all. It's always been important to me to perform my songs just as I recorded them. I don't like to break the routine of my song or have my band scattered around the stage.

But the most important reason is the time factor. For example, I was called to sing two songs on a television show. I arrived at 8:00 A.M. to accommodate the producer's schedule, and I didn't leave the studio until ten that night. That's fourteen hours to do two songs that I've been doing for many years. Does this make sense to you? I can use my precious time in a more creative way than that. To be perfectly honest, I've possibly turned down more offers to do guest spots on TV shows than any other artist in country music.

Friends, I'd like to tell you some of my philosophy about country music and the changes it has gone through in recent years. These are my opinions only, and I realize that other artists will have their different opinions, too.

Some of the artists these days are getting out-of-sight prices, like $25,000 or more a day. Some get 60 percent of the gross or a guarantee of $50,000, whichever is greater. They don't give proper consideration to the buyers of the programs, who have done so much for their music, and to the hundreds of thousands of dollars they have spent in hiring country talent and taking business risks. To some of our artists money means more than concern for their fans. But thank goodness most country artists are not that way. They are humble. Oh, there are a few dudes who make it big and won't talk to you. But most artists are true to their roots and true to their fans. On the other hand, country music fans are the most loyal of any type in the entertainment world. Usually there's a genuine closeness between the artists and their fans.

Even with unusually strong record sales, I've never let my prices to the buyers and promoters of the shows get out of line. They have big expenses and a lot to worry about, too, such as the artist getting stuck somewhere because of a transportation problem, or bad weather that would keep the fans home, or a dozen other things.

Sometimes you'll hear people refer to an artist as great, or the greatest, or legend, or superstar, or some other hyped-up term that's used entirely too much. This is misleading. The fact that an entertainer sells a lot of records does not make him or her a legend. Only history can tell us who the legends will be. Most of us are not concerned about a legendary status. We're hoping our luck lasts a little longer and our fans continue to buy our records and attend our concerts. Some of today's artists may be big in music now, but they will disappear from sight within a short time, and many others will stay in the limelight for many years to come.

The artists who add to the rich heritage of country music and are loyal to their fans are the ones I admire the most. There are a few who just want to make all the money they can and don't give a damn about keeping the country music tradition alive. I don't admire them.

Before I get off this kick, there's something very important I want to mention. Twenty-five years ago there were numerous people who turned up their noses at country music. They didn't want anybody to know they had a country record in their house. They were ashamed of our music. Some of those same people, I learned later, were on the board of directors of the Country Music Association. I could also mention a few artists in the pop field who felt the same way—until country music became so popular. Then they were quick to jump on the bandwagon and reap the income from country music, the number-one music of America today.

A few of these pop artists who are doing interviews across the country for the press, radio stations, and television can't tell you one thing about Hank Williams, Sr., Red Foley, Cowboy Copas, Ernest Tubb, or even myself. They know nothing about the history of country music, and some of them can't sing country music any more than I can sing like Caruso.

I have been real concerned in recent years that our people would lose a great part of our heritage if we permitted traditional country music to become a relic of the past. Our great fans over the years didn't leave us. We in country music left them.

I noticed a sudden change in country music around 1974, the same year I had a number-one hit across many parts of the world entitled "Hello, Love." Record companies began recording pop music, and they called it country. They felt the companies and the artists could make more money if they appealed to both the country and the pop audiences. I'm not criticizing the executives for trying an experiment to increase profits, but my beef is trying to pass pop music off as good country music.

Another influence was a popular 1980 movie, *Urban Cowboy,* which brought a lot of new people into the country music scene. Folks began to wear cowboy hats and boots and listen to country radio stations. But in order to keep this new audience, some in the industry tried to change the music to fit what they thought the audience wanted to hear, and the music became more pop oriented. Much of the music didn't have an honest, real-life feeling, and we lost many of these new listeners.

Also, around that time, X-rated movies and X-rated magazines became commonplace in this country, and I believe this encouraged some writers to write songs with suggestive lyrics that many of the old artists did not and would not sing. I strongly disapproved of these kinds of lyrics. If I were beginning to raise children and build a family, I wouldn't want them to listen to some of the trash that was being written. Those songwriters had a lot of nerve in writing filth! Fortunately, we had a few country artists who did not sell out to the big money. Some of the artists who stuck to clean lyrics included Willie Nelson, Randy Travis, George Strait, Rodney Crowell, and Emmylou Harris, among others. Of course, television and motion pictures are even worse than the songs, because there this filth is visible. I'm concerned about the lack of morality that young people are constantly exposed to. My slogan in dealing with child abuse and neglect over the years has always been and always will be "The future of the world tomorrow depends on today's little children." So the environment of the mass media these days still worries me.

Many people continue to ask me, "Why did you stop writing songs?" Well, I didn't want to write suggestive lyrics, and I didn't know anything about writing pop material. But I did write a couple of songs after "Hello, Love" was released. They came from my heart, and each contained a good message. I thought they had the potential of becoming hits. I recorded them, but they didn't make it to first base. This was highly disappointing to me, and I didn't want to write anymore.

I also believe that with the exception of a few writers such as Irving Berlin and Stephen Foster each writer has only so many songs in his brain, and after that, forget it. I thank the Good Lord that He let me live long enough to record the one hundred fifty that I wrote.

Changes at the radio stations affected our music, too. For years country music disc jockeys throughout the nation used to come to Nashville in October to the Disc Jockey Convention, cosponsored by the Grand Ole Opry and the Country Music Association. We often had upward of six thousand deejays in the city as the artists, record companies, and publishers celebrated "DJ Week." This was to thank the deejays across the U.S.A. and from other countries for playing down-to-earth country music. I know the deejays played a tremendous part in the success I've had over the years and helped account for the fact that my records are still in demand.

Gradually, there were fewer deejays coming to Nashville, until finally there was no more DJ Week. From then on we, the older artists, began losing contact with our deejay friends. The closeness between the artists and the deejays is almost gone, and some of the disc jockeys today don't even remember the names of the old artists like Red Foley, Cowboy Copas, and Ernest Tubb.

Today the deejays are expected to play records from a "short playlist," rather than play their choices and what the listeners want. Owners and directors of radio stations, trade papers, record producers, and the record companies all got together and came up with a bright idea—"top forty." This meant that those people would select around forty country songs, or what they called country songs, to play each day. Each song would be rotated on the playlist. So if you listened to the country stations you would hear the same songs from this short playlist being played over and over. We lost the biggest part of our supporters because they got bored listening to the same so-called country music over and over again.

Radio stations ran this brilliant idea into the ground, and it hurt the record industry. Think about it, friends, how many different artists on a country station do you hear every day? Remember, there are hundreds and hundreds of artists cutting records. In most cases you'll never have the opportunity to hear most of these entertainers, whether they are new or old artists, and you will not be able to hear some of the finest country songs. How long has it been since you heard a song by Bob Wills, the Sons of the Pioneers, Jimmie Rodgers, the Delmore Brothers, Carson Robison, Slim Whitman, Jimmie Davis, Webb Pierce, Ray Price, Faron Young, and yes, Hank Snow? If you drive across this great country of ours and listen to country music radio stations, you'll hear the "top forty." These large record companies and radio stations are doing a great disservice to country music and have denied the country fans their right to have a choice. Fortunately, a few of the smaller stations do play country music that people want to hear.

The producers, recording companies, and trade papers pick out around one hundred forty stations from the thousands that play country music, and they decide which records are to be played. They determine the chart positions of country songs, which everybody in the business follows. This is their Bible. Many of the other stations copy the selections from the hundred and forty because they want to be included with the big brass, so they can claim they're playing the country hit songs just like the bigger stations.

Radio stations receive hundreds of records each week, and program directors throw them in the trash can unless they are the same songs that the major labels are promoting. In many cases the artists, and the business people supporting the artist, may have invested thousands of dollars in a project, but they might not even get it played on the radio. The audience never hears most of these songs. You can see that something is dreadfully wrong in this system.

Remember when all the so-called payola was going on years ago, and under-the-counter money was being paid by certain people to play their songs? Even the U.S. Congress picked up on the charges, and they did an investigation and condemned payola. Do you suppose this same type of unfairness still exists? I heard from a pretty reliable source that a certain artist paid up to fifty thousand dollars to get his record in the number-one spot.

Or consider this. Let's say that a talented country artist comes along, and he's not associated with one of the major leagues. What chance does he have to get his songs heard? If the public does not hear the songs or even know they exist, they can't buy the records. How can this artist get started in the business? The stations won't even consider playing a new artist's record on an independent label, let alone making him or her a number-one artist. To get that record to number one in the trade papers, wouldn't that take a hell of a lot of convincing, or a lot of money, or a damn strong song? Also, if an artist on a small label seems to have either a strong song or a heap of potential to make people money, wouldn't a major record company be quick to jump in and buy his or her contract from the small independent label? This, remember, is what happened to Elvis when he was under contract with Sam Phillips in Memphis. RCA Victor stepped in and bought his contract from Sun Records.

In the past several years I've heard many of the artists say the record companies and the radio stations have created a monster, and now they don't know what to do with it. Frankly, I saw it coming for a long time, and that part of the music business still concerns me.

But friends, there is some good news. A few years after the trend toward dirty lyrics and the pop music craze, something remarkable has happened. Country music is returning to its roots. Good ole country music, with somewhat different arrangements, is back in style, thanks to a host of new artists who write and sing about honesty and real-life situations—people like Randy Travis, Clint Black, Garth Brooks, George Strait, Ricky Skaggs, Vince Gill, Ricky Van Shelton, Alan Jackson, Marty Stuart, Paulette Carlson, Lorrie Morgan, Holly Dunn, Patty Loveless, and many more, too numerous to mention. These are among the young artists who keep my hopes alive for the future of wholesome country music.

I'd like to tell you about some of the organizations and people I've been associated with. I'll start with the one that I will never give the first good word to, and you have probably guessed its name already. It's the American Federation of Musicians. Remember the story about the gang from Philadelphia that I brought to Canada to work a summer's tour with me? I advanced them money, and they went back to Philadelphia with my money, without playing even the first show date with me. The union held me responsible for the whole affair and took my union card a couple of times when I couldn't make the payments on the fine they placed on me. You'll remember, too, that messy situation that began in Vancouver, British Columbia, when I got involved with the musicians who were always late for the shows, and I had to let them go. Again the AF of M held me responsible, and it cost me hundreds of dollars that I didn't have. I've been a member of that organization for over fifty-five years, so I talk from experience. During all these years I can truthfully say the AF of M had nothing to do with any success that I've had. They simply made life more difficult for me.

I would venture to say that just about all the members of AF of M feel the same way as I do, if they're not afraid to speak out. Country great Hank Thompson can tell you of his run-in with them years ago. I believe all of us musicians would have been a hell of a lot better off if we'd never heard tell of the AF of M.

I joined the federation in the late 1930s in Canada, and I joined the Nashville local when I first came to Nashville in 1950. I was told that any member who is in the organization for thirty years automatically becomes a lifetime member, relieving him or her of paying additional union dues, and a lifetime member is issued a gold card. When I realized a few years ago that I'd been in the union for some forty years, I called the local in Nashville and advised them that I felt I qualified for a lifetime membership. I was told, "You have to be a thirty-year member in the same local for thirty years." Since the AF of M is an international union and I had been with them well over the required years, I felt I deserved the lifetime card. A few years later I did get my gold card, and I damn sure earned it.

Now I'll tell you about some of the organizations in which my involvement has been positive. I was one of the first artists to join the Country Music Association, and my membership card was signed by the late Tex Ritter. Around that time, the CMA formed the Walkway of Stars around the Hall of Fame, and I was thrilled to have my name inscribed on the walkway, with a huge star in the middle.

Next, I want to express my feelings about AFTRA, which stands for American Federation of Television and Radio Artists. This organization has done an outstanding job. They established one of the finest insurance programs you could possibly ask for in hospital care, home care, dental benefits, and medicine. Plus, they have quadrupled salaries for the performers on the Opry over the years, and I believe every two years they renegotiate a new contract with the Opry. Regardless of what part of the entertainment world you're involved in, belonging to AFTRA is truly a privilege. They protect their membership to the end of the world and have done many great things and continue to do so.

Another national treasure in Nashville is Ralph Emery. For many years now he's promoted country artists and their music on his radio and television shows. Not only does he expose new talent on his programs, he continues to recognize the older artists and their contributions. Ralph has played a major role in the resurgence of country music.

But the Grand Ole Opry is number one of any organization that promotes country music around the world. It started in 1925 and is the oldest all-country show in existence. It's a household word around the entire world.

The Opry enjoyed a number of homes before locating in the Ryman Tabernacle in downtown Nashville. It's interesting to me that I made my first record in an old vacant church in Montreal, Canada, and my first appearance on the Grand Ole Opry was done in what used to be a religious tabernacle. I've always thought they both brought me good luck.

In 1974 the Opry moved into its brand new home at Opryland, into an eleven-million-dollar beautiful auditorium, with first-class dressing rooms, air-conditioning, and the finest of sound equipment and lighting. Let's just say that the Opry has the best of everything. We had none of this down at the old Ryman Auditorium.

The Opry cosponsors with the CMA the popular Fan Fair week, which is usually held in June each year. Country music fans come here to meet the artists, talk with them, get autographs, take pictures, and attend country shows provided especially for them. Thousands of Americans along with visitors from many foreign countries come to Nashville each summer to vacation and to attend Fan Fair.

One of the major factors in the Opry's continuing success has been the fine people who run it. There have been several changes in personnel management, but they all have been, and are, extremely good people to get along with. Nobody says you have to do this or you have to do that. They leave it to our discretion, and we appreciate that very much. This has worked out well over the years, because I think the performers can do a better job without being subjected to constant pressure. W. E. "Bud" Wendell is president and CEO of Gaylord Entertainment Corporation. Among his responsibilities he oversees the Opry, the Opryland Hotel, WSM Radio, and the Nashville Network. The manager of the Opry is Hal Durham. Mr. Wendell and Mr. Durham are fine, easy-going people. They are not pushy in any way. We never have any problems to speak of, and I personally praise both of them.

All of us in the Opry family take a great deal of pride just being part of it. In my forty-four years as a member, I have never experienced the first bit of jealousy among the Opry family. If there is sickness or the loss of a loved one, we are all right there to offer any assistance we can. The Opry has established a trust fund for artists in country music, whether Opry members or not, so that people in the country field who might be down on their luck or ill can receive financial help through this fund.

Most of the members stay on the Opry as long as they want to, and most choose to do so. Unfortunately, Roy Acuff, Ernest Tubb, and many of our great artists in country music have passed on, but their music still lives, and they are missed by us all. I'm also proud that periodically some of our popular younger artists are becoming members. They will tell you, as I have said many times, that being a part of the Opry is truly the pinnacle of country music.

The Opry has done a lot for country music, and country music has done a lot for the city of Nashville and the state of Tennessee over the past forty years, and I'm proud to have been a part of it. Country music built the National Life and Accident Insurance Company into a huge insurance empire, which was later sold to American General in Houston, Texas. Country music also built Opryland U.S.A., a tremendous theme park and tourist attraction, which brings in over two million people every year. It also built one of the finest hotels in the United States, the Opryland Hotel, and of course, the Grand Ole Opry. It also built the Nashville Network, which reaches millions of people daily. So country music brings tens of millions of dollars to the city every year and creates innumerable jobs.

After the twists and turns of country music during the last two decades, I'm hopeful that good ole country music has a strong future. In 1993 there were about twenty-four hundred radio stations playing country music exclusively. This is about two hundred more than the previous year. For this and other reasons I believe the increasing popularity of country music today is more than a fad. I think it's a trend—and a mighty good one.

I became an Opry member on January 7, 1950, and I hope I will be able to stay a bit longer, because I love it, and I love the people. I still host two half-hour shows each Friday and Saturday night, direct from the modern Opry House at the Opryland Theme Park.

I'm still movin' on.

39

Among My Souvenirs

There's a mighty train a-comin',
You will hear it by and by.
And you'll hear that screamin' whistle
As it thunders through the sky.

"I'm Movin' On to Glory,"
by Hank Snow

❧

"I'M MOVIN' ON" HAS BEEN MY SIGNATURE song since I recorded it in 1950, and it's still my most requested number forty-four years later.

I've been asked many times just how many artists have recorded "I'm Movin' On," as well as some of my other songs. I don't know the number or the names of all the artists, but I'll mention a few of them. But first I'd like to say that once a song has been publicly recorded and released, anyone has the right to record it without having to get permission from the writer or the publisher of the song. This is good because the songwriter receives royalties if the record sells, as well as royalties for public performances, such as when it's played on radio and television.

I don't always hear about who has recorded my songs unless someone happens to tell me. When I receive a royalty check from BMI (Broadcast Music, Inc.), their statements list the songs generating income, but they do not tell the name of the artist. And many of the releases come from the foreign-country markets like Australia, Japan, New Zealand, West Germany, France, and even Czechoslovakia.

Anyway, I know the following artists have recorded "I'm Movin' On": Ray Charles, Elvis Presley, Allan Flatt, Tiny Hill, Hank Garland, Hoagie Carmichael, Billy Vaughn, Al Hirt, Jeannie Gail, Boyd Bennett, Les Paul and Mary Ford, Don Gibson, Jim Lowe, Johnny Nash (not Cash), Connie Francis, Mac Wiseman, and Emmylou Harris. There was a comedy version by Lonzo and Oscar and by Homer and Jethro. They called it "I'm Movin' On #2." Some of the artists in foreign countries who have recorded it include Eddie Mitchell, Marie Vincent, Chris Duggan, Ron Clay, and the LeGard Twins (who came to the U.S.A. from Australia). I know "I'm Movin' On" was recorded in the French and Czech languages.

Three of my hits were recorded behind the Iron Curtain, and I have Czechoslovakian versions by a Czech artist on these songs: "I'm Movin' On," "My Mother," and "I've Been Everywhere."

Those who recorded "The Golden Rocket" include Pat Boone, Grandpa Jones, Stoney Cooper, Johnny Horton, and Roy Acuff. "Rhumba Boogie" was recorded by Spade Cooley's band, featuring the Fontaine Sisters, by the Three Browns (Jim Ed, Maxine, and Bonnie), and by Jimmie Rodgers (the singer of "Honeycomb," not the daddy of our music). "Just a Faded Petal from a Beautiful Bouquet" was recorded by Carl and Pearl Butler. Ernest Tubb recorded "My Filipino Rose." "Music-Makin' Mama from Memphis" was cut by Joe Fingers Carr. "I'm Gonna Bid My Blues Good-bye" was cut by several artists, both as an instrumental and as a song.

I get asked many times, especially when I'm on tour or doing interviews, if I remember all the musicians who have worked with me over the years. This kind of puts me on the spot, because there were quite a few over a period of fifty-eight years. But I've given this a lot of thought since I began writing my book, and I'm going to try to name them all. First, however, I want to make it perfectly clear that the musicians deserve a lot of credit for the success of an artist. Through the influence of creative musicians the artists are inspired to put their heart and soul into their songs in the studio and to do likewise on stage.

I sure hit it lucky in picking out real good musicians and real good people throughout the years. Oh, we've had problems now and then. We've gotten into arguments every once in a while, but that's normal when you're on the road from twenty to forty days straight, doing one-nighters as we sometimes did. But we never had serious or long-lasting conflicts. And that's saying a lot, because I've always expected punctuality and professionalism from my musicians. I never had anybody quit because we didn't get along or they didn't like their job. The only member I ever remember firing was the leader of the group I took from Vancouver, British Columbia, to Winnipeg, Canada. He was always late.

So here I go with the names. The Lambert Lamplighters, sponsored by Lambert Cough Medicine, at good ole CHNS in Halifax, were as follows: Morris Jollymore, fiddle; Jimmy Reid, acoustic Hawaiian guitar; Ken Doyle, accordion; Richard "Dick" Frye, piano. Our announcer, Cecil Landry, was the chief engineer of the station, and he sometimes played the jew's harp with us. Clyde Connors, tenor singer, sang pretty Irish songs; and I sang and played guitar.

Here are the musicians who played on my early RCA Victor Bluebird records in Canada: Eugene "Johnny" Beaudoin, a fine French fellow from Montreal, played electric steel guitar; Teddy Miller was on upright bass; and Irving Schultz was an accomplished violinist. Johnny was the one who actually gave my music direction a sense of uniqueness. Later, when I came to Nashville, Joe Talbot continued on with that basic steel guitar sound, and he refined it into the style that became associated with my music. When Tommy Vaden joined with Joe on my records, they established the Hank Snow style for the future.

Another Frenchman, Eugene Beaulieau, from New Carlisle, Quebec, worked with me a few times in the 1940s. He was an old-time fiddle player. Other musicians from Canada included Art "Bob" Hickey, piano accordion and piano player; Bill Davidson played fiddle; Estwood Davidson played fiddle and guitar; Gordon Wilkie, Donny Whynot, and George Chappell all played fiddle; Ross Parker was a rhythm guitar player and a singer; Scotty Winston Fitzgerald was one of the outstanding fiddle players from Cape Breton, Nova Scotia, and he was great on those jigs and reels and other square-dance music; Bernie O'Connell and Art Rhyno were steel guitar players; Lawrence Kelly played rhythm guitar; Eugene McCabe was a drummer; and Morris Boulieau played several instruments extremely well.

During my first Canadian tour with Big Slim and Hazel, Earl Langley played guitar and sang; Pete Palcic played piano accordion and doubled on piano; Lew Wade played bass and did comedy.

In the U.S.A. I was fortunate to have Tommy Vaden and Robert "Chubby" Wise. They were two great fiddle players in the Rainbow Ranch band. First was Tommy and then Chubby. For a while I used both of these gentlemen to play twin fiddles, and their creative playing on my recordings was beautiful. Buddy Spicher is an accomplished violinist, and he played on several of my RCA Victor records and albums. He did various tours with me and at times played twin fiddle with Chubby. It would be hard to choose among these three greats on the fiddle, Tommy, Chubby, and Buddy.

Steel players included Bob Foster, Jerry Merher, and Buford Gentry. Buford took up where Joe Talbot left off. Hillous Butrum played bass in the early years of personal appearances and the Opry. Rhythm guitar players included Sherman Collins, Johnny Johnson, and Ed Hyde. Jimmy Widener was both a fine bass man and a rhythm player.

Additional players include Curt Gibson and Roy Curry on rhythm guitar. Jimmy Crawford, Verle Ayres, and Howard White all played steel guitar. Bobby Wright played bass.

I sincerely hope I haven't left anybody out. If I did, it was not on purpose. Some of these musicians played with my band for a lengthy period, others for a brief time. Gentlemen, take a bow. You all did a great job.

The present Rainbow Ranch Boys are as follows: Kayton Roberts, steel guitar player, who has been in my band for twenty-seven years; Bobby Sykes, rhythm guitar; Roger Carroll, bass; and Tommy Vaden, fiddle. These are all excellent musicians and perfect gentlemen. It's a pleasure to be associated with them.

It's interesting how Tommy Vaden rejoined my band after many years. Tommy worked with me from 1950 up into the mid-1960s. Then he had a sad experience that left him devastated. His wonderful wife, Marie, passed away. It was an untimely death due to a heart problem. Tommy and his wife were so devoted to each other, her death hit him so hard that he laid his fiddle down and didn't pick it up again for fourteen years. About thirteen years ago I called Tommy and tried to get him to play on my recordings and on the Opry again. He was carrying so much sadness deep inside, I thought that getting back into music would do him good. He was working at a boat dock, on the all-night shift, up on Old Hickory Lake. Tommy replied, "Hank, I wouldn't even know how to hold a fiddle bow after all these years." But about five years later, on a hunch, I called him again. After a little persuasion, he said he'd give it a try. "I'm just sitting here in this old rocking chair every day by myself. Since I don't work the dock anymore, it does get pretty lonesome here, and I never go anywhere. My life is just wasting away, so music might do me good. But remember, Hank, it's going to take me a couple of months to get the feel of things again."

He got his fiddle worked on by an expert in Nashville, and within about six weeks he was sounding like the Tommy Vaden of years ago. So after not playing the fiddle for many years and not playing with me for about twenty years, he rejoined the Rainbow Ranch Boys and me on the Grand Ole Opry. My band was complete again! He recaptured the beautiful mellow tone he used to have, which goes so well with my style.

Back in the 1950s, Tommy was real funny. And when Chubby and he were with me together as twin fiddlers, I really had a pair of humorous people. There was never a dull moment. Tommy's back having fun and kidding people just like he used to do. It makes me feel good that he has adjusted to the past and is going on with his life, as his wife would have wanted him to do. He needed encouragement, and I'm glad I was there when he needed someone.

Here's another question people have asked me through the years. "Hank, who makes those beautiful rhinestone suits that you wear on stage?" I've always appreciated that question, because my jewel-studded suits and bow ties have been my trademark over many years. Very few times have I gone on stage without wearing a fancy suit. It's always been my belief that the audience wants to see and deserves a little flash by the artist on stage, rather than him looking like the neighbor next door.

My designer tailors made my wardrobe, but they also made wardrobes for many other country music artists. My first western suit was made by Globe Western Tailors. Globe made me two or three suits and did fine tailor work on them. Nathan Turke in Hollywood was my second western tailor. He made my fancy suits and western-styled wardrobe, and he always did extremely fine work. Mr. Turke also made wardrobes for both Gene Autry and Roy Rogers and for a lot of the western movie stars. Next came Harris Tailoring in Fort Worth, Texas. I believe the gentleman's name is Leon Harris. He made several of my costumes until he went out of business. Then I switched to my old friend Nudie, in North Hollywood. Nudie is known throughout the world for his fine tailoring. After Nudie passed away, Harvey Krantz in Hollywood made my fancy, beautiful wardrobe. Harvey comes to Nashville periodically and takes a suite at one of the hotels. He makes appointments for me and others he makes wardrobes for. He always brings the latest in beautiful materials from Italy, China, Japan, and Mexico, and it's exciting to choose from his large selection.

Overall, friends, I must say that my whole career has been highly rewarding. I've played in many parts of the world to all kinds of audiences. I've played my share of honky-tonks, and I've played in prestigious places like the London Palladium, the Copacabana in Tokyo, the Hollywood Bowl, and Madison Square Garden in New York City. I've sung my songs to the working people and to presidents, to poor people and to royalty. Even with the hard traveling, I wouldn't have missed it for the world!

Who would have thought that an abused little boy, with less than a fifth-grade education, and living at times in the depths of poverty, would achieve every goal that he ever dreamed about? The Good Lord has sure been good to me.

In addition to the personal satisfaction and the prestige I received from my long association with RCA, at the Opry, and from personal appearances, my income has continued to be consistent. And because of self-schooling in financial matters, I learned much about good management, especially during the poverty years. I've made some excellent investments, and I've made a few bad ones. But I've always tried to learn from my mistakes, and I usually proceeded in business with caution.

I read the Gene Autry story and heard Gene do many radio and television interviews, and I've tried to handle business affairs in the same manner he did. One important lesson I took from Gene's experiences was to always surround myself with good, honest, and professional business people. I've done that. I use the same certified public accountant that I've had for over forty years, Dave Hirsberg, of the Hirsberg accounting firm. I've also kept in touch with a well-established attorney from a well-known and reputable law firm. I've been doing business with the same bank, Third National Bank, for over forty years. I've stayed with Hill and Range Songs since 1948, even though it changed hands a couple of times during those years. I was with RCA Victor for forty-five years, and I've entered my forty-fifth year with the Grand Ole Opry. I've lived in the same home for forty-three years. And I have had the same beautiful wife for fifty-eight years! You can easily see that I'm a person who doesn't believe in constant changes.

I've read Napoleon Hill's book, *Think and Grow Rich,* about six times. He also refers to surrounding oneself with professional people. He says this is one's mastermind to draw information from, regardless of what form it might take. And I've always believed in a positive and confident approach in dealing with life's hardships and business affairs. I offer the same advice to you, my friends. Surround yourself with talented and knowledgeable people, and be loyal to them. Don't change with the wind, and listen to the experts.

Even though I'm semi-retired and not recording these days, I still get royalties from many parts of the world on my first RCA Victor Bluebird record in 1936, as well as my later recordings. I spend lots of time practicing my music, answering my mail, and handling my business affairs as if I were still at the prime of life. I still look forward to playing on the Grand Ole Opry every Friday and Saturday nights, and I do the best job I can possibly do.

Music to me is like food. If I go any length of time without music and singing, I get starved for it and feel empty. It is, I guess one would say, a soul-feeding food. I still have my own eight-track studio, and these days I use it mostly for rehearsal sessions. I once heard that Bing

Crosby would practice three hours every day. I try to sing and play every day, too, or as often as I can. This keeps my larynx in shape, my vocal cords strong, and my fingers limber for playing the guitar. Chet Atkins once said something I've never forgotten: "If I don't pick up my guitar and play it for a week or so, the next time I pick it up, it don't even know me."

Sometimes I practice the old tunes that I used to sing years ago, to see if they might be good for the Opry. I find a lot of songs from the older days that the people seem to like, such as "The Prisoner's Song," "Moonlight and Skies," and "You Nearly Lose Your Mind," among others.

Music has been more than a business to me. It has been my whole life. Shortly before Roy Acuff passed away, he told me one night at the Opry, "Hank, I just want you to know how much I have appreciated you throughout all of these years at the Opry. You're a professional in every sense of the word, and you're a real gentleman. I love you." I place comments like this among my most prized souvenirs.

I also want to give sincere thanks to those persons who did so much in helping me reach my every dream—playing and singing the music I so dearly love. There must be hundreds who played a role in my success in music, but I can name only a few of them. These are persons who went out of their way for me many times, and I owe them all a strong debt of gratitude. C. A. Landry, chief announcer of radio station CHNS in Halifax, Nova Scotia, was a most kind gentleman and like a father to me in many ways. He taught me a lot about show business, especially how to properly pronounce my words and to enunciate clearly and precisely.

Next I want to thank Julian and Jean Aberbach, owners of Hill and Range Songs, Inc., in Hollywood and New York. They believed in me from the first time I met them, when a lot of other people were afraid to take a chance on me. They advanced me money when I was down on my luck, and they continued to support me and sent me many hit songs.

I give special thanks to Jack Howard, the little guy in Philadelphia who did so much to encourage me to come to the United States. He also ran my fan club for several years and did a great job. In addition, he helped to promote me all across the country. Jack was the one who took me to see Big Slim, the Lone Cowboy, who I had been corresponding with a year or so before that. Many thanks to Big Slim and Jack, who made it possible for me to get a spot one winter on the big 50,000-watt station, WWVA, in Wheeling, West Virginia, so my music could be heard by millions of people.

Thanks to Bea Terry, who is solely responsible for bringing me from the West Coast to Dallas, Texas. She too believed in me, promoted me, and introduced me to others who would play a role in my career. Thanks to Johnny Hicks, my disc-jockey friend from Dallas, Texas, who had the Top Ten Hit Parade on the powerful 50,000-watt radio station, KRLD. Thanks to Fred Edwards, another disc jockey on the same station. He played my song "Brand on My Heart," which stayed number one on that nightly hit parade for sixteen straight weeks. This was a big step forward in launching my career in the U.S.A. The late Pappy Hal Horton, who I never had the pleasure of meeting, was also a fine disc jockey on the same station. Pappy Hal passed away before I came to Dallas, but he loved country music, and I thank him for doing so much to promote it. Betty Goudie from British Columbia, bless her heart, sent my first Bluebird records down to Texas, where they were constantly played on the Texas stations.

My thanks to Lucky Moeller. He was more than a booking agent. He and his dear wife, Bernice, became lifelong friends. Many thanks to Billy Deaton. He booked me on my most recent tours, and he's still active with his reputable booking agency in Nashville. He is an honest and a good man, and he is a special and lifelong friend.

My three A&R men and producers, A. H. Joseph, Steve Sholes, and Chet Atkins, deserve a lot of credit for getting me many hit records.

Here are two names that should be engraved in gold in my life story. They deserve to share my awards and my achievements as much as I do. Number one is Dennis Arnett, whom I met in Flagstaff, Arizona, on my first trip to the West Coast, back in the mid-1940s. He had enough faith and trust in me, over the short period of time we were acquainted, to go out on a limb for my family and me. And he became our sponsor so we could come to the United States on permanent visas. Through this, Min, Jimmie, and I became citizens of this great United States of America.

Number two is my special friend, the late Ernest Tubb, who was responsible for getting me on the Grand Ole Opry. I've mentioned him frequently in this book. He was, without a doubt, one of the most unselfish people I've ever met and one of the kindest. Without these two gentlemen, Dennis Arnett and Ernest Tubb, I probably would not have had this story to write.

In addition to all these beautiful people I've mentioned and all the help they gave me, it would have meant nothing without the support of my dear fans. All of you, throughout the world who have supported my music, I thank you kindly. You have been a wonderful audience.

Most of all, I owe my dear wife a huge debt of gratitude. Min has been my best friend, and she has always understood my complex personality and my unusual drive to succeed. Without her I never could have accomplished a fraction of what I've achieved. She has endured many hardships with me, but she has never lost her smile and she never complains. We've laughed a lot through the years, when we could have just as easily cried. Min has helped me keep life's frustrations in proper perspective, and she has a wonderful sense of humor. She has been a hard worker, a fine cook, a good homemaker, and a loving wife.

I thank my beloved mother for her undying support and encouragement. She endured her hardships with a smile and a sense of humor. She never blamed other people for the hard times, and she never criticized. Her philosophy has been a strong influence on me throughout my life. I've never forgotten one of Mother's favorite sayings, "We should all take a broom and sweep our own doorsteps clean before we go sweeping others." I've tried to follow that, and I hope throughout my life I have been true to her Christian values that she believed in so much.

During the 1950s my family and I became citizens of the United States, but I'm proud to count good ole Canada as our native country. We felt that as long as we were going to make the United States our permanent home, we should become citizens. We wanted to vote and not just be citizens, but be good citizens. Naturally, we hated to give up the Canadian citizenship, but after all, it was our good Canadian people who encouraged me to come to the U.S.A., and I shall never forget my many Canadian friends for their continuing support. Anytime I go back to Canada, they are always there to give me a great big welcome. I've returned to Canada just about every year since I came to the States.

Canada has done many good things for us. One of the highest honors ever bestowed upon me was my induction into the Canadian Academy of Recording Arts and Sciences Hall of Fame in Toronto, during the Juno Awards in 1979. On that occasion the prime minister of Canada, Pierre Trudeau, honored me by making a trip by plane from Ottawa to be with us, along with the man who made my first record, Hugh Joseph from Montreal.

A great tribute was paid to me on July 21, 1986, when the premier of Nova Scotia, the Honorable John M. Buchanan, hosted a big dinner for me in Halifax. He invited about five hundred guests as a special tribute commemorating my fifty years in country music and show business. On this night, too, a letter of commendation from the prime minister of Canada, Brian Mulroney, was read to me and the audience.

In 1989 I made a ten-day tour in the western provinces of Canada. We played in Alberta, Saskatchewan, and Manitoba, and we had wonderful crowds. Those good Canadian people, bless their hearts, gave me standing ovations on each of the ten shows I played. We finished the tour by doing the famous Tommy Hunter television show in Toronto, and again I got a standing ovation.

The Friends of Hank Snow Society are now in the planning stages of acquiring the old Canadian National railroad station and grounds in Liverpool for the establishment of the Hank Snow Home Town Museum and Country Music Centre. As a kid I ran away many times from my cold-hearted grandmother in nearby Brooklyn to visit my mother, who was living in Liverpool. I spent many nights in that same station just to keep warm, and it's ironic that the good people of Canada are seeking to establish a permanent museum where I often took refuge. That possibility thrills me to no end, and it will be among the greatest honors I will have ever received.

So I would like to say a special thanks to you, my millions of friends across Canada. We made it, you and I.

* * *

After years of working on my book it's finally a reality. It's taken a lot of effort, and I hope my story is an inspiration to you, my friends.

Now, a few words to my coauthors, Jack Ownbey and Bob Burris. We have spent hundreds of hours over the past several years working on this project, and now that it's finished, I want you both to know how very much I appreciate your untiring efforts. I feel I made an excellent choice in selecting my cowriters. It's been painful reliving some of the early events in my life, but writing this book also brought back many wonderful memories of a career that has extended far beyond my wildest dreams. Thanks for helping me tell the story in my own words. I'm satisfied that this factual, in-depth account of the way I've lived my life has been told in a simple, straightforward manner, and we can now share our work with all my devoted fans who have waited so patiently for its completion.

To my assistant, Sherry Blackwood, a million thanks! You have worked closely with Jack, Bob, and me from the time we started writing my story several years ago, and we join together in thanking you for your outstanding contribution to this project.

Thank you, Graham "Buzz" Baker, for your many hours of research on fishing vessels and procedures.

A very special thanks to our literary agent, Gary Buck.

And my sincere thanks to Judith McCulloh and all the folks at the University of Illinois Press. It's been great working with you!

* * *

Now to all of you, my friends, wherever you may be—so long, good luck, good health, and may the Good Lord always be proud of you!

A Hank Snow Photo Album

Hank's mother, Marie Alice Snow, taken in 1929.

Hank's father, George Lewis Snow, taken in 1925.

Hank (Jack) at the age of five, pictured with his youngest sister, Marion, in 1920. Hank is wearing the outfit made by his mother from his uncle's World War I army parka.

George Wright, a police officer in Liverpool, Nova Scotia, during the time Hank lived with his grandmother. Courtesy of Dorothy Slauenwhite of Bridgewater, Nova Scotia.

Constance Gardner with five-year-old Hank, leaving for school.

Hank practicing target shooting with his .22 rifle in 1929.

Hank at the age of fourteen, holding a bunny. Taken at Stonehurst, Lunenburg County, Nova Scotia, 1928.

Sixteen-year-old Hank with his mother's guitar in 1930.

Left to right: Hank's Grandfather Godfrey, Hank's Grandmother Godfrey (the mean grandmother), others unknown. Taken in 1920.

Jimmie Rodgers, the Father of Country Music. Rodgers inscribed this publicity photo to the Carter Family during their recording sessions together in Louisville in the summer of 1931.

Carrie (Mrs. Jimmie) Rodgers.

Hank's first band in 1937. *Left to right:* Bill Davidson, Ross Parker, Eugene McCabe, Hank, George Legere.

The Lambert Lamplighters in 1939. *Left to right:* Hank, Ken Doyle, Clyde Connors, Jimmy Reid, Cecil Landry, Dick Fry, Morris Jollymore.

Hank's first homemade trailer and his 1938 Plymouth. Taken outside one of the small halls he played in 1939.

A 1943 photograph of Hank and Min taken in Moncton, New Brunswick.

One of Hank's early publicity shots. Taken in 1943 in Montreal.

Hank posing in front of his new 1947 Cadillac convertible and the van built especially for Shawnee, his trained horse.

Hank (on Shawnee) and A. H. Joseph, taken in front of Hank's van at RCA Victor in Montreal.

Hank trickriding Shawnee.

Hank and Shawnee in promotional shot taken at the Rainbow Ranch.

Shawnee rearing.

Shawnee saying his prayers.

Shawnee doing the "camel crawl."

Hank balancing Shawnee.

Shawnee untying a hankie from his front ankle.

Shawnee untying a hankie from his back ankle.

Shawnee spinning his little lasso.

Shawnee marching.

Shawnee whispering in Hank's ear during a stage show. Hank would reply, "Can't you wait until after the show?!"

Shawnee taking a bow.

Shawnee taking home an intoxicated Hank.

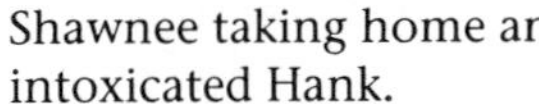

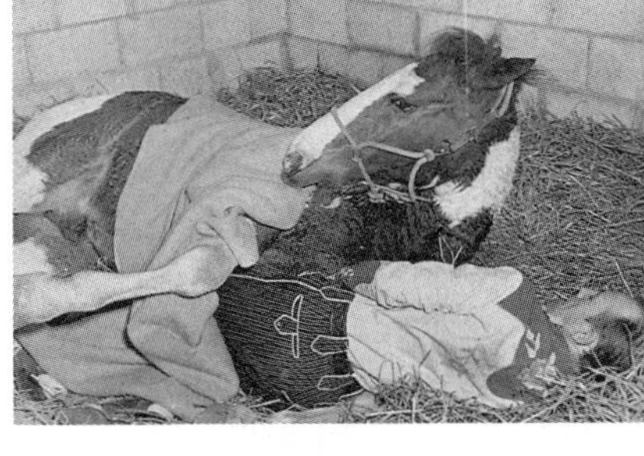

Hank singing Shawnee to sleep.

Shawnee covering Hank with a blanket.

Hank and Shawnee having breakfast. (This picture was taken across the road from Betty Grable's ranch in Calabasas, California.)

Hank, little twelve-year-old Jimmie, and Min at the Roundup Club in Dallas, Texas, in 1948.

Billy King, a juggler in one of Hank's 1949 tours.

On stage in St. John's, Newfoundland, in 1949. *Left to right:* Roy Curry, Hank, Jimmie Snow, Bernie O'Connell.

Hank and Gus Winter in Winter's St. John's, Newfoundland, record store in 1949.

Ernest Tubb and Hank posing with a Jimmie Rodgers picture record.

Spade Cooley, Hank, and Rex Allen in the 1950s.

Group picture of the Grand Ole Opry family on the stage of the old Ryman Auditorium in the late 1950s. Hank is at the microphone to the left of center stage.

Left to right: Buford Gentry, Tommy Vaden, James "Sleepy" McDaniel, Hank, and Hillous Butrum on the stage of the Grand Ole Opry.

Hank at an autograph session in Hartney's Department Store in Montreal. To his right is Elwood Glover, a famous 1950s talk show host.

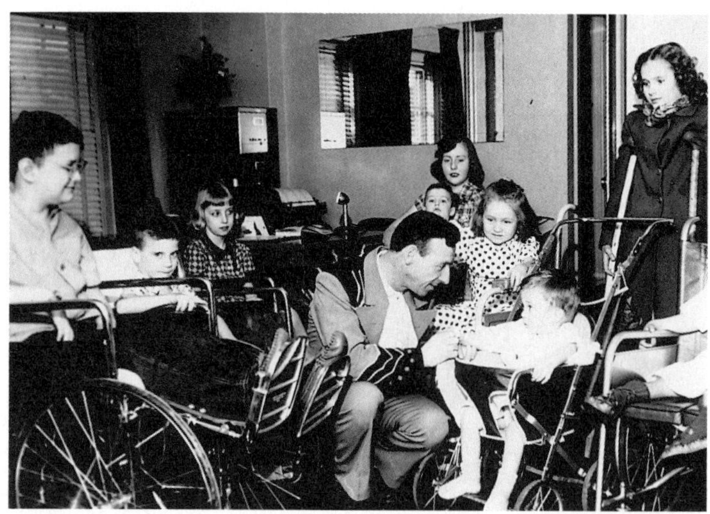

Entertaining children at the Children's Hospital in Winnipeg, Manitoba.

Steve Sholes (manager of the RCA Victor recording department in New York City), Hank, and WSM station manager Harry Stone in 1951. Stone and Hank are shaking hands.

Major William Borrett (manager of radio station CHNS in Halifax, Nova Scotia), Hank, and Clarence Bowers (salesman for RCA Victor Records in the Halifax area). The photograph is inscribed: "To my good friend 'Hank' Snow, with best wishes! May your shadow never grow less!"

Standing, left to right: Hank, Bill McDaniel, Ernest Tubb, Danny Dill, and Lou Childre; *front row:* Tommy Vaden, Hillous Butrum, and Dickie Harris. Taken during refueling operations at Wake Island en route to Korea in 1953.

"Sleepy" McDaniel, Hank, and Lou Childre pose in front of the Rice Paddy Theater sign during the 1953 Korean trip.

Hank entertaining GI's during the Korean conflict, 1953.

Hank and the Rainbow Ranch Boys entertaining the troops in Korea.

Entertaining Japanese civilians at the Ernie Pyle Theater in Tokyo, Japan. *Left to right:* "Sleepy" McDaniel, Tommy Vaden, Hank, Hillous Butrum, and Buford Gentry.

May 26, 1953: Justin Tubb and Hank unveil the Jimmie Rodgers Monument in Meridian, Mississippi, on the twentieth anniversary of the singer's death.

Hank laying a wreath on Jimmie Rodgers's grave in Meridian.

Hank pictured among the twenty-two thousand get-well cards and letters he received after his severe automobile accident in August, 1951.

At a benefit concert for the relief of flood victims in Winnipeg, Manitoba.

An appearance on the Perry Como show in 1953. The bass player is an unknown member of Como's band.

Left to right: Hank, Goldie Hill, promoter Smokey Smith of Des Moines, Iowa, and Jim Reeves in 1953.

Hank with Mickey (*left*) and Pal.

Hank, Tennessee Governor Frank Clement, and Ernest Tubb.

Left to right: Hank, Carrie Rodgers, Ernest Tubb, Anita Rodgers Court (daughter of Jimmie Rodgers), and Carrie's brother Nathan Williamson (Mr. Nate) in front of the Jimmie Rodgers Monument in 1954.

Left to right: Hank, Tennessee Governor Frank Clement, Carrie Rodgers, Ernest Tubb, and Louisiana Governor Jimmie Davis at the 1954 Jimmie Rodgers Celebration in Meridian, Mississippi.

Huge banner outside a Tampa, Florida, auditorium in 1955. Notice the name "Elvis Presley" in small letters; he was just starting his career.

Hank played to more than 12,000 people in the large Denver Auditorium in 1956.

Hank and Lucky Moeller in 1957.

Left to right: Hugh Cherry, Roy Acuff, Hank, Audrey Williams, and Hank Williams, Sr., at radio station WMPS in Memphis, Tennessee.

Hank, Audrey Williams, and Nudie.

Hank and Elvis in 1959.

Long line of people waiting to hear Hank's 1959 concert in the Hippodrome Theater, Baltimore, Maryland.

Hank, piano player Jerry Byers, and Ott Devine backstage at the Grand Ole Opry in 1960.

Hank greets Edwin Craig and "Dizzy" Dean at one of his shows in the 1960s.

Left to right: Richard "Dick" Fry, Min, Major Borrett, and Hank in 1964.

Japanese singer Masaka Hara on stage with Hank and his band during his concert in Japan.

Hank receiving roses during the 1964 show in Tokyo, Japan.

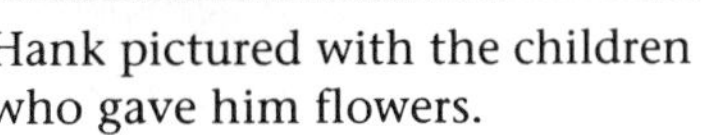

Hank pictured with the children who gave him flowers.

Entertaining at the Blind Children's Orphanage in Yokohama, Japan.

Hank presenting guitars at the Blind Children's Orphanage.

Hank introduces Fusako Kawahara to the audience at the Grand Ole Opry in the mid-1960s. Also pictured is Ott Devine, at that time the manager of the Opry.

Hank introduces Masemi Uyeda at the Grand Ole Opry in the 1960s.

Wild Bill Reed prepares Hank for the high jump in Tampa, Florida, in 1963.

Hank making the high jump.

Hank and Vito Pellettieri in 1965.

Hank and an unidentified GI in Vietnam, holding a twenty-two-foot-long python.

Left to right: Kayton Roberts, Hank, Jimmy Widener, and Bobby Wright in England in 1967.

W. E. "Bud" Wendell, then Executive Director of Opryland, poses with Hank and Vito Pellettieri in 1967.

Hank and W. F. "Squirlie" Carter in 1968. Squirlie worked for Hank for twenty-six years.

Hank and his three A&R men. *Left to right:* Steve Sholes, Min, A. H. Joseph, Hank, and Chet Atkins.

A. H. Joseph presents Hank with a gold record in Montreal in the 1960s.

Hank with Julian and Jean Aberbach.

Ernest Tubb, Hank, and Nudie in 1961.

Left to right: Joe Talbot, Tommy Vaden, Charlie Greon, Jimmie Snow, Hank, and Jack Schook at a 1961 recording session for RCA.

Left to right: Jimmie Snow, Hank, Min, Larry Kanaga, and Steve Sholes in 1956. Kanaga, then a vice-president at RCA, is presenting Hank with a bronze Nipper in honor of his twentieth anniversary with the company.

Hank and Min aboard the forty-one-foot-long *Golden Rocket* in 1962.

To honor the twenty-fifth anniversary of Hank's first recording, A. H. Joseph presented Hank with a Canadian Award in Nashville. The plaque reads, in part, "Admired from sea to sea."

Hank visits with A. H. Joseph backstage at a 1962 show in Ottawa, Canada.

Ringo Starr poses with Hank backstage after Hank's 1972 performance at the London Palladium.

Hank with Dolly Parton.

Canadian Prime Minister Pierre Trudeau, Hank, and A. H. Joseph.

During the April, 1979, Juno Awards, Canadian Prime Minister Pierre Trudeau inducted Hank into the Canadian Academy of Recording Arts and Sciences Hall of Fame.

Hank meets President Jimmy Carter in the Oval Office at the White House.

Hank and the Rainbow Ranch Boys today. *Left to right:* Kayton Roberts, steel guitar; Hank; Roger Carroll, bass; Tommy Vaden, fiddle; Bobby Sykes, rhythm guitar. Photo by Bill McCutcheon.

Signing the book contract, May 10, 1993. *Left to right:* Bob Burris, Judith McCulloh, Gary Buck, Hank, Jack Ownbey. Photo by Judy Mock.

Hank and his assistant, Sherry Blackwood, at the Rainbow Ranch in September, 1993. Photo by Ruth Bauer.

A Note on the Recordings

Charles K. Wolfe

THE RECORDED LEGACY OF HANK SNOW is one of the largest and most impressive in country music history. It spans the early makeshift studios of depression-era Canada to the digital sophistication of contemporary Nashville, and its formats run the gamut of fragile old 78s through the earliest "doughnut" discs of the 45 rpm age, from the eight-track tape to the compact disc. Hank Snow's music has, over the years, appeared on every recorded format except possibly the old Edison cylinder. The complexity of the Snow discography testifies not only to the quality and variety and richness of his repertoire, but also to the impact he has made on listeners in both the United States and Canada and in the many other countries where his records have been released. The complete listing of all the Snow recordings, with all master numbers, personnel, and release or catalog numbers, would constitute a book in itself. While such a book should some day be published, perhaps this sketch may serve as a cursory overview of the Snow "collected works."

Fortunately, the vast bulk of Hank Snow's recordings are well documented. RCA Victor, unlike many other companies, followed the practice of making out a "session sheet" for each of its recording sessions. In addition to technical information, each of these sheets contained personnel, composer credits, master numbers, and catalog numbers. The sheets for Hank Snow reveal that between October, 1936, when he made his recording debut, to November, 1980, when he did his last session for RCA, the singer recorded a total of 833 commercial sides—quite possibly the largest discography of any country singer. In addition to these commercial recordings, Hank recorded dozens of songs for Thesaurus transcriptions (for exclusive use by radio stations), as well as many pieces for other transcription services. In 1985 he also recorded an album with Willie Nelson for Columbia. Over the years many of these songs have been issued and reissued on a long series of LPs—a series dramatized by the title of his 1977 album, *No. 104, Still Movin' On,* reflecting RCA's count that this was the 104th Hank Snow album.

The first Snow recordings were done for RCA's Canadian label. From 1936 through 1942, these sides were issued on the Canadian Bluebird label, and from 1943 through 1947 in their RCA Victor 55,000 series. Hank did a total of ninety-eight Canadian titles, all of them recorded in Montreal, most of them done with a small band or with Hank's guitar as the accompaniment. Few of these early records were released to the American market, though Hank's fans found ways to order them from Canadian friends or bring them in from visits there. It was not until 1948, just before Hank began recording in the United States himself, that some of his Canadian discs were reissued in the States.

Hank's first American session was held on March 8, 1949, in Chicago, and yielded his first *Billboard* chart hit, Jenny Lou Carson's song "Marriage Vow." By the following year (March 28, 1950), Hank was recording in Nashville, at Brown Radio Productions, and was using his regular stage band to back him: steel guitarist Joe Talbot, bass player Ernie Newton, and fiddler Tommy Vaden. These musicians, who helped craft the distinctive "Hank Snow sound," would remain the core of his recording bands through 1953. In these early days the primary goal of a country session was to produce hit singles. Most of the sessions ran for three hours and were expected to produce four usable masters—an astounding feat by modern studio time frames.

Hank and his musicians, however, knew and understood this system and used it with amazing success. During their first five years with Victor they produced no fewer than twenty top-ten singles. Eventually, some eighty-five Hank Snow singles would make *Billboard's* prestigious best-seller list between 1949 and 1980. The biggest of these—the songs that broke into the top-five positions over the years—are shown on the accompanying chart.

Title (composer)	Chart date	Weeks on chart	Highest position
"I'm Moving On" (Clarence E. Snow)	July 1, 1950	44	1
"The Golden Rocket" (Clarence E. Snow)	Nov. 25, 1950	23	1
"Rhumba Boogie" (Clarence E. Snow)	Mar. 3, 1951	27	1

"Bluebird Island" (Clarence E. Snow) (with Anita Carter)	Apr. 21, 1951	11	4
"Down the Trail of Achin' Hearts" (Jimmy Kennedy—Nat Simon) (with Anita Carter)	May 19, 1951	14	2
"Music-Makin' Mama from Memphis" (Clarence E. Snow)	Dec. 15, 1951	9	4
"The Gold Rush Is Over" (Cindy Walker)	Apr. 5, 1952	15	2
"Lady's Man" (Cy Coben)	July 5, 1952	13	2
"I Went to Your Wedding" (Jessie Mae Robinson)	Sept. 27, 1952	11	3
"The Gal Who Invented Kissin'" (Charles Orr—Earl Griswald)	Dec. 13, 1952	10	4
"(Now and Then, There's) A Fool Such as I" (Bill Trader)	Dec. 27, 1952	16	3
"Spanish Fire Ball" (Dan Welch)	June 6, 1953	8	3
"I Don't Hurt Anymore" (Don Robertson—Jack Rollins)	May 29, 1954	41	1
"Let Me Go, Lover" (Jenny Lou Carson—Al Hill)	Dec. 25, 1954	16	1
"Yellow Roses" (Ken Divine—Sam Nichols)	Mar. 30, 1955	27	3
"Would You Mind" (Cy Coben)	Mar. 30, 1955	17	3
"Mainliner (The Hawk with Silver Wings)" (Stuart Hamblen)	Oct. 26, 1955	8	5
"Born to be Happy" (Stuart Hamblen)	Oct. 26, 1955	4	5
"These Hands" (Eddie Noack)	Feb. 1, 1956	10	5
"Conscience, I'm Guilty" (Jack Rimmings—Dick Reynolds—Jack Rhodes)	July 25, 1956	22	4
"Hula Rock" (Dusty Rose—Betty Rose)	Aug. 14, 1956	5	5
"Tangled Mind" (Ted Daffan—Herman Shoes)	July 13, 1957	19	4
"The Last Ride" (Robert Halcomb—Ted Daffan)	Oct. 18, 1959	20	3
"Beggar to a King" (J. P. Richardson)	May 21, 1961	20	5
"I've Been Everywhere" (Geoff Mack)	Sept. 15, 1962	22	1
"Ninety Miles an Hour (Down a Dead-End Street)" (Don Robertson—Hal Blair)	Oct. 26, 1963	22	2
"Hello, Love" (Betty Jean Robinson—Aileen Mnich)	Feb. 9, 1974	15	1

During the early 1950s the *Billboard* charts listed only ten or fifteen positions but divided them into three categories: best-sellers, disc-jockey play, and jukebox sales. It is a tribute to Hank's popularity that he often placed his hit singles high on all three charts. Many of the songs listed here also became country standards, done over and over by Hank and others, and their sales would extend over a period of years. Some songs were instant smashes, though. In its first five months out, "I Don't Hurt Anymore" had sales approaching six hundred thousand.

During the mid-1950s Hank and his producer Steve Sholes began to realize that the LP was starting to have an impact on country music the way it had on popular music, and during this time Hank became the first country singer to fully exploit the idea of the album as a basic medium for his music. In 1952 and 1953 Hank released three ten-inch LPs, including a tribute to Jimmie Rodgers and a collection of Hank's own biggest hits, *Country Classics* (LPM 3026). A third set, *Hank Snow Sings* (LPM 3070), was unusual in that it contained material cut especially for the album and was not just a collection of older items. (For a time, these early albums appeared not only on LP, but on 45, EP, and 78 formats as well.) Early in 1955 appeared Hank's first full twelve-inch LP, *Just Keep a-Movin'* (LPM 1113), which reissued a number of singles, but also included several songs recorded especially for the LP.

From 1954 through 1958 Hank went on to release seven full LPs. About half of the cuts on these albums were new material, designed especially for the albums. A number of these early albums were what today we call "concept albums," sets built around a specific theme, a specific type of music, or a special instrumental sound. The first highly defined concept album was 1955's *Old Doc Brown* (LPM 1156), a set of recitations and talking blues. Another set was *Country Guitar* (LPM 3267), the first of a series that would spotlight Hank's guitar virtuosity. A collection of older sentimental songs called *When Tragedy Struck* (LPM 1861) was released in 1958.

Throughout the 1960s Hank would continue to devote one or two sessions a year to material for singles, but increasingly his medium was the LP album. By 1962 he had fallen into a pattern in which he would do two or three albums a year, usually completing a whole album in two recording sessions. Several albums were instrumentals, featuring Hank's unique guitar work. *The Guitar Stylings of Hank Snow* (LSP 3548), released in 1966, was a natural sequel to the earlier solo efforts, and two albums spotlighting duets by Hank and Chet Atkins followed up their earlier experiments (*Reminiscing,* LSP 2952, 1964, and *C. B. At-*

kins and C. E. Snow, By Special Request, LSP 4254, 1970). By Hank's own estimation, the best-selling album from this era was *Spanish Fireball* (LSP 3857, 1967). This brought together some of the finest guitarists in Nashville: Chet Atkins, Grady Martin, Harold Bradley, Pete Wade, Joe Talbot. The songs included a cross section of Latin-flavored songs like "El Paso," "Vaya Con Dios," and "Senorita Rosalita" and spotlighted, on half the selections, the harmony of the Glaser Brothers.

Hank's fondness for vintage songs found outlet in a follow-up to *When Tragedy Struck* called *Songs of Tragedy* (LSP 2901) in 1964. Even more impressive was 1961's *Souvenirs* (LSP 2285). The plan here had been to re-record some of Hank's 1950s hits in better sound, and the album eventually sold over one hundred thousand copies, making it one of the biggest-selling Snow LPs of the decade. A follow-up, *More Hank Snow Souvenirs* (LSP 2812), came out in 1964, as well as two collections of "cover" songs that featured Hank interpreting hits by other singers (*Big Country Hits [Songs I Hadn't Recorded Til Now],* LSP 2458, 1961, and *Hits Covered by Snow,* LSP 4166, 1969). He paid tribute to his musical heroes in *Hank Snow Sings Jimmie Rodgers Songs* (LSP 2042), released in 1959, and in his salute to the Sons of the Pioneers (done with the Jordanaires) in *Heartbreak Trail* (LSP 3471) in 1965. *Railroad Man* (LSP 2705, 1963) was a collection of railroad pieces that included songs of Rodgers as well as other early singers. Gospel songs, which Hank had started recording in the early 1950s, were featured in *Sacred Songs* (LPM 1968, issued in 1958, redone in 1973), *Gloryland March* (LSP 3378, issued in 1965), and *Gospel Train* (LSP 3595, issued in 1966).

The 1970s saw a new direction in Hank Snow albums, one that was still rooted in Snow tradition, but that used some of the best and brightest of Nashville's younger studio players. *Cure for the Blues* (LSP 4379, 1970) re-emphasized the singer's lifelong love of the blues, while *No. 104, Still Movin' On* (APLI 2400, 1977) was widely hailed by critics for its use of some younger "outlaw" musicians as backup. Produced by Chuck Glaser, featuring men like fiddler Buddy Spicher and drummer Larrie London, the album had a strong jazz and blues feel and sported special lyrics to the title song by Shel Silverstein. *Award Winners* (LSP 4601, 1971) included more recognition of the "outlaw" side of Nashville, with Hank doing versions of songs by Kris Kristofferson, Gordon Lightfoot, and others. *Hello Love* (APLI 0441, 1974) was a fine set of new songs built around the singer's number-one hit of 1974, while *Mysterious Lady* (AHLI 3208, 1979) was characterized by the singer's most elaborate studio arrangements yet—vocal choirs, overdubs, even a string section. Another duo session with Chet Atkins yielded

Instrumentally Yours (AHLI 3511, 1979), while two albums with new duet partner Kelly Foxton rounded out the era (*Lovingly Yours,* AHLI 3496, 1980, and *Win Some, Lose Some, Lonesome,* AYLI 3987, 1981).

With the demise of the LP in the late 1980s, many of the older Hank Snow albums went out of print. They are still findable, though, from collectors' stores and out-of-print specialists. Much of the Snow catalog, however, is available on a well-produced series of boxed compact-disc sets issued by the German company Bear Family under license from BMG, the corporation that now owns the Victor masters. Though expensive and difficult to obtain, these sets include virtually all the Snow recordings, including unissued performances, from 1936 through 1969. The first box contains all the Canadian recordings; it is *The Yodeling Ranger* (Bear Family BCD 15587 E1). The first American recordings, including the early hits like "I'm Movin' On," encompassing the period from 1949 through 1953, are found in *Hank Snow, the Singing Ranger* (BCD 15426). A complete set of the Thesaurus transcriptions, from the early 1950s, is found in a five-CD collection, *The Thesaurus Transcriptions* (BCD 15488). *Hank Snow, the Singing Ranger, Vol. 2* (BCD 15476) picks up the commercial recordings in chronological order and includes material from late 1953 to early 1958. A final set, consisting of the twelve CDs including most of the material from the 1960s, is *Hank Snow, the Singing Ranger, Vol. 3* (BCD 15502 LI). Though available only on an import basis, these sets are sometimes available from mail-order specialists like County Sales, P.O. Box 191, Floyd, VA 24091; Roundup Records, P.O. Box 154, North Cambridge, MA 02140; or Roots & Rhythm, 6921 Stockton Avenue, El Cerrito, CA 94530.

Two domestic CDs reissue some of the original 1950s recordings. These are *Hank Snow Collector's Series,* RCA-Nashville 07863-52279-2, and *All Time Greatest Hits,* RCA 9968-2-R.

Index

Photographs are indicated by boldface page numbers.

Grateful acknowledgment is made to the copyright owners and publishers of the following material:

"Act 1, Act 2, Act 3" by Charles Tebbetts. Copyright © 1954 by UniChappell Music, Inc. Copyright renewed. All rights reserved. Used by permission.

"Bluebird Island" by Clarence E. Snow. Copyright © 1951 by UniChappell Music, Inc. Copyright renewed. All rights reserved. Used by permission.

"Brand on My Heart" by Clarence E. Snow. Copyright © 1947 by UniChappell Music, Inc. Copyright renewed. All rights reserved. Used by permission.

"Christmas Roses" by N. A. Catsos and Paula Frances Ianello. Copyright © 1949 by Catsos Music. Copyright renewed 1977. All rights reserved. Used by permission.

"(For Every Inch I've Laughed) I've Cried a Mile" by Tompall Glaser and Harlan Howard. Copyright © 1965 by Tree Publishing Co., Inc. All rights administered by Sony Music Publishing. All rights reserved. Reprinted by permission.

"The Gold Rush Is Over" by Cindy Walker. Copyright © 1951 by Unichappell Music, Inc. Copyright renewed. All rights reserved. Used by permission.

"The Golden Rocket" by Clarence E. Snow. Copyright © 1950 by UniChappell Music, Inc. Copyright renewed. All rights reserved. Used by permission.

"Hello, Love" by Betty Jean Robinson and Aileen Mnich. Copyright © 1970 by Acuff-Rose Music, Inc. All rights administered by Opryland Music Group. All rights reserved. Used by permission.

"The Highest Bidder" by Clarence E. Snow, Mary Shurtz, and Boudleaux Bryant. Copyright © 1951 by UniChappell Music, Inc. Copyright renewed. All rights reserved. Used by permission.

"Human" by Gary Usher. Copyright © 1963 by Acuff-Rose Music, Inc. Copyright renewed. All rights administered by Opryland Music Group. All rights reserved. Used by permission.

"I Don't Hurt Anymore" by Don Robertson and Jack Rollins. Copyright © 1953 by Chappell & Co. Copyright renewed. All rights administered by UniChappell Music, Inc. All rights reserved. Used by permission.

"I'm Gonna Bid My Blues Good-bye" by Clarence E. Snow. Copyright © 1949 by Hank's Music, Inc. Copyright renewed. All rights administered by UniChappell Music, Inc. All rights reserved.

"I'm Movin' On" by Clarence E. Snow. Copyright © 1950 by UniChappell Music, Inc. Copyright renewed. All rights reserved. Used by permission.

"I'm Movin' On to Glory" by Clarence E. Snow. Copyright © 1953 by UniChappell Music, Inc. Copyright renewed. All rights reserved. Used by permission.

"I've Been Everywhere" by Geoff Mack. Copyright © 1962 by Rightsong Music, Inc. Copyright renewed. All rights administered by UniChappell Music, Inc. All rights reserved. Used by permission.

"In the Misty Moonlight" by Cindy Walker. Copyright © 1964 by Acuff-Rose Music, Inc. Copyright renewed. All rights administered by Opryland Music Group. All rights reserved. Used by permission.

"Just a Faded Petal from a Beautiful Bouquet" by Clarence E. Snow. Copyright © 1948 by Hank's Music, Inc. Copyright renewed. All rights administered by UniChappell Music, Inc. All rights reserved. Used by permission.

"Let Me Go, Lover" by Jenny Lou Carson and Al Hill. Copyright © 1954 by UniChappell Music, Inc., and Pamasons Publishing Co. All rights reserved.

"Little Children (Hope of the World)" by Paul Mitchell. Copyright © 1953 by UniChappell Music, Inc. Copyright renewed. All rights reserved.

"Marriage Vow" by Jenny Lou Carson. Copyright © 1949 by UniChappell Music, Inc. Copyright renewed. All rights reserved. Used by permission.

"Married by the Bible, Divorced by the Law" by Johnny Rector, Neva Starns, and Pee Wee Truehitt. Copyright © 1952 by UniChappell Music, Inc. Copyright renewed. All rights reserved. Used by permission.

"A Message from the Tradewinds" by Clarence E. Snow. Copyright © 1953 by UniChappell Music, Inc. Copyright renewed. All rights reserved. Used by permission.

"Miller's Cave" by Jack Clement. Copyright © 1959 by Songs of Polygram, Inc. All rights reserved.

"Music-Makin' Mama from Memphis" by Clarence E. Snow. Copyright © 1951 by UniChappell Music, Inc. Copyright renewed. All rights reserved. Used by permission.

"My Filipino Rose" by Clarence E. Snow. Copyright © 1948 by UniChappell Music, Inc. Copyright renewed. All rights reserved. Used by permission.

"My Mother" by Clarence E. Snow. Copyright © 1950 by UniChappell Music, Inc. Copyright renewed. All rights reserved. Used by permission.

"My Nova Scotia Home" by Clarence E. Snow. Copyright © 1959 by Hank's Music, Inc. Copyright renewed. All rights administered by UniChappell Music, Inc. All rights reserved. Used by permission.

"The Next Voice You Hear" by Cindy Walker. Copyright © 1953 by UniChappell Music, Inc. Copyright renewed. All rights reserved. Used by permission.

"The Night I Stole Ole Sammy Morgan's Gin" by Clarence E. Snow. Copyright © 1949 by UniChappell Music, Inc. Copyright renewed. All rights reserved. Used by permission.

"Nobody's Child" by Cy Coben and Mel Foree. Copyright © 1949 by Milene Music, Inc., and Delmore Music Co. Copyright renewed. All rights administered by Opryland Music Group. All rights reserved. Used by permission.

"(Now and Then, There's) A Fool Such as I" by Bill Trader. Copyright © 1952 by MCA, Inc. All rights reserved.

CLARENCE EUGENE "HANK" SNOW was born in Nova Scotia in 1914. He faced a difficult childhood and went to sea at the age of twelve. Developing his natural talents, he has enjoyed a lengthy career as a singer, guitarist, and songwriter in Canada, the United States, and throughout the world.

ROY GLENN "JACK" OWNBEY is a devoted Hank Snow fan and a songwriter. He attended David Lipscomb College (now University) in Nashville and the University of Tennessee at Chattanooga and received his master's degree from San Diego State University. He recently retired as a history teacher to work on music and to play tennis just about every day.

ROBERT DEE "BOB" BURRIS has lived all of his life in Cleveland, Tennessee. He graduated from Cleveland State Community College and Lee College in Cleveland. He is a Farm Bureau agent and president of a small chain of laundry and dry cleaners. He served six years in the U. S. Army Reserve and is active in civic affairs.

CHARLES K. WOLFE is a professor of English at Middle Tennessee State University and an eminent country music authority. He is the author of many articles and books, most recently *The Life and Legend of Leadbelly* (with Kip Lornell), and has edited or annotated many recordings, including the Bear Family boxed sets of Hank Snow's works.

Books in the Series Music in American Life

Only a Miner: Studies in Recorded Coal-Mining Songs
Archie Green

Great Day Coming: Folk Music and the American Left
R. Serge Denisoff

John Philip Sousa: A Descriptive Catalog of His Works
Paul E. Bierley

The Hell-Bound Train: A Cowboy Songbook
Glenn Ohrlin

Oh, Didn't He Ramble: The Life Story of Lee Collins, as Told to Mary Collins
Edited by Frank J. Gillis and John W. Miner

American Labor Songs of the Nineteenth Century
Philip S. Foner

Stars of Country Music: Uncle Dave Macon to Johnny Rodriguez
Edited by Bill C. Malone and Judith McCulloh

Git Along, Little Dogies: Songs and Songmakers of the American West
John I. White

A Texas-Mexican *Cancionero:* Folksongs of the Lower Border
Américo Paredes

San Antonio Rose: The Life and Music of Bob Wills
Charles R. Townsend

Early Downhome Blues: A Musical and Cultural Analysis
Jeff Todd Titon

An Ives Celebration: Papers and Panels of the Charles Ives Centennial Festival-Conference
Edited by H. Wiley Hitchcock and Vivian Perlis

Sinful Tunes and Spirituals: Black Folk Music to the Civil War
Dena J. Epstein

Joe Scott, the Woodsman-Songmaker
Edward D. Ives

Jimmie Rodgers: The Life and Times of America's Blue Yodeler
Nolan Porterfield

Early American Music Engraving and Printing: A History of Music Publishing in America from 1787 to 1825, with Commentary on Earlier and Later Practices
Richard J. Wolfe

Sing a Sad Song: The Life of Hank Williams
Roger M. Williams

Long Steel Rail: The Railroad in American Folksong
Norm Cohen

Resources of American Music History: A Directory of Source Materials from Colonial Times to World War II
D. W. Krummel, Jean Geil, Doris J. Dyen, and Deane L. Root

Tenement Songs: The Popular Music of the Jewish Immigrants
Mark Slobin

Ozark Folksongs
Vance Randolph; edited and abridged by Norm Cohen

Oscar Sonneck and American Music
Edited by William Lichtenwanger

Bluegrass Breakdown: The Making of the Old Southern Sound
Robert Cantwell

Bluegrass: A History
Neil V. Rosenberg

Music at the White House: A History of the American Spirit
Elise K. Kirk

Red River Blues: The Blues Tradition in the Southeast
Bruce Bastin

Good Friends and Bad Enemies: Robert Winslow Gordon and the Study of American Folksong
Debora Kodish

Fiddlin' Georgia Crazy: Fiddlin' John Carson, His Real World, and the World of His Songs
Gene Wiggins

America's Music: From the Pilgrims to the Present
Revised Third Edition
Gilbert Chase

Secular Music in Colonial Annapolis: The Tuesday Club, 1745–56
John Barry Talley

Bibliographical Handbook of American Music
D. W. Krummel

Goin' to Kansas City
Nathan W. Pearson, Jr.

"Susanna," "Jeanie," and "The Old Folks at Home": The Songs of Stephen C. Foster from His Time to Ours
Second Edition
William W. Austin

Songprints: The Musical Experience of Five Shoshone Women
Judith Vander

"Happy in the Service of the Lord": Afro-American Gospel Quartets in Memphis
Kip Lornell

Paul Hindemith in the United States
Luther Noss

"My Song Is My Weapon": People's Songs, American Communism, and the Politics of Culture
Robbie Lieberman

Chosen Voices: The Story of the American Cantorate
Mark Slobin

Theodore Thomas: America's Conductor and Builder of Orchestras, 1835–1905
Ezra Schabas

"The Whorehouse Bells Were Ringing" and Other Songs Cowboys Sing
Guy Logsdon

Crazeology: The Autobiography of a Chicago Jazzman
Bud Freeman, as Told to Robert Wolf

Discoursing Sweet Music: Brass Bands and Community Life in Turn-of-the-Century Pennsylvania
Kenneth Kreitner

Mormonism and Music: A History
Michael Hicks

Voices of the Jazz Age: Profiles of Eight Vintage Jazzmen
Chip Deffaa

Pickin' on Peachtree: A History of Country Music in Atlanta, Georgia
Wayne W. Daniel

Bitter Music: Collected Journals, Essays, Introductions, and Librettos
Harry Partch; edited by Thomas McGeary

Ethnic Music on Records: A Discography of Ethnic Recordings Produced in the United States, 1893 to 1942
Richard K. Spottswood

Downhome Blues Lyrics: An Anthology from the Post–World War II Era
Jeff Todd Titon

Ellington: The Early Years
Mark Tucker

Chicago Soul
Robert Pruter

That Half-Barbaric Twang: The Banjo in American Popular Culture
Karen Linn

Hot Man: The Life of Art Hodes
Art Hodes and Chadwick Hansen

The Erotic Muse: American Bawdy Songs
Second Edition
Ed Cray

Barrio Rhythm: Mexican American Music in Los Angeles
Steven Loza

The Creation of Jazz: Music, Race, and Culture in Urban America
Burton W. Peretti

Charles Martin Loeffler: A Life Apart in Music
Ellen Knight

Club Date Musicians: Playing the New York Party Circuit
Bruce A. MacLeod

Opera on the Road: Traveling Opera Troupes in the United States, 1825–60
Katherine K. Preston

The Stonemans: An Appalachian Family and the Music That Shaped Their Lives
Ivan M. Tribe

Transforming Tradition: Folk Music Revivals Examined
Edited by Neil V. Rosenberg

The Crooked Stovepipe: Athapaskan Fiddle Music and Square Dancing in Northeast Alaska and Northwest Canada
Craig Mishler

Traveling the High Way Home: Ralph Stanley and the World of Traditional Bluegrass Music
John Wright

Carl Ruggles: Composer, Painter, and Storyteller
Marilyn Ziffrin

Never without a Song: The Years and Songs of Jennie Devlin, 1865–1952
Katharine D. Newman

The Hank Snow Story
Hank Snow, with Jack Ownbey and Bob Burris